CANADIAN EDITION

criminology

Freda Adler
Rutgers University

Gerhard O. W. Mueller
Rutgers University

William S. Laufer
University of Pennsylvania

Jana Grekul
University of Alberta

McGraw-Hill Ryerson

Toronto Montréal Boston Burr Ridge, IL Dubuque, IA Madison, WI New York San Francisco St. Louis Bangkok Bogotá Caracas Kuala Lumpur Lisbon London Madrid Mexico City Milan New Delhi Santiago Seoul Singapore Sydney Taipei

Criminology
Canadian Edition

Statistics Canada information is used with the permission of Statistics Canada. Users are forbidden to copy this material and/or redisseminate the data, in an original or modified form, for commercial purposes, without the expressed permission of Statistic Canada. Information on the availability of the wide range of data from Statistics Canada can be obtained from Statistics Canada's Regional Offices, its World Wide Web site at http://www.statcan.ca and its toll-free access number 1-800-263-1136

ISBN-13: 978-0-07-06408-8
ISBN-10: 0-07-06408-5

1 2 3 4 5 6 7 8 9 10 TCP 0 9

Printed and bound in Canada

Care has been taken to trace ownership of copyright material contained in this text; however, the publisher will welcome any information that enables them to rectify any reference or credit for subsequent editions.

Vice-President and Editor-In-Chief: *Joanna Cotton*
Publisher: *Nicole Lukach*
Sponsoring Editor: *Nick Durie*
Marketing Manager: *Michele Peach*
Developmental Editor: *James Booty*
Editorial Associate: *Marina Seguin*
Photo/Permissions Research: *Shelley Wickabrod*
Supervising Editor: *Elizabeth Priest*
Copy Editor: *Valerie Adams*
Senior Production Coordinator: *Jennifer Hall*
Cover & Interior Design: *Liz Harasymczuk*
Cover Image: *Corbis Premium RF/Alamy*
Page Layout: *Aptara®, Inc.*
Printer: *Transcontinental Printing Group*

Library and Archives Canada Cataloguing in Publication

Criminology / Freda Adler ... [et al.]. —Canadian ed.

Includes bibliographical references and indexes.
ISBN 978-0-07-076408-8

1. Criminology—Textbooks.   I. Adler, Freda

HV6025.C7395 2008   364   C2008-903628-X

ABOUT THE AUTHORS

FREDA ADLER is Distinguished Professor of Criminal Justice at Rutgers University, School of Criminal Justice. She received her BA in sociology, her MA in criminology, and her PhD in sociology from the University of Pennsylvania. Dr. Adler began her career in criminal justice as an evaluator of drug and alcohol treatment programs for U.S. federal and state governments. Since 1968, she has taught such subjects as criminal justice, criminology, comparative criminal justice systems, statistics, and research methods. She has served as criminal justice advisor to the United Nations, as well as to various governments. Dr. Adler's published works include 17 books as author or co-author, nine books as editor or co-editor, and more than 90 journal articles. She has served on the editorial boards of the *Journal of Criminal Justice, Criminology,* and the *Journal of Research on Crime and Delinquency.* Dr. Adler serves as editorial consultant to the *Journal of Criminal Law and Criminology* and co-editor of *Advances in Criminological Theory.* She also has served as president of the American Society of Criminology (1994–1995).

GERHARD O. W. MUELLER was Distinguished Professor of Criminal Justice at Rutgers University, School of Criminal Justice. After earning his JD degree from the University of Chicago, he went on to receive a master of laws degree from Columbia University. He was awarded the degree of DrJur (hc) by the University of Uppsala, Sweden. His career in criminal justice began in 1945, when he served as a chief petty officer in the British Military Government Water Police, where he commanded a Coast Guard cutter. As Chief of the United Nations Crime Prevention and Criminal Justice Branch, he was responsible for all United Nations programs dealing with problems of crime and justice worldwide. He continued his service to the United Nations as Chairman ad interim of the Board of the International Scientific and Professional Advisory Council of the United Nations Crime Prevention and Criminal Justice Programme. Professor Mueller was a member of the faculties of law at the University of Washington, West Virginia University, New York University, and the National Judicial College. He was the author or editor of some 50 books and close to 300 scholarly articles.

JANA GREKUL is Assistant Professor of Sociology and Director of Criminology at the University of Alberta. After completing her BA degree in sociology at the University of Alberta, Dr. Grekul, went on to complete her MA in 1995 and her PhD in 2002. Her master's thesis research was conducted at a maximum-security prison where she investigated the impact of group processes on the misperceptions and misunderstandings that occur between correctional officers and inmates, and how these processes contribute to prison violence. Her doctoral research was a case study of the eugenics movement in Alberta. Dr. Grekul's current research interests include studying street and prison gangs, and particularly Aboriginal gangs. She is involved with the Community Solution to Gang Violence as part of the Research and Evaluation team. She is also working on a research project that focuses on the experiences of women in academia. Dr. Grekul teaches a variety of sociology and criminology courses and recently published *Sociology Matters*.

WILLIAM S. LAUFER is Associate Professor of Legal Studies and Business Ethics, Sociology, and Criminology at the Wharton School of the University of Pennsylvania. He is Director of the Carol and Lawrence Zicklin Center for Business Ethics Research and Associate Director of the Jerry Lee Center of Criminology. Dr. Laufer received his BA in Social and Behavioural Sciences at the Johns Hopkins University, his JD at Northeastern University School of Law, and his PhD at Rutgers University School of Criminal Justice. Since 1987, he has taught such subjects as corporate and white-collar crime, business ethics, criminal law and criminal procedure, and criminology. His most recent book, *Corporate Bodies and Guilty Minds,* was published by University of Chicago Press in 2006. He is co-editor of the *Handbook of Psychology and Law; Personality Theory, Moral Development and Criminal Behaviour;* and *Crime, Values and Religion.* Dr. Laufer is co-editor with Freda Adler of *Advances in Criminological Theory.*

DEDICATION

Canadian Reviewers

Dr. Jon Frauley   *York University*
Marilyn Bell-McQuillan   *University of Calgary*
Oliver R. Stoetzer   *Fanshawe College*
Deidre Way Consulting   *Loyalist College*
Carla Hotel   *Douglas College*
Shahid Alvi   *University of Ontario Institute of Technology*
Amy Walther   *Georgian College*
Lorne Landry   *Sheridan College*
David Ryan/Animated Resolutions   *Seneca College*
Dale Dearden   *Kwantlen University College*
Dr. Randy Lippert   *University of Windsor*

CONTENTS IN BRIEF

CONTENTS

■ CHAPTER 8

Labelling, Conflict, Radical, and Feminist Theories   182

■ CHAPTER 9

Environmental Theory   212

PART III

Types of Crimes   235

■ CHAPTER 10

Violent Crimes   236

PREFACE

Criminology is a young discipline—in fact, the term "criminology" is only a little over a century old. But in this brief time, criminology has emerged as an important social and behavioural science devoted to the study of crime as a social phenomenon. Criminology fosters theoretical debates, contributes ideas, and suggests solutions to a crime problem that many consider intolerable. Problems as vital and urgent as those addressed in this book are challenging, exciting, and, at the same time, disturbing and tragic. Moreover, these problems are immediately relevant to students' lives. This is especially true today, where we witness reports of increasing gang activity, revelations of new corporate scandals, and consequences of environmental crimes.

Our goal with this book is to discuss these problems, their origins, and their possible solutions in a clear, practical, straightforward fashion that brings the material to life for students. It is critical that we situate the behaviours labelled as criminal within the broader social, economic, political, and cultural frameworks within which they take place. This means that integral to explaining crime is an understanding that our definition and perception of behaviours as criminal is influenced by the time period within which we live, the culture of which we are a part, and inequalities based on ethnicity, class, gender, and age.

The image on the cover of this text is fitting for a variety of reasons. First, as you will see throughout the text, criminal acts are the result of a chain of events. Socialization and processes based in the family influence behaviours, as do experiences at school, among peers, in the workplace, and in broader society. Media is a critical factor here too. Second, for criminologists who focus their attention on precursors to crime, prevention or targeting a particular link in the chain, such as family violence or poverty, can effectively prevent the criminal act from occurring. Third, the chain serves as a reminder to us that there are institutions in place that reinforce the divisions in our society between those who have crossed the legal line and those who

haven't. Criminal labels are one way of creating insider-outsider boundaries that serve to separate us from each other.

We invite teachers and students alike to join us in travelling along criminology's path, exploring the intricacies of its domain, and mapping out its future.

THE FIRST CANADIAN EDITION

This first Canadian edition builds on the strengths of six previous American editions. A major focus of these foundational editions was the preparation of criminology students to understand the contemporary problems with which criminology is concerned and to anticipate those issues that society would have to face in the twenty-first century. We have now entered that century and are faced with new developments and issues that pertain directly to the work of criminologists.

While Canada shares many of the same social and crime problems as the United States, this country is unique in many respects. For example, the rate of violent crime in Canada is significantly lower than it is in the United States, and gun-related violence is not as prevalent. Canada's multicultural society, and the prominent place in that society of the two Charter groups (the English and the French), as well as First Nations peoples, means that our cultural heritage presents interesting and important contexts to crime-related issues in society. Gangs, long established in many U.S. states, have only recently become a cause for concern in Canada. These differences influence the work of Canadian criminologists and, along with a variety of other differences discussed throughout the text, make Canadian criminology a unique enterprise.

Also providing context to the work of Canadian criminologists is the traditionally more progressive Canadian public. Canada has legalized same-sex unions and taken steps toward the decriminalization of marijuana. The work of Canadian criminologists is influenced by the relatively liberal nature of public opinion in the country and public understanding of crime and social problems. As a result, the emphases in this Canadian edition differ somewhat from the American editions.

First, we focus on the socially constructed nature of crime in Chapter 1 and to some extent throughout the text, pointing to the relativity of crime: Behaviour considered criminal in one time period, or one cultural context, may in another context be labelled "normal." The underlying theme is that a variety of social structural factors often interact to produce the kinds of behaviours that tend to be labelled criminal in society. In some ways, criminals are not all that different from non-criminals, except that environmental, social, and other factors have joined together in a particular configuration that produces their criminal behaviours. In other words, criminals are sometimes not really so different from the rest of us: We are all interconnected. It follows then, that a more humanistic stance toward understanding and dealing with deviant and criminal behaviours is in the best interest of society's members.

The Canadian edition provides a more integrated feminist perspective on various criminological issues. As well, the work of Canadian critical criminologists is discussed in some detail. Chapter 12, "White-Collar, Corporate, and Organized Crime," in particular, draws on many Canadian examples, from Conrad Black's exploits, to the Walkerton tragedy, and the mercury poisoning suffered by First Nations groups in Canada. Many would argue that white-collar and corporate offences have been on the periphery of the field of criminology—but not for much longer.

We have vigorously researched, refined, and updated every chapter of the text—and, wherever possible, have integrated Canadian research and examples, not only to maintain the book's scholarly integrity, but also to ensure its relevance for today's students. While all chapters are critical to understanding crime and criminology today, four chapters in particular add depth to this text:

- Chapter 1, "The Changing Boundaries of Criminology," introduces students to the relativity of crime, and the ways in which power and inequality, as well as historical, political, temporal, and cultural contexts influence the definition of crime.

- Chapter 2, "Counting Crime and Measuring Criminal Behaviour," focuses on what crime is *and* how we measure it. This organization makes the material on crime measurement—which can sometimes be difficult for students to grasp—more meaningful, relevant, and understandable by presenting it alongside the more inherently concrete discussion of what crime is.

- Chapter 12, "White-Collar, Corporate, and Organized Crime," addresses the problems of white-collar and corporate crime. This is a welcome change from a field that often has as its focus more traditional violent and property offences.

- Chapter 14, "International and Comparative Criminology," focuses on criminology from a global perspective and highlights comparative criminology, its history, purpose, and goals.

Inasmuch as developments in criminology influence and are influenced by media reports of national significance, the student will find discussion and analysis of recent major current events.

We have endeavoured in this edition not only to reflect developments and changes, but to anticipate them on the basis of the latest Canadian criminological data. After all, those who study criminology with our text today must be ready to address and resolve new criminological issues tomorrow when they are decision makers, researchers, teachers, and planners. The aim, however, remains constant: to reach a future as free from human suffering as possible.

ORGANIZATION

Part I, "Understanding Criminology," presents an overview of criminology and describes the vast horizon of this science. It explains what crime is and techniques for measuring the amount and characteristics of crime and criminals. It also traces the history of criminological thought through the era that witnessed the formation of the major schools of criminology, classicism and positivism (eighteenth and nineteenth centuries).

Part II, "Explanations of Crime and Criminal Behaviour," includes explanations of crime and criminal behaviour on the basis of the various theories developed in the twentieth century. Among the subjects covered are theories that offer biological, psychological, sociological, sociopolitical, and integrated explanations. Coverage of research by radical, socialist, and feminist criminologists has been Canadianized and updated. Theories that discuss why offenders choose to commit one offence rather than another at a given time and place are also covered in this part.

Part III, "Types of Crimes," covers the various types of crimes from a legal and sociological perspective. The familiar street crimes, such as homicide and robbery, are assessed, as are other criminal activities such as white-collar and corporate crime, which are so much in the spotlight these days, as well as other high-tech crimes that have been highlighted by researchers only in recent years. Chapter 14, "International and Comparative Criminology," which deals with an area with vastly increased practical and policy implications, has been expanded and updated in light of the growing research in the field.

PEDAGOGICAL AIDS

Working together, the authors and the editors have developed a format for the text that supports the goal of a readable, practical, and attractive text. In addition to all the changes already mentioned, we include plentiful, current photographs to make the book even more approachable. Redesigned and carefully updated tables and figures highlight and amplify the text coverage. Chapter outlines, chapter review sections, and a comprehensive glossary all help students to master the material. Always striving to help students see the relevance of criminology in their lives, we also include unique, innovative features such as:

- *Did You Know?* Surprising factual realities that provide eye-opening information about chapter topics.
- *Research Informs Policy.* Brief sections at the end of theory chapters that demonstrate how problems identified by criminologists have led to practical solutions.

- *Criminology & Public Policy* exercises. Activities at the end of each chapter that challenge students to explore policy issues related to criminology.

We are particularly proud of our "box" program. In these boxes, we highlight criminologically significant issues that deserve special discussion:

- *Debatable Issues* boxes highlight current controversies that challenge us to come up with a resolution.
- *Of Immediate Concern* boxes highlight problems "of the moment," due to their technological nature or human implications, which challenge us to come up with specific effective responses right now. Thus, in the wake of school killings, should we create maximim-security schools? In light of our experience with hate-motivated crimes, are harsher laws called for?
- *Window to the World* boxes examine developments abroad that affect Canada's crime situation. Now that ethnic gangs have emerged around the world and are, among other things, forcibly transporting women and young girls to be sex slaves, how can nations deal with the problem?
- *From the Media* boxes discuss current issues and problems reported in the media. These boxes are doubly beneficial to students: Not only do they relate chapter material to what students see every day on the news, they provide yet another means of keeping students focused on all important policy issues in criminology.

SUPPLEMENTS PACKAGE

As a full-service publisher of quality educational products, McGraw-Hill Ryerson does much more than just sell textbooks. The company creates and publishes an extensive array of print, video, and digital supplements for students and instructors. This edition of *Criminology* is accompanied by an extensive, comprehensive supplements package:

For the Student

Online Learning Centre Website. An innovative website features unique *Interactive Explorations* that allow students to explore some of the hottest topics in criminal justice today—terrorism, serial killers, gangs, and so on. The website also features PowerWeb, online access to articles from the popular and scholarly press, weekly updates, daily newsfeeds, a search engine, and more. All of this material—plus flashcards that can be used to master vocabulary and a wealth of other review materials—is organized by chapter for ease of use when studying for exams or writing papers.

For the Instructor

- *Instructor's Manual/Testbank.* The manual includes detailed chapter outlines, key terms, overviews, lecture notes, and a complete testbank.

- *Computerized Testbank.* Easy-to-use computerized testing program is compatible with both Windows and Macintosh computers.

- *PowerPoint Slides.* Complete, chapter-by-chapter slide shows feature text, art, and tables.

- *Online Learning Centre Website.* Password-protected access to supplements and other important instructor support materials and additional resources.

- *Full-Length Videotapes.* A wide variety of videotapes from the *Films for the Humanities and Social Sciences* series is available to adopters of the text.

- *Primis Online.* This unique database publishing system allows instructors to create their own custom text from material in *Criminology* or elsewhere and deliver that text to students electronically as an e-book or in print format via the bookstore.

All of the above supplements are provided free of charge to students and instructors. Orders of new (versus used) textbooks help us defray the cost of developing such supplements, which is substantial. Please contact your local McGraw-Hill Ryerson representative for more information on any of these supplements.

IN APPRECIATION

I would like to acknowledge the many people who have contributed in one way or another to the completion of this project. There are too many to list here, but I do want to make special mention of Karen Ritcey and Jodi Lewchuk who started this whole thing. Nicole Lukach and Nick Durie, an absolute pleasure to work with, are also incredibly perceptive and thoughtful individuals. Marcia Luke and James Booty are very diligent and conscientious developmental editors. I would also like to acknowledge the careful attention the manuscript received from Elizabeth Priest and Valerie Adams. Alison Derry is someone I would love to bargain shop with sometime—thank you! Shelley Wickabrod did so much more than she needed to: Her strength, wisdom, and sense of humour were a true gift throughout the process. Thanks also to Joanna Cotton, Marina Seguin, Edith Smith, and the entire team at McGraw-Hill Ryerson.

I am very fortunate to work in a sociology department filled with talented and personable individuals who are supportive. In particular, I want to acknowledge the superb mentorship of Harvey Krahn and Tim Hartnagel. Flora Webber, Charlene Marshall, and Bev Wald are an absolute joy to work with. Kim Sanderson, my "partner in crime" at work, deserves thanks for her (more than) capable help, patience, and ear over the past year.

Thanks to Patti and Allen Benson, whom I can always count on.

I am surrounded by the most sincere, clever, and forgiving students, who mean a great deal to me and whose insights have contributed in one way or another to this book. I can't thank each and every one, but I want to thank a special few: Kiara, Lara, Andrea, Emily, Eman, Candace, Rena, Keith, Timm, and Justin. And all the BA Criminology students!

Bill and Connor: Thank you for tip-toeing around in the morning and letting me sleep in after a late night of writing and for putting up with a workaholic.

Though many think their parents are the best, mine really are. My brother is the sweetest soul who breaks traditional gender norms, while at the same time maintaining the best of them. My sister-in-law is a rare gem. They all defy proper acknowledgment or description. And my sister? Not only is she my idol and best friend, but she really gets it. Thank you, Lisa.

—Jana Grekul

THE CHANGING BOUNDARIES OF CRIMINOLOGY

CHAPTER 1

CHAPTER OUTLINE

The Changing Boundaries of Criminology
The Importance of Perspective
Why Do Perspectives and Boundaries Change?
Moral Entrepreneurs and Context
Media
Public Opinion
Consequences of Boundary Changes

What Is Criminology?

The Making of Laws
Deviance
The Concept of Crime

The Consensus and Conflict Views of Law and Crime

The Breaking of Laws

Society's Reaction to the Breaking of Laws
Criminology and the Criminal Justice System
The Global Approach to the Breaking of Laws

Research Informs Policy

REVIEW

CHAPTER QUESTIONS

1. How do the boundaries of criminology change?
2. Who are criminologists and what do they do?
3. What influences the ways in which laws are created?
4. What causes people to break the law?
5. How does society deal with lawbreakers?
6. How do criminologists influence policy changes?

Protestors show their support for Robert Latimer, the Saskatchewan father who was convicted of second-degree murder for taking the life of his 12-year-old severely handicapped daughter.

Plymouth, Nova Scotia, witnessed the worst mining disaster in Canadian history when a methane explosion ignited a build-up of coal dust in the mine early in the morning on May 9, 1992. Twenty-six miners died in the Westray mining disaster. The province's Labour Department warned the mining company (Westray) about a variety of safety violations in the months prior. Following the tragedy, the RCMP launched a criminal investigation into the incident; the government commissioned a provincial inquiry to determine whether neglect resulted in the disaster. Six years later, the issue of criminal responsibility remained unresolved; the inquiry revealed extensive problems with government regulation in the mining industry. The mine was permanently sealed (with 11 miners' bodies trapped within) and a memorial erected in honour of the 26 victims.

On October 24, 1993, Robert Latimer, a farmer from Saskatchewan, killed his daughter Tracy. Tracy, an 18-kilogram, 12-year-old quadriplegic, suffered from a severe form of cerebral palsy and functioned at the level of a three-month-old. Though she responded to affection and occasionally smiled, she was in constant, excruciating pain. Her father, who could no longer watch her suffer, piped carbon monoxide into his truck and watched her die. He was convicted of second-degree murder and sentenced to life in prison; 25 years with no parole before ten years.

September 13, 2006, Kimveer Gill stormed onto the Dawson College campus and proceeded to kill one student and injure 20 others in a shooting rampage. The self-described "Angel of Death" posted pictures of himself, clothed in a black trench coat, flashing his weapons, including a Beretta CX4 Storm semi-automatic rifle, on his profile on the website vampirefreaks.com.

By now you may well be asking, What do all these disparate events have in common? What do they have to do with criminology? A great deal. Each of these incidents raises issues and debates of concern to the public and policy makers. Is a prison term "cruel and unusual punishment" for a loving father who "euthanized" his daughter to end her suffering? Is taking another life considered murder no matter what the motivation? Who should make these decisions? Canadians have been debating gun control, most notably the gun registry introduced by the former Liberal federal government, for over a decade. Yet Gill, the gunman who terrorized hundreds of college students and shocked the nation, had legally purchased his weapons.

The first lesson of this book is that criminology is not just a theoretical science. Rather, it is a science that should inform policy—policy aimed at protecting the community from harm and making clear the boundaries for acceptable behaviours. There is a second lesson. As the Westray mine example illustrates, criminology is not just concerned with street crimes. Criminal actions can result when company executives put profit before human lives. Much of what happens on earth has criminological significance. Indeed, we may well (and prematurely) suggest that there is not just one criminology, but many criminologies, such as a criminology of white-collar and corporate crime (Chapter 12), and a criminology of violence and human rights (Chapter 10), among others. And this is where our story begins. . . .

3

Chapter-Opening Previews

Succinct chapter-opening outlines and overviews help students focus on the chapter's critical theories, concepts, and terminology.

FROM THE MEDIA

Youth Jail Terms Less Common after 2003 Law

Far fewer young offenders are being found guilty of crimes and sentenced to jail terms since the Youth Criminal Justice Act came into being in 2003, according to a study of recent trends in youth crime.

"What is remarkable is that for both minor assaults and all other violent charges, the rate appears to have dropped rather dramatically with the coming into force of the YCJA," the study states. It notes there was a similar decrease for property offences such as theft.

A surprise finding was that verdicts of guilt in Alberta and B.C. plummeted to a level traditionally occupied exclusively by Quebec, the most liberal of the provinces when it comes to crime and imprisonment.

"Quebec is no longer distinct in the manner in which it uses its youth court," states the study, which was conducted for the federal Department of Justice in March [2006]. "This is an important finding in that it was assumed, we think, that the low rate of using youth court in Quebec related to a special tradition that existed only in Quebec of using other social systems to deal with offending youths."

The study, conducted by University of Toronto criminologist Anthony Doob and University of Guelph criminologist Jane Sprott, compared the last five years of the Young Offenders Act—1998 to 2003—with the first year after it was replaced by the YCJA.

The issue of youth crime leapt up on the political agenda . . . after a Supreme Court ruling that judges must not stiffen sentences for young offenders in the hope of discouraging the offender or potential lawbreakers.

Justice Minister Vic Toews, a long-time critic of the youth justice system, responded by blasting the YCJA as "a very badly drafted act" that needs to be reviewed.

"Accountability and responsibility for serious crimes needs to be enforced in our youth justice system," he said.

The YCJA replaced the Young Offenders Act after 18 years of inflamed debate. Where the YOA was marred by undefined principles and could result in wildly differing sentences, the new act had a strong philosophical base.

It mandated that sentences should be proportional to the severity of the crime and the maturity level of the perpetrator. It discouraged judges from using jail for less serious offences, and promoted the use of alternatives such as probation, mediation sessions with victims and victim compensation or restitution.

Speaking on condition of anonymity [in 2006], an Ontario judge said a Supreme Court ruling . . . hammered home the dramatic changes the YCJA has brought about. "The significance of this decision and other appellate cases is that judges and lawyers are definitely getting the message that we are in a new paradigm, and that we have to stop thinking about 'jail versus no jail' as our only alternatives," the judge said.

Prof. Doob and Prof. Sprott observed . . . that Mr. Toews is apparently unaware that the new law was tailored to treat serious crime relatively harshly while finding more enlightened—and less costly—ways to deal with minor offenders.

They also noted that, in keeping with the aims of Parliament, the overall proportion of those being sentenced to jail for violent offences has increased under the new act.

"Who knows what this government is going to do?" Prof. Sprott said. . . . "They want to talk tough and sound tough, but I'm not sure they want to raise taxes to pay for it."

"The irony is that the minister keeps saying, 'We want accountability,' " Prof. Doob added. "That is exactly what's in the act."

The study attributed part of the drop in findings of guilt to the fact that police are charging fewer youths.

"Over all, in Canada, there was a 41-per-cent decrease in the custody rate—from 6.4 to 3.78 per 1,000 in the population," the study adds. "Obviously, some of this decrease was the result of fewer cases being brought to youth court."

It said that in the first year of the YCJA, all 13 provinces and territories decreased their rate of sentencing youths into custody.

Source
http://www.theglobeandmail.com/servlet/story/RTGAM.20060623.wyouth24.V124/BNStory/BabyBoomers/, accessed May 8, 2008. Reprinted with permission from the Globe and Mail.

Questions for Discussion

1. How did the change in youth justice legislation affect youth crime rates?
2. In what ways can politics affect statistics? Has youth crime really gone down?

From the Media Boxes

Detailed discussion of the very issues and problems students hear about in the news helps them relate these issues to chapter and lecture material.

the extent of harm done during the commission of an offence. There is significant qualitative difference between an attempted and completed armed robbery, for example. Yet, this detail is lost when both acts are conflated into one category.

Another serious limitation is the fact that when several crimes are committed in one event, only the most serious offence is included in the UCR; the others go unreported. The end result for researchers is that a number of crimes go uncounted. At the same time, there are differences in the ways that personal and property crimes are counted. For personal crimes, the counting system is such that one crime equals one victim. If a person assaults six people, the UCR lists six assaults. When property crimes are committed, each individual act is counted as a separate offence. If a person robs a group of six people, for example, the UCR lists one robbery (see Figure 2.1). In addition, the UCR collects limited information about reported crimes (type of offence,

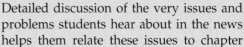

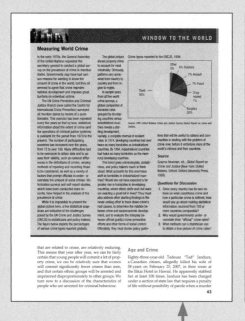

Classic *Window to the World* and *Of Immediate Concern* Boxes

Acclaimed thematic box program—one box devoted to highlighting the international dimensions of criminology, another to introduce criminological problems that are "of the moment."

Fascinating *Did You Know?* Facts

Intriguing, little-known facts related to specific chapter topics engage students' natural curiosity about criminology.

Easy-to-Use End-of-Chapter Review

Review section that summarizes the chapter in a clear and concise fashion, incorporating notable key terms.

Unique *Criminology & Public Policy* Exercises

End-of-chapter activities that challenge students to explore and think critically about policy issues.

Unique *You Be the Criminologist* Exercises

Chapter-ending exercises challenge students to use their critical thinking skills to apply what they have read about in the chapter.

Online Learning Centre Website

Unique, book-specific website features *Interactive Explorations* that enable students to think about and explore some of the latest issues in criminal justice today. The website also includes online access to scholarly articles, the media, flashcards that can be used to master vocabulary, and many other chapter review tools.

UNDERSTANDING CRIMINOLOGY

PART **I**

Criminology is the scientific study of the making of laws, the breaking of laws, and society's reaction to the breaking of laws. Sometimes these laws are arrived at by the consensus of most members of a community; sometimes they are imposed by those in power. Communities have grown in size, from village to world, and the threats to communities have grown accordingly. World-level threats necessitated that criminological research and crime prevention strategies become globalized. Criminological research contributes to an understanding of the processes and factors that influence the making and breaking of laws, and is influential in policy making (Chapter 1).

Criminologists have adopted methods of study from all the social and behavioural sciences. Like all other scientists, criminologists measure. They assess crime over time and place, and they measure the characteristics of criminals and crimes (Chapter 2).

Throughout history, thinkers and rulers have written about crime and criminals and the control of crime. Yet the term "criminology" is little more than a century old, and the subject has been of scientific interest for only two centuries. Two schools of thought contributed to modern criminology: the classical school, associated predominantly with Cesare Beccaria (eighteenth century), which focused on crime, and the positivist school, associated with Cesare Lombroso, Enrico Ferri, and Raffaele Garofalo (nineteenth and early twentieth centuries), which focused on criminals (Chapter 3). While contemporary Canadian criminology owes much to these European roots, Canadian criminologists have also contributed to the development of the discipline.

THE CHANGING BOUNDARIES OF CRIMINOLOGY

CHAPTER 1

CHAPTER QUESTIONS

1. How do the boundaries of criminology change?

2. Who are criminologists and what do they do?

3. What influences the ways in which laws are created?

4. What causes people to break the law?

5. How does society deal with lawbreakers?

6. How do criminologists influence policy changes?

Protestors show their support for Robert Latimer, the Saskatchewan father who was convicted of second-degree murder for taking the life of his 12-year-old severely handicapped daughter.

lymouth, Nova Scotia, witnessed the worst mining disaster in Canadian history when a methane explosion ignited a build-up of coal dust in the mine early in the morning on May 9, 1992. Twenty-six miners died in the Westray mining disaster. The province's Labour Department warned the mining company (Westray) about a variety of safety violations in the months prior. Following the tragedy, the RCMP launched a criminal investigation into the incident; the government commissioned a provincial inquiry to determine whether neglect resulted in the disaster. Six years later, the issue of criminal responsibility remained unresolved; the inquiry revealed extensive problems with government regulation in the mining industry. The mine was permanently sealed (with 11 miners' bodies trapped within) and a memorial erected in honour of the 26 victims.

On October 24, 1993, Robert Latimer, a farmer from Saskatchewan, killed his daughter Tracy. Tracy, an 18-kilogram, 12-year-old quadriplegic, suffered from a severe form of cerebral palsy and functioned at the level of a three-month-old. Though she responded to affection and occasionally smiled, she was in constant, excruciating pain. Her father, who could no longer watch her suffer, piped carbon monoxide into his truck and watched her die. He was convicted of second-degree murder and sentenced to life in prison: 25 years with no parole before ten years.

September 13, 2006, Kimveer Gill stormed onto the Dawson College campus and proceeded to kill one student and injure 20 others in a shooting rampage. The self-described "Angel of Death" posted pictures of himself, clothed in a black trench coat, flashing his weapons, including a Beretta CX4 Storm semi-automatic rifle, on his profile on the website vampirefreaks.com.

By now you may well be asking, What do all these disparate events have in common? What do they have to do with criminology? A great deal. Each of these incidents raises issues and debates of concern to the public and policy makers. Is a prison term "cruel and unusual punishment" for a loving father who "euthanized" his daughter to end her suffering? Is taking another life considered murder no matter what the motivation? Who should make these decisions? Canadians have been debating gun control, most notably the gun registry introduced by the former Liberal federal government, for over a decade. Yet Gill, the gunman who terrorized hundreds of college students and shocked the nation, had legally purchased his weapons.

The first lesson of this book is that criminology is not just a theoretical science. Rather, it is a science that should inform policy—policy aimed at protecting the community from harm and making clear the boundaries for acceptable behaviours. There is a second lesson. As the Westray mine example illustrates, criminology is not just concerned with street crimes. Criminal actions can result when company executives put profit before human lives. Much of what happens on earth has criminological significance. Indeed, we may well (and prematurely) suggest that there is not just one criminology, but many criminologies, such as a criminology of white-collar and corporate crime (Chapter 12), and a criminology of violence and human rights (Chapter 10), among others. And this is where our story begins. . . .

THE CHANGING BOUNDARIES OF CRIMINOLOGY

There is a third lesson that emerges from the stories in the opening section: perspective matters. From the perspective of the law, each of these examples represents an instance of criminal behaviour. At the same time, members of the public react differently to the events. In the Latimer case, Canadians became embroiled in a debate over the sanctity of life versus the efforts of a father to save his daughter from a lifetime of suffering. The Westray mine disaster raised issues surrounding the effectiveness of government in regulating the activities of business and holding companies accountable for their unlawful actions.

Our reaction to these kinds of incidents is influenced by a variety of factors, including media coverage of the events. In the Latimer case, the *relationship* between offender and victim influenced peoples' reaction to what happened. In the case of school shootings like the Dawson College incident and, more recently, the Virginia Tech shooting in the United States, it is the *context*—educational institutions where young people should be able to learn in a safe environment—that shakes us up. *Characteristics* of victims and offenders affect public reaction to crimes as well.

What is a crime? Take a moment to think about how you would define it. Does your definition include a reference to the violation of social norms? Does it focus on harm inflicted on victims? Would it include the real-life scenarios described in the preceding paragraphs? Is your definition based on formal punishments for the act, meted out by the state? Or is your definition of crime broader in scope, citing the violation of social norms, moral codes, and the contravention of human rights and responsibilities?

For many of us, it seems that "crime" is a very clear-cut phenomenon. Images of Clifford Olson, Karla Homolka, armed robbers cloaked in balaclavas, pimps, gang members, and thieves might pop into our heads. But as the examples above illustrate, criminals do not conform to any one stereotype. Crime encompasses a variety of behaviours, and to make things even more complex, perspectives on what crime is vary.

The Importance of Perspective

Working as a correctional officer years ago, one of the authors of this book met an Aboriginal inmate who shared a story with her. He had, a few years earlier, received a rather large sum of money (legitimately) from his band council. Within days he spent the entire amount: He bought a new stereo system, new furniture and appliances, and a new car. One day about a week later he returned home from work to an empty house: Everything was gone—all of his new possessions had disappeared! The author was shocked when she heard the story, and exclaimed to him, "Well?! Did you report the break-and-enter and theft to the police? Did they find the thieves? Did they lay charges?" She was horrified by the injustice that had occurred. This person had been truly victimized. The inmate looked at her, puzzled. "No, Jana. Why would I call the police? I knew who had my stereo—it was my auntie. My furniture was at my sister's. My cousin was using my car. In our [Aboriginal] culture, we share everything. These items were not stolen. I knew exactly where they were and if I wanted them back, all I would have to do is go and get them." The author sat and stared at him blankly, feeling silly for her overreaction, but at the same time wondering about this scenario. Had a crime occurred? Can we talk about a crime taking place when the victim doesn't see himself or herself as a victim at all? In this sense, perspective matters and influences our understanding of events we call *criminal*.

Perspectives of individuals vary and change, as does the perspective of the state when laws change over time. Picture this scenario: It's 1968. Police are called to a domestic disturbance. The husband clearly has severely beaten his wife. The officers ask her if she would like to lay charges. She looks over at her husband, who glares at her threateningly. She stops and thinks about the repercussions of following through with charges, including the prospect of future violent victimization from her now very angry husband who will want revenge for the charge. She thinks about the possibility of him spending time in jail, and wonders about supporting her three children (she is a stay-at-home mother). Weighing the costs and benefits of going ahead with the charge, she chooses not to press charges against her husband.

In the early 1980s Canadian law went through significant changes, particularly with respect to laws relating to sexual assault and domestic violence. Police were given the responsibility to lay charges in domestic violence situations. No longer was it up to the beaten wife to do so; it was now out of her hands. The perspective of the law on these kinds of events changed: If police could determine that spousal violence had in fact occurred, charges were to be laid. How is it that perspectives, legal or otherwise, change?

Why Do Perspectives and Boundaries Change?

Our definitions of criminal behaviours change because crime is closely connected to notions of morality. As our morals change, so do our definitions of appropriate and inappropriate actions. We respond to these changes by encoding our beliefs about appropriateness in the law. In this sense, then, the criminal law is a living organism; its boundaries change as society changes. Certainly, these changes don't occur overnight and often there is much conflict and debate among interest groups, politicians, and the public over whether such changes are in fact warranted. Changes are usually the end product of a long interactive process between interested parties, but are also influenced by the economy, history, politics, science, and international events among other factors. Let us illustrate the fluidity of criminal boundaries, the role that context plays in this process, and the influence it has on the study of crime, the domain of criminology.

Moral Entrepreneurs and Context

In a democratic society like Canada, citizen concerns and views are reflected in the decision-making process of our governments. Because of this consultative system, interest groups can and do play a significant role in the definitions, normative and legal, of appropriate behaviours. Pick up any newspaper today and you will witness this process in action, whether the focus is on same-sex marriage legislation, anti-smoking regulations, environmental protectionism, or the decriminalization of marijuana. Think about the group MADD. What does it stand for? We are familiar with this particular interest group because its media campaigns over the years have increased our sensitivity to the issue of drinking and driving. Have you ever wondered how and why MADD gained such prominence and influence as an interest group? There wasn't always a MADD! In fact, prior to the 1980s, impaired driving did not invoke the disapproval it does today. It wasn't unheard of for individuals, after a night of drinking with friends, to remark that they had to "drive

Mothers Against Drunk Driving, a very successful interest group, has significantly changed the way society views drinking and driving.

home because they were too drunk to walk"! MADD is an example of an interest group, run by individuals who want to effect change. People who are passionate about a cause and who use their political, economic, or educational influence to raise awareness about an issue and who work toward making changes in laws are termed **moral entrepreneurs.**

Media

A large part of the success of the MADD campaign is its use of the media. Media reports from around the world enter into our living rooms every night. Not only are we aware of the goings-on in our city, province, or country, but we are bombarded with reports of crime incidents across the globe, reports on the latest attacks and casualties in Afghanistan, the most recent school shootings, the latest weather-related tragedies, the anti-terrorism activities of a variety of nations, and the policy and legislative changes that result from awareness of these events. The boundaries of criminology change and grow in response to real acts and behaviours, the response to such behaviours, and the media reporting of such behaviours.

Clearly, media is an important part of the context within which criminology operates. Media shapes public and private understandings and perceptions of criminal events. Often though, media distorts the truth, presenting a particular version of the story, usually the version that will sell the most newspapers.

Think for a moment about the "gang problem." Who makes up the "gangs" we are afraid of? Is it outlaw motorcycle groups? Is it "Asian gangs" or maybe "Aboriginal gangs" (particularly if you live in the Prairie provinces)? Depending on where in the country you live, it might be the "Jamaicans" who are most likely to come to mind. Why don't we ever hear reports of drive-by shootings linked to a local "Caucasian" gang? In rural Alberta, police gang unit officials report the existence of a gang called the "White Boy Posse," yet this group never makes the headlines. Why not? Probably because reports of gang-related activities committed by Caucasians won't sell as many newspapers as reports of "ethnic gangs." The gang problem has been constructed as something to be blamed on ethnic minorities. Some of this construction may be based on truth, but the ethnic composition of gangs and the targeting of particular ethnic groups is to some extent an exaggerated media construction.[1]

Media, then, can shape public perceptions and understandings of crime problems by sharing information but also by exaggerating the facts. Criminologists include in their domain of study the role of the media and other powerful interest groups in the construction of crime, the creation of perceptions surrounding what crime is and how it should be dealt with.

Public Opinion

Media influences public opinion, which in turn influences the activities of politicians, who in turn voice the concerns of the populace in government and make laws. But the influence of the public doesn't end here. The public can influence definitions of criminal behaviour in at least two other ways as well. Frequency of behaviour is one way that the public can influence the making of laws. Drug use in Canada is such an example. It is illegal for Canadians to use a variety of mind-altering substances, including marijuana, yet the Canadian Medical Association estimates that 1.5 million of us smoke marijuana recreationally. The Canadian Addiction Survey reports that 14 percent of Canadians said they had used pot in 2003 (about double the number from 1994).[2] Norms change and these changes can impact on changes to the law. Beginning July 31, 2002, Canada became the first country to regulate the medicinal use of marijuana. The push for decriminalization of small amounts of cannabis and recreational use of the substance resulted in the introduction of a bill in Parliament by the Liberals in 2004 that would decriminalize some aspects of use. However, this bill was scrapped by Stephen Harper's

Conservative government in April 2006. Marijuana use is a hotly contested issue in which the public certainly continues to play a big role.

American sociologist Jack Gibbs asked, "With what frequency must a type of act occur before it is considered a norm?"[3] How *many* people must smoke pot before we as a society change our definitions of it from "criminal" behaviour to something else? Or, from a slightly different perspective, how many (primarily young) people must bear the burden of a criminal record for partaking in behaviour whose criminal status is up for debate? In this sense, the role of the public as active participants in shifting moral, normative, and criminal boundaries, and as influences on the government in the form of interest groups are an area of study for criminologists.

Education and awareness provide another avenue through which the public influences definitions of behaviour, whether normal, deviant, or criminal. Touted by many as a neo-temperance movement, the anti-smoking drive has ignited a new definition of deviance and criminal behaviour based on health consciousness. In Canada, we have witnessed in recent years the passage of municipal regulations that make smoking in public places illegal. The crusade is framed in health terms, focusing on the damage produced by nicotine not only to smokers but to innocent and unsuspecting victims forced to inhale second-hand smoke. Criminologists are affected by these kinds of changes because of the creation of new categories of deviants and criminals. Shifts in boundaries relating to normalcy, deviancy, and criminality mean shifts in subject areas of study for criminologists.

Consequences of Boundary Changes

As moral entrepreneurs and activists work toward changing laws, our understanding of behaviours also changes. These changing definitions have consequences for criminology but also, and importantly, for people's lives. In the 1980s, students could smoke in many university classrooms. Imagine your criminology professor lighting up a cigarette as he or she delivers your next lecture! As recently as 1976, individuals convicted of committing murder in Canada could have been executed. Many American states continue to execute convicted murderers.

Canada's youth justice system is another example of the ways in which boundary changes affect lives. Prior to 1908 we didn't have a separate

Adam Trotter, the young offender convicted of manslaughter for the beating death of his fellow inmate, James Lonnee, at the Wellington Detention Centre in Guelph, Ontario, in 1996.

justice system for youths. Rather, children aged seven and older who committed crimes were often dealt with in the same manner as adult criminals. Our first youth justice legislation came into effect in 1908, and since then the Young Offender Act (1984) and the Youth Criminal Justice Act (2003) have influenced the treatment of young people in trouble with the law. Each is informed by a different philosophy that influences the manner in which youth are dealt with.

These types of changes are not just abstract, theoretical, or historical in nature; they have real implications and consequences for us all, and form the basis of research for many criminologists. As boundaries, definitions, and laws change, so do the research activities of criminologists.

By this time, you may be asking, is there no limit to the reach of criminological inquiry? There is not, since every human activity is capable of abusive action, thus requiring criminological scrutiny. Not even the ocean is the limit. It is the oceans, covering nearly three-quarters of the world's surface, that make life on earth possible. Yet the oceans are being threatened by many types of criminality, of which the most deadly is pollution. Consider the case of the supertanker *Exxon Valdez,* which negligently ruptured her hull in Alaska waters, spilling more than 40 million litres of crude oil in 1989. This caused the greatest environmental disaster North America had known. At the time, many expressed the hope that this criminally caused disaster would lead to greater efforts to prevent recurrences. But no. Oil spill disasters that should have been prevented have

occurred with heightening regularity off the coasts of China, South Africa, the Galapagos Islands, the United States, American Samoa, Denmark, Thailand, Brazil, Finland, Germany, the Netherlands, and Vietnam, among other countries.[4] This criminality, destroying the environment, is called "ecocide." There is yet another task for criminologists.

As far as the reach of criminology is concerned, do not be deceived by the media and their symbiotic relationship with legislatures. Today's focus of the media on a given crime problem is no indication of the extent of criminology's tasks. In the 1960s, the emphasis was on juvenile delinquency; in the 1970s, attention turned to street crime in general and drugs, in particular, which led, in the 1980s, to a focus on prison overcrowding, on the one hand, and target hardening, on the other. Then, in the 1990s, more attention was being paid to foreign influences on our crime rates, in the wake of globalization. Domestic violence (such as school shootings) and foreign violence, along with terrorism, dictated the market for ideas, along with the competing attention on computer, white-collar, and corporate criminality. Today, well into the first decade of the twenty-first century, it is clear that these problems demand more of criminology than it is capable of delivering as yet. The principal crime problems are totally globalized. Criminology has to become equally globalized.

Seemingly, we have neglected street crimes in this survey of the reach of criminology. These topics are, and will remain, a major focus of criminologists—in competition with all the other forms of criminality to which we have alluded. Now that you are acquainted with the changing boundaries of criminology, we next introduce you to what this discipline is all about.

WHAT IS CRIMINOLOGY?

In the Middle Ages, human learning was commonly divided into four areas: law, medicine, theology, and philosophy. Universities typically had four faculties, one for each of these fields.

For centuries, all the knowledge the universities recognized continued to be taught in these four faculties. It was not until the eighteenth and nineteenth centuries that the natural and social sciences became full-fledged disciplines. In fact, the science of criminology has been known as such for only a little more than a century.

Smokers—the New Deviants

"Smokers need not apply," ran a classified ad for a job in Ireland this past May [2006].

"Why not?" asked Catherine Stihler, a British Labour party MEP, who posed the question on behalf of one of her constituents. Should women not apply, either? Or homosexuals? Muslims? What about high-functioning alcoholics, or fat people?

The answer, from the European Commission that oversees anti-discrimination legislation in the EU, came back to Stihler [in August 2006]: Smokers are fair game for discrimination.

"A job advertisement saying that 'smokers need not apply' would not seem to fall under any of the prohibited grounds (under EU legislation)," Vladimir Spidla, the commissioner for employment and equal opportunities, wrote to Stihler, who showed the letter to the press.

This would have pleased the employer who placed the ad, call-centre director Philip Tobin, who reportedly told Irish radio in May [2006], "If these people (meaning smokers) can ignore so many warnings and all that evidence then they haven't got the level of intelligence that I am looking for. Smokers are idiots."

In other words, if you're addicted to nicotine, a substance that studies have repeatedly shown to be more difficult to withdraw from than heroin, you're too dumb to answer the phone.

Joni Mitchell need not apply. Kurt Vonnegut doesn't have the brains to say, "How may I help you?" Peter Jennings, thick as a plank. C. S. Lewis, T. S. Eliot, Oscar Wilde, Winston Churchill inferior minds all around.

And we believe this. We've bought into it because health is now the basis of our prejudices. We judge one another's conduct according to how well we maintain ourselves physically.

It isn't confined to smoking. British surgeons have begun to refuse doing certain operations for obese patients. Women who drink more than a glass of wine a day are made to feel they're

Anti-smoking supporters. Increasingly, smokers are being pushed to the margins of society, making them "deviants."

alcoholics. Mothers who choose not to breast-feed are castigated as if they were amoral.

The objective of life, in this health utopia of ours, is to live it as long as possible, in mechanically perfect condition. Compare that to previous utopian cultures, where the objective of life would have been, variously, to be honourable, or spiritually sublime, or warrior-like or, in the case of Communism, a humble devotee of collective economic well-being: an impeccable worker ant.

Every culture with a utopian vision has its officially acknowledged deviants.

The Ontario government's anti-smoking website is addressed http://www.stupid.ca. It's for stupid people. Deviants addicted to nicotine.

The degree to which we have turned an addiction into a moral failing really came home to me [in 2005] when Peter Jennings died of lung cancer. On his last ABC news broadcast, when he announced his diagnosis, he explained to his viewers that he had quit smoking 20 years earlier but had fallen off the wagon after 9/11. He apologized. He actually apologized for dying of cancer.

Imagine if Jennings had said on the air: "I've got lung cancer, but I enjoyed every cigarette I ever smoked, and my life has been really full and interesting. Live fast and die at 67."

It would have been viewed as an apostasy.

Consider, by contrast, how AIDS activists have so successfully turned around

the stigma of their affliction. How someone gay or straight, male or female, young or old contracted HIV doesn't matter. As *The New York Times* reported, in a lead-up to the Toronto AIDS conference, "In 1996 in Vancouver, the audience cheered after a grandmother told the conference: 'How did I get infected? The answer is very simple: It just doesn't matter.'"

How do smokers, young or old, get addicted to nicotine? A [2006] study . . . by McGill University epidemiologist Jennifer O'Loughlin shows that some people are so susceptible to nicotine that they can begin to crave the substance after one cigarette. One cigarette. One shared needle. One night of unprotected sex. It just doesn't matter.

In the last several years, the U.S. has made available to smokers a huge arsenal of nicotine-replacement therapies, such as the lozenge, a nasal spray, and a new pill called Chantix that blocks nicotine reception in the brain, none of which is available in Canada. The Americans run in-patient rehab programs for nicotine addiction. We Canadians run public-service ads in movie theatres specifically produced to demonstrate that smokers are knuckleheads.

Are we seriously committed to helping people wrest free of nicotine? Or are we writing them off as deviants?

What the EU discrimination ruling about the Irish call centre reveals is that the door is wide open for health discrimination in the upcoming decade. Until we snap out of it and realize that there's more to life than its length, we are in for a whole new wave of prejudice.

Source

Reprinted with permission of Patricia Pearson.

Questions for Discussion

1. What influences society's changing definitions of deviance? Why are smokers the new deviants?
2. Should employers be permitted to discriminate against smokers?

In 1885, the Italian law professor Raffaele Garofalo coined the term "criminology" (in Italian, *criminologia*).[5] The French anthropologist Paul Topinard used it for the first time in French (*criminologie*) in 1887.[6] "Criminology" aptly described and encompassed the scientific concern with the phenomenon of crime. The term immediately gained acceptance all over the world, and criminology became a subject taught at universities. Unlike their predecessors in 1434—or even in 1894—today's entering students will find that teaching and learning are distributed among 20 or 30 disciplines and departments. And criminology or criminal justice is likely to be one of them.

Criminology is a science, an empirical science. More particularly, it is one of the social, or behavioural, sciences. It has been defined in various ways by its scholars. The definition provided in 1934 by Edwin H. Sutherland, one of the founding scholars of American criminology, is widely accepted:

> **Criminology** is the body of knowledge regarding crime as a social phenomenon. It includes within its scope the process of making laws, of breaking laws, and of reacting toward the breaking of laws. . . . The objective of criminology is the development of a body of general and verified principles and of other types of knowledge regarding this process of law, crime, and treatment or prevention.[7]

This definition suggests that the field of criminology is narrowly focused on crime, yet broad in scope. By stating as the objective of criminology the "development of a body of general and verified principles," Sutherland mandates that **criminologists,** like all other scientists, collect information for study and analysis in accordance with the research methods of modern science. As we shall see in Chapter 3, it was in the eighteenth century that serious investigations into criminal behaviour were first conducted. The investigators, however, were not engaged in empirical research, although they based their conclusions on factual information. It was only in the nineteenth century that criminologists began to systematically gather facts about crime and criminals and evaluate their data in a scientific manner.

Among the first researchers to analyze empirical data (facts, statistics, and other observable information) in a search for the causes of crime was Cesare Lombroso (1835–1909) of Italy (Chapter 3). His biologically oriented theories influenced American criminology at the turn of the twentieth

century. At that time, the causes of crime were thought to rest within the individual: Criminal behaviour was attributed to feeble-mindedness and "moral insanity." From then on, psychologists and psychiatrists played an important role in the study of crime and criminals.

By the 1920s, other scholars attributed the cause of crime to the influx of immigrants and their alien behaviours. The search then moved on to cultural and social interpretations. Crime was explained not only in terms of the offender but also in terms of social, political, and economic problems.

In increasing numbers, sociologists, political scientists, legal scholars, and economists have entered the arena of criminology. Architects, too, have joined the ranks of criminologists in an effort to design housing units that will be relatively free from crime. Engineers are working to design cars that are virtually theft-proof. Pharmacologists play a role in alleviating the problem of drug addiction. Satellites put into space by astrophysicists can help control the drug trade. Educators have been enlisted to prepare children for a life as free from delinquency as possible. Economists and social workers are needed to help break the cycle of poverty and crime. Biologists and endocrinologists have expanded our understanding of the relationship between biology and deviant behaviour. Geographers develop and use computer programs to help map "hotspots" for criminal behaviour. Police and social control agents then use this information to target these areas with specific enforcement tactics. Clearly, criminology is a discipline composed of the accumulated knowledge of many other disciplines. Criminologists acknowledge their indebtedness to all contributing disciplines, but they consider theirs a separate science.

Criminology in Canada tends to be a subdiscipline of sociology. Sociologists are more involved in the study of social problems than researchers from other disciplines. Because criminology concerns itself with crime and social problems that can lead to crime, the affinity between the two, criminology and sociology, seems appropriate. In Europe, however, the tendency is for criminology to be included in or affiliated with law schools, giving criminology in Europe a more legal orientation. Although criminology has its roots in European scholarship, and has undergone refinements, Canadian criminologists and Canadian criminology schools and

Terrorism Globalized

On September 27, 2005, a Spanish court sentenced a Syrian man to 27 years in prison (the only person sentenced to date) for conspiracy to commit the 9/11 attacks on the World Trade Center and the Pentagon. These attacks of 2001, which killed close to 3000 people, were not the first attacks against the United States. There had been, among others,

- the Olympic Park explosion in Atlanta, Georgia, on July 30, 1996, which killed one person and injured many;
- the Oklahoma City bombing on April 19, 1995, which killed 168;
- the 1993 bombing that tore a hole in the World Trade Center, killing 6.

But Americans were not alone in their victimization by terrorists. While Canada has not witnessed the extent of terrorist attacks that other nations have, our history in this regard is not spotless. Examples include

- the October Crisis of 1970, where the terrorist Quebec nationalist group Front de liberation du Québec (FLQ) kidnapped James Cross, British Trade Commissioner, and Pierre Laporte, Minister of Labour, who was eventually executed; the War Measures Act was invoked during this turbulent period;
- the June 22, 1985, Air India Flight 182 from Canada to India, which blew up, killing all 329 people aboard;

- the December 6, 1989, "Montreal Massacre," in which anti-feminist Marc Lépine opened fire on students at L'École Polytechnique de Montréal, shooting 26 people, killing 14 women.

Internationally, there have been, among others,

- the October 1, 2005, bombings that killed 202 and injured hundreds more as they ate and drank on a Saturday night in the crowded tourist areas on the island of Bali;
- the July 23, 2005, deadly attacks in the Red Sea resort of Sharm El-Sheik, Egypt, where two car bombs and one bomb in a knapsack destroyed an entrance to a beach promenade, a luxury hotel, and a local Egyptian neighbourhood, killing 84 and injuring 200;
- the July 7, 2005, suicide bombing of underground trains and a double-decker bus during the morning rush hour in London, killing 52 and injuring 700;
- the three February 14, 2005, bomb explosions in the Philippines that killed or injured over 100 people in one hour while they were celebrating Valentine's Day;
- the March 11, 2004, bombings of four commuter trains in Madrid during the morning rush hour, killing 191 and wounding over 1000;

Rescue workers search for survivors at the collapsed towers of the World Trade Center after September 11, 2001.

departments have contributed significantly to the discipline. Canadian criminologists work in sociology departments across the country, but also in schools of criminology, such as that at Simon Fraser University. Some of the research in the areas of criminology and criminal justice (which is a specialized area in the discipline that focuses more directly on the operation of the various agencies comprising the criminal justice system) is produced by criminologists who are affiliated with one of the several Centres for Criminological Research in the country. The Centre for Criminological Research at the University of Toronto, for example, produces research on a wide variety of topics.

Canadian criminologists are faced with a number of factors that make Canada unique and that invariably influence their work. Canada, for example, has a much lower rate of violent crime than the United States. The countries differ dramatically when it comes to firearm-related violence. American support for the "right to bear arms," which influences gun control in that country, is also indicative of other differences in values and beliefs between the nations. The United States has a justice system that is much harsher than the Canadian criminal justice system, as is reflected in a rate of incarceration several times higher than the Canadian rate, as well as use of the death penalty in several states. These differences affect Canadian criminologists both in terms of the values and beliefs they hold, but also in the focus of their research efforts, the patterns of criminal behaviours they study, and the causal explanations they develop.

- the July 9, 1999, brutal attack in Moscow that destroyed an apartment building, killing 94.

There was a time when terrorists enjoyed the support, both financial and material, of some foreign governments. That support no longer exists. Very few countries can be counted among the supporters of current terrorist groups.

In 1993, a meeting of over 200 counterterrorism experts and Pentagon officials concluded "that the proliferation of ethnic and regional conflicts will spawn new radical movements, leading inevitably to new terrorism." "We're going to see a global increase in anarchy," said one U.S. Defense Department analyst. Some at the meeting worried about what they term "mass terrorism," like that spawned by ethnic conflicts. Others were more concerned about what they are calling "single-issue" terrorism, attacks by radicals who share no ideology, only the hatred for a particular enemy.(1) The experts were right. Their conclusions, unfortunately, became reality.

Source

1. Douglas Waller, "Counterterrorism: Victim of Success?" Newsweek, July 5, 1993, pp. 22–23.

The deadly explosions that destroyed two popular nightclubs on the Indonesian resort island of Bali in 2002 comprise the worst single terrorist attack since September 11, 2001. The Bali bombings killed more than 200 people, a vast majority of whom were young Australians. Injuries exceeded 300. According to witnesses, many of the victims were burned beyond recognition or destroyed entirely by the bomb blasts.

Questions for Discussion

1. International terrorism is a criminal activity that can involve an almost limitless number of specific crimes, individuals, and countries. How would you devise a strategy to combat it at the national and international levels?

2. How would you go about studying trends in terrorism and the impact of terrorist attacks on society and the economy?

Criminologists in Canada are also influenced by regional differences within the country. As we discuss in the next chapter, crime patterns vary between, for example, the Prairies and the Maritimes, and between the West Coast and Central Canada. These differences influence the focus of criminological study and permit regional comparisons and theories about regional influences on crime causation. Perhaps the most significant regional difference that has a direct impact on criminological study is that between Quebec and the rest of the country. The province, known for its cultural distinctiveness, retains a civil legal system for issues of private law. Criminologists have long documented the differences in crime patterns between Quebec and the other provinces, as well as the significantly different manner in which Quebec treats its offenders.

Throughout this book, as we discuss "the making of laws," the "breaking of laws," and "reacting toward the breaking of laws," we will draw on Canadian scholarship and examples.

THE MAKING OF LAWS

Conjure up a picture of a crowded supermarket just after working hours when most people are eager to get home after a busy day. The checkout counters have long lines of carts overflowing with groceries. One counter—an express line—takes 10 items only. You have 15, but you get in line anyway. People behind you in the line stare. Your behaviour is not acceptable. You are a non-conformist, a deviant.

Deviance

Criminologists use the term **deviance** to describe behaviour that violates **social norms,** including laws. The customary ways of doing everyday things (like not exceeding the posted limit of items at supermarket express lines) are governed by norms other than laws. More serious deviant behaviour, like taking someone else's property, is governed by laws. Criminologists are interested in all social norms and in how society reacts to success or failure of compliance.[8] They are interested in what society does when customary ways of doing things no longer prove effective in controlling conduct perceived as undesirable. Canadians living in urban centres concerned over the problem of dog droppings provide an example.

Disciplined city dwellers had always observed the custom of curbing their dogs. But as more and more dog owners failed to comply, the cleanliness of sidewalks in cities became an important issue. Laws were enacted making it an offence not to clean up after one's dog. The current maximum penalty for failing to "stoop and scoop" in Toronto is $5000. In Beijing, China, and Reykjavik, Iceland, dogs have been severely restricted or banned from the city altogether.

The difference between crime and other forms of deviance is subject to constant change and may vary from one country to another and from one time to another. What yesterday was only distasteful or morally repugnant may today be illegal. Criminologists are therefore interested in all norms that regulate conduct. Making something that is distasteful into a crime may be counterproductive and detrimental to the social order. If everything deviant (inconsistent with the majority's norms) were to be made criminal, society would become very rigid. The more rigid a society, the more that behaviour defined as violating social norms is prohibited by law.

Jack D. Douglas and Frances C. Waksler have presented the continuum of deviance as a funnel (Figure 1.1). This funnel consists of definitions ranging from the broadest (a "feeling that something is vaguely wrong, strange, peculiar") to the narrowest (a "judgment that something is absolutely evil"). Somewhere between these two extremes, deviant behaviour becomes criminal behaviour. The criminologist's interest in understanding the process begins at the earliest point—when a behaviour is first labelled "deviant."[9]

Although criminologists are interested in all deviant behaviour—even that of no interest to the law—their primary interest is in criminal behaviour, that which violates the law.

The Concept of Crime

A **crime** is any human conduct that violates a criminal law and is subject to punishment. What leads a society to designate some deviant behaviour as a

FIGURE 1.1 The funnel of deviance.

Most inclusive

    I. Feeling that something is vaguely wrong, strange, peculiar
   II. Feelings of dislike, repugnance
  III. Feeling that something violates values or rules
  IV. Feeling that something violates moral values or moral rules
   V. Judgment that something violates values or rules
  VI. Judgment that something violates moral values or moral rules
 VII. Judgment that something violates morally legitimate misdemeanour laws
VIII. Judgment that something violates morally legitimate felony laws
  IX. Judgment that something violates moral human nature
   X. Judgment that something is absolutely evil

Least inclusive

Source: Adapted from Jack D. Douglas and Frances C. Waksler, *The Sociology of Deviance* (Boston: Little, Brown, 1980), p. 11. Copyright © 1982 by Jack D. Douglas and Frances Chaput Waksler. Reprinted by permission of the authors.

crime and leave other wrongs to be settled by private or civil remedies? For centuries, natural-law philosophers, believing in the universal rightness and wrongness of certain human behaviour, held the view that some forms of behaviour are innately criminal and that all societies condemn them equally. Homicide and theft were thought to be among these.

This notion is no longer supported. Raffaele Garofalo, who gave our discipline its name, defended the concept of natural crime, by which he meant behaviour that offends basic moral sentiments, such as respect for the property of others and revulsion against infliction of suffering. Nevertheless, he admitted that although we might think such crimes as murder and robbery would be recognized by all existing legal systems, "a slight investigation seems to dispel this idea."[10]

The Code of Hammurabi, king of ancient Babylonia, is the oldest complete legal code in existence (approximately 1750 B.C.). The 2.5-metre carving, found in Iraq in 1902, is now on display in the Louvre in Paris. The only exact replica is at the United Nations building in New York.

Garofalo was right. The earliest codes, including the Babylonian Code of Hammurabi (about 1750 B.C.) and the Roman Law of the Twelve Tables (451–450 B.C.), do not list homicide or ordinary theft as crimes. Problems like these were settled without resorting to punishment. But all early societies imposed punishment for acts detrimental to their own existence: treason. Other crimes depended on socioeconomic needs (destroying a bridge was a crime among the Incas; stealing a beehive was a crime among the ancient Germanic tribes; stealing a horse or a blanket was a crime among American Plains Indians).

> **Did You Know?**
>
> . . . that in the early days of the common law, judges made the laws? Legislatures (parliament) took over law-making only about three centuries ago.

The question arises: Who in a society decides— and when and under what circumstances—which acts that are already considered deviant in that society should be elevated to the level of gross deviance or crime, subject to punishment?

The Consensus and Conflict Views of Law and Crime

In the traditional interpretation of the historical development of legal systems, and of criminal justice in particular, law-making is an accommodation of interests in a society, whether that society is composed of equals (as in a democracy) or of rulers and ruled (as in absolute monarchies), so as to produce a system of law and enforcement to which

everybody basically subscribes. This is the **consensus model**. According to this view, certain acts are deemed so threatening to the society's survival that they are designated crimes. If the vast majority of a group shares this view, we can say the group has acted by consensus.

The model assumes that members of a society by and large agree on what is right and wrong, and that codification of social values becomes law, with a mechanism of control that settles disputes that arise when some individuals stray too far from what is considered acceptable behaviour. In the words of the famous French sociologist Émile Durkheim, "we can . . . say that an act is criminal when it offends strong and defined states of the collective conscience."[11] Consensus theorists view society as a stable entity in which laws are created for the general good. Laws function to reconcile and to harmonize most of the interests that most of us accept, with the least amount of sacrifice.

To a large extent the consensus model is applicable in the Canadian context. Most Canadians would likely agree that a pedophile should be punished for his crimes. The vast majority of Canadians would also agree that first-degree murder warrants severe punishment. People who premeditate the taking of another's life should go to jail for a very long time. There is, then, consensus, particularly with certain types of crime. However, the consensus model loses some of its explanatory power when we discuss certain "morality"-based crimes. We find much less consensus among Canadians when we consider laws surrounding prostitution, gambling, pornography, and the use and distribution of certain substances. When looking at these latter examples, we are led to ask how and why laws regulating these behaviours were passed when consensus is clearly lacking.

It is through the use of a different theoretical perspective, the **conflict model,** that we can more adequately answer these questions. From the perspective of the conflict model, the criminal law expresses the values of the ruling class in a society, and the criminal justice system is a means of controlling the classes that have no power. Conflict theorists claim that a struggle for power is a far more basic feature of human existence than is consensus. It is through power struggles that various interest groups manage to control law-making and law enforcement. Think about the current debate surrounding decriminalization of marijuana, or the move toward the "criminalization" of smoking cigarettes in public places. Accordingly, the appropriate object of criminological investigation is not the violation of laws but the conflicts within society.

Traditional historians of crime and criminal justice do not deny that throughout history there have been conflicts that needed resolution. Traditionalists claim that differences have been resolved by consensus, while conflict theorists claim that the dominant group has ended the conflicts by imposing its will. This difference in perspective marks one of the major criminological debates today, as we shall see in Chapter 8. It also permeates criminological discussion of who breaks the criminal laws and why.

THE BREAKING OF LAWS

Sutherland's definition of criminology includes within its scope investigating and explaining the process of breaking laws. This may seem simple if viewed from a purely legal perspective. A Crown prosecutor is not interested in the fact that hundreds of people are walking on Main Street. But if one of those hundreds grabs a woman's purse and runs away with it, the Crown prosecutor is interested, provided the police have brought the incident to the prosecutor's attention. What alerts the prosecutor is the fact that a law has been broken, that one of those hundreds of people on Main Street has turned from a law-abiding citizen into a lawbreaker. This event, if detected, sets in motion a legal process that ultimately will determine whether someone is indeed a lawbreaker.

Sutherland, in saying that criminologists have to study the process of law-breaking, had much more in mind than determining whether or not someone has violated the criminal law. He was referring to the process of breaking laws. That process encompasses a series of events, perhaps starting at birth or even earlier, which results in the commission of crime by some individuals and not by others.

Let us analyze the following rather typical scenario: In the maximum-security Stony Mountain Correctional Facility is an inmate we will call Rob. He is one of three robbers who held up a cheque-cashing establishment. During the robbery, another of the robbers killed the clerk. Rob has been sentenced to life imprisonment.

Born on a reserve near Winnipeg, Rob was the third child of an unwed mother. He had a succession of temporary "fathers." By age 12, he had run away from home for the first time, only to be brought back to his mother, who really did not care much whether he returned or not. He rarely went to school because, he said, "all the guys were bigger." At age 16, after failing two grades, Rob dropped out of school completely and hung around the streets of his deteriorated, crime-ridden neighbourhood. He had no job. He had no reason to go home, since usually no one was there.

One night he was beaten up by members of a local gang, the Indian Posse. He joined a rival gang, the Manitoba Warriors, for protection and soon began to feel proud of his membership in one of the toughest gangs in the province. Caught on one occasion vandalizing a vacant apartment building and on another trying to steal a car CD player, he was sentenced to two months in a young offender centre in the nearby city. By the age of 18, he had moved from petty theft to armed robbery.

Many people reading the story of Rob would conclude that he deserves what is coming to him and that his fate should serve as a warning to others. Other people would say that with his background, Rob did not have a chance. Some may even marvel at Rob's ability to survive at all in a very tough world.

To the criminologist, popular interpretations of Rob's story do not explain the process of breaking laws in Sutherland's terms. Nor do these interpretations explain why people in general break a certain law. Sutherland demanded scientific rigour in researching and explaining the process of breaking laws. As we will see later in the book (Parts II and III), scientists have thoroughly

Life Sentences for Juveniles?

Fourteen-year-old Reena Virk was a troubled British Columbia teen whose life ended tragically on Friday, November 14, 1997, when she was swarmed by eight teens, seven girls and one boy. She was repeatedly punched, kicked, and hit. Her attackers attempted to set her hair on fire and reportedly a cigarette was stubbed out on her forehead. After the beating, Virk managed to walk away, but was followed, beaten again, and ultimately drowned by two members of the group. While all of the attackers received some form of punishment, the two individuals, Kelly Ellard and Warren Glowatski, who finished the attack, received the harshest sentences: Both were charged with second-degree murder. Glowatski, the only boy among the accused, was convicted in June 1999 and sentenced to life in prison with no chance of parole for seven years. Ellard, in April 2000, received a life sentence after being convicted in adult court of second-degree murder. The decision was overturned, Ellard was retried, and was at one point released on bail and rearrested for assaulting a 58-year-old woman. Most recently, on April 12, 2005, she was found guilty and given an automatic life sentence.

On Boxing Day, 2005, 15-year-old Jane Creba was caught in gang-related crossfire and killed while holiday shopping in downtown Toronto; six others were injured. In June 2006, eight people were arrested for the Boxing Day shootings, two of whom were young people. One of the youths was charged with second-degree murder and six counts of attempted murder; another youth was charged with manslaughter in connection with the Boxing Day incident.

In Laval, Quebec, a 17-year-old will serve a life sentence as an adult for his role as ringleader of a group of teens that "pummelled, punched, pepper-sprayed, and stabbed" 19-year-old Sébastien Lacasse at a house party. The offender, who pleaded guilty to second-degree murder, was described as having little chance of being rehabilitated in a youth detention centre by the judge dealing with the case. The teen faces a minimum of ten years behind bars. If he had been sentenced as a young offender, he would have spent a minimum of four years in a youth detention centre.

As you already know, Sutherland's definition of criminology tells us that the science encompasses the making and breaking of and the reaction to the breaking of laws. Let us demonstrate using the preceding cases:

The *breaking of laws:* In all three cases, laws were broken. All three cases involved homicides. Criminology seeks to answer why the offenders committed the crimes.

The *making of laws:* These cases involve questions about laws that allow young offenders to be sentenced as adults. Is sentencing a 17-year-old to a minimum of ten years in the adult prison system beneficial to society?

The *reaction to the breaking of laws:* There are many conflicting reactions. Long sentences, and cases where young offenders are sentenced as adults, often please politicians and prosecutors who are concerned with their public image as crime fighters. Victims' families often applaud adult sentences for young offenders as well, hoping that the message is sent to other potential young offenders that they

will be held responsible for their actions. It appears that the general public seems satisfied to prohibit minors below 18 to vote, serve on a jury, or even gamble in a casino, yet it's acceptable to let them spend their life in prison. Once again, it is criminologists who need to determine whether society can bear the cost of such a policy.

Sources

1. Canadian Broadcasting Corporation (CBC) News, "Young Offender Gets Adult Sentence for Murder," September 7, 2006, www.cbc.ca/canada/montreal/story/2006/09/07, accessed April 12, 2007.
2. *The Epoch Times,* "Police Make Arrests in Boxing Day Killing," Reuters, June 13, 2006, http://en.epochtimes.com, accessed March 26, 2007.
3. Adam Liptak, "Jailed for Life after Crimes as Teenagers," *New York Times,* Oct. 3, 2005, www.nytimes.com/2005/10/03/national/03lifers.html.
4. CBC News, "The Murder of Reena Virk: A Timeline," July 20, 2004, www.cbc.ca.news/background/virk/, accessed April 12, 2007.
5. "Reena Virk," http://en.wikipedia.org/w/index.php?title=Reena_Virk/, accessed April 3, 2007.

Questions for Discussion

1. What are the pros and cons of adult and life sentences in prison for young offenders?
2. How should society deal with young people who commit murder?

---

explored Rob's story and the stories of other lawbreakers. They ask, Why are some people prone to commit crime and others are not? There is no agreement on the answer as yet. Researchers have approached the question from different perspectives. Some have examined young offenders and criminals from a biological perspective in order to determine whether some human beings are constitutionally more prone to yield to opportunities to commit criminal acts. Are genes to blame? Hormones? Diet? Others have explored the role played by moral development and personality. Is there a criminal personality? (These questions are discussed in Chapter 4.) Still others would look at Rob's ethnicity and ask questions concerning the discrimination against Aboriginal peoples that exists within the Canadian criminal justice system and that contributes to their overrepresentation at every stage in the criminal justice process.

Most contemporary criminologists look to such factors as economic and social conditions, which can produce strain among social groups and lead to law-breaking (Chapter 5). Others point to subcultures committed to violent or illegal activities (Chapter 6). Yet another argument is that the motivation to commit crime is simply part of human nature. So some criminologists examine the ability of social groups and institutions to make their rules effective (Chapter 7).

The findings of other scholars tend to show that law-breaking depends less on what the offender does than on what society, including the criminal justice system, does to the offender (Chapter 8). This is the perspective of the labelling, conflict, and radical theorists, who have had great influence on criminological thinking since the 1970s.

Scholars have also researched the question of why people who are inclined to break laws engage in particular acts at particular times. They have demonstrated that opportunity plays a great role in the decision to commit a crime. Opportunities are suitable targets inadequately protected. In these circumstances, all that is required for a crime to be committed is a person motivated to offend. These claims are made by criminologists who explain crime in terms of two perspectives: routine activities and rational choice (Chapter 9).

SOCIETY'S REACTION TO THE BREAKING OF LAWS

Criminologists' interest in understanding the process of breaking a law (or any other social norm) is tied to understanding society's reaction to deviance. The study of reactions to law-breaking demonstrates that society has always tried to control or prevent norm-breaking.

In the Middle Ages, the wayfarer entering a city had to pass the gallows, on which the bodies of criminals swung in the wind. Wayfarers had to enter through gates in thick walls, and the drawbridges were lowered only during the daylight hours; at nightfall the gates were closed. In front of the town hall, stocks and pillory warned dishonest vendors and pickpockets. Times have changed, but perhaps less than we think. Today correctional facilities exist within or on the outskirts of many cities in Canada. Signs proclaim "Drug-Free School Zone," and decals on doors announce

"Neighbourhood Crime Watch." Police patrol cars are as visible as they are audible. Some Canadian cities display police "bait car" signs, daring potential car thieves to chance stealing the "wrong" car.

These overt signs of concern about crime provide us with only a surface view of the apparatus society has created to deal with law-breaking; they tell us little of the research and policy making that have gone into the creation of the apparatus. Criminologists have done much of the research on society's reaction to the breaking of laws, and the results have influenced policy making and legislation aimed at crime control. The research has also revealed that society's reaction to law-breaking has often been irrational, arbitrary, emotional, politically motivated, and counterproductive.

Research on society's reaction to the breaking of laws is more recent than research on the causes of crime. It is also more controversial. For some criminologists, the function of their research is to assist government in the prevention or repression of crime. Others insist that such a use of science only supports existing power structures that may be corrupt. Whether their work is used to support and improve it, or to question its operation and suggest alternatives, many criminologists focus their research efforts on the Canadian **criminal justice system.**

Criminology and the Criminal Justice System

The term "criminal justice system" is relatively new. The discovery that various ways of dealing with law-breaking form a system was itself the result of criminological research. Research into the functioning of the system and its component parts, as well as into the work of functionaries within the system, has provided many insights over the last few decades.

Scientists who study the criminal justice system are frequently referred to as "criminal justice specialists." This term suggests a separation between criminology and criminal justice. In fact, the two fields are closely interwoven. Scholars of both disciplines use the same scientific research methods. They have received the same rigorous education, and they pursue the same goals. Both fields rely on the cooperation of many other disciplines, including sociology, psychology, political science, law, economics, management, and education. Their origins, however, do differ. Criminology has its roots in European scholarship; criminal justice is a recent American innovation.

The two fields are also distinguished by a difference in focus. Criminology generally focuses on scientific studies of crime and criminality, whereas criminal justice focuses on scientific studies of decision-making processes, and the collection of statistics on criminal justice system operations, and such justice-related concerns as the efficiency of police, courts, and corrections systems; the just treatment of offenders; the needs of victims; and the effects of changes in sentencing philosophy. Some criminologists rely on the data collected by criminal justice system agencies to conduct their scientific studies. Both fields, criminology and criminal justice, are united in that their underlying foundation is the criminal law.

Canadian criminal law has its roots in English common law. Under the British North American Act of 1867, the federal government was given law-making power; the provinces were granted responsibility for administering the law. The criminal justice system in Quebec, however, is different and operates under a civil law system. In 1892 English common law was codified into the Criminal Code of Canada (CCC), which has determined criminal justice in Canada ever since. The Criminal Code of Canada undergoes changes as judges set precedents through their decisions, and as laws are created to reflect changing moral and political climates. For example, in 1983 the crime of "rape" was transformed into a new category termed "sexual assault" to reflect the violence involved in sexual offences. In fact, three categories of sexual assault were created to reflect the different levels of violence that can occur during the commission of these offences. In addition, the CCC was changed to reflect the fact that some husbands sexually assault their wives. Up until this time, husbands technically could not be charged for such behaviour. As laws are created or modified, there are implications for the functioning of the criminal justice system in the provinces: They must adapt to the changes and enforce them accordingly. Increasingly, however, Canadians are affected by the criminal behaviours not only of their fellow citizens but also by international or transnational criminals. It is necessary, therefore, to place the topic of making, breaking, and reacting to the breaking of laws into perspective; specifically, we need to look at how globalization affects criminology.

The Global Approach to the Breaking of Laws

Until fairly recently, there was rarely any need to cooperate with foreign governments, because crime had few international connections. This situation has changed drastically: Crime, like life itself, has become globalized, and responses to law-breaking have inevitably extended beyond local and national borders. In the first three and a half decades after World War II, from 1945 until the late 1970s, the countries of the world gradually became more interdependent. Commercial relations among countries increased. The jet age brought a huge increase in international travel and transport. Satellite communications facilitated intense and continuous public and private relationships. The Internet added the final touch to globalization.

Beginning in the 1980s, the internationalization of national economies accelerated sharply, and with the collapse of communism in Eastern Europe in the 1990s, a global economy is being created. These developments, which turned the world into what has been called a "global village," have also had considerable negative consequences. As everything else in life became globalized, so did crime. Transnational crimes suddenly boomed. Then there are the truly international crimes—those that are

In 2005 Karl Toft completed a 13-year sentence for sexually assaulting 18 boys at a New Brunswick Youth Training Centre from the mid-1960s to the 1980s. When he was moved to a halfway house in Edmonton in 2002 to complete his sentence, his presence in the city caused concern among citizens who believed he was at risk to reoffend.

proscribed by international law—such as crimes against the peace and security of humanity, genocide, and war crimes. But even many apparently purely local crimes, whether local drug crime or handgun violence, now have international dimensions. In view of the rapid globalization of crime, we devote an entire chapter (Chapter 14) to the international dimensions of criminology. In addition, a "Window to the World" box in each chapter explores the international implications of various topics. Before we explore the international aspects of crime, we should first discuss how criminology influences global and local policy that affects, and is affected by, our understanding of crime, reactions to it, and its prevention.

RESEARCH INFORMS POLICY

Skeptics often ask: With so many criminologists at work and so many studies conducted over the last half century, why do we have so much crime, why is some of it increasing, and why do new forms of crime emerge constantly? There are several answers. Crime rates go up and down. Through the 1990s and recently, crime has actually been decreasing. The popular perception that the crime problem is increasing rests on a fear of crime that is fuelled by media portrayals. Obviously, the various elements of the mass media are very competitive, and such competitiveness determines the focus on crime. Sensational reports often sell newspapers and TV programs. Politicians, in turn, seek security in office by catering to public perceptions of crime, rather than to its reality. They therefore propose and enact measures that respond to popular demands and that often are more symbolic than result-oriented. At the moment, this means ever harsher and more punitive measures for dealing with the crime problem.

Few criminologists believe that at present enough research exists to justify such an approach. In fact, some criminological research demonstrates the futility of escalating punishments and often points to measures of quite a different nature as more promising, more humane, and more cost-beneficial. So why do criminologists not make themselves heard? The answer is that criminologists are social scientists, not politicians. Criminologists are not voted into governments. Yet criminologists have served on a variety of federal commissions and have participated in studies dealing with problems of crime or criminal justice. But criminologists cannot dictate national or provincial crime-control policies. They can, however, provide pertinent research findings that inform national policy making.[12] In subsequent chapters that deal with the causes of crime, we continue this discussion under the heading "Theory Informs Policy."

REVIEW

1. How do the boundaries of criminology change?
Very little happens on earth that does not concern **criminology** (p. 9). **Criminologists** (p. 9) study behaviour that violates all **social norms** (p. 12), including laws. Explaining **deviance** (p. 12) and criminal behaviours also means taking into account the activities of **moral entrepreneurs** (p. 5); interest groups; social, political, economic, and historical contexts; and public opinion. It means considering the role played by the media, as well as scientific advancements and international factors that influence our understanding of appropriate human behaviours. The province of criminology today is the entire world: Every aspect of life, including crime, has become increasingly globalized in recent years as a result of both rapid advances in technology and economic integration.

2. Who are criminologists and what do they do?
Criminology as a science is only a century old. Edwin H. Sutherland provided the most widely accepted definition:
"The body of knowledge regarding crime as a social phenomenon. It includes within its scope the process of making laws, of breaking laws, and of reacting toward the breaking of laws." Criminologists come from a variety of backgrounds and disciplines but are united in their focus on the topics listed by Sutherland years ago.

3. What influences the ways in which laws are created?
Criminologists distinguish between two conflicting views of the history of criminal law: the **consensus model** (p. 13), which regards law-making as the result of communal agreement about what is to be prohibited, and the **conflict model** (p. 14), according to which laws are imposed by those with power over those without power.

4. What causes people to break the law?
The breaking of laws (the subject to which much of this book is devoted) is not merely a formal act that may lead to arrest and prosecution, but an intricate process by which some people violate some laws under some

circumstances. Many disciplines contribute to understanding the process of breaking laws or other norms, but as yet there is no consensus on why people become criminals. Society has always reacted to law-breaking, although the scientific study of law-breaking is of very recent origin.

5. How do societies deal with lawbreakers?

Today criminologists analyze the methods and procedures society uses in reacting to **crime** (p. 12); they evaluate the success or failure of such methods, and on the basis of their research, they propose more effective ways of controlling crime.

Criminologists have discovered that the various agencies society has created to deal with law-breaking constitute a system that, like any other system, can be made more efficient. Research on the **criminal justice system** (p. 16) depends on the availability of a variety of data, especially statistics. The gathering and analysis of statistics on crime and criminal justice are among the primary tasks of some criminologists. The effectiveness of their work depends on reliable data.

6. How do criminologists influence policy changes?

Criminology is a politically sensitive discipline. Its findings inform public policy. While criminologists cannot dictate what the various levels of government—municipal, provincial, and federal—should do about crime, their research findings are increasingly being used in making governmental decisions.

CRIMINOLOGY & PUBLIC POLICY

Crime waves always carry with them calls for more law enforcement authority. The September 11, 2001, terrorist attack on American soil was, among other things, a crime wave—that one day caused the number of homicides in the United States in 2001 to be 20 percent higher than the year before. It is no surprise, then, that even before the fires in the rubble that was the World Trade Center burned out, politicians in both the U.S. and Canada were calling for broader powers for law enforcement and greater restrictions on citizens, all in the effort to fight this particular crime wave.

Law enforcement authority varies with the nature and size of the crime problems police must combat, and with changes in the definition, perception, and understanding of crime. A glance at the recent history of criminal procedure shows as much. Most legal restrictions on policing date from the criminal procedure revolution of the 1960s, which itself can be seen as a consequence of the low-crime 1950s. Higher crime rates led to cutbacks in those legal protections in the 1970s and 1980s, just as lower crime rates have led to some expansion in the past few years. In the wake of the September 11 attacks, both Canadian and U.S. governments increased restrictions on citizens. The Canadian government fast-tracked changes to its immigration law, which resulted in policies that permit indefinite detention of immigrants and refugees suspected of a variety of behaviours, even if there is little concrete evidence to support the charges. Accusations of racial profiling have increased, with certain groups (particularly Muslims) being targeted for their "suspicious activities." Canadians generally have been affected by stricter controls relating to air travel, including an increased list of restricted carry-on items, more invasive search procedures, and the necessity of providing a passport when travelling to the United States.

Laws and their enforcement vary with crime as they must if the law is to reflect a sensible balance between the social need for order and individuals' desire for privacy and liberty. The terrorist attacks on New York and Washington raised the demands on law enforcement. Those increased demands have led to some increases in law enforcers' legal authority, and that trend will likely continue, at least for awhile. (*Sources:* Lori Wilkinson, "Are Human Rights Jeopardized in 21st Century Canada? An Examination of Immigration Policies Post 9/11, in *Security vs. Freedom: Playing a Zero-Sum Game in the Post-9/11 Era,* ed. Sandra Rollings-Magnuson [Halifax: Fernwood, 2008]"; William J. Stuntz, "Local Policing after Terror." Reprinted by permission of The Yale Law Journal Company and William S. Hein Company from the *Yale Law Journal,* 111, 2002: 2137.)

Questions for Discussion Sutherland's broad definition of criminology (see p. 9) includes a critical examination of the criminal justice response to crimes. Following the spirit of his definition, how does our current moral and political climate influence the creation and enforcement of laws? What are the "hot topics" regarding crime and public policy today? How should we deal with things like hate crime, terrorism, and the decriminalization of certain substances? How much freedom are you willing to give up in the name of law enforcement?

YOU BE THE CRIMINOLOGIST

How would you teach the ideal course on criminology? (Don't answer until you have completed the course!)

Visit the Online Learning Centre: www.mcgrawhill.ca/olc/adler

COUNTING CRIME AND MEASURING CRIMINAL BEHAVIOUR

CHAPTER **2**

CHAPTER QUESTIONS

1. What elements are common to all crimes?

2. What are some of the legal defences to crime?

3. How does the typology of crime used in this text compare to other crime typologies?

4. How do criminologists measure crime?

5. How much crime is there?

6. What do we know about crime trends?

7. What are some characteristics of criminals?

Many large police departments employ policing models that emphasize community-connectedness. The use of "intelligence-led" practices that are based in the collection and analysis of crime data facilitate effective deployment of officers to areas that appear to require police attention.

In one of many versions of Aesop's fable about the three blind men and the elephant, a circus comes to town, and the residents of a home for the blind are invited to "experience" an elephant. When one blind man is led to the elephant, he touches one of its legs. He feels its size and shape. Another man happens to touch the tail, and still another feels the trunk. Back at their residence, they argue about the nature of the beast. Says the first man, "An elephant is obviously like the trunk of a tree." "No," says the second, "it's like a rope." "You're both wrong," says the third. "An elephant is like a big snake." All three are partly right, for each has described the part of the animal he has touched.

Assessment of the nature and extent of crime often suffers from the same shortcomings as the three blind men's assessments of the elephant. Researcher A may make assessments on the basis of arrest records. Researcher B may rely on conviction rates to describe crime. Researcher C may use the number of convicts serving prison sentences. None of the researchers, however, may be in a position to assess the full nature and extent of crime; each is limited by the kinds of data he or she uses.

Questions about how crime is measured and what those measurements reveal about the nature and extent of crime are among the most important issues in contemporary criminology. Researchers, theorists, and practitioners need information in order to explain and prevent crime and to operate agencies that deal with the crime problem. We begin this chapter with an explanation of the ingredients that all crimes share. We then look at the objectives and methods of collecting information on specific types of crimes. Next, we will consider the limitations of the information sources criminologists most frequently use to estimate the nature and extent of crime in Canada. We then explore measurement of the characteristics of crimes and criminals.

THE LEGAL INGREDIENTS OF A CRIME

For a particular act to qualify as a crime, several elements must occur. First and foremost, the law must define the act or behaviour as criminal. In order for the state to prove that a crime occurred and that the accused is responsible, the prosecution must show that the accused engaged in the guilty act, referred to as *actus reus,* and had the intent, or *mens rea,* to commit the act. For most crimes, both the actus reus and mens rea must be present for the act to be considered a crime.

Actus Reus

Law scholars have long agreed that one fundamental ingredient of every crime is a voluntary human act. The law is interested only in an act (*actus*) that is guilty, evil, and prohibited (*reus*). In this context, what is an "act"? Suppose a sleepwalker, in a trance, grabs a stone and hurls it at a passerby, with lethal consequences. The law does not consider this event to be a voluntary act; before any human behaviour can qualify as an act, there must be a conscious interaction between mind and body, a physical movement that results from the determination or effort of the actor. If Bob picks up a gun and shoots Mike in the head, a physical act has occurred; Bob has committed a crime. But if the shooting occurred when Bob was sleepwalking, he will not be held criminally liable. Thus a reflex or convulsion, a bodily movement that occurs during unconsciousness or sleep, conduct that occurs during hypnosis or results from hypnotic suggestion, or a bodily movement that is not determined by the actor, as when somebody is pushed by another person, are behaviours that are not considered voluntary acts.[1] It is only when choices are overpoweringly influenced by forces beyond our control that the law will consider behaviour irrational and beyond its reach.

Act versus Status The criminal law, in principle, does not penalize anyone for a status or condition. Suppose the law made it a crime to be more than 1.8 metres tall or to have red hair. Or suppose the law made it a crime to be a member of the family of an army deserter or to be of a given religion or ethnic background. That was exactly the situation in the Soviet Union under Stalin's penal code, which made it a crime to be related to a deserter from the Red Army.[2]

There is thus more to the act requirement than the issue of a behaviour's being voluntary and rational: There is the problem of distinguishing between act and status. In Canada, *being* a prostitute is not illegal. What *is* illegal is "communicating for the purposes of prostitution" (section 213 of the Criminal Code of Canada).

Failure to Act The act requirement has yet another aspect. An act requires the interaction of mind and body. If only the mind is active and the body does not move, we do not have an act: Just thinking about punching someone in the nose is not a crime. We are free to think. But if we carry a thought into physical action, we commit an act, which may be a crime.

Then there is the problem of omission, or failure to act. If the law requires that convicted sex offenders register with the police, and such a person decides not to fill out the registration form, that person is guilty of a crime by omission. But he has acted! He told his hand not to pick up that pen, not to fill out the form. Inaction may be action when the law clearly spells out what one has to do and one decides not to do it.

The law in Canada imposes no duty to be a Good Samaritan, to offer help to another person in distress. The law requires action only if one has a legal duty to act. Lifeguards, for example, are contractually obligated to save bathers from drowning; parents are obligated by law to protect their children; law enforcement officers and firefighters are required to rescue people in distress.

> **Did You Know?**
>
> . . . that the concept of guilt (guilty mind, mens rea) is so central to our sense of justice that we symbolized it in the pre-Christian era with the goddess of justice (*Justitia*) and her scales—to measure guilt and punishment? In the Christian era, Justitia became a symbol of justice, sometimes referred to as a saint, but certainly no longer a goddess. She is now the lady justice.

Mens Rea: The "Guilty Mind" Requirement

Every crime, according to legal tradition, requires **mens rea,** a "guilty mind." To be convicted of a criminal offence, it must be proven that the

The posting of "pooper-scooper" regulations has had its effect. Many city residents consider the failure to "pick up" to be a sign of disrespect and a violation of custom.

accused carried out the act intentionally, knowingly, and willingly. If Bob intended to shoot Mike and kill him and proceeded to point the loaded gun at Mike's head and pull the trigger, not only is actus reus present, but so is mens rea: the intent to kill Mike. The definition of intent, however, also includes cases of recklessness or negligence, where the accused is held to a standard of what a responsible person would think. Anyone who violently attacks another person, takes another's property, invades another's home, forces intercourse, or forges a signature on someone else's cheque knows rather well that he or she is doing something wrong. All these examples of mens rea entail an intention to achieve harm or a knowledge that the prohibited harm will result.

For some crimes, however, less than a definite intention suffices: reckless actions by which the actors consciously risk causing a prohibited harm (for example, the driver who races down a rain-slicked highway or the employer who sends his employees to work without safety equipment, knowing full well that lives are thereby being endangered). Using a rifle for target practice behind a school yard at recess, and in the process firing off a shot that hits a child is not something a reasonable person would do. Although the shooter may not have intended to kill the child, he or she acted recklessly and therefore can be held accountable for the crime.

Strict liability is an exception to the mens rea requirement. There is a class of offences for which legislatures or courts require no showing of criminal intent or mens rea. These offences are considered public welfare offences and generally apply to statutes other than the Criminal Code. For these offences, the fact that the actor makes an innocent mistake and proceeds in good faith does not affect criminal liability. Strict-liability offences range all the way from distributing adulterated food to running a red light. Typically, these offences are subject to small penalties only, but in a few cases, substantial punishments can be and have been imposed.

The Concurrence Requirement

The concurrence requirement states that the criminal act must be accompanied by an equally criminal mind. Suppose a striker throws a stone at an office window in order to shatter it, and a broken piece of glass pierces the throat of a secretary, who bleeds to death. Wanting to damage property deserves condemnation, but of a far lesser degree than wanting to kill. Act and intent did not concur in this case, and the striker should not be found guilty of murder.

Indictable and Summary Offences

The nature and severity of punishments also help us differentiate between grades of crime. In Canada there are two main categories of criminal offences distinguished by the procedure for dealing with the accused and the penalty dispensed to the convicted. **Summary offences,** such as loitering, are considered more minor; cases are heard in provincial or territorial courts, and they can result in a fine of up to $2000, a six-month jail term, or both. On the other hand, **indictable offences,** the more serious of the two, can result in much more serious punishment if the defendant is found guilty. These offences involve a trial by judge or judge and jury, depending

Did You Know?

... that in England, 200 or more years ago, all serious crimes were subject to capital punishment? If all felons had, in fact, been executed, England would have lost most of its male population. So, to save fellow citizens from the gallows, juries refused to convict and judges invented (or expanded) defences to serious charges.

on what the defendant chooses, and there is no limitation period on prosecution for these crimes. In contrast, there is a six-month limitation period for the prosecution of summary offences.

The American system uses a different categorization system, recognizing three degrees of severity. Felonies are severe crimes, subject to punishments of a year or more in prison or to capital punishment. Misdemeanours are less severe crimes, subject to a maximum of one year in jail. (For crimes of both grades, fines can also be imposed as punishments.) Violations are minor offences, normally subject only to fines.

THE DEFENCES

You will soon see that we measure the amount of crime at various stages of the criminal process. For example: How many crimes are reported to the police? For how many of these crimes have convictions been obtained? There is a huge discrepancy. Far fewer convictions have been obtained than crimes reported or even prosecuted. There are several reasons for this discrepancy. One of the principal reasons is that not all elements of the crime charged could be proven in court. Why not? Because frequently the defendant has offered one of a number of defences to the offence charged. Each of these defences simply negates the existence of one (or more) of the elements of the offence charged.

Let us take the insanity defence as an example. When the defendant pleads the existence of a mental disease or defect (a psychiatric question), he claims that he could not have acted (did not appreciate the nature and quality of the act—consequently, no *actus reus*) or he could not form the requisite mens rea (did not appreciate the wrongfulness of the act).[3] In Canada, a successful defence of this nature would result in the determination that the offender is "not criminally responsible" (NCR) for the act.

Another defence is that of mistake of fact. Here the defendant claims that by reason of a factual error (e.g., taking someone else's coat believing it to be one's own), she did not, and could not, realize that she did something wrong. Hence, there was no *mens rea* (or sometimes not even the requisite *actus reus*).

In some situations, the defendant's defence is that he or she did in fact commit the act, but was justified in doing so. If an individual kills his attacker in self-defence (his option was to kill or be killed), the law will likely accept this as a defence. The law recognizes that it is natural for people to react to this type of threat and attempt to save their own lives. The defence of necessity follows a similar rationale: The accused admits committing the criminal act but argues she was justified in doing so because of the circumstances surrounding the event. Breaking into a warehouse and "stealing" life-saving supplies and equipment in order to save lives following a hurricane is defendable on the grounds of necessity. Other defences, such as duress, provocation, and intoxication (partial defences), and automatism, all work pretty much on the same principle—they negate an essential element of the offence charged.

TYPOLOGIES OF CRIME

The general term "crimes" covers a wide variety of types of crimes, with their own distinct features. Murder and arson, for example, both are crimes but they also have unique elements. In murder, the criminal intent takes the form of intending to kill another human being, while in arson the intent is that of wrongfully burning property. Lawyers and criminologists have searched for a system of grouping the many types of crimes into coherent, rational categories, for ease of understanding, of learning, and of finding them in the law books, and for purposes of studying them from both a legal and a criminological perspective. Such categorizations are called "typologies."

The Canadian Criminal Code is made up of parts that categorize offences. For example, Part VIII includes offences against the person and reputation, while Part IX includes offences against rights of property. The typology we have chosen for this book seeks to accommodate both the established legal typology and the criminological objectives that are so important for the study of crime from a sociological and behavioural perspective. These categories are:

- Violent crimes
- Crimes against property
- White-collar and corporate crime
- Drug-, alcohol-, and sex-related crimes

We discuss these categories in Part III.

MEASURING CRIME

There are three major reasons for measuring characteristics of crimes and criminals. First of all, researchers need to collect and analyze information in order to test theories about why people commit crime. One criminologist might record the kinds of offences committed by people of different ages; another might count the number of crimes committed at different times of the year. But without ordering these observations in some purposeful way, without a **theory,** a systematic set of principles that explain how two or more phenomena are related, scientists would be limited in their ability to make predictions from the data they collect.

The types of data that are collected and the way they are collected are crucial to the research process. Criminologists analyze these data and use their findings to support or refute theories, to revise theories, or to develop new ones. In Part II, we examine several theories (including the one outlined briefly here) that explain why people commit crime, and we will see how these theories have been tested.

One theory of crime causation, for example, is that high crime rates result from the wide disparity between people's goals and the means available to them for reaching those goals. Those who lack legitimate opportunities to achieve their goals (primarily, people in the lower class) try to reach them through criminal means. To test this theory, researchers might begin with the **hypothesis** (a testable proposition that describes how two or more factors are related) that lower-class individuals engage in more serious crimes and do so more frequently than middle-class individuals. (See "Social Class and Crime" later in this chapter.) Next they would collect facts, observations, and other pertinent information—called **data**—on the criminal behaviours of both lower-class and middle-class individuals. A finding that lower-class persons commit more crimes would support the theory that people commit crimes because they do not have legitimate means to reach their goals.

The second objective of measurement is to enhance our knowledge of the characteristics of various types of offences. Why are some more likely to be committed than others? What situational factors, such as time of day or type of place, influence the commission of crime? Experts have argued that this information is needed if we are to prevent crime and develop strategies to control it (Chapter 9 deals with this subject).

Measurement has a third major objective: Criminal justice agencies depend on certain kinds of information to facilitate daily operations and to anticipate future needs. How many persons flow through remand centres and provincial correctional facilities? How many will receive prison sentences? Besides the questions that deal with the day-to-day functioning of the system (number of beds, distribution and hiring of personnel), other questions affect legislative and policy decisions. For instance, what effect does a change in law have on the amount of crime committed? Consider Canada's dangerous offender legislation. Does the prospect of serving an indefinite amount of time behind bars deter potential violent offenders from committing crimes? Does fear of crime go down if we put more police officers in a neighbourhood? Does drug smuggling move to another entry point if old access routes are cut off? These and other potential changes need to be evaluated—and evaluations require measurement.

Methods of Collecting Data

Given the importance of data for research, policy making, and the daily operation and planning of the criminal justice system, criminologists have been working to perfect data-collection techniques. Through the years, these methods have become increasingly more sophisticated.

Data can be found in a wide variety of sources, but the most frequently used sources are statistics compiled by government agencies, private foundations, and businesses. Familiarity with the sources of data and the methods used to gather data will help in understanding the studies we discuss throughout this book. The facts and observations researchers gather for the purpose of a particular study are called **primary data.** Those they find in government sources, or data that were previously collected for a different investigation, are called **secondary data.**

Surveys Most of us are familiar with surveys—in public-opinion polls, marketing research, and election-prediction studies. Criminologists use surveys to obtain quantitative data. A **survey** is the systematic collection of respondents' answers to questions asked in questionnaires or

The census is a survey that provides information on all Canadians, including those living in the far northern regions of the country, which, as this photo reveals, are not always easily accessible. Most surveys used in social science research are based on a sample that is considered representative of the population researchers are interested in studying.

interviews; interviews may be conducted face-to-face or by telephone. Generally, surveys are used to gather information about the attitudes, characteristics, or behaviour of a large group of persons, who are called the **population** of the survey. Surveys conducted by criminologists measure, for example, the amount of crime, attitudes toward police or toward the sentencing of dangerous offenders, assessment of drug abuse, and fear of crime.

Instead of interviewing the total population under study, most researchers interview a representative subset of that population—a **sample.** If a sample is carefully drawn, researchers can generalize the results from the sample to the population. A sample determined by random selection, whereby each person in the population to be studied has an equal chance of being selected, is called a **random sample.**

Surveys are a cost-effective method, but they have limitations. If a study of drug use by high school students was done one time only, the finding of a relationship between drug use and poor grades would not tell us whether drug use caused bad grades, whether students with bad grades turned to drugs, or whether bad grades and drug-taking resulted from some other factor, such as lack of a stable family. Panel studies, which repeatedly survey the same sample at various points in time, address this problem. Not surprisingly, they are more costly than cross-sectional studies.

Experiments The **experiment** is a technique used in the physical, biological, and social sciences. An investigator introduces a change into a process and makes measurements or observations in order to evaluate the effects of the change. Through experimentation, scientists test hypotheses about how two or more **variables** (factors that may change) are related. The basic model for an experiment involves changing one variable, keeping all other factors the same (controlling them, or holding them constant), and observing the effect of that change on another variable. If you change one variable while keeping all other factors constant and then find that another variable changes as well, you may safely assume that the change in the second variable was caused by the change in the first. Experiments in the real world are costly and difficult to carry out, but they have the advantage of increasing scientists' ability to establish cause and effect.

Most experiments are done in laboratories, but it is possible to do them in real-world, or field, settings (hence the name **field experiment**). In 1998 seven police officers working the Downtown Eastside beat in Vancouver embarked on a project that, while not intentionally planned as a field experiment, resulted in some interesting findings. Calling themselves the "Odd Squad," these officers set out to create an educational video on drug abuse. They spent a year documenting the lives of drug users, recording the horror of drug abuse, the extreme poverty suffered by users, and illustrating life and death on the street. The end result was a powerful award-winning film entitled *Through a Blue Lens*, which has captivated audiences for almost a decade. The film is an effective educational tool, but perhaps just as provocative is the story it tells of the interaction between the police and the subjects of the film. Using the camera as a catalyst, police officers interacted candidly with the subjects of their film, and developed friendships with them. They became more sympathetic to the people they were filming; the drug addicts, in having friendship extended to them by the police and filmmakers, developed self-esteem. In some cases, they reached out for help and cleaned up. The film is a testament to the positive social change that can result when people look past their respective labels—such as police officer or drug addict—and see each other as human beings.

Participant and Non-participant Observation
Researchers who engage in participant and non-participant observation use methods that provide detailed descriptions of life as it actually is lived—in prisons, gangs, and other settings.

Observation is the most direct means of studying behaviour. Investigators may play a variety of

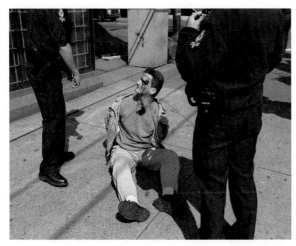

Vancouver's Downtown Eastside: An individual is handcuffed and detained after a "street fight."

roles in observing social situations. When they engage in **non-participant observation,** they do not join in the activities of the groups they are studying; they simply observe the activities in everyday settings and record what they see. Investigators who engage in **participant observation** take part in many of the activities of the groups in order to gain acceptance, but they generally make clear the purpose of their participation. After months of riding with the Rebels outlaw motorcycle group, partying with them, fighting with them against rival groups, and developing friendships with them, Daniel Wolf describes the delicate predicament he was in when it was time to ask the group if he could use his experiences with them as the basis for his doctoral dissertation. He first ran the idea by the leaders of the club, who agreed to present it to the membership for a vote at the next general meeting of the club. Wolf describes his feelings as he waited for the decision:

> For me it was the longest night of the year as I waited for the decision. The issue was hotly debated, a vote was held, and the study approved. Why? Granting me permission for the study was done as a "personal favour": "You have come into favour with a lot of the members and been nothing but good to the club. All in all you've been a pretty righteous friend of the club. But there was a lot of opposition to your study, especially from guys like T. T. [Terrible Tom] and Blues. The way I see it the vote went the way it did because you were asking us a favour. You didn't come in promising us the moon, you know, money from books and that sort of thing. You promised

us nothing so we did it as a personal favour" (Wee Albert) [Wee Albert was the first friend Wolf made when he started the study].[4]

Observations of groups in their natural setting afford the researcher insights into behaviour and attitudes that cannot be obtained through such techniques as surveys and experiments.

Case Studies A **case study** is an analysis of all pertinent aspects of one unit of study, such as an individual, an institution, a group, or a community. The sources of information are documents such as life histories, biographies, diaries, journals, letters, and other records. A classic demonstration of criminologists' use of the case-study method is found in Edwin Sutherland's *The Professional Thief*, which is based on interviews with a professional thief.

Sutherland learned about the relationship between amateur and professional thieves, how thieves communicate, how they determine whether to trust each other, and how they network. From discussions with the thief and an analysis of his writings on topics selected by the researcher, Sutherland was able to draw several conclusions that other techniques would not have yielded. For instance, a person is not a professional thief unless he is recognized as such by other professional thieves. Training by professional thieves is necessary for the development of the skills, attitudes, and connections required in the "profession."[5] One of the drawbacks of the case-study method is that the information given by the subject may be biased or wrong and by its nature is limited. For these reasons it is difficult to generalize from one person's story—in this instance—to all professional thieves.

Using Available Data in Research Besides collecting their own data, researchers often depend on secondary data collected by private and public organizations. The police, the courts, and corrections officials, for example, need to know the number of persons passing through the criminal justice system at various points in order to carry out day-to-day administrative tasks and to engage in long-range planning. It is not always feasible to collect new data for a research project, nor is it necessary to do so when such vast amounts of relevant information are already available.

To study the relationship between crime and variables such as average income or educational attainment, one might make use of the Uniform

Crime Reports (see "Police Statistics" later in this chapter), together with information found in the census and other reports of Statistics Canada. Various other agencies, among them the Canadian Centre for Justice Statistics, the Correctional Service of Canada, and the Department of Public Safety and Emergency Preparedness, are also excellent sources of statistics useful to criminologists. At the international level, United Nations' world crime surveys contain information on crime, criminals, and criminal justice systems in countries on all continents.

Researchers who use available data can save a great deal of time and expense. However, they have to exercise caution in fitting data not collected for the purpose of a particular study into their research. Many official records are incomplete or the data have been collected in such a way as to make them inadequate for the research. It is also frequently difficult to gain permission to use agency data that are not available to the public because of a concern about confidentiality. Table 2.1 provides a summary of the strengths and weaknesses of research methods available to criminologists.

Ethics and the Researcher

In the course of their research, criminologists encounter many ethical issues. Ethics review committees at most universities and government agencies check all proposals for research projects to ensure the protection of human subjects. In addition, researchers are required to inform their subjects about the nature of the study and to obtain written and informed agreement to participate. They are also required, where necessary, to ensure confidentiality.

Because of heightened awareness of the ethical issues involved in human experimentation—particularly in correctional institutions, where coercion is difficult to avoid—social science researchers, including those in the field of criminology and criminal justice, are bound by the ethical principles found in the *Tri-Council Policy Statement: Ethical Conduct for Research Involving Humans*.[6] The guidelines include respect for human dignity, free and informed consent, vulnerable persons, privacy and confidentiality, justice, and inclusiveness. In addition, researchers must balance the harms and benefits of their research and must minimize harm to their subjects.

The case of Russel Ogden, a graduate student from Simon Fraser University in British Columbia, is a fascinating example of ethics regulations in universities and their effect on both researchers and their subjects. Ogden did his master's thesis on the topic of assisted suicides among people suffering from HIV/AIDS. When he submitted his ethics proposal to the university's ethics committee, he indicated that he would offer his research subjects "absolute confidentiality," which is entirely in keeping with ethical standards of conduct among researchers. After Ogden completed his thesis, he was subpoenaed to appear in Coroner's Court and asked to provide information to the court regarding a death about which it was thought he might have knowledge. When he refused to testify, he

TABLE 2.1 Summary Table: Research Methods Used by Criminologists

Method	Advantages	Disadvantages
Surveys	Cost effective Can reach large number of respondents Ensure anonymity	Poor response rate Cannot probe beyond listed questions Difficult to establish cause-effect relationships
Experiments	Can help establish cause and effect	Contrived laboratory setting Field experiments can be costly
Participant Observer	Get a "real" look at lifestyle of subjects Can probe aspects of life that cannot be reached through a survey	Can be dangerous Gaining entry/acceptance can be difficult
Case Study	Detailed look at lives of subjects	Time-consuming Not generalizable
Secondary Data	Cost-effective way of doing research	Must depend on others' data collection Data may not have been collected with the goals of the present study in mind

was threatened with charges of contempt of court. Ogden subsequently was faced with a court battle, which he won, based on the assertion that the information he gained was subject to researcher–participant privilege. The unsettling aspect of this case for many researchers is the fact that the university's administration and ethics committee left Ogden on his own to fight to protect the confidentiality guarantee so integral to criminological research.[7]

Ogden's case also indirectly illustrates another issue that some researchers grapple with: value neutrality. Although one of the goals of the scientific method, which social scientists such as criminologists ascribe to, is value neutrality, it is difficult in some instances to achieve complete objectivity. Ogden felt compelled to respect the guarantee of confidentiality he made to his subjects, even when faced with a trial and little support from the university that had approved his ethics proposal. Wolf, in the study cited earlier in this chapter, developed bonds of friendship with his fellow bikers, who were also his research subjects. How do researchers deal with the fact that human emotions cannot be "shut off" when they conduct their research? These researchers would argue that as difficult as it is, it is possible to conduct good, criminological research that embodies the main objectives of the scientific method in spite of the fact that researchers are subjective beings. In fact, many would argue that their research has been enriched by their rejection of value neutrality.

THE NATURE AND EXTENT OF CRIME

As we have seen, criminologists gather their information in many ways. The methods they choose depend on the questions they want answered. To estimate the nature and extent of crime in Canada, they rely primarily on the Uniform Crime Reports, data compiled by the police and on national crime victimization surveys, which measure crime through reports by victims. Researchers may also use self-report surveys, which ask individuals about criminal acts they have committed, whether or not these acts have come to the attention of the authorities.

Official statistics gathered from law enforcement agencies provide information available on the crimes actually investigated and reported by these agencies. But not all crimes appear in police statistics. In order for a criminal act to be "known to the police," the act first must be *perceived* by an individual (the car is not in the garage where it was left). It must then be *defined*, or classified, as something that places it within the purview of the criminal justice system (a theft has taken place), and it must be *reported* to the police. Once the police are notified, they classify the act and often *redefine* what may have taken place before *recording* the act as a crime known to the police. Information about criminal acts may be lost at any point along this processing route, and many crimes are never discovered to begin with.

Police Statistics

Police statistics are at the top of a symbolic **crime funnel,** making them, in many ways, the best source of official crime data available to criminologists. The criminal justice system in Canada is an institution consisting of police, the courts, and the correctional apparatus. The system is widest at the top, where cases initially come to the attention of the police and enter the system. (Technically, however, the widest part of the funnel would include all the crimes that occur in a particular time period. We will never really know this number for a variety of reasons, which we will discuss shortly.) The criminal justice system is described using the metaphor of a funnel, because as we move further into the system, cases are lost, as they are filtered out by the various social control agencies. In other words, the Canadian criminal justice system is a "volume-reducing" system. In a given time period a certain number of crimes occur, but only a percentage of those crimes come to the attention of the police. In fact, police data is "report sensitive" because it relies primarily on the reporting behaviour of victims and witnesses.

Moving further into the funnel, it becomes apparent that not all crimes reported to the police result in a charge being laid. Sometimes the offender eludes detection; other times there isn't enough evidence to lay a charge. As a result, only a portion of offences known to the police move on to the court stage of the criminal justice system. We have already "lost" cases: those cases that did not move into the court system. We also know that not all court cases or trials result in a conviction. Some people plea bargain, making a compromise with the Crown prosecutor, and in other cases the accused will be acquitted. Regardless of the reason, the fact is that not everyone who goes to court will end up in prison. More cases are lost, and the end result is that the people who end up in prison make up a very small percentage of total offenders. For criminologists, depending on where and when in the process we get our data from, there are implications for our research findings. A criminologist who wants to understand what kinds of background factors (family, education, work, prior prison experiences) contribute to the repeat offending of career criminals, would do better to study offender case file records or speak with imprisoned offenders. On the other hand, a researcher who wants to investigate whether a relationship exists between location and frequency of break-and-enters would not do well to interview prisoners. Rather, he or she should probably focus on the top end of the funnel.

The data from what we have been referring to as the top end of the funnel is police recorded data. Since 1962 police departments across Canada have reported crimes substantiated through police investigation to Statistics Canada (and since 1982 to the Canadian Centre for Justice Statistics [CCJS], a division of Statistics Canada) in the form of the **Uniform Crime Reports (UCR)** survey. The objective of the UCR is to provide police departments with a standard set of procedures for the collection of crime-related information. The end result, following collection and compilation by the CCJS, is a source of uniform and comparable national data. UCR data are often presented in the form of crime rates, which also make data from different regions, provinces, and cities in Canada comparable. Crime rates also make international comparisons possible because they are a standardized way of presenting the data.

Crime Rates To analyze crime data, experts frequently present them as crime rates. Crime rates are computed by the following formula:

$$\text{Crime rate} = \frac{\text{number of reported crimes}}{\text{total population}} \times 100\ 000$$

If we say, for example, that the homicide rate is 1.9 (see Table 2.2), we mean that there were 1.9 homicides for every 100 000 persons in the population under consideration (such as the total Canadian population or all males in Canada). Expressing the amount of crime in terms of rates over time shows whether an increase or a decrease in crime results

from a change in the population or a change in the amount of crime committed.

In addition to data on reported crimes, the UCR include the number of offences cleared by arrest. Crimes may be cleared in one of two ways: by the arrest, charging, and turning over to the courts of at least one person for prosecution; or by disposition of a case when an arrest is not possible, as when the suspect has died or fled the jurisdiction. Besides reported crimes and crimes cleared by arrest, the reports contain data on characteristics of crimes (such as geographical location, time, and place), characteristics of criminals (such as gender, age, and race), and distribution of law enforcement personnel. We shall look at what these statistics reveal about the characteristics of crime and criminals in more detail later, but first we must recognize their strengths and limitations.

Strengths and Limitations of the Uniform Crime Reports The Canadian UCR is considered to be an improved version of a similar UCR system in the United States, largely because all Canadians are governed by the federal Criminal Code, which makes consistency across the country easier to achieve; in the United States, each state has a separate code. Neither system is perfect, however, and both the American and Canadian UCRs share some common problems. The Canadian UCR was revised by 1984 in an attempt to address some of the weaknesses with the original survey. First, we discuss some of the problems with the UCR and then briefly discuss the changes that occurred with the revised UCR (UCR2).

UCR data is invaluable to researchers because it is collected on a national basis and in a standard format, making national comparisons and year-to-year comparisons possible. Another advantage of this source of data is that in order for a criminal event to enter into the UCR, it must have passed through two filters—the person reporting the crime to the police and the police officer who recorded it.[8] In other words, UCR data are valid and reliable in the sense that two separate entities (victim/witness, police officer) both believe that a crime occurred. However, there are problems with the UCR as well.

Despite the fact that the UCR is among the main sources of crime statistics, its research value has been questioned. The criticisms deal with methodological problems and reporting practices. In terms of reporting, some scholars argue, for

TABLE 2.2 Crime Rate in Canada for Selected Offences, 2002–2006.

	2002	2003	2004	2005	2006
	rate per 100 000 population				
All incidents	**8 504.0**	**8 900.6**	**8 950.6**	**8 535.4**	**8 269.0**
Criminal Code offences (excluding traffic offences)	7 705.6	8 142.3	8 162.0	7 772.5	7 518.5
Crimes of violence	968.8	965.0	944.5	949.5	951.2
Homicide	1.9	1.7	2.0	2.1	1.9
Attempted murder	2.2	2.2	2.1	2.5	2.6
Assaults (level 1 to 3)[1]	751.3	747.6	732.3	732.8	734.8
Sexual assault	78.1	74.2	72.0	72.8	67.9
Other sexual offences	8.8	8.1	8.2	8.6	8.6
Robbery	85.0	89.8	86.0	89.2	94.1
Other crimes of violence[2]	41.6	41.3	42.0	41.6	41.4
Property crimes	3 973.2	4 120.6	3 970.1	3 737.2	3 587.6
Breaking-and-entering	878.4	899.5	862.4	809.2	767.8
Motor vehicle theft	516.1	550.0	531.4	495.4	487.2
Theft over $5000	63.2	61.3	53.0	53.3	52.3
Theft $5000 and under	2 127.1	2 211.8	2 106.9	1 977.4	1 888.8
Possession of stolen goods	95.8	104.7	111.7	106.7	107.7
Frauds	292.7	293.4	304.6	295.3	283.8
Other *Criminal Code* offences	2 763.6	3 056.8	3 247.4	3 085.7	2 979.7
Criminal Code offences (traffic offences)	374.8	369.7	377.1	376.4	367.7
Impaired driving	255.1	245.1	251.1	242.6	227.9
Other traffic offences[3]	119.6	124.6	126.0	133.8	139.9
Federal statutes	423.6	388.5	411.5	386.5	382.8
Drugs	295.7	274.0	305.2	290.0	294.8
Other federal statutes	127.9	114.5	106.3	96.5	88.1

[1] "Assault level 1" is the first level of assault. It constitutes the intentional application of force without consent, the attempt or threat to apply force to another person, or openly wearing a weapon (or an imitation) while accosting or impeding another person.

[2] Includes unlawfully causing bodily harm, discharging firearms with intent, abductions, assaults, against police officers, assaults against other peace or public officers, and other assaults.

[3] Includes dangerous operation of motor vehicle, boat, vessel, or aircraft, dangerous operation of motor vehicle, boat, vessel, or aircraft causing bodily harm or death, driving motor vehicle while prohibited and failure to stop or remain.

Source: Adapted from Statistics Canada, www.40.statscan.ca/101/cst01/legal02.htm, accessed April 6, 2007.

example, that figures on reported crime are of little use in categories such as breaking-and-entering, in which a majority of crime is not reported. The statistics present the amount of crime known to law enforcement agencies, but they do not reveal how many crimes have actually been committed. People do not report their victimization to the police for a variety of reasons, including the belief that the police can't or won't do anything to help, that the offender might seek revenge or reprisal, or a desire on the part of the victim to deal with the crime in his or her own way (such as forgetting it or seeking revenge). In this sense, UCR data are dependent on the reporting behaviour of the public.

Changes in laws affect crime reporting. Prior to 1983, the law did not recognize that a man could rape his wife; after 1983, it did. Changes in legislation affect crime reporting behaviour, as well as the response of the police. Public sentiment also affects police activities, including the recording of crime. Consider the case of impaired driving. Police departments are far more concerned about enforcing laws surrounding drinking and driving today than they were 40 years ago. Does an increase in impaired driving charges by police departments indicate an increase in impaired driving, or is it indicative of a change in public and official response to this kind of behaviour? UCR data are also, then, dependent on the activities of law enforcement agencies. Such data are also reliant to some extent on the public and the media.[9]

In terms of methodological problems, three loom large for the UCR. First, UCR counting rules require that attempted and completed crimes be counted in the same category, with the exception of homicide. This practice obscures detail regarding

Youth Jail Terms Less Common after 2003 Law

Far fewer young offenders are being found guilty of crimes and sentenced to jail terms since the Youth Criminal Justice Act came into being in 2003, according to a study of recent trends in youth crime.

"What is remarkable is that for both minor assaults and all other violent charges, the rate appears to have dropped rather dramatically with the coming into force of the YCJA," the study states. It notes there was a similar decrease for property offences such as theft.

A surprise finding was that verdicts of guilt in Alberta and B.C. plummeted to a level traditionally occupied exclusively by Quebec, the most liberal of the provinces when it comes to crime and imprisonment.

"Quebec is no longer distinct in the manner in which it uses its youth court," states the study, which was conducted for the federal Department of Justice in March [2006]. "This is an important finding in that it was assumed, we think, that the low rate of using youth court in Quebec related to a special tradition that existed only in Quebec of using other social systems to deal with offending youths."

The study, conducted by University of Toronto criminologist Anthony Doob and University of Guelph criminologist Jane Sprott, compared the last five years of the Young Offenders Act—1998 to 2003— with the first year after it was replaced by the YCJA.

The issue of youth crime leapt up on the political agenda . . . after a Supreme Court ruling that judges must not stiffen sentences for young offenders in the hope of discouraging the offender or potential lawbreakers.

Justice Minister Vic Toews, a long-time critic of the youth justice system, responded by blasting the YCJA as "a very badly drafted act" that needs to be reviewed.

"Accountability and responsibility for serious crimes needs to be enforced in our youth justice system," he said.

The YCJA replaced the Young Offenders Act after 18 years of inflamed debate. Where the YOA was marred by undefined principles and could result in wildly differing sentences, the new act had a strong philosophical base.

It mandated that sentences should be proportional to the severity of the crime and the maturity level of the perpetrator. It discouraged judges from using jail for less serious offences, and promoted the use of alternatives such as probation, mediation sessions with victims and victim compensation or restitution.

Speaking on condition of anonymity [in 2006], an Ontario judge said a Supreme Court ruling . . . hammered home the dramatic changes the YCJA has brought about. "The significance of this decision and other appellate cases is that judges and lawyers are definitely getting the message that we are in a new paradigm, and that we have to stop thinking about 'jail versus no jail' as our only alternatives," the judge said.

Prof. Doob and Prof. Sprott observed . . . that Mr. Toews is apparently unaware that the new law was tailored to treat serious crime relatively harshly while finding more enlightened—and less costly— ways to deal with minor offenders.

They also noted that, in keeping with the aims of Parliament, the overall proportion of those being sentenced to jail for violent offences has increased under the new act.

"Who knows what this government is going to do?" Prof. Sprott said. . . . "They want to talk tough and sound tough, but I'm not sure they want to raise taxes to pay for it."

"The irony is that the minister keeps saying, 'We want accountability,' " Prof. Doob added. "That is exactly what's in the act."

The study attributed part of the drop in findings of guilt to the fact that police are charging fewer youths.

"Over all, in Canada, there was a 41-per-cent decrease in the custody rate—from 6.4 to 3.78 per 1,000 in the population," the study adds. "Obviously, some of this decrease was the result of fewer cases being brought to youth court."

It said that in the first year of the YCJA, all 13 provinces and territories decreased their rate of sentencing youths into custody.

Source

http://www.theglobeandmail.com/servlet/story/RTGAM.20060623.wyouth24.V124/BNStory/BabyBoomers/, accessed May 8, 2008. Reprinted with permission from the Globe and Mail.

Questions for Discussion

1. How did the change in youth justice legislation affect youth crime rates?
2. In what ways can politics affect statistics? Has youth crime really gone down?

the extent of harm done during the commission of an offence. There is significant qualitative difference between an attempted and completed armed robbery, for example. Yet, this detail is lost when both acts are conflated into one category.

Another serious limitation is the fact that when several crimes are committed in one event, only the most serious offence is included in the UCR; the others go unreported. The end result for researchers is that a number of crimes go uncounted. At the same time, there are differences in the ways that personal and property crimes are counted. For personal crimes, the counting system is such that one crime equals one victim. If a person assaults six people, the UCR lists six assaults. When property crimes are committed, each individual act is counted as a separate offence. If a person robs a group of six people, for example, the UCR lists one robbery (see Figure 2.1). In addition, the UCR collects limited information about reported crimes (type of offence,

FIGURE 2.1 Counting crime in the Uniform Crime Reports.

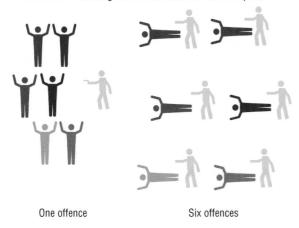

One offence   Six offences

gender of offender, young or adult offender, and clearance status of offence, for example).

Another significant problem with the UCR is the form in which data are collected. Data are collected in aggregate, which means that aggregate totals for each month are recorded. For example, all sexual assaults reported and all sexual assaults cleared by charge (i.e., solved) are reported for the month of July. This is misleading because it is entirely (and very probably) possible that some of the assaults cleared in July occurred in June or in a previous month, and that some of the assaults reported in July won't be solved until September or October!

Finally, the UCR data suffer from several omissions. Many arsons go unreported because not all fire departments report to the UCR.[10] Most white-collar offences are omitted because they are reported not to the police but to government regulatory authorities.

To deal with the limitations of the UCR, in 1984 the Canadian UCR was revised to take into account some of these problems. The UCR2 collects more detailed information about criminal events. Instead of "aggregate-based" data collection, the revised UCR is "incident-based." In addition to monthly totals, the details of each incident are recorded and reported from the initial report until completion. More detailed information in the form of location of the incident, weapons used, relationship between victim and offender, and value of stolen property is incorporated into the police reports. All of these factors increase the richness of such data for researchers. Still, one important fact remains: UCR data deal only with crimes that come to the attention of the police. What about crimes that remain unreported?

For what is called the "dark figure of crime," those crimes that are not reported to the police, we have to rely on victimization data and self-report studies.

Victimization Surveys

Victimization surveys provide researchers with the opportunity to tap into the dark figure of crime. These surveys measure the extent of crime by interviewing individuals about their experiences as victims. By accessing information from victims directly, these surveys record the perceived characteristics of criminal victimization, many of which never enter into the official record just described. The first victimization survey in Canada was conducted in 1982. The Canadian Urban Victimization Survey, carried out by the Ministry of the Solicitor General of Canada and Statistics Canada, included 60 000 respondents in seven major urban centres in the country. In 1988, Statistics Canada for the first time included a victimization component in the General Social Survey (GSS), which occurs every five years. Since then, victimization surveys have been included in the 1993, 1999, and 2004 versions of the GSS. Finally, a special topics victimization survey was conducted in 1993. The Violence Against Women Survey (VAWS) involved 12 000 women who were asked about a variety of violent victimizations they experienced as young girls and as adults.

The GSS is our main source of national victimization data in Canada. In its most recent form, in 2004, 24 000 respondents aged 15 and older were asked a series of questions, including questions about whether they have experienced crimes such as break-and-enter, motor vehicle theft, sexual assault, assault, robbery, personal theft, household property theft, and vandalism.[11] Victimization surveys are organized into two main sections. All respondents are asked to participate in the first part of the survey, which asks them to supply social and demographic information and responses to questions regarding fear of crime and attitudes toward the criminal justice system. A series of questions in this first part is used to identify respondents who have been victims of crime. These participants are then administered the second section of the survey, which asks them detailed questions about their criminal victimization. The survey covers characteristics of crimes, such as time and place of occurrence, number of offenders, use of weapons, economic loss, and time lost from work; characteristics of victims, such as gender, age, race, ethnicity, marital status, household composition, and educational attainment; perceived characteristics of offenders, such as age, gender, and race; circumstances surrounding the offences and their effects, such as financial loss and injury; and patterns of police reporting, such as rates of reporting and reasons for reporting and for not reporting. Some questions also encourage interviewees to discuss family violence.

The strengths of this method of crime data collection is that researchers can speak directly to a crucial party to the criminal event: the victim. Also, they can tap into the dark figure of crime, learning about the circumstances and characteristics of events not reported to police, which helps provide a more valid estimate of the actual crime rate. As Figure 2.2 illustrates, the discrepancy between crimes reported to police and those recorded through victimization surveys is significant. Victimization surveys also ask respondents why they do or do not report their victimization to the police, as Figure 2.3 shows. Finally, by administering the "screening questionnaire" to all participants, researchers can compare victims to non-victims in terms of such demographic characteristics as age, gender, education, and lifestyle characteristics.

Limitations of Victimization Surveys While victimization surveys give us information about crimes that are not reported to the police, these data, too, have significant limitations. Although the GSS and other victimization surveys are conducted by trained interviewers, some individual variations in interviewing and recording style are inevitable, and as a result, the information recorded may vary as well. In addition, certain categories of people are omitted when this methodology is used. For example, institutionalized populations, including the elderly, prisoners, and the mentally ill, are not accessed. Similarly, children under the age of 15 are off limits to researchers, as are homeless people. These populations experience victimization; some would argue they have higher victimization rates than the general population in Canada, and could have much to offer researchers in terms of understanding crime. Despite our efforts to reach people and events that are represented in the dark figure of crime, we cannot seem to reach them all. This, of course, affects our understanding of victimizations,

FIGURE 2.2   A comparison of number of crimes reported[1]: General Social Survey (GSS)[2] and Uniform Crime Reports

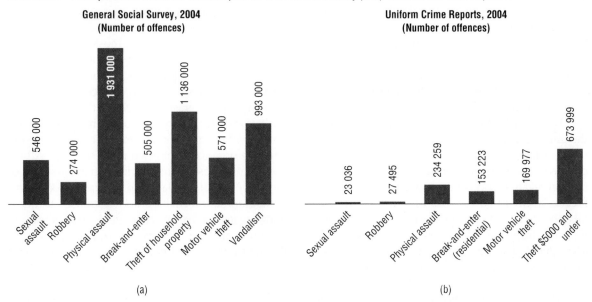

(a)

(b)

Source: Adapted from "Criminal Victimization in Canada, 2004," Maire Gannon and Karen Mihorean, *Juristat*, Statistics Canada, Catalogue No: 85-002-XPE. Vol. 25, No. 7, November 2005; "Crime Statistics in Canada, 2005," Maire Gannon, *Juristat*, Statistics Canada, Catalogue No: 85-002-XIE, Vol. 26, No. 4 July, 2006.

[1]Statistics must be interpreted with caution. Crime categories used with the GSS and the UCR are not directly comparable. GSS data do not include the Northwest Territories, the Yukon, and Nunavut.

[2]Includes all incidents of spousal and physical assault.

FIGURE 2.3   Reasons for reporting violent victimizations and reasons for not reporting violent victimizations.

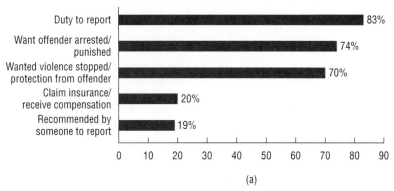

REASONS FOR REPORTING VIOLENT VICTIMIZATIONS

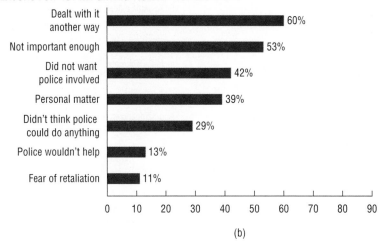

REASONS FOR NOT REPORTING VIOLENT VICTIMIZATIONS

Source: Adapted from "Criminal Victimization in Canada, 2004," Maire Gannon and Karen Mihorean, *Juristat,* Statistics Canada, Catalogue No: 85-002-XPE, Vol. 25, No. 7, November 2005.

our theories of crime, and certainly our methods of dealing with crime and victimization.

Since the victimization surveys are based on personal reporting, the method also suffers from the fact that memories may fade over time; so some facts are forgotten while others are exaggerated. Moreover, some interviewees may try to please the interviewer by fabricating crime incidents.[12] Respondents also have a tendency to telescope events—that is, to move events that took place in an earlier time period into the time period under study. All of these possibilities may affect the validity and reliability of this data collection method. Table 2.3 provides a comparison of the UCR and the GSS, and Table 2.4 outlines the advantages and disadvantages of using information collected through the use of the UCR, victimization surveys, and self-report surveys.

Self-Report Surveys

Another way to determine the amount and types of crime actually committed is to ask people to report their own criminal acts in a confidential interview or, more commonly, on an anonymous questionnaire. These investigations are called **self-report surveys.** Self-report surveys, similar to victimization surveys, aim to uncover crimes not reported to the police. Also similar to victimization surveys, self-report surveys divide respondents into those who have and have not committed offences through the use of a screening

TABLE 2.3 Differences Between the UCR and GSS

UCR	GSS
Data Collection Methods:	
Administrative police records	Personal reports from individual citizens
Census	Sample survey
100% coverage of all police agencies	Sample of approximately 10 000 persons using random digit dialling sampling technique
Data submitted on paper or in machine-readable format	Computer Assisted Telephone Interviewing (CATI); excludes households without telephones
National in scope	Excludes Yukon, Nunavut, and Northwest Territories
Continuous historical file: 1962 onwards	Periodic survey: 1988, 1993, 1999
All recorded criminal incidents regardless of victims' age	Target population: persons aged 15 and over, excluding full-time residents of institutions
Counts only those incidents reported to and recorded by police	Collects crimes reported and not reported to police
Scope and Definitions:	
Primary unit of count is the criminal incident	Primary unit of count is criminal victimization (at personal and household levels)
Nearly 100 crime categories	Eight crime categories
"Most Serious Offence" rule results in an undercount of less serious crimes	Statistics are usually reported on a "most serious offence" basis, but counts for every crime type are possible, depending on statistical reliability.
Includes attempts	Includes attempts
Sources of Error:	
Reporting by the public	Sampling error
Processing error, edit failure, non-responding police department	Non-sampling error related to the following: coverage, respondent error (e.g., recall error), non-response, coding, edit and imputation, estimation
Police discretion, changes in policy and procedures	
Legislative change	

Source: Adapted from "Comparison of the GSS and UCR," adapted from Statistics Canada publication *An Overview of the Differences Between Police-Reported and Victim-Reported Crime,* Catalogue 85-542, No.1, released May 14, 1997, www.statcan.ca/bsolc/english/bsolc?catno=85-542-X.

TABLE 2.4 Strengths and Weaknesses of Three Main Data Sources

Source of Information/Data	Advantages	Disadvantages
UCR	National comparisons Standardized format Police reported crime	Aggregate vs. incident-based reporting systems Cannot tap into "dark figure of crime"
Victimization Surveys	Taps into dark figure of crime Comparisons between victims and non-victims Can reach large number of people	Populations not reached (homeless, institutionalized) Definition of "victimization" varies by population
Self-Report Surveys	Taps into dark figure of crime Find out why people commit crime, how many of their crimes go undetected	"Missing cases" problem Tend to be conducted with youth

questionnaire. In this way, offenders and non-offenders can be compared on the basis of demographic and lifestyle characteristics.

Findings of Self-Report Surveys Self-reports of delinquent and criminal behaviour have produced several important findings since their development in the 1940s. First, they quickly refuted the conventional wisdom that only a small percentage of the general population commits crimes. The use of these measures over the last several decades has demonstrated very high rates of law-violating behaviour by seemingly law-abiding people. Almost everyone, at some point in time, has broken a law.

In 1947, James S. Wallerstein and Clement J. Wyle questioned a group of 1698 individuals on whether or not they had committed any of 49 offences that were serious enough to require a maximum sentence of not less than one year. They found that over 80 percent of the men reported committing malicious mischief, disorderly conduct, or larceny. More than 50 percent admitted a history of crimes, including reckless driving and driving while intoxicated, indecency, gambling, fraud, and tax evasion. The authors acknowledged the lack of scientific rigour of their study. No attempt was made to ensure a balanced or representative cross-section of the individuals surveyed.[13] However, these findings do suggest that the distinction between criminals and non-criminals may be more apparent than real.

Studies conducted since the 1940s have provided a great deal more information. They suggest a wide discrepancy between official and self-report data as regards the age, race, and gender of offenders.[14] Unrecorded offenders commit a wide variety of offences, rather than specializing in one type of offence.[15] It also appears that only one-quarter of all serious, chronic young offenders are apprehended by the police. Moreover, an estimated 90 percent of all youths commit delinquent or criminal acts, primarily truancy, use of false identification, alcohol abuse, larceny, fighting, and marijuana use.[16]

From 1991 to 1993, the first International Self-Report Delinquency (ISRD) study was conducted in Finland, Great Britain, the Netherlands, Belgium, Germany, Switzerland, Portugal, Spain, Italy, Greece, the United States, and New Zealand. Each country used the same questionnaire, which had been translated into the respective languages. The studies used various sampling techniques, so the results from each country are not strictly comparable. Nonetheless, the findings support much of what is found in the self-report literature. Boys commit about twice as many offences as girls. The peak age of offending in the participating countries is 16 to 17 years. Violence is strongly related to lower educational levels. No relationship was found between socioeconomic status and criminal behaviour. Drug use seems related to leaving school early and unemployment. School failure is related to violent offences.[17]

Self-report surveys in Canada include work by M. Fréchette and Marc LeBlanc, which confirms the existence of much hidden delinquency, and Julian Tanner and Scott Wortley, who surveyed 3400 high school students and 400 street youth in Toronto, asking them about a variety of issues ranging from gang participation to perceptions of crime.[18]

Limitations of Self-Report Surveys Self-report surveys have taught us a great deal about criminality. But they, like the other methods of data collection, have drawbacks. The questionnaires are often limited to petty acts, such as truancy, and therefore do not represent the range of criminal acts that people may commit. Michael Hindelang, Travis Hirschi, and Joseph Weis argue that researchers who find discrepancies with respect to gender, race, and class between the results produced by official statistics and those collected by self-report methods are in fact measuring different kinds of behaviour rather than different amounts of the same behaviour. They suggest that if you take into account the fact that persons who are arrested tend to have committed more serious offences and to have prior records (criteria that affect decisions to arrest), then the two types of statistics are quite comparable.[19]

Another drawback of self-reports is that most of them are administered to high school or college students, so the information they yield applies only to young people attending school. And who can say that respondents always tell the truth? The information obtained by repeated administration of the same questionnaire to the same individuals might yield different results. Many self-report measures lack validity; the data obtained do not correspond with some other criterion (such as school records) that measures the same behaviour. Finally, samples may be biased. People who choose not to participate in the studies may have good reason for not wanting to discuss their criminal activities. Considering that many self-report surveys are conducted with junior and high school students, it is entirely possible that the students with the most to offer in terms of self-reported delinquency are actually not in attendance when the surveys are administered.

Each of the three commonly used sources of data—police reports, victim surveys, and self-report surveys—adds a different dimension to our knowledge of crime. All of them are useful in our search for the characteristics of crimes, criminals, and victims. Awareness of advantages and limitations are of utmost importance when assessing the validity and reliability of the methods. In using crime data, researchers should always be cognizant of the importance of perspective that each of these methods brings to the counting of crime. Consider, for example, the case of Bill and Mike who both go out on a Friday night. Both consume large amounts of alcohol and become inebriated. Throw into the scenario an attractive young lady who both friends are interested in. Before long, a dispute ensues, punches are thrown, and the police are called. Upon arriving at the scene, the police officer correctly deduces this is a case of too much alcohol and testosterone among two friends. She manages to calm the men, and each is sent home in a cab. No official report is filed, so the incident does not make it into the UCR. However, six months later, Statistics Canada begins conducting its GSS victimization survey and Bill and Mike both happen to be selected as respondents. When asked if they have been punched in the past 12 months, they recall the fight and both respond "yes." Coincidentally, researchers from the local university also are conducting a self-report survey and call up Bill and Mike, asking them if they have ever hit anyone in the past 12 months. Again, they both answer that they have. So, the incident is reported in both the victimization survey and the self-report study, yet is not included in the annual UCR report. Perspectives of participants in a criminal situation, including offenders, victims, and police, then, can influence the understanding of crime, which in turn affects the crime data available to researchers.

MEASURING CHARACTERISTICS OF CRIME

Whyte Avenue in Edmonton, Alberta, is located in Strathcona, an historic part of the city dating back to the early twentieth century. Locals and tourists alike are attracted to the area, largely because of the historic atmosphere, the unique shops, the variety of pubs and bars, the coffee shops, and patios. Whyte Avenue made national news when Canada Day celebrations in 2001 turned nasty and a riot ensued. Again in June 2006, the area made headlines when rowdy behaviour during the Stanley Cup playoffs resulted in fires, fights, assaults, and riotous behaviour.[20] Only a few months later, Dylan McGillis was stabbed to death after he and his friend were swarmed by a group on Whyte Avenue. Just blocks away, another individual was stabbed. As Whyte Avenue continues to attract over 25 000 on any given Friday or Saturday night,

business owners and patrons alike are increasingly at risk of victimization and are fearful. The Edmonton Police Service and City Council now discuss Whyte Avenue as a focal concern for particular policing tactics and increased budget allowances; recently, city councillors were asked to double fines for fighting and public urination in the area (from $250 to $500) as a means of deterrence.[21] What has happened to the once safe, quaint area and source of pride in the city? It seems this area of the city is out of control.

Experts would point to the nature of the area and the types of people attracted to it: young people, participating in evening activities, consuming alcohol (and a variety of illegal substances), interacting with other young people, who represent a diversity of backgrounds and lifestyles. But Whyte Avenue has always attracted such people. What has changed? Certainly, one would have to consider the booming Alberta economy: Young people now have more money to spend on their evening activities. One would have to look at increased drug trade activities, increased use of weapons, and the manner in which group processes and anonymity can facilitate behaviours people may not normally embark on when alone. This kind of information not only gives us general insights into the crime problem on Whyte Avenue, but also enables us to examine the changes in the area over time.

Criminologists use this kind of information, including crime rates, in their research. Some investigators, for example, may want to compare drug use to crime in major cities. Others may want to explain a decrease or an increase in the crime rate in a single city (e.g., Edmonton), in a single area (e.g., Whyte Avenue), or perhaps in the nation as a whole.

Crime Trends

One of the most important characteristics of any crime is how often it is committed. From such figures we can determine crime trends, the increases and decreases of crime over time. The UCR report that about 2.6 million Criminal Code incidents (excluding traffic incidents and other federal statutes such as drug offences) were reported to the police in 2006. Of the total number of reported crimes, 12 percent were violent crimes, 43 percent were property crimes, and the remaining 45 percent were other Criminal Code offences.[22]

FIGURE 2.4   Comparison of rates of violent victimization, 1993, 1999, 2004.

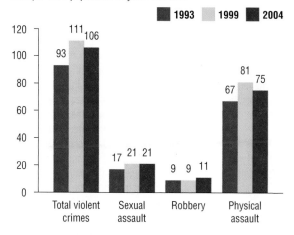

Rate per 1000 population 15 years and over

Rates of violent victimization remain unchanged.

Note: Includes incidents of spousal and physical assault.

Source: Adapted from Maire Gannon and Karen Mihorean, November, 2005, "Criminal Victimization in Canada, 2004," *Juristat,* Statistics Canada, Catalogue No: 85-002-XPE, Vol. 25, No. 7; Statistics Canada, General Social Survey, 1999 and 2004, *Juristat,* Catalogue No. 85-002, Vol. 15, No. 10.

FIGURE 2.5   Reports to police of household victimization declined, 1993–2004.

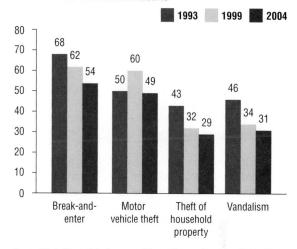

% of household victimization incidents

Source: Adapted from Maire Gannon and Karen Mihorean, November, 2005, "Criminal Victimization in Canada, 2004," *Juristat,* Statistics Canada. Catalogue No: 85-002-XPE, Vol. 25, No. 7; Statistics Canada, General Social Survey, 1993, 1999 and 2004.

Victimization survey data suggest that the rate of violent victimization has not changed significantly in recent years (see Figure 2.4).

The 2004 GSS presents a somewhat different picture (see Figure 2.2 on page 34). Though the data presented in the GSS and the UCR are not entirely comparable because the GSS collects information on eight crime types, the number of crimes reported to the police and the number reported in the victimization survey are clearly far apart. The GSS reveals that a significant number of Canadians do not report their victimizations to the police (see Figure 2.5). In fact, only about 34 percent of criminal incidents came to the attention of the police in 2004. In terms of overall victimization, 28 percent of Canadians aged 15 years and older reported being victimized one or more times in the 12 months preceding the survey. In 1999, this number was 26 percent.[23]

Let's consider Figure 2.5 for a moment. The figure clearly shows that as far as household victimization is concerned, the percentage of victims who report their victimization to the police has been decreasing over the past several years. What are possible explanations for this trend? One might at first glance feel somewhat comforted in the thought that victimization itself is declining.

Fewer victimizations might simply translate into proportionately fewer of these crimes being reported to the police. In other words, it's all relative; fewer overall crimes means less to report.

However, a more critical examination of the figure might encourage us to consider the value of goods taken or destroyed during the household victimization, including whether or not the occupants had insurance. In order to claim loss through insurance, a police report is required by the insurance company, thus providing an incentive to report the crime. Also, the greater the dollar amount loss, the more likely victims are to obtain compensation through insurance. These factors also affect the statistics. Beyond the issue of insurance, another plausible explanation for the trend we see in Figure 2.5 is the possibility that over time Canadians have lost faith in the ability of police to apprehend individuals who commit household victimizations and therefore feel little incentive to report the incident to the police. They might think that "the cops can't do anything for me anyway, so why bother reporting it." Certainly, these reasons are not exhaustive, but they should draw our attention to the importance of reading data critically and looking beyond the surface or obvious explanations.

According to UCR data, the crime rate increased between 1962 up until the early 1990s, peaking in 1991–1992. The total Criminal Code offence rate

Why Did Crime Drop?

Canadians witnessed an unprecedented drop in crime beginning in the 1990s. Between 1991 and 2000, rates of crime reported to police decreased by 26 percent. Property crime dropped by 34 percent during this period. In 1993, violent crime began to decline; between 1993 and 2000, rates of violent crime dropped by 9 percent—after 30 years of annual increases in the crime rate. Similar trends occurred in the United States during the same time period. This is a topic of great interest to criminologists, who have offered a variety of explanations for recent trends:

- Anthony Harris, Stephen Thomas, Gene Fisher, and David Hirsch suggest that improvements in medical technology and emergency services have reduced the lethality of violent crime during the last 40 years. They argue that even though there has been an increase in serious assault rates and weapons use, the murder rate has decreased over the years because improvements in medical technology have saved many assault victims from death. They found support for this explanation in a study of violent crime between 1960 and 1999. In this study, 98.8 percent of the decrease in violent crime was due to an actual decrease in lethality, as opposed to a shift to less-dangerous weapons. They also found that lethality was linked to several medical variables, including the presence of an area trauma centre.(1) The study suffers from a number of weaknesses, however, among them the failure to control for other explanations and the failure to examine the relationship between medical improvements and lethality over time. As a result, the strength of the explanation is debatable.

- One school of thought holds that demographic changes, specifically a temporary dip in the high-crime population aged 18 to 24, can account for some of the drop in youth and total violent crime. Most research has supported this explanation,(2) although there is no consensus on how much of the drop can be attributed to demographic changes.

- Others point to changes in gun control legislation in Canada and 22 U.S. states. Changes to Canadian firearm legislation in 1991, 1995, and 1998 defined restricted and prohibited weapons, instituted firearms acquisition certificates, implemented a system of licensing for firearms owners, and increased penalties for a variety of weapons offences. Over this time period there was a reduction in weapon-related crimes, but researchers point out that crime generally was decreasing during this time period, so legislative changes alone cannot account for the decrease.(3)

- Some researchers argue that a change in social values, including growing respect for social institutions, less tolerance for interpersonal violence, and a general "civilizing" has influenced the drop in crime.(3, 4) As an example, Canadian data reveal reductions in alcohol consumption and impaired driving since the 1970s. It's possible that this shift in attitude may have contributed to the reduction in other types of crime, such as assault and homicide, which often occur within the context of alcohol abuse. Data also support a shift in attitudes with respect to the equality of women, which occurred at the same time as rates of spousal assault and homicide declined. (3) The applicability of this explanation to youth may, however, be questionable. The Ontario Student Drug Use Survey reported an increase in adolescent drug use in recent years, after a lengthy period of decline in the 1980s. This may indicate a negative shift in public attitudes for this age group.(3)

- Canadian crime rates, which declined at a similar pace as those in the United States, occurred in the absence of the increases in criminal justice budgets, police strength, and rates of incarceration the U.S. experienced. While American researchers attribute some of the crime reduction in their country to crackdowns on certain types of crime, increased police presence, and higher rates of incarceration, the same degree of "get tough" policies did not occur in Canada.(3) Some criminologists

almost tripled during this time period. Following a decline throughout the 1990s, the overall crime rate witnessed a slight increase between 2002 and 2004 (see Figure 2.6 on page 42). In 2006 the crime rate decreased by 3 percent, following a drop of 5 percent in 2005. The GSS shows that victimization rates remained relatively stable between the 1999 and 2004 surveys. The 2004 overall rate of victimization of 28 percent is slightly higher than the 26 percent rate from 1999.

The gradual decline in the crime rate after 1991 is an important phenomenon that requires a bit more analysis. One important factor is the age distribution of the population. Given the fact that young people tend to have the highest crime rate, the age distribution of the population has a major effect on crime trends. After World War II, the birthrate increased sharply in what is known as the "baby boom." The baby-boom generation reached its crime-prone years in the 1960s, and the crime rate duly rose. As the generation grew older, the crime rate became more stable and in the 1990s began to decline. Some researchers claim that the children of the baby boomers may very well expand the ranks of the crime-prone ages once again and that crime will again increase.

attribute the crime rate drops in both countries to a reorganization of policing. Community policing, or problem-oriented policing, encourages police officers to work closely with community members in the identification and solution of problems, with the goal of reducing criminal justice system involvement in the process. Redefining crimes as "problems," then, keeps such incidents out of the official record of crime.(5) The association between various policing strategies and the crime drop appears promising; however, very few studies have tested it systematically. As a result, the strength of the relationship is unclear.(6)

- Canadian researchers have found support for increasing levels of education among Canadians as a possible contributing factor to the decline in crime. In looking at the broader social and economic context in tackling this issue, they also discovered that in years where inflation increased, so did financially motivated crime. In years where alcohol consumption and unemployment increased, homicide rates also went up.(3)

- These are just some of the explanations that have been offered over the years. All of them are logical, and many are supported by research. What is apparent is that the crime drop is a complicated phenomenon that involves multiple factors and

complex relationships between them. Reasons for the decrease in crime are likely to vary by crime type, across time and space, and between adults and youth. Thus, explaining crime trends requires that we consider different accounts simultaneously and in interaction with each other.

Sources

1. Anthony R. Harris, Stephen H. Thomas, Gene A. Fisher, and David J. Hirsch, "Murder & Medicine: The Lethality of Criminal Assault 1960–1999," *Homicide Studies: An Interdisciplinary International Journal* **6**(2) 2002: 128–176.
2. Robert M. O'Brien, Jean Stockard, and Lynne Isaacson, "The Enduring Effects of Cohort Characteristics on Age-Specific Homicide Rates, 1960–1995," *American Journal of Sociology* **104**(4) 1999: 1061–1095; James Alan Fox, "Demographics and U.S. Homicide," in *The Crime Drop in America,* Alfred Blumstein and Joel Wallman, eds. (Cambridge: Cambridge University Press, 2000).
3. Valerie Pottie Bunge, Holly Johnson, and Thierno A. Baldé, "Exploring Crime Patterns in Canada," *Crime and Justice Research Paper Series,* 2005, Statistics Canada, Catalogue no: 85-561-MIE—No. 005. ISBN: 0-662-40697-4. Minister of Industry, Ottawa.
4. Gary LaFree, "Social Institutions and the Crime 'Bust' of the 1990s," *Journal of Criminal Law and Criminology* **88** (1999): 1217–1232; M. Ouimet, "Explaining the American and Canadian Crime "Drop" in the 1990's," *Canadian Journal of Criminology,* 44(1) 2000: 33–50; R. Rosenfeld, "Patterns in Adult Homicide: 1980–1995" in A. Blumstein and J. Wallman, eds., *The Crime Drop in America* (Cambridge: Cambridge University Press, 2000), pp. 130–163.
5. L. W. Kennedy and D. Veitch, "Why Are Crime Rates Going Down? A Case Study in Edmonton," *Canadian Journal of Criminology,* **39** (1997): 51–69.
6. John E. Eck and Edward R. Maguire, "Have Changes in Policing Reduced Violent Crime? An Assessment of the Evidence," in *The Crime Drop in America,* Alfred Blumstein and Joel Wallman, eds. (Cambridge: Cambridge University Press, 2000).

Questions for Discussion

1. What do you think is the most important factor in the crime drop?
2. Do you think different explanations are needed for adult and youth crime?
3. What additional factors might be important for explaining the youth crime drop?
4. How might the decrease be different in urban and rural areas?

During the period when the baby-boom generation outgrew criminal behaviour, Canadian society was undergoing other changes. We adopted a get-tough crime-control policy (though not to the extent that the United States has), which may have deterred some people from committing crimes. Mandatory prison terms meant judges had less discretion in sentencing, and fewer convicted offenders were paroled before serving a minimum number of years of their sentence. In addition, crime-prevention programs, such as neighbourhood watch groups, became popular. While these and other factors have been suggested

to explain why crime rates have dropped, we have no definitive answers.

Locations and Times of Criminal Acts

Statistics on the characteristics of crimes are important not only to criminologists who seek to know why crime occurs but also to those who want to know how to prevent it (Chapter 9). Two statistics of use in prevention efforts are those on *where* crimes are committed and *when* they are committed.

Victimization data show that violent victimization rates are higher in urban areas (112 violent incidents per 1000 population, compared to 83 per

FIGURE 2.6   Reported crime rates, 1962–2006.

Rate per 100 000 population

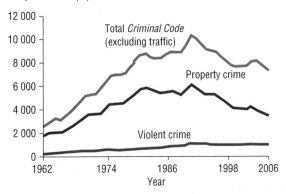

Source: Adapted from Maire Gannon, "Crime Statistics in Canada, 2005," *Juristat*, Statistics Canada, Catalogue No: 85-002-XIE, Vol. 26, No. 4. July, 2006. Minister of Industry; Statistics Canada, Canadian Centre for Justice Statistics, Uniform Crime Reporting Survey.

1000 in rural areas). But UCR data reveal that the largest cities in Canada do not necessarily have the highest per capita levels of crime, nor have they experienced the largest crime drops. Smaller cities like Winnipeg, Regina, and Saskatoon have higher crime rates than large cities like Toronto and Montreal.[24] Some of the smaller cities have, in contradiction to general crime patterns, actually witnessed increases in crime over the past decade. These patterns can be attributed to a variety of factors—population density, age distribution of residents, stability of the population, economic conditions, the quality of law enforcement, and the way these factors interact in different cities.

There are substantial regional differences in crime across Canada. An enduring trend has been the tendency for crime to increase as one moves from east to west across the country. However, in recent years this pattern has witnessed some modification. Beginning in 2002, Ontario and Quebec recorded crime rates lower than most, and by 2005, lower than all, Atlantic provinces. The western provinces and the territories continue to have the highest rates of crime in the country.[25]

GSS data tell us the safest place to be is at home, although Canadians who stay at home are not immune to crimes, particularly spousal assault and child abuse, and household-related property crimes. However, going out in the evenings puts Canadians at a greater risk of victimization. In 2004, those who reported participating in 30 or more evening activities (e.g., going to bars, visiting friends) in a given month also reported the highest level of

victimization (174 per 1000 population).[26] This rate is four times that for individuals who took part in fewer than 10 evening activities a month. These victimization rates are also related to factors such as age, marital status, and income, which we will discuss in further detail later in the text.

The number of evening activities is also related to the type of settings individuals frequent. GSS data show that victimization occurs more frequently in commercial establishments or public places (e.g., streets and parks), corroborating the fact that going out frequently places people at risk, since they are typically going to these types of public settings.

Crime rates also vary by season. Personal and household crimes are more likely to be committed during the warmer months of the year, perhaps because in summer people spend more time outdoors, where they are more vulnerable to crime. People also often leave doors and windows open when they go out in warm weather. Also, adolescents, who commit a significant proportion of property crime, are out of school and therefore have more opportunity to commit crime. There may also be a link between crime and the days when government welfare and social security cheques arrive. For some, this means more disposable income, which may relate to behaviours associated with crime, such as drinking and gambling. Alternately, cheque recipients might be victims of theft and robbery.[27]

> **Did You Know?**
>
> . . . that children and youth account for about 61 percent of the victims of sexual assaults reported to police?

MEASURING CHARACTERISTICS OF CRIMINALS

Information on the characteristics of crimes is not the only sort of data analyzed by criminologists. They also want to know the characteristics of the people who commit those crimes.

Behind each crime is a criminal or several criminals. Criminals can be differentiated by age, ethnicity, gender, socioeconomic level, and other criteria. These characteristics enable us to group criminals into categories, and it is these categories that researchers find useful. They study the various offender groups to determine why some people are more likely than others to commit crimes or particular types of crimes. Certain correlates of crime, which refer to characteristics or variables

Measuring World Crime

In the early 1970s, the General Assembly of the United Nations requested the secretary-general to conduct a global survey on the prevalence of crime in member states. Governments may have had various reasons for wanting to know the amount of crime in the world, but they all seemed to agree that crime impedes national development and imposes great burdens on individual victims.

The UN Crime Prevention and Criminal Justice Branch (now called the Centre for International Crime Prevention) surveyed all member states by means of a questionnaire. This exercise has been repeated every five years so that by now, statistical information about the extent of crime (and the operations of criminal justice systems) is available for the period from 1970 to the present. The number of participating countries has increased over the years, from 72 to over 100. Many difficulties had to be overcome to obtain data and to assess their validity, such as national differences in the definitions of crimes, varying methods of reporting and recording those to be considered, as well as a variety of factors that prompt officials to under- or overstate the amount of some crimes. Victimization surveys and self-report studies, which have been conducted more recently, have helped in the analysis of the prevalence of crime.

While it is impossible to present the global picture here, a few statistical snapshots are indicative of the challenges posed by the UN Crime and Justice Survey (UNCJS) to statisticians and policy makers. The figure below depicts the percentages of various crime types reported globally.

The global picture shows property crime to account for most criminality. Obviously, patterns vary somewhat from country to country and from region to region.

In sample years from all five world crime surveys, a global comparison of homicide rates grouped by developing countries versus industrialized countries reveals a startling development, namely, a complete reversal of incident rates. In 1974, developing countries had over twice as many homicides as industrialized countries. By 1994, industrialized countries had twice as many homicides as the more rural developing countries.

This trend gives criminologists, statisticians, and policy makers much to think about: What accounts for this enormous shift to homicides in industrialized countries? Would one not have expected a far greater rise in homicides in developing countries, where ethnic strife and civil wars are exacting a great toll in lives? They must also address other startling findings in the never-ending effort to track down crime's root causes, to determine the relation between crime and socioeconomic development, and to evaluate the interplay between official (public) crime-prevention efforts and other forms of social control. Ultimately, they must devise policy guidelines that will be useful to nations and communities in dealing with the problem of crime *now*, before it victimizes more of the world's citizens and their countries.

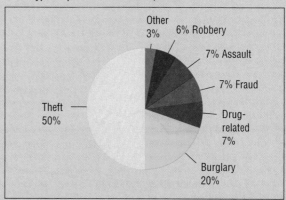

Crime types reported to the UNCJS, 1994.

Other 3%
6% Robbery
7% Assault
7% Fraud
Drug-related 7%
Burglary 20%
Theft 50%

Source: Fifth United Nations Crime and Justice Survey Global Report on Crime and Justice.

Source

Graeme Newman, ed., *Global Report on Crime and Justice* (New York: United Nations; Oxford: Oxford University Press, 1999).

Questions for Discussion

1. Since every country has its own notions on what constitutes crime and how a particular crime is defined, how would you go about making statistical information received from 100 or more countries comparable?
2. Why would governments under- or overstate their "official" crime rates?
3. What methods can a statistician use to obtain a true picture of crime rates?

that are related to crime, are relatively enduring. This means that year after year, we can be fairly certain that young people will commit a lot of property crime, we can be relatively sure that women will commit significantly fewer crimes than men, and that certain ethnic groups will be arrested and imprisoned disproportionately to other groups. We turn now to a discussion of the characteristics of people who are arrested for criminal behaviour.

Age and Crime

Eighty-three-year-old Tadeusz "Ted" Jandura, a Canadian citizen, allegedly killed his wife of 58 years on February 25, 2007, in their room at the Ilikai Hotel in Hawaii. He apparently stabbed her at least 100 times. Jandura has been charged under a section of state law that requires a penalty of life without possibility of parole when a murder

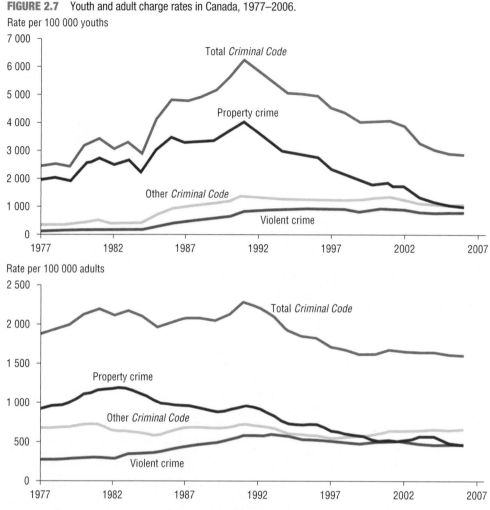

FIGURE 2.7 Youth and adult charge rates in Canada, 1977–2006.

Source: Valerie Pottie Bunge, Holly Johnson and Thierno A. Baldé, "Exploring Crime Patterns in Canada," *Crime and Justice Research Paper Series*, Statistics Canada, Catalogue no: 85-561-MIE–No. 005, ISBN:0-662-40697-4; Statistics Canada, Canadian Centre for Justice Statistics, Uniform Crime Reporting Survey; Warren Silver "Crime Statistics in Canada, 2006." *Juristat.* Statistics Canada. Catalogue No: 85-002-XIE, Vol. 27, No. 5, July, 2007; Statistics Canada, Canadian Centre for Justice Statistics, Uniform Crime Reporting Survey; Persons Charged by Type of Offence, www.40.statcan.ca/101/cst01/legal14c.htm, accessed January 31, 2008.

is "especially heinous, atrocious, or cruel, manifesting exceptional depravity."[28]

Cases involving seniors committing violent crimes are extraordinarily rare largely because crime tends to be a young person's and, specifically, a young man's game. In any given year, young people are charged with a disproportionate number of crimes. For example, in 2003, while young people aged 12 to 17 (the official age range for young offenders in Canada) made up about 8 percent of the Canadian population, they made up 17 percent of the total number of people charged with federal offences (excluding traffic offences).[29] Figure 2.7 displays the crime rates for youths for property crime, violent crimes, and total Criminal Code

offences from 1977 to 2006. Although youth commit a disproportionate amount of crime, what appears from the figure is that youth crime rates have generally been decreasing since the early 1990s.

Figure 2.8 captures the nature of the age relationship for young people charged with property and violent crimes. While the peak age for both types of crime is approximately 16 years, charges for property crime drop off quickly, while those for violent crime witness a more gradual decline. What stands out to you as you look at Figure 2.8? To start with, it is obvious that property crimes "clump" in the 15–20 year age group. Why? What is it about this age group that might help to explain the higher rate of property crime, compared

FIGURE 2.8 Age distribution of persons accused of property and violent crimes.

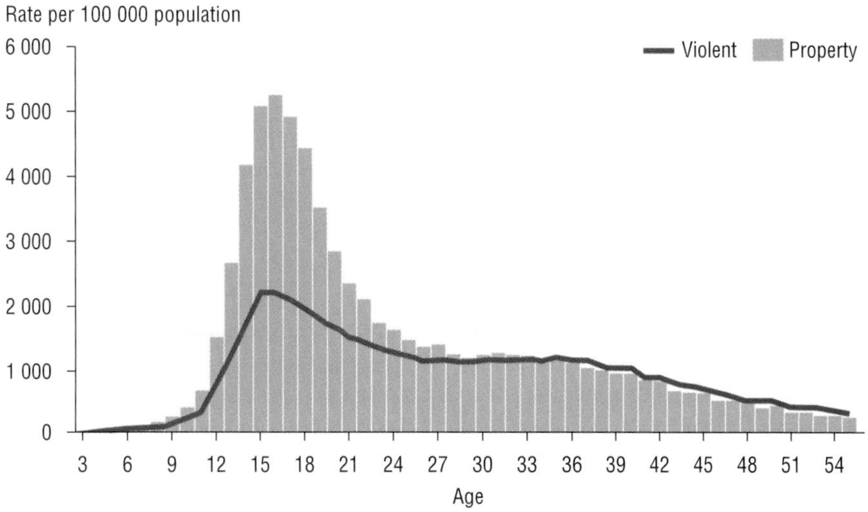

Rate per 100 000 population

Source: Valerie Pottie Bunge, Holly Johnson, and Thierno A. Baldé, "Exploring Crime Patterns in Canada," *Crime and Justice Research Paper Series*, Statistics Canada, Catalogue no: 85-561-MIE–No. 005, ISBN:0-662-40697-4; Statistics Canada, Canadian Centre for Justice Statistics, Incident-based Uniform Crime Reporting Survey.

to other ages? If we compare the pattern for property crime to that for violent crimes, two major differences exist. First, fewer violent crimes occur. Second, while there is a pronounced age drop in frequency of property offending after about age 20, the decline in age for frequency in violent criminal offending is much more gradual. What factors might explain this difference?

Age is also related to patterns in court data. Younger adults are overrepresented in criminal court statistics. In 2003–2004, adults aged 18 to 24 comprised 12 percent of the adult population but accounted for 31 percent of all cases in adult criminal court.[30] People aged 15 to 24 years of age made up 18 percent of the adult population and 28 percent of the cases in criminal court. It appears, then, that adults in the younger age range make up a disproportionate percentage of people accused of committing crimes (as is illustrated in Figure 2.8). Young offender overrepresentation is greatest for property crimes, while young adult overrepresentation is more significant for violent crimes. Still, despite the crime story mentioned at the start of this section, criminal activity for most crime types decreases with age.

This decline in criminal activities with age is known as the **aging-out phenomenon.** The reasons for it have sparked a lively scientific debate. Michael Gottfredson and Travis Hirschi contend there is a certain inclination to commit crimes that peaks in the middle or late teens and then declines

throughout life. This relationship between crime and age does not change, "regardless of sex, race, country, time, or offence."[31]

Crime decreases with age, the researchers add, even among people who commit frequent offences. Thus differences in crime rates found among young people of various groups, such as males and females or lower class and middle class, will be maintained throughout the life cycle. If lower-class youths are three times more likely to commit crimes than middle-class youths, for instance, then 60-year-old lower-class persons will be three times more likely to commit crimes than 60-year-old middle-class persons, though crimes committed by both lower-class and middle-class groups will constantly decline.[32] According to this argument, all offenders commit fewer crimes as they grow older because they have less strength, less mobility, and so on.

James Q. Wilson and Richard Herrnstein support the view that the aging-out phenomenon is a natural part of the life cycle.[33] Teenagers may become increasingly independent of their parents yet lack the resources to support themselves; they band together with other young people who are equally frustrated in their search for legitimate ways to get money, sex, alcohol, and status. Together they find illegitimate sources. With adulthood, the small gains from criminal behaviour no longer seem so attractive. Legitimate means open up. They marry. Their peers no longer endorse law-breaking. They learn to delay gratification. Petty crime is no longer adventurous. It is at this time that the aging-out process begins for most individuals. Even the ones who continue to commit offences will eventually slow down with increasing age.

The opposing side in this debate, sometimes called the "life-course perspective," argues that the decrease in crime rates after adolescence does not imply that the number of crimes committed by all individual offenders declines. In other words, the frequency of offending may go down for most offenders, but some chronic active offenders may continue to commit the same amount of crime over time. Why might this be so? Because the factors that influence any individual's entrance into criminal activity vary, the number and types of offences committed vary, and the factors that eventually induce the individual to give up criminal activity vary.[34]

According to this argument, the frequency of criminal involvement, then, depends on such social factors as economic situation, peer pressure, and lifestyle; and it is these social factors that explain the aging-out phenomenon. A teenager's unemployment, for example, may have very little to do with the onset of criminal activity because the youngster is not yet in the labour force and still lives at home. Unemployment may increase an adult's rate of offending, however, because an adult requires income to support various responsibilities. Thus the relationship between age and crime is not the same for all offenders. Various conditions during the life cycle affect individuals' behaviour in different ways.[35]

To learn how the causes of crime vary at different ages, Alfred Blumstein and his colleagues suggest that we study **criminal careers,** a concept that describes the onset of criminal activity, the types and amount of crime committed, and the termination of such activity.[36] **Longitudinal studies** follow the development and behaviours of research subjects over a period of time. Currently, the National Longitudinal Survey of Children and Youth (NLSCY), a long-term study of Canadian children which began in 1994, is following the development and well-being of these children from birth to early adulthood. Researchers collect information about factors influencing the social, emotional, and behaviour development of children, and monitor the impact of these factors on children's development over time. Several of the factors being monitored, such as family functioning and dynamics, and school support and performance, are of interest to criminologists because of their potential impact on the delinquent and criminal behaviour of children in the sample. Longitudinal studies of a particular group of people over time should enable researchers to uncover the factors that distinguish criminals from non-criminals and those that differentiate criminals in regard to the number and kinds of offences they commit.

Those who are involved in research on criminal careers assume that offenders who commit 10 crimes may differ from those who commit 1 or 15. They ask: Are the factors that cause the second offence the same ones that cause the fourth or the fifth? Do different factors move one offender from theft to rape or from assault to shoplifting? How many persons in a **birth cohort** (a group of people born in the same year) will become criminals? Of those, how many will become career criminals (chronic offenders)?

In the 1960s, researchers at the Sellin Center of the University of Pennsylvania began a search for answers. Their earliest publication, in 1972, detailed the criminal careers of 9945 boys (a cohort) born in Philadelphia in 1945. Marvin Wolfgang, Robert Figlio, and Thorsten Sellin obtained their data from school records and official police reports. Their major findings were that 35 percent of the boys had had contact with the police before reaching their 18th birthday; of those boys, 46 percent were one-time offenders and 54 percent were repeat offenders. Of those with police contact, 18 percent had committed five or more offences; they represented 6 percent of

Two very old inmates in the geriatric unit at Estelle Prison, Huntsville, Texas: an increasing burden for custodial care. The United States is not alone is dealing with an aging prisoner population. The Correctional Service of Canada has created an Older Offender Division to deal with the special needs of this population.

the total. The "chronic 6 percent," as they are now called, were responsible for more than half of all the offences committed, including 71 percent of the homicides, 73 percent of the rapes, 82 percent of the robberies, and 69 percent of the assaults.[37]

Research continued on 10 percent of the boys in the original cohort until they reached the age of 30. This sample was divided into three groups: those who had records of offences only as juveniles, those who had records only as adults, and those who were persistent offenders with both juvenile and adult records. Though they made up only 15 percent of the follow-up group, those who had been chronic juvenile offenders made up 74 percent of all the arrests. Thus, chronic juvenile offenders do indeed continue to break laws as adults.[38]

The boys in the original cohort were born in 1945. Researchers questioned whether the same behaviour patterns would continue over the years. Criminologist Paul Tracy and his associates found the answer in a second study, which examined a cohort of 13 160 males born in 1958. The two studies show similar results. In the second cohort, 33 percent had had contact with the police before reaching their 18th birthday, 42 percent were one-time offenders, and 58 percent were repeat offenders. Chronic delinquents were found in both cohorts. The chronic delinquents in the second cohort, however, accounted for a greater percentage of the cohort—7.5 percent. They also were involved in more serious and injurious acts than the previous group.

The 1945 cohort study did not contain females, so no overall comparisons can be made over time. But comparing females and males in the 1958 cohort, we see significant gender differences. Of the 14 000 females in the cohort, 14 percent had had contact with the police before age 18. Among the female delinquents, 60 percent were one-time offenders, 33 percent were repeat offenders, and 7 percent were chronic offenders. Overall, female delinquency was less frequent and less likely to involve serious charges.[39]

The policy implications of such findings are clear. If a very small group of offenders is committing a large percentage of all crime, the crime rate should go down if we incarcerate those offenders for long periods of time. Some jurisdictions in the United States have adopted "three strikes" legislation whereby offenders convicted for a third felony offence are incarcerated for life. In Canada, we have dangerous offender legislation, which similarly permits the incarceration of individuals deemed "dangerous offenders" until such time as it is believed they can be safely released. These kinds of policies are controversial because of the ongoing debate between people who support the rights of offenders to fair treatment versus those whose focus is the protection of society.

In a variation of the longitudinal study research design, A. Matarrazo, Peter J. Carrington, and Robert D. Hiscott looked at 16 636 youth court cases in Canada during 1993–1994 in an effort to discover whether prior sentences in court had an effect on current dispositions. The study is longitudinal in that the researchers looked at youth court cases where the offender had received a sentence in youth court on at least two previous occasions. The findings show that previous sentences have a significant impact on sentencing for the individual's current offence. In other words, the sentences handed out by judges in the young offender's past influence the decision making of the judge dealing with the current offence. Past labels are often more influential on sentencing than the severity of one's current offence.[40]

Gender and Crime

As mentioned earlier, males commit more crime than females at all ages. While there has been an increase in the female crime rate over the decades resulting in a narrowing of the gap, a gap between the genders does exist. Furthermore, most of the crime committed by females in Canada tends to consist of petty property offences such as shoplifting.[41] According to the UCR for 2003, women made up 16 percent of adults charged with violent offences (males made up 84 percent of arrests), 22 percent of adults charged with property offences (78 percent for males), and 19 percent of those charged with other Criminal Code offences (81 percent for males). For young people, females were charged with 26 percent of violent crimes, 25 percent of property crimes, and 30 percent of other offences. The numbers are 74 percent, 75 percent, and 70 percent respectively for male youth (see Figure 2.9). The GSS of 2004 reports a similar gendered pattern of criminal offending. For personal crimes of violence involving a single offender, 87 percent of victims reported the gender of the offender as male.[42]

Since the 1960s, however, there have been some interesting developments in regard to gender

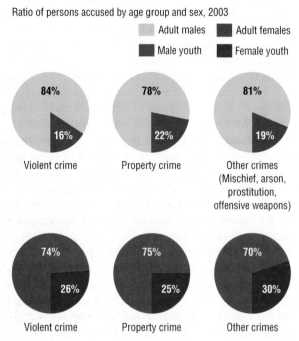

Source: Adapted from Marnie Wallace, "Crime Statistics in Canada, 2003," *Juristat*, Statistics Canada, Catalogue No: 85-002-XIE, Vol. 24, No. 6. July, 2004.

and crime data. In 1974, for example, females accounted for about 8 percent of violent crime and 18 percent of property crime, whereas they now account for 16 percent and 22 percent of violent and property crime respectively.[43] When making comparisons across time periods, we must be cautious. Looking at one year out of a 30- or 40-year time period can be misleading (think about where in the long-term trend 1974 is placed, recalling that crime rates increased generally from 1962 until 1991 and have been generally decreasing since then). Also, definitions of crime and the way crime is counted change over time. Nonetheless, women's criminal activity has increased over the years, and while the female arrest rate is still much lower than that of males, the rate of increase for women has risen faster than the rate for men.[44]

Self-report surveys, which show more similarities in male and female criminal activity than official reports do, find that males commit more offences than females. However, several of these studies also suggest that gender differences in crime may be narrowing. They demonstrate that the patterns and causes of male and female delinquent activity are becoming more alike.[45] John Hagan

and his associates agree, but only with respect to girls raised in middle-class egalitarian families in which husband and wife share similar positions of power at home and in the workplace. They argue that girls raised in lower-class, father-dominated households grow up in a cult of domesticity that reduces their freedom and thus the likelihood of their delinquency.[46] Researchers Merry Morash and Meda Chesney-Lind disagree. In a study of 1427 adolescents and their caretakers, they found gender differences in delinquency between girls and boys regardless of the type of family in which the youngsters were raised.[47]

Because women traditionally have had such low crime rates, the scientific community and the mass media had generally ignored the subject of female criminality. Both have tended to view female offenders as misguided children who are an embarrassment rather than a threat to society. Only a handful of the world's criminologists have deemed the subject worthy of independent study. Foremost among them was Cesare Lombroso (whom we shall meet again in Chapter 3). His book *The Female Offender* (co-authored by William Ferrero), which appeared in 1895, detailed the physical abnormalities that would predestine some girls to be criminal from birth.[48] Lombroso's findings on male criminals, however, have not stood the test of later scientific research, and his portrayal of the female criminal has been found to be similarly inaccurate.

A little over a generation later, in the 1930s, Sheldon and Eleanor Glueck launched a massive research project on the biological and environmental causes of crime, with a separate inquiry into female offenders. Their conclusions were decidedly sociological. They said, in essence, that in order to change the incidence of female criminality, there would have to be a change in the social circumstances in which females grow up.[49]

Otto Pollack shared the Gluecks' views on sociological determinants. In 1952, he proposed that female crime has a "masked character" that keeps it from being properly recorded or otherwise noted in statistical reports. Protective attitudes toward women make police officers less willing to arrest them, make victims less eager to report their offences, make prosecutors less enthusiastic about prosecuting them, and make juries less likely to find them guilty. Moreover, Pollack noted that women's social roles as homemakers, child rearers, and shoppers furnish them with opportunities

Audrey Black was sentenced to four years for sexual exploitation and child pornography in Saskatchewan in 2007.

for concealed criminal activity and with victims who are the least likely to complain and/or cooperate with the police. He also argued that female crime was limited by the various psychological and physiological characteristics inherent in the female anatomy.[50]

A quarter century after Pollack's work, two researchers, working independently, took a fresh look at female crime in light of women's new roles in society. In 1975, Freda Adler posited that as social and economic roles of women changed in the legitimate world, their participation in crime would also change. According to this argument, the temptations, challenges, stresses, and strains to which women have been increasingly subjected in recent years cause them to act or react in the same manner in which men have consistently reacted to the same stimuli. In other words, equalization of social and economic roles leads to similar behaviour patterns, both legal and illegal, on the part of both men and women. To steal a car, for example, one needs to know how to drive. To embezzle, one needs to be in a position of trust and in control of funds. To get into a bar fight, one needs to go to a bar. To be an inside trader on the Toronto Stock Exchange, one needs to be on the inside.[51]

Rita Simon has taken a similar position. She, too, has argued that female criminality has undergone changes. But these changes, according to Simon, have occurred only in regard to certain property crimes, such as larceny/theft and fraud/embezzlement. Women are becoming more involved in these crimes because they have more opportunities to commit them. Simon hypothesizes that since the propensity of men and women to commit crime is not basically different, as more women enter the labour force and work in a much broader range of jobs, their property crime rate will continue to go up.[52]

Some criminologists have challenged the views of Adler and Simon. Many questions have been asked about the so-called new female criminal. Does she exist? If so, does she commit more crimes than the old female criminal did? What types of crimes? Is she still involved primarily in offences against property, or has she turned to more violent offences? Researchers differ on the answers. Some contend that the extent of female criminality has not changed through the years but that crimes committed by women are more often making their way into official statistics simply because they are more often reported and prosecuted. In other words, the days of chivalry in the criminal justice system are over.[53]

Others argue that female crime has indeed increased, but they attribute the increase to nonviolent, petty property offences that continue to reflect traditional female gender roles.[54] Moreover, some investigators claim, the increased involvement in these petty property offences suggests that women are still economically disadvantaged, still suffering sexism in the legitimate marketplace.[55] Other researchers support the contention of Adler and Simon that female roles have changed and that these changes have indeed led women to commit the same kinds of crimes as men, violent as well as property offences.[56]

Though scholars disagree on the form and extent of female crime, they do seem to agree that the crimes women commit are closely associated with their socioeconomic position in society. The controversy has to do with whether or not that position has changed. In any case, the association between gender and crime has become a recognized area of concern in the growing body of research dealing with contemporary criminological issues.[57] Contemporary feminist scholarship adds to this discussion the important interaction between gender and other social characteristics that affect both criminal behaviour and criminal justice system response to individuals, as well as one's experience of crime. These researchers look at the ways in which ethnicity, age, and social class, for example, interact with gender to influence a person's involvement in crime.[58]

Social Class and Crime

Researchers agree on the importance of age and gender as factors related to crime, but they disagree strongly about whether social class is related to crime. First of all, the term "class" can have many meanings. If "lower class" is defined by income, then the category might include graduate students, unemployed stockbrokers, pensioners, single mothers requiring government support, prison inmates, and many others who have little in common except low income. Furthermore, "lower class" is often defined by the low prestige associated with blue-collar occupations. Some delinquency studies determine the class of young people by the class of their fathers, even though the young people may have jobs quite different from those of their fathers.

Another dispute focuses on the source of statistics used by investigators. Many researchers attribute the relatively strong association between class and crime found in arrest statistics to class bias on the part of the police. If the police are more likely to arrest a lower-class suspect than a middle-class suspect, they say, arrest data will show more involvement of lower-class people in criminality whether or not they are actually committing more crimes. When Charles Tittle, Wayne Villemez, and Douglas Smith analyzed 35 studies of the relationship between social class and crime rates in 1978, they found little support for the claim that crime is primarily a lower-class phenomenon. An update of that work, which evaluates studies done between 1978 and 1990, again found no pervasive relationship.[59]

Many scholars have challenged such conclusions. They claim that when self-report studies are used for analysis, the results show few class differences because the studies ask only about trivial offences. Delbert Elliott and Suzanne Ageton, for example, looked at serious crimes among a sample of 1726 young people aged 11 to 17. According to the youths' responses to a self-report questionnaire, lower-class young people were much more likely than middle-class young people to commit such serious crimes as burglary, robbery, assault, and sexual assault.[60] A follow-up study concluded that middle-class and lower-class youths differed significantly in both the nature and the number of serious crimes they committed.[61] Canadian researchers confirm that previous self-report studies masked the fact that lower-class crime tends to be more serious and persistent.[62]

Controversies remain about the social class of people who commit crimes. There is no controversy, however, about the social class of people in prison. The probability that a person such as Martha Stewart, chief executive officer of Martha Stewart Omnimedia, who was convicted of lying to the government, would face prison time is extremely low. Stewart does not fit the typical profile of the hundreds of thousands of incarcerated Americans, nor is she representative of the thousands of inmates imprisoned in Canadian provincial and federal institutions. For starters, she is a *she*. We established in the last section that crime is primarily a male activity. According to a "one-day snapshot" study of incarcerated Canadians, 98 percent of provincial/territorial and 93 percent of federal inmates are male.[63] Stewart is also unrepresentative because she is educated. Provincially, 34 percent of inmates had a grade nine education or less; federally, 46 percent were in the same situation. Stewart has a white-collar job with an income equal to that of a high-ranking corporate officer. Over half (55 percent) of provincial/territorial inmates and 43 percent of federal inmates who reported they were in the labour market at the time of incarceration were unemployed at the time they were admitted to prison. Martha Stewart committed a white-collar offence. In the United States and Canada, only a small proportion of white-collar offenders serve time for their offences, and their sentences are often less than a year. In contrast, more than one-quarter male offenders in federal custody are serving sentences for homicide, one-third for robbery, one-sixth for sex offences, and nearly one-quarter for drug offences.[64] Finally, Martha Stewart

David Radler, former chief operating officer of Hollinger International and a former associate of Conrad Black, pleaded guilty to one count of fraud for his involvement in a conspiracy. He received a sentence of 29 months in jail and a fine of US$250 000 in exchange for his testimony in the Black trial.

is white in a criminal justice system where blacks are disproportionately represented. In the Canadian criminal justice system, blacks are also overrepresented, as are Aboriginals.

Ethnicity and Crime

Statistics on race and crime show that while Aboriginal peoples constitute about 3 percent of the Canadian population, they account for approximately 17 percent of the federally incarcerated population. These numbers are even higher in the Prairie provinces; notably, in Saskatchewan the proportion of Aboriginals incarcerated is over nine times their proportion in the provincial population (72 percent of the inmate population compared to 8 percent of total population).[65] Blacks in Canada also experience overrepresentation, constituting about 2 percent of the general population and 6 percent of the federal inmate population. A study conducted by the Kingston police found that its members were 3.7 times more likely to stop a black person and 1.4 times more likely to stop an Aboriginal person than they were to stop a white individual (Chapter 7 discusses racial profiling in more detail).

Information on race and crime in Canada is limited because police do not systematically collect and release this information.[66] Debate surrounding the collection and release of race-related data centres on the value of such information for researchers and policy makers who could use it to address any issues relating to ethnicity and crime, and opponents who say that releasing this information would increase prejudice, discrimination, and labelling of ethnic or racial groups. Nonetheless, correctional data reveal the overrepresentation of Aboriginals within the system, as do various studies and inquiries conducted on the topic.[67] The correlation between Aboriginal status and involvement in the criminal justice system is not something new: The patterns we've touched on have existed for decades and indicate to criminologists the importance of systemic processes that contribute to the high rates of this group's involvement in the system. For example, 65 percent of Aboriginal offenders have had prior convictions, and they are five times as likely to be convicted of a serious assault as are non-

> **Did You Know?**
>
> ...that in Manitoba, Aboriginals represent 16 percent of 12- to 17-year-olds but make up 71 percent of youths sentenced to custody?

Aboriginals. The on-reserve rate of violence is five times higher than the off-reserve rate.[68]

As we will see later in this text, offenders and victims tend to come from similar categories; often representation in both sets of statistics is an indicator of disadvantaged social and economic status. While Aboriginals are overrepresented in the criminal justice system as offenders, they are also overrepresented in terms of particular kinds of victimization. The 2004 GSS shows that Aboriginals are three times as likely as non-Aboriginals to report being victims of violent victimization. Rates of victimization for Aboriginal women are 3.5 times higher than the rates for non-Aboriginal women. Death from violence occurs at a rate three times that of non-Aboriginals, and suicide among males is four times higher than the non-Aboriginal rate.[69]

The statistics and reports raise many questions. Do Aboriginals actually commit more crimes? Or are they simply arrested more often? Are Aboriginal communities under more police surveillance than white neighbourhoods? Do Aboriginals receive differential treatment in the criminal justice system? If Aboriginals do commit more crimes than whites, why?

Data support the argument that there are more Aboriginals in the criminal justice system because bias operates from the time of arrest through incarceration. Other data support the argument that racial disparities in official statistics reflect an actual difference in criminal behaviour. If disparity in criminal behaviour actually exists, and if we are to explain it, we have to try to discover why people commit crimes. A history of colonialism, an attempt at cultural genocide, and decades of abuse in residential schools has created a legacy of family dysfunction, high rates of family abuse, substance abuse, and alienation among many Aboriginal people. Adding to the situation is the relegation of Aboriginals to reserves marred by extreme poverty and social disorganization. High unemployment and high rates of disease and infant mortality, combined with discrimination and negative self-images, contribute to what many criminologists would consider a recipe for criminal involvement. Considering the social and economic situation of thousands of Aboriginals across the country, it might be more fitting to ask: Why don't even more Aboriginals commit crime? Part of the answer to this latter question is that Aboriginal communities are working toward improving some of the issues that have plagued them for decades. In addition, government agencies such as the Correctional Service of Canada have incorporated Aboriginal programming for inmates, including the presence of elders in institutions. Restorative justice, a topic we explore in more detail later in this book, has roots in Aboriginal culture and spirituality: Our justice system increasingly is acknowledging the importance of healing to the health of individuals, families, and communities. While we still have a long way to go, the system is more concerned with addressing some of the causal factors to crime than it was only a few years ago.

We will have more to say about the causal factors associated with high crime rates and race in Chapters 5 and 6.

REVIEW

1. What elements are common to all crimes?

There are several ingredients that usually must exist before we can say that a crime, in the legal sense, has occurred. These include **actus reus** (p. 22), **mens rea** (p. 22), and concurrence. In Canada, offences are distinguished legally on the basis of the procedures for dealing with the accused and the punishment given to the convicted. We have two broad categories of offences: **summary offences** (p. 23) and **indictable offences** (p. 23).

2. What are some of the legal defences to crime?

Depending on the circumstances surrounding a criminal event, there are several defences that negate the existence of one or more of the elements of the offence charged. For example, an accused might claim he or she acted in self-defence and therefore should be acquitted of the crime. Or, the claim might be made that the act was committed out of necessity. Other defences include a claim that the person is not criminally responsible for the act, that a mistake of fact was made, that the accused was highly intoxicated or provoked and therefore is not completely responsible, or that he or she was acting under duress when the crime was committed.

3. How does the typology of crime used in this text compare to other crime typologies?

While different ways of categorizing crimes exist, this textbook divides such behaviours into the following groups: violent crimes, crimes against property, white-collar and corporate crime, and drug-, alcohol-, and sex-related crimes.

4. How do criminologists measure crime?

Criminologists use **theory** (p. 25) to order their ideas in an organized and purposeful manner. **Hypotheses** (p. 25) are testable propositions that enable researchers to test their theories. Researchers have three main objectives in measuring crime and criminal behaviour patterns. They need (1) to collect and analyze **data** (p. 25) to test theories about why people commit crime, (2) to learn the situational characteristics of crimes in order to develop prevention strategies, and (3) to determine the needs of the criminal justice system on a daily basis. They may gather facts and observations for the purpose of a particular study. These data are referred to as **primary data** (p. 25). Or they may use information previously collected for a different investigation, called **secondary data** (p. 25). One method of collecting data is through **surveys** (p. 25), whereby researchers use **samples** (p. 26), such as **random sample** (p. 26), to generalize to a **population** (p. 26). **Experiments** (p. 26) allow scientists to test the relationship between **variables** (p. 26) by changing one variable and controlling all others. **Field experiments** (p. 26) follow the same general model but move the experiment from the laboratory to the real world. **Non-participant** (p. 27) and **participant observation** (p. 27), and **case studies** (p. 27) are more direct means of studying behaviour.

5. How much crime is there?

It is often cost-effective for researchers to use repositories of information gathered by public and private organizations for their own purposes. The three main sources of data for measuring crime are the **Uniform Crime Reports** (p. 30), data collected in **victimization surveys** (p. 33) like the General Social Survey (GSS), and **self-report surveys** (p. 35). Though each source is useful for some purposes, all three have limitations.

6. What do we know about crime trends?

By measuring the characteristics of crime and criminals, we can identify crime trends, and the places and times at which crimes are most likely to be committed.

7. What are some characteristics of criminals?

Current controversies concerning offenders focus on, for example, the relationship between crime and age throughout the life cycle. Researchers debate the nature and extent of the **aging-out phenomenon** (p. 45), which refers to the decline in criminal activities with age. Some criminologists have focused their attention on

criminal careers (p. 46), a concept that describes the onset of criminal activity, the types and amount of crime committed, and the termination of such activity. **Longitudinal studies** (p. 46) of a particular group of people over time enable researchers to study the factors that distinguish criminals from non-criminals. Such studies focus on the activities (criminal or not) of a **birth cohort** (p. 46). Also interesting to criminologists is the changing role of women in crime, and the effects of social class and race on the response of the criminal justice system. Crime is an activity disproportionately engaged in by young people, males, and minorities.

CRIMINOLOGY & PUBLIC POLICY

In the wake of the terrorist attacks of September 11, 2001, advocates of racial and ethnic profiling point to the need for heightened suspicion regarding the activities of young Arabic men. The arrests and detention of hundreds of people after the terrorist attacks have created considerable controversy—many of these people would not have been subject to this treatment were it not for ethnic characteristics. Furthermore, it is not likely that ethnic profiling will be any more useful or constitutional than racial profiling, a topic that is highly controversial, particularly in the United States where police defend their racially disparate practices by saying that, generally, minorities commit more crimes than whites. In the area in which racial profiling has been most controversial—narcotics enforcement—proponents' arguments do not withstand empirical and legal scrutiny. For example, the data do not indicate a minority-dominated drug trade. National drug abuse studies from the United States show that minorities possess and use drugs only slightly more frequently than whites do. "The typical cocaine user is white, male, a high school graduate employed full-time, and living in a small metropolitan area or suburb," former U.S. drug czar William Bennett has said.

Canadians are hesitant to collect and release information on the ethnicity of offenders. In fact, in 1990 the Canadian Centre for Justice Statistics proposed including statistics on the race of suspects and victims in crime reports, but political pressure put a stop to the idea. Arguments against collection and release of data on race and ethnicity include the difficulty of accurately categorizing ethnicity: Is it a matter of skin colour, country of origin, or self-identification? Also problematic is the existence of racism within the Canadian populace: People are more likely to report crimes to the police when the offender belongs to an ethnic minority. There is also the possibility that the collection of information regarding race and ethnicity will contribute further to the "racialization" of crime. When an entire ethnic group becomes identified with criminal activity, the danger is that the public and agents working within the criminal justice system will be more likely to label members of these groups as criminal and treat them accordingly.

There are drawbacks to not collecting data on race and ethnicity. Racial minorities, including blacks and Aboriginals, are treated differentially by the criminal justice system, as commissions investigating the problem have repeatedly shown. Proponents of race data collection argue that such data could be used to more clearly illustrate the systemic racism that occurs in the criminal justice system and bring much needed attention to addressing the issue. (*Sources:* Kevin Haggerty, *Making Crime Count* [Toronto: University of Toronto Press, 2001]; Julian V. Roberts, "Racism and the Collection of Statistics Relating to Race and Ethnicity" in *Crimes of Colour: Racialization and the CJS in Canada*, Wendy Chan and Kilran Mirchandani, eds. [Peterborough, Ontario: Broadview Press, 2002], pp. 101–112; David Rudovsky, "Breaking the Pattern of Racial Profiling," *Trial*, August 2002, Association of Trial Lawyers of America; Larry J. Siegel and Chris McCormick, *Criminology in Canada: Theories, Patterns and Typologies*, Third Edition [Toronto: Thomson/Nelson]; Scot Wortley, "Justice for All? Race and Perceptions of Bias in the Ontario Criminal Justice System—A Toronto Survey," *Canadian Journal of Criminology* [October 1996].)

Questions for Discussion Crime data are often discussed in racial terms. As we note in the "Ethnicity and Crime" section of this chapter, these data raise a host of questions, including the way in which people of colour are treated by police. Is racial profiling ever justifiable? If the answer is yes, how effective must the profiling be to remain justified? If the answer is no, do the events of 9/11 suggest a justification for other forms of ethnic profiling?

YOU BE THE CRIMINOLOGIST

Your agency has been asked by the mayor's office to develop a program to reduce youth violence. Of course, you must first determine the extent of youth violence before going out into the field to talk to people. You plan to use information that is publicly available. What specifically will you measure, and what data will you use?

Visit the Online Learning Centre: www.mcgrawhill.ca/olc/adler

SCHOOLS OF THOUGHT THROUGHOUT HISTORY

CHAPTER **3**

CHAPTER QUESTIONS

1. What was the context within which criminology developed?

2. What is positivist criminology?

3. Is there a biological link to criminal behaviours?

4. Is there a psychological link to criminal behaviours?

5. How do sociologists explain criminal behaviours?

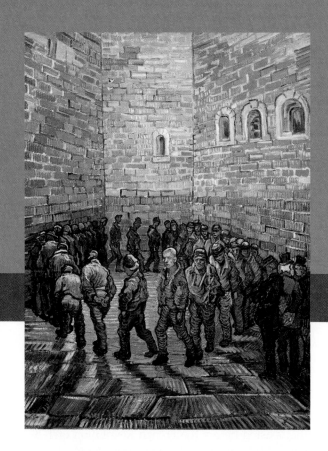

Painter Vincent van Gogh portrayed himself among the inmates in *The Prison Courtyard*, 1890. Oil on canvas. The Pushkin Museum of Fine Art, Moscow, Russia.

Criminologists traditionally consider that their field has its origins as a science in the eighteenth century, when Cesare Beccaria established what came to be known as the "classical school of criminology." But when we look at what some much earlier thinkers had to say about crime, we may have to reconsider this assumption. Take a look at this quotation: "Children now love luxury. They have bad manners, contempt for authority. They show disrespect for elders. They contradict their parents, chatter before company, cross their legs and tyrannize their teachers."[1] This may appear to be a modern description of delinquent youth, but Socrates made this observation over 2300 years ago.

Scholars, philosophers, and poets have speculated about the causes of crime and possible remedies since ancient times, and modern criminology owes much to the wisdom the ancient philosophers displayed. The philosophical approach culminated in the middle of the eighteenth century in the **classical school** of criminology. It is based on the assumption that individuals choose to commit crimes after weighing the consequences of their actions. According to classical criminologists, individuals have free will. They can choose legal or illegal means to get what they want; fear of punishment can deter them from committing crime; and society can control behaviour by making the pain of punishment greater than the pleasure of the criminal gains.

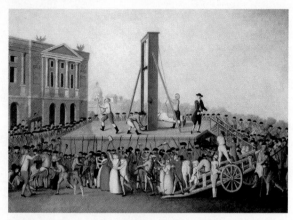

Public punishment: painting depicts beheading of the king's wife, Marie Antoinette, at the guillotine, October 16, 1793.

The classical school did not remain unchallenged for long. In the early nineteenth century, great advances were made in the natural sciences and in medicine. Physicians in France, Germany, and England undertook systematic studies of crimes and criminals. Crime statistics became available in several European countries. There emerged an opposing school of criminology, the **positivist school.** This school posits that human behaviour is determined by forces beyond individual control and that it is possible to measure those forces. Unlike classical criminologists, who claim that people rationally choose to commit crime, positivist criminologists view criminal behaviour as stemming from biological, psychological, and social factors.

The earliest positivist theories centred on biological factors, and studies of those factors dominated criminology during the last half of the nineteenth century. In the twentieth century, biological explanations were ignored (and even targeted as racist after World War II). They did not surface again until the 1970s, when scientific advances in psychology shifted the emphasis from defects in criminals' bodies to defects in their minds. Throughout the twentieth century, psychologists and psychiatrists have played a major role in the study of crime causation. A third area of positivist criminology focuses on the relation of social factors to crime. Sociological theories, developed in the second half of the nineteenth century and advanced throughout the twentieth, continue to dominate the field of criminology today.

An understanding of the foundations of modern criminology helps us understand contemporary developments in the field. Let us begin with the developments that led to the emergence of the classical school.

CLASSICAL CRIMINOLOGY

In the late eighteenth to the mid-nineteenth centuries, during what is now called the "neoclassical period," the classical culture of the ancient Mediterranean was rediscovered. This was also a period of scientific discoveries and the founding of new scholarly disciplines. One of these was criminology, which developed as an attempt to apply rationality and the rule of law to brutal and arbitrary criminal justice processes. The work of criminology's founders—scholars like Cesare Beccaria and Jeremy Bentham—became known as "classical criminology."

The Historical Context

Classical criminology grew out of a reaction against the barbaric system of law, punishment, and justice that existed before the French Revolution of 1789. Until that time, there was no real system of criminal justice in Europe. There were crimes against the state, against the church, and against the crown. Some of these crimes were specified; some were not. Judges had discretionary power to convict a person for an act not even legally defined as criminal.[2] Monarchs often issued what were called in French *lettres de cachet*, under which an individual could be imprisoned for almost any reason (disobedience to one's father, for example) or for no reason at all.

Many criminal laws were unwritten, and those that had been drafted, by and large, did not specify the kind or amount of punishment associated with various crimes. Arbitrary and often cruel sentences were imposed by judges who had unbounded discretion to decide questions of guilt and innocence and to mete out punishment. Due process in the modern sense did not exist. While there was some official consensus on what constituted crime, there was no real limit to the amount and type of legal sanction a court could command. Punishments included branding, burning, flogging, mutilating, drowning, banishing, and beheading.[3] In England, a person might receive the death penalty for any of more than 200 offences, including what we today call "petty theft."

Public punishments were popular events. When Robert-François Damiens was scheduled to

Stone Age Crime and Social Control

On a fine Thursday afternoon in September 1991, vacationers from Germany, on an alpine hiking trip, spotted a head protruding from the glacial ice. They hurried to a nearby guest house and reported their find to the innkeeper, who promptly called both the Italian and the Austrian police. It became immediately apparent that this corpse was no ordinary mountain casualty. Rather, this was an ancient mountain casualty. Experts were brought in from Austrian universities, and the body was freed from its icy embrace. It was dubbed "Oetzi," after the Oetztal Alps of the discovery.

Oetzi is 5300 years old, a robust young man, 25 to 30 years old at the time of his death. Completely mummified, he was found in the position in which he had placed himself, in a crevice, probably to escape a snowstorm. He was fully dressed, in an unlined fur robe. Originally fashioned with great skill, the robe was badly repaired with sinew and plant fibre, suggesting that he could not have relied on the services of his wife or the village seamstress for some time. Oetzi had placed his equipment by his side, most of it of the best Stone Age craftsmanship. What is surprising is that he did not carry with him a ready-to-shoot bow.

Investigators determined that Oetzi was an outdoor type, a shepherd who sought refuge in the crevice, froze to death, and was preserved for five millennia by permafrost and glacial ice. But what was Oetzi doing at 3210 metres above sea level on a fall day? Obviously, he was not a herder since he was far above the grazing range of a herd. Nor was he a trader trying to cross the Alps in the fall. So what was he doing up there, where nothing grows and where it is hard to breathe? One answer, based on all the evidence available so far, is that Oetzi may have been an outlaw.

Oetzi was a Late Stone Age (Neolithic) man, likely to have come from a herding

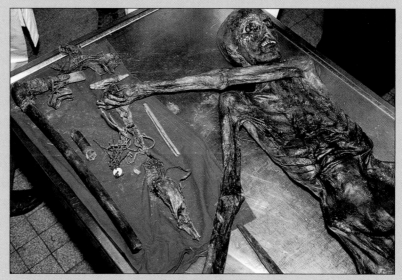

Oetzi, who was preserved in the glacial crevice in which he died 5000 years ago.

community of, at most, 200 persons. Robert Carneiro of the American Museum of Natural History has figured out that a community of 200 produces 20 000 one-on-one disagreement possibilities. Oetzi may have had such interpersonal problems.

The tasks of social control even within such a small community stagger the imagination. Fighting could have erupted within the community. Jealousy could be engendered about who deserves more respect as the best hunter, the best storyteller, the best healer, or the wisest person. A dispute could have happened over the distribution of food or the sharing of tools.

The evidence about Neolithic society permits us to conclude that these societies had no institution that we could compare with modern criminal justice, although they had problems that today might be referred to a criminal justice system. How were such problems solved? Minor problems were dealt with by the use of shaming, by dispute resolution, by compensation, and by sacrifices. Major unforgivable offences led to casting out

the wrongdoers: They would be declared outlaws. They had to leave camp instantly, without gathering weapons or tools, and flee to the wilderness. Oetzi fits the description of such an outlaw, literally, a person cast outside the protection of the laws, the customs, and the protection of his group, to take to the wilderness and perhaps to die there. If Oetzi was a criminal banished from his village, the punishment clearly was effective.

Source

Adapted from Gerhard O. W. Mueller and Freda Adler, "The Emergence of Criminal Justice: Tracing the Route to Neolithic Times," in *Festskrift till Jacob W. F. Sundberg*, Erik Nerep and Wiweka Warnling Nerep, eds. (Stockholm: Jurisförlaget, 1993), pp. 151–170.

Questions for Discussion

1. For purposes of improving modern crime-control techniques, can we learn anything from Stone Age societies?
2. What crimes do you think might result in the banishment of one of the members of such a community?

be executed on March 2, 1757, for the attempted murder of Louis XV, so many people wanted to attend the spectacle that window seats overlooking the execution site were rented for high prices. Torture to elicit confessions was common. A criminal defendant in France might be subjected to the *peine forte et dure*, which consisted of stretching him on his back and placing over him an iron weight as heavy as he could bear. He was left that way until he died or spoke. A man would suffer these torments and lose his life in order to avoid trial and therefore conviction so that his lands and goods would not be confiscated and would be preserved for his family. This proceeding was not abolished until 1772.[4]

Even as Europe grew increasingly modern, industrial, and urban in the eighteenth century, it still clung to its medieval penal practices. With prosperity came an increasing gulf between the haves and the have-nots. Just before the French Revolution, for example, a Parisian worker paid 97 percent of his daily earnings for a 2 kilogram loaf of bread.[5] Hordes of unemployed people begged by day and found shelter under bridges by night. One of the few ways in which the established upper class could protect itself was through ruthless oppression of those beneath it, but ruthless oppression created more problems. Social unrest grew. And as crime rates rose, so did the brutality of punishment. Both church and state became increasingly tyrannical, using violence to conquer violence.

The growing educated classes began to see the inconsistency in these policies. If terrible tortures were designed to deter crime, why were people committing even more crimes? Something must be wrong with the underlying reasoning. By the mid-eighteenth century, social reformers were beginning to suggest a more rational approach to crime and punishment. One of them, Cesare Beccaria, laid the foundation for the first school of criminology—the classical school.

Cesare Beccaria

Cesare Bonesana, Marchese di Beccaria (1738–1794), was rather undistinguished as a student. After graduating with a law degree from the University of Pavia, he returned home to Milan and joined a group of articulate and radical intellectuals. Disenchanted with contemporary European society, they organized themselves into the Academy of Fists, one of many young men's clubs that flourished in Italy at the time. Their purpose was to discover what reforms would be needed to modernize Italian society.

In March 1763, Beccaria was assigned to prepare a report on the prison system. Pietro Verri, the head of the Academy of Fists, encouraged him to read the works of English and French philosophers—David Hume (1711–1776), John Locke (1632–1704), Claude Adrien Helvétius (1715–1771), Voltaire (1694–1778), Montesquieu (1685–1755), and Jean-Jacques Rousseau (1712–1778). Another member of the academy, the protector of prisons, revealed to him the inhumanities that were possible under the guise of social control. Beccaria learned well. He read, observed, and made notes on small scraps of paper. These notes, Harry Elmer Barnes has observed, were destined to "assure to its author immortality and would work a revolution in the moral world" upon their publication in July 1764 under the title *Dei delitti e delle pene (On Crimes and Punishment).*[6] Beccaria presented a coherent, comprehensive design for an enlightened criminal justice system that was to serve the people rather than the monarchy.

> **Did You Know?**
>
> . . . that it took the 26-year-old Cesare Beccaria just months to write *On Crimes and Punishment*, the brief book that has influenced criminology all over the world? And did you know that he published the book anonymously out of fear that the authorities, with their interest in perpetuating the existing brutal system, would persecute him?

The climate was right: With the publication of this small book, Cesare Beccaria became the "father of modern criminology." The controversy between the rule of men and the rule of law was at its most heated. Some people defended the old order, under which judges and administrators made arbitrary or whimsical decisions. Others fought for the rule of law, under which the decision making of judges and administrators would be confined by legal limitations. Beccaria's words provided the spark that ultimately ended medieval barbarism.

According to Beccaria, the crime problem could be traced not to bad people but to bad laws. A modern criminal justice system should guarantee all people equal treatment before the law. Beccaria's book supplied the blueprint. That blueprint was based on the assumption that people freely choose what they do and are responsible

Cesare Beccaria, the young Italian nobleman-dissident who became the father of modern criminology with his monograph, *On Crimes and Punishment*.

for the consequences of their behaviour. Beccaria proposed the following principles:

• *Laws should be used to maintain the social contract.* "Laws are the conditions under which men, naturally independent, united themselves in society. Weary of living in a continual state of war, and of enjoying a liberty, which became of little value, from the uncertainty of its duration, they sacrificed one part of it, to enjoy the rest in peace and security."

• *Only legislators should create laws.* "The authority of making penal laws can only reside with the legislator, who represents the whole society united by the social compact."

• *Judges should impose punishment only in accordance with the law.* "[N]o magistrate then, (as he is one of the society), can, with justice inflict on any other member of the same society punishment that is not ordained by the laws."

• *Judges should not interpret the laws.* "Judges, in criminal cases, have no right to interpret the penal laws, because they are not legislators. . . . Every man hath his own particular point of view, and, at different times, sees the same objects in very different lights. The spirit of the laws will then be the result of the good or bad logic of the judge; and this will depend on his good or bad digestion."

• *Punishment should be based on the pleasure/pain principle.* "Pleasure and pain are the only springs of actions in beings endowed with sensibility. . . . If an equal punishment be ordained for two crimes that injure society in different degrees, there is nothing to deter men from committing the greater as often as it is attended with greater advantage."

• *Punishment should be based on the act, not on the actor.* "Crimes are only to be measured by the injuries done to the society. They err, therefore, who imagine that a crime is greater or less according to the intention of the person by whom it is committed."

• *The punishment should be determined by the crime.* "If mathematical calculation could be applied to the obscure and infinite combinations of human actions, there might be a corresponding scale of punishments descending from the greatest to the least."

• *Punishment should be prompt and effective.* "The more immediate after the commission of a crime a punishment is inflicted, the more just and useful it will be. . . . An immediate punishment is more useful; because the smaller the interval of time between the punishment and the crime, the stronger and more lasting will be the association of the two ideas of crime and punishment."

• *All people should be treated equally.* "I assert that the punishment of a nobleman should in no wise differ from that of the lowest member of society."

• *Capital punishment should be abolished.* "The punishment of death is not authorized by any right; for . . . no such right exists. . . . The terrors of death make so slight an impression, that it has not force enough to withstand the forgetfulness natural to mankind."

• *The use of torture to gain confessions should be abolished.* "It is confounding all relations to expect . . . that pain should be the test of truth, as if truth resided in the muscles and fibres of a wretch in torture. By this method the robust will escape, and the feeble be condemned."

• *It is better to prevent crimes than to punish them.* "Would you prevent crimes? Let the laws be clear and simple, let the entire force of the nation be united in their defence, let them be intended rather to favour every individual than any particular classes. . . . Finally, the most certain method

Utilitarianism Gone Astray

Few people can be credited for their contribution to Anglo-American criminal law philosophy as much as Jeremy Bentham (1748–1832), the foremost spokesperson for the utilitarian approach to the management of people in general and criminals and potential criminals in particular. Above all, he is remembered for his proposition that the purpose of all legislation is to achieve "the greatest happiness of the greatest number." Punishments, he argued, should be no greater (nor less) than necessary to achieve government's purpose to control crime.(1)

According to Princeton University professor Peter Singer, utilitarianism—the greatest good of the greatest number—implies that a child born with incurable birth defects should be killed, as its life would impose a far greater emotional and financial burden on its family and the community than its death.(2) Thus Singer argues that "some infanticide is not even as important as, say, killing a happy cat."(3) Among his principal examples for justifiable infanticide are babies born with Down's syndrome. Singer's argument fails to take into account the many adults with Down's syndrome who take a bus to work every day, earn a salary, and pay taxes on their earnings.(2) Another aspect of the utilitarian argument is illustrated by the motive of Robert Latimer, the

Demonstrators picket Princeton University over its appointment of a controversial bioethics professor, Peter Singer, in Princeton, New Jersey, April 1999.

Saskatchewan farmer who terminated his 12-year-old daughter's life in 1993. Her severe case of cerebral palsy caused her to live with excruciating pain on a daily basis. He couldn't bear to see her suffer any longer.

Putting aside the difficulty of making a prognosis about a baby's chance to have a productive and content life, how would society determine where to put the limit on legalizing infanticide? Justice Holmes ruled in *Buck v. Bell* that "three generations of

of preventing crime is to perfect the system of education."[7]

Perhaps no other book in the history of criminology has had so great an impact. Beccaria's ideas were so advanced that Voltaire, the great French philosopher of the time, who wrote the commentary for the French version, referred to Beccaria as "brother."[8] The English version appeared in 1767; by that time, three years after the book's publication, it had already gone through six Italian editions and several French editions.

After the French Revolution, Beccaria's basic tenets served as a guide for the drafting of the French penal code, which was adopted in 1791. In Russia, Empress Catherine II (the Great) convened

a commission to prepare a new code and issued instructions, written in her own hand, to translate Beccaria's ideas into action. The Prussian King Friedrich II (the Great) devoted his reign to revising the Prussian laws according to Beccaria's principles. Emperor Joseph II had a new code drafted for Austria-Hungary in 1787—the first code to abolish capital punishment. The impact of Beccaria's treatise spread across the Atlantic as well: It influenced the first ten amendments to the U.S. Constitution (the Bill of Rights).

Jeremy Bentham's Utilitarianism

Legal scholars and reformers throughout Europe proclaimed their indebtedness to Beccaria, but

imbeciles are enough" in upholding a state statute that mandated the sterilization of "imbeciles" with a family record of imbecility.(4) By those utilitarian standards, killing *all* imbecile babies would be even more cost-beneficial. Should a similar mandate apply to three generations of criminals, as determined by convictions? And would society not be better off (in terms of cost-benefit calculations) if it were to get rid of *all* troublemakers? Would Professor Singer go that far?

Between 1929 and 1972, Alberta did go that far. As one of only two provinces in Canada that implemented sexual sterilization legislation (British Columbia was the other one), Alberta's sterilization program aimed to rid the province of the "feeble-minded" who, it was thought, would lead to the downfall of the human race. Included in the categories of people targeted by the eugenics movement in the province were the so-called "mental defectives," immigrants, the poor, criminals, and the mentally ill. In the end, over 2800 people were sterilized, many without their consent, and many of whom, it was later discovered, did not fit the description of "mental defective" at all. In fact, decades later the provincial government was targeted for lawsuits by the victims of the sterilization program who claimed they were wrongfully institution-

alized and sterilized. In November 1999, the government of Alberta publicly apologized for the acts of its predecessors and provided $80 million in compensation to the hundreds of victims. Alberta's dark history with eugenics raises important questions about who has the right to live, to reproduce, and to bear children, and importantly, who has the right to make those decisions.(5)

Bentham had nothing of this sort of program in mind when he set forth his utilitarian principles. In fact, he was not even an advocate of capital punishment, considering it to be "unfrugal" and "irremissible."(1)

To demonstrate his utilitarianism, Jeremy Bentham decreed that upon his death (June 6, 1832), his body be dissected in the presence of his friends and the skeleton be reconstructed, supplied with a wax head to replace the original (to be mummified), dressed in his own clothes, and placed upright in a glass case so that he, himself, could be useful as a reminder of his principles. Until recently, once a year at meetings of the Bentham Society in London, Bentham's body was wheeled out and celebrated with a feast.

Sources

1. Jeremy Bentham, *An Introduction to the Principles of Morals and Legislation* (1789; New York: Haffner Library of Classics, 1948), esp. pp. 197, 200.
2. Peter Singer, *Rethinking Life and Death:* The Collapse of Our Traditional Ethics (New York: St. Martin's Press, 1996); *How Are We to Live? Ethics in an Age of Self-Interest* (New York: Prometheus Books, 1995).
3. George F. Will, "Life and Death at Princeton," *Newsweek,* Sept. 13, 1999, pp. 80–81.
4. *Buck v. Bell,* 274 U.S. 200, 207 (1927).
5. Jana Grekul, Harvey Krahn, and Dave Odynak, "Sterilizing the "Feeble-minded": Eugenics in Alberta, Canada, 1929–1972," *Journal of Historical Sociology,* 17 (December, 2004), pp. 358–384.

Questions for Discussion

1. According to utilitarian principles, should abortion be legalized when a baby can be profiled (by family history) as a high risk for a life in crime? Should we revisit notions of selective sexual sterilization to prevent certain types of people from reproducing?
2. Can you think of a way to use utilitarian principles to reduce the use and duration of imprisonment?

none owed more to him than the English legal philosopher Jeremy Bentham (1748–1832). Bentham had a long and productive career. He inspired many of his contemporaries, as well as criminologists of future generations, with his approach to rational crime control.

Bentham devoted his life to developing a scientific approach to the making and breaking of laws. Like Beccaria, he was concerned with achieving "the greatest happiness of the greatest number."[9] His work was governed by utilitarian principles. **Utilitarianism** assumes that all human actions are calculated in accordance with their likelihood of bringing happiness (pleasure) or unhappiness (pain). People weigh the probabilities of present and future pleasures against those of present and future pain.

Bentham proposed a precise pseudomathematical formula for this process, which he called "felicific calculus." According to his reasoning, individuals are "human calculators" who put all the factors into an equation in order to decide whether or not a particular crime is worth committing. This notion may seem rather whimsical today, but at a time when there were over 200 capital offences, it provided a rationale for reform of the legal system.[10] Bentham reasoned that if prevention was the purpose of punishment, and if punishment became too costly by creating more harm than good, then penalties needed to be set just a bit in excess of the pleasure one might derive from committing a crime, and no higher. The law exists in order to create happiness for the community. Since punishment creates unhappiness, it can be justified only if it prevents greater evil than it produces. Thus, Bentham suggested, if hanging a man's effigy produced the same preventive effect as hanging the man himself, there would be no reason to hang the man.

Sir Samuel Romilly, a member of Parliament, met Jeremy Bentham at the home of a mutual friend. He became interested in Bentham's idea that the certainty of punishment outweighs its severity as a deterrent against crime. On February 9, 1810, in a speech before Parliament, he advocated Benthamite ideas:

> So evident is the truth of that maxim that if it were possible that punishment, as the consequence of guilt, could be reduced to an absolute certainty, a very slight penalty would be sufficient to prevent almost every species of crime.[11]

Although conservatives prevented any major changes during Romilly's lifetime, the program of legislative pressure he began was continued by his followers and culminated in the complete reform of English criminal law between 1820 and 1861. During that period, the number of capital offences was reduced from 222 to 3: murder, treason, and piracy. Gradually, from the ideals of the philosophers of the Age of Enlightenment and the principles outlined by the scholars of the classical school, a new social order was created, an order that affirmed a commitment to equal treatment of all people before the law.

The Classical School: An Evaluation

Classical criminology had an immediate and profound impact on jurisprudence and legislation. The rule of law spread rapidly through Europe and the United States. Of no less significance was the influence of the classical school on penal and correctional policy. The classical principle that punishment must be appropriate to the crime was universally accepted during the nineteenth and early twentieth centuries. Yet the classical approach had weaknesses. Critics attacked the simplicity of its argument: The responsibility of the criminal justice system was simply to enforce the law with swiftness and certainty and to treat all people in like fashion, whether the accused were paupers or nobles; government was to be run by the rule of law rather than at the discretion of its

officials. In other words, the punishment was to fit the crime, not the criminal. The proposition that human beings had the capacity to choose freely between good and evil was accepted without question. There was no need to ask why people behave as they do, to seek a motive, or to ask about the specific circumstances surrounding criminal acts.

During the last half of the nineteenth century, scholars began to challenge these ideas. Influenced by the expanding search for scientific explanations of behaviour in place of philosophical ones, criminologists shifted their attention from the act to the actor. They argued that people did not choose of their own free will to commit crime; rather, factors beyond their control were responsible for criminal behaviour.

POSITIVIST CRIMINOLOGY

During the late eighteenth century, significant advances in knowledge of both the physical and the social world influenced thinking about crime. Auguste Comte (1798–1857), a French sociologist, applied the modern methods of the physical sciences to the social sciences in his six-volume *Cours de philosophie positive (Course in Positive Philosophy)*, published between 1830 and 1842. He argued that there could be no real knowledge of social phenomena unless it was based on a positivist (scientific) approach. Positivism alone, however, was not sufficient to bring about a fundamental change in criminological thinking. Not until Charles Darwin (1809–1882) challenged the doctrine of creation with his theory of the evolution of species did the next generation of criminologists have the tools with which to challenge classicism.

The turning point was the publication in 1859 of Darwin's *Origin of Species*. Darwin's theory was that God did not make all the various species of animals in two days, as proclaimed in Genesis 1:20–26, but rather that the species had evolved through a process of adaptive mutation and natural selection. The process was based on the survival of the fittest in the struggle for existence. This radical theory seriously challenged traditional theological teaching. It was not until 1871, however, that Darwin publicly took the logical next step and traced human origins to an animal of the anthropoid group—the ape.[12] He thus posed an even more serious challenge to a religious tradition that maintained that God created the first human in his own image (Genesis 1:27).

The scientific world would never be the same again. The theory of evolution made it possible to ask new questions and to search in new ways for the answers to old ones. New biological theories replaced older ones. Old ideas that demons and animal spirits could explain human behaviour were replaced by knowledge based on new scientific principles. The social sciences were born.

The nineteenth-century forces of positivism and evolution moved the field of criminology from a philosophical to a scientific perspective. But there were even earlier intellectual underpinnings of the scientific criminology that emerged in the second half of the nineteenth century.

BIOLOGICAL DETERMINISM: THE SEARCH FOR CRIMINAL TRAITS

Throughout history, a variety of physical characteristics and disfigurements have been said to characterize individuals of "evil" disposition. In the earliest pursuit of the relationship between biological traits and behaviour, a Greek scientist who examined Socrates found his skull and facial features to be those of a person inclined toward alcoholism and brutality.[13] The ancient Greeks and Romans so distrusted red hair that actors portraying evil persons wore red wigs. Through the ages, cripples, hunchbacks, people with long hair, and a multitude of others were viewed with suspicion. Indeed, in the Middle Ages, laws indicated that if two people were suspected of a crime, the uglier was the more likely to be guilty.[14]

The belief that criminals are born, not made, and that they can be identified by various physical irregularities is reflected not only in scientific writing but in literature as well. Shakespeare's Julius Caesar states:

> Let me have men about me that are fat; Sleek-headed men, and such as sleep o' nights. Yond Cassius has a lean and hungry look; He thinks too much: such men are dangerous.

Although its roots can be traced to ancient times, it was not until the sixteenth century that the

Italian physician Giambattista della Porta (1535–1615) founded the school of human **physiognomy,** the study of facial features and their relation to human behaviour. According to Porta, a thief had large lips and sharp vision. Two centuries later, Porta's efforts were revived by the Swiss theologian Johann Kaspar Lavater (1741–1801).[15] They were elaborated by the German physicians Franz Joseph Gall (1758–1828) and Johann Kaspar Spurzheim (1776–1832), whose science of **phrenology** posited that bumps on the head were indications of psychological propensities.[16] In the United States, these views were supported by the physician Charles Caldwell (1772–1853), who searched for evidence that brain tissue and cells regulate human action.[17] By the nineteenth century, the sciences of physiognomy and phrenology had introduced specific biological factors into the study of crime causation.

Lombroso, Ferri, Garofalo: The Italian School

Cesare Lombroso (1835–1909) integrated Comte's positivism, Darwin's evolutionism, and the many pioneering studies of the relation of crime to the body. In 1876, with the publication of *L'uomo delinquente (The Criminal Man),* criminology was permanently transformed from an abstract philosophy of crime control through legislation to a modern science of investigation into causes. Lombroso's work replaced the concept of free will, which had reigned for over a century as the principle that explained criminal behaviour, with that of determinism. Together with his followers, the Italian legal scholars Enrico Ferri and Raffaele Garofalo, Lombroso developed a new

A criminological examination according to an 1890 caricature.

orientation, the Italian, or positivist, school of criminology, which seeks explanations for criminal behaviour through scientific experimentation and research.

Cesare Lombroso After completing his medical studies, Cesare Lombroso served as an army physician, became a professor of psychiatry at the University of Turin, and later in life accepted an appointment as professor of criminal anthropology. His theory of the "born criminal" states that criminals are a lower form of life, nearer to their apelike ancestors than non-criminals in traits and dispositions. They are distinguishable from non-criminals by various **atavistic stigmata**—physical features of creatures at an earlier stage of development, before they became fully human.

He argued that criminals frequently have huge jaws and strong canine teeth, characteristics common to carnivores who tear and devour meat raw. The arm span of criminals is often greater than their height, just like that of apes, who use their forearms to propel themselves along the ground. An individual born with any five of the stigmata is a **born criminal.** This category accounts for about a third of all offenders.

The theory became clear to Lombroso "one cold grey November morning" while he pored over the bones of a notorious outlaw who had died in an Italian prison:

> This man possessed such extraordinary agility, that he had been known to scale steep mountain heights bearing a sheep on his shoulders. His cynical effrontery was such that he openly boasted of his crimes. On his death . . . I was deputed to make the post-mortem, and on laying open the skull I found . . . a distinct depression . . . as in inferior animals.

Lombroso was delighted by his findings:

> This was not merely an idea, but a revelation. At the sight of that skull, I seemed to see all of a sudden, lighted up as a vast plain under a flaming sky the problem of the nature of the criminal—an atavistic being who reproduces in his person the ferocious instincts of primitive humanity.[18]

Criminal women, according to Lombroso, are different from criminal men. It is the prostitute who represents the born criminal among them:

> We also saw that women have many traits in common with children; that their moral sense is different; they are revengeful, jealous, inclined to vengeance of a refined cruelty. . . . When a morbid activity of the psychical centres intensifies the bad qualities of women . . . it is clear that the innocuous semi-criminal present in normal women must be transformed into a born criminal more terrible than any man. . . . The criminal woman is consequently a monster. Her normal sister is kept in the paths of virtue by many causes, such as maternity, piety, weakness, and when these counter influences fail, and a woman commits a crime, we may conclude that her wickedness must have been enormous before it could triumph over so many obstacles.[19]

> **Did You Know?**
>
> . . . that certain Nazi anthropologists and physicians made use of Lombroso's ideas about born criminals? They proposed "scientific" classification of Aryans and non-Aryans (and ultimately death or denial of civil rights to non-Aryans) on the basis of skull measurements.

To the born criminal, Lombroso added two other categories, insane criminals and criminoloids. *Insane criminals* are not criminal from birth; they become criminal as a result of some change in

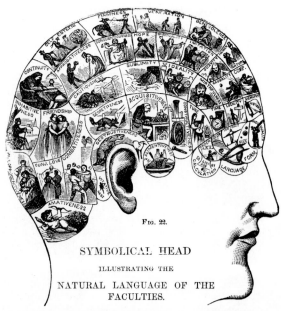

F̄ɪɢ. 22.

SYMBOLICAL HEAD

ILLUSTRATING THE

NATURAL LANGUAGE OF THE FACULTIES.

This depiction of the human brain appeared in an 1890s scientific book, *How to Read Character: A New Illustrated Hand-Book of Physiology, Phrenology and Physiognomy for Students and Examiners.*

their brains that interferes with their ability to distinguish between right and wrong.[20] *Criminoloids* make up an ambiguous group that includes habitual criminals, criminals by passion, and other diverse types.

Most scientists who followed Lombroso did not share his enthusiasm or his viewpoint. As happens so often in history, his work has been kept alive more by criticism than by agreement. The theory that criminals were lodged on the lower rungs of the evolutionary ladder did not stand up to scientific scrutiny. But the fact that Lombroso measured thousands of live and dead prisoners and compared these measurements with those obtained from control groups (however imperfectly derived) in his search for determinants of crime changed the nature of the questions asked by the generations of scholars who came after him.

His influence continues in contemporary European research; American scientists, as the criminologist Marvin Wolfgang says, use him "as a straw man for attack on biological analyses of criminal behavior."[21] Thorsten Sellin has noted: "Any scholar who succeeds in driving hundreds of fellow-students to search for the truth, and whose ideas after half a century possess vitality, merits an honourable place in the history of thought."[22] At his death, true to his lifetime pursuits, Lombroso willed his body to the laboratory of legal medicine and his brain to the Institute of Anatomy at the University of Turin, where for so many years the father of empirical criminology had espoused biological determinism.[23]

Enrico Ferri The best known of Lombroso's associates was Enrico Ferri (1856–1929). Member of Parliament, accomplished public lecturer, brilliant lawyer, editor of a newspaper, and esteemed scholar, Ferri had published his first major book by the time he was 21. By age 25, he was a university professor. Although Ferri agreed with Lombroso on the biological bases of criminal behaviour, his interest in socialism led him to recognize the importance of social, economic, and political determinants.

Ferri was a prolific writer on a vast number of criminological topics. His greatest contribution was his attack on the classical doctrine of free will, which argued that criminals should be held morally responsible for their crimes because they

must have made a rational decision to commit these acts. Ferri believed criminals could not be held morally responsible because they did not choose to commit crimes but, rather, were driven to commit them by conditions in their lives. He did, however, stress that society needed protection against criminal acts and that it was the purpose of the criminal law and penal policy to provide that protection.

Although he advocated conventional punishments and even the death penalty for individuals he assumed would never be fit to live in society, he was more interested in controlling crime through preventive measures—state control of the manufacture of weapons, inexpensive housing, better street lighting, and so forth.

Ferri claimed that strict adherence to preventive measures based on scientific methods would eventually reduce crime and allow people to live together in society with less dependence on the penal system. Toward the end of his life, he proudly admitted that he was an idealist, a statement with which generations of scholars have agreed. Though his prescription for crime reduction was overly optimistic, Ferri's importance to the development of modern criminology is undisputed. "When Enrico Ferri died on April 12, 1929," writes Thorsten Sellin, "one of the most colourful, influential figures in the history of criminology disappeared."[24]

Raffaele Garofalo Another follower of Lombroso was the Italian nobleman, magistrate, senator, and professor of law Raffaele Garofalo (1852–1934). Like Lombroso and Ferri, Garofalo rejected the doctrine of free will and supported the position that the only way to understand crime was to study it by scientific methods. Influenced by Lombroso's theory of atavistic stigmata, in which he found many shortcomings, Garofalo traced the roots of criminal behaviour not to physical features but to their psychological equivalents, which he called "moral anomalies." According to this theory, natural crimes are found in all human societies, regardless of the views of lawmakers, and no civilized society can afford to disregard them.[25]

Natural crimes, according to Garofalo, are those that offend the basic moral sentiments of probity (respect for the property of others) and piety (revulsion against the infliction of suffering on others). An individual who has an organic deficiency in these moral sentiments has no moral constraints against committing such crimes. Garofalo argued that these individuals could not be held responsible for their actions. But, like Ferri, he also emphasized that society needed protection and that penal policy should be designed to prevent criminals from inflicting harm.[26]

Influenced by Darwinian theory, Garofalo suggested that the death penalty could rid society of its maladapted members, just as the natural selection process eliminated maladapted organisms. For less-serious offenders, capable of adapting themselves to society in some measure, other types of punishments were preferable: transportation to remote lands, loss of privileges, institutionalization in farm colonies, or perhaps simply reparation. Clearly, Garofalo was much more interested in protecting society than in defending the individual rights of offenders.

Challenges to Lombrosian Theory Although Lombroso, Ferri, and Garofalo did not always agree on the causes of criminal behaviour or on the way society should respond to it, their combined efforts marked a turning point in the development of the scientific study of crime. These three were responsible for developing the positivist approach to criminality, which influences criminology to the present day. Nevertheless, they had their critics. By using the scientific method to explore crime causation, they paved the way for criminologists to support or refute the theories they had created. The major challenge to Lombrosian

Dr. Cesare Lombroso (1836–1909), professor of criminal anthropology at Turin University, founder of the Positivist School of Criminology.

theory came from the work of Charles Buckman Goring.

From 1901 until 1913, Charles Buckman Goring (1870–1919), a medical officer at Parkhurst Prison in England, collected data on 96 traits of more than 3000 convicts and a large control group of Oxford and Cambridge university students, hospital patients, and soldiers. Among his research assistants was a famous statistician, Karl Pearson. When Goring had completed his examinations, he was armed with enough data to refute Lombroso's theory of the anthropological criminal type. Goring's report to the scientific community proclaimed:

> From a knowledge only of an undergraduate's cephalic [head] measurement, a better judgment could be given as to whether he were studying at an English or Scottish university than a prediction could be made as to whether he would eventually become a university professor or a convicted felon.[27]

This evaluation still stands as the most cogent critical analysis of Lombroso's theory of the born criminal. Although Goring rejected the claim that specific stigmata identify the criminal, he was convinced that poor physical condition plus a defective state of mind were determining factors in the criminal personality.

A Return to Biological Determinism

After Goring's challenge, Lombrosian theory lost its academic popularity for about a quarter century. Then in 1939, Ernest Hooten (1887–1954), a physical anthropologist, reawakened an interest in biologically determined criminality with the publication of a massive study comparing American prisoners with a non-criminal control group. He concluded:

> [I]n every population there are hereditary inferiors in mind and in body as well as physical and mental deficients. . . . Our information definitely proves that it is from the physically inferior element of the population that native born criminals from native parentage are mainly derived.[28]

Like his positivist predecessors, Hooten argued for the segregation of those he referred to as the "criminal stock," and he recommended their sterilization as well.[29]

The Somatotype School In the search for the source of criminality, other scientists, too, looked for the elusive link between physical characteristics and crime. The **somatotype school** of criminology, which related body build to behaviour, became popular during the first half of the twentieth century. It originated with the work of a German psychiatrist, Ernst Kretschmer (1888–1964), who distinguished three principal types of physiques: (1) the *asthenic*—lean, slightly built, narrow shoulders; (2) the *athletic*—medium to tall, strong, muscular, coarse bones; and (3) the *pyknic*—medium height, rounded figure, massive neck, broad face. He then related these physical types to various psychic disorders: pyknics to manic depression, asthenics and athletics to schizophrenia, and so on.[30]

Kretschmer's work was brought to the United States by William Sheldon (1898–1977), who formulated his own group of somatotypes: the *endomorph*, the *mesomorph*, and the *ectomorph*. Sheldon's father was a dog breeder who used a point system to judge animals in competition, and Sheldon worked out a point system of his own for judging humans. Thus one could actually measure on a scale from 1 to 7 the relative dominance of each body type in any given individual. People with predominantly mesomorph traits (physically powerful, aggressive, athletic physiques), he argued, tend more than others to be involved in illegal behaviour.[31] This finding was later supported by Sheldon Glueck (1896–1980) and Eleanor Glueck (1898–1972), who based their studies of delinquents on William Sheldon's somatotypes.[32]

By and large, studies based on somatotyping have been sharply criticized for methodological flaws, including non-representative selection of their samples (bias), failure to account for cultural stereotyping (our expectations of how muscular, physically active people should react), and poor statistical analyses. An anthropologist summed up the negative response of the scientific community by suggesting that somatotyping was "a New Phrenology in which the bumps on the buttocks take the place of the bumps on the skulls."[33] After World War II, somatotyping seemed too close to **eugenics** (the science of controlled reproduction to improve hereditary qualities), and the approach fell into disfavour. During the 1960s, however, the discovery of an extra sex chromosome in some criminal samples (see Chapter 4) revived interest in this theory.

Inherited Criminality During the period when some researchers were measuring skulls and bodies of criminals in their search for the physical determinants of crime, others were arguing that criminality was an inherited trait passed on in the genes. To support the theory, they traced family histories. Richard Dugdale (1841–1883), for example, studied the lives of more than 1000 members of the family he called "Jukes." His interest in the family began when he found six related people in a jail in upstate New York. Following one branch of the family, the descendants of Ada Jukes, whom he referred to as the "mother of criminals," Dugdale found among the descendants 280 paupers, 60 thieves, 7 murderers, 40 other criminals, 40 persons with venereal disease, and 50 prostitutes.

His findings indicated, Dugdale claimed, that since some families produce generations of criminals, they must be transmitting a degenerate trait down the line.[34] A similar conclusion was reached by Henry Goddard (1866–1957). In a study of the family tree of a Revolutionary War soldier, Martin Kallikak, Goddard found many more criminals among the descendants of Kallikak's illegitimate son than among the descendants of his son by a later marriage with "a woman of his own quality."[35]

Dugdale and Goddard were not alone in their thinking. A similar argument was made about families like the Black Donnellys, an infamous Irish

Dugdale and others identified the Jukes clan as determined by heredity to be criminals, imbeciles, and paupers. Research since then has shown that the methodology was flawed and many conclusions were fabricated.

> **Did You Know?**
>
> . . . that the Alberta sterilization program was most active in the 1930s and then again in the late 1950s and 1960s (long after the horrors of Nazi Germany's sterilization program were revealed)?

family from the Lucan, Ontario, area who in the mid-1800s earned a reputation for feuding. *The Toronto Globe* reported that "the Donnelly family, to a marked degree, bore quarrelsome characteristics—when they were not fighting among their neighbours, they constantly fought among themselves."[36] Goddard or Dugdale likely would have expressed an interest in the Goler Clan, comprised of impoverished and inbred people on Nova Scotia's South Mountain as well. The family was exposed for its multigenerational practices of forced incestuous relationships and physical, sexual, and psychological abuse of children in 1984, when one the girls in the family revealed her victimization to authorities.[37] Some would suggest the family provides evidence for the transmission of degenerate traits from generation to generation, although in a case like the Golers, or any of the examples we've discussed, it is difficult to separate the influence of nature and nurture. An argument could easily be made that environment not heredity had a strong impact on the behaviours of the individuals in question.

The early studies on the issue, like those of Dugdale and Goddard, have been discredited primarily on the grounds that genetic and environmental influences could not be separated. But in the early twentieth century, they were taken quite seriously. On the assumption that crime could be controlled if criminals could be prevented from transmitting their traits to the next generation, some U.S. states permitted the sterilization of habitual offenders. Sterilization laws were held constitutional by the U.S. Supreme Court in a 1927 opinion written by Justice Oliver Wendell Holmes Jr., which included the following well-known pronouncement:

> It is better for all the world, if instead of waiting to execute degenerate offspring for crime, or to let them starve for their imbecility, society can prevent those who are manifestly unfit from continuing their kind. . . . Three generations of imbeciles are enough.[38]

Following this ruling, and under the influence of American and European sterilization programs, the government of Alberta passed its Sexual Sterilization Act in 1928. The Alberta Eugenics Board operated under this act from 1928 to 1972, when the act was repealed. During this period, over 2800 people were sterilized because they were thought to be "feeble-minded" or mentally defective. Of course,

this kind of reasoning, which leads to laws and policies to protect society from "misfits" and "degenerates," encounters problems when labelling is inaccurate, and when economic and political factors are involved. Consider the case of the "Duplessis Orphans"—thousands of orphaned children in Quebec who became economic pawns in the 1940s through to the 1960s, of the provincial government under Maurice Duplessis. The orphans were falsely labelled as mentally ill by the government, confined to psychiatric institutions, and subjected to experimental drug treatments, and sexual and other forms of abuse. A drawback of biological positivism, then, is the danger of intentional, or unintentional, diagnosis and labelling, which can have serious consequences for those subject to the labels.

Clearly the early positivists, with their focus on physical characteristics, exerted great influence. They were destined to be overshadowed, though, by investigators who focused on psychological characteristics.

PSYCHOLOGICAL DETERMINISM

On the whole, scholars who investigated criminal behaviour in the nineteenth and early twentieth centuries were far more interested in the human body than in the human mind. During that period, however, several contributions were made in the area of psychological explanations of crime. Some of the earliest contributions came from physicians interested primarily in the legal responsibility of the criminally insane. Later on, psychologists entered the field and applied their new testing techniques to the study of offenders (see Chapter 4).

Pioneers in Criminal Psychology

Isaac Ray (1807–1881), acknowledged as the first American forensic psychiatrist, was interested throughout his life in the application of psychiatric principles to the law. He is best known as the author of *The Medical Jurisprudence of Insanity*, a treatise on criminal responsibility that was widely quoted and influential.[39] In it he defended the concept of moral insanity, a disorder first described in 1806 by the French humanitarian and psychiatrist Philippe Pinel (1745–1826).[40] "Moral insanity" was a term used to describe persons who were normal in all respects except that something was wrong with the part of the brain that regulates affective

Who's Responsible?

For more than two centuries, scholars, psychologists, and criminologists have been debating the question of whether people with mental deficiencies should be held fully responsible for their crimes, especially when the death penalty is involved. According to biological positivism, individuals who are "mentally deficient" or mentally ill suffer from problems relating directly to their biological make-up. Such individuals are "sick" and in need of treatment rather than punishment. If we extend the argument to individuals with physical or mental afflictions who commit acts of deviance or crime, it follows that they should not be punished, certainly not to the same extent as those who do not suffer from such maladies. In June 2002, the U.S. Supreme Court barred the execution of mentally retarded inmates, stating that "today our society views mentally retarded offenders as categorically less culpable than the average criminal."

The decision was based on the case of a Virginia man, Daryl Atkins, with an IQ of 59, who was convicted of committing a murder and robbery at the age of 18. The generally accepted definition of mental retardation is an IQ of approximately 70, accompanied by limitations on abilities like communication or caring for oneself. Fifteen countries of the European Union filed a brief on behalf of Mr. Atkins, and a group of American diplomats told the Court that executing the retarded was out of step with the rest of the world. Amnesty International reported that since 1995, only three countries had executed mentally retarded people: Kyrgyzstan, Japan, and the United States.

The Court made its ruling based on the majority's view that a "national consensus" now rejected such executions as cruel and unusual punishment, as put forward in the Eighth Amendment of the U.S. Constitution.

In another case, decided in November 2002, the Supreme Court granted a last-minute reprieve to a death-row inmate who suffers from severe mental illness, halting his execution at 5:59 P.M., one minute before the inmate was scheduled to be led to the death chamber. In 1994, James Blake Colburn raped and murdered a woman he knew. Although he had a history of psychiatric problems, including chronic paranoid schizophrenia and 15 suicide attempts, the jury sentenced him to death. The Court granted the stay "pending the timely filing and disposition of a petition for writ of certiorari," or a request for the Court to review the case. That means they did not ban the execution of the mentally ill; instead they gave Mr. Colburn's attorneys more time to prove that he had not been given a fair trial or appropriate sentence.

These cases may seem irrelevant from a Canadian perspective because they are situations involving the death penalty, which is no longer used in this country. However, there are several underlying issues that emerge from this debate, which are relevant to the broader discussion relating to deterrence. On a continuum of increasing severity of punishment, the death penalty clearly falls on the most extreme end. Supporters of the death penalty argue that its severity serves as a deterrent to individuals contemplating crime. The argument is that if the goal is to "get tough" on crime, perhaps the best way to do so is to invoke the most severe type of punishment—the death penalty—for individuals convicted of the most heinous crimes. Of course, as illustrated in the cases just mentioned, the question remains as to whether certain categories of individuals, such as those with mental illness or other psychological disorders, can effectively be deterred. Are all criminals rational?

Some argue that all criminals are not rational, and a case in point is those whose ability to reason is affected by biological or psychological conditions. These critics also point to the lack of "swiftness," another requirement for deterrence to occur, in death penalty cases, where trials and appeals often take many years. Another argument presented by opponents is termed the "brutalization thesis": the belief that violence in the form of executions performed by the state increases the overall level of acceptance of violence in society, and actually leads to an increase in violent crimes. Perhaps one of the strongest arguments against capital punishment is the occurrence of wrongful convictions.

Despite the arguments against the use of the death penalty, about half of Canadians support the reinstatement of capital punishment.

Sources

Linda Greenhouse, "The Supreme Court: The Death Penalty; Citing 'National Consensus,' Justices Bar Death Penalty for Retarded Defendants," *New York Times,* June 21, 2002; Jim Yardley, "Court Stays Execution of Mentally Ill Texan," *New York Times,* Nov. 7, 2002, Reprinted with permission; Larry J. Siegel and Chris McCormick, *Criminology in Canada,* 3rd ed. (Toronto: Thomson Nelson, 2006).

Questions for Discussion

1. Where do we draw the line on who is responsible for his or her own behaviour and who is not? Should this be determined on a case-by-case basis, or can laws cover such instances "across the board"?

2. The U.S. Supreme Court banned the execution of mentally challenged offenders, not because it found the practice morally or legally wrong, but because it found a "national consensus" that such executions were excessive and inappropriate. Can you think of ways that such a method of determination might have both positive and negative effects?

3. James Blake Colburn was executed on March 26, 2003. In a country like the United States where capital punishment exists, do you believe that inmates with serious mental illness should be put to death?

responses. Ray questioned whether we could hold people legally responsible for their acts if they had such an impairment, because such people committed their crimes without an intent to do so.

Henry Maudsley (1835–1918), a brilliant English medical professor, shared Ray's concerns about criminal responsibility. According to Maudsley, some people may be considered either "insane or criminal according to the standpoint from which they are looked at." He believed that for many persons, crime is an "outlet in which their unsound tendencies are discharged; they would go mad if they were not criminals."[41] Most of Maudsley's attention focused on the borderline between insanity and crime.

Psychological Studies of Criminals

Around the turn of the twentieth century, psychologists used their new measurement techniques to study offenders. The administering of intelligence tests to inmates of jails, prisons, and other public institutions was especially popular at that time, because it was a period of major controversy over the relation of mental deficiency to criminal behaviour. The new technique seemed to provide an objective basis for differentiating criminals from non-criminals.

In 1914, Henry H. Goddard, research director of the Vineland, New Jersey, Training School for the Retarded, examined some intelligence tests that had been given to inmates and concluded that 25 to 50 percent of the people in prison had intellectual defects that made them incapable of managing their own affairs.[42] This idea remained dominant until it was challenged by the results of intelligence tests administered to World War I draftees, whose scores were found to be lower than those of prisoners in the federal penitentiary at Leavenworth. As a result of this study and others like it, intelligence quotient (IQ) measures largely disappeared as a basis for explaining criminal behaviour.

SOCIOLOGICAL DETERMINISM

During the nineteenth and early twentieth centuries, some scholars began to search for the social determinants of criminal behaviour. The approach had its roots in Europe in the 1830s, the time between Beccaria's *On Crimes and Punishment* and Lombroso's *The Criminal Man*.

Adolphe Quételet and André Michel Guerry

The Belgian mathematician Adolphe Quételet (1796–1874) and the French lawyer André Michel Guerry (1802–1866) were among the first scholars to repudiate the classicists' free-will doctrine. Working independently on the relation of crime statistics to such factors as poverty, age, sex, race, and climate, both scholars concluded that society, not the decisions of individual offenders, was responsible for criminal behaviour.

The first modern criminal statistics were published in France in 1827. Guerry used those statistics to demonstrate that crime rates varied with social factors. He found, for example, that the wealthiest region of France had the highest rate of property crime but only half the national rate of violent crime. He concluded that the main factor in property crime was opportunity: there was much more to steal in the richer provinces.

Quételet did an elaborate analysis of crime in France, Belgium, and Holland. After analyzing criminal statistics, which he called "moral statistics," he concluded that if we look at overall patterns of behaviour of groups across a whole society, we find a startling regularity of rates of various behaviours. According to Quételet:

> We can enumerate in advance how many individuals will soil their hands in the blood of their fellows, how many will be frauds, how many prisoners; almost as one can enumerate in advance the births and deaths that will take place.[43]

By focusing on groups rather than individuals, he discovered that behaviour is indeed predictable, regular, and understandable. Just as the physical world is governed by the laws of nature, human behaviour is governed by forces external to the individual. The more we learn about those forces, the easier it becomes to predict behaviour. A major goal of criminological research, according to Quételet, should be to identify factors related to crime and to assign to them their "proper degree of influence."[44] Though neither he nor Guerry offered a theory of criminal behaviour, the fact that both studied social factors scientifically, using quantitative research methods, made them key figures in the subsequent development of sociological theories of crime causation.

Gabriel Tarde

One of the earliest sociological theories of criminal behaviour was formulated by Gabriel Tarde (1843–1904), who served 15 years as a provincial judge and then was placed in charge of France's national statistics. After an extensive analysis of these statistics, he came to the following conclusion:

> The majority of murderers and notorious thieves began as children who had been abandoned, and the true seminary of crime must be sought for upon each public square or each crossroad of our towns, whether they be small or large, in those flocks of pillaging street urchins who, like bands of sparrows, associate together, at first for marauding, and then for theft, because of a lack of education and food in their homes.[45]

Tarde rejected the Lombrosian theory of biological abnormality, which was popular in his time, arguing that criminals were normal people who learned crime just as others learned legitimate trades. He formulated his theory in terms of **laws of imitation**—principles that governed the process by which people became criminals. According to Tarde's thesis, individuals emulate behaviour patterns in much the same way that they copy styles of dress. Moreover, there is a pattern to the way such emulation takes place: (1) Individuals imitate others in proportion to the intensity and frequency of their contacts; (2) inferiors imitate superiors—that is, trends flow from town to country and from upper to lower classes; and (3) when two behaviour patterns clash, one may take the place of the other, as when guns largely replaced knives as murder weapons.[46] Tarde's work served as the basis for Edwin Sutherland's theory of differential association, which we shall examine in Chapter 6.

Émile Durkheim

Modern criminologists take two major approaches to the study of the social factors associated with crime. Tarde's approach asks how individuals become criminal. What is the process? How are behaviour patterns learned and transmitted? The second major approach looks at the social structure and its institutions. It asks how crime arises in the first place and how it is related to the functioning of a society. For answers to these questions, scholars begin with the work of Émile Durkheim (1858–1917).

Émile Durkheim (1858–1917), one of the founders of sociology.

Of all nineteenth-century writers on the relationship between crime and social factors, none has more powerfully influenced contemporary criminology than Durkheim, who is universally acknowledged as one of the founders of sociology. On October 12, 1870, when Durkheim was 12 years old, the German army invaded and occupied his hometown, Epinal, in eastern France. Thus, at a very early age, he witnessed social chaos and the effects of rapid change, topics with which he remained preoccupied throughout his life. At the age of 24, he became a professor of philosophy, and at 29 he joined the faculty of the University of Bordeaux. There he taught the first course in sociology ever to be offered by a French university.

By 1902, he had moved to the University of Paris, where he completed his doctoral studies. His *Division of Social Labor* became a landmark work on the organization of societies. According to Durkheim, crime is as normal a part of society as birth and death. Theoretically, crime could disappear altogether only if all members of society had the same values, and such standardization is neither possible nor desirable. Furthermore, some crime is in fact necessary if a society is to progress:

> The opportunity for the genius to carry out his work affords the criminal his originality at a lower level. . . . According to Athenian law, Socrates was a criminal, and his condemnation was no more than just. However, his crime, namely, the independence of his thought, rendered a service not only to humanity but to his country.[47]

Durkheim further pointed out that all societies have not only crime but also sanctions. The rationale for the sanctions varies in accordance with the structure of the society. In a strongly cohesive society, punishment of members who deviate is used to reinforce the value system—to remind people of what is right and what is wrong—thereby preserving the pool of common belief and the solidarity of the society. Punishment must be harsh to serve these ends. In a large, urbanized, heterogeneous society, however, punishment is used not to preserve solidarity but rather to right the wrong done to a victim. Punishment thus is evaluated in accordance with the harm done, with the goal of restitution and reinstatement of order as quickly as possible. The offence is not considered a threat to social cohesion, primarily because in a large, complex society, criminal events do not even come to the attention of most people.

The most important of Durkheim's many contributions to contemporary sociology is his concept of **anomie,** a breakdown of social order as a result of a loss of standards and values. In a society plagued by anomie (see Chapter 5), disintegration and chaos replace social cohesion.

HISTORICAL AND CONTEMPORARY CRIMINOLOGY: A TIME LINE

Classical criminologists thought the problem of crime might be solved through limitations on governmental power, the abolition of brutality, and the creation of a more equitable system of justice. They argued that the punishment should fit the crime. For over a century, this perspective dominated criminology. Later on, positivist criminologists influenced judges to give greater consideration to the offender than to the gravity of the crime when imposing sentences. The current era marks a return to the classical demand that the punishment correspond to the seriousness of the crime and the guilt of the offender.

As modern science discovered more and more about cause and effect in the physical and social universes, the theory that individuals commit crimes of their own free will began to lose favour. The positivists searched for determinants of crime in biological, psychological, and social factors. Biologically based theories were popular in the late nineteenth century, fell out of favour in the early part of the twentieth, and emerged again in the 1970s (see Chapter 4) with studies of hormone imbalances, diet, environmental contaminants, and so forth. Since the studies of criminal responsibility in the nineteenth century centring on the insanity defence and of intelligence levels in the twentieth century, psychiatrists and psychologists have continued to play a major role in the search for the causes of crime, especially after Sigmund Freud developed his well-known theory of human personality (see Chapter 4). The sociological perspective became popular in the 1920s and has remained the predominant approach of criminological studies. (We will examine contemporary theories in Chapters 5 through 9.)

REVIEW

1. What was the context within which criminology developed?

In the history of criminology from ancient times to the early twentieth century, its many themes at times have clashed and at times have supported one another. There is no straight-line evolutionary track that we can follow from the inception of the first "criminological" thought to modern theories. Some scholars, like those affiliated with the **classical school** (p. 55), concentrated on criminal law and procedure and based their work on the assumption that individuals have free will and choose to commit crime. **Utilitarianism** (p. 61), which assumes that all human actions are calculated in accordance with their likelihood of bringing happiness or unhappiness, played an important role in the classical school.

2. What is positivist criminology?

Positivist school (p. 56) criminologists, influenced by scientists like Auguste Comte and Charles Darwin, moved the field of criminology from a philosophical to a scientific perspective.

3. Is there a biological link to criminal behaviours?

While the classical school scholars focused their attention on reforming the criminal justice system, other scholars, influenced by positivism, focused their attention on criminal behaviour. Some, like those who studied **physiognomy** (p. 63), took the biological route. Their work was elaborated upon by physicians who worked within the science of **phrenology** (p. 63). These early biological positivists suggested that **atavistic stigmata** (p. 64) distinguished criminals from non-criminals. An individual born with any five of the stigmata was thought to be a **born criminal** (p. 64). During the first half of the twentieth century, the **somatotype school** (p. 67) of criminology, which related body builds to behaviour, became popular, but fell into disfavour following World War II, as it seemed too close to **eugenics** (p. 67).

4. Is there a psychological link to criminal behaviours?

Some theorists focused on psychological explanations for criminal behaviours. Early approaches researched the link between intellectual capacity and criminal behaviour.

5. How do sociologists explain criminal behaviours?

Still other researchers concentrated on sociological contributors to criminal behaviours. And the work of some investigators has encompassed a combination of factors. Toward the end of the nineteenth century, a discipline began to emerge. For example, Gabriel Tarde argued that criminals were normal people who learned crime in the same way that others learned to work in legitimate fields. Tarde's theory was built around **laws of imitation** (p. 71). Durkheim, on the other hand, linked criminal behaviours to a breakdown of social order, which he referred to as **anomie** (p. 72).

Tracing the major developments back in time helps us understand how criminology grew into the discipline we know today. Many of the issues that appear on the intellectual battlefields in the twenty-first century are the same issues our academic ancestors grappled with for hundreds, indeed thousands, of years. With each new clash, some old concepts died, while others were incorporated within competing doctrinal boundaries, there to remain until the next challenge. The controversies of one era become the foundations of knowledge for the next. As societies develop and are subjected to new technologies, the crime problem becomes ever more complex. So do the questions it raises. In Part II we will see how twentieth-century theorists have dealt with those questions.

CRIMINOLOGY & PUBLIC POLICY

Politicians are known for their "tough on crime" promises. In May 2006, the newly elected Conservative government introduced two anti-crime bills as part of its law-and-order justice strategy. The mandatory minimum sentencing bill aimed to reduce judicial discretion in sentencing, making it a requirement for convicted offenders to serve a minimum of five years for a first offence involving a firearm or committed in connection with a gang, an increase to seven years for a second offence, and ten years for a third. Other changes in the proposed legislation include the elimination of statutory release, whereby inmates who have served two-thirds of their sentence are released to serve the remainder under supervision in the community. These proposed changes to sentencing draw on the deterrence philosophy that Beccaria and Bentham outlined centuries ago: People will be deterred from criminal offending if punishment is swift, certain, and severe.

However, the proposed changes will significantly increase the prison population in Canadian prisons and drive up the cost of corrections (the average cost to keep an inmate in prison for one year is $87 000). Estimates are that the changes would mean an increase in prisoner population by about 5500 inmates. The costs of keeping the additional inmates locked up are significant, but another problem is the lack of prison space to house them. New prisons would have to be built; the last federal prison constructed in Ontario in 1998 cost $62 million. Prison overcrowding presents problems for staff and inmates alike. Fewer resources to go around means frustration, anger, and the possibility of violence. Depression rates are higher in situations of overcrowding, as are rates of suicide. Neil Boyd from Simon Fraser University and Anthony Doob from the University of Toronto voice the opinion of many criminologists when they point out that "get tough" legislation is an attempt at a quick fix (that may sound good to the public) to a problem that requires re-examining social policy: providing opportunities and hope for those who live in poverty, providing legitimate alternatives to criminal ones, and putting money into social programs instead of into building more prisons.

(*Sources:* Jim Trautman, "Barring Disaster: Are Tough-on-Crime Tories Paving the Way for Private Prisons?" *This Magazine,* Red Maple Foundation, July–August, 2006, http://socialisses.wiseto.com/Articles/148319679/, accessed May 4, 2007; Curt T. Griffiths, *Canadian Corrections,* 2nd ed. [Toronto: Thomson Nelson, 2004].)

Visit the Online Learning Centre: www.mcgrawhill.ca/olc/adler

Questions for Discussion Beccaria voiced concerns over bad laws (see the "Cesare Beccaria" section on page 58. He made an inspired call for an end to medieval barbarism. Punishment should be prompt and effective. Capital punishment should be abolished—and so, too, should the use of torture. Prison overcrowding has been shown to have negative effects on inmates, physically and mentally. An alternative to the problem is the privatization of prisons. Ontario has experimented with private prisons as a way of dealing with a growing incarcerated population. What do you think of the privatization of prison? What are the alternatives?

YOU BE THE CRIMINOLOGIST

An historical society has invited you to represent criminology in a discussion group made up of experts from various disciplines. The topic is: How do the foundations of your discipline help us to understand contemporary developments in the field? What would you discuss?

EXPLANATIONS OF CRIME AND CRIMINAL BEHAVIOUR

Having explored the history of criminology, the early explanations of criminal behaviour, and the scientific methods used by criminologists, we turn now to contemporary theories and research. Current explanations of criminal behaviour focus on biological, psychological, social, and economic factors. Biological and psychological theories assume that criminal behaviour results from underlying physical or mental conditions that distinguish criminals from non-criminals (Chapter 4). These theories yield insight into individual cases, but they do not explain why crime rates vary from place to place and from one situation to another.

Sociological theories seek to explain criminal behaviour in terms of the environment. Chapter 5 examines strain theories, which focus on the social forces that cause people to engage in criminal behaviour. These theories assume that social class and criminal behaviour are related. Strain theorists argue that people commit crimes because they are frustrated by not being able to achieve their goals through legitimate means. In Chapter 6, the discussion centres on cultural deviance theories and theories that focus on the formation of subcultures. Cultural deviance theorists claim that crime is learned in socially disorganized neighbourhoods where criminal norms are transmitted from one generation to the next. We examine subcultures that have their own norms, beliefs, and values, which differ significantly from those of the dominant culture. Chapter 7 explains how people remain committed to conventional behaviour in the face of frustration, poor living conditions, and other criminogenic factors. In Chapter 8, we further discuss theoretical perspectives that focus on society's role in creating criminals and defining them as such, including the ways in which labelling helps to create future criminal behaviour. Finally, in Chapter 9, we discuss how legitimate routines and lifestyles can create opportunities for victimization. We explain why offenders choose to commit one offence rather than another at a given time and place.

PSYCHOLOGICAL AND BIOLOGICAL PERSPECTIVES

CHAPTER 4

CHAPTER QUESTIONS

1. What are some psychological explanations for criminal behaviours?

2. Is there a link between mental disorder and crime?

3. How do biological approaches explain criminal behaviours?

4. Is a biological explanation for criminality valid?

Paul Bernardo, serial rapist and murderer, was sentenced to life in prison without the possibility of parole for 25 years for the murders of Kristen French and Leslie Mahaffy. Designated a dangerous offender, Bernardo will likely never be released. Much controversy surrounded his case, particularly concerning the role played by his wife and crime partner Karla Homolka.

January 22, 2007, marked the beginning of the trial of the worst alleged serial killer in Canadian history. A 57-year-old pig farmer from Port Coquitlam, British Columbia, Robert Pickton, charged with the first-degree murders of 26 women, was being tried on six of the charges. Pickton allegedly confessed to an undercover police officer posing as Pickton's cellmate, that he had killed 49 women and "got sloppy" when going for "an even 50." Although the accused's defence team claims Pickton suffers from diminished intellectual capacity, one RCMP staff sergeant expressed grudging admiration for the way Pickton played the police during his videotaped interrogation where the apparent psychopath cleverly suggests, yet avoids, a confession when he says things like: "you're making me more of a mass killer than I am" and "I won't admit to anything, yet."[1]

Pickton apparently hosted parties at a converted farm building named "The Piggy Palace," where an ever-changing line-up of Vancouver's Downtown Eastside prostitutes would entertain. Pickton was first charged with attempted murder in 1997, but the charges were dropped. It was not until 2002 that police were able to make the charges stick. As police embarked on a massive excavation and search of Pickton's property, increasing evidence resulted in the eventual laying of 27 murder charges. The cost of the investigation is estimated to have been $70 million. During the course of the investigation, which included using two 15-metre flat conveyer belts and soil sifters to find traces of remains, it was revealed that human flesh may have been ground up and mixed with pork from the farm. Forensic analysis is very difficult because the bodies of victims may have been left to decompose, or fed directly to the pigs.

In North America, explanations of criminal behaviour have been dominated by sociological theories. These theories focus on lack of opportunity and the breakdown of the conventional value system in urban ghettos, the formation of subcultures whose norms deviate from those of the middle class, and the increasing inability of social institutions to exercise control over behaviour. Criminological texts have treated psychological and biological theories as peripheral, perhaps because criminology's disciplinary allegiance is to sociology. When psychological theories were first advanced to explain criminal behaviour, their emphasis was largely psychoanalytic, so they may have seemed not quantitative enough to some criminologists.[2] Others may have considered the early work of Lombroso, Goring, and Hooten too scientifically naïve to be taken seriously.

Sociological theories focus on crime rates of groups that experience frustration in their efforts to achieve accepted goals, not on the particular individual who becomes a criminal. Sociological theories cannot explain how one person can be born in a slum, be exposed to family discord and abuse, never attend school, have friends who are delinquents, and yet resist opportunities for crime, while another person can grow up in an affluent suburban neighbourhood in a two-parent home and end up firing a gun at the prime minister. In other words, sociologists do not address individual differences.[3] Instead, psychologists and biologists are interested in finding out what may account for individual differences.

It is clear that psychological, biological, and sociological explanations are not competing to answer the same specific questions. Rather, all three disciplines are searching for answers to different questions, even though they study the same act, status, or characteristic. We can understand crime in a society only if we view criminality from more than one level of analysis: why a certain individual commits a crime (psychological and biological

Serial killers only stop murdering when they are caught or killed.

explanations) and why some groups of individuals commit more or different criminal acts than other groups (sociological explanations).

Sociological theory and empirical research often ignore such factors as personality and human biology, almost as if they were irrelevant. And psychological theory often focuses on the individual, with little regard for the fact that while each one of us comes into the world with certain predispositions, from the moment we are born we interact with others in complex situations that influence our behaviour.

PSYCHOLOGY AND CRIMINALITY

Psychologists have considered a variety of possibilities to account for individual differences—defective conscience, emotional immaturity, inadequate childhood socialization, maternal deprivation, and poor moral development. They study how aggression is learned, which situations promote violent or criminal reactions, how crime is related to personality factors, and how various mental disorders are associated with criminality.

Psychological Development

The **psychoanalytic theory** of criminality attributes delinquent and criminal behaviour to at least three possible causes:

- A conscience so overbearing that it arouses feelings of guilt

- A conscience so weak that it cannot control the individual's impulses

- The need for immediate gratification

Consider the case of Richard. Richard was six when he committed his first delinquent act: He stole a magazine from the corner drugstore. Three months before the incident, his father, an alcoholic, had been killed in an automobile accident, and his mother, unable to care for the family, had abandoned the children.

For the next ten years, the provincial social services department moved Richard in and out of foster homes. During this time, he actively pursued a life of crime, breaking into houses during daylight hours and stealing cars at night. By age 20, while serving a five-year prison sentence for armed robbery, he had voluntarily entered psychoanalysis. After two years, Richard's analyst suggested three reasons for his criminality. It was possible that being caught and punished for stealing made him feel less guilty about hating both his father for dying and thus abandoning him as well as his mother for deliberately abandoning him. Second, stealing did not violate his moral and ethical principles. The third possible reason was that stealing resulted in immediate gratification and pleasure, both of which Richard had great difficulty resisting.

Sigmund Freud (1856–1939), the founder of psychoanalysis, suggested that an individual's psychological well-being is dependent on a healthy interaction among the id, ego, and superego—the three basic components of the human psyche. The **id** consists of powerful urges and drives for gratification and satisfaction. The **ego** is the executive of the personality, acting as a moderator between the superego and id. The **superego** acts as a moral code or conscience. Freud proposed that criminality may result from an overactive superego or conscience. In treating patients, he noticed that those who were suffering from unbearable guilt committed crimes in order to be apprehended and punished.[4] Once they had been punished, their feelings of guilt were relieved. Richard's psychoanalyst suggested that Richard's anger over his father's death and his mother's abandonment created unconscious feelings of guilt, which he sought to relieve by committing a crime and being punished for it.

The psychoanalyst also offered an alternative explanation for Richard's persistent criminal activities: His conscience was perhaps not too strong, but too weak. The conscience, or superego, was so weak or defective that he was unable to control the impulses of the id. Because the superego is essentially an internalized parental image, developed

"The first human who hurled an insult instead of a stone was the founder of civilization."
Sigmund Freud

when the child assumes the parents' attitudes and moral values, it follows that the absence of such an image may lead to an unrestrained id and thus to delinquency.[5]

Psychoanalytic theory suggests yet another explanation for Richard's behaviour: an insatiable need for immediate reward and gratification. A defect in the character formation of delinquents drives them to satisfy their desires at once, regardless of the consequences.[6] This urge, which psychoanalysts attribute to the id, is so strong that relationships with people are important only so long as they help satisfy it. Most analysts view delinquents as children unable to give up their desires for instant pleasure.

The psychoanalytic approach is still one of the most prominent explanations for both normal and asocial functioning. Despite criticism,[7] three basic principles still appeal to psychologists who study criminality. First, the actions and behaviour of an adult are understood in terms of childhood development. Second, behaviour and unconscious motives are intertwined, and their interaction must be unravelled if we are to understand criminality. Finally, criminality is essentially a representation of psychological conflict.

In spite of their appeal, psychoanalytic treatment techniques devised to address these principles have been controversial since their introduction by Freud and his disciples. The controversy has involved questions about improvement following treatment and, perhaps more important, the validity of the hypothetical conflicts the treatment presupposes.

Moral Development

Consider the following moral dilemma:

> A woman is near death from a special kind of cancer. There is one drug that the doctors think might save her. It is a form of radium that a druggist in the same town has recently discovered. The drug is expensive to make, and the druggist is charging ten times that cost. He paid $200 for the radium and is charging $2000 for a small dose of the drug. The sick woman's husband, Heinz, goes to everyone he knows to borrow the money, but he can get together only $1000. He tells the druggist that his wife is dying and asks him to sell the drug more cheaply or to let him pay later. The druggist says, "No, I discovered the drug and I'm going to make money from it." Heinz is desperate and considers breaking into the man's store to steal the drug for his wife.[8]

This classic dilemma sets up complex moral issues. While you may know that it is wrong to steal, you may believe that this is a situation in which the law should be circumvented. Or is it always wrong to steal, no matter what the circumstances? Regardless of what you decide, the way you reach the decision about whether or not to steal reveals much about your moral development.

The psychologist Lawrence Kohlberg, who pioneered moral developmental theory, has found that moral reasoning develops in three phases.[9] In the first, the preconventional level, children's moral rules and moral values consist of dos and don'ts to avoid punishment. A desire to avoid punishment and a belief in the superior power of authorities are the two central reasons for doing what is right. According to the theory, until the ages of 9 to 11, children usually reason at this level. They think, in effect, "If I steal, what are my chances of getting caught and being punished?"

Adolescents typically reason at the conventional level. Here individuals believe in and have adopted the values and rules of society. Moreover, they seek to uphold these rules. They think, in effect, "It is illegal to steal and therefore I should not steal, under any circumstances." Finally, at the postconventional level, individuals examine customs and social rules according to their own sense of universal human rights, moral principles, and duties. They think, in effect, "One must live within the law, but certain universal ethical principles, such as respect for human rights and for the dignity of human life, supersede the written law when the two conflict." This level of moral reasoning is generally seen in adults after the age of 20. (See Table 4.1.)

According to Kohlberg and his colleagues, most delinquents and criminals reason at the preconventional level. Low moral development or preconventional reasoning alone, however, does not result in criminality. Other factors, such as the presence or the absence of significant social bonds, may play a part. Kohlberg has argued that basic moral principles and social norms are learned through social interaction and role-playing. In essence, children learn how to be moral by reasoning with others who are at a higher level of moral development.[10]

Students of Kohlberg have looked at practical applications of his theory. The "just-community intervention" approach, designed for use in prisons, but extended to school systems as well, involves a structured educational curriculum stressing democracy, fairness, and a sense of community. A series of evaluations of just-community programs has revealed significant improvement in moral development.[11] Despite the positive practical developments emerging from his theory, Kohlberg's work has been subject to criticism. Carol Gilligan points out that the basis for Kohlberg's theory was a longitudinal study of 84 males. One result of the absence of females from his study is that the theory is biased in favour in males. Gilligan points out that there is variation in moral standards by gender: females take a more care-oriented approach to morality whereas males tend to use a more justice-oriented stance. This difference means that females typically reach only the second level (third stage) in Kohlberg's theory. As a result, the traits that have traditionally defined the "goodness" of women, their care for and sensitivity to others, "are those that mark them as deficient in moral development."[12]

Maternal Deprivation and Attachment Theory

In a well-known psychological experiment, infant monkeys were provided with the choice between two wire "monkeys." One, made of uncovered cage wire, dispensed milk. The other, made of cage wire covered with soft fabric, did not give milk.

TABLE 4.1 Kohlberg's Sequence of Moral Reasoning

Level	Stage	Sample Moral Reasoning	
		In Favour of Stealing	**Against Stealing**
Level 1: Preconventional morality. At this level, the concrete interests of the individual are considered in terms of rewards and punishments.	Stage 1: Obedience and punishment orientation. At this stage, people stick to rules in order to avoid punishment, and there is obedience for its own sake.	If you let your wife die, you will get in trouble. You'll be blamed for not spending the money to save her, and there'll be an investigation of you and the druggist for your wife's death.	You shouldn't steal the drug because you'll be caught and sent to jail if you do. If you do get away, your conscience will bother you, thinking how the police will catch up with you at any minute.
	Stage 2: Reward orientation. At this stage, rules are followed only for one's own benefit. Obedience occurs because of rewards that are received.	If you do happen to get caught, you could give the drug back and you wouldn't get much of a sentence. It wouldn't bother you much to serve a little jail term, if you have your wife when you get out.	You may not get much of a jail term if you steal the drug, but your wife will probably die before you get out, so it won't do much good. If your wife dies, you shouldn't blame yourself; it wasn't your fault she had cancer.
Level 2: Conventional morality. At this level, moral problems are approached by an individual as a member of society. People are interested in pleasing others by acting as good members of society.	Stage 3: "Good boy" morality. Individuals at this stage show an interest in maintaining the respect of others and doing what is expected of them.	No one will think you're bad if you steal the drug, but your family will think you're an inhuman husband if you don't. If you let your wife die, you'll never be able to look anybody in the face again.	It isn't just the druggist who will think you're a criminal; everyone else will too. After you steal it, you'll feel bad, thinking how you've brought dishonour on your family and yourself; you won't be able to face anyone again.
	Stage 4: Authority and social-order-maintaining morality. People at this stage conform to society's rules and consider that "right" is what society defines as right.	If you have any sense of honour, you won't let your wife die just because you're afraid to do the only thing that will save her. You'll always feel guilty that you caused her death if you don't do your duty to her.	You're desperate and you may not know you're doing wrong when you steal the drug. But you'll know you did wrong after you're sent to jail. You'll always feel guilty for your dishonesty and lawbreaking.
Level 3: Post-conventional morality. People at this level use moral principles that are seen as broader than those of any particular society.	Stage 5: Morality of contract, individual rights, and democratically accepted law. People at this stage do what is right because of a sense of obligation to laws that are agreed upon within society. They perceive that laws can be modified as part of changes in an implicit social contract.	You'll lose other people's respect, not gain it, if you don't steal. If you let your wife die, it will be out of fear, not out of reasoning. So you'll just lose self-respect and probably the respect of others too.	You'll lose your standing and respect in the community and violate the law. You'll lose respect for yourself if you're carried away by emotion and forget the long-range point of view.
	Stage 6: Morality of individual principles and conscience. At this final stage, a person follows laws because they are based on universal ethical principles. Laws that violate the principles are disobeyed.	If you don't steal the drug, if you let your wife die, you'll always condemn yourself for it afterward. You won't be blamed and you'll have lived up to the outside rule of the law, but you won't have lived up to your own standards of conscience.	If you steal the drug, you won't be blamed by other people, but you'll condemn yourself because you won't have lived up to your own conscience and standards of honesty.

Source: Adapted from Robert S. Feldman, *Understanding Psychology* (New York: McGraw-Hill, 1987), p. 378. Copyright (c) 1987 by The McGraw-Hill Companies, Inc. Reprinted by permission of the publisher.

The infant monkeys in the experiment gravitated to the warm cloth monkey, which provided comfort and security even though it did not provide food. What does this have to do with criminality? Research has demonstrated that a phenomenon important to social development takes place shortly after the birth of any mammal: the construction of an emotional bond between the infant and its mother. The strength of this emotional bond, or **attachment,** will determine, or at least

Experiments with young monkeys and surrogate mothers reveal the power of attachment in behavioural development. Here, a frightened baby rhesus monkey holds on to a terry-cloth mother.

materially affect, a child's ability to form attachments in the future. In order to form a successful attachment, a child needs a warm, loving, and interactive caretaker.

Studies of Attachment The British psychiatrist John Bowlby has studied both the need for warmth and affection from birth onward and the consequences of not having it. Based on his research findings Bowlby contends that a child needs to experience a warm, intimate, and continuous relationship with either a mother or a mother substitute in order to be securely attached. When a child is separated from the mother or is rejected by her, anxious attachment results. Anxious attachment affects the capacity to be affectionate and to develop intimate relationships with others.[13] Habitual criminals, it is claimed, typically have an inability to form bonds of affection.[14]

Family Atmosphere and Delinquency Criminologists also have examined the effects of the mother's absence, whether because of death, divorce, or abandonment. Does her absence cause delinquency? Empirical research is equivocal. Perhaps the most persuasive evidence comes from longitudinal research conducted by Joan McCord, who has investigated the relationship between family atmosphere (such as parental self-confidence, deviance, and affection) and delinquency.

In one study, she collected data on the childhood homes of 201 men and their subsequent court records in order to identify family-related variables that would predict criminal activity. Such variables as inadequate maternal affection and supervision, parental conflict, the mother's lack of self-confidence, and the father's deviance were significantly related to the commission of crimes against persons and/or property. The father's absence by itself was not correlated with criminal behaviour. Heather Juby and David Farrington also provide support for the importance of maternal presence. Using data from the Cambridge Study in Delinquent Development, they examined the impact of family structure on youth and adult crime and found that youth crime rates are lower among boys who live with their mother postseparation compared to those who live with their father. They also found that youth crime rates are very similar in disrupted families and high-conflict intact families.[15]

> ### Did You Know?
>
> ...that, while evidence is lacking that deprivation directly causes delinquency, research on the impact of family-based crime-prevention programs is promising? Programs that target family risk factors in multiple settings (ecological contexts) have achieved success. (See Table 4.2.)

Other studies, such as those by Sheldon and Eleanor Glueck and the more recent studies by Lee N. Robins, which were carried out in schools, youth courts, and psychiatric hospitals, suggest a moderate to strong relation between crime and childhood deprivation.[16] However, evidence that deprivation directly causes delinquency is lacking.[17]

So far we have considered psychological theories that attribute the causes of delinquency or criminality to unconscious problems and failures in moral development. Not all psychologists agree with these explanations of criminal behaviour. Some argue that human behaviour develops through learning. They say that we learn by observing others and by watching the responses to other people's behaviour (on television or in the movies, for instance) and to our own. Social learning theorists reject the notion that internal functioning alone makes us prone to act aggressively or violently.

Learning Aggression and Violence

Social learning theory maintains that delinquent behaviour is learned through the same psychological processes as any other behaviour. Behaviour is learned when it is reinforced or rewarded; it is not learned when it is not reinforced. We learn

TABLE 4.2 Family-Based Crime Prevention by Ecological Context

Ecological Context	Program	Prevention Agent
Home	Regular visits for emotional, informational, instrumental, and educational support for parents of preschool (or older) children	Nurses, teachers, paraprofessionals, preschool teachers
	Foster care outplacement for the prevention of physical and sexual abuse or neglect	Family services, social workers
	Family preservation of families at risk of outplacement of child	Private family-preservation teams
	Personal alarm for victims of serious domestic violence	Police
	In-home proactive counselling for domestic violence	Police, social workers
Preschool	Involvement of mothers in parent groups, job training, parent training	Preschool teachers
School	Parent training	Psychologists, teachers
	Simultaneous parent and child training	Psychologists, child-care workers, social workers
Clinics	Family therapy	Psychologists, psychiatrists, social workers
	Medication—psychostimulants for treatment of hyperactivity and other childhood conduct disorders	Psychiatrists, psychologists, pediatricians
Hospitals	Domestic violence counselling	Nurses, social workers
	Low-birthweight baby mothers' counselling and support	Nurses, social workers
Courts	Prosecution of batterers	Police, prosecutors
	Warrants for unarrested batterers	Police, prosecutors
	Restraining orders or "stay away" order of protection	Police, prosecutors, judges, victims' advocates
	Hotline notification of victim about release of incarcerated domestic batterer	Probation, victim advocates
Battered-women's shelters	Safe refuge during high-risk two to seven days' aftermath of domestic assault; counselling; hotlines	Volunteers, staff

behaviour in various ways: observation, direct experience, and differential reinforcement.

Observational Learning Albert Bandura, a leading proponent of social learning theory, argues that individuals learn violence and aggression through **behavioural modelling:** Children learn how to behave by fashioning their behaviour after that of others. Behaviour is socially transmitted through examples, which come primarily from the family, the subculture, and the mass media.[18]

Psychologists have been studying the effects of family violence (see Chapter 10) on children. They have found that parents who try to resolve family controversies by violence teach their children to use similar tactics. Thus a cycle of violence may be perpetuated through generations. Observing a healthy and happy family environment tends to result in constructive and positive modelling.

To understand the influence of the social environment outside the home, social learning theorists have studied gangs, which often provide excellent models of observational learning of violence and aggression. They have found, in fact, that violence is very much a norm shared by some people in a community or gang. The highest incidence of aggressive behaviour occurs where aggressiveness is a desired characteristic, as it is in some subcultures.

Observational learning takes place in front of the television set and at the movies as well. Children who have seen others being rewarded for violent acts often believe that violence and aggression are acceptable behaviours.[19] And today children can see a lot of violence. The psychologist Leonard Eron has argued that the "single best predictor of how aggressive a young man would be when he was 19 years old was the violence of the television programs he preferred when he was 8 years old."[20]

Results from the three-year landmark *National Television Violence Study* initiated in 1994 suggest that the problem is one not only of violence, but also of the portrayal of violence—the absence of consequences for violent acts and the glamorization of violence.[21]

Direct Experience What we learn by observation is determined by the behaviour of others. What we learn from direct experience is determined by what we ourselves do and what happens to us. We remember the past and use its lessons to avoid future mistakes. Thus we learn through trial and error.

Gene Combo Linked to Conduct Disorder, Antisocial Behavior

Genes strongly influence the development of both childhood conduct disorder (CD) and adult antisocial behavior, but no single gene is consistently linked to these disorders. However, a new study suggests that two genes—both involved in the brain's use of the neurotransmitter dopamine, which plays a key role in pleasure and motivation—may work in tandem to heighten the risk of CD and antisocial behavior.

Kevin Beaver and colleagues studied 872 males participating in the National Longitudinal Study of Adolescent Health. This ongoing project collected data from participants at three different times: when they were between the ages of 11 and 19, approximately two years later, and again when they were between the ages of 18 and 27. Beaver and colleagues focused on participants' responses to questions about behavior linked to conduct disorder (such as serious fighting, use of weapons, and gang membership). They also asked participants to answer the question, "Have you ever been convicted of a felony?" The researchers used data from the participants' DNA samples to determine if they possessed specific variants of two genes:

- The DRD2 gene. Carriers of one variant of this gene (the A-1 allele) have fewer brain D2 dopamine receptors, reduced dopamine activity in the central nervous system, and lower glucose metabolism in the brain. Beaver and colleagues note that this gene may contribute to "reward deficiency syndrome," in which a person does not obtain sufficient biological reward from behaviors that normally are satisfying—a problem that can lead to thrill-seeking behavior.
- The DRD4 gene. The researchers note that this gene is "found in areas of the brain that are responsible for the expression of emotions and for the stimulation of cognitive faculties." The gene is involved in attention, motivation, and exploratory behaviors. One variant of this gene (the 7-repeat allele) is tentatively linked to a variety of psychological problems.

The researchers measured participants' behaviors at each of the three study intervals. They also created a lifetime measure of conduct disorder and a separate measure of antisocial behavior.

Analyzed separately, neither the DRD2 nor the DRD4 gene variant showed a consistent effect on CD or antisocial behavior. However, the researchers say, the data showed that "DRD2 interacted with DRD4 to predict variation in adolescent conduct disorder and in adult antisocial behavior." This was true for all three study intervals, as well as for the lifetime conduct disorder scale and the antisocial behavior ratings.

The report builds on prior research showing that combinations of genes affecting dopamine function can influence novelty-seeking behavior, impulsiveness, and attention deficit hyperactivity disorder.

Sources:

"A gene x gene interaction between DRD2 and DRD4 is associated with conduct disorder and antisocial behavior in males," K. Beaver, J. P. Wright, M. DeLisi, A. Walsh, M. G. Vaughn, D. Boisvert, and J. Vaske, Behavioral and Brain Functions, June 22, 2007, full free text at http://www.behavioralandbrainfunctions.com/content/3/1/30. Address: Kevin Beaver, kbeaver@fsu.edu.

"Gene Combo Linked to Conduct Disorder, Antisocial Behavior", Crime Times, Volume 13, No. 3, 2007 located at http://www.crimetimes.org/07c/w07cp4.htm. Copyright 2007 THE WACKER FOUNDATION.

Questions for Discussion:

1. Why are genetic explanations of crime "appealing" to certain groups of people? Who would find such explanations particularly appealing?
2. What are the policy implications of gene-based research into criminal behaviour?

According to social learning theorists, after engaging in a given behaviour, most of us examine the responses to our actions and modify our behaviour as necessary to obtain favourable responses. If we are praised or rewarded for a behaviour, we are likely to repeat it. If we are subjected to verbal or physical punishment, we are likely to refrain from such behaviour. Our behaviour in the first instance and our restraint in the second are said to be "reinforced" by the rewards and punishments we receive.

The psychologist Gerald Patterson and his colleagues examined how aggression is learned by direct experience. They observed that some passive children at play were repeatedly victimized by other children but were occasionally successful in curbing the attacks by counter-aggression. Over time, these children learned defensive fighting, and eventually they initiated fights. Other passive children, who were rarely observed to be victimized, remained submissive.[22] Thus children, like adults, can learn to be aggressive and even violent by trial and error.

While violence and aggression are learned behaviours, they are not necessarily expressed until they are elicited in one of several ways. Albert Bandura describes the factors that elicit behavioural responses as "instigators." Thus social learning theory describes not only how aggression is acquired but also how it is instigated. Consider the following instigators of aggression:

- *Aversive instigators.* Physical assaults, verbal threats, and insults; adverse reductions in

Who Is Responsible for the Crime of Parricide?

J.R. was 12 years old when she and her 23-year-old boyfriend repeatedly stabbed and killed her mother and father, and strangled and slit the throat of her eight-year-old brother in Medicine Hat, Alberta. The girl was found guilty on all three counts of first-degree murder in July 2007 and is believed to be the youngest person in Canada to be convicted of multiple counts of first-degree murder. Her parents had sought family counselling to help the girl through a difficult time in her life but she was upset with them because they disapproved of her relationship with her co-accused.(1)

Two sisters, aged 15 and 16, in Mississauga, Ontario, were convicted of first-degree murder for the 2003 murder of their mother. The girls, who had no history of violence or criminal behaviour before the killing, plied their mother with Tylenol-3 pills and alcohol and then one of the girls held the mother's head under water in a bathtub until she drowned.(2)

Mark Martone was 16 when he shot his father to death. He remembers abuse back to age five, when he told his dad he was scared of the dark. "Oh, Jesus Christ," said the parent in disgust. Then he led the terrified boy down to the cellar, handcuffed his arms over a rafter, turned off the light and shut the door. Mark dangled in silence for hours. When Mark was nine, his father held the boy's hand over a red-hot burner as punishment for moving a book of matches on a bureau. And when he was 15, his dad, angered by a long-distance phone bill, stuck a gun in his son's mouth and "told me he was going to blow my brains out."(3)

Why do children kill their parents? One explanation is abuse. In a nationwide study of reported child abuse in Canada, researchers estimate that there are about 22 investigations of child abuse and neglect per 1000 children. Investigations of child abuse and neglect represent only a portion of all cases of such abuse.(4) Of the millions of North American children who are abused, maybe a few hundred each year fight back with the ultimate weapon: They kill the abusive parent. In the past, such children were regarded as particularly evil, and the law reserved the most terrible forms of capital punishment for parricides. With the growing understanding of the horrors of child abuse, however, these youths are being treated with increasing sympathy. "They know what they're doing is wrong," comments one psychologist. "But they are desperate and helpless, and they don't see alternatives."(3)

The typical case involves a 16- to 18-year-old from a white middle-class family. Sons are more likely than daughters to commit murder, and the victim is more likely to be a father than a mother. While children who kill non-abusive parents usually display some sign of mental disorder, the killers of abusive parents generally are seen as well adjusted.(5)

While in some cases sympathy for these teenagers has led to the successful use of defences (e.g., battered-child defence and self-defence) or convictions for reduced charges, in the cases of J.R. and the two Mississauga sisters maximum sentences under the Youth Criminal Justice Act were handed out. J.R. will serve part of her sentence in a psychiatric facility. Mental health experts think that treatment is more appropriate than punishment for children who kill their parents, particularly in cases where parents have abused the children. "These kids don't need to be locked up for our protection," says one attorney and psychologist. "Some may benefit in the sense that they've been able to atone and overcome some guilt. But beyond that, it's really Draconian."(3)

CHARACTERISTICS ASSOCIATED WITH ADOLESCENT PARRICIDE OFFENDERS

1. Patterns of family violence exist (parental brutality and cruelty toward child and/or toward one another).
2. Adolescent's attempts to get help from others fail.
3. Adolescent's efforts to escape family situation fail (e.g., running away, thoughts of suicide, suicide attempts).
4. Adolescent is isolated from others/fewer outlets.
5. Family situation becomes increasingly intolerable.
6. Adolescent feels increasingly helpless, trapped.
7. Adolescent's inability to cope leads to loss of control.
8. Prior criminal behaviour is minimal or non-existent.
9. Gun is available.
10. Homicide victim is alcoholic.
11. Evidence to suggest dissociative state in some cases.
12. Victim's death perceived as relief to offender/family; initial absence of remorse.

Sources

1. *CBC News,* "Medicine Hat Girl Guilty of First-Degree Murder," July 9, 2007, www.cbc.ca/canada/calgary/story/2007/07/09/med-hat.html, accessed February 9, 2008; Dawn Walton, "Alberta Girl Sentenced in Murders," *Globe and Mail,* November 8, 2007, www.theglobeandmail.com/servlet/story/RTGAM.20071108.walbertamurder1108/BN, accessed February 9, 2008.
2. *CBC News,* "2 Sisters Get Maximum Youth Penalty in Mother's Drowning," June 30, 2006, www.cbc.ca/canada/toronto/story/2006/06/30/bathtub-sisters.html, accessed February 9, 2008.
3. Hannah Bloch and Jeanne McDowell, "When Kids Kill Abusive Parents," *Time,* Nov. 23, 1992, p. 60.
4. N. Trocmé, B. MacLaurin, B. Fallon et al., *Canadian Incidence Study of Reported Child Abuse and Neglect: Final Report* (Ottawa: Minister of Public Works and Government Services Canada, 2001).
5. Kathleen M. Heide, *Why Kids Kill Parents* (Columbus: Ohio State University Press, 1992), pp. 40–41.

Questions for Discussion

1. If you were on a jury, would you be willing to consider that what appears to be a cold-blooded murder might have been a form of self-defence for a battered child?
2. A lawyer specializing in parricide feels that such cases "open a window on our understanding of child abuse." How would you go about determining which of millions of child abuse cases are likely to lead to parricide for which a standard defence should be recognized?

conditions of life (such as impoverishment) and the thwarting of goal-directed behaviour

- *Incentive instigators.* Rewards, such as money and praise
- *Modelling instigators.* Violent or aggressive behaviours observed in others
- *Instructional instigators.* Observations of people carrying out instructions to engage in violence or aggression
- *Delusional instigators.* Unfounded or bizarre beliefs that violence is necessary or justified[23]

Hockey provides an illustration of these instigators; it shows how aggression and violence are modelled, taught, and instigated in many hockey players from a young age. Although aggressiveness through body checking, for example, is considered an important part of the sport, there is a growing sense among many Canadians that the sport is becoming excessively violent. Recent incidents involving NHL players, including Marty McSorley's attack on Donald Brashear (using his hockey stick as a bat swinging at Brashear's head) and Todd Bertuzzi's attack on Steve Moore, have raised questions about the extent of violence that is condoned in the sport. Exacerbating the issue are the relatively light penalties offenders receive (McSorley was given a short suspension from playing the game; Bertuzzi, charged criminally, received a sentence that amounted to a "slap on the wrist"), sending the message to viewers, many of whom are young hockey players, that extreme violence is a natural part of the game.

In fact, minor hockey league players are learning that they have to be fighters as well as hockey players; leagues provide youngsters with "checking clinics" where they learn proper techniques for playing aggressively. While this is part of the game, it seems that the line between "proper checking" and inappropriate violence is becoming blurry. Checking clinics aside, Don Cherry's *Rock'em Sock'em* videos glamorize fighting and bloodshed as part of the game of hockey. As one grade 12 student writes:

I've often been at a St. John's Leafs game and heard children say, "Look Dad, there's my favourite hockey player. He's a great fighter." . . . Children at this age see fighting as an asset to the game. Often times coaches encourage nine- and ten-year-old children to hurt the best player on the other teams so they have a better chance to win. These same children see hockey superstars earning millions of

Mark Corry, a hockey dad who was upset over the fighting penalty his young son received, faces two charges of assault after allegedly attacking referees.

dollars a year, for being an instigator. Why wouldn't the children want to fight?[24]

Increasingly, it seems we hear reports of parents attacking coaches, players beating on referees, parents hitting parents, family members dumping hot chocolate over the heads of coaches, and in one recent case in Edmonton, a player's older brother beating up a player who had hit the younger brother during the game. The implications of these kinds of behaviours, in terms of social learning theory, are worrisome.

Differential Reinforcement In 1965, the criminologist C. Ray Jeffery suggested that learning theory could be used to explain criminality.[25] Within a year, Ernest Burgess and Ronald Akers combined

With over 15 000 fans watching, rookie Joe Thornton took on the 1.9-metre, 100-kilogram Canucks forward Dave Scatchard, who just ran him into the boards near the penalty box after some words were exchanged. What was the reaction of the fans? Violent fights are the highlight of hockey games. Fans, young and old, cheered Thornton for standing up to Scatchard.

Censoring TV Violence

Government regulations require that warnings and ratings regarding the violent and age-appropriate content of television shows be provided to viewers. Parents can purchase a "V-chip" to screen out violent programming. Of course, neither of these matters if children are watching television unsupervised. Nonetheless, North Americans have in recent years become more concerned about the content of television programming and its influence on their children's behaviour.(1)

THE RELATIONSHIP BETWEEN MEDIA VIOLENCE AND DEVIANT BEHAVIOUR AMONG YOUTH

Despite high levels of concern that exposure to violence on TV and in movies leads to violence among children, there is much debate about the nature and strength of the relationship between the two. In 1993, the American Psychological Association Commission on Youth and Violence found a correlation between higher levels of viewing violence in the mass media and increased aggression and acceptance of aggressive behaviour. Considering the findings of studies that show how much television children watch (those aged two to five watch television for an average of 28 hours per week, those 6 to 11 watch 24 hours a week, and teens watch 23 hours a week), combined with the results of a study showing that children's programming contains an average of 32 violent acts per hour (56 percent of shows had violent characters and 74 percent had characters who were victims of violence), the concern appears legitimate.(2)

More recent studies have shown that the relationship between exposure to violence in the mass media and aggressive behaviour is not universal, however. It varies by both individual and environmental characteristics. The fact is that not all children, youth, and adults who watch media violence become violent themselves; not all imitate what they see on television, in movies, or in video games. However, one of the greatest effects of viewing violence in the media is desensitization; that is, as exposure to violent content increases, the shock value of such incidents and their effects decreases.(3)

A study of students in grades 4 and 5 found that exposure to video game violence was associated with lower empathy and more intense pro-violence attitudes, which was higher than the measure for any other media, except for movies.(2) Psychologists recognize that media violence does not directly cause violent behaviour (although some studies show that watching TV violence is correlated with aggressive behaviour, at least in the short term; subjects who view violent TV shows begin to act aggressively almost immediately). Rather, they point out that watching violence might provide children with scripts for aggressive behaviour, provide situations that young people can imitate, result in increased arousal levels which are conducive to violence, promote attitudinal changes that favour violence, and reduce inhibitions to violence.(2)

DRAWING THE LINE

While many people see network ratings and V-chips as disappointingly small contributions to a big problem, others have begun to worry about freedom of expression.

Janet Jackson's "wardrobe malfunction" at the 2004 Super Bowl halftime show raised censorship concerns on both sides even further. In response to the incident, a five-second delay was instituted in all live broadcasts for screening purposes; however, it did not stop there. The American Federal Communications Commission (FCC) commissioner Michael Powell ordered an investigation into the incident and threatened fines for relevant stations, which in turn led some networks to highly scrutinize the content of their programs and make pre-emptive changes to adult programs that would not previously have been an issue. Many have argued that such restrictions on television programming constitute an infringement on free speech. "Fewer messages are sent; the diversity of views is lessened; and our communications media—in this case, television—are impoverished."(4)

It is difficult to know where to draw the line when it comes to television censorship. On the one hand, we need to be aware of the age-appropriateness of different television programs and allow for some sort of screening system, especially because evidence indicates some negative effects of children's exposure to violence in the media. On the other hand, however, there is the concern for freedom of speech. Television is one of the most important venues for communicating ideas and information, and spreading knowledge and awareness.

Sources

1. Ann Scott, "The Role of Washington in Curbing Youth Violence," *Christian Science Monitor,* May 6, 1999, p. 2.
2. Larry J. Siegel and Chris McCormick, *Criminology in Canada: Theories Patterns, and Typologies,* 3rd ed. (Toronto: Thomson Nelson, 2006), pp. 176–177.
3. Edward Donnerstein and Daniel Linz, "The Media," in *Crime,* James Q. Wilson and Joan Petersilia, eds. (San Francisco: Institute for Contemporary Studies, 1995).
4. Julie Hilden, "Jackson 'Nipplegate' Illustrates the Danger of Chilling Free Speech," *CNN.com (Find Law),* February 20, 2004.

Questions for Discussion

1. How far do you think censorship regulations should go? What are the pros and cons of such regulations?
2. Do you agree with the screening systems currently in place?
3. What do you think is the best way to balance freedom of speech concerns with the potentially harmful effects of television?
4. Whose responsibility is it to regulate children's exposure to violence in the media? The government? Parents?

Bandura's psychologically based learning theory with Edwin Sutherland's sociologically based differential association theory (see Chapter 6) to produce the theory of **differential association-reinforcement.** This theory suggests that (1) the persistence of criminal behaviour depends on whether or not it is rewarded or punished, and (2) the most meaningful rewards and punishments are those given by groups that are important in an individual's life—the peer group, the family, teachers in school, and so forth. In other words, people respond more readily to the reactions of the most significant people in their lives. If criminal behaviour elicits more positive reinforcement or rewards than punishment, such behaviour will persist.[26]

Social learning theory helps us understand why some individuals who engage in violent and aggressive behaviour do so: They learn to behave that way. But perhaps something within the personality of a criminal creates a susceptibility to aggressive or violent models in the first place. For example, perhaps criminals are more extroverted, irresponsible, or unsocialized than non-criminals. Or perhaps criminals are more intolerant and impulsive or have lower self-esteem.

Personality

Four distinct lines of psychological research have examined the relationship between personality and criminality.[27] First, investigators have looked at the differences between the personality structures of criminals and non-criminals. Most of this work has been carried out in prisons, where psychologists have administered personality questionnaires such as the Minnesota Multiphasic Personality Inventory (MMPI) and the California Psychological Inventory (CPI) to inmates. University of British Columbia professor Robert Hare and his colleagues have developed the Revised Psychopathy Checklist (PCL-R), which is used widely in the both the Canadian mental health and criminal justice systems. The evidence from these studies shows that inmates are typically more impulsive, hostile, self-centred, and immature than non-criminals.[28]

Second, a vast amount of literature is devoted to the prediction of behaviour. Criminologists want to determine how an individual will respond to prison discipline and whether he or she will avoid crime after release. The results are equivocal. At best, personality characteristics seem to be modest predictors of future criminality.[29] Yet when they are combined with such variables as personal history, they tend to increase the power of prediction significantly.[30]

Third, many studies examine the degree to which normal personality dynamics operate in criminals. Findings from these studies suggest that the personality dynamics of criminals are often quite similar to those of non-criminals. Social criminals (those who act in concert with others), for example, are found to be more sociable, affiliative, outgoing, and self-confident than solitary criminals.[31]

Finally, some researchers have attempted to quantify individual differences between types and groups of offenders. Several studies have compared the personality characteristics of first-time offenders with those of repeat or habitual criminals. Other investigators have compared violent offenders with non-violent offenders, and murderers with drug offenders. In addition, prison inmates have been classified according to personality type.[32] Generally, it seems that "the data do not reveal any significant differences between criminal and non-criminal psychology. . . . Personality testing has not differentiated criminals from noncriminals."[33]

Despite these conclusions, whether or not criminals share personality characteristics continues to be debated. Are criminals in fact more aggressive, dominant, and manipulative than non-criminals? Are they more irresponsible? Clearly, many criminals are aggressive; many have manipulated a variety of situations; many assume no responsibility for their acts. But are such characteristics common to all criminals? Samuel Yochelson and Stanton Samenow addressed these questions. In *The Criminal Personality*, this psychiatrist-psychologist team described their growing disillusion with traditional explanations of criminality. These researchers have found that criminals share abnormal thinking patterns that lead to decisions to commit crimes. They have identified as many as 52 patterns of thinking common to the criminals in their studies. According to their findings, criminals are angry people who feel a sense of superiority, expect not to be held accountable for their acts, and have a highly inflated self-image. Any perceived attack on their glorified self-image elicits a strong reaction, often a violent one.[34]

Other researchers have used different methods to study the association between criminality and personality. For example, criminologists have reviewed the findings of a large sample of studies that use the California Psychological Inventory. Their research revealed a common personality profile: The criminals tested showed remarkable similarity in their deficient self-control, intolerance, and lack of responsibility.[35]

Though studies dealing with personality correlates of criminals are important, some psychologists are concerned that by focusing on the personalities of criminals in their search for explanations of criminal behaviour, investigators may overlook other important factors, like the complex social environment in which a crime is committed.[36] A homicide that began as a barroom argument between two intoxicated patrons who backed different teams to win the Stanley Cup, for example, is very likely to hinge on situational factors that interact with the participants' personalities.

Eysenck's Conditioning Theory For over 20 years, Hans J. Eysenck has been developing and refining a theory of the relationship between personality and criminality that considers more than just individual characteristics.[37] His theory has two parts. First, Eysenck claims that all human personality may be seen in three dimensions—psychoticism, extroversion, and neuroticism. Individuals who score high on measures of **psychoticism** are aggressive, egocentric, and impulsive. Those who score high on measures of **extroversion** are sensation-seeking, dominant, and assertive. High scorers on scales assessing **neuroticism** may be described as having low self-esteem, excessive anxiety, and wide mood swings. Eysenck has found that when criminals respond to items on the Eysenck Personality Questionnaire (EPQ), they uniformly score higher on each of these dimensions than do non-criminals.

The second part of Eysenck's theory suggests that humans develop a conscience through **conditioning.** From birth, we are rewarded for social behaviour and punished for asocial behaviour. Eysenck likens this conditioning to training a dog. Puppies are not born house trained. You have to teach a puppy that it is good to urinate and defecate outside your apartment or house by pairing kind words and perhaps some tangible reward (such as a dog treat) with successful outings. A loud, angry voice will convey disapproval and disappointment when mistakes are made inside.

In time, most dogs learn and, according to Eysenck, develop a conscience. But as Eysenck also

has noted, some dogs learn faster than others. German shepherds acquire good "bathroom habits" faster than basenjis, who are most difficult to train. It is argued that the same is true of humans; there are important individual differences. Criminals become conditioned slowly and appear to care little whether or not their asocial actions bring disapproval.

Eysenck has identified two additional aspects of a criminal's poor conditionability. First, he has found that extroverts are much more difficult to condition than introverts and thus have greater difficulty in developing a conscience. Youthful offenders tend to score highest on measures of extroversion. Second, differences in conditionability are dependent on certain physiological factors, the most important of which is **cortical arousal,** or activation of the cerebral cortex.

The cortex of the brain is responsible for higher intellectual functioning, information processing, and decision making. Eysenck found that individuals who are easily conditionable and develop a conscience have a high level of cortical arousal; they do not need intense external stimulation to become aroused. A low level of cortical arousal is associated with poor conditionability, difficulty in developing a conscience, and need for external stimulation.

MENTAL DISORDERS AND CRIME

Edmond Yu attended York University studying pre-medicine from 1982 until 1984 when he was accepted into medicine at the University of Toronto. Shortly after that, in 1985 Yu was arrested by police and taken to the Clarke Institute of Psychiatry where he was diagnosed with paranoid schizophrenia. On February 20, 1997, Yu allegedly assaulted a woman at a bus stop, then boarded a bus. As police attempted to board the bus after him, according to witnesses he raised a small hammer, thought by some to be a toy. Police opened fire on the man, killing him.[38]

An official inquest into this incident cleared the police of wrongdoing. However, the report made several recommendations that focused on the need for housing for homeless men with mental health problems. In fact, in the years since Yu's death, a foundation to fund housing for mentally ill homeless men has been set up in Yu's name. The incident and the factors leading up to it are certainly distressing and raise questions about the role that one's mental state plays in criminal behaviour. How could the situation have been handled differently? How does the criminal justice system deal with mentally disordered individuals? Criminologists have conducted—and continue to conduct—a good deal of research that brings us closer to understanding more completely the relationship between mental disorder and criminal behaviour. Part of the difficulty in assessing the extent of the relationship concerns definitions of mental disorder itself.

It has been difficult for psychiatrists to derive criteria that would help them decide which offenders are mentally ill. According to psychiatrist Seymour L. Halleck, the problem lies in the evolving conceptualization of mental illness. Traditionally, the medical profession viewed mental illness as an absolute condition or status—either you are afflicted with **psychosis** or you are not. Should such a view concern us? Halleck suggests that it should. "Although this kind of thinking is not compatible with current psychiatric knowledge," he writes, "it continues to exert considerable influence upon psychiatric practice. . . . As applied to the criminal, it also leads to rigid dichotomies between the 'sick criminal' and the 'normal criminal.'"[39]

Halleck and other psychiatrists, such as Karl Menninger, conceptualize mental functioning as a process.[40] Mental illness should not be considered apart from mental health—the two exist on the same continuum. At various times in each of our lives, we move along the continuum from health toward illness.[41] For this reason, a diagnosis of "criminal" or "mentally ill" may overlook potentially important gradations in mental health and mental illness.

Still, the existence of the American Psychiatric Association's *Diagnostic and Statistical Manual of Mental Disorder* (DSM-IV) and the diagnoses and treatment of millions of North Americans annually prove that mental disorders affect peoples' lives daily. A continuum of mental health may exist, but we continue to distinguish between people who are mentally disordered and those who are not. One area of debate concerns the relationship between mental disorder and criminal behaviour.

While a variety of mental disorders (severe depression, bipolar disorder, manic depression) appear among both general and criminal populations, one condition that may be more prevalent among incarcerated offenders is schizophrenia. S. Hodgins and G. Côté conducted a study in Quebec prisons that revealed a high rate of mental disorders. The researchers report that the rate of schizophrenic disorders is approximately seven times that of non-incarcerated adult males.[42] Another researcher found that the rate of mental disorder among inmates ranges from about 5 to 12 percent for severe mental disorders and from 16 to 67 percent for more broadly defined mental illnesses.[43] Other researchers report that the rate of mental disorder among prison populations is no higher than rates in the general population.[44]

Canadian researcher R. Roesch, in his study of pre-trial population, found the prevalence of serious mental disorders to be 15.6 percent. He emphasizes the importance of "co-occurring disorders," the overlap that exists between mental disorders and drug or alcohol abuse, among prison populations.[45] Other researchers confirm both the existence of high rates of substance use disorders and the co-occurrence of these disorders with other mental disorders such as schizophrenia.[46]

Setting aside for a moment the debates surrounding the definition of mental disorder and the prevalence of such disorders among prison populations, one point that researchers do tend to agree on is the increasing number of mentally disordered offenders who are involved with the criminal justice system. The deinstitutionalization movement, which resulted in the "emptying" of mental hospitals as advancements in chemical therapies made it possible for mentally disordered individuals to live in the community, also reduced some of the discretionary powers of the police. No longer are police able to use mental hospitals as an option when dealing with mentally disordered individuals. Rather, the police often have no other option but to arrest the individual and detain him or her in prison. In other words, the behaviour of individuals likely hasn't changed much. In effect, what has happened is that the institutional response to the behaviour of individuals has changed. As mental hospitals have closed and reduced their ability to take on new patients, police turn to the criminal justice system as a way of dealing with disruptive and disturbing behaviours.[47]

Importantly, we must also consider other factors that sometimes occur concomitantly with mental disorder, and that might also be related to criminal behaviour. People with mental illness may lack the resources to obtain proper treatment, may live in impoverished areas that are conducive to crime and victimization, and may experience stress as a result of these living conditions. It may be these structural conditions that are conducive to criminal behaviour as opposed to mental illness alone.[48] The Canadian Mental Health Association reports that people with major mental illness are 2.5 times more likely to be victims of violence than other members of society, usually as a result of poverty, a transient lifestyle, and substance use.[49] These factors may make a person with mental illness more vulnerable to assault and also increase the likelihood that he or she will respond to the assault with violence.

Yet, there are cases that stand as exceptions to some of the patterns we see in the relationship between mental disorder and criminal behaviour. Consider the case of David Carmichael, a successful and nationally known Canadian fitness promoter with a wife and two children. On July 31, 2004, he took his 11-year-old son Ian to a hotel in London, Ontario, and strangled him. Carmichael was charged with first-degree murder, but was found not criminally responsible due to mental illness. He was severely depressed and had been taking antidepressants. It turns out a side effect of the drugs was psychotic delusions, which in Carmichael's case created thoughts that his son was living in hell (the son experienced some mild learning disabilities, but was well adjusted, outgoing, and athletic) and was going to become violent and hurt other children. While the drug he was using and its alleged influence on his behaviour was not brought up in court, experts are divided on what caused his psychotic state.[50]

To summarize, there is conflicting evidence regarding the relationship between mental disorder and crime. Today, most researchers agree that the majority of criminals are not mentally ill.[51] The majority of offenders know the difference between right and wrong. Certainly, some criminals exhibit symptoms of mental illness, but the majority are not mentally ill. Furthermore, most mentally disordered offenders are not violent and their risk of recidivism may be lower than that of other offenders, particularly if they receive treatment.[52]

Nonetheless, some categories of offenders with mental disorders do recidivate. One Canadian researcher mentioned earlier, Dr. Robert

David Carmichael strangled his 11-year-old son Ian because he believed Ian would become violent and harm other children. The psychotic delusions that led him to kill his son are believed to have been caused by the medication he was taking for depression. Here, Carmichael's twin brother embraces their mother after the courts came back with a not criminally responsible verdict.

Hare, has been working since the 1960s on a checklist that facilitates the prediction of violence among one such category: the psychopath.

Psychopathy

Estimates vary, but Hare found that about 39 percent of the total Canadian prison sample in his study suffered from a type of mental disorder that in the nineteenth century was described by the French physician Philippe Pinel as *manie sans délire* ("madness without confusion"), by the English physician James C. Prichard as "moral insanity," and by Gina Lombroso Ferrero as "irresistible atavistic impulses." Today such mental illness is called **psychopathy,** sociopathy, or antisocial personality—a personality characterized by the inability to learn from experience, lack of warmth, and absence of guilt. While estimates are that anywhere from 20 to 60 percent of prison populations fit the criteria, experts suggest that about 3 percent of men and less than 1 percent of women in the general population suffer from the disorder.[53]

Hare and his colleagues have devised a 20-item checklist of personality traits and behaviours that are associated with psychopathy (see Table 4.3). The checklist, which is used in identifying psychopaths involved in both the mental health and criminal justice systems, has the goal of predicting the future behaviour of such individuals. As an instrument of prediction, Hare's checklist is used in judicial decision making and in release decisions.[54]

TABLE 4.3 Items and Factors in the Hare PCL-R

Interpersonal	Affective
1. Glibness/superficial charm	6. Lack of remorse or guilt
2. Grandiose sense of self-worth	7. Shallow affect
4. Pathological lying	8. Callous/Lack of empathy
5. Conning/manipulative	16. Failure to accept responsibility for actions

Lifestyle	Antisocial
3. Need for stimulation/ prone to boredom	10. Poor behavioural controls
9. Parasitic lifestyle	12. Early behavioural problems
13. Lack of realistic long-term goals	18. Juvenile delinquency
14. Impulsivity	19. Revocation conditional release
15. Irresponsibility	20. Criminal versatility

Note: The items are from Hare (1991, 2003). Copyright 1991 R. D. Hare and Multi-Health Systems, 3770 Victoria Park Avenue, Toronto, Ontario, M2H 3M6. All rights reserved. Reprinted by permission. Note that the item titles cannot be scored without reference to the formal criteria contained in the PCL-R Manual. Item 11, Promiscuous sexual behaviour, and Item 17, Many short-term marital relationships, contribute to the Total PCL-R score but do not load on any factors.

The psychiatrist Hervey Cleckley views psychopathy as a serious illness even though patients may not appear to be ill. According to Cleckley, psychopaths appear to enjoy excellent mental health; but what we see is only a "mask of sanity." Initially, they seem free of any kind of mental disorder and appear to be reliable and honest. After some time, however, it becomes clear that they have no sense of responsibility whatsoever. They show a disregard for truth; are insincere; and feel no sense of shame, guilt, or humiliation. Psychopaths lie and cheat without hesitation and engage in verbal as well as physical abuse without any thought. It seems that individuals with antisocial personality disorder do not learn from negative experiences, largely because they seem incapable of experiencing anxiety in the manner most of us do.[55] They lack a sense of fear in terms of negative consequences for inappropriate behaviour. While as children most of us may have feared our parents' disapproval for misbehaving, the same thought process does not appear in psychopaths.

Canadian killer Clifford Olson, who tortured and murdered 11 boys and girls, and was sentenced in January 1982 to life imprisonment for his crimes, is a psychopath. According to Hare, Olson is a "prototypical psychopath." The following quotation from an article written at the time of his trial provides some insight into his character and personality:

> He was a braggart and a bully, a liar and thief. He was a violent man with a hairtrigger temper. But he could also be charming and smooth-tongued when trying to impress people. . . . Olson was a compulsive talker. . . . He's a real smooth talker, he has the gift of gab. . . . He was always telling whoppers. . . . The man was just an out-and-out liar. . . . He always wanted to test you to the limits. He wanted to see how far he could go before you had to step on him. . . . He was a manipulator. . . . Olson was a blabbermouth. . . . We learned after a while not to believe anything he said because he told so many lies.[56]

Olson's manipulative skills clearly came into play when he convinced the Crown to pay him $100 000 in return for information on the locations where he hid the bodies of seven of his victims. Hare writes the following about the psychopath:

> In the years since his imprisonment Olson has continued to bring grief to the families of his victims by sending them letters with comments about the murders of their children. He has never shown any guilt or remorse for his depredations; on the contrary, he continually complains about his treatment by the press, the prison system, and society. During his trial he preened and postured whenever a camera was present, apparently considering himself an important celebrity rather than a man who had committed a series of atrocities.

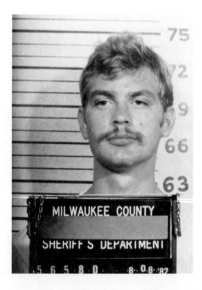

Jeffrey Dahmer murdered at least 17 boys and men before his capture. He was beaten to death by a fellow inmate on November 28, 1994.

TABLE 4.4 Psychology and Criminality: Review

Theory	Theorist(s)	Key Ideas	Explanation of Criminality
Psychoanalytic Theory	Freud	Adult behavioural patterns are rooted in childhood development; behaviour and unconscious motives are intertwined.	Criminality is a representation of psychological conflict.
Moral Development	Kohlberg	Moral reasoning develops in three phases: pre-conventional, conventional, postconventional.	Most delinquents reason at the preconventional level.
Maternal Deprivation and Attachment	Bowlby	Children need to experience a warm, intimate, and continuous relationship with a mother/mother substitute in order to be securely attached.	Habitual criminals have an inability to form bonds of affection.
Social Learning	Bandura Patterson	Individuals learn violence and aggression through behavioural modelling. Aggression is learned by direct experience.	Learned violence can lead to criminal behaviour and violence.
Personality	Yochelson and Samenow	Personality influences criminal behaviours.	Criminals are angry people who feel a sense of superiority, expect not to be held accountable for their acts, and have a highly inflated self-image.
	Eysenck		Criminals tend to score higher on psychoticism, extroversion, and neuroticism personality dimensions. Criminals are slower to develop a conscience.
Psychopathy	Cleckley and Hare	Psychopaths are pathological liars, self-centred, manipulative, and impulsive.	Psychopaths lack empathy for their victims, do not feel guilty about their criminal actions, and do not learn from or fear the consequences of their criminal behaviours.

Psychologists also have found that psychopaths, like Hans Eysenck's extroverts, have a low internal arousal level; thus psychopaths constantly seek external stimulation, are less susceptible to learning by direct experience, are more impulsive, and experience far less anxiety than non-psychopaths about any adverse consequences of their acts.[57] Some psychiatrists consider "psychopathy" to be an artificial label for an antisocial personality.[58] To Eysenck, Hare, and others, it is a major behavioural category that presents significant challenges. Eysenck sums up this view by writing that the psychopath poses the riddle of delinquency. If we could solve the riddle, then we would have a powerful weapon to fight the problem of delinquency.[59] Table 4.4 provides a summary of the psychological theories and the explanations of criminality they offer.

BIOLOGY AND CRIMINALITY

Within the last two decades, biologists have followed in the tradition of Cesare Lombroso, Raffaele Garofalo, and Charles Goring in their search for answers to questions about human behaviour. Geneticists, for example, have argued that the predisposition to act violently or aggressively in certain situations may be inherited. In other words, while criminals are not born criminal, the predisposition to be violent or commit crime may be present at birth.

To demonstrate that certain traits are inherited, geneticists have studied children born of criminals but reared from birth by non-criminal adoptive parents. They wanted to know whether the behaviour of the adoptive children was more similar to that of their biological parents than to that of their adoptive parents. Their findings play an important role in the debate on heredity versus environment. Other biologists, sometimes called "biocriminologists," take a different approach. Some ask whether brain damage or inadequate nutrition results in criminal behaviour. Others are interested in the influence of hormones, chromosomal abnormalities, and allergies.

Did You Know?

. . . that a recent study published in the *Annals of Internal Medicine* concluded that there is a strong association between low cholesterol levels and violence?

They investigate interactions between brain and behaviour, and between diet and behaviour.

Modern Biocriminology

Biocriminology is the study of the physical aspects of psychological disorders.[60] It has been known for some time that adults who suffer from depression show abnormalities in brain waves during sleep, experience disturbed nervous system functioning, and display biochemical abnormalities. Research on depressed children reveals the same physical problems; furthermore, their adult relatives show high rates of depression as well. In fact, children whose parents suffer from depression are more than four times more likely than the average child to experience a similar illness.[61] Some researchers believe depression is an inherited condition that manifests itself in psychological and physical disturbances. The important point is that until only recently, physicians may have been missing the mark in their assessment and treatment of depressed children and adults by ignoring the physiological aspects.

Criminologists who study sociology and psychology to the exclusion of the biological sciences may also be missing the mark in their efforts to discover the causes of crime. Recent research has demonstrated that crime does indeed have psychobiological aspects similar to those found in studies of depression—biochemical abnormalities, abnormal brain waves, nervous system dysfunction. There is also evidence that strongly suggests a genetic predisposition to criminality.[62]

The resurgence of interest in integrating modern biological advances, theories, and principles into mainstream criminology began two decades ago. The sociobiological work of Edward Wilson on the interrelationship of biology, genetics, and social behaviour was pivotal.[63] So were the contributions of C. Ray Jeffery, who argued that a biosocial interdisciplinary model should become the major theoretical framework for studying criminal behaviour.[64]

Criminologists once again began to consider the possibility that there are indeed traits that predispose a person to criminality and that these traits may be passed from parent to child through the genes. Other questions arose as well. Is it possible, for instance, that internal biochemical imbalances or deficiencies cause antisocial behaviour? Could too much or too little sugar in the bloodstream increase the potential for aggression? Or could a vitamin deficiency or some hormonal problem be responsible? We will explore the evidence for a genetic predisposition to criminal behaviour, the relationship between biochemical factors and criminality, and neurophysiological factors that result in criminal behaviour.

Genetics and Criminality

Today the proposition that human beings are products of an interaction between environmental and genetic factors is all but universally accepted.[65] We can stop asking, then, whether nature or nurture is more important in shaping us; we are the products of both. But what does the interaction between the two look like? And what concerns are raised by reliance on genetics to the exclusion of environmental factors? Consider the example of the XYY syndrome.

The XYY Syndrome **Chromosomes** are the basic structures that contain our genes—the biological material that makes each of us unique. Each human being has 23 pairs of inherited chromosomes. One pair determines gender. A female receives an X chromosome from both mother and father; a male receives an X chromosome from his mother and a Y from his father. Sometimes a defect in the production of sperm or egg results in genetic abnormalities. One type of abnormality is the XYY chromosomal male. The XYY male receives two Y chromosomes from his father rather than one. Approximately 1 in 1000 newborn males in the general population has this genetic composition.[66] Initial studies done in the 1960s found the frequency of XYY chromosomes to be about 20 times greater than normal XY chromosomes among inmates in maximum-security hospitals.[67] The XYY inmates tended to be tall, physically aggressive, and, frequently, violent.

Supporters of these data claimed to have uncovered the mystery of violent criminality. Critics voiced concern over the fact that these studies were done on small and unrepresentative samples. The XYY syndrome, as this condition became known, received much public attention because of the case of Richard Speck. Speck, who in 1966 murdered eight nurses in Chicago, initially was diagnosed as an XYY chromosomal male. However, the diagnosis later turned out to be wrong. Nevertheless, public concern was aroused: Were all XYY males potential killers?

Studies undertaken since that time have discounted the relation between the extra Y chromosome and criminality.[68] Although convincing evidence in support of the XYY hypothesis appears to be slight, it is nevertheless possible that aggressive and violent behaviour is at least partly determined by genetic factors. The problem is how to investigate this possibility. One difficulty is separating the external or environmental factors, such as family structure, culture, socioeconomic status, and peer influences, from the genetic predispositions with which they begin to interact at birth. A particular individual may have a genetic predisposition to be violent but be born into a wealthy, well-educated, loving, and calm familial environment. He may never commit a violent act. Another person may have a genetic predisposition to be rule-abiding and non-aggressive yet be born into a poor, uneducated, physically abusive, and unloving family. He may commit violent criminal acts. How, then, can we determine the extent to which behaviour is genetically influenced? Researchers have turned to twin studies and adoption studies in the quest for an answer.

Twin Studies To discover whether or not crime is genetically predetermined, researchers have compared identical and fraternal twins. Identical, or **monozygotic (MZ), twins** develop from a single fertilized egg that divides into two embryos. These twins share all their genes. Fraternal, or **dizygotic (DZ), twins** develop from two separate eggs, both fertilized at the same time. They share about half of their genes. Since the prenatal and postnatal family environments are, by and large, the same, greater behavioural similarity between identical twins than between fraternal twins would support an argument for genetic predisposition.

In the 1920s, a German physician, Johannes Lange, found 30 pairs of same-sex twins—13 identical and 17 fraternal pairs. One member of each pair was a known criminal. Lange found that in 10 of the 13 pairs of identical twins, both twins were criminal; in 2 of the 17 pairs of fraternal twins, both were criminal.[69] The research techniques of the time were limited, but Lange's results were nevertheless impressive.

Many similar studies have followed. The largest was a study by Karl Christiansen and Sarnoff A. Mednick that included all twins born between 1881 and 1910 in a region of Denmark, a total of 3586 pairs. Reviewing serious offences only, Christiansen

and Mednick found that the chance of there being a criminal twin when the other twin was a criminal was 50 percent for identical twins and 20 percent for same-sex fraternal twins.[70] Such findings lend support to the hypothesis that some genetic influences increase the risk of criminality.[71] A more recent American study conducted by David C. Rowe and D. Wayne Osgood reached a similar conclusion.[72]

While the evidence from these and other twin studies looks persuasive, we should keep in mind the weakness of such research. It may not be valid to assume a common environment for all twins who grow up in the same house at the same time. If the upbringing of identical twins is much more similar than that of fraternal twins, as it well may be, that circumstance could help explain their different rates of criminality.

Adoption Studies One way to separate the influence of inherited traits from that of environmental conditions would be to study infants separated at birth from their natural parents and placed randomly in foster homes. In such cases, we could determine whether the behaviour of the adopted child resembled that of the natural parents or that of the adoptive parents, and by how much. Children, however, are adopted at various ages and are not placed randomly in foster homes. Most such children are matched to their foster or adoptive parents by racial and religious criteria. And couples who adopt children may differ in some important ways from other couples. Despite such shortcomings, adoption studies do help us expand our knowledge of genetic influences on human variation.

The largest adoption study conducted so far was based on a sample of 14 427 male and female adoptions in Denmark between 1924 and 1947. The hypothesis was that criminality in the biological parents would be associated with an increased risk of criminal behaviour in the child. The parents were considered criminal if either the mother or the father had been convicted of a felony. The researchers had sufficient information on more than 4000 of the male children to assess whether or not both the biological and the adoptive parents had criminal records. Mednick and his associates reported the following findings:

- Of boys whose adoptive and biological parents had no criminal record, 13.5 percent were convicted of crimes.

- Of boys who had criminal adoptive parents and non-criminal biological parents, 14.7 percent were convicted of crimes.

- Of boys who had non-criminal adoptive parents and criminal biological parents, 20 percent were convicted of crimes.

- Of boys who had both criminal adoptive parents and criminal biological parents, 24.5 percent were convicted of crimes.[73]

These findings support the claim that the criminality of the biological parents has more influence on the child than does that of the adoptive parents. Other research on adopted children has reached similar conclusions. A major Swedish study examined 862 adopted males and 913 adopted females. The researchers found a genetic predisposition to criminality in both sexes, but an even stronger one in females.[74]

Results of adoption studies have been characterized as "highly suggestive" or "supportive" of a genetic link to criminality. But how solid is this link? There are significant problems with adoption studies. One is that little can be done to ensure the similarity of adopted children's environments. Of even greater concern to criminologists, however, is the distinct possibility of mistaking correlation for causation. In other words, there appears to be a significant correlation between the criminality of biological parents and adopted children in the research we have reviewed, but this correlation does not prove that the genetic legacy passed on by a criminal parent causes an offspring to commit a crime.

So far, research has failed to shed any light on the nature of the biological link that results in the association between the criminality of parents and that of their children. Furthermore, even if we could identify children with a higher-than-average probability of committing offences as adults on the basis of their parents' behaviour, it is unclear what we could do to prevent these children from following the parental model.

The Controversy over Violence and Genes

At the same time that advances in research on the biological bases of violence shed new light on crime, attacks on such research are calling its usefulness into question. Government-sponsored research plans have been called racist, a conference on genetics and crime was cancelled after protests, and a session on violence and heredity at a recent American Association for the Advancement of Science meeting became "a politically correct critique of the research."[75]

Few involved in such research expect to find a "violence gene"; rather, researchers are looking for a biological basis for some of the behaviours associated with violence. As one explanation put it:

> Scientists are . . . trying to find inborn personality traits that might make people more physically aggressive. The tendency to be a thrill seeker may be one such characteristic. So might "a restless impulsiveness, an inability to defer gratification." A high threshold for anxiety or fear may be another key trait. . . . Such people tend to have a "special biology," with lower-than-average heart rates and blood pressure.[76]

No one yet has found any direct link between genes and violence. In fact, Sarnoff Mednick, the psychologist who conducted adoption studies of criminal behaviour in Denmark, found no evidence for the inheritance of violence. "If there were any genetic effect for violent crimes, we would have picked it up," says Mednick, whose study included 14 427 men.

The controversy over a genetic basis for violent behaviour seems to deal less with actual research findings than with the implications of such findings. For example, Harvard psychologist Jerome Kagan predicts that in 25 years, biological and genetic tests will make it possible to identify the 15 children in every 1000 who may have violent tendencies. Of those 15, only one will actually become violent. The ethical question, then, is what to do with this knowledge. "Do we tell the mothers of all 15 that their kids might be violent?" he asks. "How are the mothers then going to react to their children if we do that?"[77]

What frightens those opposed to biological and genetic research into the causes of violence is the thought of how such research could be used by policy makers. If a violent personality can be shown to be genetically determined, crime-prevention strategies might try to identify "potential criminals" and to intervene before their criminal careers begin and before anyone knows if they would ever have become criminals. "Should genetic markers one day be found for tendencies . . . that are loosely linked to crime," explains one researcher, "they would probably have little specificity, sensitivity or explanatory power: most people with the markers will not be criminals and most criminals will not have the markers."[78] On the other hand, when environment—poverty, broken homes, and other problems—is seen as the major cause of violence, crime prevention takes the shape of improving social conditions rather than labelling individuals.

A middle-of-the-road approach is proposed by those who see biological research as a key to helping criminals change their behaviour. Studies show that risk factors statistically linked to violence include hyperactivity, impulsivity, aggression, lying, risk-taking, poor early grades, low IQ, fearlessness, an inability to defer gratification, and difficult temperament.[79] "Once you find a biological basis for a behaviour, you can try to find out how to help people cope," says one such scholar. "Suppose the link is impulsivity, an inability to defer gratification. It might be you could design education programs to teach criminals to readjust their time horizon."[80]

The IQ Debate

A discussion of the association between genes and criminality would be incomplete without paying at least some attention to the debate over IQ and crime. Is an inferior intelligence inherited, and if so, how do we account for the strong relationship between IQ and criminality?

The Research Background Nearly a century ago, scientists began to search for measures to determine people's intelligence, which they believed to be genetically determined. The first test to gain acceptance was developed by a French psychologist, Alfred Binet. Binet's test measured the capacity of individual children to perform tasks or solve problems in relation to the average capacity of their peers.

Between 1888 and 1915, several researchers administered intelligence tests to incarcerated criminals and to boys in reform schools. In Canada in the 1920s, the Canadian National Committee on Mental Hygiene administered IQ tests and conducted surveys of elementary school children and individuals in provincial mental institutions, looking for a link between mental abnormality (which

included low intelligence) and social inefficiency. Not surprisingly, in surveying "troublesome" school children, and in conducting follow-up interviews with them, they found a link between low IQ and "less sound moral values." Tests of this kind in Alberta eventually led to the enactment of a sexual sterilization act, which aimed to rid the province of such "mental defectives."[81]

Initial studies of the relationship between IQ and crime revealed some surprising results. The psychologist Hugo Munsterberg estimated that 68 percent of the criminals he tested were of low IQ. Using the Binet scale, Henry H. Goddard found that between 25 and 50 percent of criminals had low IQs.[82] What could account for such different results?

Edwin Sutherland observed that the tests were poor and there were too many variations among the many versions administered. He reasoned that social and environmental factors caused delinquency, not low IQ.[83] In the 1950s, the psychologist Robert H. Gault added to Sutherland's criticism. He noted particularly that it was "strange that it did not occur immediately to the pioneers that they had examined only a small sample of caught and convicted offenders."[84]

For more than a generation, the question about the relationship between IQ and criminal behaviour was not studied, and the early inconsistencies remained unresolved. Then in the late 1970s, the debate resumed.[85] Supporters of the view that inheritance determines intelligence once again began to present their arguments. The psychologist Arthur Jensen suggested that race was a key factor in IQ differences; Richard J. Herrnstein, a geneticist, pointed to social class as a factor.[86] Both positions spurred a heated debate in which criminologists soon became involved. More recently, University of Western Ontario psychology professor J. P. Rushton argued in his evolutionary theory that race, IQ, and sexuality are linked. The long-term consequence of the interconnections of these factors results in higher crime rates among members of races with smaller brains and larger penises. Understandably, this view has sparked debate among criminologists and geneticists.[87] Although Rushton's work has been discredited on a variety of grounds, the debate surrounding IQ and crime continues.

Travis Hirschi and Michael Hindelang evaluated the existing literature on IQ and crime.[88]

They cited the following three studies as especially important:

- Travis Hirschi, on the basis of a study of 3600 California students, demonstrated that the effect of a low IQ on delinquent behaviour is more significant than that of the father's education.[89]

- Marvin Wolfgang and associates, after studying 8700 Philadelphia boys, found a strong relationship between low IQ and delinquency, independent of social class.[90]

- Albert Reiss and Albert L. Rhodes, after an examination of the juvenile court records of 9200 white Tennessee schoolboys, found IQ to be more closely related to delinquency than is social class.[91]

Hirschi and Hindelang concluded that IQ is an even more important factor in predicting crime than is either race or social class. They found significant differences in intelligence between criminal and non-criminal populations within like racial and socioeconomic groups. A lower IQ increases the potential for crime within each group. Furthermore, they found that IQ is related to school performance. A low IQ ultimately results in a youngster's associating with similar non-performers, dropping out of school, and committing delinquent acts. Hirschi and Hindelang's findings were confirmed by James Q. Wilson and Richard Herrnstein but rejected by criminologist Deborah Denno, who conducted a prospective investigation of 800 children from birth to age 17. Her results failed to confirm a direct relationship between IQ and delinquency. A recent review of research on IQ and delinquency suggests an indirect link as well, mediated by academic competence.[92]

The Debate: Genetics or Environment? The debate over the relationship between IQ and crime has its roots in the controversy over whether intelligence is genetically or environmentally determined. This is a debate whose policy implications haunt us from the past. Alberta experimented with eugenics in an effort to rid certain genetic "deficiencies" from the gene pool. Low IQ along with immorality and "feeble-mindedness" generally were the targets of the sterilization campaign in the province. When discussing the possibility of a genetic link to crime, it is critical to pay heed to Canadian criminologist Jim Hackler's comment:

"there is no gene that codes directly for social behaviour, such as crime."[93] For example, IQ tests, many people believe, measure cultural factors rather than the innate biological makeup of an individual.[94] Therefore, using the results of such tests to definitively label individuals as biologically inferior in some way is dangerous, particularly when policies are implemented to target such "deficiencies." Studies by psychologists Sandra Scarr and Richard Weinberg of black and white adopted children confirmed that environment plays a significant role in IQ development. They found that both black and white children adopted by white parents had comparable IQs and performed similarly.[95] With evidence of cultural bias and environmental influence, why not abandon the use of intelligence tests? The answer is simple: Many psychologists believe they do predict performance in school and so have utility. As a result, it appears that this debate will be with us for a long time to come.

Biochemical Factors

Biocriminologists' primary focus has been on the relationship between criminality and biochemical and neurophysical factors. Biochemical factors include food allergies, diet, hypoglycemia, and hormones. Neurophysical factors include brain lesions, brain wave abnormalities, and minimal brain dysfunction.

Food Allergies In 1993, by the time Rachel was two years old, she displayed a pattern of behaviour that went way beyond the "terrible twos." Without warning, her eyes would glaze over, her speech would develop a lisp, and she'd kick and hit and thrash about wildly until her mother swaddled her tightly and she fell asleep, exhausted. She even developed a "kitty-cat" routine, complete with meowing, stalking, and growling, that often went on for hours.

When Rachel's sister Emma was born later that year, she nursed poorly and never slept through the night. After their mother introduced baby corn into her diet, Emma experienced severe intestinal distress, for which she was hospitalized. After a battery of medical tests proved inconclusive, she was sent home, but the symptoms continued intermittently, without apparent reason.

The following year, in desperation, their mother had Rachel and Emma, then three years and 15 months, tested for food allergies. Both showed marked sensitivity to corn, wheat, sugar, preservatives, and dairy products. After those foods were eliminated, Emma's health and well-being improved, and Rachel's perplexing and worrisome behaviour all but disappeared.[96]

Over the last decade, researchers have investigated the relation between food allergies and aggression and antisocial behaviour. In fact, since 1908 there have been numerous medical reports indicating that various foods cause such reactions as irritability, hyperactivity, seizures, agitation, and behaviour that is "out of character."[97] Investigators have identified the following food components as substances that may result in severe allergic reactions:

- Phenylethylamine (found in chocolate)
- Tyramine (found in aged cheese and wine)
- Monosodium glutamate (used as a flavour enhancer in many foods)
- Aspartame (found in artificial sweeteners)
- Xanthines (found in caffeine)

Each of these food components has been associated with behavioural disorders, including criminality.

Diet

- Susan had been charged with 16 offences, including criminal damage, solvent abuse, and vehicle theft, by the time she was 13. She had no friends, showed no affection toward her parents, and frequently hit her mother. Her schoolwork deteriorated, and she played truant most days. After six months on a changed diet, which excluded burgers, bananas, and chocolate, the number of her offences dropped to zero. And for the first time since she was a young child, Susan gave her mother a hug.

- Craig, 15, vandalized his home several times and committed numerous petty crimes. He was a bully and was virtually impossible to teach. And his eight-year-old brother was beginning to follow in his footsteps. Both were put on a special diet, cutting out fizzy drinks and sweets, and including more green vegetables and fresh fruit. Within months, says their mother, both were more pleasant and easier to deal with. But Craig has since quit the diet and has reoffended. The bullying and the violence have started again.

- Graham, an 11-year-old, turned from an uncontrollable delinquent into a normal, pleasant boy when pizzas, baked beans, and chocolate in his diet were replaced by fresh vegetables, coconut milk, and carrots. He became less aggressive and argumentative and, reportedly, was "happy" for the first time in his life. Graham's schoolwork improved, and he began to make friends.

Anecdotal reports, in addition to more scientific investigations, link criminality to diets high in sugar and carbohydrates, to vitamin deficiency or dependency, and to excessive food additives.

Criminologist Stephen Schoenthaler conducted a series of studies on the relation between sugar and the behaviour of institutionalized offenders. In these investigations, inmates were placed on a modified diet that included very little sugar. They received fruit juice in place of soda and vegetables instead of candy. Schoenthaler found fewer disciplinary actions and a significant drop in aggressive behaviour in the experimental group.[98] Some individuals charged with crimes have used this finding to build a defence like that of Dan White.

In 1979, San Francisco city supervisor Dan White was on trial for the murder of his fellow supervisor, Harvey Milk, and Mayor George Moscone. White defended himself with testimony on the impact of sugar on his behaviour. The testimony showed that when White was depressed, he

The National Council Against Health Fraud is critical of the diet-crime link. "Valid evidence is lacking to support the claim that diet is an important determinant in the development of violence and criminal behaviour" (see www.ncahf.org).

departed from his normal, healthy diet and resorted to high-sugar junk food, including Twinkies, Coca-Cola, and chocolates. Thereafter, his behaviour became less and less controllable. The jury found White guilty of manslaughter, rather than murder, due to diminished capacity. White served five years in prison and committed suicide after his release. His defence was promptly dubbed the "junk-food defence," "Dan White's defence," or the "Twinkie defence." Most subsequent attempts to use the junk-food defence have failed.

Other researchers have looked for the causes of crime in vitamin deficiencies. One such study found that 70 percent of criminals charged with serious offences in one Canadian jurisdiction had a greater-than-normal need for vitamin B_6.[99] Other studies have noted deficiencies of vitamins B_3 and B_6 in criminal population samples.

Some investigators have examined the effects of food additives and food dyes on behaviour. Benjamin Feingold has argued that between 30 and 60 percent of all hyperactivity in children may be attributable to reactions to food colouring.[100] There is additional support for this hypothesis.[101] Some studies have suggested that a diet deficient in protein may be responsible for violent aggression.

Hypoglycemia   What prompted an otherwise loving father to throw his 20-month-old daughter into a nearby lake? Neighbours knew that something was amiss when they noticed their 22-year-old neighbour climb on the roof of his duplex in a quiet suburb. He then proceeded to dance, touching power lines in the course of his pantomime. No one sounded the alarm, however, until he disappeared into his lakeside apartment, returning momentarily with his daughter Ashley in his arms. The police arrived on the scene to find the father in a state of agitation and Ashley facedown in the nearby lake. Seated in the back of a police car, handcuffed, the bewildered the young man had no recollection of the preceding events. When his blood was tested, he had a glucose level of 20 milligrams per decilitre of blood. The average is 80 to 120 milligrams. He was suffering from severe hypoglycemia. According to the police spokesperson, "he had virtually no thought process."[102]

Hypoglycemia is a condition that occurs when the level of sugar in the blood falls below an acceptable range. The brain is particularly vulnerable to hypoglycemia, and such a condition can impair its function. Symptoms of hypoglycemia include anxiety, headache, confusion, fatigue, and even aggressive behaviour. As early as 1943, researchers linked the condition with violent crime, including murder, rape, and assault. Subsequent studies found that violent and impulsive male offenders had a higher rate of hypoglycemia than non-criminal controls.

Consider the work of Matti Virkkunen, who has conducted a series of studies of habitually violent and psychopathic offenders in Finland. In one such study done in the 1980s, he examined the results of a glucose tolerance test (used to determine whether hypoglycemia is present) administered to 37 habitually violent offenders with antisocial personalities, 31 habitually violent offenders with intermittent explosive disorders, and 20 controls. The offenders were found to be significantly more hypoglycemic than the controls.[103]

Hormones   Experiments have shown that male animals are typically more aggressive than females. Male aggression is directly linked to male hormones. If an aggressive male mouse is injected with female hormones, he will stop fighting.[104] Likewise, the administration of male hormones to pregnant monkeys results in female offspring who, even three years after birth, are more aggressive than the daughters of non-injected mothers.[105]

While it would be misleading to equate male hormones with aggression and female hormones with non-aggression, there is some evidence that abnormal levels of male hormones in humans may prompt criminal behaviour. Several investigators have found higher levels of testosterone (the male hormone) in the blood of individuals who have committed violent offences.[106] Some studies also relate premenstrual syndrome (PMS) to delinquency and conclude that women are at greater risk of aggressive and suicidal behaviour before and during the menstrual period. After studying 156 newly admitted adult female prisoners, Katherina Dalton concluded that 49 percent of all their crimes were committed either in the premenstrual period or during menstruation.[107] Recently, however, critics have challenged the association between menstrual distress and female crime.[108] Feminists' concerns are that, notwithstanding the reality of PMS for many women, and in particular the suffering that results from extreme forms of the condition, there is a danger that all women will be

Lisa Thompson of Niagara Falls appears in court after a failed "mercy killing" of her six-year old disabled daughter. How is this case different from that of Dr. Suzanne Killinger-Johnson, a 37-year-old medical doctor with a successful psychotherapy practice, who jumped off a subway station platform in Toronto, with her six-month-old baby boy in her arms? He died instantly; she died eight days later. The only plausible explanation was that Killinger-Johnson was suffering from a severe case of postpartum depression. Thompson's behaviour, on the other hand, was likely not connected to hormones or other biological factors.

affected by the recognition by the courts of PMS as a legitimate defence to crime. The danger is that society will revisit past understandings of women as beings controlled by their biology not their rationality, and therefore inferior to men. Another concern is the stigmatization of an entire group of people (women generally or women who suffer from PMS) based on the activities of a few.[109]

Neurophysiological Factors

In England in the mid-1950s, a father hit his son with a mallet and then threw him out of a window, killing him instantly. Instead of pleading insanity, as many people expected him to do, he presented evidence of a brain tumour, which, he argued, resulted in uncontrollable rage and violence. A jury acquitted him on the grounds that the brain tumour had deprived him of any control over and knowledge of the act he was committing.[110] Brain lesions or brain tumours have led to violent outbursts in many similar cases. Neurophysiological studies, however, have not focused exclusively on brain tumours; they have included a wide range of investigations: MRI studies of cerebral structure, brain wave studies, clinical reports of minimal brain dysfunction, and

theoretical explorations into the relationship between the limbic system and criminality.[111]

EEG Abnormalities Sam recalled that his wife, Janet, looked slightly different and that the house smelled funny, and he felt out of sorts. During an intimate moment in bed, Janet made a funny remark, after which Sam flew into a rage, choked her, and slashed her throat. When he came to his senses, he immediately went to the police and admitted to the crime, although he had little memory of his violent acts. Can EEG (electroencephalogram) tracings explain the behaviour of this young military man who had returned home on leave? Subsequent tracings were found to be abnormal—indicative of an "intermittent explosive disorder." After reviewing this evidence, the court reduced Sam's charges from first-degree murder to manslaughter.

The EEG is a tracing made by an instrument that measures cerebral functioning by recording brain wave activity with electrodes placed on the scalp. Numerous studies that have examined the brain activity of violent prisoners reveal significant differences between the EEGs of criminals and those of non-criminals. Other findings relate significantly slow brain wave activity to young offenders and adult murderers.[112] When Sarnoff A. Mednick and his colleagues examined the criminal records and EEGs of 265 children in a birth cohort in Denmark, they found that certain types of brain wave activity, as measured by the EEG, enabled investigators to predict whether convicted thieves would steal again.[113]

When Jan Volavka compared the EEGs of juvenile delinquents with those of comparable nondelinquents, he found a slowing of brain waves in the delinquent sample, most prominently in those children convicted of theft. He concluded that thievery "is more likely to develop in persons who have a slowing of alpha frequency than in persons who do not."[114]

Fetal Alcohol Syndrome Fetal alcohol syndrome (FAS) and **fetal alcohol spectrum disorders (FASD)** refer to conditions caused by exposure to alcohol in the womb. FAS always involves brain damage, impaired growth, and head and face anomalies. FASD refers to the range of birth defects caused by prenatal alcohol damage. Estimates are that approximately 5 percent of all fetal defects are due to alcohol consumption during pregnancy.

TABLE 4.5 Biology and Criminality: Review

Theory	Theorists	Key Ideas	Explanation of Criminality
Genetics	Christiansen Mednick et al.	XYY Syndrome Twin studies and adoption studies	Suggests a link between genetic predisposition and some types of criminal behaviour.
IQ	Goddard Rushton Hirschi and Hindelang	Some studies provide support for a link between low IQ scores and criminality, although there is debate among scholars.	Individuals with lower IQs are more prone to criminal behaviours.
Biochemical Factors (food allergies, diet, hypoglycemia, hormones)	Various researchers including Schoenthaler and Dalton	The ingestion of certain substances influences criminality.	Testosterone may be linked to male aggression; PMS to female criminality.
Neurophysiological Factors (EEG abnormalities, FAS/FASD, minimal brain dysfunction)	Mednick et al. Volarka	Brain activity of criminals may differ from non-criminals.	Criminals exhibit slower brain activity than non-criminals.

The rates are higher in certain areas of the country and among specific groups of people, and are affected by the nature of diagnosis for this disorder. For example, studies conducted on Aboriginal peoples in Canada show higher rates of FAS and FASD. Studies have found the prevalence of FASD within the Aboriginal community to range from 25 to 200 per 1000 births. The rate for the general population in Canada is 1 to 10 per 1000 births.[115] The higher incidence of these disorders is very likely linked to structural factors that are more pronounced for Aboriginals.[116]

Children with FASD may exhibit poor coordination, hyperactivity, learning disabilities, developmental disabilities (speech and language delays), low IQ, and poor reasoning and judgment skills. They are also at risk for a range of psychiatric problems, criminal behaviours, unemployment, low levels of education, and victimization. Some research reports that 60 percent of children over 12 with FAS had been suspended, been expelled, or dropped out of school. Recent studies in Saskatchewan and Manitoba revealed that at least 50 percent of young offenders had been born with FASD. One study conducted in British Columbia found that of 415 individuals with FASD, 60 percent aged 12 and over had been in trouble with the law.[117]

Minimal Brain Dysfunction   **Minimal brain dysfunction (MBD)** includes a wide variety of conditions and behaviours linked to abnormality in cerebral structures. MBD produces such asocial behavioural patterns as impulsivity, hyperactivity, aggressiveness, low self-esteem, and temper outbursts.[118] In its more serious forms, MBD has been linked to serious antisocial behaviours, including explosive rage, chemical imbalances and abnormalities, and an imbalance in the urge-control mechanisms of the brain.

Attention deficit/hyperactivity disorder (AD/HD), which affects 3 to 5 percent of children (most often boys), is a relatively common form of minimal brain dysfunction. Symptoms of AD/HD include lack of attention, poor school performance, poor concentration, acting without thinking, lack of organizational skills, constant fidgeting, bullying, and lack of response to discipline. Research links AD/HD to the onset and sustenance of a delinquent career; the disorder is nine times more likely to be found in delinquent children.[119] Early detection and treatment of AD/HD, often through the use of stimulants such as Ritalin, can significantly increase children's ability to deal effectively with the condition and increase life chances. Table 4.5 provides a summary of the various biologically based explanations for criminal behaviour we've discussed in this section.

CRIME AND HUMAN NATURE

The criminologist Edward Sagarin has written:

> In criminology, it appears that a number of views . . . have become increasingly delicate and sensitive, as if all those who espouse them were inherently evil,

or at least stupidly insensitive to the consequences of their research. . . . In the study of crime, the examples of unpopular orientations are many. Foremost is the link of crime to the factors of genes, biology, race, ethnicity, and religion.[120]

Criticisms of Biocriminology

What is it about linking biology and criminality that makes the subject delicate and sensitive? Why is the concept so offensive to so many people? One reason is that biocriminologists deny the existence of individual free will. The idea of predisposition to commit crimes fosters a sense of hopelessness. But this criticism seems to have little merit. As Diana H. Fishbein has aptly noted, the idea of a "conditioned free will" is widely accepted.[121] This view suggests that individuals make choices in regard to a particular action within a range of possibilities that is "preset" yet flexible. When conditions permit rational thought, one is fully accountable and responsible for one's actions. It is only when conditions are somehow disturbed that free choice is constricted. The child of middle-class parents who has a low IQ might avoid delinquent behaviour. But if that child's circumstances changed so that he lived in a lower-class, single-parent environment, he might find the delinquent lifestyle of the children in the new neighbourhood too tempting to resist.

Critics have other concerns as well. Some see a racist undertone to biocriminological research. If there is a genetic predisposition to commit crime and if minorities account for a disproportionate share of criminal activity, are minorities then predisposed to commit crime? In Chapter 2, we learned that self-reports reveal that most people have engaged in delinquent or criminal behaviour. How, then, do biocriminologists justify their claim that certain groups are more prone than others to criminal behaviour? Could it be that the subjects of their investigations are only criminals who have been caught and incarcerated? And is the attention of the police disproportionately drawn to members of minority groups?

How do biocriminologists account for the fact that most criminologists see the structure of our society, the decay of our neighbourhoods, and the subcultures of certain areas as determinants of criminality? Are biocriminologists unfairly de-emphasizing social and economic factors? (In Chapters 5 through 9, we review theories that attribute criminality to group and environmental forces.)

These issues raise a further question that is at the core of all social and behavioural science: Is human behaviour the product of nature (genetics) or nurture (environment)? The consensus among social and behavioural scientists today is that the interaction of nature and nurture is so pervasive that the two cannot be viewed in isolation.

Supporters of biocriminology also maintain that recognizing a predisposition to crime is not inconsistent with considering environmental factors. In fact, some believe that predispositions are triggered by environmental factors. Even if we agree that some people are predisposed to commit crime, we know that the crime rate would be higher in areas that provide more triggers. In sum, while some people may be predisposed to certain kinds of behaviour, most scientists agree that both psychological and environmental factors shape the final forms of those behaviours.

An Integrated Theory

In recent years, the debate has found a new forum in integrated biocriminological theories, such as the one proposed by James Q. Wilson and Richard Herrnstein. These scholars explain predatory street crime by showing how human nature develops from the interplay of psychological, biological, and social factors. It is the interaction of genes with environment that in some individuals forms the kind of personality likely to commit crimes. An individual may be born with a genetic predisposition toward aggression, for example, but if raised in a caring, loving environment with parent role models who solve conflicts by talking and reasoning rather than using violence, the individual may learn not to act upon his or her predisposition toward aggression and/or violence. Similarly, the interaction between biological and environmental factors is illustrated by the child born with a genetic predisposition for being tall. However, if during pregnancy the mother was malnourished, and then once born the child also suffered from poor nutrition, the "height" gene might be counteracted by a less-than-ideal environment. The argument takes into account such factors as IQ, body build, genetic makeup, impulsiveness, ability to delay gratification, aggressiveness, and even the drinking and smoking habits of pregnant mothers as factors that interact to produce characteristics and behaviours in people.

According to Wilson and Herrnstein, the choice between crime and conventional behaviour is closely linked to individual biological and psychological traits and to such social factors as family and school experiences. Their conclusion is that "the offender offends not just because of immediate needs and circumstances, but also because of enduring personal characteristics, some of whose traces can be found in his behaviour from early childhood on."[122] In essence, they argue that behaviour results from a person's perception of the potential rewards and/or punishments that go along with a criminal act. Perception develops through a combination of genetic and environmental factors. A child born with a predisposition to impulsivity who never learns self-control (from parents or others), is less likely to defer gratification or to think about consequences for behaviour. If the potential reward (such as money) is greater than the expected punishment (say, a small fine), the chance that a crime will be committed increases.

REVIEW

1. What are some psychological explanations for criminal behaviours?

When psychologists have attempted to explain criminality, they have taken several general approaches. First, they have focused on failures in psychological development—an overbearing or weak conscience, inner conflict, insufficient moral development, and maternal deprivation, with its concomitant failure of **attachment** (p. 81). Freud, in his **psychoanalytic theory** (p. 78), for example, speculated on the importance of the development of the **id** (p. 79), **ego** (p. 79), and **superego** (p. 79) to the healthy psychological development of individuals. Psychologists have studied the development of moral reasoning and point to the lower level of moral reasoning that seems to characterize many criminals. Studies on maternal deprivation suggest that habitual criminals lack the ability to form bonds of affection. Second, they have investigated the ways in which aggression and violence are learned through **behavioural modelling** (p. 83), **differential association-reinforcement** (p. 88), and direct experience. **Social learning theory** (p. 82) maintains that delinquent behaviour is learned through the same psychological processes as any other behaviour. Third, they have investigated the personality characteristics of criminals and found that criminals tend to be more impulsive, intolerant, and irresponsible than non-criminals. Eysenck found that an individual's placement on continuums of **extroversion** (p. 89), **neuroticism** (p. 89), and **psychoticism** (p. 89) predicts the possibility of future criminality. He also suggests that humans develop a conscience through conditioning. Susceptibility to conditioning is dependent on physiological factors such as **cortical arousal** (p. 89).

2. Is there a link between mental disorder and crime?

Psychologists have investigated the relationship of criminality to such mental disorders as **psychosis** (p. 90) and **psychopathy** (p. 91). Hare has created a psychopathy checklist that is used to predict the future criminal behaviour of offenders. While research on the relationship between mental disorder and criminal behaviour is mixed, most criminologists agree that the majority of criminals do know the difference between right and wrong. Complicating the relationship between mental disorder and crime are other factors such as substance use and poverty.

3. How do biological approaches explain criminal behaviours?

Biocriminology (p. 94) investigates the biological correlates of criminality, including a genetic predisposition to commit crime. The XYY syndrome, though now generally discounted as a cause of criminality, suggests that aggressive and violent behaviour may be at least partly determined by genetic factors such as **chromosomes** (p. 94). Studies of the behaviour of **monozygotic** (p. 95) and **dizygotic twins** (p. 95) and of the rates of criminality among adopted children with both criminal and non-criminal biological and adoptive parents tend to support this hypothesis. Investigators have also found a strong correlation between low IQ and delinquency. Criminologists are still debating what public policy issues are raised by the possible role of genetics in crime.

Biocriminologists' most recent and perhaps most important discovery is the relation of criminal behaviour to biochemical factors (food allergies, dietary deficiencies, **hypoglycemia** [p. 100], and hormonal imbalances) and neurophysiological factors (EEG abnormalities, **minimal brain dysfunction** [p. 102], **attention deficit/ hyperactivity disorder** [p.102], and **fetal alcohol disorder/fetal alcohol spectrum disorder** [p. 101]).

4. Is a biological explanation for criminality valid?

Most scientists agree that if some people are biologically predisposed to certain behaviours, both psychological and environmental factors shape the forms of those behaviours.

CRIMINOLOGY & PUBLIC POLICY

Sexual predators fall into the gap between criminal and civil confinement. They are routinely held fully responsible and blameworthy for their behaviour because they almost always retain substantial capacity for rationality, they remain entirely in touch with reality, and they know the applicable moral and legal rules. Consequently, even if their sexual violence is in part caused by a mental abnormality, they do not meet the usual standards for an NCR (not criminally responsible) defence. For the same reason, they do not meet the usual non-responsibility standards for civil commitment and retain the competence to make rational decisions about treatment.

In Canada, the designation of "dangerous offender" (DO) is reserved for individuals with a history of extremely violent, brutal behaviour and who are deemed to be at risk of recidivating because of a distinct pattern of this type of behaviour. In addition, DOs are either unresponsive to treatment or are unwilling to participate in treatment programming. Approximately 85 percent of dangerous offenders have been convicted of a sexual offence. In order to be declared a dangerous offender, a Crown prosecutor must initiate a DO hearing for an offender convicted of a serious personal injury offence punishable by at least ten years of imprisonment. Such offences include manslaughter, attempted murder, aggravated assault, and aggravated sexual assault. Canadian legislation makes it possible for dangerous offenders to receive an indeterminate sentence, which essentially is a life sentence with no possibility of parole for at least seven years.

This legislation is a recognition that some offenders are "beyond help" or reform. They might be psychopathic or exhibit other personality disorders, but because they are legally "sane," they cannot be confined in mental health institutions. Dangerous offender legislation is a policy initiative that aims to keep such dangerous individuals out of society indefinitely—to incapacitate them by removing opportunities for them to continue to victimize members of society. (*Source:* Michael Weinrath, "Dangerous offender FAQ" *CBC News Viewpoint,* July 8, 2004, www.cbc.ca/news/viewpoint/vp_weinrath/; Stephen J. Morse, "Uncontrollable Urges and Irrational People," *Virginia Law Review,* 88, 2002: 1025. Copyright 2002 by *Virginia Law Review.* Reproduced by permission of *Virginia Law Review* in the format Textbook via Copyright Clearance Center.)

Questions for Discussion How should criminologists view the commitment of "sexual predators" or "dangerous offenders" to prison for an indefinite term? Does this indeterminate commitment amount to a second round of punishment? If not, and little treatment takes place, how is this additional term of incapacitation justified? Should sexual predators be diverted from the criminal justice system in the first place?

YOU BE THE CRIMINOLOGIST

For many years, psychologists searched for the criminal personality, a common set of personality characteristics associated with criminals. If you were asked to assist in this effort, what methods would you use to capture the criminal personality? Would you use objective personality inventories? If you were successful, what would you do with your findings? How could this common personality profile be used in the criminal justice system?

Visit the Online Learning Centre: www.mcgrawhill.ca/olc/adler

STRAIN THEORIES

CHAPTER 5

CHAPTER QUESTIONS

1. How are sociological theories connected?

2. How does Durkheim's concept of anomie contribute to an understanding of crime?

3. What does Merton's strain theory add to our understanding of crime?

4. How is status deprivation connected to strain and crime?

5. What is differential opportunity?

This Toronto area gang member is taken into police custody. What draws individuals to gang involvement?

The early decades of the twentieth century brought major changes to North American society. In both Canada and the United States large numbers of settlers explored and developed untamed lands, but many of these immigrants settled in cities. One of the most significant changes was in the composition of the populations of cities. Between 1840 and 1924, 45 million people—Irish, Swedes, Germans, Italians, Poles, Armenians, Bohemians, Russians—left the Old World; two-thirds of them were bound for the United States.[1] Canada witnessed large influxes of immigrants around 1911 and then again between 1921 and 1931. While Canada and the United States experienced many of the same developments and challenges during this time, the United States dealt with the issues on a larger scale. For example, during this time, increased mechanization deprived many American farmworkers of their jobs and forced them to join the ranks of the foreign-born and the black labourers who had migrated from the South to northern and midwestern industrial centres.

During the 1920s, large U.S. cities swelled with 5 million new arrivals.[2]

Chicago's expansion was particularly remarkable: Its population doubled in 20 years. Many of the new arrivals brought nothing with them except what they could carry. The city offered them only meagre wages, 12-hour working days in conditions that jeopardized their health, and tenement housing in deteriorating areas. Chicago had other problems as well. In the late 1920s and early 1930s, it was the home of major organized crime groups, which fought over the profits from the illegal production and sale of liquor during Prohibition (as we shall see in Chapter 12).

Teeming with newcomers looking for work, corrupt politicians trying to buy their votes, and bootleggers growing more influential through sheer firepower and the political strength they controlled, Chicago also had a rapidly rising crime rate. The city soon became an inviting urban laboratory for criminologists, who began to challenge the predominant theories of crime causation of the time, which were based on biological and psychological factors.

Many of these criminologists were associated with the University of Chicago, which has the oldest sociology program in North America (begun in 1892). By the 1920s, these criminologists began to measure scientifically the amount of criminal behaviour and its relation to the social turmoil Chicago was experiencing. In Canada, the first sociology department emerged in the 1920s at McGill University. Influenced by the structural functionalism associated with the Chicago school, early Canadian sociologists focused their research efforts on historical and political sociology rather than criminology. By the 1960s, sociology departments existed across the country. Denis Szabo introduced the teaching of criminology at the University of Montreal with his creation of the Department of Criminology. This department became the model for other Canadian criminologists to follow. While sociology and criminology were developing in Canada, the Chicagoans continued developing the theories that form the foundation for criminological research in both countries. Since the development of these initial ideas, sociological theories have remained at the forefront of the scientific investigation of crime causation.

THE INTERCONNECTEDNESS OF SOCIOLOGICAL THEORIES

The psychological and biological theories of criminal behaviour (Chapter 4) share the assumption that such behaviour is caused by some underlying physical or mental condition that separates the criminal from the non-criminal. They seek to identify the kind of person who becomes a criminal and to find the factors that caused the person to engage in criminal behaviour. These theories yield insight into individual cases, but they do not explain why crime rates vary from one neighbourhood to the next, from group to group, within large urban areas, or within groups of individuals. Sociological theories seek the reasons for differences in crime rates in the social environment. These theories can be grouped into three general categories: strain, cultural deviance, and social control.[3]

The strain and cultural deviance theories formulated between 1925 and 1940, and still popular today, focus on the social forces that cause people to engage in criminal activity. These theories, some of which we discuss in the next chapter, laid the foundation for the subcultural theories (also discussed in Chapter 6). Social control theories (Chapter 7) take a different approach: They are based on the assumption that the motivation to commit crime is part of human nature. Consequently, social control theories seek to discover why people do not commit crime. They examine the ability of social groups and institutions to make their rules effective.

Strain and cultural deviance theories both assume that social class and criminal behaviour are related, but they differ about the nature of the relationship. **Strain theory,** the focus of this chapter, argues that all members of society subscribe to one set of cultural values—that of the middle class. One of the most important middle-class values is economic success. Since lower-class persons do not have legitimate means to reach this goal, they turn to illegitimate means in desperation.

ANOMIE: ÉMILE DURKHEIM

Imagine a clock with all its parts finely synchronized. It functions with precision. It keeps perfect time. But if one tiny weight or small spring breaks down, the whole mechanism will not function properly. One way of studying a society is to look at its component parts in an effort to find out how they relate to each other. In other words, we look at the structure of a society to see how it functions. If the society is stable, its parts operating smoothly, the social arrangements are functional. Such a society is marked by cohesion, cooperation, and consensus. But if the component parts are arranged in such a way as to threaten the social order, the arrangements are said to be dysfunctional. In a class-oriented society, for example, the classes tend to be in conflict.

The Structural-Functionalist Perspective

The structural-functionalist perspective was developed by Émile Durkheim (1858–1917) before the end of the nineteenth century.[4] At the time, positivist biological theories, which relied on the search for individual differences between criminals and non-criminals, were dominant. So at a time when science was searching for the abnormality of the criminal, Durkheim was writing about the normality of crime in society. To him, the explanation of human conduct, and indeed human misconduct, lies not in the individual but in the group and the social organization. It is in this context that he introduced the term "anomie," the breakdown of social order as a result of the loss of standards and values.[5]

Throughout his career, Durkheim was preoccupied with the effects of social change. He believed that when a simple society develops into a modern, urbanized one, the intimacy needed to sustain a common set of norms declines. Groups become fragmented, and in the absence of a common set of rules, the actions and expectations of people in one sector may clash with those of people in another. As behaviour becomes unpredictable, the system gradually breaks down, and the society is in a state of anomie.

Anomie and Suicide

Durkheim illustrated his concept of anomie in a discussion, not of crime, but of suicide.[6] He suggested several reasons why suicide was more common in some groups than in others. For our purposes, we are interested in the particular form of suicide he called "anomic suicide." When he analyzed statistical data, he found that suicide rates increased during times of sudden economic change, whether that change was major depression or unexpected prosperity. In periods of rapid change, people are abruptly thrown into unfamiliar situations. Rules that once guided behaviour no longer hold.

Consider the events of the 1920s. Wealth came easily to many people in those heady, prosperous years. Toward the end, through July, August, and September of 1929, the New York stock market soared to new heights. Enormous profits were made from speculation. But on October 24, 1929, a day history records as Black Thursday, the stock market crashed. Thirteen million shares of stock were sold. As more and more shares were offered for sale, their value plummeted. In the wake of the crash, a severe depression overtook the United States and then the world. Banks failed. Mortgages were foreclosed. Businesses went bankrupt. People lost their jobs. Lifestyles changed overnight. Many people were driven to sell apples on street corners to survive, and they had to stand in mile-long breadlines to get food to feed their families. Suddenly the norms by which people lived were no longer relevant. People became disoriented and confused. Suicide rates rose.

It is not difficult to understand rising suicide rates in such circumstances, but why would rates also rise at a time of sudden prosperity? According to Durkheim, the same factors are at work in both situations. What causes the problems is not the amount of money available but the sudden change. Durkheim believed that human desires are boundless, an "insatiable and bottomless abyss."[7] Since nature does not set such strict biological limits on the capabilities of humans as it does on those of other animals, he argued, we have developed social rules that put a realistic cap on our aspirations. These regulations are incorporated into the individual conscience and thus make it possible for people to feel fulfilled.

But with a sudden burst of prosperity, expectations change. When the old rules no longer determine how rewards are distributed among members of society, there is no longer any restraint on what people want. Once again the system breaks down. Thus, whether sudden change causes great prosperity or great depression, the result is the same—anomie.

STRAIN THEORY

A few generations after Durkheim, the American sociologist Robert Merton (1910–2002) also related the crime problem to anomie. But his conception differs somewhat from Durkheim's. The real problem, Merton argued, is created not by sudden social change but by a social structure that holds out the same goals to all its members without giving them equal means to achieve them. This lack of integration between what the culture calls for and what the structure permits, the former encouraging success and the latter preventing it, can cause norms to break down because they no longer are effective guides to behaviour.

Merton borrowed the term "anomie" from Durkheim to describe this breakdown of the normative system. According to Merton,

> it is only when a system of cultural values extols, virtually above all else, certain common symbols of success for the population at large while its social structure rigorously restricts or completely eliminates access to approved modes of acquiring these symbols for a considerable part of the same population, that antisocial behaviour ensues on a considerable scale.[8]

From this perspective, the social structure is the root of the crime problem (hence the approach Merton takes is sometimes called a "structural explanation"). "Strain theory," the name given by contemporary criminologists to Merton's explanation of criminal behaviour, assumes that people are law-abiding but when under great pressure will resort to crime. Disparity between goals and means provides that pressure.

Consensus vs. Conflict

Strain theories are consensus-based theories: They assume society-wide general agreement on the definition of behaviours as criminal. Conflict theories, on the other hand, assume little consensus and focus their attention on how some groups are able to influence the definition of behaviours as criminal.

Merton's Theory of Anomie

Merton argued that in a class-oriented society, opportunities to get to the top are not equally distributed. Very few members of the lower class ever get there. His anomie theory emphasizes the importance of two elements in any society: (1) cultural

A Social System Breaks Down

The American anthropologist Kenneth Good committed—for anthropologists—the unpardonable sin of marrying a young woman of the tribe he studied, the Yanomamö. The young bride returned with her husband to suburban Pennsylvania in 1988, and there they raised their children.(1) But in 1993, the Yanomamö wife slipped back into the Amazon jungle to live among her own people.

Who are the Yanomamö?

When another anthropologist, Robert Carneiro, went to the Amazon jungle in 1975 to study the Yanomamö, he found them to be a remote, Stone Age people dedicated to frequent intervillage warfare.(2)

Indeed, the Yanomamö are the last major remaining Stone Age people on earth, living their lives in harmony with nature but also engaging in tribal warfare, according to their customs.

But all went awry in the 1980s, when gold was discovered in the Yanomamö territory.(3) As many as 40 000 prospectors had invaded by 1987, clearing the jungle for airstrips, bringing diseases—venereal and others—against which the Yanomamö had no immunity, importing modern weapons to replace Stone Age clubs, and raising the homicide rate.(4) What once was a nation of 100 000 was reduced to 22 000 (9400 in Brazil; 12 600 in Venezuela). A severe drought in the late 1990s added to the suffering of the Yanomamös, who use ancient incantations to bring rain as well as to quench forest fires and to drive out invaders.(2)

Help is underway and more is promised. The United Nations sent an emergency team of firefighters to deal with the forest fires. The Brazilian government clamped down on encroachments by rogue miners. The U.S. Congress made some assistance available to protect the rain forests but did not designate preservation of the Yanomamö territory and lifestyle a priority.

Too little, too late? The Yanomamö's traditional way of life has broken down. The chances that they can withstand the attack of the Western culture invasion are slim. The large deposits of gold, diamonds, tin, and other minerals in the soil of their land will continue to attract invaders, with their

A Yanomamö man with the trappings of modern civilization.

attack on the traditional culture. Yanomamö are dying faster than ever before, hunting and fishing are increasingly difficult, alcohol and prostitution are taking their toll, firearms are escalating the death rate, and infant mortality is about 28 times that of Canada.(5) In Durkheim's terms, the outside influence on this society has eroded the intimacy required to sustain the group's common set of norms. Group fragmentation results in clashes over actions and expectations among members of this once unified group. In other words, behaviour becomes unpredictable, deviance ensues, and the society is in a state of anomie.

What are we to do about the Yanomamö? It does not seem possible to transplant Yanomamö into Montreal or Ottawa. Forcing modern capitalism on them is even more destructive.

Should we just build a fence around the Yanomamö territory and allow them to live their accustomed lifestyle? The spectre of an entrepreneur flying in tourists in jumbo jets and charging admission to view "unspoiled," Stone Aged Yanomamö is just too daunting.

Are we witnessing a genocide in the making?

Are you wondering about the Yanomamö wife? Well, you can see her adorned with tribal decoration in a photo at the American Museum of Natural History, Amazon exhibit.

Sources

1. Kenneth Good with David Chernoff, *Into the Heart* (New York: Simon and Schuster, 1991).
2. Robert L. Carneiro, "War and Peace: Alternating Realities in Human History," in *Studying War—Anthropological Perspectives*, S. P. Reyna and R. E. Downs, eds. (Langhorn, PA: Gordon and Breach, 1994), pp. 3–27.
3. Lynne Wallis, "Quiet Genocide: Miners Seeking Precious Metals Are Causing Deaths of the Yanomami," *Ottawa Citizen,* June 28, 1993, p. A6.
4. "Aid for an Ancient Tribe," *Newsweek,* Apr. 9, 1990, p. 34.
5. "Genocide in the Amazon," *Newsweek,* Aug. 30, 1993, p. 61; www.geographyiq.com/ranking/ranking_Infant_Mortality_Rate.aall.htm.

Questions for Discussion

1. Traditionally, stringent norms determined the manner in which the Yanomamö dealt with deviance. For example, disagreements between men were resolved through a series of "fighting" ceremonies (e.g., the chest-pounding duel and the club fight), the rules of which were known to all and were followed carefully. As the Yanomamö culture is being destroyed, how would you expect the group's traditional ways of dealing with deviance and crime to be affected? Explain.
2. What measures might be effective in protecting indigenous peoples in all parts of the world from suffering a fate similar to that of the Yanomamö? First Nations groups in Canada suffered a similar imposition of European culture on traditional ways of life centuries ago. How have Aboriginal communities and the Canadian government dealt with the cultural, economic, and spiritual devastation that occurred at the hands of colonizers?

aspirations, or goals that people believe are worth striving for, and (2) institutionalized means or accepted ways to attain the desired ends. If a society is to be stable, these two elements must be reasonably well integrated; in other words, there should be means for individuals to reach the goals that are important to them. Disparity between goals and means fosters frustration, which leads to strain. The theory focuses on the criminogenic, or crime-producing nature of the interaction between social structure and socialization processes. When individuals are socialized to believe that hard work will "pay off" in terms of material success, but then find it difficult to access the means to achieving success, some of these frustrated individuals will turn to crime as an alternative to reaching their goals.

Merton's theory explains crime in Canada in terms of the wide disparities in income among the various classes. Statistics clearly demonstrate that such disparities exist. Canadian families had a median income of $54 560 in 1990; in 2004 it was $54 100. Statistics indicate that the rich are getting richer and the poor are getting poorer. Since 1990, the richest 10 percent of Canadian families experienced a 14.6 percent increase in income (in real dollars, which means that adjustments have been made for inflation), while the bottom 10 percent saw an increase of less than 1 percent. To phrase the information differently, the 10 percent of families with the highest incomes have an income of $18 for every $1 of income for families in the lowest 10 percent.[9]

> **Did You Know?**
>
> . . . that 16 percent of Canadians live in poverty? Compared to this national average, 36 percent of visible minorities and 43 percent of Aboriginal people live in poverty.

Canada In our society, opportunities to move up the social ladder exist, but they are not equally distributed. A child born to a single, uneducated, 13-year-old girl living in a poverty-stricken area has a significantly reduced chance to move up, whereas the child of a middle-class family has a better-than-average chance of reaching a professional or business position. Yet many people in the society share the same goals. And those goals are shaped by billions of advertising dollars spent each year to spread the message that everyone can drive a sports car, take a well-deserved exotic vacation, and record the adventure with a camcorder.

The mystique is reinforced by instant lottery millionaires, the earnings of superstar athletes, and rags-to-riches stories of such people as the Bronfmans, one of Canada's best-known and wealthiest families. Samuel Bronfman, the legendary whiskey magnate and founder of Seagram's, was the son of a struggling farmer. The young Sam told his father, "the bar makes more profits than we do. Instead of selling horses, we should be selling the drinks." Sam and his brothers eventually had distilleries in Yorkton and Regina; during Prohibition in the 1920s, their empire flourished when they became a major supplier of liquor to American bootleggers.

Hockey players provide another example of the extraordinary payoff for hard work and talent, providing successful NHL players with their own "rags to riches" stories: Mats Sundin, for example, made $7.6 million during the 2006–07 season. While perhaps less frequent, stories like that of movie star Jim Carrey provide yet another example. Carrey came from meagre beginnings in Ontario. In a *Hamilton Spectator* interview, Carrey remarked that if his career in show business "hadn't panned out" he would "probably be working today in the circus industry or dealing crack in the streets of Ontario." He went on to say that when he would look across the Burlington Bay towards Hamilton, he could see the mills and thought "those are where the great jobs are."[10] Though Merton argued that lack of legitimate means for everyone to reach material goals like these does create problems, he also made it clear that the high rate of deviant behaviour cannot be explained solely on the basis of lack of means.

India The world has produced class systems that are more rigid than our own and societies that place much stricter limitations on people's ability to achieve their goals, without causing the problems Canada faces. In the traditional society of India, for example, the untouchables at the bottom of the caste system are forbidden by custom (although no longer by law) even to enter the temples and schools used by those above them, while those at the top enjoy immense privileges.

All Hindu castes fall within a hierarchy, each one imposing upon its members duties and prohibitions covering both public and private life. People of high status may give food to people of lower status, for example, but may not receive

These women are members of one of the lowest castes in India.

TABLE 5.1 A Typology of Modes of Individual Adaptation

Mode of Adaptation	Culture Goals*	Institutionalized Means*
Conformity	+	+
Innovation	+	−
Ritualism	−	+
Retreatism	−	−
Rebellion	±	±

*+ = acceptance; − = rejection; ± = rejection and substitution.

Source: Robert K. Merton, *Social Theory and Social Structure* (New York: Free Press, 1957). p. 140. Copyright © 1957 by The Free Press. Copyright © renewed 1985 by Robert K. Merton. All rights reserved.

food from them. One may eat in the home of a person of lower status, but the food must be cooked and served by a person of equal or higher status. Members of such a rigid system clearly face many more restraints than we do. Why, then, does India not have a very high crime rate?

The answer lies in the fact that Indians learn from birth that all people do not and cannot aspire to the same things. In Canada, the egalitarian principle denies the existence of limits to upward mobility within the social structure.[11] In reality, everyone in society experiences some pressures and strains, and the amounts are inversely related to position in the hierarchy: the lower the class, the higher the strain.

Modes of Adaptation

To be sure, not everyone who is denied access to a society's goals becomes deviant. Merton outlined five ways in which people adapt to society's goals and means. Individuals' responses (modes of adaptation) depend on their attitudes toward the cultural goals and the institutional means of attaining those goals. The options are conformity, innovation, ritualism, retreatism, and rebellion (see Table 5.1).

Merton does not tell us how any one individual chooses to become a drug pusher, for example, and another chooses to work on an assembly line. Instead, he explains why crime rates are high in some groups and low in others.

Conformity Conformity is the most common mode of adjustment. Individuals accept both the culturally defined goals and the prescribed means for achieving those goals. They work, save, go to school, and follow the legitimate paths. Look around you in the classroom. You will see many children of decent, hard-working parents. After university or college they will find legitimate jobs. Some will excel. Some will walk the economic middle path. But all those who are conformists will accept (though not necessarily achieve) the goals of our society and the means it approves for achieving them.

Innovation Individuals who choose the adaptation of innovation accept society's goals, but since they have few legitimate means of achieving them, they design their own means for getting ahead. The means may be burglary, robbery, embezzlement, or a host of other crimes. Youngsters who have no parental attention, no encouragement in school, no way to the top—no future—may scrawl their signatures on subway cars and buildings and park benches in order to achieve recognition of a sort. Such illegitimate forms of innovation are certainly not restricted to the lower classes, as evidenced by such crimes as stock manipulation, sale of defective products, and income tax evasion.

Ritualism People who adapt by ritualism abandon the goals they once believed to be within reach and resign themselves to their present lifestyles. They play by the rules; they work on assembly lines, hold middle-management jobs, or follow some other safe routine. Many workers have been catching a bus at the same street corner at the same hour every day for 20 years or more. They have long forgotten why, except that their jobs are where their paycheques come from. Their great relief is a two-week vacation in the summer.

Retreatism   Retreatism is the adaptation of people who give up both the goals (can't make it) and the means (why try?) and retreat into the world of drug addiction or alcoholism. They have internalized the value system and therefore are under internal pressure not to innovate. The retreatist mode allows for an escape into a non-productive, non-striving lifestyle. Some members of the anti-war movement of the 1960s opted to drop out entirely. The pressure was too great; the opportunities were unacceptable. They became addicts or followers of occult religions.

Rebellion   Rebellion occurs when both the cultural goals and the legitimate means are rejected. Many individuals substitute their own goals (get rid of the establishment) and their own means (protest). They have an alternative scheme for a new social structure, however ill-defined. Many of the so-called militias operating in North America today have lost faith in the legitimacy of government and are trying to establish their own alternative quasi-governmental structures.

Merton's theory of how the social structure produces strain that may lead to deviant behaviour is illustrated in Figure 5.1. His theory has challenged researchers for half a century.

Tests of Merton's Theory

Merton and his followers (whom we will discuss shortly) predict that the greatest proportion of crime will be found in the lower classes because lower-class people have the least opportunity to reach their goals legitimately. Many research studies designed to test the various propositions of strain theory focus on the association between social class and delinquency (an association that evokes considerable controversy). Some studies report a strong inverse relationship: As class goes up, crime rates go down. Others find no association at all between the two variables (see Chapter 2).

Social Class and Crime   The controversy over the relationship between social class and crime began when researchers, using self-report questionnaires, found more serious and more frequent delinquency among lower-class boys than among those of higher classes.[12] In Chapter 2, we saw that other researchers seriously questioned those findings.[13] When Charles Tittle and his colleagues attempted to clarify the relationship by analyzing 35 empirical studies, they concluded that "class is not now and has not been related to criminality in the recent past."[14] Summarizing the research literature on social class and crime, Gary Jensen and Kevin Thompson wrote, "The safest conclusion concerning class structure and delinquency is the same one that has been proposed for several decades: Class, no matter how defined, contributes little to explaining variation in self-reports of common delinquency."[15]

Once again there was a critical reaction. A summary of more than 100 projects concluded that "lower-class people do commit those direct interpersonal types of crime which are normally handled by the police at a higher rate than middle-class people."[16] But isn't it possible that crimes committed by lower-class people more readily come to the attention of the police? Observers point out that

FIGURE 5.1   Modes of deviant behaviour.

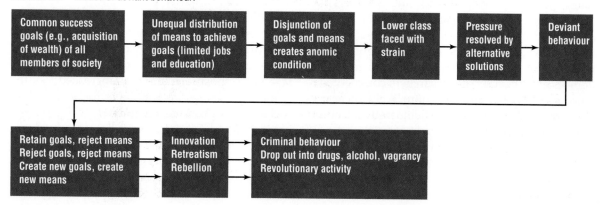

inner-city areas are policed more than higher-class areas. If we combine the greater police presence in areas inhabited primarily by lower-class individuals, and if we consider that street crimes like public muggings, drug trafficking, prostitution, and assaults are more likely to be detected by police or other social control agents (i.e., more likely to be reported) than, for example, the white-collar crimes committed by higher-class individuals behind the closed doors of their corporate boardrooms, doesn't it make sense that lower-class individuals are more likely to show up in crime statistics? Take, for example, the case of prostitution. Who is more likely to come to the attention of the police, be arrested, and enter into crime statistics—the street prostitute desperate for a "date" to pay for her next drug-induced high, or the high-priced escort with several regular private customers?

The suggestion of a connection between lower-class status and criminal behaviour raises an additional question. If low social status creates frustration that pushes people to commit crime, why don't all the people in the lowest class commit crimes, or drop out into the drug world, or become revolutionaries? Since they clearly do not, there must be some limitations to the causal relationship between crime and social class.

According to a number of studies, we may be able to learn more about the relationship between social class and crime if we look closely at specific types of offences rather than at aggregate crime (or delinquency) rates. In two large cross-national studies, two teams of Canadian researchers explored the relationship between income inequality and national homicide rates.[17] Both teams reported results that support strain theory. When opportunities or means for success are not provided equally to all members of society (as indicated by crime rates), pressure is exerted on some members of that society to engage in deviant behaviour (in this case, homicide). Further analyses by one of the teams showed that the effects of inequality on homicide may be even more pronounced in more democratic societies. The researchers commented, "Income inequality might be more likely to generate violent behaviour in more democratic societies because of the coexistence of high material inequality and an egalitarian value system."[18]

John Hagan argues that youngsters who grow up in a culture where friends are delinquent, parents are criminals, and drug abuse is common, and where early experiences with delinquent activities are widespread, become "embedded" in behaviours that result in later adult unemployment. They are excluded from employment by events that begin early in life. Steve Baron surveyed 200 male street youth under the age of 24 and found that they committed a total of 334 636 crimes during the previous year, an average of 1673 per respondent. Drug offences were responsible for 72 percent of the reported crime, suggesting that these youth were faced with economic strain and were very likely "innovating" in terms of Merton's typology. Violent offences, which are of little utility in terms of dealing with strain, accounted for only 5 percent of their reported crimes and were most often directed against each other in the context of disputes, horseplay, or in situations requiring revenge (e.g., getting "ripped off" in a drug deal).[19] Hagan and Bill McCarthy also report economic pressure among homeless youth in Canada, which can produce strains that then lead to desperation and anger, often precursors to crime.[20] The Toronto and Vancouver street youth in Hagan and McCarthy's study came from families characterized by poor parenting, violence and abuse, neglect, and economic marginalization. The youth described their own poor experiences in school with teachers and low grades. The limited resources available to these youth and their families led them to life on the street, which then further eroded chances of educational or employment success, and further propelled them into a life of crime, further abuse and victimization, prostitution, drugs, and violence.

Of course, youngsters can become equally "embedded" in a culture of middle-class values, economic stability, and early work experiences—the foundation for job stability and career success.[21]

Ethnicity and Crime Some evidence shows that class interacts with race and ethnicity to affect adult criminality. Individuals who are racial and ethnic minorities and come from disadvantaged class positions are at an increased risk for crime.[22] Other researchers have found that low social status promoted delinquency by increasing individuals' strain and by decreasing educational and occupational aspirations, whereas high social status promoted individuals' delinquency by increasing risk taking and decreasing conventional values.[23] Terence Thornberry and

Margaret Farnsworth argue that there is no simple connection between class and crime. The relationship, they say, is highly complex; it involves race, seriousness of the offence, education of family and offender, and many other factors.[24]

In a democratic society that stresses equal opportunities for individual achievement but in reality distributes resources on the basis of race, there is bound to be conflict. The most disadvantaged are precisely those who cannot change their situation through political action. In such circumstances, the frustrations created by racial inequalities tend to be expressed in various forms of aggression, such as violent crime and self-harm. Several researchers have supported these findings. For example, in Canada, Aboriginal peoples as a group occupy the lowest socioeconomic position in the country. The suicide rate of young Aboriginals is four times that of the general population. Rates of violence among this group are three times that of Canadians generally. Aboriginals have high rates of substance abuse and are overrepresented in prison populations. Some strain theorists would argue that Aboriginal status in Canada places individuals in a position of social structural disadvantage, which in turn contributes to their higher rates of both victimization and offending behaviour. Ethnic status interacts with educational opportunity, job opportunity, and class in ways that contribute to increased strain for ethnic minorities. Increased strain can lead to criminal behaviour, certainly not for all Aboriginal people, but it does seem to increase the chances of either committing criminal acts or attracting the attention of authorities. However, not all researchers are in agreement when it comes to the discussion of ethnicity and crime.

John Braithwaite examined Uniform Crime Report statistics for a sample of 175 American cities. He compared the rates of violent crime with racial inequality, as measured by the incomes of black families and the incomes of all other families in his sample cities. He concluded that racial inequality does not cause specific crime problems.[25] Perhaps the crucial point is not whether one actually has an equal chance to be successful but, rather, how one perceives one's chances. According to this reasoning, people who feel the most strain are those who have not only high goals but also low expectations of reaching them. So far, however, research has not supported this contention.

Nikos Passas points out that not all those persons exposed to the same problems respond in the same way. In fact, not all people perceive the same situation as a problem. He explains that anomie theorists base their arguments on rates of crime, rather than on individual behaviour.[26] In a similar vein, Gwynne Nettler questions the notion of "opportunity"; more specifically, he ponders the distinction, if any, between perceived opportunities and real ones.[27] It may be that, as Stephen Cernkovich and his colleagues suggest, ethnic minorities subscribe to different goals from the majority.[28] If this is in fact the case, then the notion of the "American dream" and the idea that we are all chasing wealth, fame, and fortune becomes questionable, as does Merton's explanation for criminal behaviour. It may be the case that, for example, Aboriginals are not in fact pursuing the same goals as mainstream society, which would suggest they are not strained in the same way as other Canadians. In turn, this would indicate that perhaps something other than strain contributes to their overrepresentation in the criminal justice system. It might also mean that they experience strains beyond economic strain (e.g., cultural strain, racism, discrimination, and issues relating to colonialism). We discuss revisions of strain theory that can account for this different conceptualization of strain later in this chapter.

Evaluation: Merton's Theory

The strain perspective developed by Merton and his followers has influenced both research and theoretical developments in criminology.[29] Yet, as popular as this theory remains, it has been

Corinne Williams describes how dangerous it is . . . outside the Fredericton Emergency Shelter.

questioned on a variety of grounds.[30] By concentrating on crime at the lower levels of the socio-economic hierarchy, for example, it neglects crime committed by middle- and upper-class people. Radical criminologists (see Chapter 8), in fact, claim that strain theory "stands accused of predicting too little bourgeois criminality and too much proletarian criminality."[31]

Feminist theorists point out that Merton's strain theory is inadequate in its explanation of women's criminal behaviour. Strain theory takes account of blocked opportunities based on social class, but not on gender.[32] Generally speaking, women tend to occupy relatively disadvantaged positions in society, which is linked in the theory to high degrees of strain. It follows that women, strained by their economic position in society and limited access to institutionalized means, would innovate and commit a lot of crime. Yet, as we saw in Chapter 2, they don't. The rate of female offending is significantly lower than that for males. Strain theory implies that women's low rate of offending must be linked to lower aspirations: If they don't strive to achieve the "American dream," then they won't feel the strain associated with trying to reach this goal. Feminist scholars argue that women experience strain in accessing institutionalized means and reject this reasoning as based on assumptions and biases that simply aren't true.[33]

Other critics question whether a society as heterogeneous as ours really does have goals on which everyone agrees. Are we all really chasing the "American dream"? Do we all aspire to money and status to the exclusion of other goals? Some theorists argue that subcultures have their own value systems (see Chapter 6). If that is the case, we cannot account for deviant behaviour on the basis of Merton's cultural goals. There are also other questions about the theory. If we have an agreed-upon set of goals, is material gain the dominant one? If crime is a means to an end, why is there so much useless, destructive behaviour, especially among teenagers? Some researchers suggest that offenders may have a different belief system than members of mainstream society. As James Hackler reports, Herman and Julia Schwendinger (two well-known criminologists, who have extensively researched youth and crime) speculate that the philosophy of serious offenders might go something like this: "Do unto others as they would do unto you . . . only do it first."[34] Baron asked the

homeless youth in his study about why they don't look for legitimate work. One individual responded that he was too "busy being a criminal. Looking for work you just get broke and have no place to live." Another said about finding a job: "[I] just don't want one now. Found other ways to survive instead of working."[35]

No matter how it is structured, each society defines goals for its members. Canada is far from being the only society in which people strive for wealth and prestige. Yet, while some people in other cultures have limited means for achieving these goals, not all these societies have high crime rates. Two such societies—Japan and Switzerland—are among the most developed and industrialized in the world. Although Canada has quite a bit in common with them, it does not share their very low crime rates.[36]

Despite the many critical assessments, strain theory, as represented primarily by Merton's formulation of anomie, has had a major impact on contemporary criminology. It dominated the delinquency research of the 1950s and 1960s. During the 1970s, the theory lost its dominant position as criminologists paid increasing attention to how crime and delinquency were related to individuals' loss of attachment to their social institutions—the family, the school, or the government (see Chapter 7). Then, in the mid-1980s and continuing unabated into the 2000s, there was a resurgence of interest in empirical research and theorizing based on strain concepts.

Institutional Imbalance and Crime

In their book *Crime and the American Dream*, Steven Messner and Richard Rosenfeld agree with Merton that the material success goal is pervasive in North American culture. In essence, the American dream is quite clear—succeed by any means necessary, even if those means are illegitimate.[37] The American dream, then, encourages high crime rates. Messner and Rosenfeld expand on Merton's ideas on the relationships among culture, social structure, anomie, and crime rates. High crime, they contend, is more than a matter of striving for monetary gains. It also results from the fact that our major social institutions do not have the capacity to control behaviour. These institutions fail to counterbalance the ethos of the American dream. The dominance of economic institutions manifests

A Head Start Really Does Help

Canadian educational researchers Bill Maynes and Rosemary Foster in their article "Educating Canada's Urban Poor Children" critically evaluate the state of Canada's educational poverty programs. One of the largest looming questions for Canadian policy makers and educators, according to these researchers, is whether we are making a serious effort to equalize educational opportunities for poor and non-poor children, or whether we are simply trying to mollify the poor in an effort to prevent social unrest. The authors' second major point is that we haven't funded or implemented the kinds of long-term early intervention programs that research in the United States has shown to be effective. Rather, we seem to be moving forward with our programs in a relatively haphazard fashion without seriously considering evaluation research on American educational programming. One such evaluation is discussed in the following excerpt from the New York Times.

In the longest study of its kind, researchers at the University of Wisconsin tracked 1500 school children from the age of 5 to the age of 20, and announced their results in the May 2001 *Journal of the American Medical Association.* The conclusion? Poor children who attend intensive preschool classes are more likely to graduate from high school and less likely to be arrested than poor children who have not participated in such programs.

The study followed 989 children who were living at or below the poverty level. Their educational careers were compared with 550 other children from the same neighbourhoods who did not attend any preschool at all, or who attended schools with less intensive programs. The study found that 16.9 percent of those who graduated from the Chicago preschool program had been arrested for juvenile crimes, while 25.1 percent of those who did not attend preschool had been arrested. They also found that 49.7 percent of the Chicago preschool students graduated from high school, as compared to 38.5 percent of those with little or no preschool experience.

Edward Ziglar, a founder of the Head Start program in the 1960s, commented that the Chicago findings "contradict the naysayers who believe that public schools cannot be fixed or that poor children cannot be helped because of nature or nurture."

The caveat, however, is that the programs must be highly structured and that parents must be involved in order to achieve the desired results. The children studied all attended child-care centers run by the public school system of Chicago, which require parents to participate in their children's homework assignments. The Center also helps families arrange medical care and social services.

In other words, they focus on more than just learning to read. Arthur J. Reynolds, professor of social work at Wisconsin, added, "You've got to put

parents in classrooms, as well as kids." Outside of the classroom, teachers are responsible for working with parents or guardians, helping them with projects like finding family photographs children might use to make a journal.

"We're providing a foundation for academic success," said Armando Almendarez, chief officer for early education at the Chicago public schools. "We know that success is tied to what is happening in the home environment, and that we can impact that environment."

Source

Adapted from Jacques Steinberg, "Gains Found for the Poor in Rigorous Preschool," *New York Times,* May 9, 2001. Reprinted with permission. Introduction based on Bill Maynes and Rosemary Foster, "Educating Canada's Urban Poor Children," *Canadian Journal of Education,* 25 (2000): 56–61.

Questions for Discussion

1. What can we learn from American evaluation research into programs such as Head Start? Should the federal government in Canada become more actively involved in funding such programs? Should guidelines be put in place to require more parental input in all government funded child-care programs?

2. What do these findings say about nature versus nurture? About how to design child-care programs that are effective in preventing future crime?

---

itself in three ways: devaluation of other institutions, their accommodation to economic institutions, and the penetration of economic norms.

- *The devaluation of non-economic roles and functions.* Performance in the economic world takes precedence over performance in other institutional settings: Non-economic functions are devalued. Education is important, for example, only because it promises economic gains. Learning for its own sake is relatively unimportant. In the context of the family, the home owner is more important

than the homemaker. In politics, too, there is a devaluation: If a citizen does not vote, there may be mild disapproval; if an adult citizen does not work, he or she loses status.

- *The accommodation of other institutions to economic needs.* In situations where institutions compete, non-economic ones **accommodate.** Family life is generally dominated by work schedules. Individuals go to school primarily to get a "good" job. Once out of school, those who return usually do so to get a better job. In political accommodation, government strives to maintain an environment hospitable to business.

- *The penetration of economic norms.* Penetration of economic norms into those of other institutions is widespread. Spouses become partners in "managing" the home, businesspeople/politicians campaign for public office, claiming they will "run the country like a corporation," and economic terms such as "accountability" are adopted by educators.

Messner and Rosenfeld contend that as long as there is a disproportionate emphasis on monetary rewards, the crime problem will increase. In fact, if economic opportunities increase, there may be an increase in the preoccupation with material success. Crime will decrease only when non-economic institutions have the capacity to control behaviour.[38]

Hackler describes a *Reader's Digest* informal study where 1100 wallets were "lost" in several countries. Each wallet contained $50 in local currency, as well as the name and phone number of the owner. While approximately 44 percent of the wallets disappeared, in Norway and Denmark *every single wallet* was returned.[39] The study raises questions concerning value systems of countries and the ability of such value systems to either support or counteract illegitimate opportunities. Freda Adler's study of ten countries with low crime rates supports this argument. She demonstrates that where economic concerns have not devalued informal social control institutions such as family, community, or religion, crime rates are relatively low and stable. This finding held for non-industrialized *and* highly industrialized societies.[40]

General Strain Theory

Sociologist Robert Agnew substantially revised Merton's theory in order to make it more broadly explanatory of criminal behaviour.[41] The reformulation is called **general strain theory.** Agnew argues that failure to achieve material goals (the focal point of Merton's theory) is not the only reason for committing crime. Criminal behaviour may also be related to the anger and frustration that result when an individual is treated in a way he or she does not want to be treated in a social relationship. General strain theory explains the range of strain-producing events.

- *Strain caused by failure to achieve positively valued goals.* This type of strain is based on

Merton's view that lower-class individuals are often prevented from achieving monetary success goals through legitimate channels. When people do not have the money to get what they want, some of them turn to illegitimate means to get it.

- *Stress caused by the removal of positively valued stimuli from the individual.* This type of strain results from the actual or anticipated loss of something or someone important in one's life: death of a loved one, breakup with a boyfriend/girlfriend, divorce of parents, move to a new school. Criminal behaviour results when individuals seek revenge against those responsible, try to prevent the loss, or escape through illicit drug use.

- *Strain caused by the presentation of negative stimuli.* The third major source of strain involves stressful life situations. Adverse situations and events may include child abuse, criminal victimization, bad experiences with peers, school problems, or verbal threats. Criminal behaviour in these situations may result when an individual tries to run away from the situation, end the problem, or seek revenge.[42]

According to Agnew, each type of strain increases an individual's feelings of anger, fear, or depression. The most critical reaction for general strain theory is anger, an emotion that increases the desire for revenge, helps justify aggressive behaviour, and stimulates individuals into action.

General strain theory acknowledges that not all persons who experience strain become criminals. Many are equipped to cope with their frustration and anger. Some come up with rationalizations ("don't really need it anyway"); others use techniques for physical relief (a good workout at the gym); and still others walk away from the condition causing stress (get out of the house). The capacity to deal with strain depends on personal experience throughout life. It involves the influence of peers, temperament, attitudes, and, in the case of pressing financial problems, economic resources. Recent empirical tests show preliminary support for general strain theory.[43] By broadening Merton's concepts, general strain theory has the potential to explain a wide range of criminal and delinquent behaviour, including aggressive acts, drug abuse, and property offences, among individuals from all classes in society.

Strain theory has helped us develop a crime-prevention strategy. If, as the theory tells us, frustration builds up in people who have few means for reaching their goals, it makes sense to design programs that give lower-class people a bigger stake in society.

Aboriginal Head Start   It was in the 1960s in the United States that President Lyndon Johnson inaugurated the Head Start program as part of a major anti-poverty campaign. The goal of Head Start is to make children of low-income families more socially competent, better able to deal with their present environment and their later responsibilities. The youngsters get a boost (or a head start) in a preschool developmental program that is intended to prevent them from dropping out of society. In 1995 Canadians created Aboriginal Head Start in Urban and Northern Communities, a version of Head Start that focuses specifically on the needs of First Nations, Inuit, and Métis children and their families. In 1998 Aboriginal Head Start (AHS) was expanded to serve First Nation communities on reserves. As one of the most disadvantaged and strained groups in Canadian society, Aboriginal communities appear to have much to gain from this kind of programming.

The primary goal of AHS is to demonstrate that locally controlled and designed early intervention strategies can provide Aboriginal children with a positive sense of themselves, a desire for learning, and opportunities to develop fully as successful young people. This early childhood development initiative is funded by Health Canada, but individual projects are locally designed and controlled and administered by non-profit Aboriginal organizations. AHS projects provide half-day preschool experiences for children up to age six, with emphasis on children three to five years old, and are intended to prepare young Aboriginal children for their school years by meeting their spiritual, emotional, intellectual, and physical needs. All projects provide programming in the following six core areas: Aboriginal culture and language, education and school readiness, parental involvement, health promotion, nutrition, and social support.[44]

There are approximately 140 Aboriginal Head Start programs in operation across Canada. About 4500 children are enrolled, representing about 8 percent of the three- to five-year-old Aboriginal children living off-reserve in Canada.[45] Local evaluations as well as comments and reports from parents, kindergarten teachers, and community members report major gains in all areas of children's development, improved family relationships, and parenting skills. Reports indicate that many AHS projects have become the community's centre on which to focus energy on improving the lives of Aboriginal children, and a foundation on which to build other child and family related services. Aboriginal Head Start programming is one aspect of the government's response to one of the recommendations of the Royal Commission on Aboriginal Peoples, which states: "By seeking greater control over schooling, Aboriginal people are asking for no more than what other communities already have: the chance to say what kind of people their children will become."

Ontario Public Service Learn and Work Program   Another program that tries to ameliorate the disparity between goals and means in society is the Ontario Public Service (OPS) Learn and Work Program. The program gives young people aged 16 to 19 who have left high school without a diploma the opportunity to earn up to 10 credits and gain up to 27 weeks of paid work experience in the Ontario Public Service and its related agencies.[46] Work placements include more than 10 government ministries and related agencies, the Ontario Rental Housing Tribunal, and the Ontario Science Centre. The OPS Learn and Work Program is part of the Ontario government's $28.5 million Youth Opportunities Strategy, "a broad plan to help young people faced with significant challenges achieve individual success and promote stronger and safer communities."

As a result of the perceived success of the initial 18-week pilot project, in January 2007, the Ontario government announced plans to expand the OPS Learn and Work Program to provide the opportunity to participate to an increasing number of students.

Job Corps   An ad for the Toronto Youth Job Corps reads as follows: "Have you dropped out of school, lack work experience, have a learning disability, and/or face other barriers to employment such as past or present involvement with the criminal justice system or homelessness?" The program, aimed at people aged 15 to 29, provides participants with a five-week pre-employment preparation phase that works to enhance participants' employment potential through life skills workshops and workability assessments as well as increasing confidence and self-esteem. Next, Job Corps members work in a subsidized work placement with an employer for 16–24 weeks to obtain work experience.[47]

The Alberta Job Corps is run in a similar manner, aimed at the same target population, with the exception that participants must be 18 years of age. The primary goal of the program is to "get hard-to-employ people job-ready" by providing training and workplace experience to clients unable to get, or maintain, work in the competitive job market.[48]

ALBERT COHEN: STATUS DEPRIVATION

Albert Cohen was a student of Robert Merton and of Edwin Sutherland (whose work we discuss in more detail in the next chapter), both of whom had made convincing arguments about the causes of delinquency. Sutherland persuaded Cohen that differential association and the cultural transmission of criminal norms led to criminal behaviour. From Merton he learned about structurally induced strain. Cohen combined and expanded these perspectives to explain how the delinquent subculture arises, where it is found within the social structure, and why it has the particular characteristics that it does.[49] Because Cohen's approach draws on both the importance of social structural strain and of cultural/subcultural concepts, Cohen's theory is considered by many to fall under the "strain" heading as well as the "subcultural" theory heading. We choose to discuss his theory here, but his ideas have relevance for Chapter 6 as well.

The Middle-Class Measuring Rod

According to Cohen, delinquent subcultures emerge in the slum areas of large cities. They are rooted in class differentials in parental aspirations, child-rearing practices, and classroom standards. The relative position of a youngster's family in the social structure determines the problems the child will face throughout life.

Lower-class families who have never known a middle-class lifestyle, for example, cannot social-ize their children in a way that prepares them to enter the middle class. The children grow up with poor communication skills, lack of commitment to education, and an inability to delay gratification. Schools present a particular problem. There, lower-class children are evaluated by middle-class teachers on the basis of a **middle-class measuring rod.** The measures are based on such middle-class values as self-reliance, good manners, respect for property, and long-range planning. By such measures, lower-class children fall far short of the standards they must meet if they are to compete successfully with middle-class children. Cohen argues that they experience status frustration and strain, to which they respond by adopting one of three roles: corner boy, college boy, or delinquent boy.

Corner Boy, College Boy, Delinquent Boy

"Corner boys" try to make the best of bad situations. The corner boy hangs out in the neighbourhood with his peer group, spending the day in some group activity, such as gambling or athletic competition. He receives support from his peers and is very loyal to them. Most lower-class boys become corner boys. Eventually, they get menial jobs and live a conventional lifestyle.

There are very few "college boys." These boys continually strive to live up to middle-class standards, but their chances for success are limited because of academic and social handicaps.

"Delinquent boys" band together to form a subculture in which they can define status in ways that to them seem attainable. Cohen claims that even though these lower-class youths set up their own norms, they have internalized the norms of the dominant class and they feel anxious when they go against those norms. To deal with this conflict, they resort to **reaction formation,** a mechanism that relieves anxiety through the process of rejecting with abnormal intensity what one wants but cannot obtain. These boys turn the middle-class norms upside down, thereby making conduct right in their subculture precisely because it is wrong by the norms of the larger culture (see Figure 5.2).

Consequently, their delinquent acts serve no useful purpose. They do not steal things to eat them, wear them, or sell them. In fact, they often discard or destroy what they have stolen. They appear to delight in the discomfort of others and in breaking taboos. Their acts are directed against people and property at random, unlike the goal-

FIGURE 5.2   The process of reaction formation among delinquent boys.

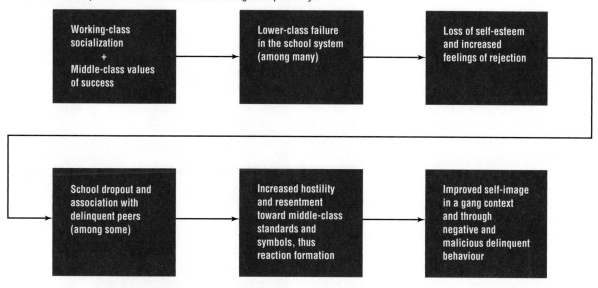

oriented activities of many adult criminal groups. The subculture is typically characterized by short-run hedonism, pure pleasure seeking, with no planning or deliberation about what to do, nor where or when to do it. The delinquents hang out on the street corner until someone gets an idea; then they act impulsively, without considering the consequences. The group's autonomy is all-important. Its members are loyal to each other and resist any attempts on the part of family, school, or community to restrain their behaviour.

Tests of Cohen's Theory

Criminological researchers generally agree that Cohen's theory is responsible for major advances in research on delinquency.[50] Among them are researchers who have found a relationship between delinquency and social status in our society. Much evidence also supports Cohen's assumption that lower-class children perform more poorly in school than middle-class children.[51] Teachers often expect them to perform less ably than their middle-class students, and this expectation is one of the components of poor performance.

Researchers have demonstrated that poor performance in school is related to delinquency. When Travis Hirschi studied more than 4000 California schoolchildren, he found that youths who were academically incompetent and performed poorly in school came to dislike school. Disliking it,

they rejected its authority; rejecting its authority, they committed delinquent acts (Chapter 7).[52] Delbert Elliott and Harwin Voss also investigated the relationship between school and delinquency. They analyzed annual school performance and delinquency records of 2000 students from ninth grade to one year after the expected graduation date. Their findings indicated that those who dropped out of school had higher rates of delinquency than those who graduated. They also found that academic achievement and alienation from school were closely related to dropping out of school.[53] Similarly, in his research on adolescents in Ontario, Ian Gomme found that self-reported delinquency and official rates of delinquency are strongly correlated with school failure.[54] Other Canadian research supports these conclusions.[55] Linda Pagani and her colleagues, using data from the Montreal Longitudinal-Experimental Study, found that family poverty predicted both academic failure among boys by the age of 16, as well as serious delinquency. These researchers report that while family poverty did not have an effect on more minor types of self-reported delinquency, it reliably predicted severe academic failure and extreme delinquency. They speculate that adolescents who experience financial hardship during their childhood may be more at risk of poor academic performance because of limited exposure to environmental stimuli. Interestingly, it was not persistent poverty that was related to these outcomes, but rather intermittent poverty: Family situations characterized by bouts of poverty interspersed with periods where they moved out of poverty seemed to have a more negative effect on the boys' behaviours.[56]

From analysis of the dropout-delinquency relationship among over 5000 persons, G. Roger Jarjoura concluded that while dropouts were more likely to engage in delinquent acts than graduates, the reason was not always simply the fact that they had dropped out. Dropping out because of a dislike for school, poor grades, or financial reasons was related to future involvement in delinquency; dropping out because of problems at home was not. Dropping out for personal reasons such as marriage or pregnancy was significantly related to subsequent violent offending.[57] All these findings support Cohen's theory.

Other findings, however, do not. Scott Davies discovered that gender matters when it comes to the relationship between school failure and offending. For boys, dropping out is linked to rebellion and resistance, whereas for girls dropping out is linked to marriage and motherhood.[58] In another study, Davies surveyed high school students in Ontario and found that, contrary to Cohen's theory, resistance to or rebellion against school systems is not specifically a working-class behaviour. He found that problematic behaviours like drinking and doing drugs and disrespect toward police and authority are related to tracking and academic problems but not to class background.[59] P. Solomon, based on his study of student resistance in a Toronto high school, found that for some students, school resistance is at least in part racially based. Black male students in his study reported resentment to school based on conflict between the cultural assumptions on the part of the school system and their own cultural background and experiences.[60]

In a study of 12 524 students Albert Reiss and Albert Rhodes found only a slight relationship between delinquency and status deprivation.[61] This conclusion was supported by the research of Marvin Krohn and his associates.[62] Furthermore, several criminologists have challenged Cohen's claim that delinquent behaviour is purposeless.[63] They contend that much delinquent behaviour is serious and calculated and often engaged in for profit.[64] Others have also questioned the consistency of the theory: Cohen argues that the behaviour of delinquent boys is a deliberate response to middle-class opinion; yet he also argues that the boys do not care about the opinions of middle-class people.[65]

Boredom in class, as demonstrated by this ninth-grade student, may lead to dropout and delinquency.

Evaluation: Cohen's Theory

Researchers have praised and criticized Cohen's work. Cohen's theory answers a number of questions left unresolved by other theories. It explains the origin of delinquent behaviour and why some youths raised in the same neighbourhoods and attending the same schools do not become involved in delinquent subcultures. His concepts of status deprivation and the middle-class measuring rod have been useful to researchers. Yet his theory does not explain why most delinquents eventually become law-abiding even though their position in the class structure remains relatively fixed. Some criminologists also question whether youths are driven by some serious motivating force or whether they are simply out on the streets looking for fun.[66] Moreover, if delinquent subcultures result from the practice of measuring lower-class boys by a middle-class measuring rod, how do we account for the growing number of middle-class gangs? Questions are also raised about lower-class girls and whether they are judged by the same middle-class measuring rod as their male counterparts? If they are, as

Multicultural macho advertisements appeal to young males concerned with showing toughness through masculinity. This billboard suggests that Converse sneakers are not for kids' playgrounds.

feminists would argue, how do they cope with status frustration? We return to the critique of Merton when it comes to gender: Is the lower crime rate among females a result of lowered expectations and less strain, different coping mechanisms, or are these theories simply inadequate in addressing the behaviour of females today?

Other questions concern the difficulty of trying to test the concepts of reaction formation, internalization of middle-class values, and status deprivation, among others. To answer some of his critics, Cohen, with his colleague James Short, expanded the idea of delinquent subcultures to include not only lower-class delinquent behaviour but also such variants as middle-class delinquent subcultures and female delinquents.[67] Cohen took Merton's strain theory a step further by elaborating on the development of delinquent behaviour. He described how strain actually creates frustration and status deprivation, which in turn fosters the development of an alternative set of values that give lower-class boys a chance to achieve recognition. Since the mid-1950s, Cohen's theory has stimulated not only research but also the formulation of new theories.

DELINQUENCY AND OPPORTUNITY

Like Cohen's theory, the theory of differential opportunity developed by Richard Cloward and Lloyd Ohlin combines strain, differential association, and social disorganization concepts (discussed in Chapter 7).[68] Both theories begin with the assumption that conventional means to conventional success are not equally distributed among the socioeconomic classes, that lack of means causes frustration for lower-class youths, and that criminal behaviour is learned and culturally transmitted. Both theories also agree that the common solution to shared problems leads to the formation of delinquent subcultures. They disagree, however, on the content of these subcultures. As we have noted, norms in Cohen's delinquent subcultures are right precisely because they are wrong in the dominant culture. Delinquent acts are negative and non-utilitarian. Cloward and Ohlin disagree; they suggest that lower-class delinquents remain goal-oriented. The kind of delinquent behaviour they engage in depends on the illegitimate opportunities available to them.

According to Cloward and Ohlin's **differential opportunity theory**, delinquent subcultures flourish in lower-class areas and take the particular forms they do because opportunities for illegitimate success are no more equitably distributed than those for conventional success. Just as means—opportunities—are unequally distributed in the conventional world, opportunities to reach one's goals are unequally distributed in the criminal world. A person cannot simply decide to join a theft-oriented gang or, for that matter, a violence-oriented one. Cloward and Ohlin maintain that the types of subcultures and the youth gangs that flourish within them depend on the types of neighbourhoods in which they develop (see Figure 5.3).

In areas where conventional and illegitimate values and behaviour are integrated by a close connection of illegitimate and legitimate businesses, "criminal gangs" emerge. Older criminals serve as role models. They teach youngsters the kinds of people to exploit, the necessary criminal skills, the importance of loyal relationships with criminal associates, and the way to make the right connections with shady lawyers, crooked politicians, and corrupt police officers. Adolescent members of criminal gangs, like adult criminals in the neighbourhood, are involved in extortion, fraud, theft, and other activities that yield illegal income.

Recruitment into gangs varies, but as Michael Chettleburgh points out in his book *Young Thugs: Inside the Dangerous World of Canadian Street Gangs*, in some areas and for some gangs,

FIGURE 5.3 Factors leading to development of three types of delinquent gangs.

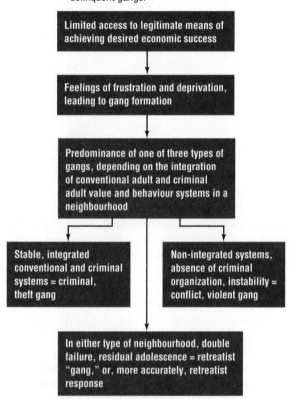

Source: Donald J. Shoemaker, *Theories of Delinquency: An Examination of Explanations of Delinquent Behavior*, 3rd ed. (New York: Oxford University Press, 1996), p. 115. Copyright © 1984, 1990, 1996, 2000 by Oxford University Press, Inc. Used by permission of Oxford University Press, Inc.

recruitment flows naturally, based on community characteristics:

> We Canadians, by our actions and by our decisions, have produced street gangs. When he is faced with a future flipping burgers at McDonald's for minimum wage, a troubled home life, an absent dad, a crime-infested community and stifled dreams, the pull of a gang and all that it offers may be just too strong for a young man. . . . Youths with gang-involved older siblings may simply grow into a gang from a young age—as young as eight in some places, such as in Winnipeg and Regina's large Aboriginal communities. If a street gang is established, has sufficient critical mass, enjoys steady proceeds from crime and is not involved in any heated rivalries, it may not need to recruit new members, preferring them to come through existing members.[69]

Neighbourhoods characterized by transience and instability, Cloward and Ohlin argue, offer few opportunities to get ahead in organized crimi-

nal activities. This world gives rise to "conflict gangs," whose goal is to gain a reputation for toughness and destructive violence. Thus "one particular biker would catch a bird and then bite off its head, allowing the blood to trickle from his mouth as he yelled 'all right!'"[70] It is the world of the warrior: Fight, show courage against all odds, defend and maintain the honour of the group. Above all, never show fear.

Violence is the means used to gain status in conflict gangs. Conventional society's recognition of the "worst" gangs becomes a mark of prestige, perpetuating the high standards of their members. Conflict gangs emerge in lower-class areas where neither criminal nor conventional adult role models exercise much control over youngsters.

A third subcultural response to differential opportunities is the formation of "retreatist gangs." Cloward and Ohlin describe members of retreatist gangs as double failures because they have not been successful in the legitimate world and have been equally unsuccessful in the illegitimate worlds of organized criminal activity and violence-oriented gangs. This subculture is characterized by a continuous search for getting high through alcohol, atypical sexual experiences, marijuana, hard drugs, or a combination of these.

The retreatist hides in a world of sensual adventure, borrowing, begging, or stealing to support his habit, whatever it may be. He may peddle drugs or work as a pimp or look for some other deviant income-producing activity. But the income is not a primary concern; he is interested only in the next high. Belonging to a retreatist gang offers a sense of superiority and well-being that is otherwise beyond the reach of these least-successful dropouts.

Not all lower-class youngsters who are unable to reach society's goals become members of criminal, conflict, or retreatist gangs. Many choose to accept their situation and to live within its constraints. These law-abiding youngsters are Cohen's corner boys.

Tests of Opportunity Theory

Cloward and Ohlin's differential opportunity theory presented many new ideas, and a variety of studies emerged to test it empirically.

The first of Cloward and Ohlin's assumptions—that blocked opportunities are related to delinquency—has mixed support. Travis Hirschi, for example, demonstrated that "the greater one's acceptance of conventional (or even quasi-conventional) success goals, the less likely one is to be delinquent, regardless of the likelihood these goals will someday be attained."[71] In other words, the youngsters who stick to hard work and education to get ahead in society are the least likely to become delinquent, no matter what their real chances of reaching their goals. John Hagedorn disagrees. In late 1992 and early 1993, he conducted interviews with 101 founding members of 18 gangs. His conclusion: "Most of those we were trying to track appeared to be on an economic merry-go-round, with continual movement in and out of the secondary labour market. Although their average income from drug sales far surpassed their income from legal employment, most male gang members apparently kept trying to find licit work."[72] There is also evidence that both gang and non-gang boys believe the middle-class values of hard work and scholastic achievement to be important. Gang boys, however, are more ready to approve of a wide range of behaviours, including aggressive acts and drug use.[73]

An interesting extension of this perspective is provided by John Hagan and Bill McCarthy's research on street youth in Toronto and Vancouver.[74] The researchers found that negative family experiences, including parental unemployment, marital problems, neglect, and abuse, increased the likelihood of youth turning to the streets to escape problematic home situations. Leaving one negative environment for another, the youth, now on the street, were forced to seek food and shelter, which often led them to interaction with seasoned criminals. Such seasoned criminals were good sources of "training" for the youth, offering them tutelage in criminal behaviours. On the other hand, youth from functioning families do well in school and in finding legitimate employment.

The second assumption of differential opportunity theory—that the type of lower-class gang depends on the type of neighbourhood in which it emerges—has also drawn the attention of criminologists. Empirical evidence suggests that gang behaviour is more versatile and involves a wider range of criminal and non-criminal acts than the patterns outlined by Cloward and Ohlin. Ko-lin Chin's research on New York gangs in 1993 demonstrates that Chinese gangs are engaged in extortion, alien smuggling, heroin trafficking, and the running of gambling establishments and houses of prostitution.[75] A recent report from the Denver Youth Survey showed

that while the most frequent form of illegal activity is fighting with other gangs, gang members are also involved in robberies, joyriding, assaults, stealing, and drug sales.[76] Aboriginal gangs, which are increasing in influence on a growing number of prairie reserves, are a response by generations of Aboriginals to social structural problems, including lack of legitimate and often illegitimate opportunities. While gangs such as the Indian Posse, Redd Alert, and Alberta and Manitoba Warriors certainly are active in illicit money-making activities such as drug trafficking, they are also known for their violence, to which they subject both insiders and outsiders.[77]

The RCMP 2006 study *Youth Gangs & Guns*, which broadly describes "youth" as individuals aged 30 and under, reports that as of 2002 there were 434 youth gangs active across Canada, with approximately 7000 members. The 2006 annual report of the Criminal Intelligence Service Canada (CISC) estimated that there were 11 000 street-gang members and associates in Canada, located in every province except Prince Edward Island and Newfoundland and Labrador, as well as in the Northwest Territories[78] (see Figure 5.4). Gangs are active in large and small Canadian jurisdictions and their prominent financial drive is illicit drug distribution. As a research participant in a study by the University of Toronto's Scot Wortley and Julian Tanner states: "It's like the only jobs they got for poor black people is like McDonald's or Wendy's or other bullshit like that. Low, low pay, no respect. . . . I'm my own boss, make way more money and don't sell myself out to shit like that. I'd rather die than embarrass myself like that."[79] In Toronto, at least 25 gangs are estimated to have ties to organized crime, often playing the role of "foot soldier" and doing the "dirty work" for more organized groups. Collaboration with organized crime groups is highest with respect to drug trafficking, intimidation/extortion, and auto theft.

Research does support Cloward and Ohlin's argument that criminal gangs emerge in areas where conventional and illegitimate behaviours have a close connection with illegitimate and legitimate businesses. Chinatowns in the United States, for example, are social, economic, political, and cultural units.[80] All types of organizations, including those that dominate illegal activities, play an important role in the maintenance of order in the community. The illegitimate social order has control of territorial rights, gambling places, heroin trafficking, alien smuggling, and loan-sharking. The illegal order

FIGURE 5.4 Gang presence in Canada.

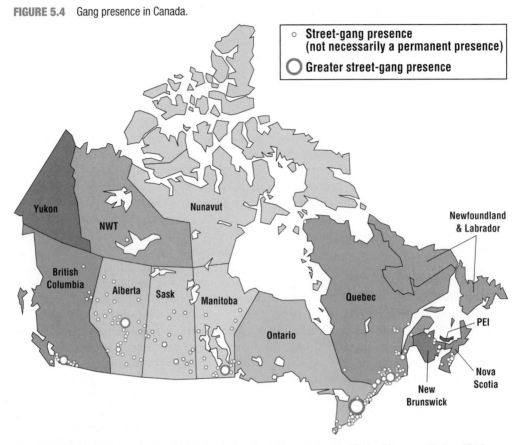

○ **Street-gang presence**
   (not necessarily a permanent presence)

◯ **Greater street-gang presence**

Source: 2006 CISC Annual Report on Organized Crime in Canada. Reproduced with permission of the Ministry of Government Works and Public Services, Canada 2008.

defines who is in control of particular restaurants, retail shops, garment factories, and the like. Business owners pay a "membership fee" for protection. Adult criminals maintain control of youth gang members by threatening to exclude them from work that pays well. They also resolve conflicts, provide recreational facilities, lend money, and give the young gang members a chance to climb the illegitimate career ladder within the criminal organization. Gang activities are closely supervised by their leaders, who work with the adult crime groups. Elaborate initiation rites are conducted by an adult the youngsters call "uncle"—the link between the gang and the adult sponsoring organization.

Evaluation: Differential Opportunity Theory

For three decades, criminologists have reviewed, examined, and revised the work of Cloward and Ohlin.[81] One of the main criticisms is that their theory is class-oriented. If, as Cloward and Ohlin claim, delinquency is a response to blocked opportunities, how can we explain middle-class delinquency? Another question arises from contradictory statements. How can delinquent groups be non-utilitarian, negativistic, and malicious

Outlaw motorcycle gang members are arrested in 2002.

(Cohen)—and also goal-oriented and utilitarian? Despite its shortcomings, however, differential opportunity theory has identified some of the reasons lower-class youngsters may become alienated. Cloward and Ohlin's work has also challenged researchers to study the nature of the subcultures in our society, the focus of the next chapter.

REVIEW

1. How are sociological theories connected?
Contemporary criminologists tend to divide the socio-logical explanation of crime into three categories: strain, cultural deviance, and social control. The strain and cul-tural deviance perspectives focus on the social forces that cause people to engage in deviant behaviour. They assume that there is a relationship between social class and criminal behaviour.

2. How does Durkheim's concept of anomie contrib-ute to an understanding of crime?
Strain theories have their roots in the structural-functionalist perspective developed by Durkheim. **Strain theory** (p. 108) holds that all people in society share one set of cultural values and that since lower-class persons often do not have legitimate means to attain society's goals, they may turn to illegitimate means instead.

3. What does Merton's strain theory add to our understanding of crime?
Robert Merton argued that strain in the form of a social structure that holds out the same goals to all members but then withholds the means of achieving them, can lead to criminal behaviours. Messner and Rosenfeld ex-pand on Merton's ideas. They contend that crime also results from the fact that our major social institutions do not have the capacity to control behaviour. These institu-tions fail to counterbalance the ethos of the "American dream." **General strain theory** (p. 118), a revision of Merton's theory, relates criminal behaviour to the anger that results when an individual is treated in a way he or she does not want to be treated in a social relationship.

4. How is status deprivation connected to strain and crime?
Albert Cohen built on these ideas by suggesting that lower-class males, frustrated by their inability to measure up to the **middle-class measuring rod** (p. 120), set up their own norms by which they could gain status. They resort to **reaction formation** (p. 120), whereby they reject with abnormal intensity what they want but cannot gain.

5. What is differential opportunity?
Cloward and Ohlin's **differential opportunity theory** (p. 123) adds another dimension to strain theories: dif-ferential opportunity refers to the socially structured na-ture of illegitimate opportunities. Cohen and Cloward and Ohlin's theories are also considered cultural deviance theories, the focus of the next chapter. Cultural deviance theorists maintain that the lower class has a distinctive set of values and that these values often conflict with those of the middle class.

CRIMINOLOGY & PUBLIC POLICY

In North American society, people are evaluated on the basis of achievement and success (or the lack thereof) rather than on the basis of who they are or how they are connected to others. "'Success' is to a large extent the ultimate measure of social worth. Quite understandably, then, there are pervasive cultural pressures to achieve at any cost. A strong achievement orientation, at the level of basic cultural values, thus cultivates and sustains a mentality that "it's not how you play the game; it's whether you win or lose." (*Source:* Richard Rosenfeld and Steven F. Messner, "Crime and the American Dream: An Institutional Analysis," in *The Legacy of Anomie: Advances in Criminological Theory,* F. Adler and W. S. Laufer, eds. [New Brunswick, NJ: Transaction, 1999].)

Questions for Discussion Robert Merton's no-tion of strain may be traced to the same values upon which the "American dream" rests, in particular a strong achievement orientation. What are the ramifications of such a theoretical premise? What kind of social pro-grams address this orientation? Do programs grounded in this success orientation promote an unrealistic and unattainable goal? Given the rich diversity of Canadian culture, does the concept of the "American dream" hold stead? Or has it been eroded by the influence of other cultures?

YOU BE THE CRIMINOLOGIST

A major funding agency has given a large grant for changing the quality of life in a high-crime in-ner-city neighbourhood where residents are afraid to let their children play outside. You are the project director. Whom would you hire as consultants? Would you work with law enforcement? And, finally, what would be your goals, and how would you reach them?

Visit the Online Learning Centre: www.mcgrawhill.ca/olc/adler

CULTURAL DEVIANCE AND THE FORMATION OF SUBCULTURES

CHAPTER 6

Two 15-year-olds suspected of committing a break-and-enter are searched by members of the Winnipeg police street gang unit. Winnipeg is ranked near the top in the list of Canadian cities with a large number of gang-affiliated individuals.

Vancouver's 626 gang. Rock Machine. Redd Alert. Crazy Cambodian Killers. White Boy Posse. These are just a few of the gangs that have affected Canadians in one way or another. The gang phenomenon is not a new one; historical reports indicate that groups of people, youth and adults, have caused mainstream society problems since the days of the fur trade. Yet it seems we are becoming more concerned about what has been described as an increasingly serious problem. Who are these gang members? What is their problem?

Criminologists suggest "their" problems are actually "our" problems too. The media help to construct the gang issue in ways that are misleading and that help to create some inaccurate perceptions about gang members. Vancouverites were plagued in 1992 by the "626 gang," known for committing armed robberies of banks, stores, and credit unions. Once they were apprehended, police discovered the "gang" wasn't a gang at all; members didn't consider themselves as such. Rather they were a group of eight young people who were drawn together by friendship and a common interest in crime. They decided to try their luck at armed robbery. Their "gang name" was actually created by police (and reported by the media) because they used stolen Mazda 626 automobiles to commit their crimes.[1]

Canadians are aware of the so-called "ethnic" gang problem. Yet, reports from gang members, ex-members, and gang experts indicate that most gangs are ethnically mixed, and although a group like the "Crazy Cambodian Killers" suggests an ethnic connection, the fact is that there are usually as many "white" members as there are ethnically distinct members. An exception to the rule is Aboriginal gangs, which are less likely to be ethnically mixed, although they can be. Aboriginal gangs, more prevalent in the Prairie provinces, have very strong and direct links to prison gangs. In fact, the Redd Alert was initially formed as a means of protection for individuals in prison who were afraid of being coerced into gangs! Interestingly, the White Boy Posse, a gang that has roots in rural Alberta, only recently made the news. Yet it, too, is an "ethnic gang."

The fact is that gangs—whether relatively unorganized street gangs or more organized groups like Quebec's biker group the Rock Machine—exist because they fill a need. For members, street gangs provide a substitute for families that have failed their children, protection for young people who feel they need it, and the promise of big money for youth growing up surrounded by disadvantage. Whether the gangs "deliver" is another issue—most don't. For non-members, gangs also fill a need. Biker gangs and other groups that provide drugs and prostitutes to willing customers are supplying goods and services for which there is a demand.

Gangs are indicative of a society that is failing its citizens. An economy that shuts youth and adults out, offers them meagre wages while expecting them to literally buy into consumerism, dysfunctional families, and increasing rates of poverty contribute to a situation where gangs become a viable option for some, who often start their involvement at a young age. This chapter investigates issues surrounding gangs by surveying several classic criminological theories whose genesis is based on explaining youth gang membership and activities. While these theories focus on youth, gang involvement is a phenomenon not restricted to any particular age group.

CULTURAL DEVIANCE THEORIES

As we saw in Chapter 5, strain theorists attribute criminal behaviour to the striving of all citizens to conform to the conventional values of the middle class, primarily financial success. Criminal behaviour is a result of the frustrations suffered by lower-class individuals deprived of legitimate means to reach their goals. The programs that emanate from strain theory attempt to give underprivileged children ways to achieve middle-class goals.

Cultural deviance theories attribute crime to a set of values that exist in disadvantaged neighbourhoods. These theories claim that lower-class people have a different set of values, which tends to conflict with the values of the middle class. Consequently, when lower-class persons conform to their own value system, they may be violating conventional or middle-class norms. Programs based on cultural deviance theories concentrate on teaching middle-class values. Strain and cultural deviance theories locate the causes of crime in the marginalized position of those at the lowest stratum in a class-based society. Both perspectives form the foundation for subcultural theory, which emerged in the mid-1950s and which we discuss later in this chapter.

Two major cultural deviance theories are differential association and culture conflict. **Differential association theory** maintains that people learn to commit crime as a result of contact with antisocial values, attitudes, and criminal behaviour patterns. **Culture conflict theory** states that different groups learn different **conduct norms** (rules governing behaviour) and that the conduct norms of some groups may clash with conventional middle-class rules.

Both theories contend that criminals and delinquents in fact do conform—but to norms that deviate from those of the dominant middle class. Before we examine the specific theories that share the cultural deviance perspective, we need to explore the nature of cultural deviance.

The Nature of Cultural Deviance

Jacob is a typical teenager in his Hutterite community near Brandon, Manitoba. At 15 he is in his final year of schooling. Over the next few years he will become a full-time worker on the colony farm, contributing to its mixed-farming economy. When he is a bit older, Jacob may meet a young woman in a neighbouring colony; if they marry, the couple will live in a private apartment in the row houses traditionally built on the colonies. Jacob and his family live in a manner very similar to their ancestors, members of the conservative Anabaptist church who migrated to North America from Europe in the nineteenth and twentieth centuries. Jacob is well aware of the rather different way of life of the mainstream. Hutterian beliefs promote a simple, austere lifestyle. They are a *non-conformist* community within a highly materialistic culture.

Motorcycle gangs made their appearance shortly after World War II. The Hell's Angels was the first of many outlaw biker gangs to be established in slum areas of cities across the United States, and then in Canada. To become a member of this gang, initiates are subjected to gruelling and revolting degradations. They are conditioned to have allegiance only to the gang. Contacts with middle-class society are usually antagonistic and criminal. Motorcycle gangs finance their operations through illegal activities, such as dealing drugs, running massage parlours and gambling operations, and selling stolen goods. The members' code of loyalty to one another and to their national and local groups makes the gangs extremely effective criminal organizations.

The normative systems of Hutterites and the bikers are at odds with the conventional norms of the society in which they live. Both deviate from middle-class standards. Sociologists define **deviance** as any behaviour that members of a social group define as violating their norms. As we can see, the concept of deviance can be applied to non-criminal acts that

Wearing a pendant made out of bullet, this individual is participating in a neo-Nazi gathering.

Cults—Culture Conflict—Crime

In Hamilton, Ontario, in 2006, a family is ripped apart when Mirella Brun del Re ostracizes her family and attends the Dominion Christian Centre (DCC) on a daily basis. She is one of many followers of Pastor Peter Rigo, who demands complete compliance from his followers and encourages them to break ties with family members who do not understand the "truth." Mirella's parents were charged with kidnapping and forcible confinement as a result of their attempts to remove her from what they perceive as the dangerous and "cultish" practices of Rigo and the DCC and have her deprogrammed. Mirella believes it's her parents and other concerned families who are being manipulated by "the enemy."(1)

A cult is defined as "a great devotion to a person, idea, object, [or] movement; . . . a usually small group of people characterized by such devotion" (*Merriam Webster's Collegiate*® Dictionary, Tenth Edition). Most cults are marked by

- a dynamic leader;
- the willingness of members to surrender their worldly possessions;
- strict obedience to the leader;
- a communal social structure, with its own set of norms and values that are in conflict with those of conventional societies.

Experts estimate that there are 1000 to 2000 cults in North America, with as many as 4 to 6 million members.

Criminologists are interested primarily in destructive cults such as these:
- An Indian cult has its devotees "marry" their little daughters to a goddess. Upon reaching puberty, the little girls are sold into prostitution for about $200 each.(2)
- Members of the Japanese cult Aun Shinrikyo launched a nerve gas attack in the Tokyo subway system—for unknown reasons—killing 12 and injuring over 5000 (March 20, 1995).
- The Reverend Jim Jones led his cult followers to death at their Jonestown,

Shoko Asahara, leader of the Japanese cult Aun Shinrikyo.

Guyana, encampment: 914 died; those who refused to take the poison were shot (November 18, 1978).
- The Solar Temple cult followers committed 74 murder/suicides in Canada and in Switzerland (1994–1997).
- Of the 107 members of the cult group of David Koresh—called the Branch Davidians—80 died (most committed suicide) in a standoff with U.S. federal authorities in Waco, Texas (April 1993).(3)

Some governments (China, Germany, and Russia) have outlawed some cults. The Vatican has issued a strong report exhorting the church to fulfill the spiritual needs of the people to keep them from seeking salvation in cults.(4) In Canada the debate centres around our constitutional right to religious freedom. What governments, theologians, and criminologists have in common is their determination to bring alienated members of society into the mainstream to keep them out of destructive cults. But what is a destructive cult? Where should we draw the line between the freedom to exercise one's religious beliefs and the government's legitimate interest in protecting its citizens from coercive, destructive, and often violent religious groups?

Sources

1. "Pied Piper of Hamilton," *W-Five*, CTV.ca, Nov. 17, 2006, www.ctv.ca/servlet/ArtcileNews/print/CTVNews/20061027/wfive_pied_piper_0610, accessed February 18, 2008.
2. "India Sex Cult's 'Handmaidens' Join Tribute to Hindu Goddess, Secret Society Forces Girls Who 'Marry' Yelamma into Prostitution," *Toronto Star*, Jan. 23, 1997, p. A16.
3. Richard Lacayo, "Cult of Death," *Time*, Mar. 15, 1993, p. 36; Sophfionia Scott Gregory, "Children of a Lesser God," *Time*, May 17, 1993, p. 54.
4. E. J. Dionne, "Vatican, Taking Some Blame, Cites Threat of Cults," *New York Times*, May 4, 1986, p. A10.

Questions for Discussion

1. Where and how can we draw the line between those cults that engage in violations of the criminal law (such as murder, arson, incitation to suicide, sexual assault, child abuse, and prostitution) and those that have not (yet) committed any criminal acts and therefore enjoy constitutional rights to religious freedom?
2. Both theologians and criminologists advocate narrowing the gap between conduct norms of deviant cultures (cults, sects) and the rules of mainstream society. How could either group practically accomplish that goal?

members of a group view as peculiar or unusual (the lifestyle of the Hutterites) or to criminal acts (behaviour that society has made illegal). The Hell's Angels fit the expected stereotype of deviance as negative; Hutterian culture demonstrates that deviance is not necessarily bad, just different.

Cultural deviance theorists argue that our society is made up of various groups and subgroups, each with its own standards of right and wrong. Behaviour considered normal in one group may be considered deviant by another. As a result, those who conform to the standards of cultures considered deviant are behaving in accordance with their own norms but may be breaking the law—the norms of the dominant culture.

Differential Association Theory

What we eat, what we say, what we believe—in fact, the way we respond to any situation—depends on the culture in which we have been reared. Socialization plays a significant role in the way we think and act. In other words, to a very large extent, the social influences that people encounter determine their behaviour. Whether a person becomes law-abiding or criminal, then, depends on contacts with criminal values, attitudes, definitions, and behaviour patterns. Growing up in a neighbourhood heavily influenced by the Hell's Angels, where many adults are members of the group, could potentially influence a child growing up in that neighbourhood. This proposition underlies one of the most important theories of crime causation in criminology—differential association.

Sutherland's Theory In 1939, Edwin Sutherland introduced differential association theory in his textbook *Principles of Criminology.* Since then, scholars have read, tested, re-examined, and sometimes ridiculed this theory, which claimed to explain the development of all criminal behaviour. The theory states that crime is learned through

Latin Kings gang member teaches gang hand symbols to a child. Social interactions like these are learned and transmitted from one generation to the next.

social interaction. People come into constant contact with "definitions favourable to violations of law" and "definitions unfavourable to violations of law." The ratio of these definitions—criminal to non-criminal—determines whether a person will engage in criminal behaviour.[2] In formulating this theory, Sutherland relied heavily on findings from other research suggesting that delinquent values are transmitted within a community or group from one generation to the next. Cultural transmission refers to the process whereby these values, beliefs, and behaviours are passed from generation to generation through the process of socialization.

Sutherland's Nine Propositions Nine propositions explained the process by which this transmission of values takes place:

1. Criminal behaviour is learned.
2. Criminal behaviour is learned in interaction with other persons in a process of communication. A person does not become a criminal simply by living in a criminal environment. Crime is learned by participation with others in verbal and non-verbal communications.
3. The principal part of the learning of criminal behaviour occurs within intimate personal groups. Families and friends have the most influence on the learning of deviant behaviour. Their communications far outweigh those of the mass media.
4. When criminal behaviour is learned, the learning includes (a) techniques of committing the crime, which are sometimes very complicated, sometimes very simple, and (b) the specific direction of motives, drives, rationalizations, and attitudes. Young delinquents learn not only how to shoplift, crack a safe, pick a lock, or roll a joint but also how to rationalize and defend their actions. One safecracker accompanied another safecracker for a year before he cracked his first safe.[3] In other words, criminals, too, learn skills and gain experience.
5. The specific direction of motives and drives is learned from definitions of the legal codes as favourable or unfavourable. In some societies, an individual is surrounded by persons who invariably define the legal codes as rules to be observed, while in others he or she is surrounded by persons whose

definitions are favourable to the violation of the legal codes. Not everyone in our society agrees that the laws should be obeyed; some people define them as unimportant. In North American society, where definitions are mixed, we have a culture conflict in relation to legal codes.

6. A person becomes delinquent because of an excess of definitions favourable to violation of law over definitions unfavourable to violation of law. This is the key principle of differential association. In other words, learning criminal behaviour is not simply a matter of associating with bad companions. Rather, learning criminal behaviour depends on how many definitions we learn that are favourable to law violation as opposed to those that are unfavourable to law violation.

7. Differential associations may vary in frequency, duration, priority, and intensity. The extent to which associations and definitions will result in criminality is related to the frequency of contacts, their duration, and their meaning to the individual.

8. The process of learning criminal behaviour by association with criminal and anti-criminal patterns involves all the mechanisms that are involved in any other learning. Learning criminal behaviour patterns is very much like learning conventional behaviour patterns and is not simply a matter of observation and imitation.

9. While criminal behaviour is an expression of general needs and values, it is not explained by those general needs and values, since noncriminal behaviour is an expression of the same needs and values. Shoplifters steal to get what they want. Others work to get money to buy what they want. The motives—frustration, desire to accumulate goods or social status, low self-concept, and the like—cannot logically be the same because they explain both lawful and criminal behaviour.

Tests of Differential Association Theory

Since Sutherland presented his theory more than 50 years ago, researchers have tried to determine whether his principles lend themselves to empirical measurement. James Short tested a sample of 126 boys and 50 girls at a training school and reported a consistent relationship between delinquent behaviour and frequency, duration, priority, and intensity of interactions with delinquent peers. Similarly, Travis Hirschi demonstrated that boys with delinquent friends are more likely to become delinquent.[4] Research over the years has consistently found that association with delinquent peers is the single most important predictor of "official" delinquency.[5] Research on seventh- and eighth-grade students attending public schools in the late 1980s and early 1990s shows that gang membership is strongly associated with peer delinquency and the amount of delinquency and drug use.[6] Recent studies show that among at-risk youth, gang membership is a greater predictor of delinquency than association with deviant peers.[7] Mark Warr demonstrated that while the duration of delinquent friendships over a long period of time has a greater effect than exposure over a short period, it is recent friendships rather than early friendships that have the greatest effect on delinquency.[8]

Differential association theory principles also point to the importance of learning skills and rationalizations for delinquent behaviour from one's close "associates." Research on Aboriginal youth at risk for gang involvement illustrates the importance of family, peers, and the strain of life on impoverished reserves that can contribute to gang involvement. As one ex-gang member says, "I grew up on a reserve surrounded by gang members. My family was involved and sold drugs. I started drug running at 12 and started selling at 14. I wanted the money." Another ex-gang member states that "the strongest link in a gang is when it is made up of the people that you grow up with."[9]

Adults have also been the subjects of differential association studies. Two thousand residents of New Jersey, Oregon, and Iowa were asked such questions as how many people they knew personally had engaged in deviant acts and how many were frequently in trouble. They were also asked how often they attended church (assumed to be related to definitions unfavourable to the violation of law). This differential association scale correlated significantly with such crimes as illegal gambling, income tax cheating, and theft.[10] Daniel Wolf, a researcher who rode with the Rebels, an Edmonton biker gang, revealed the importance of the "brotherhood" to members: "When a patch holder defends his colours, he defends his personal identity, his community, his lifestyle. . . . What matters is that, for patch holders, the brotherhood emerges as a necessary feature of their continued existence as individuals and as a group."[11]

Evaluation: Differential Association Theory

Many researchers have attempted to validate Sutherland's differential association theory. Others have criticized it. Much of the criticism stems from errors in interpretation. Perhaps this type of error is best demonstrated by the critics who ask why it is that not everyone in heavy, prolonged contact with criminal behaviour patterns becomes a criminal. Take, for argument's sake, corrections officers, who come into constant contact with more criminal associations than non-criminal ones. How do they escape from learning to be law violators themselves?

The answer, of course, is that Sutherland does not tell us that individuals become criminal by associating with criminals or even by association with criminal behaviour patterns. He tells us, rather, that a person becomes delinquent because of an "excess of definitions favourable to violation of law over definitions unfavourable to violation of law." The key word is "definitions." Furthermore, unfavourable definitions may be communicated by persons who are not robbers or murderers or tax evaders. They may, for example, be law-abiding parents who, over time, define certain situations in such a way that their children get verbal or non-verbal messages to the effect that antisocial behaviour is acceptable.

Several scholars have asked whether the principles of differential association really explain all types of crime. They might explain theft, but what about homicide resulting from a jealous rage?[12] Why do some people who learn criminal behaviour patterns not engage in criminal acts? Why is no account taken of non-social variables, such as a desperate need for money? Furthermore, while the principles may explain how criminal behaviour is transmitted, they do not account for the origin of criminal techniques and definitions. In other words, the theory does not tell us how the first criminal became a criminal.

Differential association theory suggests there is an inevitability about the process of becoming a criminal. Once you reach the point where your definitions favourable to law violation exceed your definitions unfavourable to law violation, have you crossed an imaginary line into the criminal world? Even if we could add up the definitions encountered in a lifetime, could scientists measure the frequency, priority, duration, and intensity of differential associations?

Other critics have pointed to the importance of situational factors that contribute to criminal events. How a crime is committed and which crimes are committed depend at least in part on how a particular offender is thinking, feeling, and processing the information around him or her at that moment. In other words, while motivations, rationalizations, and skills may be learned through association with others, what a particular individual does with that information is variable and depends on factors other than group membership.[13]

Despite these criticisms, the theory has had a profound influence on criminology.[14] Generations of scholars have tested it empirically, modified it to incorporate psychologically based learning theory (see Chapter 4), and used it as a foundation for their own theorizing (see Chapter 5). The theory has also had many policy implications.

THEORY INFORMS POLICY

If, according to differential association theory, a person can become criminal by learning definitions favourable to violating laws, it follows that programs that expose young people to definitions favourable to conventional behaviours should reduce criminality. Such educational efforts as Head Start, Aboriginal Head Start, and Job Corps have attempted to do just that. The same theory underlies many treatment programs directed at young people at risk of dropping out of school, young people generally who may be tempted by delinquent peers who use and abuse substances, or those who otherwise push the boundaries of acceptable behaviours.

Full Impact was a program created by an inmate serving time in a federal prison in Drumheller, Alberta. Along with a group of other inmates from the institution, he created a videotape documenting the reality of life behind bars. The inmates eventually were granted permission to embark on a tour of elementary and junior high schools in the area, showing the video to students and then talking frankly with their audiences about life as an inmate. The goal of the program was to encourage children to make good decisions, abide by the law, and avoid criminal behaviour, thereby avoiding the mistakes these inmates had made.

While the program was not evaluated, Richard, an inmate, involved in the program, tells a story of the kind of impact the program had on at least one young girl. Having listened to the inmates, the girl, in grade 5 at the time, approached Richard during the after-presentation socializing session. She tugged at his jacket. As he engaged in conversation with her she said, "You sure have had a tough life."

"Yes," he responded, "I have, but a lot of that was because of my own bad decisions."

"Yet, you continue to trust people, like by coming here and talking to us. . . ."

As she continued talking to Richard, she revealed to him—and for the first time to anybody—that her stepfather had been molesting her for the past five years. Richard took her, holding her hand, as they went together and reported the abuse to the principal and a police officer, who was in attendance at the session.

Richard recalled the van ride back to prison after this particular Full Impact session and reflected on how there is nothing more powerful or touching than seeing six large, tattooed, hardened inmates sobbing their eyes out as they left the school and the little girl behind them to return to prison. They had all been deeply touched by the effect of the visit on the little girl, and on themselves.

Richard has since resurrected the Full Impact program in the form of his "Choices" program, where he continues to visit school classrooms—in Sutherland's terms, "providing definitions favourable to conventional behaviour" to young people, by sharing with them the perils of a life of delinquent behaviour, and by showing them that the choices people make have consequences for themselves and others.

Culture Conflict Theory

Differential association theory is based on the learning of criminal (or deviant) norms or attitudes. Culture conflict theory focuses on the source of these criminal norms and attitudes. According to

Serving as a positive role model and breaking down barriers that often exist between police and citizens, this Kingston police officer plays goalie in a local roller hockey tournament.

Thorsten Sellin, conduct norms—norms that regulate our daily lives—are rules that reflect the attitudes of the groups to which each of us belongs.[15] Their purpose is to define what is considered appropriate or normal behaviour and what is inappropriate or abnormal behaviour.

Sellin argues that different groups have different conduct norms and that the conduct norms of one group may conflict with those of another. Individuals may commit crimes by conforming to the norms of their own group if that group's norms conflict with those of the dominant society. According to this rationale, the main difference between a criminal and a non-criminal is that each is responding to different sets of conduct norms.

Consider the recent spate of conflicts between Aboriginal peoples and the Canadian government. In 1990 the country witnessed the Oka Crisis: a land dispute between the Mohawk nation and the town of Oka, Quebec. Starting on July 11 and lasting until September 26, the standoff resulted in three deaths. More recently, Aboriginal protestors in Caledonia, Ontario, blocked the road to a construction site in an effort to protect what they believe is land that is rightfully theirs. Members of the Six Nations Confederacy (which includes the Seneca, Onondaga, Oneida, Tuscarora, Cayuga, and Mohawk) camped out at the site and persevered through a police raid that included tear gas, cannons, stun guns, and numerous arrests, all in an effort to reclaim the land, which the protestors claim was granted to Six Nations more than 200 years ago and never officially transferred to non-natives. If we consider that the "deviant"

Ron Cross, also known as "Ron Lasagna," displays his archery skills while on guard at Kanesatake Reserve during the Oka Crisis.

group in this instance—the First Nations members—were fighting for what they believe is theirs, then suddenly their "criminal" behaviour becomes more understandable, and less criminal.

Another example—far more criminal—was the Solar Temple, founded by a former Gestapo officer, which flourished in Switzerland and Canada. This mystic cult attracted wealthy members who "donated" all their property to the cult, perhaps $93 million in all; much of it was spent for the personal benefit of two cult leaders. Cult members were heavily armed (and engaged in arms trading) in anticipation of the end of the world. Their end of the world came in the fall of 1994, when the two cult leaders murdered nearly all their followers and then committed suicide.

Sellin distinguishes between primary and secondary conflicts. "Primary conflict" occurs when norms of two cultures clash. A clash may occur at the border between neighbouring cultural areas; a clash may occur when the law of one cultural group is extended to cover the territory of another; or it may occur when members of one group migrate to another culture. In a widening gap between cultural norms and generations, Southeast Asian immigrant children are running away from home in increasing numbers. They often run into an informal network of "safe houses." No one knows how many runaways there are, but it is estimated that at least one-third of all refugee families have had at least one child vanish for days, months, or even longer.

"Secondary conflict" arises when a single culture evolves into a variety of cultures, each with its own set of conduct norms. This type of conflict occurs when the homogeneous societies of simpler cultures become complex societies in which the

number of social groupings multiplies constantly and norms are often at odds. Your university or college may make dormitory living mandatory for all first-year students, for example, but to follow the informal code of your peer group, you may seek the freedom of off-campus housing. Or you may have to choose whether to violate work rules by leaving your job half an hour early to make a mandatory class or to violate school rules by walking into class half an hour late. Life situations are frequently controlled by conflicting norms, so no matter how people act, they may be violating some rule, often without being aware that they are doing so.

In the next section, which deals with the formation and operation of subcultures, we expand our discussion of norm conflict. We also examine the empirical research that seeks to discover whether there is indeed a multitude of value systems in our society and, if so, whether and how they conflict.

SUBCULTURAL THEORIES OF DELINQUENCY AND CRIME

A **subculture** is a subdivision within the dominant culture that has its own norms, beliefs, and values. Subcultures typically emerge when people in similar circumstances find themselves isolated from the mainstream and band together for mutual support. Subcultures may form among members of racial and ethnic minorities, among prisoners, among occupational groups, and among ghetto dwellers. Subcultures exist within a larger society, not apart from it. They therefore share some of its values. Nevertheless, the lifestyles of their members are significantly different from those of individuals in the dominant culture.

Subcultural theories in criminology were developed to account for delinquency among lower-class males, especially for one of its most important expressions—the teenage gang. According to subcultural theorists, delinquent subcultures, like all subcultures, emerge in response to special problems that members of the dominant culture do not face. Theories developed by Albert Cohen and by Richard Cloward and Lloyd Ohlin, which we discussed in Chapter 5, are extensions of the strain, social disorganization (see in Chapter 7), and differential association theories. They explain why delinquent subcultures emerge in the first place (strain), why they take a particular form (social disorganization), and how they are passed on from one generation to the next.

The explanations of delinquency developed by Marvin Wolfgang and Franco Ferracuti and by Walter Miller are somewhat different from those previously mentioned. These theorists do not suggest that delinquency begins with failure to reach middle-class goals. Their explanations are rooted in culture conflict theory. The **subculture of violence thesis** argues that the value systems of some subcultures demand the use of violence in certain social situations. This norm, which affects daily behaviour, conflicts with conventional middle-class norms. Along the same lines, Miller suggests that the characteristics of lower-class delinquency reflect the value system of the lower-class culture and that the lower-class values and norms conflict with those of the dominant culture.

Although Miller contends that the lower-class culture as a whole—not a subculture within it—is responsible for criminal behaviour in urban slums, his theory is appropriate to our discussion because it demonstrates how the needs of young urban males are met by membership in a street gang. Miller's street gangs condone violent criminal activity as one of the few means of attaining status in a slum.

THE SUBCULTURE OF VIOLENCE

Like Cohen, and like Cloward and Ohlin, whose theories were discussed in Chapter 5, Marvin Wolfgang and Franco Ferracuti turned to subcultural theory to explain criminal behaviour among lower-class young urban males. All three theories developed by these five researchers assume the existence of subcultures made up of people who share a value system that differs from that of the dominant culture. And they assume that each subculture has its own rules or conduct norms that dictate how individuals should act under varying circumstances. The three theories also agree that these values and norms persist over time because they are learned by successive generations. The theories differ, however, in their focus.

If you recall, Cohen and Cloward and Ohlin focus on the origin of the subculture, specifically, culturally induced strain. The thrust of Wolfgang and Ferracuti's work is culture conflict. Furthermore, the earlier theories encompass all types of delinquency and crime; Wolfgang and Ferracuti concentrate on violent crime. They argue that in some subcultures, behaviour norms are dictated by a value system that demands the use of force or violence.[16] Subcultures that adhere to conduct norms conducive to violence are referred to as **subcultures of violence.**

Violence is not used in all situations, but it is frequently an expected response. The appearance of a weapon, a slight shove or push, a derogatory remark, or the opportunity to wield power undetected may very well evoke an aggressive reaction that seems uncalled for to middle-class people. Fists rather than words settle disputes. Knives or guns are readily available, so confrontations can quickly escalate. Violence is a pervasive part of everyday life. Childrearing practices (hitting), gang activities (street wars), domestic quarrels (battering), and social events (drunken brawls) are all permeated by violence.

Violence is not considered antisocial. Members of this subculture feel no guilt about their aggression. In fact, individuals who do not resort to violence may be reprimanded. The value system is transmitted from generation to generation, long after the original reason for the violence has disappeared. The pattern is very hard to eradicate.

When Wolfgang and Ferracuti described population groups that are likely to respond violently to stress, they posed a powerful question to the criminal justice system. How does one go about changing a subcultural norm? This question becomes increasingly significant with the merging of the drug subculture and the subculture of violence.

> **Did You Know?**
>
> ... that 71 homicides in Canada in 2004 were "gang-related"? Fifty of those involved a firearm.

Tests of the Subculture of Violence

Howard Erlanger, using nationwide data collected in the United States, found no major differences in attitudes toward violence by class or race. Erlanger concluded that though members of the lower class show no greater approval of violence than middle-class persons do, they lack the sophistication necessary to settle grievances by other means. Not all studies support this idea, however. In *Code of the Street*, Elijah Anderson presents ethnographic evidence that violence is part of a complex street culture in impoverished communities that develops in response to structural obstacles. Other quantitative and review studies provide mixed evidence on the race/class/subculture of violence hypothesis.[17]

The subculture of violence thesis has also generated a line of empirical research that looks at regional differences in levels of violent crime.

In Canada, crime rates tend to increase as one moves from east to west. It has been suggested that in the past migrating to the West required a "frontier mentality" that was adventuresome, independent, and individualistic, all of which might lead to more daring, sometimes criminal behaviours. Timothy Hartnagel suggests that geographic mobility leads to weakened social controls in communities, which in turn can lead to crime.[18] In provinces like Alberta and British Columbia, which host an influx of Canadians migrating from eastern provinces, this type of heterogeneity may decrease social control, thus "freeing people up" to commit crimes. It is, after all, easier to commit crimes where you are an anonymous stranger than committing the same behaviour in your small hometown in Nova Scotia where everyone knows you.

Large-scale changes in economy can contribute to high crime rates in particular regions of the country. The problem with some studies is that it is difficult to separate the effects of economic and social factors from those of cultural values. Several researchers have sought to solve this problem. Colin Loftin and Robert Hill, for example, using a sophisticated measure of poverty, found that economic factors, not cultural ones, explained regional variation in homicide rates.[19]

Researchers who support the subculture of violence thesis point to statistics on characteristics of homicide offenders and victims. In Canada, Aboriginals are overrepresented in UCR reports on violent crime and in statistics on violent victimization. In her study of female gang involvement in Winnipeg, Melanie Nimmo reports that female gang members tend to be charged with more violent offences than other female offenders generally.[20] While early theorists focused their research attention on male gang members and males generally, Nimmo's research lends support to the argument that females and males alike are influenced by subcultural norms promoting violent behaviour.

Support exists for a connection between subcultural values that promote violence and violent behaviours. The 2006 RCMP study on youth gangs reports that most of the gang-related and gun-related homicides occur in at-risk neighbourhoods,

such as the Jane-and-Finch area in Toronto. While 11 percent of high school youth report having been a gang member at some point, this figure is more than double for homeless youth (27 percent).[21] At the same time, though, self-report data from the National Longitudinal Study of Children and Youth (NLSCY) suggests that violence is not restricted to members of violent subcultures. For example, by the age of 13, approximately 55 percent of boys and 27 percent of girls report having been in a fight. Another study reveals that one in ten students reports involvement in all of the following behaviours in the past 12 months: assault, fighting at school, and carrying a weapon.[22] Studies show that some children who begin to exhibit antisocial and violent behaviours at an early age move into more serious criminal behaviour as they grow older. Research also shows that one of the best predictors of committing a violent act is whether the individual has been the victim of a violent crime. Though most young people who fight and get into trouble during adolescence "grow out of it," and most who are victims of violence do not commit a criminal act in response, it may be that members of disadvantaged groups, often impoverished males, alternate the roles of victim and offender in a way that maintains the values and attitudes of a violent subculture.[23]

Evaluation: The Subculture of Violence Theory

Though empirical evidence remains inconclusive, the subculture of violence theory is supported by the distribution of violent crime in American society and to some extent in Canada.[24] The number of gangs and the violence associated with their activities is growing.[25] Jeffrey Fagan noted that "drug use is widespread and normative" among gangs.[26] Gang warfare, which takes the lives of innocent bystanders in ghetto areas, is a part of life in most of the impoverished, densely populated neighbourhoods in such major American cities as Los Angeles, New York, Chicago, Miami, Washington, D.C., and Atlanta, and in smaller urban centres as well. For example, over the three years between 1985 and 1988, Jamaican "posses"—gangs transplanted from Kingston, Jamaica, to the United States—have been involved in 1400 homicides.[27]

In Canada, major urban centres like Montreal, Toronto, Ottawa, Edmonton, and Vancouver are witnessing an increased gang presence and certainly increased public perception of gang threats. Street gangs and organized crime groups are not contained by national or provincial boundaries and are therefore capable of moving into new territories. However, there do appear to be some general regional patterns when it comes to some of these gangs. While reports indicate that traditional Italian organized crime groups are more likely to operate in regions of Ontario and in Montreal, Aboriginal and "Asian" gangs are considered more problematic in the west. Furthermore, reports from official sources indicate gangs are moving into small towns and rural areas.[28] And although outlaw biker gangs are present nationwide, the chapters operating in Quebec and Ontario have attained notoriety among police, media, and the public because of their open displays of gang warfare, and because of police sting operations that have impacted on their leadership and membership.[29]

Though not all persons in these subcultures follow the norm of violence, it appears that a dismaying number of them attach less and less importance to the value of human life and turn increasingly to violence to resolve immediate problems and frustrations. (We return to this issue later in the chapter.)

FOCAL CONCERNS: MILLER'S THEORY

All the theorists we have examined thus far explain criminal and delinquent behaviour in terms of subcultural values that emerge and are perpetuated from one generation to the next in lower-class urban slums. Walter Miller reasons differently. According to Miller,

> in the case of "gang" delinquency, the cultural system which exerts the most direct influence on behaviour is that of the lower-class community itself— a long-established, distinctively patterned tradition with an integrity of its own—rather than a so-called "delinquent subculture" which has arisen through conflict with middle-class culture and is oriented to the deliberate violation of middle-class norms.[30]

To Miller, juvenile delinquency is not rooted in the rejection of middle-class values; it stems from lower-class culture, which has its own value system. This value system has evolved as a response to living in disadvantaged neighbourhoods

TABLE 6.1 Some Facts about Poverty among Canadian Families

- Data from the 2006 census show that increases (from 2001) in common-law-couple families (18.9 percent) and lone-parents families (7.8 percent) outpaced that of married-couple families (3.5 percent).

- An estimated 655 000 Canadian families were living in low income in 2005; 7.4 percent of all families.

- 788 000 children under 18 were living in low-income families; 11.7 percent of the total.

- In 2005, the median income of two-parent families with children was $72 800; the median income of female lone-parent families was $22 200.

- The incidence of low income for female lone-parent families remained more than four times as high as that of two-parent families with children.

- An estimated 50 percent of Aboriginal children are living in poverty.

Sources: Richard Schaefer and Jana Grekul, *Sociology Matters* (Toronto: McGraw-Hill Ryerson, 2007), p. 151; National Council of Welfare, *The Cost of Poverty* (Ottawa: Minister of Public Works and Government Services, 2001); Statistics Canada, "Income of Canadians," *The Daily*, May 3, 2007, www.statcan.ca./Daily/English/070503/d070503a.htm, accessed February 18, 2008; Statistics Canada, "2006 Census: Families, Marital Status, Households and Dwelling Characteristics," *The Daily*, September 12, 2007, www.statcan.ca/Daily/English/070912/d070912a.htm, accessed February 18, 2008.

characterized by single-parent households (see Table 6.1). Gang norms are simply the adolescent expression of the lower-class culture in which the boys have grown up. This lower-class culture exists apart from the middle-class culture, and it has done so for generations. The value system, not the gang norms, generates delinquent acts.

Miller has identified six focal concerns, or areas, to which lower-class males give persistent attention: trouble, toughness, smartness, excitement, luck, and autonomy. Concern over *trouble* is a major feature of lower-class life. Staying out of trouble and getting into trouble are daily preoccupations. Trouble can get a person into the hands of the authorities, or it can result in prestige among peers. As an ex-gang member from Winnipeg states, "I wanted a reputation. I spent time in neighbourhood parks and earned a reputation from dealing drugs and standing up to other gang members."[31] Lower-class individuals are often evaluated by the extent of their involvement in activities such as fighting, drinking, and sexual misbehaving. In this case, the greater the involvement or the more extreme the performance, the greater the prestige or "respect" the person commands.

These young men are almost obsessively concerned with *toughness;* the code requires a show of

Cohen vs. Miller

Both Albert Cohen and Walter Miller argue that deviant subcultures develop among disadvantaged segments of society. Their theories diverge, however, when it comes to the association of these subcultures with the values of mainstream society. According to Cohen, delinquent subcultures are formed when disadvantaged youths cannot adhere to the same middle-class standards as their more-advantaged peers. In other words, deviant subculture develops in response to mainstream culture. Miller, on the other hand, hypothesizes that the subculture of violence develops in isolation from mainstream society. It is part of a more general culture that exists among the lower class, but it is not formed as a symbolic rejection of middle-class values and goals.

Overall, a comparison of Cohen and Miller's theories raises the question of whether it is disadvantage itself that leads to the formation of deviant subcultures or disadvantage *relative* to other segments of society.

In general, Canadian and U.S. census data on poverty favour Cohen's theory. The United States has one of the highest violent-crime rates in the world, and it is also characterized by a mix of wealthy and impoverished segments of society. In 2000, 9.2 percent of families and 12.4 percent of individuals were living below the poverty line. At the same time, 12.3 percent of households were earning an annual income of US$100 000 or more. In Canada, the total amount of income of the 10 percent of Canadian families in the highest income bracket accounted for 28 percent of all family income, yet the 10 percent of families with the lowest income made up less than 2 percent of all family income. Canada has a lower violent crime rate,

with a homicide rate of 2.04 per 100 000 population per year, compared to 5.63 per 100 000 in the United States. Canada's score on the Gini Index of income inequality is 32.6, somewhat lower than the American score of 40.8.(1) Lower inequality rating, lower violent crime rate—this seems to make sense in light of Cohen's theory.

In the United States, concentrated poverty—or the proportion of individuals living in high-poverty areas—declined between 1990 and 2000, but in 2000 it was still substantial at 10 percent.(2) In Canada the Aboriginal population (which makes up about 3 percent of the general population) living in inner cities and in reserves generally experiences much higher levels of poverty. This can be interpreted as support for Miller or Cohen, depending on your perspective. On the one hand, it indicates that a significant proportion of the United States, and a somewhat smaller proportion of Canada, is covered by clusters of impoverished communities where lower-class culture is likely to flourish in isolation from mainstream culture. On the other hand, the clustering of these communities together in space may make inhabitants more aware of the gap between themselves and the middle class.

International data is equally contradictory. Some international data support Cohen's theory. Between 1998 and 2001, South Africa had an average yearly homicide rate of 55.86 per 100 000 individuals, which is more than 10 times higher than that of the United States during roughly the same time period.(3) South Africa also has one of the largest wealth gaps in the world as measured by the Gini index of income inequality.(4) Other countries, such as China, have high in-

come inequality but low crime rates.(5, 6) It appears that the direction of the relationship between inequality and crime varies by nation. However, an additional complication to the relationship might be perception of inequality. For example, in a socialist regime where the perception is that everyone is equal (with the exception of a small elite), perhaps that perception works toward promoting ideas of similarity, equality, and solidarity, which preclude victimizing one another. On the other hand, in a country like South Africa, which continues to experience disharmony and violence as a result of racial tension spawned by apartheid and its demise, perhaps the perception regarding equality is one very dissimilar from that in China. Similarly, in a democratic-socialist country like Canada (where most individuals would place themselves in the middle class), compared to a free enterprise country like the United States, perception of inequality may mean something different.

Aside from the international evidence, which provides no clear conclusions, one may ask which theory makes more intuitive sense. Does it seem possible for disadvantaged segments of society to not only be indifferent to mainstream culture, but to be completely unaware of it as well? On the other hand, doesn't rejection of middle-class values suggest that disadvantaged youths have internalized them to some degree? In other words, if they do not care about mainstream values at all, wouldn't they retreat from them without hostility?

One may also point out that Cohen and Miller focus on the development of different types of subcultures—Cohen's theory explains delinquent subcultures while Miller's explains violent subcultures.

masculinity, a denial of sentimentality, and a display of physical strength. Miller argues that this concern with toughness is related to the fact that a large proportion of lower-class males grow up in female-dominated households and have no male figure from whom to learn the male role. They join

street gangs in order to find males with whom they can identify.

Recent theorizing describes this process and the result as *hegemonic masculinity*: the ways men create cultural ideas of dominance, control and independence.[32] Hegemonic versions of masculinity

However, neither scholar offers any insight into why the two types of subcultures may develop differently from each other. **Is this difference enough to reconcile the disparities between the two lines of thinking? Why might violent subcultures develop solely from lower-class culture and delinquent subcultures develop in response to middle-class standards?**

If, according to Cohen, it is the inadequacy felt by disadvantaged youths when they are measured against the middle class that leads to delinquency, then **why is this mentality limited to those individuals? Why does it not extend to middle-class youths when they compare themselves to upper-class peers, for example, or to upper-class youths when they compare themselves to celebrity children?** Cohen would argue that the expectations of society are grounded in middle-class rather than upper-class standards and that it is the expectations of society rather than those of the individual that influence subculture formation. Does this mean that awareness of an even higher standard has no influence, though? In other words, is it only expectations that matter, or do individual desires play a role as well? According to Miller, the question is irrelevant because deviant subculture is a product of membership in the lower class and thus does not apply to other individuals, regardless of their aspirations.

Recent developments in subcultural theory in the United Kingdom question the very notion of subcultures as Cohen and Miller described them. Critics argue that the category of subculture homogenizes the practices of youth and fails to allow for local variation. These postmodern critics suggest that the term "subculture" is outdated and meaningless today. Using terms such as "neo-tribe" and "lifestyle" instead, these theorists move away from models of social constraint in explaining behaviour and instead emphasize agency in the actions of young people searching for individual meaning in their subcultural practices. Neo-tribes are characterized by fluidity and occasional gatherings and dispersal (e.g., Internet chat groups) rather than the concrete day-to-day interactions that underlie Cohen's or Miller's subculture.(7) In these neo-tribes, there are no rules—rather, youth focus on individualistic consumerism. Resistance to authority is not about necessarily rejecting the "middle class measuring rod." It's about doing what feels good and right at the time and about expressing oneself; post-subculturalists are critical of the influence of social structures.

Defenders of the classic notions of subculture (and critics of this post-subcultural view) argue that class, gender, ethnicity, and sexuality matter: They continue to structure the choices and behaviours of young people. To avoid addressing the importance of these social forces and reduce youthful behaviour to narcissistic individualism ignores the fact that youth differ on these social structural dimensions and that this influences their economic stability and the choices they have.(8) Other theorists argue that while subcultures may no longer be the tightly knit working-class youth groups Cohen and Miller described, they do maintain some of these elements. Choices are influenced by social class position, but at the same time youth today are more able to consume global forms of youth culture, thus broadening their exposure to ideas, behaviours, leisure activities, and choices than youth in the 1950s. Surely, this must have some impact on the structure and composition of youth subcultures.

Sources

1. United States Census, 2000.
2. Paul Jargowsky, "Stunning Progress, Hidden Problems: The Dramatic Decline of Concentrated Poverty in the 1990s," *Living Cities Census Series*, Center on Urban and Metropolitan Studies (Washington, D.C.: Brookings Institute, 2003).
3. Gordon Barclay and Cynthia Tavares, "International Comparisons of Criminal Justice Statistics 2001," Home Office and Council of Europe, October 24, 2003.
4. Jens Martins, "A Compendium of Inequality: The Human Development Report 2005," FES briefing paper, October 2005.
5. Michael Yates, "Poverty and Inequality in the Global Economy," *Monthly Review* **55**(9), February 2004, www.monthlyreview.org/0204yates.htm.
6. Yuri Andrienko, "Crime, Wealth, and Inequality: Evidence from International Crime Victim Surveys," Economics Education and Research Consortium, Moscow, November 2002.
7. Shane Blackman, "Youth Subcultural Theory: A Critical Engagement with the Concept, Its Origins and Politics, from the Chicago School to Postmodernism," *Journal of Youth Studies*, **8**(1) (March 2005): 1–20.
8. Tracey Greener and Robert Hollands, "Beyond Subculture and Post-subculture? The Case of Virtual Psytrance," *Journal of Youth Studies*, **9**(4) (September 2006): 393–418.

are those dominant and dominating forms of masculinity that claim the highest status and exercise the greatest influence and authority and which represent the standard-bearer of what it means to be a "real" man or boy. Hegemonic masculinity is about male dominance—over women, and over other men who do not fit the ideal type of "real man." Miller's lower-class boys, Cohen's young men and boys who were rejecting the middle-class school system, and men and boys who grow up in a subculture of violence are all attempting to embody this form of masculinity. Being tough, fighting,

Rapper 50 Cent, pictured here in February 2003, expressed his values with his debut record, *Get Rich or Die Tryin'*, which sold 892 000 copies in four days. His follow-up record, *Massacre*, sold 771 000 copies in its first full week of release.

joining a gang, participating in criminal behaviour may all in some way provide the opportunity for some males to engage with and play out dominant versions of masculinity. For those who come from disadvantaged environments, or those who fail in the school system, expressing their masculinity in this way is a source—perhaps the only source—of power, control, and confidence. Being tough and getting in trouble are practices that permit boys and young men to express their masculinity.

Another focal concern is *smartness*—the ability to gain something by outsmarting, outwitting, or conning another person. In lower-class neighbourhoods, youngsters practise outsmarting each other in card games, exchanges of insults, and other trials. Prestige is awarded to those who demonstrate smartness.

Many aspects of lower-class life are related to another focal concern, the search for *excitement*. Youngsters alternate between hanging out with peers and looking for excitement, which can be found in fighting, getting drunk, and using drugs. Risks, danger, and thrills break up the monotony of their existence.

Fate, particularly *luck*, plays an important role in lower-class life. Many individuals believe that their lives are subject to forces over which they have little control. If they get lucky, a rather drab life could change quickly. Miller's last focal concern, *autonomy*, stems from the lower-class person's resentment of external controls, whether parents, teachers, or police. This desire for personal freedom is expressed often in such terms as "No one can push me around" and "I don't need nobody."[33]

According to Miller, status in every class is associated with the possession of qualities that are valued. In the lower class, the six focal concerns define status. It is apparent that by engaging in behaviour that affords status by these criteria, many people will be breaking the laws of the dominant society (see Figure 6.1).

Tests of Miller's Theory

An obvious question is whether in our urban, heterogeneous, secular, technologically based society any isolated pockets of culture are still to be found. The pervasiveness of mass advertising, mass transit, and mass communication makes it seem unlikely that an entire class of people could be unaware of the dominant value system. Empirical research on opportunity theory has found that lower-class boys share the conventional success goals of the dominant culture. This finding suggests that the idea of isolation from the dominant system does not fit with reality. Empirical research has also found, however, that while gang boys may support middle-class values, they are willing to deviate from them. If an opportunity arises to gain prestige in a fight, gang boys are willing to take the chance that their act will not result in punishment.

Most empirical tests of values question young people on their attachment to middle-class values. Stephen Cernovich expanded this type of research

FIGURE 6.1 The relationship between delinquency and lower-class focal concerns.

Source: Donald J. Shoemaker, *Theories of Delinquency: An Examination of Explanations of Delinquent Behaviour,* 3rd ed. (New York: Oxford University Press, 1996), p. 122. Copyright © 1984, 1990, 1996, 2000 by Oxford University Press, Inc. Used by permission of Oxford University Press, Inc.

by investigating attachment to lower-class focal concerns.[34] He found that toughness, excitement, trouble, and pleasure-seeking were related to self-reported delinquency in all classes. His findings also showed that boys of all classes were committed to delayed gratification, hard work, and education. Cernovich concluded that it is values, rather than class, that are associated with delinquency.

Evaluation: Miller's Theory

Criminologists have been disturbed by Miller's assumption that the lower-class lifestyle is generally focused on illegal activity. In making such an assumption, they say, Miller disregards the fact that most people in the lower class do conform to conventional norms. Moreover, some criminologists ask, if lower-class boys are conforming to their own value system, why would they suffer guilt or shame when they commit delinquent acts?[35]

Perhaps the best support for Miller's ideas is found in qualitative, rather than quantitative, accounts of life in a lower-class slum. In our discussion of cultural deviance and subcultural theories, we noted that the values and norms that define behaviour in these areas do not change much over time or from place to place. Successive generations have to deal with the same problems. They typically demonstrate similar responses. Angela D'Arpa-Calandra, a former probation officer who now directs a Juvenile Intensive Supervision program, says she recently walked into a courtroom and "saw a mother and grandmother sitting with the 14-year-old offender. 'I had the grandmother in criminal court in 1963,' D'Arpa-Calandra says. 'We didn't stop it there. The grandmother was 14 when she was arrested. The mother had this child when she was 14. It's like a cycle we must relive.'"[36]

By and large, descriptions of life in poverty-stricken areas, whether written by people who have lived in them or by people who have studied them, reveal dreary routine, boredom, constant trouble, and incessant problems with drugs, alcohol, and crime. "Derek," an ex-gang member featured in the documentary *Gang Aftermath,* describes growing up in poverty in an inner-city neighbourhood in the Prairies:

> When I look around (at the place I grew up) . . . this was the community league for the hood—this is where gang members came, the drug dealers, the drunks, drug addicts, the people from the street. . . .

When I was 10 . . . that was a hard thing to deal with—having mom taking off and not being there . . . you get up in the morning, sometimes she would be there, sometimes she wouldn't. When she was there, she wouldn't be up to get us ready for school, to cook us breakfast. I would slap something together for me and my little brother, get my little brother dressed and away we went.[37]

Two other ex-gang members add to Derek's description of the lifestyles that contributed to their gang involvement:

> My family was involved in the gang lifestyle. My mother was a prostitute. I was taken away from her at 7. I started doing petty crime and moved up to selling drugs by age 12. I hung around with a group of other kids, mostly my cousins.

> I grew up in Saskatoon and was surrounded by family members who were gang members. Other than this I had no real connection to my family otherwise. They were alcoholics or drug addicts. I had no role models and no support in the community.[38]

GANGS AT THE TURN OF THE TWENTY-FIRST CENTURY

In Toronto:
Jane Creba, a 15-year-old shopping with her sister is gunned down in a gang-related shooting incident that also injures six others.[39]

In Quebec:
A turf war between the Rock Machine and the Hell's Angels in the late 1990s claimed 150 lives, including two prison guards and 11-year-old Daniel Desroches, who died when a car bomb exploded outside a biker hangout.[40]

In British Columbia:
In August 2003, Bobby Johal was shot to death outside his parents' Cordova Bay home. He had survived a gangland-style attack three years earlier outside a Port Coquitlam gym in which his brother was killed and he was shot in the leg.[41]

The new subculture that emerged in the 1980s and continues into the new century combines violence, which has become more vicious than in earlier years, with big business in drug trafficking.[42] While gang-related issues have plagued the United States for decades, the extent of gang activity in

TABLE 6.2 Bill C-24: Criminal Organization Definition

A criminal organization means:

1. a group, however organized, that is composed of three or more persons and,

2. that has as one of its main purposes or main activities the facilitation or commission of one or more serious offences,

3. that, if committed, would likely result in the direct or indirect receipt of a material benefit, including a financial benefit, by the group or by any one of the persons who constitute the group.

Source: Edmonton Police Service, Who Are Your Children Hangin' With? A Resource Guide on Youth and Gangs, p. 2.

Several Aboriginal ex-gang members in recent years have developed programs aimed at helping gang members sever their ties to gangs.

Canada has not been as prevalent, nor have Canadian researchers studied the phenomenon to the extent that American scholars have. In fact, it was only in 2002 that the federal government of Canada formally recognized criminal organization in the passage of Bill C-24 (see Table 6.2). This is not to deny that Canada has gangs. It clearly does. For example, in Toronto, early in June, 2007, 700 police officers, including members of the Toronto Police, the RCMP, and the Ontario Provincial Police, launched a raid entitled Project Kryptic, which resulted in more than 60 alleged gang members of the Driftwood Crips being arrested.[43] In this sting operation, police seized dozens of firearms and drugs with a street value well in excess of $1 million.

But if we compare, for example, the Bloods and Crips, long established California-based gangs with Blood and Crip affiliates in Canada, we realize that Canada does not have the same history of gangs that the United States does. In some instances, the gangs appearing in Canada are offshoots of American-based gangs. In other instances, Canada has its own gangs, some of which actually base their structure and organization on American-style gangs. In recent years, Canadian gang researchers have added to the research on gangs, and as gangs grow in numbers and influence, we will likely see an increase in research and policy on the topic. A recent study by Scott Wortley and Julian Tanner that was conducted on Toronto high school and street youth revealed that there is a difference between identifying with a gang (often for "social purposes") and being involved in a "criminal gang." While one out of ten high school students report they have been a member of a gang at some point in their lives, current membership in a criminal gang is much less

prevalent. The authors found that 6 percent of their high school sample, compared to 16 percent of the street youth sample, admitted current gang membership. The researchers also found that the factors influencing gang membership are complex and include interactions among ethnicity, social class, family structure, social alienation, age, and gender. In short, there are no quick fixes to gang involvement among young people because there is no single cause for membership. Rather, involvement in gangs is often a result of a variety of other social issues.[44]

Rival gangs kill for more than simply turf. In cities around the world, teenagers are driving BMWs with Uzi submachine guns concealed under the driver's seat and thousands of dollars in their pockets so that they can make bail at any moment. Classic movies like *Colors, Scarface,* and *The Godfather,* and more recent movies and television shows like *The Sopranos* provide models for their activities. Recent Canadian research suggests that American movies and music appear to influence the formation and activities of Canadian gang members. Youth coming from families plagued with poverty and dysfunction, lacking in role models, turn to images provided by American pop culture idols and by gang stereotypes often portrayed in popular culture. In the video *Gang Aftermath,* another ex-gang member speaks about the effect "gangsta" music and movies had on him as a young boy:

I got all mine [role models] from movies. . . . I found that [movie] *Blood In Blood Out* . . . watched it . . . it was straight gangster man . . . it was awesome man. . . . [I thought] that's it, right there.[45]

Gangs: Guns, Prison, Violence

American estimates are that between 50 and 70 percent of gang members own or have access to weapons. In fact, gangs often judge each other by their firepower. Despite stricter gun controls in Canada, guns find their way into the hands of gang members and other criminals. Their arsenal of weapons includes sawed-off rifles and shotguns, semi-automatic weapons, all types of handguns, body armour, and explosives.[46] Gangs have "treasuries" to buy the sophisticated weapons that are now used on the street for resolving conflicts, for demonstrating bravery, for self-defence, and for protecting turf.

In Canada it is difficult to make these kinds of estimates because municipal, provincial, and federal police forces don't amalgamate their information into one main gang database. In fact, it was only in 2002 with the passage of Bill C-24 that Canadian police organizations had a clear definition of an organized crime group. Bill C-24 is an example of the passage of laws in response to changes in society (increasing gang activity and frustration on the part of social control agencies to do something about it). Despite issues relating to definitions and jurisdiction, we do have some statistics regarding gang activities in Canada:

- The 2002 Canadian Police Survey on Youth Gangs estimated the number of youth gangs in Canada at 434, with an estimated membership of 7071.[47]

- Approximately 59 percent of the national population is served by law enforcement agencies reporting active youth gangs.[48]

- Saskatchewan, Manitoba, and British Columbia have the highest percentage of jurisdictions reporting active youth gangs.

- No youth gang activity was reported in the three northern territories, or in New Brunswick, Prince Edward Island, or Newfoundland and Labrador.

- On a per capita basis, Saskatchewan reported the highest concentration of youth gang members—1.34 per 1000 population, or approximately 1315 in total.[49]

- There are at least 12 known adult and youth gangs operating in Saskatchewan. Approximately 70 percent of the gang members in

Saskatoon are 18 years or older, and in Regina the average age is 24.[50]

- Based on the criminal history of a sample of 56 known gang members in Saskatchewan, a large percentage (87.5 percent) had previous youth court convictions and multiple property-related offences. The severity of their offences escalated with age.[51]

- The vast majority of youth gang members are male (94 percent) under the age of 24.[52]

- The largest proportion of youth gang members in Canada are African-Canadian (25 percent), followed by First Nations (22 percent), and Caucasian (18 percent).[53]

- Across the country, 40 percent of respondents believe that the return of adult or youth gang-involved inmates from prison has affected youth gangs very much.[54]

There is little doubt among researchers that street gangs and prison gangs are connected. In fact, prisons often serve as recruiting grounds for street gangs. Canadian research indicates that some gangs were formed in prisons and then spilled onto the streets as gang members were released.[55] When we consider the overrepresentation of Aboriginal inmates in the federal and provincial prison systems (particularly in the prairies) and the prison–street gang connection, the increasing presence of Aboriginal gangs in communities is more clearly understood. Certainly, Aboriginal gangs are not the only groups to illustrate this connection; others, including outlaw biker groups and white supremacist groups, have street and prison connections.

While gang-related conflicts in prisons can involve a diverse array of homemade and smuggled in weapons, the use of guns rather than knives and clubs turns violent events into life-and-death situations on the street; gangs battle gangs in a kind of street guerrilla warfare. Drive-by shootings, in particular, have become a favoured method of operation. A "drive-by" involves members of one gang driving into a rival gang's turf to shoot at someone, followed by a high-speed escape. Gang members take great pride in this hit-and-run technique. Often these encounters occur spontaneously, but they easily spiral into planned events. The sequence may be the following:

> A gang member shoots a rival gang member during an argument. The surviving rival or his friends get a gun and conduct a drive-by on the initial instigator or members of his gang at their home(s). During this retaliatory strike, a friend, family member or gang member is killed or seriously wounded. The original instigatory gang now views itself as the "passive victim" and sets out to get back at the new aggressor. This spiral which, in real time, can result in several drive-by shootings or other murders within a few hours, can and often does lead to protracted gang wars.[56]

Some drive-bys are for "fun," some for defending gang honour, and others for getting rid of competition in the drug business.

FEMALE DELINQUENT SUBCULTURES

Traditionally, gang membership has been limited primarily to young, inner-city males. Theoretical and empirical studies in this area therefore focused on that population. More recently, however, gang membership has been changing. There are increasing numbers of white participants, members younger than 14, members older than 18, and females. There is less information on female gang members in Canada, in part because Canada does not have the extent of gang membership as does the United States, and also because research on gangs, male or female, in Canada is relatively limited. As mentioned earlier, research does suggest that gang presence and membership varies by region of the country. Research, police reports, and reports from community workers also indicate that the gang landscape tends to change over time, with certain groups dominating at one point, and others coming to the fore at a different time. Gang membership, including the membership and roles of females also varies. Until recently, little was known about female subcultures. Researchers are now focusing more attention on two types of female gangs—those that are affiliates of male gangs and those that consist of all females.

Early Research

In one of the few early studies, done in 1958, Albert Cohen and James Short suggested that female delinquent subcultures, like their male counterparts, were composed of members who had been frustrated in their efforts to achieve conventional goals (respectability, marriage, status). The girls had drifted into a subculture that offered them substitute status, albeit outside legitimate society. Drug use and prostitution became all but inevitable. Since the research that led to this finding was conducted among mostly lower-class black females, Cohen and Short admitted that their findings probably could not be generalized to all female delinquent subcultures.[57]

Recent Studies

Twenty-six years after these tentative findings, Anne Campbell published the first major work on the lifestyle of female gang members in New York. She spent two years with three gangs: one Hispanic (the Sex Girls), one black (the Five Percent Nation), and one racially mixed (the Sandman Ladies). Campbell's findings demonstrate that girls, like boys, join gangs for mutual support, protection, and a sense of belonging. They, too, gain status by living up to the value system of their gang. Campbell also noted that these youngsters will probably end up, as their mothers have, living in a neighbourhood marred by poverty, requiring social assistance to make ends meet, and after leaving the gangs, constantly feeling threatened by the isolation often felt by single mothers living in such circumstances.[58]

A recent Canadian study on female gang members was conducted in Winnipeg, Manitoba, which by the late 1990s had been dubbed the "gang capital" of Canada. In 1998, Melanie Nimmo interviewed 24 frontline workers in the community. The respondents represented criminal justice agencies (e.g., police and correctional officers), inner-city schools, social services organizations, and community groups whose occupation involved intervening in the lives of gang women. Respondents, in their in-depth interviews, suggest that female gang members typically come from socially and economically disadvantaged backgrounds, similar to their male counterparts. In addition, these young gang-involved girls and women are predominantly Aboriginals, have suffered physical, sexual, and emotional abuse, and turn to gangs for the sense of family such groups promise. The gangs also supply them with a promise of protection, money, drugs, and instant gratification. In the words of Nimmo, gang life "gives marginalized, alienated, and disenfranchised women a sense of power. The comfort, excitement and clout that the gang provides may seem to be the best they can hope for."[59]

However, because of the highly patriarchal nature of gang life, this power is fleeting and elusive: the temporary relief from abuse and the pains of marginalization that gang affiliation appears to offer actually leads to more abuse and danger for female gang members.[60] It is difficult to determine the generalizability of Nimmo's findings on female gang members in Winnipeg in the late 1990s to other gangs, to other parts of the country, or to the present. However, many of her findings are similar to American research findings and certainly offer a starting point for comparison between gangs in the two countries, and also offer suggestions for future, much needed research on the topic.

Respondents in Nimmo's study estimate that between 10 and 50 percent of gang members are female, but this number varies depending on the occupation of the respondent.[61] In the United States, the estimate is that between 10 and 25 percent of gang members nationwide are female, with the number being higher in major cities.

American research reports that many female gangs are affiliates of male gangs, often offering support for the young men they refer to as their "homeboys." Nimmo's Canadian study confirms that, at least in the case of Aboriginal gangs in Winnipeg at the time of her study, female gang members were affiliated with male gangs and as such were never really identified as "gang members" per se. As one respondent explains,

> A male that's acting up is gang affiliated, gang involved . . . very rarely would someone refer a youth to me, and let's say her name was Tara. "Tara is heavily involved with I.P. [Indian Posse]" or "Tara is an I.P. member." You don't hear that. You hear, "Tara's boyfriend is I.P. . . . You rarely hear someone say, "So and so is a gang member" when it comes to females, at least with the youth. "They're going out with a gang member."[62]

Initiation rites for females involve either a "jump-in, jump-out," in which they are beaten by four or five gang members, or a "sex-in, sex-out," in which they have sexual relations with all male members.[63] Nimmo found no evidence for this latter initiation rite in her Manitoba study, though Roberta, an Aboriginal female who was once gang

Candles are lit for missing Aboriginal women during a vigil in Vancouver in 2006. For females, gang life is often associated with violence, including sexual and physical abuse, and prostitution. It is a high-risk lifestyle that, for many, ends in death.

involved, talks openly in the documentary film *Gang Aftermath* about female gang members being beaten frequently, being treated as the property of male members, and living with the expectation that they were to be shared sexually with whichever other gang members their boyfriends demanded.[64]

Interviews with ex-gang members indicate that the primary roles for females in street gangs, Aboriginal and other, are as sexual property and as drug runners. One male ex-gang member describes women affiliated with the gang as "pin cushions." A gang unit police officer confirms that in his experience women are never really considered real gang members, but rather fill the role of "nominee." They help with the criminal work of the gang by registering vehicles in their names, for example.[65] Nimmo adds that women, because of their lower status in the gang hierarchy, are often used as "bait" to fool people into being robbed, or to set up rival gang members for an assault.

The processes and practices that comprise hegemonic masculinity help explain the role of women in gangs, and the role of female gangs. Male gang members use notions of what "real men" are as a means of maintaining power, dominance, and control over others. Constructions of masculinity are developed in contrast to femininity. A defining feature of hegemonic masculine performance is its opposition to girls/women and men who don't fit the "real man" stereotype. As a result, women are put down, humiliated, and objectified in the gang ethos.[66] Hegemonic masculinity as embodied by some men, including gang members, legitimates men's domination over women as a group.[67] Moreover, all forms of femininity (including those expressed by female gang members) are "constructed in the context of the overall subordination of women to men."[68]

Despite the processes that place female gang members at a much lower rung in the gang hierarchy, this does not stop them from forming their own groups. Nimmo did find evidence, similar to that in the United States, for female stand-alone gangs that have their own initiation rites (which mimic male ceremonies but are usually much less violent) and their own gang colours.[69] However, such stand-alone female gangs like the Sisterhood and Ace have within a short period of time, in Winnipeg at least, been absorbed back into the male gangs Indian Posse and Deuce.[70]

Although female and male gang members share in the violence and criminal activities associated with gang involvement, the gang experience appears to be quite different for female members. In addition to occupying lower-status positions in the group, females have the added responsibility that comes with the expectation of unprotected sexual activity and multiple partners, common within the gang, according to Nimmo's respondents. One respondent estimates that 50 percent or more of female gang members are mothers, with 100 percent of those pregnant with the children of gang members. Another respondent from the Winnipeg study said,

> We have an awful lot of females in the program who are pregnant, and often carrying a gang member's baby. When the kid is born, he'll probably end up with a rag [gang bandanna] on his head, or a little [Manitoba] Warrior's jacket on. I don't know if you've ever seen that, but it's rather scary, seeing little babies wearing Warrior jackets. And what are we talking already, that's a fourth or a third generation Warrior.[71]

Nonetheless, despite the crime, violence, and abuse, girls in the gang are less likely than male members to leave.[72] The alternative for many is worse: a life filled with poverty and uncertainty. For many, despite the drawbacks, the gang offers a sense of family. Adding to the complexity of the situation is the fact that many family members, including parents, uncles, aunts, cousins, and siblings, are gang-involved. Nimmo reports a pronounced lack of programming available to female gang members who may want to leave. Policy and programming are directed primarily at males, since they make up the bulk of gang members. Female gang members, though in many ways more disadvantaged than their male counterparts, seem to be invisible, not only in research efforts but in terms of policy and programming as well.[73]

Overall, research suggests that the extent and nature of female participation has changed considerably over the last few decades. Research findings show increased participation in gangs (in one study, about equal to that of males) and in gang-related activities, including serious delinquent acts and drug abuse.[74]

MIDDLE-CLASS DELINQUENCY

Most people think of gangs and criminal behaviour as synonymous with low-income city neighbourhoods, turf wars, and a membership that often comes into conflict with law enforcement. But now gang lifestyle is moving to suburbia.[75] Affluent youngsters are joining established gangs such as Toronto's Jamestown Crew or the Malvern Crew or forming their own gangs, sometimes referred to as "yuppie gangs."[76] Their activities can be as harmless as adherence to a particular dress code or as violent as a drive-by shooting. Experts have identified several types of suburban gangs, two of which we briefly describe here.[77]

Street Gangs Criminal activities include physical assaults, theft, burglary, and distribution of illegal drugs. The members seek money, peer recognition, the thrill of high-risk behaviour, or even protection: "If you want to be able to walk the mall, you have to know you've got your boys behind you."[78] They typically adopt hand signals, dress in certain colours, and mark their territory with graffiti, and they are increasingly making linkages with more organized crime groups. Often the street gangs serve as foot soldiers, carrying out the dirty work of more organized gangs. There are, however, several street gangs that operate independently, specializing in particular areas of criminal activity. For example, a police sweep conducted by the Toronto Police Service in 2006 targeted the Jamestown Crew, resulting in over 1000 charges being laid against more than 125 people. A similar sweep in that city in 2004 targeted the Malvern Crew, which specialized in drugs, guns, and telemarketing scams.[79]

The Girls in the Gang

Psychologist Anne Campbell studied female gangs in New York City and published her findings in her 1984 book, *The Girls in the Gang.* She summarizes some of her observations here:

All the girls in the gang come from families that are poor. Many have never known their fathers. Most are immigrants from Puerto Rico. As children the girls moved from apartment to apartment as they were evicted or burned out by arsonists. Unable to keep any friends they managed to make and alienated from their mothers, whose lack of English restricted their ability to control or understand their daughters' lives, the girls dropped out of school early and grew up on the streets. In the company of older kids and street-corner men, they graduated early into the adult world. They began to use drugs and by puberty had been initiated into sexual activity. By fifteen many were pregnant. Shocked, their mothers tried to pull them off the streets. Some sent their daughters back to relatives in Puerto Rico while they had their babies. Abortion was out of the question in this Catholic world.

Those who stayed had "spoiled their identity" as good girls. Their reputations were marred before they ever reached adulthood. On the streets, among the gang members, the girls found a convenient identity in the female gang. Often they had friends or distant relatives who introduced them as "prospects." After a trial period, they could undertake the initiation rite: they had to fight an established member nominated by the godmother. What was at issue was not winning or losing but demonstrating "heart," or courage. Gangs do not welcome members who join only to gain protection. The loyalty of other gang members has to be won by a clear demonstration of willingness to "get down," or fight.

Paradoxically, the female gang goes to considerable lengths to control the sexual behaviour of its members. Although the neighbourhood may believe they are fast women, the girls themselves do not tolerate members who sleep around. A promiscuous girl is a threat to the other members' relationships with their boyfriends. Members can take a boyfriend from among the male gang members (indeed, they are forbidden to take one from any other gang) but they are required to be monogamous. A shout of "Whore!" is the most frequent cause of fistfights among the female members.

A portrait of Hispanic teen female members of the Pico Rivera gang with one member holding her child.

On the positive side, the gang provides a strong sense of belonging and sisterhood. After the terrible isolation of their lives, the girls acquire a ready-made circle of friends who have shared many of their experiences and who are always willing to support them against hostile words or deeds by outsiders. Fighting together generates a strong sense of camaraderie and as a bonus earns them the reputation of being "crazy." This reputation is extremely useful in the tough neighbourhoods where they live. Their reputation for carrying knives and for solidarity effectively deters outsiders from challenging them. They work hard at fostering their tough "rep" not only in their deeds but in their social talk. They spend hours recounting and embroidering stories of fights they have been in. Behind all this bravado it is easy to sense the fear they work so hard to deny. Terrified of being victims (as many of them have already been in their families and as newcomers in their schools), they make much of their own "craziness"—the violent unpredictability that frightens away anyone who might try to harm them.(1)

Campbell demonstrates the commonality of violence in the lives of female gang members in the early 1980s. Today there is a growing concern over the increasing prevalence and severity of violence in some areas.(2) The number of female gang members and the extent of changes in the use of violence are, however, still debated among researchers.(3)

Sources

1. Written by Anne Campbell. Adapted from Anne Campbell, *The Girls in the Gang* (New York: Basil Blackwell, 1984).
2. John M. Hagedorn, "Gang Violence in the Postindustrial Era," in *Youth Violence, Crime and Justice: A Review of Research,* vol. 24, Michael Tonry and Mark H. Moore, eds. (Chicago: University of Chicago Press, 1998), pp. 365–419.
3. Margaret O'Brien, "At Least 16,000 Girls in Chicago's Gangs More Violent than Some Believe, Report Says," *Chicago Tribune,* Sept. 17, 1999, p. 5.

Questions for Discussion

1. How similar are Campbell's female gangs to the female Aboriginal gangs that were the focus of Melanie Nimmo's study discussed earlier in this chapter? How similar are they to the male gangs described in this chapter? Are there any significant differences?
2. Would you expect female gangs to become as involved in criminal activity as male gangs? Why or why not?

Hate Gangs   Hate gangs, such as skinheads, attach themselves to an ideology that targets racial and ethnic groups. Physical assaults and even murder are justified by their belief system. According to some reports and estimates, their numbers are growing rapidly. One type of hate group, neo-Nazi skinheads, experienced a decline in membership in the 1980s but witnessed an increase beginning in the 1990s. One estimate places their membership at approximately 600 in Canada.[80] Recent years have witnessed an explosion of websites promoting hate based on ethnicity and race, which means membership in such groups may be rising. For example, there were at least 2000 of these websites in existence in 1999, but one expert reports that the number of websites used to promote terrorism and hate increased by 20 percent between 2005 and 2006; his group monitors 6000 websites of this nature.[81] During 2001 and 2002, 12 major Canadian police forces reported a total of 928 hate crime incidents. About 57 percent of these hate crimes were motivated by race or ethnicity, while 43 percent were motivated by religion. Of these incidents, one-quarter were directed against Jewish people or institutions.[82] Because of the difficulties in gathering statistics on hate crime, these numbers most likely represent only a small percentage of the actual figure.[83]

Explanations

Most explanations of middle-class delinquency are extensions of subcultural explanations of

Ernst Zundel, Holocaust denier, pleads his case before being sent to prison in Germany.

lower-class delinquency. Albert Cohen, who contributed significantly to the elaboration of subcultural formation (see Chapter 5), suggested that changes in the social structure have weakened the value traditionally associated with delay of gratification.[84] Some criminologists say that a growing number of middle-class youngsters no longer believe that the way to reach their goals is through hard work and delayed pleasure. They prefer reaping profits from quick drug sales or shoplifting goods that attract them. Michael Chettleburgh, in *Young Thugs*, describes the perceived immediate gratification—monetary and personal—that ostensibly comes with gang involvement:

> The job is considered a pretty good one by those who hold it. . . . You are required to work eight-hour shifts in teams of two, one driver and one "runner." You are each paid $100 per shift for five shifts a week. . . . As well, it is understood among those who hold this job that you can skim a little of the product off the top to resell later on your own account. By doing so you can increase your weekly net earnings to maybe $1000, almost double the gross pay of an unattached Canadian male worker. . . . Your employer . . . happily supplies you with all the tools you need to do your job well. On-the-job training, ongoing mentoring, an ample supply of product, security, and collection services if you need them, a comfortable prepaid rental car, as well as one or several cell phones or BlackBerry devices—all provided for free. . . . You can get a job like this when you are as young as thirteen or fourteen. . . . The only downside of the position, of course, is that it is illegal. It makes you part of a street gang "dial-a-dope" operation.[85]

Behaviour has become more hedonistic and more peer-oriented. While most of this youth subculture exhibits non-delinquent behaviour, sometimes the pleasure-seeking activities have led to delinquent acts. Bored and restless, these youngsters seek to break the monotony with artificial excitement and conspicuous indulgence: fast cars, trendy clothes, alcohol, drugs, and sexual activity. Experts note that many affluent gang members come from broken, unstable, or extremely dysfunctional homes. Their problems stem from divorce, separation, physical or sexual abuse, or a drug- or alcohol-addicted parent.[86]

Subcultural theory assumes that individuals engage in delinquent or criminal behaviour because (1) legitimate opportunities for success are blocked, and (2) criminal values and norms are learned in lower-class subcultures. Several programs in Canada attempt to address both points, but we describe two programs that work toward changing the values and norms of gang-involved individuals both on the street and in prison.

Gang Prevention and Intervention: On the Streets and in Prison

Many programs based on subcultural theory have attempted to change the attitudes and behaviours of youth at risk of criminal behaviour, young offenders, and gang-involved individuals, who have spent most of their lives learning unconventional street norms. In one type of programming, change is accomplished by setting up an extended-family environment for high-risk youths, one that provides positive role models, academic and vocational training, strict rules for behaviour, drug treatment, health care, and other services. Programs that target multiple sources of difficulty for young people offer promise for success, as illustrated by work done with multisystemic therapy in Ontario.[87]

Another program, "Gang Prevention and Intervention," established in 2005, is run by two ex-gang members and deals with gang-involved youth and adults. The program is based on a similar approach used by Troy Rupert in Winnipeg beginning in the early 1990s. Rupert, who knows life on the street and in prison, started his Winnipeg Native Alliance to help young Aboriginal people in the city leave gangs and the street life. Following his lead, Rob Papin started his own program with similar goals in Edmonton. Eventually, he brought Derek Powder, another ex-gang member, on board and together they visit classrooms and groups across the country, relaying to them their gang-related experiences and illustrating through their stories and experiences the perils of gang life. The two draw on personal experience and childhood events, and describe how criminal lifestyles lead to a dead end. The two program facilitators also speak with professional groups, social workers, police officers, correctional officers, educators, and a variety of groups and individuals who work in the field, with the stated goal of preventing young people from joining gangs, and also educating people generally about gangs. In addition to the prevention and educational components to the program, the facilitators also work with gang-involved individuals, offering networks of support and programming should members decide to leave their gangs. To help raise community awareness about the impact of gangs, the program coordinators created a *Gang Handbook*, which serves as a stand-alone resource for social workers, police officers, parents, and other community members, and, in 2005, a powerful documentary film entitled *Gang Aftermath.*

Yet another program operates within a maximum-security federal correctional facility. The Long-Term Offender Program is for offenders serving sentences for serious violent crimes, which are often gang related. Recognizing the strong link between street and prison gangs, program staff attempt to educate offenders through group therapy and individual counselling sessions, dealing with the causal factors that led to their gang involvement, crime, and violent behaviours. Addressing issues of family dysfunction, poverty, drug use and abuse, sexual and physical child abuse, and gang involvement, counsellors work toward undoing antisocial values and beliefs and replacing them with prosocial values and behavioural norms. This is not an easy task, as the following scenario reveals:

Group members have just completed a family tree and are sharing the information with each other. They are getting to know each other by talking about family. The psychologist probes each offender about his past, his upbringing, his childhood. One inmate relays his story: his mother was a prostitute who would lock him up in a closet, sometimes for days at a time, with little or no food, while she was out turning tricks and partying. After the individual finishes telling his story, the psychologist thanks the inmate for sharing his story and during the course of their discussion makes the following statement:

"Your mom wasn't a very good parent."

"What the fuck did you say?"

Out of the Gang, Back to the Tribe

"Did he tell you the story about how I started public speaking?" I'm sitting in a downtown Tim Hortons with former native gang member Derek Powder, who's gesturing across the table toward Rob Papin, the man who inspired him not just to leave gang life behind but to help other aboriginal youth follow his example. These days, Powder, the veteran of several stints in jail on a variety of assault charges, is one of Papin's biggest successes, having appeared alongside Papin at dozens of workshops and in-school seminars, telling his life story and hopefully disabusing a few naïve young people of their illusions about gang life in the process. "The only positive thing I'll say about having been in a gang," Powder says, "is that it let me do the work I'm doing now."

You can get a glimpse of the polished public speaker Powder has become in *Gang Aftermath,* a sobering educational video about native gangs (created by Edmonton production company Bearpaw Media). . . . But when Papin first pushed Powder in front of a microphone [in 2003], the young former drug dealer couldn't have been more unprepared for the experience.

"Rob told me he was doing a presentation at a teachers' convention at Shaw Conference Centre," Powder recalls, "and he asked me if I wanted to come down and check it out and see what he did for a living. And I said, 'Sure, why not?' So I go down and I'm sitting in the front row, and Rob's talking to all these teachers, and then out of the blue he looks at me and says, 'Now I'd like to introduce a friend of mine by the name of Derek Powder who's a former gang member and who's going to tell you his story.' And he gives me the mic, and now I'm standing in front of 300 people, and I'm scared shitless. But as time went on, I just told my story and started to loosen up—and I've been doing it ever since."

As Powder tells his anecdote, Papin's face breaks into a rare smile. With his powerful build, his chiselled, somewhat severe good looks, the tattoos on his chest, his neck and the backs of his hands and a cut across the bridge of his nose, Papin is an intimidating figure (he works part-time as a nightclub bouncer to make ends meet), but it's the seriousness of purpose that underlies his entire demeanour—that implacable, thousand-yard stare that he can conjure up even gazing out the window of a donut joint—that really commands your respect. You get the feeling that, having thrown away so much of his life already on crime, drugs and violence, he has no patience whatsoever for anyone who wants to waste any more of his time.

A Cree from Enoch First Nation, Papin became a gang member when he was still a teenager, but by the time he was 24, he decided he'd had enough and embarked on a dramatically different career path. He re-enrolled in school, completed a tough three-year program in criminal justice and in 2000 he founded the Edmonton Native Alliance, a grassroots organization designed to promote a healthy, constructive, drug-free, family-oriented lifestyle for native youth, reconnect them with traditional aboriginal culture and deter them from getting involved in gang activity. (That program has since morphed into a new privately funded initiative he and Powder operate together called the Gang Awareness Intervention Network, or GAIN, whose functions include everything from drug counseling to court advocacy to school appearances.)

"I was tired of reading the papers and seeing people saying that [in order to fight the gang problem] we need more money for policing and this and that bullshit," Papin says, "when the simplest thing to do is to take the time to ask these people why they're involved in gangs at all. A lot of these individuals, including myself, are products of our environment—family violence, physical abuse, mental and emotional abuse. So I decided it was time to take the bull by the horns. I took that criminal justice course, but it was in order to educate myself about the system, not to become a part of it."

Working largely outside the system, Papin, now 32, has racked up plenty of accomplishments he could boast about, including a mention alongside the likes of Roméo Dallaire, Stephen Lewis and Vancouver mayor Larry Campbell in a list of "Canada's Heroes" published [in 2004] in the Canadian edition of *Time* magazine. And yet Papin doesn't do a lot of boasting—to his mind, Powder's decision to abandon gang life is Powder's victory, not his. "I don't buy into my own publicity," he

---

The psychologist matter-of-factly repeats his comment: "I said your mom wasn't a very good parent."

"Well, fuck you," the inmate says as he stands up angrily, lifting and turning over the table he is sitting behind in the process.

As the other seven inmates push their chairs back, arms crossed, the psychologist calmly states, "Look if you want me to lie to you and tell you your childhood was wonderful, your mom was a great parent, I can do that. But that would be a lie and we are here to talk about the truth. It's up to you. Do you want the truth or a bunch of lies?"

As the inmate reluctantly sits back down again, he mumbles, "Well, the truth I guess."

The psychologist, trembling inside, tells the group, "time for a coffee break." And so begins another session of "Group."[88]

says. "I let people take credit for their own successes."

"I've seen guys come up to Rob and say they want help," Powder agrees, "but he's not going to hold your hand. It's all up to you, because when you come right down to it, you've got your own mind. Myself, I chose to be a different person. I chose to learn about traditional ways and take on that responsibility. There's no turning back to that old lifestyle for me just because something fucked up in my life; there's no time for me to sit there feeling sorry for myself and going, 'Poor me,' and still behaving like a victim. . . . Sure, in the beginning, there are going to be times where you want to fuck up. People are scared of things they don't understand, and at first I felt like I'd jumped into something way too fast—I'm a recovering alcoholic, I'm a recovering drug addict and I just quit cold turkey. I didn't know when I started working with my [elder] and Rob that I'd have to quit everything! I thought I could just slow down and have a social drink now and then, but for a recovering alcoholic, there's no such thing as a social drink.

"But now," he continues, "I've cut all ties with my past. It's done. The way I like to put it is, I'm reborn. I'm a new person at heart with new values and beliefs and new things to learn. It's only been two years since I went into recovery and I'm amazed at how far I've come in that short amount of time. I'm amazed that I'm a single dad, I'm amazed that I actually have custody of my daughter Caylin and am taking care of her. I'm amazed that I'm being paid to work with youth when just two years ago, I was selling crack to my

people and killing them off and hurting them. I work in the inner city and a couple of years ago, I'd see native prostitutes all over the fucking place and I didn't give a shit about them. 'Who cares,' right? 'They're just hos.' But now I get off work late at night and see a native prostitute on every corner, man, and I feel for them. And I'm only one person and Rob's only one person, but now I just want to help all these people who have been living this life for so many years that they're afraid to take the next step into recovery."

If the *Gang Aftermath* video is any indication, Powder and Papin have their work cut out for them—it's filled with testimonials from young men and women, many of them now incarcerated, who never seemed to consider for a moment doing anything with their lives except become part of a gang. "I grew up in a gang lifestyle," says one. "When I was a little kid, I grew up looking up to these gang members and thinking, 'Okay, I want to be just like that.'" "As I got older," says another, "I realized that I liked [being in a gang] and wanted to stay in it because I had respect. People never bad-mouthed me, people never talked back to me. If I raised a finger, somebody would jump. I like power."

Powder says that glamorous, powerful image is mostly an illusion, but 10 years went by before he figured it out and realized that the only rewards he was earning for his gangster lifestyle were repeated stabbings, jail sentences and strained relations with his family. It's a pattern that repeats itself with tragic regularity, and he and Papin have to

take their victories where they can find them. The workload has definitely taken a toll on Papin, to the point where he's thinking seriously about getting out of the gang intervention business—"It's a thankless job," he sighs with regret, "and I've got bills to pay"—but he says he can retire happily knowing that he can look at Powder and see one person whose life he's unmistakably helped change for the better. And yet, he could have had an even bigger effect with just a little more official assistance. "To me," Papin says, "true success would be if City Hall, if the politicians actually did something to help people, if they sat down and asked these guys in jails and prisons what kind of program would work for them, what kind of program would have prevented them from getting into a gang." "They spend so much money to repair the fucking roads," Powder says. "Big fucking deal! Those are roads! We're trying to repair lives! You'll spend hundreds of thousands of dollars on road construction but you aren't willing to fund a gang intervention program to help save people's lives? I mean, what the fuck is wrong with today's society?"

Source

Paul Matwychuk, "Out of the Gang, Back to the Tribe," *Vue Weekly,* **516,** September 8, 2005.

Discussion Questions:

1. What are some explanations for gang involvement among youth and young adults?
2. How can we address gangs and gang violence?

Getting Out: Gang Banging or the Morgue

The most difficult problem that counsellors and street workers face is the power of gangs over their members. Gangs, through loyalty and terror, make it almost impossible for members to quit. Many gang members would gladly get out, but any move to leave leads to gang banging or the morgue. Increasingly, groups and organizations across the country whose aim to help gang members leave

are being created. Some police gang units offer help for gang-involved individuals wanting to leave.[89] They also provide a resource for parents who are concerned that their children are at risk for gang involvement and want to know what the signs are and how to deter their children from joining.[90] Gang Prevention and Intervention, a program run by ex-gang members, is an example of another kind of program that works to reduce gang membership. Community-based projects like the Community Solution to Gang Violence in Edmonton (see www.csgv.ca) and a similar project in Saskatoon provide examples of communities coming together to prevent gang involvement through education and the development of a multi-layered community-based approach to deal with gang issues. These strategies build upon existing community- and justice-related resources such as employment programs, education, recreation, substance-abuse treatment programs, corrections-based interventions, and law enforcement, and have the support of federal, provincial, and municipal governments.[91]

Gangs, once a local problem, have become a national concern. In 2006 the federal government announced it would be spending, over the next two years, $161 million for 1000 more RCMP officers and federal prosecutors to focus on such law enforcement priorities as drugs, corruption and border security (which includes gun smuggling); $37 million for the RCMP to expand its training program to accommodate the influx of new officers; and $20 million for communities to prevent youth crime, with a focus on guns, gangs, and drugs. In January 2007, the federal government announced an additional $16.1 million funding for programs that deal with youth at risk.[92] In addition, the Correctional Service of Canada in recent years has conducted several research studies dealing specifically with prison gangs and the link between street and prison gangs, in an effort to inform policy and programming.

Experts agree that unless we put more money into educational and socioeconomic programs, there is little likelihood that our gang problems will lessen in years to come.

REVIEW

1. What is cultural deviance?
Cultural deviance theories (p. 130)—**differential association** (p. 130) and **culture conflict** (p. 130)—relate criminal behaviour to the learning of criminal values and norms.

2. How do people become deviant or criminal?
Differential association theory concentrates on the processes by which criminal behaviour is taught and learned.

3. How do cultural differences contribute to deviance and crime?
Culture conflict theory focuses on the specifics of how the **conduct norms** (p. 130) of some groups may clash with those of the dominant culture. **Deviance** (p. 130) refers to any behaviour that members of a social group define as violating their norms.

4. How are subcultures linked to deviant behaviour?
In the decade between the mid-1950s and mid-1960s, criminologists began to theorize about the development and content of youth **subcultures** (p. 136) and the gangs that flourish within them. Often these norms clashed with those of the dominant culture. Other investigators have refuted the idea that delinquent behaviour stems from a rejection of middle-class values. They claim that lower-class values are separate and distinct from middle-class values and that it is the lower-class value system that generates delinquent behaviour.

5. Can the subculture of violence thesis explain crime?
The **subculture of violence thesis** (p. 137) argues that in some subcultures, behaviour norms are dictated by a value system that demands the use of force or violence.

6. What do Miller's focal concerns contribute to the explanation of crime?
Miller identified six focal concerns that lower-class males give persistent attention to: trouble, toughness, smartness, excitement, luck, and autonomy. By acting in accordance with these values, it is very likely that these individuals will come into conflict with authority figures.

7. Why should we be concerned about gangs?
Gangs of the 1990s and now in the 2000s show increasing violence and reliance on guns. They are involved in large profit-making activities such as drug distribution. Canadian studies on gangs are not as numerous as American studies, partly because gangs in this country are not as prevalent or as long-lived as those in the United States. However, some observers claim this is changing. There appear to be some regional patterns to the types of gangs that exist in Canada, although no region is completely immune from gang influence. Studies in Canada have described this regional variation and have also investigated the link between street and prison gangs.

8. Are female delinquent subcultures unique?
Explanations of female delinquent subcultures are unique in that gender adds an interesting component to subcultural groups and, for example, gangs. Notions of masculinity and femininity contribute to the inferior treatment of females by male gang members, but also influence the formation of female gangs as a response to such treatment.

9. Is middle-class delinquency unique?

Middle-class delinquency is an extension of subcultural explanations of lower-class delinquency. While the subculture of violence thesis and differential opportunity theory from Chapter 5 differ in some respects, they share one basic assumption—that delinquent and criminal behaviours are linked to the values and norms of the areas where youngsters grow up. Middle-class youth may be attracted to street gangs or hate groups because involvement in such groups fulfills a need not being fulfilled in the home, whether it be a feeling of belonging, a need for excitement, money, or an escape from a dysfunctional family.

10. How can gang members be persuaded to leave the gang?

A variety of programs have been created to deal with both the prevention of and intervention in gang involvement. Some of these programs are run by ex-gang members, others involve helping professionals and community members, and some involve work in correctional institutions. Recent initiatives work to create multi-level, multi-agency approaches that target issues involving family, schools, employment, drug and alcohol abuse, poverty, homelessness, and discrimination.

CRIMINOLOGY & PUBLIC POLICY

"Many aspects of female gang functioning and the lives of female gang members remain a mystery because relatively few researchers have considered female gangs worthy of study. In addition, researchers face serious obstacles to the study of female gangs and, because of these obstacles, they often settle for unrepresentative samples. Gangs are highly suspicious of researchers and cooperate with them only under unusual circumstances. Female gang members, in particular, have been averse to talking about sexual abuse, whether it occurred at home or within the gang. . . . Unfortunately, female gang members have received little programmatic attention." (*Source:* Joan Moore and John Hagedorn, *Female Gangs: A Focus on Research* [Washington, D.C.: OJJDP, 2001]; Melanie Nimmo, *The "Invisible" Gang Members: A Report on Female Gang Association in Winnipeg.* [Canadian Centre for Policy Alternatives, June 2001].)

Questions for Discussion Can you conceive of other reasons why female gangs have been overlooked? After reviewing the work of Prof. Anne Campbell (see the "Of Immediate Concern: The Girls in the Gang" box on page 149) and reading about Melanie Nimmo's research in Winnipeg, what kinds of programs do you suppose would help female gang members make a transition to prosocial activities and lifestyles? In what ways must these programs differ from those proposed for male gang members?

YOU BE THE CRIMINOLOGIST

You are a consultant called in to address the rise in female gang activity and violence. On what theory or theories would you base your intervention? Are the theories based on male delinquency sufficient? Are gender-based theories necessary?

Visit the Online Learning Centre: www.mcgrawhill.ca/olc/adler

SOCIAL CONTROL THEORY

CHAPTER 7

CHAPTER QUESTIONS

1. What are the controlling forces in our lives?

2. How do social control theories explain criminal behaviour at both the microsociological and macrosociological levels?

3. How do external and internal structures insulate people from delinquency?

4. Is it possible for individuals to "drift" into and out of criminal behaviour?

5. How has social control influenced recent theoretical developments?

North Korean Communist Party in May Day Stadium as 100 000 spectators witness a 25 000-person display of political might.

Obedience, respect for authority, shared goals and values, commitment to and investment in custom and convention—this is the glue that makes a successful sports team, no less a powerful social order.

In William Golding's novel *Lord of the Flies,* a group of boys are stranded on an island far from civilization. Deprived of any superior authority—all the grown-ups, their parents, their teachers, the government, that have until now determined their lives—they begin to decide on a structure of government for themselves. Ralph declares:

"We can't have everybody talking at once. We'll have to have 'Hands up' like at school . . . . Then I'll give him the conch."

"Conch?"

"That's what this shell is called. I'll give the conch to the next person to speak. He can hold it when he's speaking!" . . .

Jack was on his feet.

"We'll have rules!" he cried excitedly. "Lots of rules!"[1]

But do rules alone guarantee the peaceful existence of the group? Who and what ensure compliance with the rules? Social control theorists study these questions.

Strain theories, as we noted, study the question of why some people violate norms, for example, by committing crimes. Social control theorists are interested in learning why people conform to norms. Control theorists take it for granted that drugs can tempt even the youngest schoolchildren; that truancy can lure otherwise good children onto a path of academic failure and lifetime unemployment; that petty fighting, petty theft, and recreational drinking are attractive features of adolescence and young adulthood. They ask why people conform in the face of so much temptation and peer pressure. The answer is that juveniles and adults conform to the law in response to certain controlling forces in their lives. They become criminals when the controlling forces are weak or absent.

WHAT IS SOCIAL CONTROL?

What are those controlling forces? Think about the time and energy you have invested in your school, your job, your extracurricular activities. Think about how your academic or vocational ambition would be jeopardized by persistent delinquency. Think about how the responsibility of homework has weighed you down, setting limits on your free time. Reflect on the quality of your relationships with your family, friends, and acquaintances and on how your attachment to them has encouraged you to do right and discouraged you from doing wrong.

Social control theory focuses on techniques and strategies that regulate human behaviour and lead to conformity, or obedience to society's rules—the influences of family and school, religious beliefs, moral values, friends, and even beliefs about government. The more involved and committed a person is to conventional activities and values and the greater the attachment to parents, loved ones, and friends, the less likely that person is to violate society's rules and to jeopardize relationships and aspirations.

The concept of social control emerged in the early 1900s in a volume by E. A. Ross, one of the founders of American sociology. According to Ross, belief systems, rather than specific laws, guide what people do and universally serve to control behaviour. Since that time, the concept has taken on a wide variety of meanings. Social control has been conceptualized as representing practically any phenomenon that leads to conformity. The term is found in studies of laws, customs, mores, ideologies, and folkways describing a host of controlling forces.[2]

Is there danger in defining social control so broadly? It depends on your perspective. To some sociologists, the vagueness of the term—its tendency to encompass almost the entire field of sociology—has significantly decreased its value as a concept.[3] To others, the value of social control lies in its representation of a mechanism by which society regulates its members. According to this view, social control defines what is considered deviant behaviour, what is right or wrong, and what is a violation of the law.

Theorists who have adopted this orientation consider laws, norms, customs, mores, ethics, and etiquette to be forms of social control. Donald Black, a sociologist of law, noted that "social control is found whenever people hold each other to standards, explicitly or implicitly, consciously or not: on the street, in prison, at home, at a party."[4]

If an example would help, consider that as recently as 20 years ago, there were no legal restrictions, norms, or customs regulating the smoking of cigarettes in public places. The U.S. surgeon general's declaration in 1972 that second-hand smoke poses a health hazard ushered in three decades of controls over behaviour that not too long ago was considered sociable—if not sophisticated and suave.

At present, the number of provinces and cities in Canada that ban smoking in public places continues to grow. Increasingly, it is becoming the norm for workplaces, whether government or public, to ban smoking. Ontario, Quebec, Saskatchewan, and Newfoundland and Labrador banned smoking in all public places in 2006. Cities across the country are also taking the lead in prohibiting smoking in public establishments, including bars, restaurants, and casinos.

This smoking example illustrates an interesting discussion concerning the nature of social control in society. Smoking is clearly an example of an individual behaviour—people choose to smoke. Norms and laws prohibit smoking, but individuals choose to ignore these prohibitions and exercise their right to choose to smoke. What will the situation be like ten years from now? Twenty? Will norms that prohibit smoking become so engrained

Learning to play by the rules: Olympic athlete Ben Johnson was stripped of his gold medal in 1988 when it was discovered he used steroids to enhance his performance.

in our society and socialization practices that smokers will become obsolete? The question really becomes one concerning the influence of society in defining deviance and in reacting to it. What are the broader patterns and trends that influence deviance and social control in society?

Erving Goffman was one of the first sociologists to suggest that there is something that unites the manner in which society deals with deviance.[5] In other words, the way a community deals with youth crime, and another deals with drug users, and yet another deals with sex offenders, is united by a broader understanding of deviance and its control. Others have picked up this theme and added a historical dimension to the analysis. These theorists ponder the historical and contemporary changes in society's approach to defining and dealing with deviants, and how a society enforces or encourages conformity or order. We briefly discuss some of the explanations offered by these theorists before examining theories that focus more explicitly on the relationship between criminal behaviour and social control among individuals and within communities.

Theorists such as Stanley Cohen, Michel Foucault, and David Garland posit stages in the way society has responded to deviance, and the way it has attempted to exert control over deviants. Foucault, for example, has described in detail the transformation that occurred in nineteenth-century France, and how that transformation has affected modern society. For Foucault, penal reforms during this period in Europe moved from public displays of capital punishment (e.g., hangings, drawing and quartering) to more private and ostensibly more humane forms of punishment (e.g., being confined to a prison cell, solitary confinement). Routinized prison structure and constant surveillance by guards helped transform deviants into docile, well-behaved, compliant, and disciplined individuals. Foucault suggested that the disciplined nature of prison life was mirrored in other institutions in society; all worked to create insidious control over individuals, whether students in a classroom, patients in a hospital, soldiers in the military, or anyone else in society. The modern era is marked by discipline, which is integral to social control.

Cohen offers a version of social control that similarly constructs control as more pervasive than we might think. Focusing on the move toward "destructuring" within the criminal justice system that was initiated in the mid-1960s, Cohen illustrates how

what was supposed to result in less government and criminal justice system control over citizens has actually had the opposite effect. Destructuring refers to the process whereby decriminalization, diversion, and deinstitutionalization result in fewer people being arrested, detained, and imprisoned. The goal of destructuring is essentially to keep as many people as possible out of the criminal justice system to reduce the costs of the system, and to protect individuals from the damaging effects of criminal justice system involvement (e.g., labelling, criminal record, loss of employment etc.).

Cohen's argument, however, is that despite the underlying good intentions of this move, the result has actually been an increase in state involvement in the lives of citizens. The introduction of community-based programming has actually brought new, soft-core deviants who, under the "old system," would never have become involved with the system at all into its reach (e.g., someone who would have been "let off" with a police warning only, now might have to participate in an alternative measures program or community service). Termed "net-widening," the process describes how the social control apparatus has actually extended its grip on more people. At the same time, prisons still exist; the social control system has expanded because community control has supplemented rather than replaced formal institutions.[6]

Adding to the discussion and further illustrating the growth in social control, David Garland illuminates the role of educated middle classes and professionals in this process. It was these same middle-class professionals who, during the 1960s and 1970s, advocated for the destructuring just described. Informed by the ideals of liberal penal welfarism (the idea that changes to the penal system that focused more on helping criminals to rehabilitate rather than treating them punitively is positive), these groups have since accepted the failure of their efforts. One result of their disillusionment with the ideals they once fought so hard for has been a subdued presence. No longer actively working to affect policy, and hesitant to oppose the influx of increasingly punitive social policies, Garland has described them as "the dog that didn't bark." In other words, the once active proponents of destructuring and rehabilitation have stopped dissenting against harsh social policies. In fact, they have come to espouse more punitive social views.[7] In an era characterized by punitiveness and increasing fear of crime (whether or not this fear is based on actual crime rates), these groups have contributed to "an increasingly punitive, control-focused culture."[8]

Cohen, Foucault, and Garland offer some historical context and depth to our understanding of social control today. Within this context of criminal justice system control, we turn now to a variety of theories of social control that offer explanations for the development of social control within individuals and communities.

> **Did You Know?**
>
> . . . that it costs $95 826.37 to imprison a young person for a year?[9] The same amount of money would fund a full year's worth of recreational activities and equipment for almost 50 youth.

THEORIES OF SOCIAL CONTROL

We have, already, been exposed to a variety of descriptions of social control. Why is it conceptualized in such different ways? Perhaps because social control has been examined from both a macrosociological and a microsociological perspective. **Macrosociological studies** explore formal systems for the control of groups:

- The legal system, laws, and particularly law enforcement

- Powerful groups in society

- Social and economic directives of governmental or private groups

These types of control can be either positive—that is, they inhibit rule-breaking behaviour by a type of social guidance—or negative—that is, they foster oppressive, restrictive, or corrupt practices by those in power.[10]

The microsociological perspective is similar to the macrosociological approach in that it, too, explains why people conform. The **microsociological approach,** however, focuses on informal systems. Researchers collect data from individuals (usually by self-report methods), are often guided by hypotheses that apply to individuals as well as to groups, and frequently make reference to or examine a person's internal control system. Macrosociological research, on the other hand, focuses on broader social structures, such as community structure, economic factors, ethnic or racial composition of a community, and other patterns that characterize groups of people.

We turn now to an example of a macrosociological approach to explaining criminal behaviour, social disorganization theory, and then discuss the microsociological approach.

The Macrosociological Perspective: Social Disorganization Theory

Early versions of social control theory explained how social structure contributed to high rates of crime and deviance. Communities that were disorganized or characterized by poverty, physical deterioration, high rates of mobility (people moving in and out), and racial or ethnic conflict were too disorganized to exert effective social control over residents. In Émile Durkheim's terms, such communities, as a result of their social disorganization, were also anomic. People lacked social bonds to each other and to social structures, and were thus free to deviate. Strong social norms were not in place to control behaviour.

Social disorganization theory focuses on the development of high-crime areas in which there is a disintegration of conventional values caused by rapid industrialization, increased immigration, and urbanization. The theory is based on notions of social control, and how the lack of such controls, formal and informal, contribute to delinquency and crime. Social disorganization theory clearly has links to anomie theory, but it also overlaps with the cultural deviance theoretical perspective discussed in Chapter 6 because it explains how cultural differences between groups and neighbourhoods contribute to conflicts, which in turn work against the development of strong social controls.

Scholars associated with the University of Chicago in the 1920s became interested in socially disorganized Chicago neighbourhoods where criminal values and traditions replaced conventional ones and were transmitted from one generation to the next. In their classic work *The Polish Peasant in Europe and America,* W. I. Thomas and Florian Znaniecki described the difficulties Polish peasants experienced when they left their rural life in Europe to settle in an industrialized city in the United States.[11] The scholars compared the conditions the immigrants had left in Poland with those they found in Chicago. They also investigated the immigrants' assimilation.

Older immigrants, they found, were not greatly affected by the move because they managed, even within the urban slums, to continue living as they

FIGURE 7.1 Social disorganization.

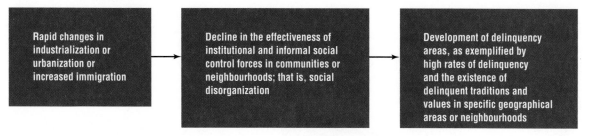

Source: Donald J. Shoemaker, *Theories of Delinquency*, 2nd ed. (New York: Oxford University Press, 1990), p. 82. Copyright © 1984, 1990, 1996, 2000 by Oxford University Press, Inc. Used by permission of Oxford University Press, Inc.

had lived in Poland. But the second generation did not grow up on Polish farms; these people were city dwellers, and they were American. They had few of the old Polish traditions but were not yet assimilated into the new ones. The norms of the stable, homogeneous folk society were not transferable to the anonymous, materially oriented urban settings. Rates of crime and delinquency rose. Thomas and Znaniecki attributed this result to *social disorganization*—the breakdown of effective social bonds, family and neighbourhood associations, and social controls in neighbourhoods and communities (see Figure 7.1).

More recently, Matthew Yeager conducted a meta-survey on the topic of immigrants and criminality and reached similar conclusions to those of Thomas and Znaniecki. Yeager reports that, in general, first-generation immigrants have lower propensities for crime than their native-born counterparts, and second- and third-generation immigrants. First-generation immigrants tend to be older than the crime-prone generation, and are often better educated, better employed, and desirous of assimilation, all of which contribute to their higher level of conformity and reduced crime rate. On the other hand, second- and third-generation children of immigrants have much more serious crime problems than their immigrant parents. Yeager attributes this to severe, cultural marginality in the adopted country. Cultural anomie, in the form of conflict with the traditional customs of their parents, leads to a loosening of social controls, which in turn leads to criminal behaviour:

The children are no longer able to identify with their parents. Tensions and quarrels ensue in the family. Parental authority is being questioned. . . . Many children are incapable of coming to terms with the conflicting norms and of integrating them

into their personality. . . . Parents lose control over their children who join a group of delinquents of the same age, in which they get acquainted with delinquent behaviour patterns and models.[12]

The precursors to criminal behaviour for these young people look much like those identified by Thomas and Znaniecki decades ago: poverty, racism, school failure, unemployment, family disorganization, and drug addiction. Social structural factors, which 1920s criminologists identified as those leading to criminal behaviour, continue to play a role in such behaviour. As Yeager concludes, this finding is perhaps more of a comment on the host country than on immigration. The findings raise questions about the impact of criminological theorizing on policy. Why are we still struggling with causal factors that were identified as precursors to crime so many years ago?

The Park and Burgess Model Thomas and Znaniecki's study greatly influenced other scholars at the University of Chicago. Among them were Robert Park and Ernest Burgess, who advanced the study of social disorganization by introducing ecological analysis into the study of human society.[13] Ecology is the study of plants and animals in relation to each other and to their natural habitat, the place where they live and grow. Ecologists study these interrelationships, how the balance of nature continues, and how organisms survive. Much the same approach is used by social ecologists, scholars who study the interrelationships of people and their environment.

In their study of social disorganization, Park and Burgess examined area characteristics instead of criminals for explanations of high crime rates. They developed the idea of natural urban areas, consisting of concentric zones extending out from

FIGURE 7.2 Park and Burgess's conception of the "natural urban areas" of Chicago.

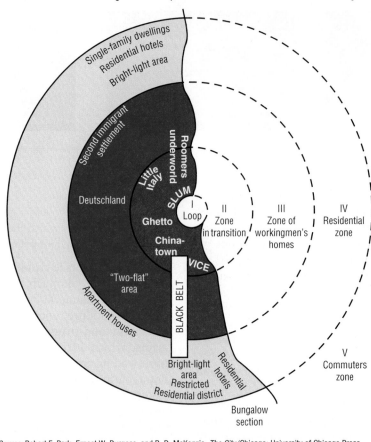

the downtown central business district to the commuter zone at the fringes of the city. Each zone had its own structure and organization, its own cultural characteristics and unique inhabitants (see Figure 7.2). Zone I, at the centre, called the "Loop" because the downtown business district of Chicago is demarcated by a loop of the elevated train system, was occupied by commercial headquarters, law offices, retail establishments, and some commercial recreation. Zone II was the zone in transition, where the city's poor, unskilled, and disadvantaged lived in dilapidated tenements next to old factories. Zone III housed the working class, people whose jobs enabled them to enjoy some of the comforts the city had to offer at its fringes. The middle class— professionals, small-business owners, and the managerial class—lived in Zone IV. Zone V was the commuter zone of satellite towns and suburbs.

Shaw and McKay's Work Clifford Shaw and Henry McKay, two researchers at Chicago's Institute

for Juvenile Research, were particularly interested in the model Park and Burgess had created to demonstrate how people were distributed spatially in the process of urban growth. They decided to use the model to investigate the relationship between crime rates and the various zones of Chicago.[14]

Shaw and McKay demonstrated that the highest rates of delinquency persisted in the same areas of Chicago over the extended period from 1900 to 1933, even though the ethnic composition changed (German, Irish, and English at the turn of the twentieth century; Polish and Italian in the 1920s; an increasing number of blacks in the 1930s). This finding led to the conclusion that the crucial factor was not ethnicity but, rather, the position of the group in terms of economic status and cultural values. Finally, through their study of three sets of juvenile court records—1900 to 1906, 1917 to 1923, and 1927 to 1933—they learned that older boys were associated with younger boys in various offences and that the same techniques for committing delinquent acts had been passed on through the years. The evidence clearly indicated to them that delinquency was socially learned behaviour, transmitted from one generation to the next in disorganized urban areas.[15] This phenomenon is called **cultural transmission.**

Tests of Social Disorganization Theory

Social disorganization, like early strain theory, was overshadowed in the 1970s by social control theorists who turned to explanations of why people do *not* break laws in the face of poor social environments with few means of becoming successful. While these explanations still have widespread impact on the scholarly community, the 1980s and 1990s saw a major resurgence of interest in how neighbourhoods affect people's lives. Modern-day social ecologists have once again begun to focus on the interrelationship between individuals and their environment. What are the consequences of rising crime rates in a neighbourhood? Ralph Taylor suggests separating these consequences into three categories: psychological and social, behavioural, and economic.[16]

Psychological and Social Effects Life in physically deteriorated neighbourhoods, with their rat-infested buildings, graffiti-ridden streets, trash-strewn vacant lots, boarded-up windows, and openly conducted drug selling, takes its psychological toll on residents.[17] They feel less emotional investment in their communities, mistrust their neighbours, and harbour increasing desires to "get out." Frustration mounts because they are unable to do so. Many parents are so worried about violence on their streets that they confine their youngsters to the home except for school attendance. Young people refer to this confinement as "lockdown" (a term used to describe the locking of prison cells for security reasons). This desperate move to protect their children from getting hurt physically has had harmful psychological effects. According to one professor of developmental psychology, in a world where a simple altercation can end as an assault or even a murder,[18] these "protected" children are at a disadvantage. When they eventually go back on the streets, they don't know how to survive.

Researchers are questioning whether people living in socially disorganized neighbourhoods become more fearful. The answer is, they usually do.[19] When word of victimization begins to spread, fear can reach epidemic proportions. Residents begin to stay off the streets, abandoning them to the gangs, drug sellers, and others involved in illicit activities. Fear becomes greatest in communities undergoing rapid age and racial-composition changes.[20]

Fear increases when there is a perception that the police care little about a neighbourhood. Community policing is a model of policing that is decentralized and has officers working with community members to increase feelings of safety in communities. In simplistic terms, rather than driving around in police cars, waiting for crimes to occur, and then dealing with them (reactive policing), police officers, often on foot patrol, proactively police neighbourhoods by interacting with community members. Officers are assigned to mini-stations, located throughout a community. This encourages interaction between officers and the community they police, thus contributing to increased feelings of safety among residents. Research shows that police officers are less likely to file reports of crime incidents in high-crime areas than in low-crime areas and that they are more likely to assist residents and initiate contacts with suspicious-looking people in low-crime neighbourhoods, examples of proactive policing—attempting to solve potential problems before they escalate.[21]

Dina Rose and Todd Clear link social disorganization to high incarceration rates. They suggest that when large numbers of males are removed through incarceration, local social, political, and economic systems in already disorganized communities become even weaker. In these areas, children are more likely to experience lack of supervision, more single-parent families, and few effective guardians.[22] Research has documented the socially disorganized nature of many Aboriginal communities and reserves in Canada. Poverty-stricken, with poor health care and educational structures in place, high rates of infant mortality, substance abuse, and family violence, these communities often witness the incarceration of many of its members. In Saskatchewan alone, where about 8 percent of the population is Aboriginal, over 75 percent of the adult prison population comes from this group.[23] Rose and Clear do not advocate policies that allow those who threaten the personal safety of residents to be on the streets. But, they argue, there are many offenders who can be regulated in the community through various neighbourhood-based approaches monitored by collaborative efforts of the police, probation and parole officers, and local groups, leaders, and residents. This crime-control strategy, one that ties the offender to the community, could then strengthen, rather than weaken, already socially disorganized neighbourhoods.[24]

Behavioural Effects The broken windows model posits that social incivilities (loitering and drinking in public) and physical incivilities (vacant lots and abandoned buildings) are an invitation to further crime, because criminals perceive that no one cares enough about the neighbourhood to take care of it.[25] By extension, the reasoning is that residents of such neighbourhoods also then will not actively resist crime. Residents living in these neighbourhoods are fearful of crime; research shows that residents consider substance abuse and fist fighting "very wrong" to "extremely wrong." Broken down by racial and ethnic groups, minority-group members are more intolerant of deviance than were whites.[26] Regardless of the level of residents' intolerance and fear, however, widespread deviance in a community generally tends to make people limit their participation in efforts to "clean up" the neighbourhood. There are, however, communities that fight back with community patrols, anti-crime programs, and various activities to protect children. Many would prefer to move away, but few do. Factors besides crime come into play: low income, stage of life cycle, an affordable place to live, or location of employment.[27] Those moving in usually do so because it is the only place they can find an inexpensive place to live.[28]

Economic Effects Estimates are that crime costs Canadians between $59 and $70 billion a year.[29] This figure includes the financial costs of victimization, police and criminal justice service expenditures, security devices, and protection services. But these are conservative estimates since they do not include factors such as the influence of high crime rates on property values in particular neighbourhoods.

Middle- and working-class people tend to escape the urban ghetto, leaving behind the most disadvantaged. When you add to those disadvantaged the people moving in from outside who are also severely disadvantaged, over time these areas become places of concentrated poverty, isolated from the mainstream.

Some social ecologists argue that communities, like people, go through life cycles. Neighbourhood deterioration precedes rising crime rates. When crime begins to rise, neighbourhoods go from owner-occupied to renter-occupied housing,

with a significant decline in the socioeconomic status of residents and an increase in population density. Later in the community life cycle, there is a renewed interest on the part of investors in buying up the cheap real estate with the idea of renovating it and making a profit (gentrification).[30]

Evaluation: Social Disorganization Theory

Though their work has made a significant impact, social ecologists have not been immune to challenges. Their work has been criticized for its focus on how crime patterns are transmitted, not on how they start in the first place. The approach has also been faulted for failing to explain why delinquents stop committing crime as they grow older, why most people in socially disorganized areas do not commit criminal acts, and why some bad neighbourhoods seem to be insulated from crime. Finally, critics claim that this approach does not come to grips with middle-class delinquency.

Clearly, however, modern criminology owes a debt to social disorganization theorists, particularly to Shaw and McKay, who in the 1920s began to look at the characteristics of people and places and to relate both to crime. There is now a vast body of research for which they laid the groundwork.

THEORY INFORMS POLICY

Theorists of the Chicago school were the first social scientists to suggest that most crime is committed by normal people responding in expected ways to their immediate surroundings, rather than by abnormal individuals acting out individual pathologies. If social disorganization is at the root of the problem, crime control must involve social organization. The community, not individuals, needs treatment. Helping the community, then, should lower its crime rate.

Vancouver's Downtown Eastside Community Development Area Project Social disorganization theory was translated into practice between 1999 and 2006 with the establishment of the Vancouver Downtown Eastside Community Development Project (DTESCDP), a federally and locally funded community mobilization project. In February 1999, the federal National Crime Prevention Centre provided a five-year, $5 million grant to the City of Vancouver and the Vancouver Coalition for Crime Prevention and Drug

Treatment. The goal was to mobilize the community and ultimately increase the quality of life and level of safety in the area.

The Downtown Eastside of Vancouver is a community of diverse neighbourhoods with rich histories, where difference is accepted and valued. To outsiders, the community is known as one of the poorest districts in Canada and for having an open drug market at Main and Hastings. It is the "shameful part of a prosperous city where drug addicts, sex workers and poor people are thrown away."[31]

The purpose of the project was to mobilize the Downtown Eastside community by bringing together residents, local agencies, and businesses in an effort to address the risk factors for crime and victimization that plagued the community. These risk factors include poverty, homelessness, addiction, and family issues. The project was made up of five major components, each bringing a different emphasis to the project, each addressing one or more of the various social disorganization factors thought to be linked to crime and victimization:

- *Community Directions.* The focus was on mobilizing the low-income community, especially those who are excluded from decision-making processes.

- *Vancouver's Chinatown Revitalization Committee.* This group formed to strengthen the cohesiveness and capacity of Chinatown businesses, as well as family associations and community agencies in an effort to actively revitalize their community.

- *Coordination and Community Cohesion.* This body worked to facilitate communication between the various partners and players in the initiative.

- *Youth Employment.* This group in the initiative provided training opportunities for youth at risk.

- *Communication.* The role of this group was to educate the broader community about the root causes of crime.

The project generally and specifically through these five components drew on a risk-protective framework, which ties directly to social disorganization theory. The goal is to reduce risk factors like poverty, addictions, and unemployment, and to increase the positive (social control) characteristics of a community: positive role models, strong friend and family networks, employment opportunities, stable housing and availability of services. Was it successful?

Graffiti covers this wall in Saint Louis Square in Montreal. Cities struggle to find ways of deterring vandals from damaging property in this way. In Winnipeg, youth are encouraged to display their artwork in a legitimate venue that benefits the community and the youth themselves.

Some of the successes of the project outlined in the evaluation report indicate that employment opportunities increased, as did the quality of life of residents. Sixty-five percent of key respondents agreed or strongly agreed that the quality of life in the community had improved since the initiation of the program. In particular, access to sports for low-income children had increased and parents were more involved in this aspect of their children's lives. Furthermore, the Aboriginal Front Door, a First Nations traditional culture and healing centre, had been established, thus building support and involvement for this particular community. In the terms of social disorganization theory, social controls were established, linking individuals to each other and to the broader community. Overall, the program has been applauded for its reduction in crime in the area, and the increase in citizen participation and involvement in the community. Community safety has also reportedly increased.[32]

Winnipeg Graffiti Gallery (Graffiti Art Programming) Steve Wilson started the Graffiti Gallery in an old pickle factory in Winnipeg's Point Douglas neighbourhood, home to a largely Aboriginal population. The gallery is a youth community art centre where young artists can meet, work, research, exchange their ideas, learn skills, and show their work in an environment that both encourages and sees the value in their work. The gallery views art as a powerful tool for community development, social change, and individual growth. In criminological terms, this translates into an opportunity for disenfranchised youth to connect with broader society, to see value and connectedness in themselves, and to make linkages with mainstream society. Rather than committing vandalism by spray-painting graffiti over home-owners' property, these individuals now have a safe place to express their artistic talents, without the threat of social disapproval. In fact, they receive quite the opposite: accolades and respect for their talent and hard work. Beyond these benefits, the Graffiti Gallery brings at-risk youth and young adults back into the community, providing them with confidence, self-esteem, and a feeling of accomplishment, and reducing their criminal activity.[33]

> **Did You Know?**
>
> . . . that it costs $150 867 to keep a woman in prison for a year and $110 223 per year to keep a man in prison? It costs about $16 000 to support a university student for one year.[34]

Programs based on social disorganization theory attempt to bring conventional social values to disorganized communities. They provide an opportunity for young people to learn norms other than those of delinquent peer groups. Let us see how such learning takes place.

PERSONAL AND SOCIAL CONTROL

Over the last 40 years, support has increased for the idea that both social (external) control systems like those described by social disorganization theory, and personal (internal) control systems are important forces in keeping individuals from committing crimes. Influenced by the works of classical school thinkers like Cesare Beccaria and Jeremy Bentham, social control theorists emphasize the rational nature of human beings. They point out the importance of cost-benefit analyses that precede human behaviours. However, they add to classical school explanations of behaviour, criminal and conforming, by suggesting that both internal and external controls influence the decision-making process. For example, in contemplating a theft, a young person might think about the "cost" of losing his or her parents' respect. Control, in the form of external or social controls and internal/personal controls, contributes to an understanding of both criminal and conforming behaviours. Early work on the importance of "control" as an explanatory factor for criminal behaviour influenced the development of more contemporary versions of control theory.

Failure of Control Mechanisms

Albert J. Reiss, a sociologist, was one of the first researchers to isolate a group of personal and social control factors. According to Reiss, delinquency is the result of (1) a failure to internalize socially accepted and prescribed norms of behaviour; (2) a breakdown of internal controls; and (3) a lack of social rules that prescribe behaviour in the family, the school, and other important social groups.

Using data from the court files of 1110 male youth probationers, Reiss concluded measures of both personal and social control seem "to yield more efficient prediction of delinquent recidivism than items which are measures of the strength of social control."[35]

Stake in Conformity

Imagine that your earliest childhood memory conjures up the sound of splintering wood as the police break down your front door and the image of your grandmother being led away in handcuffs. You are four years old. What impact would such an image have on you? What if your formative years were spent in an impoverished urban environment where your mother and grandmother sold heroin out of your living room; your closest friends were high school dropouts with criminal records; and your adolescent confrontations did not involve the school bully demanding your lunch money, but rather the neighbourhood drug dealer stopping by to settle overdue debts? Where would you be today?

Six years after the publication of Reiss's study, Jackson Toby proposed a different personal and social control model. Toby discussed the complementary role of neighbourhood social disorganization and an individual's own stake in conformity. He agreed that the social disorganization of the slums explains why some communities have high crime rates while others do not: In slums, both the community and the family are powerless to control members' behaviour. Thieves and hoodlums usually come from such neighbourhoods. But a great many law-abiding youngsters come from slums as well. Toby questioned how a theory that explained group behaviour could account for individual differences in response to a poor environment. In other words, how can the theory of social disorganization explain why only a few among so many slum youths actually commit crimes?[36]

According to Toby, the social disorganization approach can explain why one neighbourhood has a much higher crime rate than another, but not why one particular individual becomes a hoodlum while another does not. What accounts for the difference is a differing stake in **conformity,** or correspondence of behaviour to society's patterns, norms, or standards. One person may respond to conditions in a "bad" neighbourhood by becoming hostile to conventional values, perhaps because he or she knows that the chances for legitimate success are poor. Another person in the same neighbourhood may maintain his or her stake in conformity and remain committed to abiding by the law. Toby reminds us that when we try to account for crime in general, we should look at both group-level explanations (social disorganization) and individual-level explanations (stake in conformity).

Containment Theory

A broad analysis of the relationship between personal and social controls is found in Walter Reckless's presentation of containment theory.[37] **Containment theory** assumes that for every individual, there exists a containing external structure and a protective internal structure, both of which provide defence, protection, or insulation against delinquency.

According to Reckless, "outer containment," or the structural buffer that holds the person in bounds, can be found in, for example, cohesion among the members of a group, a sense of belongingness (identification with the group), identification with one or more persons within the group, a set of reasonable limits and responsibilities, and a role that provides a guide for a person's activities.[38] "Inner containment," or personal control, is ensured by a good self-concept, self-control, a strong ego, a well-developed conscience, a high frustration tolerance, and a high sense of responsibility.

Reckless suggests that the probability of deviance is directly related to the extent to which internal pushes (such as a need for immediate gratification, restlessness, and hostility), external pressures (such as poverty, unemployment, and blocked opportunities), and external pulls are controlled by one's inner and outer containment. The primary containment factor is found in self-concept, or the way one views oneself in relation to others and to the world. A strong self-concept, coupled with some additional inner controls (such as a strong conscience and sense

of responsibility), plus outer controls, makes delinquency highly unlikely.

The idea that both internal and external factors are involved in controlling behaviour has interested a number of scholars. Francis Ivan Nye, for example, developed the notion that multiple control factors determine human behaviour. He argued that **internalized control,** or self-regulation, was a product of guilt aroused in the conscience when norms have been internalized. **Indirect control** comes from an individual's identification with non-criminals and a desire not to embarrass parents and friends by acting against their expectations.

Nye believes that social control involves "needs satisfaction," by which he means that control depends on how well a family can prepare the child for success at school, with peers, and in the workplace. Finally, **direct control,** a purely external control, depends on rules, restrictions, and punishments.[39]

Other researchers have looked at direct controls in different ways. Parental control, for example, may depend on such factors as a broken home, the mother's employment, and the number of children in the family; such factors indicate some loss of direct control. Once again we find mixed results. Some studies indicate very little relationship between a broken home and delinquency, except for minor offences such as truancy and running away.[40] The same can be said about the consequences of a mother's employment and of family size. Other studies, however, have shown that direct control is a mediating factor between family structure and delinquency. Recent research on family structure and social control indicates that the relationship between social control and delinquency is complex—it varies by the type of control being measured and the type of delinquency as well.[41]

Containment theory has received significant criticism.[42] The most damaging has come from Clarence Schrag, who contends that the terminology used is vague and poorly defined, that the theory is difficult to test empirically, and that the theory fails to consider why some poorly contained youths commit violent crimes while others commit property crimes.[43] These criticisms are not easy to answer. And because little empirical research has been done to test the findings of Reckless and his colleagues over the intervening 30 years, there is little evidence of the validity of containment theory. Nonetheless, the idea of control, particularly the importance of external controls at the individual

Wilderness camps like "Outward Bound" teach at-risk youth survival skills and emphasize physical fitness. They work to increase internal controls through discipline and structure, as well as external controls by building bonds between camp participants.

or personal level, has influenced contemporary social control theorists. These theorists continue to ask the question Reckless and others have sought to answer: What makes people conform?

The Microsociological Perspective: Hirschi

Travis Hirschi has been the spokesperson of the microsociological perspective since the publication of his *Causes of Delinquency* in 1969. As we saw earlier, however, he is not the first scholar to examine the extent of individual social control and its relationship to delinquency. Like the control-based theorists from earlier, Hirschi was less interested in the source of an individual's motivation to commit delinquent acts than in the reasons people do not commit such acts. He claimed that social control theory explains conformity and adherence to rules, not deviance. It is thus not a crime-causation theory in a strict sense but a theory of prosocial behaviour used by criminologists to explain deviance.

Social Bonds

Hirschi posited four social bonds that promote socialization and conformity: attachment, commitment, involvement, and belief. The stronger these bonds, he claimed, the less likelihood of delinquency.[44] To test this hypothesis, he administered a self-report questionnaire to 4077 junior and senior high school students in California (see Table 7.1) that measured both involvement in delinquency and the strength of the four social bonds. Hirschi found that weakness in any of the bonds was associated with delinquent behaviour.

TABLE 7.1 Items from Travis Hirschi's Measure of Social Control

1. In general, do you like or dislike school?
   A. Like it
   B. Like it and dislike it about equally
   C. Dislike it

2. How important is getting good grades to you personally?
   A. Very important
   B. Somewhat important
   C. Fairly important
   D. Completely unimportant

3. Do you care what teachers think of you?
   A. I care a lot
   B. I care some
   C. I don't care much

4. Would you like to be the kind of person your father is?
   A. In every way
   B. In most ways
   C. In some ways
   D. In just a few ways
   E. Not at all

5. Did your mother read to you when you were little?
   A. No
   B. Once or twice
   C. Several times
   D. Many times, but not regularly
   E. Many times, and regularly
   F. I don't remember

6. Do you ever feel that "there's nothing to do"?
   A. Often
   B. Sometimes
   C. Rarely
   D. Never

Source: Travis Hirschi, *Causes of Delinquency* (Berkeley: University of California Press, 1969). Copyright © 2002 by Transaction Publishers. Reprinted by permission of the publisher.

Attachment The first bond, **attachment,** takes three forms: attachment to parents, to school (teachers), and to peers. According to Hirschi, youths who have formed a significant attachment to a parent refrain from delinquency because the consequences of such an act might jeopardize that relationship. The bond of affection between a parent and a child thus becomes a primary deterrent to criminal activities.[45] Its strength depends on the depth and quality of parent-child interaction. The parent-child bond forms a path through which conventional ideals and expectations can pass. This bond is bolstered by:

- The amount of time the child spends with parents, particularly the presence of a parent at times when the child is tempted to engage in criminal activity

- The intimacy of communication between parent and child
- The affectional identification between parent and child[46]

Next Hirschi considered the importance of the school. As we saw in Chapter 6, Hirschi linked inability to function well in school to delinquency through the following chain of events: Academic incompetence leads to poor school performance; poor school performance results in a dislike of school; dislike of school leads to rejection of teachers and administrators as authorities. The result is delinquency. Thus attachment to school depends on a youngster's appreciation for the institution, perception of how he or she is received by teachers and peers, and level of achievement in class.

Hirschi found that attachment to parents and school overshadows the bond formed with peers:

> As was true for parents and teachers, those most closely attached to or respectful of their friends are least likely to have committed delinquent acts. The relation does not appear to be as strong as was the case for parents and teachers, but the ideas that delinquents are unusually dependent upon their peers, that loyalty and solidarity are characteristic of delinquent groups, that attachment to adolescent peers fosters nonconventional behaviour, and that the delinquent is unusually likely to sacrifice his personal advantage to the "requirements of the group" are simply not supported by the data.[47]

Commitment Hirschi's second group of bonds consists of **commitment** to or investment in conventional lines of action—that is, support of and participation in social activities that tie the individual to the society's moral or ethical code. Hirschi identified a number of stakes in conformity or commitments: vocational aspirations, educational expectations, and educational aspirations.

Many programs and institutions currently strive to nurture and encourage such aspirations. For example, Tim Onyschuk of Sheridan College in Brampton, Ontario, started a program that aims to keep at-risk young boys in the community out of trouble with the law. Onyschuk, who has received an award for his work with the Police Foundations Program at the college, emphasizes the importance of community involvement for police officers, present and future. His Iron John program is an example of social control theory in practice: College students

mentor boys at risk in the community, provide positive role models for them, and encourage conventional behaviour among them. In this way, social bonds are created and reinforced.[48]

Though Hirschi's theory, and programs based on it, are at odds with the competing theories of Albert Cohen and Richard Cloward and Lloyd Ohlin (see Chapter 5), Hirschi provided empirical support for the notion that the greater the aspiration and expectation, the more unlikely delinquency becomes. Also, "students who smoke, those who drink, and those who date are more likely to commit delinquent acts; . . . the more the boy is involved in adult activities, the greater his involvement in delinquency."[49]

Involvement Hirschi's third bond is **involvement,** or preoccupation with activities that promote the interests of society. This bond is derived from involvement in school-related activities (such as homework) rather than in working-class adult activities (such as smoking and drinking). A person who is busy doing conventional things has little time for deviant activities.

With this premise in mind, many Big Brothers/Big Sisters (BBBS) groups, like the BBBS of Halton, Ontario, offer tutoring programs for children experiencing academic difficulties or who require help in maintaining their grades. Volunteers are adults or high school students who have a minimum average of 70 percent. The program matches volunteers with one student for a full school year.[50] The Study Buddy program in Edmonton, Alberta, offers another example of the kind of programming that increases students' involvement in conventional society by pairing university and college students with elementary, junior high, and high school students who require help with their studies.

Belief "We should be able to do what we want and we should be able to go home whenever we want." "They can't really enforce it . . . no one's going to even listen to them."[51] "This type of prejudice insults me as an individual, but I am helpless because I can't vote. Then again, it's not as if any of the new legislation is affecting me, right? Why should I have any say in my own life? After all, I'm just a teen."

As of 2002, 15 communities in New Brunswick had teen curfews. For example, in Salisbury, it was against the law for teens under 16 to be in a public place past 10 P.M. The reason curfews were implemented was because of high rates of vandalism, mischief, and theft in the communities. Teens were outraged by the restrictions on their time. As one young person states: "It's a joke if they think that kids under the age of 18 are going to be home by 10:30 P.M."[52] At base in these communities are issues whose solutions run deeper than imposing a curfew on teens.

While curfews are not a major issue in Canada, by 2004 the town of Huntington, Quebec, had one in place, and in 2006 residents in Strathcona County, Alberta, were vehemently debating the issue. As of July 2007, teens in Lambton County, Ontario, were subjected to a curfew as well. The contentious nature of curfews raises questions about the imposition of laws and practices on groups resistant to the rules, particularly when the groups in question may not have committed a crime but are treated with a blanket solution.

The last of the bonds, **belief,** consists of assent to the society's value system. The value system of any society entails respect for its laws and for the people and institutions that enforce them. The results of Hirschi's survey lead to the conclusion that if young people no longer believe laws are fair, their bond to society weakens, and the probability that they will commit delinquent acts increases.

Empirical Tests of Hirschi's Theory

Hirschi's work has inspired a vast number of studies. We can examine only a small selection of some of the more significant research.

Michael Hindelang studied rural boys and girls in grades 6 through 12. His self-report delinquency measure and questionnaire items were very similar to those devised by Hirschi. Hindelang found few differences between his results and those of Hirschi. Two of those differences, however, were significant. First, he found no relationship between attachment to mother and attachment to peers. Hirschi had observed a positive relationship (the stronger the attachment to the mother, the stronger the attachment to peers). Second, involvement in delinquency was positively related to attachment to peers.[53] Hirschi had found an inverse relationship (the stronger the attachment to peers, the less the involvement in delinquency).

Social control theory places a good deal of emphasis on family relationships. Support for this connection comes from a study conducted with Edmonton youth, which reports that boys who found their families attractive and who wanted to please their parents were less likely to engage in delinquency than were boys who did not share these close ties to their parents.[54] In another study from the same city, the researchers found that parental attachment was the strongest predictor of delinquent or law-abiding behaviours.[55] It may be that teens who are attached to their parents have developed the social skills required to maintain positive relationships with a variety of people, which in turn insulates them from life stress.[56] However, the type of peers an individual is attached to may influence the direction of behaviour, prosocial or antisocial. As Leslie Samuelson, Timothy Hartnagel, and Harvey Krahn found in their study of school dropouts, attachment to deviant peers helps motivate dropouts to commit crime. In others words, attachment to deviant peers facilitates delinquent behaviours.[57]

Some researchers influenced by social control theory have focused their research efforts on the nature of parental relationships and parenting style. Research conducted in Edmonton and Montreal has found that supervision is the family variable most strongly related to delinquency.[58] The National Longitudinal Survey of Children and Youth (NLSCY), which is following the development of more than 23 000 children, revealed that children exposed to ineffective or hostile parenting in 1994 and 1996 are nine times more likely to have behavioural problems than children exposed to effective parenting styles.[59] John Hagan and Bill McCarthy, in their study of homeless youth in Toronto, found that abusive parents contribute to delinquency by making life at home unbearable for some youth, forcing them onto the street to

Girl Guide groups across the country teach their young members positive values and the importance of structured activities.

Are Human Beings Inherently Bad?

One of the most notable distinctions between Hirschi's social control theory and other criminological theories that explain delinquency is the assumption made about human nature. It is most apparent when we compare social control theory to Merton's theory of anomie. Merton argues that individuals commit crimes when they experience strain as a result of their inability to meet society's goals with the resources available to them. Merton thus assumes that humans do not have a natural tendency to engage in offending behaviour, but that it is strain that causes them to do so. Social control theory, on the other hand, makes the opposite assumption. Hirschi argues that individuals will engage in crime and delinquency unless they are bonded to society in four ways: attachment to family, peers, and school; commitment to conventional goals; involvement in conventional activities; and belief in the legitimacy of society's laws and norms. In other words, human beings are inherently criminal. Social control theory thus explains what prevents individuals from committing crimes rather than what causes them to commit crimes.

Although research provides support for the idea that individuals with strong social bonds are less likely to engage in crime and delinquency,(1) it is impossible to test Hirschi's underlying assumption about human nature because we cannot examine human behaviour in a vacuum, removed from all social and environmental influences. The best we can do is speculate on the question based on knowledge about patterns of juvenile delinquency and criminal offending.

The most convincing argument in support of Hirschi's assumption is one that is often used to criticize other theories of delinquency. This argument points out that not all individuals who experience "causes" of crime, such as economic stress or educational failure, engage in delinquency. Some individuals who are exposed to risk factors commit crimes while others do not. A good theory of crime must explain why this happens. Social control theory is consistent with this line of thinking because it is based on the idea that there are no causes of crime—that all humans will commit crime unless they are adequately bonded to society. Thus, the behaviour of individuals who are exposed to the "causes" alleged by other scholars but do not commit crimes can be explained by stronger social bonds among these individuals.

On the other hand, a similar type of argument can be made against Hirschi's assumption about human nature. If all human beings will commit crimes without social bonds, then why don't all juveniles with weak bonds engage in delinquency? And why do some juveniles with strong bonds engage in delinquency? Studies show that college students engage in illegal behaviours.(2) How can this be explained? Arguably, these students have relatively strong social bonds. The fact that they are in college suggests that they at least have a commitment to conventional aspirations. We could also ask why some offenders engage in some types of criminal activities but refrain from others. Evidence indicates that although juvenile offenders tend to engage in a variety of offences, offence specialization increases with age.(3) Offence specialization is inconsistent with Hirschi's assumption about human nature. If humans have an inherent predisposition toward criminal behaviour, then offenders should not be selective about their criminal endeavours. In contrast, they should have a natural tendency toward all types of crime.

Sources

1. Stephen Demuth and Susan L. Brown, "Family Structure, Family Processes, and Adolescent Delinquency: The Significance of Parental Absence versus Parental Gender," *Journal of Research in Crime and Delinquency*, **41**(1), 2004: 58–81; Wendy D. Manning and Kathleen A. Lamb, "Adolescent Well-Being in Cohabiting, Married, and Single-Parent Families," *Journal of Marriage and Family,* **65** 2003: 876–893.
2. R. Tewksbury and E. E. Mustaine, "Lifestyles of the Wheelers and Dealers: Drug Dealing Among American College Students," *Journal of Crime and Justice,* **21**(2), 1998: 37–56.
3. Alex Piquero, Raymond Paternoster, Paul Mazerolle, Robert Brame, and Charles W. Dean, "Onset Age and Offence Specialization," *Journal of Research in Crime and Delinquency,* **36**(3), 1999: 275–299.

Questions for Debate

1. Do you think humans have an inherent inclination to commit crimes? Explain why or why not.
2. What are the implications of your perspective for crime prevention initiatives and laws? What is the best way to reduce crime?

escape the abuse. Once on the street, these youth are forced into delinquency out of necessity.[60]

Other researchers have focused on different aspects of the bond. In one study, criminologists administered a self-report questionnaire to 3056 male and female students. The researchers were critical of Hirschi's conceptualization of both commitment and involvement, finding it difficult to understand how he separated the two. Serious involvement, they argued, is quite unlikely without

commitment. They combined commitment and involvement items and ended up with only three bonds: attachment, commitment, and belief.[61]

The study related these bonds to alcohol and marijuana use, use of strong drugs, minor delinquent behaviour, and serious delinquent behaviour. The results suggested that strong social bonds were more highly correlated with less-serious deviance than with such delinquent acts as motor vehicle theft and assault. Also, the social bonds were more predictive of deviance in girls than in boys. Moreover, criminologists who conducted this study noticed that the commitment bond (now joined with involvement) was more significantly correlated with delinquent behaviour than were attachment and belief.

Other researchers administered questionnaires to 2213 grade 10 boys at 86 schools, seeking to answer three questions: First, are Hirschi's four bonds distinct entities? Second, why did Hirschi name only four bonds? Third, why were some factors that are related to educational and occupational aspiration (such as ability and family socioeconomic status) omitted from his questionnaire? The researchers constructed new scales for measuring attachment, commitment, involvement, and belief. They used a self-report measure to assess delinquency. These researchers found little that is independent or distinctive about any of the bonds.[62]

Robert Agnew provided the first longitudinal test of Hirschi's theory by using data on 1886 boys in grades 10 and 11. Eight social control scales (parental attachment, grades, dating index, school attachment, involvement, commitment, peer attachment, and belief) were examined at two periods in relation to two self-report scales (one measuring total delinquency and the other measuring seriousness of delinquency). Agnew found the eight control scales to be strongly correlated with the self-reported delinquency, but the social control measures did little to predict the extent of future delinquency reported at the second testing. Agnew concluded that the importance of Hirschi's control theory has probably been exaggerated.[63]

Most of the recent empirical work on Hirschi's theory explores the relationship between social bonds and other competing theories.[64] Researchers have discovered that the explanatory power of social control theory is enhanced dramatically when joined with other structural and process theories.

Evaluation: Hirschi's Social Control Theory

While social control theory has held a prominent position in criminology for several decades, it is not without weaknesses. For example, social control theory seeks to explain delinquency, not adult crime. It concerns attitudes, beliefs, desires, and behaviours that, though deviant, are often characteristic of adolescents. This is unfortunate because there has long been evidence that social bonds are also significant explanatory factors in post-adolescent behaviour.[65]

Questions also have been raised about the bonds. Hirschi claims that antisocial acts result from a lack of affective values, beliefs, norms, and attitudes that inhibit delinquency. But these terms are never clearly defined.[66] Critics have also faulted Hirschi's work for other reasons:

- Having too few questionnaire items that measure social bonds
- Failing to describe the chain of events that results in defective or inadequate bonds
- Creating an artificial division of socialized versus unsocialized youths
- Suggesting that social control theory explains why delinquency occurs, when in fact it typically explains no more than 50 percent of delinquent behaviour and only 1 to 2 percent of the variance in future delinquency[67]

Questions have also been raised about the application of social control theory to female criminality. Hirschi and others have been faulted for not looking explicitly at sex differences in the degree of adherence to social bonds and how this may help explain gender differences in criminal behaviours.[68] It is particularly useful to apply social control theory to female criminality since females, as we have seen, commit far fewer crimes than males, and their offences tend to be less serious. Social control theory prompts us to ask why this is the case? Is it possible that girls are controlled differently than boys, and women differently from men? How does social control operate to influence the different offending patterns of the genders?

We might want to assume, for the sake of exploring social control as it relates to women, that women's higher rate of conformity (and lower rate of criminality) implies they have stronger attachments to conventional society: They are more "socially controlled." In addition, girls and young women tend to experience higher levels of parental supervision than boys, thus contributing to higher levels of social control. John Hagan, A. R. Gillis, and John Simpson build on this type of reasoning in their extension to social control theory. Their power control theory (discussed in Chapter 8) combines socially structured differences in sex roles with parental supervision and occupation in an explanation of delinquency. Essentially, their argument is that in some types of families parents are more likely to place more stringent controls on daughters in comparison to sons, which results in lower delinquency rates for girls.[69]

Feminist research and theorizing by Merry Morash, Meda Chesney-Lind, and Randall Shelden introduces the concept of *ethic of care* as a means of explaining female criminality among girls and young women. Ethic of care refers to strong bonds created through nurturing between parent and child. Children raised in an ethic of care develop identities that involve concern for others; those who are strongly bonded to parents will exhibit higher rates of conformity. These researchers explain female delinquency as the outcome of situations of family-related sexual abuse where girls and women are doing the caring but are not cared for or about. Girls in these situations might attempt to escape the abuse by running away from home, which places them in vulnerable situations (living on the street, becoming involved in prostitution) and increases their risk of involvement with the criminal justice system.[70]

Marge Reitsma-Street found that female offenders are primarily those young women who resist caring and put themselves first. Tired of forfeiting their own physical, psychological, social, and economic needs for others, some girls struggle against caring for others more than themselves. However, those who resist the expectations others have of them risk various techniques of regulation or social control. Increasing in level of intensity, these techniques include judgments of the girl's reputation (e.g., being called a slut when she breaks up with a boyfriend), physical force or the threat of it from men in her life, and involvement with the justice system. Girls experience strong pressure to conform to stereotypes of what a nurturing, caring young woman should be; should she resist, there is social control of various levels of intensity in place to encourage her to rethink her non-conformity:[71]

> Acts of resistance are interpreted by parents, teachers, and others in authority as signs of disturbance. The girls who undertake them are seen as needing help, protection, or correction—anything that will enable them "to act like a normal girl."[72]

Official statistics show support for this line of theorizing: Judges and criminal justice system personnel over the years have tended to be more lenient with girls who commit common delinquencies such as theft than with girls who exhibit independence though such actions as running away from home or a group home.[73]

Related to the suggestion that norms concerning appropriate behaviours for females are more stringent and restrictive than those for males, research findings indicate that girls and women are more susceptible to the threat of shame—an informal social control—than are males. Brenda Sims Blackwell suggests that this finding holds regardless of family type, providing evidence that shame may be an important control factor for girls in general.[74]

Reacting to theories that locate female conformity in traditional gender role socialization, feminist scholar Ngaire Naffine suggests that women are bonded to conventional society, in the realm of family and child-care, but also increasingly in the workforce. In other words, "liberated" women who work outside the home rather than becoming more criminal, as some theorists suggest, actually continue in their conformity. In fact, they may become more conforming as their involvement in their careers increases. Why? Quite simply, they stand to lose a great deal by deviating from law-abiding behaviour.[75] Not only do they risk losing family and children, but they risk losing a job and career. In other words, modern women, involved in both work and childrearing, are powerfully attached to conventional society. This may help to explain the lower crime rates for women. Crime is irrational behaviour when one has a great deal to lose by being thrown in jail. Nonetheless, this line of research has yet to be more fully explored. Generally, control theorists have tended to neglect the issue of gender differences in social control and crime.

Despite the criticisms, Hirschi's work has made a major contribution to criminology. The mere fact that a quarter-century of scholars have tried to validate and replicate it testifies to its importance. Hirschi's conception of social bonds has complemented competing explanations of group-level criminality such as gang behaviour (see discussion of subcultural theories in Chapter 6). Social control is now discussed in relation to community, family, school, peer group, and individual-level factors (see Table 7.2).

SOCIAL CONTROL AND DRIFT

In the 1960s, David Matza developed a different perspective on social control that explains why some adolescents drift in and out of delinquency. According to Matza, juveniles sense a moral obligation to be bound by the law. A "bind" between a person and the law, something that creates responsibility and control, remains in place most of the time. When it is not in place, the youth may enter into a state of **drift,** or a period when he or she exists in limbo between convention and crime, responding

TABLE 7.2 Risk Factors for Youth Gang Membership
How powerful is social control theory? Consider the premise of this theory in relation to the risk factors for gang membership.

Domain	Risk Factors
Community	Social disorganization, including poverty and residential mobility Organized lower-class communities Underclass communities Presence of gangs in the neighbourhood Availability of drugs in the neighbourhood Availability of firearms Barriers to and lack of social and economic opportunities Lack of social capital Cultural norms supporting gang behaviour Feeling unsafe in neighbourhood; high crime Conflict with social control institutions
Family	Family disorganization, including broken homes and parental drug/alcohol abuse Troubled families, including incest, family violence, and drug addiction Family members in a gang Lack of adult male role models Lack of parental role models Low socioeconomic status Extreme economic deprivation, family management problems, parents with violent attitudes, sibling antisocial behaviour
School	Academic failure Low educational aspirations, especially among females Negative labelling by teachers Trouble at school Few teacher role models Educational frustration Low commitment to school, low school attachment, high levels of antisocial behaviour in school, low achievement test cores, and identification as being learning disabled
Peer group	High commitment to delinquent peers Low commitment to positive peers Street socialization Gang members in class Friends who use drugs or who are gang members Friends who are drug distributors Interaction with delinquent peers
Individual	Prior delinquency Deviant attitudes Street smartness; toughness Defiant and individualistic character Fatalistic view of the world Aggression Proclivity for excitement and trouble *Locura* (acting in a daring, courageous, and especially crazy fashion in the face of adversity) Higher levels of normlessness in the context of family, peer group, and school Social disabilities Illegal gun ownership Early or precocious sexual activity, especially among females Alcohol and drug use Drug trafficking Desire for group rewards, such as status, identity, self-esteem, companionship, and protection Problem behaviours, hyperactivity, externalizing behaviours, drinking, lack of refusal skills, and early sexual activity Victimization

Source: James C. *Howell, Youth Gangs: An Overview* (Washington, D.C.: U.S. Department of Justice, 1998).

in turn to the demands of each, flirting now with one, now with the other, but postponing commitment, evading decision. Thus, the person drifts between criminal and conventional actions.[76]

If adolescents are indeed bound by the social order, how do they justify their delinquent acts? The answer is that they develop techniques to rationalize their actions. These techniques are defence mechanisms that release the youth from the constraints of the moral order:

- Denial of responsibility. ("It wasn't my fault; I was a victim of circumstances.")

- Denial of injury. ("No one was hurt, and they have insurance, so what's the problem?")

- Denial of the victim. ("Anybody would have done the same thing in my position—I did what I had to do given the situation.")

- Condemnation of the condemner. ("I bet the judge and everyone on the jury has done much worse than what I was arrested for.")

- Appeal to higher loyalties. ("My friends were depending on me and I see them every day—what was I supposed to do?")[77]

Empirical support for drift theory has not been clear. Some studies show that delinquents consider these rationalizations valid,[78] while other research suggests that they do not. More recent investigations also demonstrate that delinquents do not share the moral code or values of non-delinquents.[79]

RECENT THEORETICAL EXPLORATIONS

Over the past several years, a number of attempts have been made to reconceptualize social control by joining, merging, and testing of different theoretical hypotheses and propositions.[80] As Table 7.3 reveals, theoretical criminologists have relied on social control theory to propose developmental, integrated, and general theories of crime.

Developmental/Life Course Theory

All developmental theories share one thing in common: explanations for why offending starts (onset), why it continues (continuance), why it becomes more frequent or serious (escalation), why it de-escalates (de-escalation), and why, inevitably, it stops (desistance). Rather than focusing exclusively on childhood, adolescence, young adulthood, or adulthood, these theories consider each developmental period in relation to the life span of an offender. In an extension of Hirschi's theory to the "life course," for example, Robert J. Sampson and John H. Laub found that family, school, and peer attachments were most strongly associated with delinquency from childhood to adolescence (through

TABLE 7.3 Examples of Recent Theoretical Explanations

Life Course/Developmental Theory	
Farrington	A combination of multiple personal (e.g., impulsivity), social (e.g., poor parental supervision), and environmental (e.g., low income) factors are associated with crime over the course of a lifetime.
Thornberry	Crime is a function of a dynamic social process that is determined by learning variables (e.g., association with delinquent peers), boundary variables (e.g., attachment and commitment to conventional activities), as well as social class, race, and gender.
Moffitt	Life-course-persistent offending is explained by faulty interactions between children and their parents, resulting in poor self-control and impulsivity. Adolescent-limited offending is traced to social mimicry, antisocial reinforcements, and models.
LeBlanc	An integrative, multilayered control theory that borrows heavily from competing perspectives explains criminality, the criminal, and the criminal event in both static and developmental terms.
Laub and Sampson	Crime causation must be viewed developmentally—in the context of the turning points in a criminal career.
Integrated Theory	
Weis	Crime results from an interaction between diminished social controls and influences from delinquent peers.
Elliott	Delinquency is traced to strain, weak social bonds, and deviant subcultures.
General Theory	
Hirschi and Gottfredson	Individual differences in crime commission may be attributed to levels of self-control.
Agnew	Individual differences in offending behaviour can be explained by interactions between five clusters of causes (self, family, peer group, work, and school).

age 17).[81] From the transition to young adulthood through the transition to middle adulthood, attachment to work (job stability) and family (marriage) appears most strongly related to crime causation. Sampson and Laub found evidence that these positive personal and professional relationships build a "social capital" in otherwise vulnerable individuals that significantly inhibits deviance over time.

Another life-course theory combines control with learning theory (see Chapter 4). Terence Thornberry argues that the potential for delinquency begins with the weakening of a person's bonds to the conventional world (parents, school, and accepted values). For this potential to be realized, there must be a social setting in which to learn delinquent values. In this setting, delinquents seek each other out and form common belief systems. There is nothing

Hobbema RCMP officer Doug Reti speaks hopefully about the addition of nine additional officers to the detachment. Hobbema, Alberta, is a reserve that is known for gang violence. In an effort to provide Aboriginal youth in the community with an alternative to gang involvement, RCMP officers started the Hobbema Community Cadet Corps, which emphasizes discipline, structure, and a feeling of belonging for Aboriginals. A prerequisite for participating is school attendance. By its second year of operation, the Cadet Corps had over 900 members.

static about this kind of learning. Criminality, according to Thornberry, is a function of a dynamic social process that changes over time.[82]

David Farrington's work with the data from the Cambridge Study of Delinquent Development reveals different explanations for the general tendency to engage in crime (long-term variables) over time, as well as the influences that prompt an individual, at any given time, to engage in crime (short-term variables) (see Table 7.3 on page 175). The former include impulsivity, low empathy, and belief systems favourable to law violation. The latter consider momentary opportunities and situationally induced motivating factors, such as alcohol consumption and boredom.[83]

In one of the most elegant developmental theories to date, Marc LeBlanc employs social control theory to provide both static (pertaining to a particular time and place) and dynamic (occurring over time) explanations of criminality (the total number of infractions), the criminal (personal characteristics of an offender), and the crime (the criminal event). To construct his models, LeBlanc borrows from a host of disciplines (see Figure 7.3).

Integrated Theory

Integrated theory combines a criminological theory, such as differential association, with a number of social controls. Delbert Elliott and his colleagues have integrated the social bonds of Hirschi's theory of social control with strain theories. These researchers suggest that limited or blocked opportunities and a subsequent failure to achieve cultural goals would weaken or even destroy bonds to the

FIGURE 7.3 Control theory at the level of the criminality.

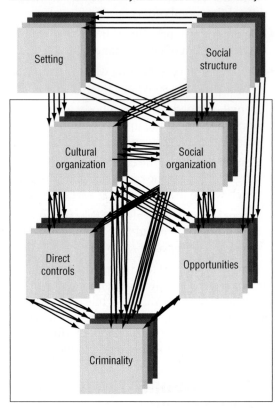

Source: Marc LeBlanc, "A Generic Control Theory of the Criminal Phenomenon: The Structural and Dynamic Statements of an Integrative Multilayered Control Theory," in *Developmental Theories of Crime and Delinquency: Advances in Criminological Theory*, vol. 7, T. P. Thornberry, ed. (New Brunswick, NJ: Transaction, 1997), p.238. Copyright © 1997 by Transaction Publishers. Reprinted by permission of the publisher.

conventional or social order. In other words, even if someone establishes strong bonds in childhood, a series of negative experiences in school, in the community, and at home, along with blocked access to opportunity, would be likely to lead to a weakening of those social bonds. As strain weakens social bonds, the chance of delinquency increases.[84]

Joseph Weis has proposed a social development model of crime, which is an elegant integration of social control and social learning theory. He proposes that delinquency is minimized when youths who are at risk to commit crime have the opportunity to engage in conforming activities and are rewarded for doing so. Consistent reinforcement maximizes the social bonds, which, in turn, diminish associations with delinquent peers and reduce crime.[85]

General Theories

In *A General Theory of Crime*, Travis Hirschi and Michael Gottfredson propose a new model of personal and social control—one designed to explain an individual's propensity to commit crime.[86] Hirschi and Gottfredson claim that their model, unlike earlier conceptualizations, explains the tendency to commit all crimes, from crimes of violence such as robbery and sexual assault to white-collar offences such as mail fraud and federal securities violations.[87]

This "general theory" of propensity to commit crimes, shown in Figure 7.4, assumes that offenders have little control over their own behaviour and desires. When the need for momentary pleasure and immediate gratification outweighs long-term interests, crime occurs. In short, crime is a function of poor self-control.

What leads to poor self-control? Inadequate socialization and poor childrearing practices, coupled with poor attachment, increase the probability of impulsive and uncontrolled acts. According to Hirschi and Gottfredson, individuals with low self-control also tend to be involved in non-criminal events that result in harm, such as drinking, smoking, and most types of accidents, including auto crashes, household fires, and unwanted pregnancies.

Evidence in support of this theory is mixed. Recent studies have shown that low self-control is linked to violent offending, homicide victimization, and delinquent behaviour and that the link holds across different genders, races, and cultures.[88] Canadian researchers have explored the link between self-control and criminal behaviours and have found mixed evidence for the relationship. In Quebec, Marc LeBlanc found that young people with "egocentric personalities," essentially a type of low self-control, have weaker social bonds and higher levels of delinquency than other youth of the same age.[89] In Edmonton, Teresa LaGrange and Robert Silverman found that self-control explained part of the difference in delinquent behaviours between males and

females.[90] While there is support for the theory, other research suggests that self-control is just one of several psychological traits that should be considered in a more comprehensive theory of criminal behaviour. One study found, however, that the effect of parental efficacy on delinquency is primarily due to factors other than self-control.[91] LaGrange and Silverman and others suggest that self-control provides a partial explanation for certain crimes, and certainly not all crimes. In other words, this "general theory of crime" may do a better job of explaining certain types of crimes than others.

Robert Agnew has recently developed another general theory of crime. In his theory, Agnew combines the main arguments from social control, social learning, self-control, strain, labelling, social support, and biopsychological theories to explain the major parameters of criminal offending. The crux of his argument is that causes of crime can be grouped into five clusters (self, family, peer group, work, and school) that interact in complex ways to influence offending behaviour.[92]

It is important to remember that all of these recent explanations of criminality share one common variable—the social bonds that are at the foundation of social control theory. The ingredients of social control theory have been used quite effectively over the last decade as building blocks for these recent developments.

THEORY INFORMS POLICY

Social control theory tells us that people commit crimes when they have not developed adequate attachments, have not become involved in and committed to conventional activities, and have not internalized the rules of society (or do not care about them). Efforts to prevent crime must therefore include the teaching of conventional values. It is also necessary to find ways to strengthen individual bonds to society, commitment to the conventional order, and involvement in conventional activities. One way is to strengthen the institutions that socialize people and continue to regulate their behaviour throughout life—the family, the school, and the workplace.[93]

The Community Solution to Gang Violence (CSGV) in Edmonton, Alberta, is an initiative comprised of a diverse group of private citizens, community organizations, and all levels of government, working collaboratively on a strategic, community-wide approach to gang violence.[94]

FIGURE 7.4   The Hirschi-Gottfredson self-control model. Hirschi and Gottfredson's model assumes that poor self-control is an intervening variable that explains all crime, as well as differences in crime rates, by age, gender, and race.

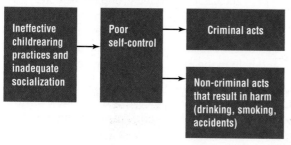

Nations with Low Crime Rates

Most criminologists devote their efforts to learning why people commit crime and why there is so much crime. A few have looked at the question from the opposite perspective: In places with little crime, what accounts for the low crime rate? Using the United Nations' first World Crime Survey (1970–1975), Freda Adler studied the two countries with the lowest crime rates in each of five general cultural regions of the world:(1)

Western Europe: Switzerland and the Republic of Ireland

Eastern Europe: The former German Democratic Republic (East Germany) and Bulgaria

Arab countries: Saudi Arabia and Algeria

Asia: Japan and Nepal

Latin America: Costa Rica and Peru(2)

This is an odd assortment of countries. They seem to have little in common. Some are democratic, others authoritarian. Some are republics, others monarchies. Some were ruled by dictators, others by communal councils. Some are rural, others highly urbanized. Some are remote and isolated;

Workers in Japan showing solidarity in an early morning exercise ritual.

others are in the political mainstream. Some are highly religious, some largely atheistic. Some have a very high standard of living, others a very low one. What explains their common characteristic of low crime rates?

Investigations slowly revealed a common factor in all ten countries: Each appeared to have an intact social control system, quite apart from whatever formal control system (law enforcement) it had.

The objectives of the initiative, informed by social control theory, are to:

- Enhance a sense of community responsibility and commitment to address gang violence
- Promote positive youth development and develop conditions to prevent young people from becoming involved in gangs
- Create a community-wide plan and network of support to find solutions to gang violence

The project participants and organizers subscribe to the notion that while the police and the justice system play a major role in the enforcement and suppression of gang violence, it is the community that is best positioned to address the underlying causes of gang violence and mobilize people to take measures to prevent young people from being drawn into gangs. The initiative has grown and now includes close to 100 individuals representing over 40 community agencies. The ultimate

goal is to strengthen community social institutions and to build bonds between these institutions, and between individuals in order to provide the kind of environment that will prevent involvement of young people in crime and in gangs.

Comprised of a steering committee, a project manager who oversees, organizes, and directs all activities of the project, an evaluation team whose mandate is to track the changes effected by the initiative, and four working groups that meet individually to work on specific goals, the CSGV has been expanding and evolving since its inception in 2003. Each working group focuses on goals specific to its domain, striving to increase awareness and promote policies and programs that directly affect at-risk youth and their families and help in the prevention of gang involvement.

Government and Policy Group This group of community members has as its mandate infrastructure, research, and policy impacting the

Here are brief descriptions of the types of social control systems identified:

Western Europe: Switzerland fostered a strong sense of belonging to and participating in the local community.(3) The family was still strong in the Republic of Ireland, and it was strengthened by shared religious values.

Eastern Europe: The former German Democratic Republic involved all youths in communal activities, organized by groups and aimed at having young people excel for the glory of self and country. In Bulgaria, industrialization focused on regional industry centres so that the workers would not be dislodged from their hometowns, which served as continuing social centres.

Arab countries: Islam continued to be strong as a way of life and exercised a powerful influence on daily activities, especially in Saudi Arabia. Algeria had, in addition, a powerful commitment to socialism in its post-independence era, involving the citizens in all kinds of commonly shared development activities.

Asia: Nepal retained its strong family and clan ties, augmented by councils of elders that oversaw the community and resolved problems. Highly industrialized Japan had lost some of the social controls of family and kinship, but it found a substitute family in the industrial community, to which most Japanese belonged: Mitsubishi might now be the family that guides one's every step.

Latin America: Costa Rica spent all the funds that other governments devoted to the military on social services and social development, caring for and strengthening its families. Peru went through a process of urbanization in stages: Village and family cohesion marked the lives of people in the countryside, and this cohesion remained with the people as they migrated from Andean villages to smaller towns and then to the big city, where they were received by and lived surrounded by others from their own hometowns.

The study concluded that **synnomie,** a term derived from the Greek *syn* meaning "with" and *nomos* meaning "norms," marked societies with low crime rates.

Sources

1. United Nations, *Report of the Secretary General on Crime Prevention and Control*, A/32/199 (popularly known as the First U.N. World Crime Survey) (New York: United Nations, 1977).
2. Freda Adler, *Nations Not Obsessed with Crime* (Littleton, CO: Fred B. Rothman, 1983).
3. Marshall B. Clinard, *Cities with Little Crime: The Case of Switzerland* (Cambridge, MA: Cambridge University Press, 1978).

Questions for Discussion

1. People in North America work in factories, live in family groups, go to church, and join youth groups. Why do these institutions not function effectively as forms of social control to keep the crime rate low?
2. How could government or community decision makers use the information presented by this study to help solve crime problems in Canada?

---

prevention and intervention of gang violence and the promotion of positive youth development. The group is bringing organizations and government together to develop policies, programs, and services for the prevention, intervention, and suppression of gang violence.

Community Awareness Group Working to provide information to increase the community's understanding of gangs and gang activity, this group has developed bridges and working relationships with a variety of community agencies. Information about the dynamics, conditions and realities of gangs drawn from other working groups, law enforcement officials, field workers, and government is integrated and then provided to citizens in the city so the community can engage in action.

Early Intervention Group This working group actively promotes and supports positive family communication and healthy family development

with the ultimate goal of preventing children from being drawn into gangs. An example of the kinds of programs the early intervention group supports and promotes are similar to the experimental school-based parent training programs offered in many U.S. states. The major premise of these programs is that a child's bond to a family is crucial. To develop this bond, parents learn to provide opportunities to help the child participate and succeed in a social unit such as the school (e.g., by demonstrating good study habits) and to reinforce conformity or punish violations of the group's norms. Results suggest that these initiatives decrease children's aggressiveness and increase parental skills.[95]

Youth Group Made up of young people whose voice is an integral part of the initiative, this group provides support for youth to avoid the drug/gang lifestyle and opportunities for positive engagement in the environments surrounding young people (school, clubs organizations, community, work settings). The group is building relationships with young people and youth service organizations to create a network of support.

Currently, the working groups are creating a strategy to reduce risk factors among youth. There is considerable evidence that the most effective approach for preventing young people from becoming involved with gangs is to reduce risk factors associated with risk-taking behaviours and increase the protective factors around young people that promote positive, healthy development. Risk factors are the conditions in the individual and the social environment that predict an increased likelihood of engaging in risk-taking behaviours such as gang involvement, while protective factors are conditions that buffer or moderate the effects of risks or increase resistance to them.

A similar initiative has recently begun in Saskatoon, Saskatchewan.

Do you recall the opening segment to this chapter? The excerpt from *Lord of the Flies* illustrates the importance of norms and rules to govern human behaviour. Are norms and rules enough? Having read this chapter, how would you answer this question? What encourages people to conform to rules? How is social control created and enforced?

REVIEW

1. What are the controlling forces in our lives?

The term "social control" has taken on a wide variety of meanings. In general, it describes any mechanism that leads to **conformity** (p. 167) to social norms. Theorists such as Cohen, Foucault, and Garland provide explanations of the ways in which historical, systemic changes have influenced the nature of society's control over individuals.

2. How do social control theories explain criminal behaviour at both the microsociological and macrosociological levels?

Mainstream studies of social control take one of two approaches. **Macrosociological studies** (p. 160) focus on formal systems of social control. **Social disorganization theory** (p. 160) focuses on the breakdown of social institutions as a precondition for the establishment of criminal norms. **Cultural transmission** (p. 163) refers to the manner in which delinquency is learned and passed on from one generation to the next in disorganized urban areas.

3. How do external and internal structures insulate people from delinquency?

Most investigators today believe that personal (inner) controls are as important as social (external) controls in keeping people from committing crimes. Albert Reiss found that personal controls reinforce social controls. Jackson Toby stressed the importance of a stake in conformity in keeping a person from responding to social disorganization with delinquent behaviour. According to the **containment theory** (p. 167) of Walter Reckless, every person has a containing external structure (a role in a social group with reasonable limits and responsibilities and alternative means of attaining satisfaction). In addition, each individual has a protective internal structure that depends on a good self-concept, self-control, a well-developed conscience, a tolerance for frustration, and a strong sense of responsibility. Nye argued that **internalized control** (p. 167), or self-regulation, was a product of guilt aroused in the conscience when norms have been internalized. **Indirect control** (p. 167) comes from an individual's identification with law-abiding citizens. **Direct control** (p. 167) depends on rules, restrictions, and punishments.

4. Is it possible for individuals to "drift" into and out of criminal behaviour?

Most contemporary criminological research takes the **microsociological approach** (p. 160), which focuses on informal systems. Travis Hirschi's **social control theory** (p. 158) has had a long-lasting impact on the scholarly community. Hirschi identified four social bonds that promote adherence to society's values: **attachment** (p. 168), **commitment** (p. 169), **involvement** (p. 169), and **belief** (p. 170). The stronger these bonds, Hirschi claimed, the less the likelihood of delinquency. When the "bind" between a person and the law falters, a person might **drift** (p. 173) between convention and crime. One study found that societies with low crime rates seem to have **synnomie** (p. 179).

5. How has social control influenced recent theoretical developments?

Recent efforts to integrate social control theories with other theories have resulted in developmental, integrated, and general theories of crime. All share one common variable—the social bonds that constitute social control theory.

As part of an effort to reduce delinquency, a variety of programs at the local and regional levels help parents, schools, and neighbourhood groups develop social controls.

CRIMINOLOGY & PUBLIC POLICY

In recent years, lawmakers in both Canada and the United States have initiated and in many instances passed legislation increasing penalties for criminal offences, particularly violent crimes. These actions came in response to public concerns about crime and the belief that many serious offenders are released from prison too soon. In the United States, many such laws have come under the general label of "three strikes and you're out."

In Canada, the federal government, under the leadership of Stephen Harper, is moving toward similar legislation. In the fall of 2006, the government tabled a Canadian version of the American "three-strikes" law, which proposed that an offender who commits three sex offences or other violent crimes be presumed to be a dangerous offender unless that person can convince a judge otherwise. Such offenders receive an indeterminate sentence and are not eligible for parole for at least seven years. Furthermore, they could have certain restrictions and conditions added upon release.

The proposed bill became law on February 28, 2008. The purpose of such laws is simple: Offenders repeatedly convicted of serious offences should be removed from society for long periods of time, in many cases for life. In social control theory terms, such laws reflect a belief among lawmakers that after a certain point—in this case, after committing three serious crimes—individuals are clearly beyond social control. Canada currently has dangerous offender legislation, but the onus is on the prosecution to initiate the procedure that designates a serious offender as dangerous. The new law makes the label of dangerous offender easier to attach procedurally and places the responsibility on the accused to show why he or she should not be considered a dangerous offender. There are about 340 designated dangerous offenders in Canada.

Yet, at the same time that these types of "get tough" laws are being passed, there is also an effort to divert young people from the criminal justice system. Representative of similar programs across the country, the Durham Pre-Charge Diversion Program is the result of a partnership between the Durham Region Police Service, Eastview Boys and Girls Club, John Howard Society of Durham, and Pinewood Centre of Lakeridge Health Corporation. The preventive and rehabilitation program provides early intervention and meaningful consequences for youth who commit crimes, by diverting them from the formal court process to community programs. The goal is to help youth accept responsibility for their criminal behaviour and to make amends to victims. The program focuses on giving youth a second chance by keeping them out of the criminal justice system. However, it also works to increase the supports and opportunities for young people to bond to conventional society, learn to make better choices, and avoid criminal behaviour in the future. As one of the individuals involved in the Durham program states:

> Research in the area of youth justice tells us that providing community-based programs that are meaningful to youth—and hold them accountable for their actions—steer them away from crime. That's why we are investing in these programs and services that give troubled youth a better opportunity to succeed and become productive members of society.

Three-strikes legislation and the pre-charge diversion offer two different perspectives on the issue of crime control and social control. The former seems to offer little hope for offenders who lack bonds to society; the other attempts to "catch" offenders early in their careers and make a difference in their lives. Each focuses on a different aspect of the criminal career—and raises interesting questions about the importance of social controls to criminal behaviour. (*Sources:* John Clark, James Austin, and D. Alan Henry, *Three Strikes and You're Out: A Review of State Legislation* [Washington, D.C.: NIJ, 1997]; Janice Tibbetts, "Government to Deliver Canadian Version of 'Three-Strikes' Law," *CanWest News Service,* September 21, 2006, accessed at www.canada.com.)

Questions for Discussion Three-strikes laws can be harsh. In some jurisdictions in the United States, offenders committing petty thefts as their third strike may, for example, receive 25 or more years in prison, as courts and prosecutors take their prior record into consideration. What concerns with three-strikes laws are raised by recent extensions to Hirschi's notion of social control—life course theories of offending? If the fundamental rationale of three-strikes laws is to protect the community from habitual offenders, are life course theories supportive? If we know what best predicts future offending, and programs may be created to address these causal factors, why rely on long prison sentences?

YOU BE THE CRIMINOLOGIST

The desire for stability, involvement, belief, and conformity can have a dark side. Consider how mechanisms of social control, narrowly conceived, can support new religious, political, and psychosocial cults or sects. How does social control theory help explain the attraction to Heaven's Gate, the Order of the Solar Temple, or the Branch Davidians?

LABELLING, CONFLICT, RADICAL, AND FEMINIST THEORIES

CHAPTER **8**

CHAPTER QUESTIONS

1. How does labelling act as a type of control?

2. How are conflict theories different from the other theories we've looked at?

3. What is "radical" about radical theories?

4. How do criminologists explain female offending and victimization?

Investigators line up while searching for remains at Robert Pickton's former "Piggy Palace."

Robert Pickton was convicted of six counts of second degree murder in January 2008 and sentenced to 25 years in prison before being eligible for parole. He is suspected in the murders of at least another 20 sex trade workers from Eastside Vancouver. The murders are thought to have occurred between about 1995 and 2002.[1] Why did it take this long to apprehend him? Some criminologists would suggest that perhaps the occupation and social status of the victims affected the manner in which this case was handled. They encourage us to ask whether more resources and effort might have been spent on the case if the victims had been the daughters of wealthy corporate executives.

Doreen Leclair and Corrine McKeown were Métis sisters in their early 50s who lived in Winnipeg's north end. Over the course of an evening in 2000, problems erupted between the sisters and the boyfriend of one of them. After five phone calls to 911 in Winnipeg, in which the sisters called for assistance, all except the last of which were ignored, disregarded, or shuffled to other departments in the police service, both sisters died of stab wounds at the hands of the boyfriend.[2] Accusations ensued and it became obvious to many that the sisters had been labelled by social control agents as "just another couple of drunk Indians" living in a seedy part of town, notorious for its high Aboriginal population, its violence, and crime. As a result, their cries for help were put on the backburner, until it was too late.

Instances of labelling and the use of power to discriminate in the treatment of individuals were not really considered in criminology until the 1960s. It was only after the development of labelling, conflict, and critical theories that criminologists began to ponder the impact of inequalities in power and privilege on the manner in which the criminal justice system operated.

These criminologists turned away from theories that explained crime by characteristics of the offender or of the social structure. They set out to demonstrate that individuals become criminals because of what people with power, especially those in the criminal justice system, do. Their explanations largely reject the consensus model of crime, on which all earlier theories rested. Their theories not only question the traditional explanations of the creation and enforcement of criminal law but also blame that law for the making of criminals (see Table 8.1).

It may not sound so radical to assert that unless an act is made criminal by law, no person who performs that act can be adjudicated a criminal. The exponents of contemporary alternative explanations of crime grant that much. But, justifiably, they also ask, Who makes these laws in the first place? And why? Is breaking such laws the most important criterion for being a criminal? Are all people who break these laws criminals? Do all members of society agree that those singled out by the criminal law to be called "criminals" are criminals and that others are not? How do the powerful use the law to protect their interests? How are those lacking in power discriminated against through the passage and enforcement of laws?

TABLE 8.1 Comparison of Five Criminological Perspectives

Perspective	Origin of Criminal Law	Causes of Criminal Behaviour	Focus of Study
Traditional/consensus	Laws reflect shared values.	Psychological, biological, or sociological factors.	Psychological and biological factors (Chap.4); unequal opportunity (Chap. 5); learning criminal behaviour in disorganized neighbourhoods (Chap. 6, 7); subculture values (Chap. 6); social control (Chap. 7).
Labelling	Those in power create the laws, decide who will be the rule breakers.	The process that defines (or labels) certain persons as criminals.	Effects of stigmatization by the label "criminal"; sociopolitical factors behind reform legislation; origin of laws; deviant behaviour (Chap. 8.)
Conflict	Powerful groups use laws to support their interests.	Interests of one group do not coincide with needs of another.	Bias and discrimination in criminal justice system; differential crime rates of powerful and powerless; development of criminal laws by those in power; relationship between rulers and ruled (Chap. 8).
Feminist	Men use their power to create laws that reflect their interests.	Gender inequality.	Differential opportunities between the genders; gender and economic oppression of women by men; creation of laws that favour male interests; enforcement of laws that favour male interests; gendered nature of victimization (Chap. 8).
Radical (Marxist)	Laws serve interests of the ruling class.	Class struggle over distribution of resources in a capitalist system.	Relationship between crime and economics; ways in which state serves capitalist interests; solution to crime problem based on collapse of capitalism (Chap. 8).

LABELLING THEORY

The 1950s was a period of general prosperity and pride for North Americans. Yet some social scientists, uneasy about the complacency they saw, turned their attention to the social order. They noted that some of the ideals fought for in World War II had not been achieved at home. Human rights existed on paper but were often lacking in practice. The civil rights movement brought attention to the fact that blacks continued to live as second-class citizens; neither the law nor the socioeconomic system provided them with equal opportunities. Social scientists and liberal lawyers attacked the criminal justice system for violation of the concepts and principles of **due process,** under which a person cannot be deprived of life, liberty, or property without lawful procedures; and **equal protection,** under which no one can be denied the safeguards of the law.

In this social climate, a small group of social scientists, known as "labelling theorists," began to explore how and why certain acts were defined as criminal or, more broadly, as deviant behaviour and others were not, and how and why certain people were defined as criminal or deviant. These theorists viewed criminals not as inherently evil persons engaged in inherently wrong acts but, rather, as individuals who had had criminal status conferred upon them by both the criminal justice system and the community at large.

Viewed from this perspective, criminal acts themselves are not particularly significant; the social reaction to them, however, is. Deviance and its control involve a process of social definition in which the response of others to an individual's behaviour is the key influence on subsequent behaviour and on individuals' views of themselves. The sociologist Howard S. Becker has written:

> Deviance is not a quality of the act the person commits, but rather a consequence of the application by others of rules and sanctions to an "offender." The deviant is one to whom that label has successfully been applied; deviant behaviour is behaviour that people so label.[3]

In focusing on the ways in which social interactions create deviance, **labelling theory** declares that the reactions of other people and the subsequent effects of those reactions create deviance. Once it becomes known that a person has engaged in deviant acts, he or she is segregated from conventional society, and a label ("thief," "whore," "junkie") is attached to the transgressor. This process of segregation creates "outsiders" (as Becker called them), or outcasts from society, who begin to associate with others like themselves.[4]

As more people begin to think of these people as deviants and to respond to them accordingly, the deviants react to the response by continuing to engage in the behaviour society now expects of them. Through this process, their self-images gradually change as well. So the key factor is the label that is attached to an individual: "If men define situations as real, they are real in their consequences."[5]

The Origins of Labelling Theory

The intellectual roots of labelling theory can be traced to the work of Charles Horton Cooley, William I. Thomas, and George Herbert Mead. These scholars, who viewed the human self as formed through a process of social interaction, were called **symbolic interactionists.** These sociologists focused their attention on microsociological processes; they suggested that people construct their reality through face-to-face interactions. It is through our interactions with others that we learn the symbolic meanings of the world around us, learn how to assign meaning to objects and behaviours, and learn how to react to others. Part of this learning process includes learning labels, and how to label others. Mead, for example, compared the impact of social labelling to "the angel with the fiery sword at the gate who can cut one off from the world to which he belongs."[6]

Labelling separates the good from the bad, the conventional from the deviant. Mead's interest in deviance focused on the social interactions by which an individual becomes a deviant. The person is not just a fixed structure whose action is the result of certain factors acting upon it. Rather, social behaviour develops in a continuous process of action and reaction.[7] The way we perceive ourselves, our self-concept, is built not only on what we think of ourselves but also on what others think of us.

Somewhat later, the historian Frank Tannenbaum (1893–1969) used the same argument in his study of the causes of criminal behaviour. He described the creation of a criminal as a process: Breaking windows, climbing onto roofs, and playing truant are all normal parts of the adolescent search for excitement and adventure. Local merchants and others who experience these activities may consider them a nuisance or perhaps even evil. This conflict is the beginning of the process by which the evil act transforms the transgressor into an evil individual. From that point on, the evil individuals are separated from those in conventional society. Given a criminal label, they gradually begin to think of themselves as they have been officially defined.

Tannenbaum maintained that it is the process of labelling, or the "dramatization of evil," that locks a mischievous boy into a delinquent role ("the person becomes the thing he is described as being"). Accordingly, "the entire process of dealing with young delinquents is mischievous insofar as it identifies him to himself and to the environment as a delinquent person."[8] The system starts out with a child in trouble and ends up with a juvenile delinquent.

Basic Assumptions of Labelling Theory

In the 1940s, the sociologist Edwin Lemert elaborated on Tannenbaum's discussion by formulating the basic assumptions of labelling theory.[9] He reminded us that people are constantly involved in behaviour that runs the risk of being labelled delinquent or criminal. But although many run that risk, only a few are so labelled. The reason, Lemert contended, is that there are two kinds of deviant acts: primary and secondary.[10]

"Primary deviations" are the initial deviant acts that bring on the first social response. These acts do not affect the individual's self-concept. It is the "secondary deviations," the acts that follow the societal response to the primary deviation, that are of major concern. These are the acts that result from the change in self-concept brought about by the labelling process.[11] The scenario goes somewhat like this:

1. An individual commits a simple deviant act (primary deviation)—throwing a stone at a neighbour's car, for instance.
2. There is an informal social reaction: The neighbour gets angry.
3. The individual continues to break rules (primary deviations)—he lets the neighbour's dog out of the yard.
4. There is increased, but still primary, social reaction: The neighbour tells the youth's parents.

5. The individual commits a more serious deviant act—he is caught shoplifting (still primary deviation).

6. There is a formal reaction: The youth is adjudicated a "young offender" in youth court.

7. The youth is now labelled an "offender" by the court and "bad" by the neighbourhood, by his conventional peers, and by others.

8. The youth begins to think of himself as an "offender"; he joins other unconventional youths.

9. The individual commits another, yet more serious, deviant act (secondary deviation)—he robs a local grocery store with members of a gang.

10. The individual is returned to youth court, has more offences added to his record, is cast out further from conventional society, and takes on a completely deviant lifestyle.

According to Lemert, secondary deviance sets in after the community has become aware of a primary deviance. Individuals experience "a continuing sense of injustice, which [is] reinforced by job rejections, police cognizance, and strained interaction with normals."[12] In short, deviant individuals have to bear the stigma of the "delinquent" label, just as English and American convicts, as late as the eighteenth century, bore stigmas, in the form of an "M" for murder or a "T" for thief, burned or cut into their bodies to designate them as persons to be shunned.[13] Once such a label is attached to a person, a deviant or criminal career has been set in motion. The full significance of labelling theory was not recognized, either in Europe or in North America, until political events provided the opportunity.[14]

Labelling in the 1960s

The 1960s witnessed a movement among students and professors to join advocacy groups and become activists in the social causes that were rapidly gaining popularity on university campuses, such as equal rights for minorities, liberation for women, and peace for humankind. The protests took many forms—demonstrations and rallies, sit-ins and teach-ins, beards and long hair, rock music and marijuana, dropping out of school, and (in the United States) burning draft cards.

Arrests of middle-class youths increased rapidly; crime was no longer confined to the ghettos. People asked whether arrests were being made for behaviour that was not really criminal. Are the real criminals the legislators and policy makers who create and enforce laws that protect their own interests while violating the rights of others? While examples from the 1960s abound, some would argue that things haven't changed much from that tumultuous time period to today. Whether drawing on examples from the 1960s or situations like the relatively recent death of Dudley George (an Aboriginal activist who was shot by police during an occupation of Ipperwash Provincial Park in Ontario), labelling theory draws our attention to the importance of power in the deviance defining process. In the hours leading up to the shooting of George, a senior police official who met with the premier and other government officials reportedly described Ontario's government as "gun-loving rednecks who couldn't care less about aboriginals."[15] Labelling theorists provide insight into such events. Sociologist Kai Erickson has put it well:

> Deviance is not a property inherent in certain forms of behaviour; it is a property conferred upon these forms by audiences which directly or indirectly witness them. The critical variable in the study of deviance, then, is the social audience rather than the individual actor, since it is the audience which eventually determines whether or not any episode or behaviour or any class of episodes is labelled deviant.[16]

Edwin Schur, a leading labelling theorist of the 1960s, elaborated on Erickson's explanation:

> Human behavior is deviant to the extent that it comes to be viewed as involving a personally discreditable departure from a group's normative expectation, and it elicits interpersonal and collective reactions that serve to "isolate," "treat," "correct," or "punish" individuals engaged in such behavior.[17]

Schur also expanded on Lemert's secondary deviance with his own concept of "secondary elaboration," by which he meant that the effects of the labelling process become so significant that individuals who want to escape from their deviant groups and return to the conventional world find it difficult to do so. Schur points to members of the gay and drug cultures.[18] The strength of the label, once acquired, tends to exclude such people permanently from the mainstream culture.[19] Schur found that involvement in activities that are disapproved of may very well lead to more participation in deviance than one had originally planned, and so increase the social distance between the person labelled "deviant" and the conventional world.[20]

Six Nations protestors occupy a construction site they believe belongs to the Six Nations Confederacy in Ontario. In this situation, First Nations protestors, standing up for what they believe in and believe is rightfully (and legally) theirs, are constructed as the enemy in the eyes of the government and land developers. Who is right? Who is the deviant?

The labelling theorists then asked, Who makes the rules that define deviant behaviour, including crime? According to Howard Becker, it is the "moral entrepreneurs"—the people whose high social position gives them the power to make and enforce the social rules by which members of society have to live. By making the rules that define the criminal, Becker argues, certain members of society create outsiders.

The whole process thus becomes a political one, pitting the rule makers against the rule breakers. Becker goes even further, suggesting that people can be labelled simply by being falsely accused. As long as others believe that someone has participated in a given deviant behaviour, that individual will experience negative social reaction. If the negative social reaction continues, the individual may eventually experience continuance commitment, which is the awareness of the impossibility of choosing a different social identity.[21] In essence, the negative labels have become a part of the person's identity and make choosing another identity or lifestyle difficult if not impossible. People can also suffer the effects of labelling when they have committed a deviant act that has not been discovered. Since most people know how they would be labelled if they were caught, these secret deviants may experience the same labelling effects as those who have been caught.[22]

Empirical Evidence for Labelling Theory

Empirical investigations of labelling theory have been carried out by researchers in many disciplines using a variety of methodologies. One group of investigators arranged to have eight sane volunteers apply for admission to various mental hospitals. In order to get themselves admitted, the subjects claimed to be hearing voices, a symptom of schizophrenia. Once admitted to the hospital, however, they behaved normally. The experiences of these pseudopatients clearly reveal the effects of labelling.

Doctors, nurses, and assistants treated them as schizophrenic patients. They interpreted the normal everyday behaviour of the pseudopatients as manifestations of illness. An early arrival at the lunchroom, for example, was described as exhibiting "oral aggressive" behaviour; a patient seen writing something was referred to as a "compulsive notetaker." Interestingly enough, none of the other patients believed the pseudopatients were insane; they assumed they were researchers or journalists. When the subjects were discharged from the hospital, it was as schizophrenics "in remission."

The findings support criminological labelling theory. Once the sane individuals were labelled "schizophrenic," they were unable to eliminate the label by acting normally. Even when they supposedly had recovered, the label stayed with them in the form of "schizophrenia in remission," which implied that future episodes of the illness could be expected.[23]

Researchers have also looked at how labels affect people and groups with unconventional lifestyles, whether prohibited by law or not—"gays," "public drunks," "junkies," "strippers," "streetwalkers."[24] The results of research, no matter what the group, were largely in conformity: "Once a ———, always a ———." Labelling by adjudication may have lifelong consequences. Richard Schwartz and Jerome Skolnick, for example, found that employers were reluctant to hire anyone with a court record even though the person had been found not guilty.[25]

The criminologist Anthony Platt has investigated how certain individuals are singled out to receive labels. Focusing on the label "juvenile delinquent," he shows how the social reformers of the late nineteenth century helped create delinquency by establishing a special institution, the juvenile court, for the processing of troubled youths. The Chicago society women in the United States and the middle-class Protestant women in Canada who lobbied for the establishment of juvenile courts may have had the best motives in trying

Racial Profiling—Labelling before the Fact

It's one thing to be labelled a criminal after you've broken the law, but what happens when you're targeted for arrest before you've done anything?(1) Racial profiling is defined from a law enforcement perspective as "a racial disparity in police stop and search practices, custom searches at airports and border-crossings, in police patrols in minority neighbourhoods and in undercover activities or sting operations which target particular ethnic groups."(2) The Ontario Human Rights Commission defines it more broadly as "any action undertaken for reasons of safety, security or public protection that relies on stereotypes about race, colour, ethnicity, ancestry, religion, or place of origin rather than on reasonable suspicion, to single out an individual for greater scrutiny or different treatment."(2)

Leaving official definitions for a moment and looking at anecdotal evidence supporting the existence of racial profiling in Canada, one would include the experiences of some black Canadians who have been frequently pulled over while driving for no other reasons than what they refer to as "DWB—driving while black."(2)

Aboriginals in Saskatoon refer to the far-too-frequent "rides in the country," "scenic tours," or "starlight tours" members of this group have been subjected to. Starlight tours involve the police in that city picking up and driving intoxicated Aboriginals outside the city limits, sometimes as far as 50 kilometres away, dumping them off in a field with nothing but the clothes on their back (sometimes removing their shoes first) and telling them to walk home to sober up. This alleged practice was called into question after several Aboriginal men froze to death after being taken on such a "tour."(3)

Does racial profiling exist in a country known for its multiculturalism and pride in diversity? That depends on whom you ask. Aboriginal communities, well aware of Aboriginal overrepresentation in correctional facilities, well aware of what they consider police harassment and overpolicing (as in the case of the Saskatoon police force), would argue that racial profiling definitely happens. A recent study initiated by the Kingston police reports that its members were 3.7 times more likely to stop a black

person as a Caucasian, and 1.4 times more likely to stop an Aboriginal than a white person. The report also found that police were less likely to stop other minorities such as Asians or South Asians.(4)

Since September 11, 2001, racial profiling has extended to people of Middle Eastern descent in Canada and the United States as well. The most common example of this is on airplanes—many individuals claim they were kicked off flights after they had passed vigorous security checks just because another passenger or flight attendant felt uncomfortable with them on board. It is not limited to airline transportation, however, as the following case reveals.

Kassim Mohamed works in Toronto and visits Egypt, where his children go to school. Mohamed made the mistake of videotaping Toronto landmarks, including the CN Tower, for his children to see. When leaving Canada shortly after filming the "souvenir" tape for his children, officials from the Canadian Security Intelligence Service (CSIS) found the videos and confiscated them. Mohamed ended up being detained in Athens during a stopover

to help immigrants' children who, by their standards, were out of control. But by getting juvenile courts established, they simply widened the net of state agencies empowered to label some children as deviant.

The state thus aggravated the official problem of juvenile delinquency, which until then had been a neighbourhood nuisance handled by parents, neighbours, priests, the local grocer, or the police officer on the street. Juvenile delinquency, according to Platt, was invented. Through its labelling effect, it contributed to its own growth.[26]

The criminologist William Chambliss also studied the question of the way labels are distributed. Consider the following description:

> Eight promising young men [the Saints]—children of good, stable, white upper-middle-class families, active in school affairs, good pre-college students— were some of the most delinquent boys at Hanibal High School. . . . The Saints were constantly occupied with truancy, drinking, wild driving, petty

theft and vandalism. Yet not one was officially arrested for any misdeed during the two years I observed them.

This record was particularly surprising in light of my observations during the same two years of another gang of Hanibal High School students, six lower-class white boys known as the Roughnecks. The Roughnecks were constantly in trouble with police and community even though their rate of delinquency was about equal with that of the Saints.[27]

What accounts for the different responses to these two groups of boys? According to Chambliss, the crucial factor is the social class of the boys, which determined the community's reaction to their activities. The Roughnecks were poor, outspoken, openly hostile to authority, and highly visible because they could not afford cars to get out of town. The Saints, on the other hand, had reputations for being bright, they acted apologetic when authorities confronted them, they

and was sent back to Toronto. Upon his return, CSIS officials questioned him about possible terrorist connections. When he finally was able to return to Egypt to see his family, he was detained in a Cairo jail for two weeks: Egyptian officials were suspicious about the questioning that had occurred in Canada. Mohamed has gone on to sue the Canadian government for the wrongful accusation and the time he spent in jail.(5)

As Kassim Mohamed's case illustrates, the events of September 11, 2001, have heightened our awareness and sensitivity to terrorist and security threats of all types and have, as Kevin Haggerty and Amber Gaszo suggest, resulted in our unquestioning acceptance of the use of a wide variety of surveillance techniques, all of which make our private lives and personal information more readily accessible, particularly when agencies and organizations work together and share this information. What many of us do not realize is that this "surveillance assemblage," which involves institutions ranging from government agencies, to schools, banks, medical

institutions, and immigration and travel organizations, has the potential to extend profiling beyond its current form and status.(6) This concern certainly raises issues about whom, exactly, profiling will be directed to/against in the future.

Sources

1. Richard Lezin Jones, "New Jersey Prosecutors Cite Racial Profiling in Dismissal of 86 Criminal Cases," *New York Times,* April 20, 2002. Reprinted with permission.
2. CBC News Online, "Indepth: Racial Profiling," May 26, 2005, www.cbc.ca/ news/background/racial_profiling/, accessed July 23, 2007.
3. Joyce Green, "From *Stonechild* to Social Cohesion: Anti-Racist Challenges for Saskatchewan," *Canadian Journal of Political Science,* **39** (September 2006): 507–527.
4. CBC News, "Police Stop More Blacks, Ont. Study Finds," May 27, 2005, www.cbc.ca/canada/story/2005/ 05/26/race050526.html, accessed July 23, 2007.
5. CTV.ca News Staff, "Canadian Suing Ottawa for Time in Egyptian Jail," Sept. 20, 2004, www.ctv.ca/servlet/ ArticleNews/print/CTVNews/20040920/ kaddim_mohamed-04092, accessed March 3, 2008.
6. Kevin D. Haggerty and Amber Gazso, "Seeing Beyond the Ruins: Surveillance as a Response to Terrorist Threats," *Canadian Journal of Sociology,* **30** (2005): 169–187.

Questions for Debate

1. Are there any circumstances under which racial profiling is justified? If so, where do you draw the line?
2. Should offenders who have been detained as a result of racial profiling have their cases dismissed as a result?
3. What do you think is the best way to minimize racial profiling among criminal justice and law enforcement officials?
4. What do you think are the effects of racial profiling among those who are profiled? How do you think it influences their respect for the criminal justice system and the law?

held school offices, they played on athletic teams, and they had cars to get them out of town. Their behaviour went undiscovered, unprocessed, and unpunished.

Chambliss's research reveals what many believe is the inherent discrimination in the youth justice system that causes the police and courts to identify the behaviour of some as problematic more so than others. These criminologists state that young minority males are more likely to be arrested and officially processed. This is also true of members of the lower economic classes. Those with wealth or political power, on the other hand, are more likely to be given simply a warning. In this way, a Roughneck who spends all his time around other Roughnecks, but does not engage in criminal behaviour, would be more likely to be arrested and processed than a Saint who was engaged in illegal activity. Research also seems to indicate that the level of seriousness of the crime committed and the prior record of the individual

committing the crime have much influence on who gets processed.

Up to this point, the contentions of labelling theorists and the evidence they present provide a persuasive argument for the validity of labelling theory. But despite supportive scientific evidence, labelling theory has been heavily criticized.

Evaluation: Labelling Theory

Critics ask, Why is it that individuals, knowing they might be labelled, get involved in socially disapproved behaviour to begin with? Most labelled persons have indeed engaged in some act that is considered morally or legally wrong.[28] According to sociologist Ronald Akers, the impression is sometimes given that people are passive actors in a process by which the bad system bestows a derogatory label, thereby declaring them unacceptable or different or untouchable.[29] Critics suggest that the labels may identify real behaviour rather than create it. After all, many delinquents have in fact had a long history of deviant behaviour, even though they have never been caught and stigmatized. These critics question the overly active role labelling theory has assigned to the community and its criminal justice system and the overly passive role it has assigned to offenders.

Some criminologists also question how labelling theory accounts for individuals who have gone through formal processing but do not continue deviant lifestyles. They suggest that punishment really does work as a deterrent.[30] The argument is that labelling theorists are so intent on the reaction to behaviour that they completely neglect the fact that someone has defied the conventions of society.[31] The criminologist Charles Wellford reminds us that, by and large, offenders get into the hands of authorities because they have broken the law. Furthermore, the decisions made about them are heavily influenced by the seriousness of their offences. He concludes:

> The assumption that labels are differentially distributed, and that differential labeling affects behavior, is not supported by the existing criminological research. In sum, one should conclude that to the degree that these assumptions can be taken to be basic to the labeling perspective, the perspective must be seriously questioned; and criminologists should be encouraged to explore other ways to conceptualize the causal process of the creation, perpetuation, and intensification of criminal and delinquent behavior.[32]

While most critics believe that labelling theorists put too much emphasis on the system, others of a more radical or Marxist persuasion believe that labelling theorists have not gone far enough. They claim that the labelling approach concentrates too heavily on "nuts, sluts, and perverts," the exotic varieties of deviants who capture public imagination, rather than on "the unethical, illegal and destructive actions of powerful individuals, groups, and institutions of our society."[33] We will look at this argument more closely in a moment.

Empirical evidence that substantiates the claims of labelling theory has been modest. All the same, the theory has been instrumental in calling attention to some important questions, particularly about the way defendants are processed through the criminal justice system. Labelling theorists have carried out important scientific investigations

of that system that complement the search of more traditional criminologists for the causes of crime and delinquency.

Some of the criticism of labelling theory can best be countered by one of its own proponents. Howard Becker explains that labelling is intended not as a theory of causation but, rather, as a perspective, "a way of looking at a general area of human activity, which expands the traditional research to include the process of social control."[34] Labelling theory has provided this perspective; it has also spawned further inquiry into the causes of crime.

In a recent extension of labelling theory to a developmental control theory, Robert Sampson and John Laub conclude that some delinquency persists because of the reactions that offenders receive to their criminal behaviour. Add significant socioeconomic disadvantage, and the result is often a breakdown in social control.[35]

CONFLICT THEORY

The labelling theorists are as well aware as other criminologists that some people make rules and some break them. Their primary concern is the consequences of making and enforcing rules. One group of scholars has carried this idea further by questioning the rule-making process itself. They claim that a struggle for power is a basic feature of human existence. It is by means of such power struggles that various interest groups manage to control lawmaking and law enforcement.[36] To understand the theoretical approach of these conflict theorists, we must go back to the traditional approach, which views crime and criminal justice as arising from communal consensus.

The Consensus Model

Sometimes members of a society consider certain acts so threatening to community survival that they designate these acts as crimes. If the vast majority of a group's members share this view, the group has acted by consensus. This is the **consensus model** of criminal lawmaking. The model assumes that members of society by and large agree on what is right and wrong and that law is the codification of these agreed-upon social values. The law is a mechanism to settle disputes that arise when individuals stray too far from what the community considers acceptable.

Among recent targets of "anti-capitalist" and "anti-imperialist" demonstrators is the International Monetary Fund (IMF), from which many developing countries had to borrow for development. These demonstrators want these debts to be cancelled.

In Durkheim's words, "We can . . . say that an act is criminal when it offends strong and defined states of the collective conscience."[37] Consensus theorists view society as a stable entity in which laws are created for the general good. The laws' function is to reconcile and to harmonize most of the interests that most members of a community cherish, with the least amount of sacrifice.

Deviant acts not only are part of the normal functioning of society but in fact are necessary, because when the members of society unite against a deviant, they reaffirm their commitment to shared values. Durkheim captured this view:

> We have only to notice what happens, particularly in a small town, when some moral scandal has been committed. They stop each other on the street, they visit each other, they seek to come together to talk of the event and to wax indignant in common. From all the similar impressions which are exchanged, for all the temper that gets itself expressed, there emerges a unique temper, more or less determinate according to the circumstances, which is everybody's without being anybody's in particular. That is the public temper.[38]

Societies in which citizens agree on right and wrong and the occasional deviant serves a useful purpose are scarce today. Such societies could be found among primitive peoples at the very beginning of social evolution. By and large, consensus theory recognizes that not everyone can agree on what is best for society. Yet consensus theory holds

that conflicting interests can be reconciled by means of law.[39]

The Conflict Model

With this view of the consensus model, we can understand and evaluate the arguments of the conflict theorists. In the 1960s, while labelling theorists were questioning why some people were designated as criminals, another group of scholars began to ask who in society has the power to make and enforce the laws. Conflict theory, already well established in the field of sociology, thus became popular as an explanation of crime and justice as well.

Like labelling theory, **conflict theory** has its roots in rebellion and the questioning of values. But while labelling theorists and traditional criminologists focused on the crime and the criminal, including the labelling of the criminal by the system, conflict theorists questioned the system itself. The clash between traditional and labelling theorists, on the one hand, and conflict theorists, on the other, became ideological.

Conflict theorists asked, If people agree on the value system, as consensus theorists suggest, why are so many people in rebellion, why are there so many crimes, so many punitive threats, so many people in prison? Clearly conflict is found everywhere in the world, between one country and another, between gay rights and anti-gay groups, between people who view abortion as a right and others who view it as murder, between suspects and police, between family members, and between neighbours. If the criminal law supports

Conflict: Pro-choice advocates confront right-to-life supporters over the explosive issue of abortion.

The Rights of the Poorest

The poorest and least powerful have had little influence on the making of laws and on society's reaction to the breaking of laws. Somehow, the poorest have to survive in a society on which they have no apparent impact. The implementation of the Safe Streets Act in Ontario in 2000 has sparked the debate in Canada over what for some is a basic question of survival: Do the poor have a constitutional right to beg?

THE SAFE STREETS ACT

Panhandling is legal in Canada. The Supreme Court of Canada ruled that asking someone for something on the streets of our country is protected under the Charter of Rights and Freedoms. The Safe Streets Act, passed in Ontario in 1999, prohibits soliciting in an "aggressive manner" and soliciting a "captive audience." The act has been linked to what many perceived to be a growing problem in Toronto and other major cities—"squeegee kids," who dash in and out of busy intersections where they solicit motorists for spare change, in exchange for washing windshields.(1) In 2004 British Columbia passed its own version of the Safe Streets Act.

CRITICAL COMMENTARY

Many individuals and groups in Ontario and across the country consider the Safe Streets Act a visible manifestation of the Ontario government's neo-conservative agenda. The act, from this perspective, is just another mechanism at the disposal of the government and crime control agencies to police the poor. People with money and power have long attempted to control individuals and groups considered "disorderly" and therefore a threat to social order. Canada's vagrancy laws of the late nineteenth and early twentieth centuries had the same effect. "Disorderly" people through this kind of legislation are constructed as a threat to public order and therefore as warranting added social control. At the same time, homeless and poor individuals who fall under the control of the legislation are excluded from public space, public discourse, public view, and participation in public processes like lawmaking.(1)

In addition to critiques centring on the Safe Street Act's objective of controlling and criminalizing the behaviours of poor people, the act has been subjected to criticism surrounding its arbitrary interpretation and enforcement. The act limits "aggressive panhandling" but defines "aggressive manner" as "a manner that is likely to cause a reasonable person to be concerned for his or her safety or security." This wording is open to interpretation since people vary in terms of what they perceive as threatening. Also of note is the fact that police officers are accused of poorly enforcing the act. Some have made a point of enforcing it almost to the extreme, while others, though mentioning the act by name, prove relatively ignorant of what it actually encompasses. As a result, many panhandlers have taken to carrying around a copy of the Safe Streets Act in preparation for conflict with law enforcers.(2)

The Safe Streets Act has been legally challenged on two main grounds. One issue surrounds the jurisdiction over criminal law in this country. The federal government has sole control over passing criminal law in Canada, yet the Safe Streets Act, arguably a Criminal Code law, was passed by a provincial government. The second basis for legal challenge concerns the Safe Streets Act's infringement on freedom of expression, one of the rights guaranteed by the Charter.(3)

In the Safe Streets Act's first constitutional challenge in 2001, Justice William Babe found 13 people guilty under the act. He upheld the act claiming that any infringement on freedom of expression is justified in the name of public safety. At the same time, Babe stated that the act does not discriminate against the poor.(3)

EXCERPTS FROM ONTARIO'S SAFE STREETS ACT: PROHIBITED ACTS

Solicitation in aggressive manner prohibited

(2) No person shall solicit in an aggressive manner. 1999, c. 8, s. 2(2).

---

the collective communal interest, why do so many people deviate from it?

Conflict theorists answered that, contrary to consensus theory, laws do not exist for the collective good; they represent the interests of specific groups that have the power to get them enacted.[40] The key concept in conflict theory is power. The people who have political control in any given society are the ones who are able to make things happen. They have power. Conflict theory holds that the people who possess the power work to keep the powerless at a disadvantage. The laws thus have their origin in the interests of the few;

these few shape the values, and the values, in turn, shape the laws.[41]

It follows that the person who is defined as criminal and the behaviour that is defined as crime at any given time and place mirror the society's power relationships. The definitions are subject to change as other interests gain power. The changing of definitions can be seen in those acts we now designate as "victimless" crimes. Possession of marijuana, prostitution, gambling—all have been legal at some times, illegal at others. We may ask, then, whether any of these acts is inherently evil. The conflict theorist would answer that all are *made*

Examples

1. Threatening the person solicited with physical harm, by word, gesture or other means, during the solicitation or after the person solicited responds or fails to respond to the solicitation.
2. Obstructing the path of the person solicited during the solicitation or after the person solicited responds or fails to respond to the solicitation.
3. Using abusive language during the solicitation or after the person solicited responds or fails to respond to the solicitation.
4. Proceeding behind, alongside, or ahead of the person solicited during the solicitation or after the person solicited responds or fails to respond to the solicitation.
5. Soliciting while intoxicated by alcohol or drugs.
6. Continuing to solicit a person in a persistent manner after the person has responded negatively to the solicitation. (1999, c. 8, s. 2 (3)).

Solicitation of captive audience prohibited

(2) No person shall,

a. solicit a person who is using, waiting to use, or departing from an automated teller machine;
b. solicit a person who is using or waiting to use a pay telephone or a public toilet facility;
c. solicit a person who is waiting at a taxi stand or a public transit stop;
d. solicit a person who is in or on a public transit vehicle;
e. solicit a person who is in the process of getting in, out of, on or off a vehicle or who is in a parking lot; or
f. while on a roadway, solicit a person who is in or on a stopped, standing or parked vehicle. (1999, c. 8, s. 3 (2)). (4)

Sources

1. Joe Hermer and Janet Mosher, eds., *Disorderly People: Law and the Politics of Exclusion in Ontario* (Halifax: Fernwood Publishing, 2002).
2. "Safe Streets Act," Wikipedia, http://en.wikipedia.org/wiki/Safe_Streets_Act, accessed June 23, 2007.
3. "'Squeegee Kids'' Law upheld in Ontario," CBC News, August 3, 2001, www.cbc.ca/canada/story/2001/08/03/squeegee_010803.html, accessed June 23, 2007.
4. Safe Streets Act, 1999. S. O. 1999, Chapter 8.

Do aggressive panhandlers like squeegee kids have a constitutional right to beg? Is asking for money "symbolic" speech protected by the Charter?

Questions for Discussion

1. Do you think the Safe Streets Act in Ontario and others like it will withstand the constitutional challenges being levelled against such legislation? Is panhandling an example of freedom of expression?
2. Are the actions of squeegee kids different from others types of panhandling or is it all the same?

---

evil when they are so designated by those in power and thus defined as crimes in legal codes.

The legal status of victimless crimes is subject to change. But what about murder, a crime considered evil in all contemporary societies? Many conflict theorists would respond that the definition of murder as a criminal offence is also rooted in the effort of some groups to guard their power. A political terrorist may very well become a national hero.

Conflict theorists emphasize the relativity of norms to time and place: Capital punishment is legal in some countries, outlawed in others; alcohol consumption is illegal in Saudi Arabia but not in Canada. Powerful groups maintain their interests by making illegal any behaviour that might be a threat to them. Laws thus become a mechanism of control, or "a weapon in social conflict."[42]

Conflict Theory and Criminology

The sociologist George Vold (1896–1967) was the first theorist to relate conflict theory to criminology. He argued that individuals band together in groups because they are social animals with needs that are best served through collective action. If the group serves its members, it survives; if not, new groups form to take its place. Individuals constantly clash as they try to advance the interests of their particular group over those of all the others. The result is that society is in a constant state of conflict, "one of the principal and essential social processes upon which the continuing ongoing of society depends." For Vold, the entire process of lawmaking and crime control is a direct reflection of conflict between interest groups, all trying to get laws passed in their favour and to gain control of the police power.[43]

The sociologist Ralf Dahrendorf and the criminologist Austin Turk are major contemporary contributors to the application of conflict theory to criminology. To Dahrendorf, the consensus model of society is utopian. He believes that enforced constraint, rather than cooperation, binds people together. Whether society is capitalist, socialist, or feudal, some people have the authority and others are subject to it. Society is made up of a large number of interest groups. The interests of one group do not always coincide with the needs of another—unions and management, for instance.

Dahrendorf argues that social change is constant, social conflicts are ever-present, disintegration and change are ongoing, and all societies are characterized by coercion of some people by others. The most important characteristics of class, he contends, are power and authority. The inequities remain for him the lasting determinant of social conflict. Conflict can be either destructive or constructive, depending on whether it leads to a breakdown of the social structure or to positive change in the social order.[44]

Austin Turk has continued and expanded this theoretical approach. "Criminality is not a biological, psychological, or even behavioural phenomenon," he says, "but a social status defined by the way in which an individual is perceived, evaluated, and treated by legal authorities." Criminal status is defined by those he calls the "authorities," the decision makers. Criminal status is imposed on the "subjects," the subordinate class. Turk explains that this process works so that both authorities and subjects learn to interact as performers in their dominant and submissive roles. There are "social norms of dominance" and "social norms of deference." Conflict arises when some people refuse to go along, and they challenge the authorities. "Law breaking, then, becomes a measure of the stability of the ruler/ruled relationship."[45] The people who make the laws struggle to hold on to their power, while those who do not make laws struggle to do so.

People with authority use several forms of power to control society's goods and services: police or war power, economic power, political power, and ideological power (beliefs, values).[46] The laws made by the "ins" to condemn or condone various behaviours help shape all social institutions—indeed, the entire culture. Where education is mandatory, for example, the people in power are able to maintain the status quo by passing on their own value system from one generation to the next.[47]

History seems to demonstrate that primitive societies, in their earliest phases of development, tend to be homogeneous and to make laws by consensus. The more a society develops economically and politically, the more difficult it becomes to resolve conflict situations by consensus. For an early instance of criminal law making by the conflict model, we can go back to 1530, when King Henry VIII of England broke away from the Roman Catholic Church because the pope refused to annul Henry's marriage to Catherine of Aragon so that he could marry Anne Boleyn. Henry confiscated church property and closed all the monasteries. Virtually overnight, tens of thousands of people who had been dependent on the monasteries for support were cast out, to roam the countryside in search of a living. Most ended up as beggars. This huge army of vagrants posed a burden on and danger to the establishment. To cope with the problem, Parliament revived the vagrancy laws of 1349, which prohibited the giving of aid to vagrants and beggars. Thus the powerful, by controlling the laws, gained control over the powerless.[48]

Empirical Evidence for the Conflict Model

Researchers have tested several conflict theory hypotheses, such as those pertaining to bias and discrimination in the criminal justice system, differential crime rates of powerful and powerless groups, and the intent behind the development of the criminal law. The findings offer mixed support for the theory.

Alan Lizotte studied 816 criminal cases in the Chicago courts over a one-year period to test the assumption that the powerless get harsher sentences.

His analysis relating legal factors (such as the offence committed) and extralegal factors (such as the race and job of the defendant) to length of prison sentence pointed to significant sentencing inequalities related to race and occupation.[49] When Freda Adler studied the importance of non-legal factors in the decision making of juries, she found that the socio-economic level of the defendants significantly influenced their judgment.[50]

While these and similar studies tend to support conflict theory by demonstrating class or racial bias in the administration of criminal justice, others, unexpectedly, show an opposite bias.[51] When we evaluate the contribution of conflict theory to criminological thought, we must keep in mind Austin Turk's warning that conflict theory is often misunderstood. The theory does not, he points out, suggest that most criminals are innocent or that powerful persons engage in the same amount of deviant behaviour as do powerless persons or that law enforcers typically discriminate against people without power. It does acknowledge, however, that behaviours common among society's more disadvantaged members have a greater likelihood of being called "crimes" than the activities in which the more powerful typically participate.[52]

Conflict theory does not attempt to explain crime; it simply identifies social conflict as a basic fact of life and as a source of discriminatory treatment by the criminal justice system of groups and classes that lack the power and status of those who make and enforce the laws. Once we recognize this, we may find it possible to change the process of criminalizing people to provide greater justice. Conflict theorists anticipate a guided evolution, not a revolution, to improve the existing criminal justice system. Another group of theories that advocates for changes to the criminal justice system, society, and the discipline of criminology are radical theories. Their goals and expectations, however, are slightly more drastic or "radical" than those of the conflict theorists. We turn to a discussion of this group of theories next.

RADICAL THEORY

While labelling and conflict theorists were developing their perspectives, social and political conditions in North America and Europe were changing rapidly and drastically. Youth were deeply disillusioned about a political and social

structure that had brought about the assassinations of John F. Kennedy, Robert Kennedy, and Martin Luther King Jr.; the war in Vietnam; and the Watergate debacle. Many looked for radical solutions to social problems, and a number of young criminologists searched for answers to questions about crime and criminal justice. They found their answers in Marxism, a philosophy born in similar social turmoil a century earlier.

The Intellectual Heritage of Marxist Criminology

The major industrial centres of Europe suffered great hardships during the nineteenth century. The mechanization of industry and of agriculture, heavy population increases, and high rates of urbanization had created a massive labour surplus, high unemployment, and a burgeoning class of young urban migrants forced into the streets by poverty. London is said to have had at least 20 000 individuals who "rose every morning without knowing how they were to be supported through the day or where they were to lodge on the succeeding night, and cases of death from starvation appeared in the coroner's lists daily."[53] In other cities, conditions were even worse.

Engels and Marx

It was against this background that Friedrich Engels (1820–1895) addressed the effects of the Industrial Revolution. A partner in his father's industrial empire, Engels was himself a member of the class he attacked as "brutally selfish." After a two-year stay in England, he documented the awful social conditions, the suffering, and the great increase in crime and arrests. All these problems he blamed on one factor—competition. In *The Condition of the Working Class in England*, published in 1845, he spelled out the association between crime and poverty as a political problem:

> The earliest, crudest, and least fruitful form of this rebellion was that of crime. The working man lived in poverty and want, and saw that others were better off than he. . . . Want conquered his inherited respect for the sacredness of property, and he stole.[54]

Though Karl Marx (1818–1883) paid little attention to crime specifically, he argued that all aspects of social life, including laws, are determined by economic organization. His philosophy reflects the economic despair that followed the Industrial Revolution. In his *Communist Manifesto* (1848), Marx viewed the history of all societies as a documentation of class struggles: "Freeman and slave, patrician and plebeian, lord and serf, guildmaster and journeyman, in a word, oppressor and oppressed, stood in constant opposition to one another."[55]

Marx went on to describe the most important relationship in industrial society as that between the capitalist bourgeoisie, who own the means of production, and the proletariat, or workers, who labour for them. Society, according to Marx, has always been organized in such a hierarchical fashion, with the state representing not the common interest but the interests of those who own the means of production. Capitalism breeds egocentricity, greed, and predatory behaviour; but the worst crime of all is the exploitation of workers. Revolution, Marx concluded, is the only means to bring about change, and for that reason it is morally justifiable.

Many philosophers before Marx had noted the link between economic conditions and social problems, including crime. Among them were Plato, Aristotle, Virgil, Horace, Sir Thomas More, Cesare Beccaria, Jeremy Bentham, André Guerry, Adolphe Quételet, and Gabriel Tarde (several of whom we met in Chapter 3). But none of them had advocated revolutionary change. And none had constructed a coherent criminological theory that conformed with economic determinism, the cornerstone of the Marxist explanation that people who are kept in a state of poverty will rebel by committing crimes. Not until 1905 can we speak of Marxist criminology.

Willem Adriaan Bonger

As a student at the University of Amsterdam, Willem Adriaan Bonger (1876–1940) entered a paper in a competition on the influence of economic factors on crime. His entry did not win; but its expanded version, *Criminality and Economic Conditions*, which appeared in French in 1905, was selected for translation by the American Institute of Criminal Law and Criminology. Bonger wrote in his preface, "[I am] convinced that my ideas about the etiology of crime will not be shared by a great many readers of the American edition."[56] He

was right. Nevertheless, the book is considered a classic and is invaluable to students doing research on crime and economics.

Bonger explained that the social environment of primitive people was interwoven with the means of production. People helped each other. They used what they produced. When food was plentiful, everyone ate. When food was scarce, everyone was hungry. Whatever people had, they shared. People were subordinate to nature. In a modern capitalist society, people are much less altruistic. They concentrate on production for profit rather than for the needs of the community. Capitalism encourages criminal behaviour by creating a climate that is less conducive to social responsibility. "We have a right," argued Bonger, "to say that the part played by economic conditions in criminality is predominant, even decisive."[57]

Willem Bonger died as he had lived, a fervent antagonist of the evils of the social order. An archenemy of Nazism and a prominent name on Hitler's list of people to be eliminated, he refused to emigrate even when the German army was at the border. On May 10, 1940, as the German invasion of Holland began, he wrote to his son: "I don't see any future for myself and I cannot bow to this scum which will now overmaster us."[58] He then took his own life. He left a powerful political and criminological legacy. Foremost among his followers were German socialist philosophers of the progressive school of Frankfurt.

Georg Rusche and Otto Kirchheimer

Georg Rusche and Otto Kirchheimer began to write their classic work at the University of Frankfurt. Driven out of Germany by Nazi persecution, they continued their research in exile in Paris and completed it at Columbia University in New York in 1939. In *Punishment and the Social Structure*, they wrote that punishments had always been related to the modes of production and the availability of labour, rather than to the nature of the crimes themselves.

Consider galley slavery. Before the development of modern sailing techniques, oarsmen were needed to power merchant ships; as a result, galley slavery was a punishment in antiquity and in the Middle Ages. As sailing techniques were perfected, galley slavery was no longer necessary, and it lost favour as a sanction. By documenting the real purposes of punishments through the ages, Rusche and Kirchheimer made **penologists,** who study the penal system, aware that severe and cruel treatment of offenders had more to do with the value of human life and the needs of the economy than with preventing crime.

The names Marx, Engels, Bonger, and Rusche and Kirchheimer were all but forgotten by mainstream criminologists of the 1940s and 1950s, perhaps because of the relative prosperity and conservatism during those years. But when tranquillity turned to turmoil in the mid-1960s, the forgotten names provided the intellectual basis for North American and European radical criminologists, who explicitly stated their commitment to Marxism.

Radical Criminology since the 1970s

Radical criminology (also called "critical," "new," and "Marxist criminology") made its first public appearance in 1968, when a group of British sociologists organized the National Deviancy Conference (NDC), a group of more than 300 intellectuals, social critics, deviants, and activists of various persuasions. What the group members had in common was a basic disillusion with the criminological studies being done by the British Home Office, which they believed was system-serving and "practical." They were concerned with the way the system controlled people rather than with traditional sociological and psychological explanations of crime. They shared a respect for the interactionist and labelling theorists but believed these theorists had become too traditional. Their answer was to form a new criminology based on Marxist principles.

The conference was followed by the publication in 1973 of *The New Criminology,* the first textual formulation of the new radical criminology. According to its authors, Ian Taylor, Paul Walton, and Jock Young, it is the underclass, the "labor forces of the industrial society," that is controlled through the criminal law and its enforcement, while "the owners of labor will be bound only by a civil law which regulates their competition between each other." The economic institution, then, is the source of all conflicts. Struggles between classes always relate to the distribution of resources and power, and only when capitalism is abolished will crime disappear.[59]

About the time that Marxist criminology was being formulated in England, it was also developing in the United States, particularly at the School of Criminology of the University of California at Berkeley, where Richard Quinney, Anthony Platt, Herman and Julia Schwendinger, William Chambliss, and Paul Takagi were at the forefront of the movement. These researchers were also influenced by interactionist and labelling theorists, as well as by the conflict theories of Vold, Dahrendorf, and Turk.

Though the radical criminologists share the central tenet of conflict theory, that laws are created by the powerful to protect their own interests, they disagree on the number of forces competing in the power struggle. For Marxist criminologists, there is only one dominating segment, the capitalist ruling class, which uses the criminal law to impose its will on the rest of the people in order to protect its property and to define as criminal any behaviour that threatens the status quo.[60] The leading American spokesperson for radical criminology is Richard Quinney. His earliest Marxist publications appeared in 1973: "Crime Control in Capitalist Society" and "There's a Lot of Us Folks Grateful to the Lone Ranger."[61] The second of these essays describes how Quinney drifted away from capitalism, with its folklore myths embodied in individual heroes like the Lone Ranger. He asserts that

the state is organized to serve the interests of the dominant economic class, the capitalist ruling class; that criminal law is an instrument the state and the ruling class use to maintain and perpetuate the social and economic order; that the contradictions of advanced capitalism . . . require that the subordinate classes remain oppressed by whatever means necessary, especially by the legal system's coercion and violence; and that only with the collapse of capitalist society, based on socialist principles, will there be a solution to the crime problem.[62]

In *Class, State, and Crime,* Quinney proclaims that "the criminal justice movement is . . . a state-initiated and state-supported effort to rationalize mechanisms of social control. The larger purpose is to secure a capitalist order that is in grave crisis, likely in its final stage of development."[63] Quinney challenges criminologists to abandon traditional ways of thinking about causation, to study what could be rather than what is, to question the assumptions of the social order, and to "ultimately develop a Marxist perspective."[64]

The Forgotten Criminology of Genocide

Why has criminology forgotten the systematic decimation of 1.5 million Armenians by the Young Turks during World War I, as well as the systematic killing of 6 million Jews and the extermination of another 5 million, including Gypsies, political opponents, mentally ill, retarded, and other "inferior" peoples, between 1941 and 1945? How could criminology have neglected an examination of the crimes against humanity that resulted in an estimated 7 million to 16 million deaths over the past 60 years since World War II? You would think that criminology, an academic field concerned with violence, aggression, power, and victimization, would focus on the crime of genocide.

If not in the violence literature, one would expect to find this scholarship in the efforts of conflict, critical, and Marxist theorists in their explanations of organized, state-sanctioned violence and oppression. Criminologists whose life's work is crime prevention also must regularly discuss the causal factors that lead to acts of genocide. If you search through every issue of the journals *Criminology* and *Journal of Criminal Law and Criminology* since their inception, however, you will find only one article on genocide, the most serious of all crimes, and that article was written over 40 years ago. So, why is there no criminology of genocide? Our answers to this question, regrettably, are inadequate.

1. *Genocide is a political act reflecting the will of sovereignty.* Genocide, it has been said, is a political rather than criminal act, most often employed to enhance a country's solidarity and unification. Decisions to liquidate, exterminate, and cleanse a minority population are matters of political policy reflecting the will of sovereignty. The immorality of genocide is tempered by a moral generosity to a sovereign's motivation. The effect of shrouding genocide in a political cloth is to see the annihilation of certain populations as something less than or different from a crime.(1)

2. *Genocide is a breach of international norms and international law.* Several years ago, two groups of victims and representatives of victims from Bosnia-Herzegovina brought an action in federal court under the Alien Tort Claims Act against the president and leader of the Bosnian Serb forces for aggravated sexual

How is it that so many people in countries around the world live in shadows of past genocides and seemingly choose to ignore it?

assault, forced prostitution and impregnation, various acts of extreme torture, and mass execution.(2) The case carried significant symbolic value. Are acts of

---

Marxist theory also can be found in the writings of other scholars who have adopted the radical approach to criminology. William Chambliss and Robert Seidman present their version in *Law, Order, and Power*:

> Society is composed of groups that are in conflict with one another and . . . the law represents an institutionalized tool of those in power (ruling class) which functions to provide them with superior moral as well as coercive power in conflict.[65]

They comment that if, in the operation of the criminal justice system by the powerful, "justice or fairness happen to be served, it is sheer coincidence."[66]

To Barry Krisberg, crime is a function of privilege. The rich create crimes to distract attention from the injustices they inflict on the masses. Power determines which group holds the privilege, defined by Krisberg as that which is valued by a given social group in a given historical time.[67] Herman and Julia Schwendinger supported this idea in their summary of the causes of delinquency. They stated that legal relations secure a capitalistic mode of production, while laws are created to secure the labour force. The bourgeoisie are always in a state of being threatened by the proletariats; therefore, while some laws may secure lower-class interests, capitalist interests underlie the basic constitutional laws. Laws in general, according to the Schwendingers, contradict their stated purpose. The Schwendingers went even further in proposing that the state fails to control delinquency because lower-class deviants supply factories with a ready pool of low-wage labourers.[68]

Anthony Platt, in a forceful attack on traditional criminology, has even suggested it would

genocide torts or crimes violations of international norms or international law? The answers to these questions are far from simple.

3. *Genocide is committed by the state.* Of the many revelations over the past 50 years, criminologists seem to have the most difficulty with the notion that an organization or entity, whether a corporation or nation-state, may commit a crime. When crimes are imputed from an individual to an inanimate entity, the intellectual challenge becomes: Should an individual be blamed as well? The equivocation with bringing those responsible for ethnic cleansing and planned mass murder to justice may be explained, at least in part, by a resistance to the notion that individuals within a "guilty" collective are to blame.

4. *The magnitude of victimization in genocide defies belief.* The extent of victimization and harm in genocide strains any assessment of seriousness. Who appreciates differences in seriousness when the offence is, for example, 100 000, 250 000, or 500 000 butchered Hutus or Tutsis? Is there a difference in judgments of offence seriousness between the

planned killing of 6 million versus 7 million people?

5. *Problems arise regarding both denying and admitting atrocity.* Two prominent themes that emerge from the literature on genocide capture an ambivalence hard felt by some survivors and refugees of genocide. This ambivalence is captured in the titles of two recently published books on the Holocaust—Deborah Lipstadt's *Denying the Holocaust* and Lawrence L. Langer's *Admitting the Holocaust.*(3) The problem of admission is with the casting of genocide as a historical problem requiring serious study; the effects of intellectualizing mass torture and death; the packaging of the Holocaust neatly into a social science; and the elevation of genocide to a respectable academic discipline of its own, with courses that fit a core curriculum and endow Holocaust professorships. The problem with denial comes from historical revisionists.

Many have commented that the field of criminology has matured. Unfortunately, it has done so without considering the most serious of all crimes.(4)

Sources

1. Irving Louis Horowitz, *Taking Lives: Genocide and State Power* (New Brunswick, NJ: Transaction, 1997).
2. *Kaic v. Karadzic,* 70 F.3d 232 (2d Cir. 1995).
3. Deborah Lipstadt, *Denying the Holocaust: The Growing Assault on Truth and Memory* (New York: Free Press, 1993); and Lawrence L. Langer, *Admitting the Holocaust: Collected Essays* (New York: Oxford, 1996).
4. William S. Laufer, "The Forgotten Criminology of Genocide," *Advances in Criminological Theory,* 8 (1999): 45–58.

Questions for Discussion

1. How satisfactory are these answers to you?
2. What could conflict and radical theorists contribute to this dialogue?

not be "too farfetched to characterize many criminologists as domestic war criminals" because they have "serviced domestic repression in the same way that economics, political science, and anthropology have greased the wheels and even manufactured some of the important parts of modern imperialism."[69]

He suggests that traditional criminology serves the state through research studies that purport to "investigate" the conditions of the lower class but in reality only prove, with their probes of family life, education, jobs, and so on, that the members of the lower class are in fact less intelligent and more criminal than the rest of us. Platt claims that these inquiries, based as they are on biased and inaccurate data, are merely tools of the middle-class oppressors.

A number of other areas have come under the scrutiny of Marxist criminologists.[70] They have

studied how informal means of settling disputes outside courts actually extend the control of the criminal justice system by adjudicating cases that are not serious enough for the courts; how juvenile court dispositions are unfairly based on social class; how sentencing reform has failed to benefit the lower class; how police practices during the latter half of the nineteenth century were geared to control labour rather than crime; how rape victims are made to feel guilty; how penitentiary reform has benefited the ruling class by giving it more control over the lower class; and how capitalist interests are strengthened by private policing.[71]

Evaluation: Marxist Criminological Theory

Critiques of Marxist criminology range from support for the attention the approach calls to the crimes of the powerful to accusations that it is nothing more than a revival of the Robin Hood myth, in which the poor steal from the rich in order to survive.[72] By far the most incisive criticism is that of sociologist Carl Klockars, who points out that the division of society into social classes may have a beneficial effect, contrary to Marxist thought. Standards, he argues, are created by some people to inspire the remainder of society. In present-day North America, Klockars claims, poverty has lost some of its meaning because luxuries and benefits are spread out over classes. To him, ownership and control of industry are two different things. Anyone who buys a share of stock, for example, can be an owner, while control is handled by bureaucrats who may or may not be owners.[73]

Class Interests versus Interest Groups
Klockars attacks Marxists for focusing exclusively on class interests and ignoring the fact that society is made up of many interest groups. This Marxist bias has yielded results that are untrustworthy and predictable, ignore reality, explain issues that are self-evident (some businesspeople are greedy and corrupt), and do not explain issues that are relevant (why socialist states have crime).[74]

Not without a note of sympathy, Richard Sparks summed up the criticism when he said,

> Marxist criminologists tend to be committed to praxis and the desire for radical social reform; but this commitment is not entailed by the scientific claims which Marxists make, and it has sometimes led to those claims being improperly suspect.[75]

Opposition to the new criminology follows many paths, but the most popular, in one way or another, is concerned with its oversimplification of causation by the exclusive focus on capitalism.[76] Critics also attack Marxist criminologists for their assertion that even by studying crime empirically, criminologists are supporting the status quo. That puts Marxist criminologists on the defensive, because if they are not ideologically in a position to expose their theories to empirical research or are unwilling to do so, their assertions will remain just that—assertions with no proof.[77]

Collapse of the Economic Order Even sharper criticism of Marxist theory can be anticipated in the wake of the collapse of the Marxist economic order in the Soviet Union, Poland, Czechoslovakia, Hungary, the German Democratic Republic, Bulgaria, Albania, and Romania, as well as in countries in Africa and Latin America.[78] Many East European criminologists are no longer quoting Marx in their publications, which tend increasingly to focus on the classical rule-of-law concept. But Quinney has never seen the conditions in those countries as representative of Marxism. According to him, a true Marxist state has not yet been attained, but the ideal is worth pursuing.[79]

To the credit of radical criminologists, it must be said that they have encouraged their more traditional colleagues to look with a critical eye at all aspects of the criminal justice system, including the response of the system to both poor and rich offenders. Their concern is the exercise of power. They ask, Whose power? On whose behalf? For whose benefit? What is the legitimacy of that power? And who is excluded from the exercise of power, by whom, and why? Criminologists have had to address all these questions. Many may not have changed their answers, but the fact that the questions have been raised has ensured clearer answers than had been offered before. One group that was excluded from the criminological enterprise for far too long is women. It is to a discussion of feminist theory that we now turn.

FEMINIST THEORY

As you may have noticed, the traditional criminological theories we have discussed so far in this text were created, tested, and critiqued primarily by male criminologists. Criminology has been a male-dominated discipline. It was only in the past 30 years or so that female criminologists have called attention to what Canadian criminologist Elizabeth Comack refers to as "criminology's amnesia" regarding women.[80] Women, if included at all in early criminological theories and studies, were on the outskirts. Marie-Andrée Bertrand and Frances Heidensohn were two of the first female criminologists to draw attention to the male bias in criminology.[81] Since then, others have critiqued the intellectual sexism that exists in criminology. Sandra Bell, for example, points out the androcentric or male-centred nature of early criminological theorizing, as well as the tendency of early criminologists to fall back on stereotypes of women, some of which bordered on misogynistic.[82]

Androcentric and Misogynistic Criminological Theorizing

This intellectual sexism appears in the form of traditional theorizing about female criminality that located women's deviance in their biology. Early theorists like Lombroso suggested women were less intelligent than men and this was linked to criminal behaviours.[83] Others argued women needed more love than men, so their criminal behaviours were linked to this drive for sexual attention and sexuality.[84] Otto Pollak provided "evidence" for the fact that women were inherently more deceitful, vengeful, and manipulative than men; woman's devious nature was rooted in her biology, in particular her ability to conceal/ fake orgasm (which permitted women to "practise" the art of deception).[85] Still others focused on the "natural" caring, nurturing, submissive character of women and the "naturally" occurring aggressiveness characteristic of men as explanations for the difference in offending rates between men and women. Although some of these early theories sound ridiculous today, the point to emphasize is that when it came to explaining criminal behaviour for women (and for men too in the earlier theories), social and economic inequality and social structural conditions were ignored. While Merton was writing about the importance of socially structured strain in explaining male deviance, standard explanations for female deviance, if they existed at all, still focused on biological factors and emotional motivations.

These types of explanations have not completely disappeared (e.g., the PMS argument discussed in Chapter 4). However, feminist theories in criminology have brought to light the importance of social structural factors in explanations of female crime, as well the differences in offending rates between men and women. Feminists have also brought much needed attention to the sexist nature of the criminal justice system, where double standards exist. Women have been frequently criminalized for sexual deviance and "immorality," behaviours not considered criminal for men.[86] More proof of the institutionalized sexism that creates differential treatment for men and women is the greater likelihood of women being labelled "sick" for deviating from social norms, and then being treated medically or psychiatrically for their "sickness."[87] Meda Chesney-Lind and others agree that traditional theories ignored the way agencies of social control reinforced women's place in a patriarchal society.[88]

Feminists affiliate with a number of different perspectives. In other words, there really is not one single "feminist perspective" but rather a number of perspectives with different emphases. However, they are united in their focus on addressing the situation of women in society. A feminist approach understands "difference" between the genders as rooted in the structure of society. For scholars who use this approach, understanding the lives of criminalized women means contextualizing experience within structures characterized by inequalities of race, class, and gender.[89] For example, discussion regarding the discriminatory treatment of women at the hands of social control agents and society generally would be remiss if it did not include the recognition that different women experience these situations differently. Earlier in this text we discussed the overrepresentation of Aboriginals in Canada's correctional institutions. The fact is that Aboriginal *women* experience this overrepresentation to a greater extent than Aboriginal men.[90] To lump all women (or all men for that matter) together in our analyses and theories obscures the importance of context to the different lived experiences of different categories of people.

We discuss several feminist perspectives next.

Liberal Feminist Approaches

The 1970s witnessed the creation of approaches to explaining gender differences in crime that focused on the importance of gender role socialization. In contrast to earlier theorists, who focused on the "naturalness" (biological roots) of gendered behaviour, these theorists emphasized the manner in which young boys and young girls are socialized to fit into "traditional" behavioural patterns. Boys learn independence, assertiveness, and risk-taking; girls learn to be passive, dependent, and cautious.[91] Learning these gender roles sets boys up for the possibility of criminal behaviour, which itself often requires risk-taking, assertive, aggressive behaviour. On the other hand, the feminine role is not conducive to criminal behaviour; women who commit crime were perceived as being poorly socialized or as having taken on masculine traits.[92]

Carol Smart suggests that role theory can only act as a partial explanation for differences in behaviour between the genders.[93] She stresses the importance of situating gender roles in broader structural terms. We should look at why socialization patterns are different for the genders and how they have come to be that way.[94] If we do not look at this broader setting within which gendered behaviour occurs, we risk falling back on biological explanations. In other words, "role is destiny" simply replaces "biology is destiny."[95]

Freda Adler and Rita Simon situate role socialization in the broader context of the women's liberation movement.[96] The liberation hypothesis posits that as women's participation and equality in society increases, so should their crime rate. In others words, as women gain equality in the legitimate workforce, so should they gain equality in the "illegitimate workforce." As opportunities to work outside the home open up for women, increased opportunities to commit crime should also occur. As a result, the convergence in gender roles for men and women would result in a convergence in crime rates as well. The liberation thesis has been hotly debated and criticized. While women's criminal offending has increased, statistics indicate that the nature and extent of role convergence predicted by Adler has not occurred.[97] In terms of statistical increases in the number of women offenders, critics draw attention to the fact that because there was such a small absolute number of female offenders to start with, any increase, if described as a percentage, will appear larger than it is. Holly Johnson and Karen Rogers illustrate this point well. Between 1970 and 1991, the reported percentage increase in charges against women for homicide was 45 percent. In practical terms, this means that the number of women charged with homicide in Canada increased by 15 during this time period.[98] In other words, because of the small base number of women offenders, reporting increases in charges against women in percentages inflates actual increases.

The liberation hypothesis is also problematic because of the fact that the women's movement primarily affected privileged white women. As we have discussed throughout this text, poor people and people of colour are more likely to appear in official crime statistics—men and women. The majority of female offenders continue to come from socially and economically disadvantaged backgrounds and continue to commit what are considered traditionally female crimes (petty property offences). In fact, feminist criminologists are quick to suggest that the increase in female criminal involvement is more directly related to the feminization of poverty (the increasing number of females, such as single mothers, in the ranks of the poor) than to female emancipation. Furthermore, feminists have critiqued the thesis because of its primary assumption: that maleness or masculinity is the norm to which women should be compared.[99] Nonetheless, the thesis certainly sparked discussion about women's offending and placed such behaviour in its social structural and economic context: Criminological theorizing could no longer emphasize women's biology as the main link to criminal behaviour.

Power Control Theory

John Hagan and his colleagues created power control theory, which offers an explanation of the gendered nature of criminal behaviour by integrating gender with economic and social structural factors.[100] The theory focuses on the relative power of men and women in families and how that power is related to roles within the capitalist economic system. For example, *patriarchal families* are comprised of men who work outside the home and women who are stay-at-home moms. In this family type, both fathers and mothers supervise the activities of sons and daughters, but daughters are more closely supervised. Being socialized into the "cult of domesticity" is considered appropriate for girls in these families. Boys, on the other hand, are granted more freedom, since the goal is that one day they will also be patriarchs. Boys in patriarchal families have more independence and freedom and, as a result, are more likely to get into trouble than their sisters.

In contrast, *egalitarian families* are made up of mothers and fathers who both work outside the home and who both supervise their children. Single-parent, female-headed households are also included in this category. Girls are supervised in a similar manner as their brothers and are granted more freedom and independence. In addition, daughters in these families have independent, "liberated" mothers as role models. As a result, daughters in egalitarian families, with similar ranges of freedom as their brothers, are as likely to share in the independence, experimentation, and possible trouble as their male siblings. The result is higher rates of delinquency and crime among daughters raised in egalitarian families. Overall, the theorists predict that we should witness greater differences in delinquency in patriarchal than egalitarian families when looking at boys' and girls' behaviours.

While power control theory certainly addresses weaknesses with other theories by situating gender roles in the broader social structural context, critics contend that the theory makes the assumption that if a woman is working outside the home for wages there will be equality within the household. This may not be the case. As Elizabeth Comack points out, attention must be paid to the nature of women's work outside the household and how this might affect gender relations at home.[101]

Radical Feminist Theory

Radical feminists locate the cause of many of women's problems, including crime and victimization, in patriarchy. This system of male domination includes both a structure and an ideology that privileges men over women. Most radical feminists argue that patriarchy is rooted in biological differences; these differences led to a division of labour that accords more importance to men's paid labour. Many claim that the division of labour by sex was actually the first class structure in society.[102] As a result of their dominant position, men are able to control women's reproductive labour and their labour power generally.

Radical feminist research locates the cause of female crime in women's subordination and victimization at the hands of males. For example, they suggest that in patriarchal societies boys are socialized to be aggressive and exploitive of women in relationships. Exploitation is obvious in sexual assault and domestic violence situations, but gendered violence also exists in family situations where molestation and incest occur, in instances of date rape, and when girls and women are sexually harassed at school, university, or work. Sexual and physical abuse and exploitation may cause girls to run away from home; they may end up on the streets where further abuse and criminal behaviour is a likely outcome.[103] Radical feminists argue

that in many cases the precursor to female criminal involvement includes abusive relationships: The female criminal is a victim—of a patriarchal system and of men in her life.

Radical feminists also show how the justice system itself contributes to female crime and delinquency. Because of the tendency to sexualize the deviance of females, young girls and women have been brought under the control of the criminal justice system for their sexually precocious behaviours. These researchers provide evidence illustrating how the criminal justice system is used as a line of defence against women who act outside of traditional gender roles. For example, under early systems of juvenile justice, like Canada's Juvenile Delinquents Act, girls were more likely to be prosecuted for sexual promiscuity and what are considered self-destructive behaviours than were boys. Research indicates that this pattern of double standards in the treatment of girls and young women, compared to boys, continues.[104]

Radical feminist scholarship also focuses on the ways in which the passage and enforcement of laws favour the interests of men. Canadian law prior to 1983 did not permit a man to be charged with raping his wife. Wife battering, child abuse, and incest, for example, are all behaviours that traditionally were perceived as "private" troubles occurring behind closed doors and not the business of outside agencies. Law enforcement officials in the past were reluctant to get involved in such incidents and often did not take allegations of assault seriously unless severe physical victimization was evident. By treating wife abuse as a private problem and turning a blind eye, police effectively contributed to the problem by permitting husbands to beat their wives over prolonged periods without fear of repercussion.

Critics of radical feminism suggest that patriarchy alone cannot explain women's offending behaviour and their victimization. These critics argue that the division of labour by sex was not always hierarchical, but became so only when men's labour began to be associated with the public realm and women's work with the private realm.[105] Other critics argue that violence against women cannot be solely linked to patriarchal relations, since many marriages are void of such exploitative relations. Rather, violence against women is the result of a combination of factors, all of which contribute to inequality between men and women.[106]

Socialist Feminism

Socialist or Marxist feminism is able to address some of the criticisms of radical feminist theorizing by merging radical feminist theory with Marxist theory. Socialist feminists argue that both patriarchy and capitalism are to blame for women's criminal behaviours and the kinds of victimization they experience. In a sense, women are "double oppressed" by both systems; the result is a lower crime rate for women in capitalist societies. According to James Messerschmidt, capitalists control the labour of workers, while men control women both economically and biologically.[107] Isolated in families, women have fewer opportunities to commit crimes, while males, working the public realm, have more such opportunities, and therefore have a higher crime rate. This is reflected in the types of crime committed, in general, by the genders. Men are more involved in elite deviance as well as street crimes like assault, break-and-enter, and drug offences, while women's deviance continues to include primarily petty property offences and non-violent crimes. Powerless and doubly oppressed, women are more likely to express their subordinated status through drug use and other self-destructive behaviours.

Because of their powerlessness, women are more likely to experience personal victimization at the hands of males, often a spouse or intimate partner. In particular, lower-class males, themselves victims of the capitalist state, attempt to regain feelings of power and status by "picking on" the only target left available to them—women.[108]

Many socialist feminists recognize the interaction of class, race, and gender in explanations of crime and victimization. Some Canadian criminologists study the impact of the legal system in reproducing the sexist, racist, and class-based social structure in the country. The interaction of these factors contributes to the different patterns of criminal behaviours among different segments of the population as well as their differential treatment by the law and criminal justice system. Life experiences are indeed different for a young, Aboriginal woman from a Prairie reserve compared to those of a white female from upper-class Richmond Hill, Ontario, or White Rock, British Columbia.[109]

Despite the contributions of socialist feminism to criminology, in particular its recognition that any explanation of criminal behaviour requires an investigation into multiple factors, including race, gender, and class, critics of the perspective exist. Radical feminists are displeased with socialist feminism's goal of uniting Marxism with radical feminism. Uniting the two reduces patriarchy to just another tool used by capitalists to oppress. In other words, radical feminists express concern that the explanatory power of patriarchy is lost by bringing capitalism into the picture. According to these critics, the two systems are different and should be treated separately.[110]

Research by both radical and socialist feminists provides important insights into our conceptualization of law, social control, power relationships, and crime-causation theory. They include

- Reframing the way sexual assault is conceptualized (see Chapter 10)
- Acknowledging the fact that the way criminologists conceive of and define violence is male-centred
- Uncovering the relationship between male power, female economic dependency, and battery (e.g., spouse abuse)
- Revealing the powerful effect of gender on justice processing[111]

Feminist theorizing has certainly added to the discipline of criminology. By bringing women "into the picture"—by researching women's offending, victimization, and situation in society—feminist theorists have broadened our understanding of crime. Importantly, these theories have impacted on the way the criminal justice system operates and the way society views women, although many would argue we still have a long way to go toward achieving equality. Comack describes the transformation of feminist theorizing and research since feminist criminology first appeared on the scene over 40 years ago. Initially concerned with bringing women into the picture, *empiricist feminists* used scientific research methods to investigate women's criminality. One of the major weaknesses these feminists sought to rectify was the absence of women from mainstream criminological research and theories. The questions they sought to answer were, first, whether theories created by and about men could also explain women's offending and, second, whether these mainstream ("malestream") theories could explain the significant gender gap in criminal behaviour.[112]

Over time, feminist criminologists recognized that using scientific research methods, which were also developed by the male academic mainstream, may not be the best way to help female offenders find their "voice" and access their stories. *Standpoint feminism,* with its recognition of the importance of race, ethnicity, class, as well as gender, also worked to provide avenues for long-silenced women offenders to express their experiences in their own words. Through the voices of their subjects, standpoint feminists were able to draw attention to the complex ways in which victimization, poverty, discrimination, family responsibilities, and a variety of other factors contributed to women's criminal behaviour in direct and indirect ways.

Postmodernist feminism focuses on the importance of discourse—"historically specific systems of meaning which form the identities of subjects and objects"[113]—in understanding the way in which female offenders have been constructed by experts, professionals, and official processes as the "other." When constructed in this manner, it is easy to lose sight of the fact that these women are mothers, daughters, sisters, and aunts, who are in many ways very similar to their non-criminalized sisters. Danielle Laberge proposes that when we consider that crime is the outcome of interactions between individuals and the criminal justice system, it might be better to think not in terms of criminal women but of criminalized women.[114]

These feminists draw on the work of Michel Foucault, whose writing focuses on the relation between power and knowledge and how the growth of new knowledges or discourses (e.g., psychology, psychiatry, criminology) contributed to a "disciplinary society" and new modes of surveillance of the population. Postmodern feminists prefer to investigate the *how* questions rather than the *why* questions.[115] Rather than asking why women commit crimes, they are more interested in examining how women and girls are defined and constituted by professional discourses, and how particular techniques of control contribute to women's continued exclusion from and marginalization in society.

Through their work, and over the years, feminist criminologists have generally worked to counteract stereotypes constructed around female offenders. Female offenders in early criminological theories, in media representations, and in the minds of many members of the public, are thought of as monsters. Feminist criminologists made great strides toward tearing down the stereotypes and providing a more realistic and accurate portrait of female offenders. However, several events in the 1990s—most notably Karla Homolka's involvement in a series of sexual assaults and homicides alongside her husband Paul Bernardo, as well as the beating and drowning death of Reena Virk, which involved several girls—essentially undid some of the successes feminists had accomplished. The backlash against feminist criminologists' portrayal of female offenders was criticized; public reaction to the nasty and violent female offender as described in the media dominated public opinion.

Feminist criminology has increased the knowledge about women and crime. We know far more about the lives of criminalized women than ever before. However, a large part of the feminist program is to continue to work toward dispelling myths about criminalized women. Many feminists concur with Elizabeth Comack and Laureen Snider, who point out that "it is one thing for feminists to produce particular discourses about women and crime, and it is quite another to have those discourses heard."[116] Feminists share this concern with several other emerging explanations, all of which offer a more critical perspective on crime and criminology.

Emerging Explanations

Over the last few decades, a number of important critical perspectives have emerged that are worthy of attention. These perspectives, which have broadened the scope and influence of criminology, include left realism, restorative justice, peacemaking criminology, and critical perspectives.

Left Realism Left realism is an example of a critical perspective.[117] This school of thought emerged during the early 1970s in the United Kingdom as a response to the perception that radical criminologists (called "radical idealists" by left realists) place far too much weight on the evils of elite deviance, largely ignoring the fact that the disenfranchised lower classes are persistently

The Ontario Coalition Against Poverty (OCAP) is a direct-action anti-poverty organization that campaigns against regressive government policies as they affect poor and working people. It also provides direct-action advocacy for individuals against eviction, termination of welfare benefits, and deportation. In this photo an activist affiliated with OCAP protests in support of affordable housing.

victimized by street crime.[118] Left realists recognize street crime as an inevitable outcome of social and political deprivation. They seek a crime-control agenda, capable of being implemented in a capitalist system that will protect the more vulnerable members of the lower classes from crime and the fear of crime. According to left realists, fear of crime has given conservative right-wing politicians a green light to promote a repressive law-and-order agenda.

Although left realists point out the flaws of official statistics, they also note that crime tends to be intra-class as opposed to inter-class. This means that working- and lower-class individuals are victimizing each other. In other words, there is universal opposition to crime: It hurts members of all classes and all classes have a vested interest in effective crime control policies and practices. According to left realists, greater effort must be exerted toward investigating and penalizing the crimes of the powerful, which are far more costly than the crimes of the lower classes, but at the same time something must be done to protect members of all classes from crime.

Left realists are concerned with policies that will help reduce crime in the short term. Street crime is real and people require protection from its devastating effects. According to these scholars, the police and criminal justice system do serve a useful purpose and, although flawed, can be adapted to provide more just, equitable crime control to all classes. With greater sensitivity to the public, and with a reduction in the force used against lower-class criminals, the police and criminal justice system generally could truly become a beneficial service to society. Left realism has as its objective the adjustment and reworking of the system to reduce crime through the implementation of effective policies. However, it is leftist and not conservative right-wing thinking that should inform the creation of these policies.

As far as policy goes, left realists argue for greater involvement of the working class in the creation of crime reduction and social control policies. Co-opting the target of crime control (the working class) and including this class in the creation of crime control agendas might risk making the state apparatus more effective in controlling the working class. However, left realists are optimistic that working-class input into crime control policies would result in crime control that genuinely addresses their needs and concerns. Aboriginal peoples in Canada have long been calling for more involvement in the administration of justice in their communities. The rationale behind either separate Aboriginal systems of justice, or the inclusion of Aboriginal-based programming in the system as it now exists, is that such systems would be more effective than the alien system of justice that has been imposed upon them.

Restorative justice is an example of a philosophy that is compatible with left realism. Restorative justice views crime as behaviour that is injurious to social relationships and to the community. As such, restorative justice-based programming focuses on the resolution of conflict between parties through a holistic and peaceful approach. This emphasis on peace is shared with another recent approach in criminology: peacemaking criminology.

Peacemaking Criminology A recently articulated critical perspective, peacemaking promotes the idea of peace, justice, and equality in society. For peacemaking criminologists, the current obsession with punishment and the war on crime suggests an orientation to criminology that

As his regime toppled, so did this statue of Saddam Hussein in Iraq. Opposing coercive state control, like that exercised in Iraq under Hussein's control, peacemaking criminologists argue that peace, justice, and equality in society will reduce the amount of violence and thus criminal behaviours.

only encourages violence. The state's current attempt at dealing with crime is crime-encouraging rather than crime-discouraging. As Larry Tifft and Dennis Sullivan put it, "The violent punishing acts of the state and its controlling professions are of the same genre as the violent acts of individuals. In each instance these acts reflect an attempt to monopolize human interaction."[119]

Scholars such as Harold Pepinsky and Richard Quinney advocate for mediation and conflict resolution policies as an alternative to punishment and prison. Peacemakers suggest that mutual aid, mediation, and conflict resolution, rather than coercive state control, are the best means to achieve a harmonious, peaceful society.[120] In short, peacemaking criminology advocates humanistic, non-violent, and peaceful solutions to crime, all of which fall directly in line with restorative justice. As such, the peacemaking perspective is part of an intellectual and social movement toward restorative justice. What is restorative justice? According to John Braithwaite, restorative justice means "restoring victims, a more victim centered criminal justice system, as well as restoring offenders and restoring community." This includes restoring

- property loss;
- sense of security;
- dignity;
- sense of empowerment;
- deliberative democracy;

- harmony based on a feeling that justice has been done;
- social support.[121]

The Canadian criminal justice system currently incorporates some restorative justice–based programs as part of its method of working with offenders and victims of crime. For example, victim-offender mediation programs, first devised in Elmira, Ontario, in 1974, have spread across the country. Family group conferencing is another restorative justice–based approach used widely across Canada. The basic format of restorative justice–based programs includes face-to-face confrontation between offenders, victims, relatives, respective community members, members of the criminal justice system, and others. While the meetings may start with hostility on the part of victims or others, the tendency is for offenders to feel ashamed and become apologetic and for participants to express their feelings regarding the incident. Through the course of the meetings, the objectives of understanding, communication, healing, and eventually reintegration of the offenders are usually achieved.[122]

Restorative justice principles are not new; Aboriginal peoples have practised them for centuries. Healing and sentencing circles, which form the basis of many current restorative justice programs, are based on the inclusiveness characteristic of small-scale communities where restoration of order through successful dispute resolution was essential.

THEORY INFORMS POLICY

Youth Restorative Action Project Restorative justice has as its goal the reintegration of offenders into the community. Victims and offenders are involved in the process, the ultimate objective of which is to restore a sense of balance between offender, victim, and the community within which the offence took place. The Youth Restorative Action Project (YRAP) is an example of the creative integration of theory and policy to achieve these goals. Restorative justice–based approaches are endorsed by the Youth Criminal Justice Act under Section 18.

The first YRAP program was developed in Edmonton, Alberta, by 16-year-old Jasmina

Sumanac, an immigrant from Serbia, who was struck by the need to deal with the rampant racism and hate she witnessed among youth. With the help of youth worker Mark Cherrington, she and several other youth developed YRAP. Made up of young people between the ages of 14 and 21, YRAP is described by one of its long-serving members as "youth being there for other youth, wanting to help other youth out."[123] As with other Youth Justice Committees, the group receives referrals from judges and lawyers. YRAP is unique in that it involves a panel of youth that hears cases involving other youth usually charged with offences involving issues relating to racism, homelessness, prostitution, and intolerance. As one YRAP member explains, "I vote to include a case when it is something that I feel is a racially motivated crime, something with abuse. Usually, I try to vote yes for that because I think it is important to get that issue in the forefront."[124]

Youth members decide on sentencing issues, are responsible for bail hearings, and public education. As Bryan Hogeveen puts it, "all facets are administered and run by the youth. Through a democratic process, participants decide on what cases they will hear, make any and all court appearances, arrange for venues, apply for funding, and mentor youth after a panel hearing."[125] Importantly, YRAP members come from diverse backgrounds, ranging from honours students to ex-offenders and recovering drug addicts.[126] Furthermore, adults' role in the group is minimal, "except in the rare instance when they are called up on to provide clarification on technical points of law."[127]

YRAP held its first meeting in October 2002 and has since earned a name for itself among the courts and the media, who applaud the program for the creativity of its dispositions. Youth participants work to provide solutions that are closely related to the crime committed. As one member states, "not that they will necessarily fix the crime, but something that will give the youth a way to express why they committed the crime that they did." Examples of "solutions" include the use of music to express the underlying conditions leading to their offence, the production of full-length documentaries, speaking to groups about social justice issues, and organizing youth groups around social justice concerns.[128] By 2006,

YRAP had been involved with 110 cases; only a handful were unsuccessful (the matter was referred back to court). In 2004 YRAP was awarded the prestigious international Royal Commonwealth Gold Youth Service Award. YRAP currently exists in Ottawa as well.

Critical Criminology   What does it mean to be "critical"? Marxism and left realism are examples of critical thinking. Left realists are critical in that they think the system needs to be "tweaked" or modified to improve the manner in which the police and criminal justice system deal with criminals and victims. They critique the way the system currently works and call for improvements to it so that, for example, policing and the criminal justice system will more effectively protect *both* upper- and lower-class victims of crime. Their goal is not a complete overhaul of the way we deal with crime but rather changes that will make the system more fair and just. Some scholars argue there are different kinds of "critique" and therefore different branches of "critical criminology."[129]

Recent developments in critical criminology have focused on the very nature of the criminological enterprise. These critical theorists show that the discipline of criminologist is a "dominated science" whose "tools, instruments, and objects do not derive from an autonomous intellectual engagement with the social world but are instead predetermined by the logic of the criminal-justice field."[130] By this, they mean that criminology operates within the confines of a certain definition of reality; definitions of what is and is not deviant or criminal are set in place by the criminal justice system and its affiliated agencies. In other words, a certain "worldview" regarding crime and justice has been set in place and has a life of its own. When people talk about what is normal and what is criminal, it is in the context of these already set-in-place definitions. Criminology is no different.

Critical theorists who work within this perspective point out how traditional criminology and even more recent attempts at critical criminology (such as peacemaking criminology and restorative justice) still operate within the foundations and assumptions of "the system." In this sense, then, criminology is dominated by traditional views of crime, criminal behaviour, criminals, and even by the classic theories of crime. Tinkering with the system assumes that the system is good, but just needs to be fixed up a bit. According to George Pavlich, restorative justice is thus "paradoxical" in nature: Opposing the criminal justice system and field from within is challenging indeed.[131] To put it another way:

> In claiming its opposition to the formal criminal-justice system, restorative justice employs the language of this system, thereby reproducing its underlying logic. Moreover, in practice, restorative justice has shown a decided tendency toward supplementing and complementing the criminal-justice game rather than challenging it or transforming it in any fundamental sense.[132]

The new critical criminology asks us to think beyond the confines of these conceptions of crime and justice. R. S. Ratner, for example, argues that to be truly critical, critical criminology must "take the system to task rather than tinker with its parts."[133] Similarly, Bryan Hogeveen and Andrew Woolford call for critique that must "extend critique and thought beyond current ontological limits into the open spaces beyond criminal justice and law."[134] The difficulty with this type of critique is institutional hostility to it, which is realized in lack for funding for research, roadblocks to disseminating research findings, and lack of coverage in criminology textbooks.[135] Ratner describes the difficulty early Canadian critical theorists faced in their attempts to develop the field. She provides a "keyhole" glimpse of some of the trials endured in constructing an alternative to the ruling paradigm of a state-saturated field."[136] Ratner exposes the personal and professional challenges she faced because of her critical work, including being rejected

for a promotion, battling to have her work published, struggling to develop an academic journal in the field, and attempting to gain acceptance at major conferences.

Joane Martel similarly writes about the problems she experienced when government agencies obstructed her research on federal women offenders.[137] Funding for research projects based in this critical perspective is hard to come by. This is understandable: "for institutional arrangements to receive such scholarship favourably would be to invite their own destruction."[138] Yet, as critical theorists argue, it is time for criminology to break away from its history of being a part of the oppression of certain (marginalized) groups, to focus on contextualizing its existence in order to self-reflexively critique the role it has played as an agent of social control.

Critical criminologists focus on the importance of exploring crime- or law-related issues within political, social, economic, and cultural frameworks, using sociological, philosophical, anthropological, and legal perspectives and methodologies.[139] Furthermore, critical criminology "pursues reflection within such areas as colonial, ecological, environmental, indigenous, human-rights, and global studies, and characteristically attempts to bring the least-heard, most-violated voices into the social conversation."[140]

In addition, critical criminology is characterized by a commitment to radical social change. As Hogeveen and Woolford succinctly put it, "The time has come (again!) for an honest reflection on our scholarly self-absorption, our political impotence, and our disconnection from the people and social movements we study."[141]

REVIEW

Labelling theory, conflict theory, and radical and feminist theories offer alternative explanations of crime, in the sense that they do not restrict their inquiry to individual characteristics or to social or communal processes. These theories examine the impact of social control, gender, lawmaking, and law enforcement processes on the creation of offenders. The labelling and conflict theories, as critical as they are of the existing system of social control and criminal justice, envisage a system made

more just and equitable by reform and democratic processes; radical theory demands revolutionary change. Some feminists favour the former approach, others the latter. With long historical antecedents, all of these theories gained prominence in the 1960s and early 1970s, during an era of rebellion against social, political, and economic inequities. They represent an alternative to the **consensus model** (p. 190), which assumes that members of society generally agree on what is right and wrong and share the values on which the criminal code is based.

1. How does labelling act as a type of control?

Labelling theorists offer an alternative explanation of crime and the link to social control. **Labelling theory** (p. 184) has its intellectual roots in **symbolic interactionism** (p. 185). Initially created in an atmosphere that stressed the importance of **due process** (p. 184) and **equal protection** (p. 184) under the law, labelling theory argues that powerful groups, including the criminal justice system, control certain segments of the population through powerful labels. Labelling theory does not presume to explain all crime, but it does demonstrate that the criminal justice system is selective in determining who is to be labelled a criminal. It explains how labelling occurs, and it blames the criminal justice system for contributing to the labelling process and, therefore, to the crime problem.

2. How are conflict theories different from the other theories we've looked at?

Conflict theory (p. 191) goes a step beyond labelling theory in identifying the forces that selectively decide in the first place what conduct should be singled out for condemnation—usually, so it is claimed, to the detriment of the powerless and the benefit of the powerful. **Penologists** (p. 197) study the penal system.

3. What is "radical" about radical theories?

Radical theory singles out the relationship between the owners of the means of production and the workers under capitalism as the root cause of crime and of all social inequities. **Radical criminology** (p. 197) demands the overthrow of the existing order, which is said to perpetuate criminality by keeping the oppressed classes under the domination of the capitalist ruling class.

4. How do criminologists explain female offending and victimization?

Feminist theories focus on the social, economic, and political status of women in society and how that impacts their criminal behaviour, their victimization experiences, and the way they are treated by the criminal justice system. Feminists also investigate the way that gender interacts with social class, age, and ethnicity to create different lived experiences for different categories of people. In recent decades, a variety of new perspectives on crime and criminology have emerged, including feminist theories, restorative justice and peacemaking criminology, and critical criminology.

Conflict, feminist, and radical theories have adherents and opponents. Research to demonstrate the validity of the theories has produced mixed results. More important, all these theories have challenged conventional criminologists to rethink their approaches and to provide answers to questions that had not been asked before.

CRIMINOLOGY & PUBLIC POLICY

The Conservative Party in the 2006 federal election included in its long list of promises to the Canadian electorate the promise to pass a constitutional amendment to deprive federal prisoners of their right to vote. The right to vote for prisoners has been a subject of debate in Canada for years. In fact, in 1985 and then again in 1993, attempts were made to do the same thing. Prisoners' right to vote is guaranteed under the Canadian Charter of Rights and Freedoms. As the Charter states, "every citizen of Canada has the right to vote in an election of members of the House of Commons or of a legislative assembly." During the most recent failed attempt to amend the constitution in order to deprive federal inmates of their right to vote, Chief Justice Beverley McLachlin said, "The idea that certain classes of people are not morally fit or morally worthy to vote and to participate in the law-making process is ancient and obsolete. . . . [T]he legitimacy of the law and the obligation to obey the law flows directly from the right of every citizen to vote." Proponents of the ban on inmate voting rights argue that lawbreakers should not be permitted to elect lawmakers.

Yet, Canada is one of the few western democracies to include voting as a constitutional right. The United States, for example, restricts inmate voting. In fact, in some states, felons are disenfranchised for the rest of their lives. Current estimates place the total number of disenfranchised felons and ex-felons at approximately 3.9 million voting-age citizens. Of this number, approximately 1.4 million have completed their sentences. Over one-third of the total disenfranchised population are black men. Recently, felon disenfranchisement laws have received considerable attention from a variety of studies and in the popular press. Some commentators discuss felon disenfranchisement in terms of altered electoral outcomes; others emphasize its effect on democratic representation. Still others focus on felon disenfranchisement's disparate impact, contending that such laws deny the vote to over 10 percent of the black voting-age population in 15 states.

In the United States it is difficult to deny that skyrocketing incarceration rates have raised the stakes of criminal disenfranchisement, altering the composition of the American electorate. In Canada there are about 12 000 federal inmates. Regulations surrounding voting dictate that inmates are permitted to vote in the riding where they lived before being incarcerated or where they were convicted, not where they are serving their sentence. This means that, on average, there are about

40 inmate voters per federal riding. And considering voter turnout for this group is well below the national average, at this time it seems that Canada isn't faced with the same issues as those in the United States. (*Source:* Ira Basen, "Reality Check: Voting No to Prisoners," CBC Reality Check Team, www.cbc.ca/canadavotes/realitycheck/prisoners.html, accessed June 23, 2007; "Developments in the Law: One Person, No Vote: The Laws of Felon Disenfranchisement," *Harvard Law Review,* **115**, 2002: 1939. Reprinted by permission of the Harvard Law Review Association and William S. Hein Company.)

Questions for Discussion   Should inmates be permitted to vote? Do you think Canada should follow the lead of some U.S. states in disenfranchising offenders for life? What is the justification for these laws? What do you think is the effect of taking away an ex-offender's voting rights? Does it unfairly contribute to the labelling of ex-offenders? What role does race play in the effect of these laws? Do you support law reform in this area? If so, what would you propose?

YOU BE THE CRIMINOLOGIST

What kind of crime-prevention program is suggested by critical, Marxist, and feminist theories? How would you go about designing such a program? How would you evaluate its effectiveness?

Visit the Online Learning Centre: www.mcgrawhill.ca/olc/adler

ENVIRONMENTAL THEORY

CHAPTER **9**

CHAPTER QUESTIONS

1. How do situational theories explain crime?

2. What do theories of victimization add to the explanation of crime?

3. How do these theories help to inform techniques, practices, and programs to help prevent crime?

Airports in Canada have increased security in recent years. These security officers are monitoring checkpoints throughout the facility.

David Milgaard spent over 20 years in prison for the sexual assault and murder of a nursing assistant named Gail Miller in Saskatoon. When the case was reopened, geographic profilers submitted evidence to the Supreme Court of Canada that suggested Milgaard was not the offender. Rather, the "hunting" habits of Larry Fisher more closely fit the location and timing of the offence.[1]

Sizzler's Steak House was twice victimized within a two-week period, apparently by the same "scruffy" white male in his mid-30s or early 40s. The assailant, who claimed to be armed with a Magnum revolver, is also a suspect in several other robberies in the area.[2]

There were 19 of them, and together they made up one of the more sophisticated and organized auto theft rings in Ontario. They focused on moving high-end luxury vehicles (and other property), including Lincolns, BMWs, Hummers, Cadillac Escalades and Mini Coopers, to West Africa and the Middle East.[3]

Here we have three different types of crime, committed in three different locations involving three different types of harm: non-consensual intercourse and homicide, the taking of property by force and violence, and the loss of automobiles. The Crown prosecutors in these jurisdictions will know what to do. They will identify

these crimes under the Criminal Code and they will file charges accordingly. But the criminologist, looking more deeply into these crime scenarios, will consider something in addition, something seemingly not of interest to the law—namely, that each of the three crimes occurs at a specific time, at a specific place. The presence of an offender is only one of the necessary components: Crimes require many conditions that are independent of the offender, such as the availability of a person to be assaulted or of goods to be stolen.

The three scenarios enable us to see how, up to the actual moment of the crime, the events were a part of everyday life: People go to and from work; stores are open for business; and people own BMWs, which must be parked when not being driven. For a full understanding of crime, it is necessary to find out how offenders view the scenes and situations around them as they exercise an option to commit a crime.

In other chapters, we have focused on factors explaining why individuals and groups engage in criminal behaviour. Now we look at how, in recent years, some criminologists have focused on why offenders choose to commit one offence rather than another at a given time and place. They identify conditions under which those who are prone to commit crime will in fact do so. Current criminological re-

search shows that both a small number of victims and a small number of places experience a large amount of all crime committed. Crimes are events. Criminals choose their targets. Certain places actually attract criminals. Think about the community you live in. Are there some places you hesitate to go to alone? If so, you recognize that some spaces are more dangerous than others. Are there areas that are safe during the day but not at night? Crime has temporal patterns—some crimes happen more often at night than during the day; others happen more on the weekend than during the rest of the week. There are even what criminologists call "seasonal patterns." Certain lifestyles increase people's chances of being victimized. For example, is a drunk person walking alone more likely to be attacked than a sober one? Although victims of crime rarely are to blame for their victimization, they frequently play a role in the crimes that happen to them.

In this chapter, we discuss theories of crime and theories of victimization. We will demonstrate how various environmental, opportunity, and victimization theories are interrelated. We will also explore the prevention of crimes against people, places, and valuable goods, presenting current criminological research. In this discussion, we include situational crime prevention, diffusion of benefits, routine precautions, and the theoretical and practical implications of focusing on the victims and targets of crime.

SITUATIONAL THEORIES OF CRIME

Among the theories of crime that focus on the situation in which a crime occurs, three distinct approaches have been identified: environmental criminology, the rational-choice perspective, and the routine-activity approach. These theoretical approaches to crime are sometimes called "opportunity theories" because they analyze the various situations that provide opportunities for specific crimes to occur (see Table 9.1).

Environmental Criminology

Environmental criminology examines the location of a specific crime and the context in which it occurred in order to understand and explain crime patterns. Environmental criminologists ask, Where and when did the crime occur? What are the physical and social characteristics of the crime site? What movements bring offender and target together at the crime site? They want to know how physical "location in time and space" interacts with the offender, the target/victim, and the law that makes the crime an illegal act.[4]

Contrary to the established criminological theories that explain criminal motivation, environmental criminology begins with the assumption that some people are criminally motivated. Through

mapping crimes on global, country, province, county, city, or site-specific levels, such as a particular building or plot of land, environmental criminologists can see crime patterns. They then relate these crime patterns to the number of targets; to the offender population; to the location of routine activities, such as work, school, shopping, or recreation; to security; and to traffic flow.

Mapping crimes and analyzing the spatial crime patterns is not new (Chapter 3). In the nineteenth century, André Guerry examined the spatial patterning of crime through his comparison of conviction rates in various regions in France.[5] Adolphe Quételet tried to establish links between seasonal differences and the probability of committing crime. He found, for instance, that property crimes increase in the winter months in France, whereas "the violence of the passions predominating in summer, excites to more frequent personal collisions" and a rise in crimes against persons (Chapter 3).[6] Contemporary research takes a more focused, crime-specific approach. While current research was foreshadowed by the work of nineteenth-century theorists, the analysis of spatial crime patterns owes much of its recent popularity to the emergence of the rational-choice perspective.

Rational-Choice Perspective

The **rational-choice perspective,** developed by Ronald Clarke and Derek Cornish, is based on two main theoretical approaches.[7] The first of these—utilitarianism—was addressed in Chapter 3. It assumes that people make decisions with the goal of maximizing pleasure and minimizing pain. The second basis for the rational-choice perspective is traditional economic choice theory, which argues that people evaluate the options and choose what they believe will satisfy their needs. According to this perspective, a person decides to commit a

TABLE 9.1 Ten Principles of Opportunity and Crime

1. Opportunities play a role in causing all crime.
2. Crime opportunities are highly specific.
3. Crime opportunities are concentrated in time and space.
4. Crime opportunities depend on everyday movements.
5. One crime produces opportunities for another.
6. Some products offer more tempting crime opportunities.
7. Social and technological changes produce new crime opportunities.
8. Opportunities for crime can be reduced.
9. Reducing opportunities does not usually displace crime.
10. Focused opportunity reduction can produce wider declines in crime.

Source: Marcus Felson and Ronald V. Clarke, *Opportunity Makes the Thief: Practical Theory for Crime Prevention*, Police Research Series Paper 98 (London: Home Office, 1998), p. 9. © Crown Copyright 1998. Reprinted by permission of Her Majesty's Stationery Office.

Ex-Vancouver police detective and world-renowned expert Dr. Kim Rossmo explains the concept of geographical profiling to help solve criminal cases.

particular crime after concluding that the benefits (the pleasure) outweigh the risks and the effort (the pain).[8]

The rational-choice perspective assumes that people make these decisions with a goal in mind and that they are made more or less intelligently and with free will. This contrasts with the theories of criminality that have an underlying assumption that when people commit a crime, forces beyond their control drive them. Rational choice implies a limited sense of rationality. An offender does not know all the details of a situation; rather, he or she relies on cues in the environment or characteristics of targets. This means the offender may not be able to calculate the costs and benefits accurately, and in hindsight, the decision may seem foolish. Further, an offender may have an impaired ability to make wise choices, perhaps because of intoxication from drugs or alcohol.

According to the rational-choice perspective, most crime is neither extraordinary nor the product of a deranged mind. Most crime is quite ordinary and committed by reasoning individuals who decide that the chances of getting caught are low and the possibilities for a relatively good payoff are high. Since the rational-choice perspective treats each crime as a specific event and focuses on analyzing all its components, it looks at crime in terms of an offender's decision to commit *a specific* offence at *a particular* time and place.

A variety of factors (or characteristics) come into play when an offender decides to commit a crime. These factors are called "choice structuring properties." With the emphasis of rational-choice theory on analyzing each crime on a crime-specific basis, each particular type of crime has its own set of choice structuring properties (see Figure 9.1). Those for sexual assault differ from those for computer crime, and those for burglary differ from those for theft. Nevertheless, these properties tend to fall into the same seven categories. Thus, a potential thief, before committing a theft, is likely to consider the following aspects (categories):

- The number of targets and their accessibility
- Familiarity with the chosen method (e.g., fraud by credit card)
- The monetary yield per crime
- The expertise needed

FIGURE 9.1   Event model (*example:* break-and-enter in a middle-class suburb).

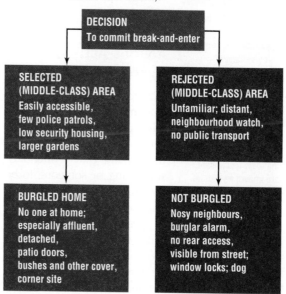

Source: Adapted from Ronald V. Clarke and Derek B. Cornish, *"Modeling Offenders' Decisions: A Framework for Research and Policy,"* in *Crime and Justice,* vol. 6, Michael Tonry and Norval Morris, eds. (Chicago: University of Chicago, 1985), p. 169. © 1985 by The University of Chicago. All rights reserved. Reprinted by permission of the University of Chicago Press.

- The time required to commit the act
- The physical danger involved
- The risk of apprehension

Characteristics fall into two distinct sets: those of the offender and those of the offence. The offender's characteristics include specific needs, values, learning experiences, and so on. The characteristics of the offence include the location of the target and the potential yield. According to rational-choice theory, involvement in crime depends on a personal decision made after one has weighed available information.

Rational-choice theory, unlike traditional theories, is not concerned with strategies of overall crime prevention. (It leaves those problems to others.) Rather, it is concerned with reducing the likelihood that any given offence will be committed by somebody "involved" in criminal activity. This theory, therefore, has its greatest potential in developing strategies to frustrate perpetrators and to prevent them from committing a crime then and there. It has its greatest challenge in demonstrating that such prevention will not lead to the commission of the intended crime later on or to the commission of other crimes (displacement). We turn to both of these issues shortly.

Routine-Activity Approach

According to Lawrence Cohen and Marcus Felson, a crime can occur only if there is someone who intends to commit a crime (likely offender), something or someone to be victimized (a suitable target), and no other person present to prevent or observe the crime (the absence of a capable guardian) (see Figure 9.2). Later revisions added a fourth element—no person to control the activities of the likely offender (personal handler). When a suitable target that is unguarded comes together in time and space with a likely offender who is not "handled," the potential for a crime is there.[9] This explanation is called the **routine-activity approach.** It does not explore the factors that influence the offender's decision to commit a crime. Instead, Cohen and Felson focus on the routine or everyday activities of people, such as going to work, pursuing recreation, running errands, and the like. It is through routine activities that offenders come into contact with suitable victims and targets.

The routine-activity approach began with an analysis of crime rate increases in the post–World War II era (1947 to 1974), when socioeconomic conditions had improved in North America. The increase was puzzling, since the general public (and some criminologists) expected crime rates to decrease with an increase in prosperity. But the authors of the routine-activity approach demonstrated that certain technological changes and alterations in the workforce create new crime opportunities. They referred to increases in female participation in the labour force, out-of-town travel, automobile usage, and technological advances as factors that account for higher risks of predatory victimization. Further advances in technology create more opportunities for the commission of crime. For example, as television sets, DVD players, personal and laptop computers, and CD players have become more common and lighter to carry, they have become attractive targets for thieves and burglars. The chance that a piece of property will become the target of a theft is based on the value of the target and its weight.[10] One need only compare the theft of washing machines and of electronic goods. Although both washing machines and electronic goods (such as television sets, laptop computers, and compact disc players) are expensive, washing machines are so heavy that their value is estimated at $8 per kilogram, compared with roughly $800 per kilogram for a laptop computer. And, of course, cellular phones have increasingly been subject to theft—for resale, for unauthorized telephone use, and for the facilitation of other crimes. Thus, cellular phones, as useful as they are in helping potential crime victims feel more secure, are also used increasingly by drug dealers to reduce the risk of having their calls traced.[11] It may be concluded that while technological developments help society run more smoothly, they also create new targets for theft, make old targets more suitable, or create new tools

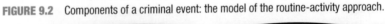

FIGURE 9.2 Components of a criminal event: the model of the routine-activity approach.

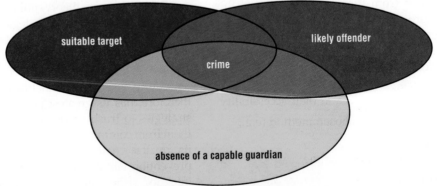

Decresting the Lovebug, Worldwide

It happened long before rational choice and routine activities had been created. Environmental design and situational crime prevention had yet to be invented. Yet there were Volkswagen Beetles the world over.

By 1961, Volkswagen (VW) had produced more than 4 million of these cars, fondly known as "lovebugs," according to a popular movie of that time. Close to a million were being driven in the United States, and the rest all over the world. On their hoods, these cars had the distinctive crest of the town of their manufacture: Wolfsburg.

It so happens that soon after the Beetles reached the American market, they lost their crests. Research conducted in 1961 established that 80 percent of the Beetles in the United States had been decrested. The question naturally arose: Who did it (and why)? Police statistics were useless, since VW owners did not feel inclined to report a loss amounting to a little over $3, even though some cars had body damage (the result of removal) many times that amount. Nor did VW owners report the loss to their insurance companies—the value being below the deductible.

The researchers got the help of industry. VW of America made available its sales figures for replacement crests. These figures, statistically analyzed, showed an amazing pattern: The crest thefts started in the east and travelled west within a little over two years. The thefts also travelled from the outer perimeters of cities to the suburbs (in less time).

Top photo: VW with crest popular with young males. Bottom photo: decrested VW.

Research established that decrestings were highest in the neighbourhood of junior high schools. In collaboration with junior high school administrators and police officials, it was learned that many students had amassed quantities of VW crests (but not those of other motor vehicles). Some were wearing them as necklaces; others had presented them to girlfriends.

Further statistical analysis showed that the fad—for that is what it seemed to

be—had spread all over the world—except Brazil. It turned out that VW Beetles manufactured in Brazil were not adorned with the Wolfsburg crest, but with the totally different crest of São Paolo, which apparently was not attractive to pubescent males.

A copy of the research report was sent to the VW company. Now everybody knows how reluctant VW was to change its lovebug. But it did: Within a few months, the Beetles rolled off VW's assembly line without the crest but with a slightly longer chrome strip. Problem solved, no more decrestings, no more body damage to the hood.

Source

Gerhard O. W. Mueller, *Delinquency and Puberty: Examination of a Juvenile Delinquency Fad* (New York: Criminal Law Education and Research Center, 1971; Fred B. Rothman, Distr.).

Questions for Discussion

1. Which of the theories discussed in this chapter best explains the decresting of VW Beetles?
2. More recently, young people have been known to steal the hood ornaments from Mercedes and BMWs, and wear them around their necks as status symbols. What can and should manufacturers of any product do at the design stage to prevent their products from becoming the targets (or instruments) of crime?

for criminals to use in committing their crimes. As people's daily work and leisure activities change with time, the location of property and personal targets also changes.

The logic of the routine-activity argument is straightforward: Routine patterns of work, play, and leisure time affect the convergence in time and place of motivated offenders who are not "handled," suitable targets, and the absence of guardians. If one component is missing, crime is not likely to be committed. And if all components are in place and one of them is strengthened, crime is likely to increase. Even if the proportions of motivated offenders and targets stay the same, changes in routine activities alone—for example, changes of the sort we have experienced since World War II—will raise the crime rate by multiplying the opportunities for crime. This approach has helped explain, among other things, rates of victimization for specific crimes, rates of urban

A male thief shoplifts from a music store by stuffing CDs into his pants as an employee appears to be guarding the merchandise.

homicide, and "hot spots"—areas that produce a disproportionate number of calls to police.[12]

Practical Applications of Situational Theories of Crime

The trio of approaches discussed here—environmental criminology, rational choice, and routine activities—often work together to explain why a person may commit a crime in a particular situation. We look now at how these theories of crime are used to explain specific varieties of crime, and how the ideas that arise from these theories have practical applications.

Break-and-Enter Criminologists are increasingly interested in the factors that go into a decision to commit break-and-enter (termed burglary in the United States): the location or setting of the building, the presence of guards or dogs, the type of alarms and external lighting, and so forth. Does a car in the driveway or a radio playing music in the house have a significant impact on the choice of home to break into? George Rengert and John Wasilchick conducted extensive interviews with suburban burglars in an effort to understand their techniques. They found significant differences with respect to several factors:[13]

- *The amount of planning* that precedes a break-and-enter. Professionals plan more than do amateurs.

- *Systematic selection of a home.* Some offenders examine the obvious clues, such as presence of an alarm, a watchdog, mail piled up in the mailbox, or newspapers on a doorstep. More experienced burglars look for subtle clues—for example, closed windows coupled with air conditioners that are turned off.

- The extent to which an offender pays *attention to situational cues.* Some routinely choose a corner property because it offers more avenues of escape, has fewer adjoining properties, and offers visibility.

Rengert and Wasilchick have also examined the use of time and place in break-and-enters (see Figure 9.3). Time is a critical factor to those committing break-and-enter, for three reasons:

- They must minimize the time spent in targeted places so as not to reveal their intention to break-and-enter.

- Opportunities for break-and-enter occur only when a dwelling is unguarded or unoccupied; that is, during daytime. (Many burglars would call in sick so often that they would be

FIGURE 9.3 Crime day of burglar #26.

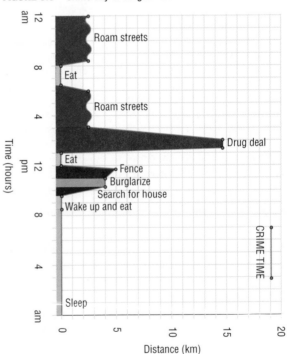

Source: George Rengert and John Wasilchick, *Suburban Burglary: A Time and a Place for Everything* (Springfield, IL: Charles C. Thomas, 1985), p. 35. Courtesy of Charles C Thomas Publisher, Ltd., Springfield, Illinois.

fired from their legitimate jobs; others simply quit their jobs because the jobs interfered with their criminal activities.)

- Burglars have "working hours"; that is, they have time available only during a limited number of hours (if they have a legitimate job).

Before committing their offences, they take into account familiarity with the area, fear of recognition, concern over standing out as somebody who does not belong, and the possibility (following some successful break-and-enters) that a particular area is no longer cost-beneficial. Season, too, plays an important role. One experienced burglar stated that because neighbourhoods are populated with children in the summer, he opted for winter months: "The best time to do crime out here is between 8:00 and 9:00 [A.M.]. All the mothers are taking the kids to school. I wait until I see the car leave. By the time she gets back, I've come and gone."[14]

Recent research demonstrates how important it is for burglars to have prior knowledge of their targets. They obtain such knowledge by knowing the occupants, by being tipped off about the occupants, or by observing the potential target. There are others, however, who come across break-and-enter opportunities during the course of their daily routine instead of planning them. For these offenders, rational-choice decisions are made right before the criminal event.[15]

Robbers and Robberies Richard Wright and Scott Decker conducted in-depth interviews with street robbers and found that they frequently victimize other street-involved individuals—drug dealers, drug users, and gang members—people who, because they are criminals themselves, are unlikely to go to the police. These people are also targeted because they are believed to have a lot of money, jewellery, and other desirable items. When women are targeted, it is because robbers believe they will not resist and are not armed. On the other hand, women are not the desirable targets men are because robbers think women do not carry as much money.[16]

Criminologists also study whether commercial robbers operate the same way as street robbers in their selection of targets. Robbers who target business establishments are interested in some of the same factors that concern burglars. Perpetrators carefully examine the location of the potential robbery, the potential gain, the capability of security personnel, the possibility of intervention by bystanders, and the presence of guards, cameras, and alarms.[17]

Criminologists have found that potential victims and establishments can do quite a bit to decrease the likelihood of being robbed. Following a series of convenience-store robberies in Gainesville, Florida, in 1985, a city ordinance required store owners to clear their windows of signs that obstructed the view of the interior, to position cash registers where they would be visible from

Thomas Crown (portrayed by Pierce Brosnan) crafted an extremely clever and well-planned theft of a painting from a well-guarded museum. Of course, not all burglars are so affluent and calculative.

the street, and to install approved electronic cameras. Within a little over a year, convenience-store robberies had decreased 64 percent.[18] We will return to this discussion later in this chapter.

Hot Products Why do thieves decide to steal some things and not others? What makes targets attractive? We have examined how burglars select which homes to burglarize, but once they have broken into a residence, how do they decide what to steal? When robbers target victims, they do so believing their chances of making off with something valuable are greater than their chances of not being successful in the robbery attempt. But what is it about things that make them valuable to robbers? Cohen and Felson argued that items are attractive if they are visible, easy to take away, valuable, and accessible.[19] Twenty years later, Ronald Clarke expanded this idea with his discussion of hot products—those consumer goods that are attractive to thieves. Using an acronym (CRAVED) to organize this idea, Clarke claims that goods are attractive if they are concealable, removable, available, valuable, enjoyable, and disposable (i.e., can be easily fenced). This approach takes into account what thieves do with goods after they are stolen, because that factor figures into their decisions about the attractiveness of items.[20]

College Campus Crime Crime on college campuses follows patterns that routine-activity theorists would expect; that is, if you engage in a risky and deviant lifestyle, your risk is significantly increased. Students who go out frequently and use recreational drugs regularly are at risk. You are more likely to be a victim of property crime if you

This woman, walking alone in a dark, deserted area, demonstrates how a victim can play a significant part in a criminal event.

are a male aged 17 to 20. If you live in an all-female dorm, you are less likely to experience a theft. Not surprisingly, students who spend several nights per week on campus and full-time students are more vulnerable to property crime than part-time students or those who do not spend as many nights on campus. With respect to target attractiveness, people who spend large amounts of money on non-essential items have a higher risk of on-campus theft than those who spend less.[21]

THEORIES OF VICTIMIZATION

Although the victim is mentioned in many theories of crime, direct consideration of the role that victims play in the criminal event has been of secondary significance. As a result of the "missing victim" in basic criminology, **theories of victimization** have recently been developed for the purpose of understanding crime from the victim's perspective or with the victim in mind.

The history of victims in criminology can be traced to Hans von Hentig's first article on the subject of victims, in 1941, in which he postulated that crime was an "interaction of perpetrator and victim."[22] Von Hentig, a highly respected scientist, had been a victim of Nazi persecution. It was that experience that made him focus on the significance of the victim. By carefully gathering and analyzing information, he demonstrated that tourist resorts were attractive to criminals who wanted to prey on unsuspecting vacationers. Von Hentig, through his book *The Criminal and His Victim*, published in 1948, founded the criminological subdiscipline of victimology, which examines the role played by the victim in a criminal incident.[23] Nevertheless, it must be acknowledged that the term "victimology" is a year older than von Hentig's book. The term was coined in 1947 by the Romanian lawyer Beniamin Mendelsohn.[24] In 1948, Frederic Wertham, an American psychiatrist, first used the term "victimology" in the United States.[25]

According to Canadian criminologist Ezzat Fattah, "von Hentig insisted that many crime victims contribute to their own victimization be it by inciting or provoking the criminal or by creating or fostering a situation likely to lead to the commission of the crime."[26] Thus, the entire event is regarded as crucial, because criminal behaviour involves both the action of the offender and interaction between offender and victim. Nor is it tenable to regard "criminals and victims . . . as different as night and day," because there is an undeniable link between offending and victimization.[27] Many offenders are victimized repeatedly, and victims are frequently offenders.

Such findings may be deemed highly controversial in a time when victims' rights groups have been active, and successful, in securing rights for victims of crimes. It must be understood, however, that *guilt* is not shared by offender and victim. Criminal guilt belongs to the perpetrator of a crime—and it must be proved at trial beyond a reasonable doubt. The victim is free of guilt. Victimology, however, can demonstrate how potential victims, by acting differently, can decrease the risk of being victimized.[28]

We turn now to a discussion of the dominant victimological theories.

Lifestyle Theories

A "lifestyle theory of victimization" was developed by Michael Hindelang, Michael Gottfredson, and James Garofalo in 1978. It argues that because of changing roles (working mother versus homemaker) and schedules (a child's school calendar), people lead different lifestyles (work and leisure activities). Variations in lifestyle affect the number of situations with high victimization risks that a person experiences.[29] The kinds of people someone associates with, such as co-workers, friends, and sexual partners, also affect victimization rates. For instance, someone who has a drug dealer or an inside trader as a friend has a greater chance of being victimized than a person who associates only with law-abiding people. (The similarity of the lifestyle theory of victimization and the routine-activities approach is quite apparent.)

The lifestyle theory of victimization centres on a number of specific propositions that outline the essence of the theory and signal directions for future research:[30]

Proposition 1: The probability of suffering a personal victimization is directly related to the amount of time that a person spends in public places (e.g., on the street, in parks), and particularly in public places at night.

Proposition 2: The probability of being in public places, particularly at night, varies as a function of lifestyle.

Proposition 3: Social contacts and interactions occur disproportionately among individuals who share similar lifestyles.

Proposition 4: An individual's chances of personal victimization are dependent upon the extent to which the individual shares demographic characteristics with offenders (such as young urban males).

Proposition 5: The proportion of time that an individual spends among non-family members varies as a function of lifestyle.

Proposition 6: The probability of personal victimization, particularly personal theft, increases as a function of the proportion of the time that an individual spends among non-family members (such as a young man who works a double shift at a factory versus a middle-aged woman who stays home to take care of an elderly parent).

Proposition 7: Variations in lifestyle are associated with variations in the ability of individuals to isolate themselves from persons with offender characteristics (being able to leave high-crime urban areas for sheltered suburbs).

Proposition 8: Variations in lifestyle are associated with variations in the convenience, the desirability, and visibility of the person as a target for a personal victimization (people who pass within the view of offenders, seem to have what the offender wants, appear unable to resist, or would probably not report the crime to the police).

Both the lifestyle theory of victimization and the routine-activity approach present some basic guidelines for reducing one's chances of victimization. And just as these theories themselves tend to embody common sense, so do the preventive measures derived from them. For instance, people in Canadian society are told not to drive while intoxicated, not to smoke or abuse alcohol or drugs, and not to eat too much greasy food. All these messages are intended to reduce the risks of dying in a motor vehicle accident, or from lung or liver cancer, or from an overdose, or from a heart attack. Although public-service messages designed to protect health may not always be heeded, people do not see them as "blaming the victim." Similarly, messages to prevent criminal victimization, like not walking alone and not frequenting deserted or unfamiliar places late at night, should not be viewed as overly restrictive and intrusive or as blaming victims who did not heed the advice. The messages directed at preventing victimization are based on theory and research and merely promote living and acting responsibly to ensure a more crime-free existence.

Victim-Offender Interaction

Marvin Wolfgang, one of the pre-eminent criminologists of his time, in his study of homicides found that many of the victims had actually brought upon themselves the attack that led to their murder. He coined the term "victim precipitation" to refer to situations where victims initiate the confrontations that lead to their death.[31]

Statistics indicate several trends in homicide in Canada; for example, the number of homicides committed with a firearm has increased. Increasingly, it seems, homicides, particularly those deemed gang-related, involve victims who are gang-involved. Ronal Shakeel Raj and Ali Abhari were gunned down in their Mercedes in an early morning attack in Vancouver in November 2007. Kyle Wong met a similar fate in March 2008. These are only two instances where victims have been targeted because of gang involvement. In a very real sense, victim actions (gang involvement) can lead to their eventual demise.[32]

James Tedeschi and Richard Felson put forward a theory of "coercive actions," which stresses that the way victims and offenders interact plays a large role in violent crime.[33] They argue that people commit violence purposefully. In other words, people don't just lose control. When they are violent, it is with a particular goal in mind. They make a decision to be violent (note the similarity between this theory and the rational-choice perspective) and tend to choose targets who are less powerful than themselves. In unarmed attacks, males are more likely to injure their opponents, while females are more likely to be injured. Gender is not the determinant as much as body size.[34] There are also victims who instigate attacks by irritating others. Schoolyard bullies are a good example.[35]

Patterns of Victimization

Most of the theories we've discussed thus far have focused on explaining offender behaviours: Why do some people commit crimes? Routine-activity theory and theories of victimization focus their attention on another key element in a crime event: the victim. How do the activities and behaviours of individuals going about their regular routine activities, living out their daily lifestyles, contribute to their potential victimization? What do we know about victimization?

Victimization surveys reveal to us that people's fear of victimization and their perception of victimization are much greater than actual victimization rates suggest. For example, a poll in Toronto found that people were very concerned about child abductions (43 percent), drugs and dealers (42 percent), sexual assault (36 percent), and police chases (24 percent). In another poll conducted in British Columbia, 60 percent of people reported being afraid of a home break-in.[36] Yet, according to the 2004 General Social Survey (GSS), the rate of victimization in Canada is 28 percent, a number that has remained relatively stable for the past two decades.[37]

There are a variety of reasons that help explain our exaggerated perception of criminal victimization and our fear of crime. One component is media overrepresentation of stranger victimizations and more serious crimes like homicide and aggravated assault.[38] If we look to research rather than television and movies, we find that victimization, like offending behaviour, is not random. There are patterns to victimization.

Lifestyle theories focus on peoples' routines and daily activities—their lifestyle—as contributing factors to their possible victimization. Leslie Kennedy and David Forde found support for the lifestyle approach to explaining victimization. They found that young, lower-class males who go out late at night to bars, work, or for a walk or drive have higher rates of victimization than other groups.[39] Further support comes from Vincent Sacco and Holly Johnson in their discovery that individuals who spend 30 or more evenings a month outside of the home are at a higher risk of victimization.[40]

Lifestyle is influenced in part by characteristics such as gender, age, social status, and relationships, which in turn can influence victimization. For example, GSS data indicate that men are more likely to be victims of robbery and assault, while women are more likely to be victims of sexual assault and theft. Women are more at risk of being victimized by someone they know, whereas men are more likely to be victimized by a stranger.[41]

Age influences victimization as well; young people, who make up a large proportion of offenders for certain crimes, also experience higher rates of victimization. In 2004, members of the 15-to-24 age group (who make up about 20 percent of the Canadian population) experienced a violent crime rate that was 1.5 to 19 times greater than the rate recorded for other age groups. In fact, the risk of violent victimization decreased steadily as age increased. While those aged 25 to 34 had a violent victimization rate of 157 per 1000, those aged 35 to 44 had a rate of 115 per 1000. Rates of violent victimization were lowest among the oldest age group: those 65 and older.[42] Evidence supports a connection between offending and victimization for younger age groups, as well as sharing in a particular lifestyle. Young people tend to go out with friends more, and are more likely to interact with strangers who are also within the same age group. Based on a study that found that young people between the ages of 16 and 24 are responsible for about 45 percent of property crimes and 32 percent of violent crimes, it follows that offenders and victims will be coming together more as they share in certain lifestyle-related activities.[43]

Social status creates lifestyle opportunities for some and closes these opportunities for others. Lower-class Canadians are more at risk for criminal victimization because they live in lower-class, often crime-prone areas. Similarly, street youth experience high rates of victimization because of their lifestyle. While the rate of assault among high school students is 39 percent, for street youth it is 69 percent.[44]

Single people are at a high risk of victimization, a pattern that is related to the fact that young people are likely to be single and participating in public activities, all of which interact to increase risk of victimization. However, for women, being in a relationship may increase the risk of victimization more so than for men. They are four times more likely to be killed by a spouse.[45]

Lifestyle factors interact with personal characteristics in ways that put different categories of people at risk for certain types of victimization. Lifestyle theories imply that modifying one's lifestyle may reduce one's chances of victimization. On the other hand, lifestyle-related characteristics such as gender, age, and social class are difficult and often impossible to change. Repeat victimizations provide further evidence for a lifestyle-based explanation for victimization.

Homeless individuals, like this man in Toronto's Chinatown, are at an increased risk of victimization. Such individuals are particularly vulnerable because they are often forced to live in neighbourhoods that are "hot spots" for crime.

Repeat Victimization

Not unlike the lifestyle theory of victimization, theories of repeat victimization also focus on the specific characteristics of situations in order to determine which factors account for the initial, as well as for repeat, victimization.[46] Theories of repeat victimization, also called "multiple victimization," dispel the myth that crime is uniformly distributed. Research shows that a small number of people and places account for a large amount of the crimes committed. For example, Canadian victimization survey data show that four out of ten victims have been victimized multiple times over the past year. If we break down the information further, about 19 percent of victims experienced two incidents in the year previous to the survey and 20 percent were victimized three or more times.[47]

The research literature on repeat victimization is increasing rapidly. This research reveals that prior victimization is a strong predictor of future victimization. Research has found that risks of a repeat break-and-enter are highest immediately after a previous invasion.[48] In their analysis of repeat victimization for crimes ranging from the repeated physical and sexual abuse of children to repeated credit card fraud, researchers concluded that the rational-choice theory of offender decision making is useful in understanding repeat victimization. Offenders choose targets based on the knowledge they gained in the previous victimization about the risks and rewards of a particular offence.[49] A recent study also found that repeat burglary victimization is a bigger problem in disadvantaged areas compared to well-off areas.[50]

Formulating strategies to deal with repeat victimizations would certainly be cost-beneficial.

Several innovative researchers have created databases of repeat victimization, starting a whole new line of research, called "hot-spots" research.

Hot Spots of Crime

In 1987, the Edmonton Police Service analyzed 153 000 calls for service and identified 21 of the "hottest" areas of the city. These "**hot spots**" for crime represented areas where a significant proportion of the calls for service were coming from. The analysis indicated that over 80 percent of the calls from these areas came from repeat addresses.[51] As this study and others show, crime does not occur randomly. Josée Savoie, Frédéric Bédard and Krista Collins focused on crime on the Island of Montreal and found that crime is indeed more prevalent in neighbourhoods characterized by an economically disadvantaged population, comprised primarily of single persons, single-parent families, recent immigrants, and a smaller proportion of people with higher levels of education. In addition, these higher crime neighbourhoods have a higher proportion of their land set aside for commercial or multi-family uses, which means less private ownership.[52]

Research findings such as these lead to the conclusion that attempts to prevent victimization should be focused not on victims, but on the places themselves by making them less vulnerable to crime. Change places, not people! We should identify neighbourhood hot spots, reduce social disorder and physical "incivilities," and promote housing-based neighbourhood stabilization. Subsequent research provides support for this idea by showing the crime and disorder reduction effects of hot-spots policing.[53]

Geography of Crime

Recently, new research based on the idea of hot spots has come into existence. It is labelled **geography of crime.** Researchers found that more crime occurs around high schools[54] and blocks with bars,[55] liquor stores,[56] the city centre,[57] and abandoned buildings.[58] Higher crime in areas that border high schools and bars is readily explainable: High schools contain a highly crime-prone age group. Bars attract, among others, offenders.[59] Abandoned buildings that are open and unsecured attract illegal users. In city centres, there are more opportunities to commit crime and generally fewer social controls in place.

A study on the vulnerability of ports and marinas to vessel and equipment theft found that the proximity of a port or marina to a high-crime area is significant in predicting boat theft.[60] Research on drug markets shows that areas with illicit drug markets account for a disproportionate amount of arrests and calls for police service.[61] In sum, the discovery that a large amount of crime occurs at a small number of places, and that such places have distinct characteristics, has led criminologists to explain crime in terms of not only who commits it, but also where it is committed.[62]

Interrelatedness of Theories

Environmental criminology, the rational-choice perspective, and the routine-activity approach focus on the interactions among the victim (or target), the offender, and the place. Recently, there has been an integration of these theories of crime with theories of victimization.[63] For example, one study using the lifestyle theory of victimization and the routine-activity approach explores how drinking routines are linked with victimization.[64] It found that alcohol contributed to victimization by making potential victims less able to protect themselves (more suitable targets). Motivated offenders also knew where to find their targets (in bars). Although the evidence on the relationships of alcohol, lifestyle, and increased risks of victimization is not conclusive, this research represents an important attempt at testing the interaction of lifestyle and routine-activity theories.

A further study on the relationship of alcohol and risks of victimization focuses specifically on the "suitable target" portion of routine-activity theory as it relates to sexual assault against women on college campuses.[65] It found that women who were sexually victimized went out more often and drank more when they were out than other women. Moreover, many of the women surveyed had experienced "uncomfortable advances in a bar or restaurant" or "on the street" or had "received obscene or threatening phone calls." In sum, by successfully combining theories of crime, like routine-activity theory, with lifestyle theory, situational factors (e.g., alcohol), and place considerations (e.g., bars and college settings) to examine victimization rates, criminological research has added a new dimension to explaining crime.[66]

As recognition of the victim and his or her role in the crime event in criminological theories grew, so too did recognition of the victim in the criminal justice system process. From a legal perspective, the two parties involved in the criminal justice process are the offender and the state. At most the victim served as a witness for the prosecution. However, as a result of the greater recognition of the role of the victim in this process, largely a result of the activities of the victims' rights movement in Canada (which in turn has its foundation in the women's movement), we have witnessed much progress in victims' rights in this country. Table 9.2 lists some of the major events that have contributed to victims' rights in Canada.

TABLE 9.2 Significant Dates in the Canadian Victim's Movement

1967	Saskatchewan enacts victims compensation program
1974	First victim-offender reconciliation takes place in Kitchener, Ontario
1974	First sexual assault centres open in Vancouver
1975	Criminal Code amended to limit questions about complainant's sexual history
1979	Edmonton Police Victim Service Unit founded; Brampton Victim Witness Program established
1982	Victims of Violence is formed in Ontario
1982	First Victimization Survey in Canada
1986	Manitoba enacts Justice for Victims of Crime Act
1987	New Brunswick passes Victim Services Act
1988	Newfoundland, Northwest Territories, Prince Edward Island, and Quebec all pass versions of Victims of Crime Act
1988	Federal, provincial, and territorial governments adopt the Statement of Basic Principles of Justice for Victims of Crime
1989	Nova Scotia passes Victims Rights and Services Act
1993	Yukon passes Victim Services Act
1998	Ontario passes Victims Bill of Rights
1996	British Columbia and Alberta pass Victims of Crime Act
1997	British Columbia allows victims to give oral impact statements at provincial parole hearings
1998	Ontario government creates the Office for Victims of Crime
2001	Manitoba passes new Victims Bill of Rights
2001	Victims permitted to provide oral statements at federal parole hearings
2005	Creation of National Office for Victims of Crime

Source: Canadian Resource Centre for Victims of Crime, "Victim's Rights in Canada," January 2006.

PREVENTING CRIMES AGAINST PLACES, PEOPLE, AND VALUABLE GOODS

Situational crime prevention seeks to protect places, people, and valuable goods from victimization. It is rooted in the 1971 work of C. Ray Jeffery's "crime prevention through environmental design" (CPTED)[67] and in Oscar Newman's concept of defensible space.[68] CPTED posits that environments can be altered, often at little expense, to decrease victimizations. "Defensible space" refers to improved architectural designs, particularly of public housing, in order to provide increased security. Canadian researchers have contributed significantly to the development of crime prevention approaches that focus on urban planning and architecture as *place improvements*. These place or environmental improvements reduce crime by reducing the attractiveness of areas as potential places to commit crimes and also reduce crime generators.[69] By focusing on situational design, "urban planners, health planners, and urban designers work towards reducing crime potential, nuisance behaviour, and fear in public and private spaces."[70] Design can enhance surveillance, reduce offenders' escape possibilities, and give residents a feeling of ownership that encourages them to protect their own space.[71] CPTED and defensible space have converged with rational choice and routine activity to form a new approach called "situational crime prevention."

Situational Crime Prevention

Rational-choice theory provides the foundation for designing situational-crime-prevention techniques and their classification (see Table 9.3). Situational crime prevention consists of the knowledge of how, where, and when to implement a specific measure that will alter a particular situation in order to prevent a crime from occurring. It begins with an understanding of crime as a complex phenomenon; crimes are products of a filtering process that channels some people to sites and situations amenable to criminal behaviour. Situational crime prevention is a planning process that uses this filter as a guide to construct techniques and interventions for the prevention of crime.[72] The routine-activity approach also aims at situational crime prevention by reducing the opportunities for likely offenders to commit crimes. Techniques include protecting

TABLE 9.3 Sixteen Techniques of Situational Prevention

Increasing Perceived Effort	Increasing Perceived Risks	Reducing Anticipated Rewards	Inducing Guilt or Shame
1. *Target hardening:* Slug-rejector device Steering locks Bandit screens	5. *Entry/exit screening:* Automatic ticket gates Baggage screening Merchandise tags	9. *Target removal:* Removable car radio Women's refuges Phone card	13. *Rule setting:* Harassment codes Customs declaration Hotel registrations
2. *Access control:* Parking lot barriers Fenced yards Entry phones	6. *Formal surveillance:* Burglar alarms Speed cameras Security guards	10. *Identifying property:* Property marking Vehicle licensing Cattle branding	14. *Strengthening moral condemnation:* "Shoplifting is stealing" Roadside speedometers "Bloody idiots drink and drive"
3. *Deflecting offenders:* Bus stop placement Tavern location Street closures	7. *Surveillance by employees:* Pay phone location Park attendants CCTV systems	11. *Reducing temptation:* Gender-neutral phone lists Off-street parking 12. *Denying benefits:* Ink merchandise tags PIN for car radios Graffiti cleaning	15. *Controlling disinhibitors:* Drinking-age laws Ignition interlock Server intervention
4. *Controlling facilitators:* Credit card photo Caller ID Gun controls	8. *Natural surveillance:* Defensible space Street lighting Cab driver ID		16. *Facilitating compliance:* Improved library checkout Public lavatories Trash bins

Source: Ronald V. Clarke and Ross Homel, "A Revised Classification of Situational Crime Prevention Techniques," in *Crime Prevention at a Crossroads,* Steven P. Lab, ed. (Cincinnati, OH: Anderson, 1997), with permission. Copyright 1997 Matthew Bender & Company, Inc., a member of the LexisNexis Group. All rights reserved.

suitable targets (making them less suitable) and increasing the presence of capable guardians. Measures such as steering-column locks, vandal-resistant construction, enhanced street lighting, and improved library checkout systems demonstrably decrease opportunities for crime. These are **target-hardening** techniques.

Cornish and Clarke have recently reformulated the situational prevention model by focusing more directly on the decision-making sequence of potential offenders. They list five strategic sets of techniques that are useful to consider when working to prevent offenders from choosing to commit a crime.[73] The first group of techniques must *increase the effort* required to commit a crime. As Patricia Brantingham, Paul Brantingham, and Wendy Taylor suggest, a program such as the "Doorsteps Neighbourhood Program" in Toronto, which provides after-school programs for elementary school children in high-risk neighbourhoods, is a good example of this tactic. When children attend this type of program and are kept busy completing homework and participating in structured playtime activities, extra effort is required to sneak away from the program and become involved in delinquent activities.[74]

Techniques that *increase the risks* of committing a crime include increasing guardianship as a means of reducing crime. Programs that train teachers and parents in the skills to identify at-risk youth and intervene in aggressive behaviour, as well as programs that increase surveillance of areas or groups, increase the risks of committing a crime. The third technique that may help prevent the commission of crimes includes techniques that *reduce the reward* an offender derives from the crime. For example, using dummy goods on display in a store, or making goods unusable if stolen. Techniques that *reduce provocation* target behaviours that can escalate into troublesome situations. For example, Operation Red Nose, a free driving service offered to impaired drivers during the holiday season, works to reduce impaired driving. Finally, techniques that *remove excuses* for doing crime make it difficult for someone to use "but I didn't know" or " but I couldn't find" as an excuse for criminal behaviour.[75] Ample garbage cans in a public area and speed limit signs make it more difficult for offenders to excuse their littering or speeding behaviours. For these suggested techniques and programs to effectively prevent crime, collaboration between different levels of government and adequate funding and support are required. To this end, effectiveness evaluation and cost-benefit analyses of these approaches are also necessary.[76]

In reviewing their situational-crime-prevention techniques, rational-choice theorists have also added aspects of the offender's *perception* of a crime

Situational Crime Prevention—Pros and Cons

Despite the increasing popularity of situational crime prevention (SCP), the perspective has been the target of criticism by more traditional-minded criminologists. The debate on the merit of SCP techniques centres on a number of issues, including the following:

1. *SCP excludes "undesirables" from public places:*(1) For example, excluding would-be offenders from a mall by limiting shopping hours makes it more difficult for them to buy needed material goods.(2)

Response: The exclusion of "troublemakers" from public and semipublic places falls under order-maintenance duties of police officers, so it is not considered SCP.(1) "Deflecting offenders," which is one SCP technique identified by theorists, does have some exclusionary potential, but it is not meant to exclude undesirables; rather, the aim is to keep likely offenders away from suitable targets.

2. *SCP will only displace crime to new locations and times:*(1, 3) It may also lead to the escalation of crime to a more serious level, and the benefits of SCP are skewed toward more-advantaged classes who can afford security measures.(1)

Response: Behaviour is influenced by situational factors, so there is no reason to assume that blocked crime at one location will lead to the commission of crime in a different situation. There will be different factors at play. Evidence also suggests that displacement is not as prevalent as critics claim, and the idea of escalation is inconsistent with many types of crime. For example, it is unlikely that reduced opportunities for shoplifting would lead offenders to start stealing shopping baskets from other customers.(3, 1)

3. *SCP inconveniences law-abiding citizens and infringes on their freedom:*(1) Crime-prevention efforts should focus on offenders—the burden should not be placed on law-abiding citizens.(4)

Response: Many SCP measures are unobtrusive, and human beings generally accept the need for implementing security measures in their own lives.(1)

4. *SCP treats the symptoms of the crime problem rather than the causes:*(4) Crime prevention should focus on the root causes of crime—unemployment, racial discrimination, and inadequate schooling, among others. Along the same lines, it is questionable whether the end (lower crime) justifies the means.(2) SCP is not necessarily the most appropriate way to deal with crime just because it is more efficient than other methods; it may not be if it prevents crime for the wrong reasons. For example, one way to reduce crime is by excluding everyone under the age of 21 from shopping malls because they are at highest risk for shoplifting. This measure reduces crime, but the means are questionable because they exclude these individuals from being able to shop freely.

Response: SCP avoids stigmatizing certain groups of individuals as likely criminals because it acknowledges that everyone is vulnerable to temptation.(4, 5) Also, people change in response to their experiences, so SCP has the potential to minimize or promote particular social practices.(6)

Despite the criticism, Felson and Clarke(4) argue that situational crime prevention meets the three goals of crime control required by democratic standards—to provide crime prevention equally to all social groups, to respect individual rights, and to share responsibility for crime prevention with all parts of society—better than other crime policies. Do you agree?

Sources

1. Ronald V. Clarke, "Situational Prevention, Criminology and Social Values," in *Ethical and Social Perspectives on Situational Crime Prevention,* A. von Hirsch, D. Garland, and A. Wakefield, eds. (Portland, OR: Hart Publishing, 2000).

2. R. A. Duff and S. E. Marshall, "Benefits, Burdens and Responsibilities: Some Ethical Dimensions of Situational Crime Prevention," in *Ethical and Social Perspectives on Situational Crime Prevention,* A. von Hirsch, D. Garland, and A. Wakefield, eds. (Portland, OR: Hart Publishing, 2000).

3. Richard Wortley, "Reconsidering the Role of Opportunity in Situational Crime Prevention," in *Rational Choice and Situational Crime Prevention,* G. Newman, R. V. Clarke, and S. G. Shoham, eds. (Aldershot, U.K.: Dartmouth, 1997).

4. Marcus Felson and Ronald V. Clarke, "The Ethics of Situational Crime Prevention," in *Rational Choice and Situational Crime Prevention,* G. Newman, R. V. Clarke, and S. G. Shoham, eds. (Aldershot, U.K.: Dartmouth, 1997).

5. Graeme Newman, "Introduction: Towards a Theory of Situational Crime Prevention," *in Rational Choice and Situational Crime Prevention,* G. Newman, R. V. Clarke, and S. G. Shoham, eds. (Aldershot, U.K.: Dartmouth, 1997).

6. David J. Smith, "Changing Situations and Changing People," in *Ethical and Social Perspectives on Situational Crime Prevention,* A. von Hirsch, D. Garland, and A. Wakefield, eds. (Portland, OR: Hart Publishing, 2000).

Questions for Discussion

1. Overall, do you think SCP is preferable to other methods of crime control that focus more on offenders?

2. What do you think is the best strategy for crime prevention?

3. Should the characteristics of a community population be taken into account when applying SCP techniques? How so? What are the potential problems with applying one policy the same way across multiple communities?

4. Should individual interpretations be a consideration when implementing SCP practices? In other words, do we need to think about the message they might send to particular groups?

Even Goofy is part of the Disney crime prevention and control strategy, making Disneyland and Disney World two of the safest locations in the United States.

opportunity to the catalogue of relevant factors, as well as the element of guilt or shame.[77] The addition of the category of "perception" of opportunity was self-evident. After all, offenders act only in accordance with what they perceive. The addition of a category called "inducing guilt or shame," on the other hand, is a significant expansion of rational choice.[78] Techniques that induce guilt or shame include the installation of signs saying "shoplifting is stealing" or other measures calculated to prevent common crimes by increasing the personal and social cost in terms of shaming—especially after being caught in the act.

There are a number of successful examples of situational crime prevention. For example, situational-crime-prevention techniques have been successfully implemented to prevent crime at Disney World, to stop auto theft, to deter robberies at convenience stores, and to lessen crime in parking facilities.

The Phantom Crime Prevention at Disney World Disney World, home of Donald Duck, Mickey and Minnie Mouse, Goofy, and their friends, provides us with an example of environmental/situational crime prevention. Illegal behaviour is successfully controlled, yet in an environment that does not have the sterile, fortresslike appearance so often associated with security. How has this been accomplished?[79]

The intricate web of security and crowd control (not visible to the untrained eye) starts at the parking lot with advice to lock your car and remember that you have parked at a particular lot, for example, "Donald Duck 1." With friendly greetings of "have a good time," watchful eyes surround visitors on the rubber-wheeled train into never-never land. Crowd control is omnipresent yet unobtrusive. Signs guide you through the maze of monorails, rides, and attractions. Physical barriers prevent injury and regulate the movement of adults and children alike. Mickey Mouse and Goofy monitor movements. Flower gardens, pools, and fountains are pretty to look at; they also direct people toward particular locations. Yet with all these built-in control strategies, few visitors realize the extent to which their choices of movement and action are limited.

> **Did You Know?**
>
> . . . that closed-circuit television (CCTV) surveillance tapes record over 75 percent of all crimes investigated by Canadian authorities.[80]

Situational Prevention: Auto Theft Rates of property crime generally have dropped in Canada for the past two decades. However, as Rick Linden and Renuka Chaturvedi point out, vehicle theft has been increasing. In their study on vehicle theft in Canada, these researchers show that auto theft rates differ by city: Winnipeg's rates have quadrupled between 1992 and 2001, while Regina's rates have tripled.[81] As an illustration of the range in rates of car theft across the country, consider these 2001 statistics: Regina's rate was 1996 thefts per 100 000, Winnipeg had 1581, Vancouver had 1149, Quebec City had 290, and St. John's had 183.[82]

In addition to the wide city and provincial variation in rates of vehicle theft, the statistics indicate that a high proportion occur in low-income, high-crime communities. And although most stolen vehicles are recovered (75 percent in Canada), this number changes by region of the country and by time period. Likely this is due to regional variation in reason for vehicle theft: Data suggest that joyriding is the typical pattern in the west, while professional vehicle theft is more likely in the east. Joyriders target older vehicles because they are more easily stolen. For example, in Winnipeg about one in 12 1990–1994 Dodge Caravans and Plymouth Voyagers are stolen each year. Finally, it appears that vehicle theft is a young man's activity; in 2001 42 percent of those arrested for vehicle theft were young offenders, the majority of them male (about 16 percent were female).[83]

Based on the characteristics of offenders and the nature of vehicle theft, Linden and Chaturvedi suggest a variety of situational crime prevention measures that should result in a reduction in this crime type. Situational measures include steering column locks, vehicle immobilizers, and the marking of parts (making it difficult for thieves to dismantle vehicles in "chop shops" and then sell the parts). In addition to situational measures, social programming for offenders and at-risk youth is also important. The community can contribute to the solution as well by sensitizing the public to the problem and educating citizens on prevention measures they can take, by improving parking lot security, and by encouraging residents to use curfew decals.

Police officers and the criminal justice system can also contribute to the reduction of vehicle theft by targeting chronic offenders with special programming, by using bait cars to deter potential thieves, and by increasing surveillance and police presence in "hot spots." Linden and Chaturvedi describe a successful approach used in Regina. Regina initiated a comprehensive program aimed at reducing vehicle theft that involved a variety of citizen groups and organizations, including the police, criminal justice agencies, schools, the media, and members of the public. Utilizing techniques like those just mentioned, the initiative helped reduce vehicle theft in the city by 33 percent between 2001 and 2003.[84]

Devising situational prevention measures, however, is most effective when researchers and practitioners have a good understanding of the pattern of criminal behaviour—for example, whether stolen vehicles are being used for joyriding or for resale. It is important that a researcher also analyze the type of offenders who steal cars (see Table 9.4).

TABLE 9.4 Typologies of Frequent Auto Theft Offenders

Acting-out Joyrider

- Most emotionally disturbed of the offenders—derives status from having his peers think he is crazy and unpredictable.
- Engages in outrageous driving stunts—dangerous to pursue—possesses a kamikaze attitude.
- Vents anger via car—responsible for large proportion of the totalled and burned cars.
- Least likely to be deterred—doesn't care what happens.

Thrill-seeker

- Heavily into drugs—doing crime is a way to finance the habit—entices others to feel the "rush" of doing crime.
- Engages in car stunts and willful damage to cars, but also steals them for transportation and to use in other crimes.
- Steals parts for sale in a loosely structured friendship network.
- Thrill-seeking behaviour likely to be transferred to other activities and might be directed to legitimate outlets.

Instrumental Offender

- Doing auto theft for the money—most active of the offenders (five or more cars a week) but the smallest proportion of the sample—connected to organized theft operations.
- Rational, intelligent—does crimes with least risk—may get into auto theft from burglary—thinks about outcomes.
- Doing crime while young offender status affords them lenient treatment—indicate that they will quit crime at age 18.

Source: Zachary Fleming, Patricia Brantingham, and Paul Brantingham, "Exploring Auto Theft in British Columbia," in *Crime Prevention Studies*, vol. 3, Ronald V. Clarke, ed. (Monsey, NY: Criminal Justice Press, 1994), p. 62. Reprinted by permission of the publisher.

Prevention of School Violence?

A rash of high school shootings during the 1998–1999 academic year (see "Violence in Schools" in Chapter 10) caused great concern across North America. A week after the April 1999 Columbine High School massacre in Littleton, Colorado, a 14-year-old boy in Taber, Alberta, opened fire with a .22 calibre rifle inside the local high school and killed a 17-year-old student. Recently, Toronto witnessed a school shooting that resulted in the death of a 15-year-old boy. The tragedy has sparked politicians to call for a "real ban" on handguns.

Criminologists, police, educators, lawmakers, and parents struggle to figure out why these young men and boys decide to pick up firearms and destroy the lives of their teachers and classmates. Many blame the easy access to guns; others point to the social isolation these students experience; still others look to broader sociological explanations.

Although you would not know it, given all the media coverage surrounding these school-shooting incidents, as well as experts' premonitions of doom and gloom, we are actually in the midst of a decline in youth violent crime. Youth and adult crime in Canada has generally been declining for the past two decades. Yet, on September 13, 2006, the nation witnessed a horrific shooting at Dawson College in Montreal, which resulted in the death of 18-year-old Anastasia DeSousa, as well as the shooter, and the wounding of 19 others.

The shooting brought up painful memories of another shooting in the city that occurred in 1989 when Marc Lépine murdered 14 young female engineers before turning the gun on himself.(1) Youth in high schools or young adults at post-secondary institutions, the question remains the same: Why?

Despite the fact that students are safer in school than they are on the street or at home, these incidents induce fear and apprehension among young people, their families, and the public. Young people in Canada are far more likely to die in alcohol-related automobile accidents; of those who died as a result of trauma in a motor vehicle collision, and had a positive alcohol level, 43 percent were under the age of 25. Furthermore, of all road fatalities that occurred among youth, 42 percent involved alcohol.(2) Even so, deaths related to school violence get much more press coverage—much of it sensationalized. As a result, parents, and the community at large, tend to panic.

Target hardening and situational crime prevention in schools are nothing new. Schools in some cities have had metal detectors, doors with alarms, and locker searches for years. Although the likelihood of a shooting in any particular school is small, officials are not taking any chances. Across the country, lockdowns are increasingly common in elementary and high schools, as are lockdown drills that provide practice should a real lockdown

On September 13, 2006, Dawson College in Montreal was the scene of a tragic shooting that shocked the nation.

be required. Police or principals can impose lockdowns when schools cannot be evacuated safely in the event of an emergency and when they deem it is safer for students to remain in rooms behind locked doors. Visitors are required to register with office personnel. These tactics are not new. Of the 109 high schools in the Toronto District School Board, 65 have security cameras.(3)

Americans have taken matters a step further. Interestingly, the prevention measures listed here fall squarely into Clarke and Homel's situational-crime-prevention model (see Table 9.3 on page 226).

Access control
• Intercom systems are being used at locked doors to buzz in visitors.(4)

Convenience Stores One very successful U.S. crime-prevention study focused on crime prevention in convenience stores. This research launched the concept of crime prevention through environmental design. It had long been known that convenience stores, like the 7-Eleven shops, had been prime robbery targets. Researchers studied the vulnerability of these stores in great detail, assessing risks as well as losses, in terms of lives and property. The researchers recommended that stores have two or more clerks on duty, post "limited cash" signs, increase exterior lighting, and restrict

escape routes and potential hiding places for robbers. Convenience stores that implemented these changes witnessed a significant drop in robberies: in some cases robberies dropped by two-thirds.[85]

Liquor Stores Drawing on crime prevention through environmental design, the City of Edmonton's zoning bylaws requires liquor stores to be at least 100 metres from parks, school facilities, and community recreation services. The goal is to reduce the possible negative impact of liquor stores, including public drunkenness, vandalism,

- Students have to flash or swipe computerized identification cards to get into school buildings.
- Perimeter fences delineate school property and secure cars after hours.

Controlling facilitators
- Students in some schools get an extra set of books to leave at home. The schools have banned backpacks and dismantled lockers to eliminate places to stash weapons. Other school districts are encouraging see-through lockers and backpacks.
- Some school boards have banned trench coats and other oversized garments, apparently to prevent students from hiding weapons on their bodies or in their clothing.

Entry/exit screening
- Handheld and walk-through metal detectors keep anyone with a weapon from entering schools.

Formal surveillance
- Uniformed police officers and private security guards, some of them armed, patrol school halls.
- Schools are installing surveillance cameras in hallways and on school buses.

Surveillance by employees (or, in this case, students)
- Students are carrying small notebooks so that they can log and then report overheard threats.

Identifying property
- Tiny microfilm is hidden inside expensive school property so that it can be identified if stolen.

On the face of it, these measures seem to make good sense. They can prevent people from bringing weapons into schools and keep unauthorized people out. They increase the ability of school officials to detect crime, identify evildoers, and prevent criminal incidents from happening.

But will this work? Kimveer Gill, the Dawson College shooter, had legally purchased his guns. Marc Lépine was out to get feminists—he singled out women in his shooting spree. Rational-choice and routine-theory theorists posit that offenders are rational individuals who weigh the costs and benefits of an action before taking it. What about those offenders who are irrational? Suicidal? Is there any amount of situational crime prevention and target hardening that will deter individuals who are depressed, mentally ill, or intent on accomplishing an irrational goal? In the wake of Lépine's massacre, the call was sounded for tighter gun control measures in Canada. Yet, 17 years later, Gill succeeded in terrorizing students at Dawson College, despite the creation of a national gun registry.

Sources

1. CBC News, "Attacks on Students and Staff," April 17, 2007, www.cbc.ca/ news/background/school-shootings/, accessed July 27, 2007.
2. MADD Canada, "More than Half of All Alcohol-Related Severe Injuries Due to Motor Vehicle Collisions," Canadian Institute for Health Information, June 22, 2005, www.madd.ca/english/news/ stories/n05jun22.htm, accessed March 14, 2008.
3. "School Shooting Sparks Concern for Rising Gun Violence in Canada," May 25, 2007, http://english/ peopledaily.com.cn/200705/25/ eng20070525_377949.html, accessed July 30, 2007.
4. Jacques Steinberg, "Barricading the School Door," *New York Times,* Aug. 22, 1999, New York section, p. 5.

Questions for Discussion

1. Did your high school or does your university or college campus have any security measures in place? If so, how do they fit into Clarke and Homel's 16 techniques of situational prevention?
2. Is there a point where security measures in schools become so extreme that they can no longer be justified? Can security measures adequately address the issue of depressed or disgruntled students who are acting out on rage and are not thinking rationally?

fighting, and criminal behaviour near facilities associated with children. Furthermore, the bylaw may also require liquor store owners to consider crime prevention, including the assessment of lighting, landscaping, and customer parking surrounding the store. These factors have been found to affect the ease with which potential offenders commit criminal activities. Having liquor store owners consider these factors prior to locating in a particular area is the city's attempt to incorporate crime prevention through environmental design for what could potentially be crime "hot spots."

Parking Facilities[86] Parking garages are said to be dangerous places: Individuals are alone in a large space, there are many hiding places, the amount of valuable property (cars and their contents) is high, they are open to the public, an offender's car can go unnoticed, and lighting is usually poor. Yet statistics indicate that because of the small amount of time and the relatively limited number of trips that each person takes to and from parking facilities, an individual's chances of being sexually assaulted, robbed, or assaulted in a parking facility are very low. Nevertheless,

THE FAR SIDE® By GARY LARSON

Inconvenience stores

the fear of victimization in these facilities is high. Efforts to improve conditions include better lighting, stairways and elevators that are open to the air or glass-enclosed, ticket-booth personnel monitoring drivers exiting and entering, colour-coded signs designating parking areas, elimination or redesign of public washrooms, panic buttons and emergency phones, closed-circuit television, and uniformed security personnel.

Displacement

One important question concerning crime-prevention measures remains. What will happen, for example, if these measures do prevent a particular crime from being committed? Will the would-be offender simply look for another target? Crime-prevention strategists have demonstrated that **displacement**—the commission of a quantitatively similar crime at a different time or place—does not always follow. German motorcycle helmet legislation demonstrates the point. As a result of a large number of accidents, legislation that required motorcyclists to wear helmets was passed and strictly enforced. It worked:

Head injuries decreased. But there were additional, unforeseen consequences. Motorcycle theft rates decreased dramatically. The risks of stealing a motorcycle became too high because a would-be offender could not drive it away without wearing a helmet. At this point, researchers expected to see a rise in the numbers of cars or bikes stolen. They did not. In other words, there was very little displacement. Studies of "hot spots policing" provide evidence against displacement as well.[87] Of course, some offenders will look for other crime opportunities, but many others will quit for some time, perhaps forever.

THEORY INFORMS POLICY

Detective Kim Rossmo was a Vancouver detective with 20 years' policing experience and a doctoral student working with Paul and Patricia Brantingham at Simon Fraser University's School of Criminology when he invented a computer program that revolutionized the hunt for serial criminals. The Brantinghams had developed a theoretical model that used information about a potential offender's routine activities, focusing on the individual's awareness of his or her surroundings, as a key to crime prevention. The researchers argued that the commission of crime is based in a multi-stage decision-making process that takes into account the offender's home, recreational activities, work-related activities, and generally the familiarity he or she has of an area. They suggest that offenders generally commit crimes in areas familiar to them, called their "awareness space."[88]

While the Brantinghams use their theory to inform crime prevention efforts, Rossmo says he was interested in "reversing what they had done, answering the opposite question: if we know the location of the crimes, what can we say about where the offender might live?"[89] Rossmo's computer program, "Rigel," does exactly that. It is used as an investigative tool to aid police officers in tracking down predatory criminals whose behaviour is characterized by hunting tactics: serial rapists, murderers, arsonists, robbers. The program constructs three-dimensional maps based on the sites where crimes are committed and then narrows the search for the offender's place of residence to within tenths of a mile. It works because of the existence of patterns to human behaviours, which routine-activity theorists and rational-choice theorists discuss.

Criminals tend to commit their crimes relatively close to where they live and to areas they are familiar with. Rossmo discusses the theory and practice behind this investigative tool in his book *Geographic Profiling*.[90] He has helped solve cases such as the Paul Bernardo case, the case of the Washington, DC, snipers in 2002, and many others in Canada, the United States, and Europe. Police forces around the world use the theory and practice behind geographic profiling to assist in their investigations of some of the

most horrific crimes that occur. Many police forces use technology that permits them to identify crime "hot spots" and then deploy officers accordingly. Other forces have moved in the direction of "intelligence-led" policing, which uses the kinds of profiling techniques discussed by Rossmo. Geographic profiling provides us with an example of the extension of the theories used to inform situational crime prevention to the investigation of criminal events and the apprehension of serious, violent offenders. In a sense, this is situational crime prevention: Catching dangerous offenders and imprisoning them will reduce, at least in the short term, their chances of reoffending.

Visit the Online Learning Centre: www.mcgrawhill.ca/olc/adler

REVIEW

1. How do situational theories explain crime?

This chapter focuses on situational theories of crime. These theories, which assume that there are always people motivated to commit crime, try to explain why crimes are committed by a particular offender against a particular target. They analyze opportunities and environmental factors that prompt a potential perpetrator to act.

We discussed the three most prominent situational approaches to crime: **environmental criminology** (p. 214), the **rational-choice perspective** (p. 214), and the **routine-activity approach** (p. 216). We noted that they have merged somewhat, particularly insofar as all of these approaches aim at preventing victimization by altering external conditions that are conducive to crime. **Target-hardening** (p. 226) techniques reduce the chances of a crime occurring.

2. What do theories of victimization add to the explanation of crime?

Theories of victimization (p. 220) view crime as the dynamic interaction of perpetrators and victims (at a given time and place). These theories draw attention to the fact that a criminal event involves both the action of the offender and interaction between offender and victim. Research on victimization has also established that there is a link between offending and victimization as well. Many offenders are victimized repeatedly and victims are frequently offenders. Lifestyle theories contribute to understanding victimization patterns by showing that variations in lifestyle affect the number of situations with high victimization risks that a person experiences. Research that focuses on crime **hot spots** (p. 224) and the **geography of crime** (p. 224) has found that certain areas are more crime prone than others. Theories of victimization and places where crime occurs focus on the fact that victimization tends not to be a random event. Attempts to prevent victimization should focus on victims' lifestyle factors, including routine activities, but also on the places themselves by making them less vulnerable to crime. Overall, the aim is to find ways for potential victims to protect themselves. Situational theories of crime and theories of victimization are interrelated.

3. How do these theories help to inform techniques, practices, and programs to help prevent crime?

Research into lifestyles, victim-offender interaction, repeat victimization, hot spots, and geography of crime has vast implications for crime control in entire cities or regions. Crime prevention through environmental design (CPTED) posits that environments can be altered, often at little expense, to decrease victimizations. "Defensible space" suggests that improved architectural designs, particularly of public housing, can help to provide increased security. **Situational crime prevention** (p. 225) consists of the knowledge of how, where, and when to implement a specific measure that will alter a particular situation in order to prevent a crime from occurring. **Displacement** (p. 232), which may or may not occur, refers to the commission of a quantitatively similar crime at a different time or place.

CRIMINOLOGY & PUBLIC POLICY

The study of targets and victims is crucial to preventing crime. Understanding how offenders make decisions helps policy makers allocate resources efficiently. For example, if it is possible to significantly reduce convenience-store robbery by relatively simple measures, isn't it better to spend time and money doing those things rather than trying to prevent crime by focusing exclusively on troubled people (who may or may not rob convenience stores anyway)? If we know that repeat victimization can be prevented by intervening with high-risk people and properties, isn't that the most cost-beneficial way to proceed?

We usually think of crime policy as being made by governments, for only they can control the police, courts, and corrections. Decisions about crime prevention, on the other hand, can be made by small communities, neighbourhoods, schools, businesses, and individuals. We discussed how simple precautions lower the risk of convenience-store robbery. This knowledge not only encouraged governments to pass certain laws mandating that stores take those precautions, but led many in private industry to adopt the measures as well. Knowledge about crime prevention is especially valuable to all people because everyone can use these tools to reduce the chances of being a victim.

Questions for Discussion Should governments pass laws making situational crime prevention measures at the business and individual level mandatory? For example, should stores be required to arrange their displays and use their space in a particular way? Should private home owners be required by law to implement the techniques and strategies suggested by the theories we've covered in this chapter? Should shopping malls have curfews controlling who shops at particular times? Who is responsible for crime prevention?

YOU BE THE CRIMINOLOGIST

Imagine you are a security consultant working for a major department store chain. Recently, one of the stores, located in the downtown area of a large city, has experienced very high levels of shoplifting and employee theft. You must design a comprehensive program to protect merchandise from theft by customers and by people who work at the store. First, identify some of the store's most vulnerable areas (it may help to visit a local department store to observe how it operates). Then, using the 16 techniques of situational crime prevention as a model, prepare a list of prevention strategies.

TYPES OF CRIMES

The word "crime" conjures up many images: mugging and murder, cheating on taxes, and selling crack. The Criminal Code defines hundreds of different crimes. These crimes are grouped into convenient and comprehensive categories for access and understanding.

In this part, we are examining the specific categories of crimes. Violent crimes (Chapter 10) are crimes against the person, ranging from assault to homicide. Many of these crimes have been well established for centuries, though modern codes have transformed them, however slightly. Most of the crimes against property (Chapter 11) have been well defined over the centuries. Yet, recent developments in commerce and technology have prompted legislatures to define new forms of crimes against property. With a spate of corporate scandals, reports of white-collar and corporate crime (Chapter 12) fill the pages of newspapers and news magazines. In this chapter, we discuss how white-collar crime and corporate crime are defined and measured. We also discuss another type of business-related crime: organized crime. In the next chapter (Chapter 13), we address the controversial types of crime related to drug and alcohol trafficking and consumption, as well as crimes that violate the sexual mores of the establishment and significant segments of the population. Finally, the occurrence of these types of crime is discussed in comparison with their occurrence elsewhere in the world (Chapter 14). This chapter is concerned with comparative criminology and, inevitably, the emergence of transnational and international criminality.

VIOLENT CRIMES

CHAPTER **10**

CHAPTER QUESTIONS

1. What is the extent and nature of homicide?

2. What is the nature and extent of assault?

3. What types of crime occur in families?

4. What are robbers like?

5. What are some current examples of criminal behaviours we are concerned about?

6. To what extent do Canadians use guns to commit crimes?

Mark of violence: one of the first shots in a sniper spree that numbed the Washington, D.C., area in October 2002.

To millions of North Americans, few things are more pervasive, more frightening, more real today than violent crime and the fear of being assaulted, mugged, robbed, or sexually assaulted. The fear of being victimized by criminal attack has touched us all in some way. People are fleeing their residences in cities to the expected safety of suburban living. Residents of many areas will not go out on the street at night. Others have added bars and extra locks to windows and doors in their homes. Bus drivers in major cities do not carry cash because incidents of robbery have been so frequent. In some areas, local citizens patrol the streets at night to attain the safety they feel has not been provided. . . .

There are numerous conflicting definitions of criminal violence as a class of behaviour. Police, Crown attorneys, correctional personnel, and behavioural scientists all hold somewhat different viewpoints as to what constitute acts of violence. All would probably agree, however, as the police reports make abundantly clear, that criminal violence involves the use of or the threat of force on a victim by an offender.[1]

The Criminal Code defines types of violent crime, and each is distinguished by a particular set of elements. We concentrate on criminological characteristics: the frequency with which each type of violent crime is committed, the methods used in its commission, and its distribution through time and place. We also examine the people who commit the offences and those who are its victims. If we can determine when, where, and how a specific type of crime is likely to be committed, we will be in a better position to reduce the incidence of that crime by devising appropriate strategies to prevent it.

We begin with homicide, since the taking of life is the most serious harm one human being can inflict on another. Serious attacks that fall short of homicide are assaults of various kinds, including serious sexual assault and the forceful taking of property from another person (robbery). Other patterns of violence are not defined as such in the Criminal Code but are so important in practice as to require separate discussion. Family-related violence and terrorism, both of which encompass a variety of crimes, fall into this category.

HOMICIDE

Homicide is the killing of one human being by another. Some homicides, such as homicides committed by law enforcement officers in the course of carrying out their duties, and homicides committed by soldiers in combat, are sanctioned by law and are therefore considered **justifiable.** Criminologists are most interested in *criminal homicides—* unlawful killings, without justification or excuse. Criminal homicides are subdivided into four separate categories: first-degree murder, second-degree murder, manslaughter, and infanticide.

Degrees of Murder

At common law, **murder** was defined as the intentional killing of another person with **malice aforethought.** Courts have struggled with an exact definition of "malice." To describe it, they have used such terms as "evil mind" and "abandoned and malignant heart." Actually, malice is a very simple concept. It is the defendant's awareness that he or she had no right to kill but intended to kill anyway.[2]

Originally, the malice had to be "aforethought": The person had to have killed after some contemplation, rather than on the spur of the moment. The concept eventually became meaningless because some courts considered even a few seconds sufficient to establish forethought. The dividing line between planned and spur-of-the-moment killings disappeared. But many legislators believed contemplation was an appropriate concept, because it allowed us to distinguish the various types of murder. They reintroduced it, calling it "premeditation and deliberation." A premeditated, deliberate, intentional killing became murder in

A memorial created to honour the 14 victims of the Montreal Massacre in 1989.

the **first degree.** First-degree murder also applies when the victim is employed in an occupation concerned with the preservation and maintenance of public order (e.g., police officer, correctional worker) and acting in that capacity, or when the killing occurs in connection with certain specific offences (e.g., sexual assault, kidnapping, or hijacking). An intentional killing without premeditation and deliberation became murder in the **second degree.**

Manslaughter

Manslaughter is the unlawful killing of another person without malice. It occurs when one person kills another in the heat of passion caused by sudden provocation, or when a person is too intoxicated to form intent. Manslaughter may be either voluntary or involuntary.

Voluntary Manslaughter   Voluntary manslaughter is a killing committed intentionally but without malice—for example, in the heat of passion or in response to strong provocation. Persons who kill under extreme provocation cannot make rational decisions about whether they have a right to kill or not. They therefore act without the necessary malice.[3]

Just as passion, fright, fear, or consternation may affect a person's capacity to act rationally, so may drugs or alcohol. In some cases, a charge of murder may be reduced to voluntary manslaughter when the defendant was so grossly intoxicated as not to be fully aware of the implications of his or her actions. All voluntary-manslaughter cases have one thing in common: The defendant's awareness of the unlawfulness of the act was dulled or grossly reduced by shock, fright, consternation, or intoxication.

Involuntary Manslaughter   A crime is designated as **involuntary manslaughter** when a person has caused the death of another unintentionally but recklessly by consciously disregarding a substantial and unjustifiable risk that endangered another person's life. In such instances, as when a drunk driver causes the death of a pedestrian, a death occurs because of the offender's negligent behaviour. The offender, in acting negligently, does not consider the harm he or she may cause others.[4]

Infanticide

Infanticide is a category of homicide that applies to the killing of a newborn child by a woman who is in a disturbed state of mind as a consequence of giving birth. Infanticide is a relatively rare event: In 2005 there were two recorded incidents of infanticide in Canada. Most killings in 2005 were classified as either first-degree murder (45 percent) or second-degree murder (44 percent). Eleven percent fell into the category of manslaughter.[5]

The Extent of Homicide

Social scientists who look at homicide have a different perspective from that of the legislators who define such crimes. Social scientists are concerned with rates and patterns of criminal activities.

Homicide Rates in Canada Today The rate of homicide in Canada is about 1.85 per 100 000 population per year. The homicide rate is not equally distributed over the whole country. Figure 10.1 illustrates the homicide rate by province for 2006.

Your chance of becoming a murder victim is much higher if you are male than if you are female: Of all murder victims in 2006, almost three-quarters (73 percent) were male. Age also plays a role—the victimization rate for males peaks at 25 to 29 years of age, while female victimization rates are highest

A victim of the infamous Washington, D.C., area snipers. This scene of the 2002 murder rampage is the Silver Spring post office located next to the Leisure World retirement community.

between 18 to 39 years of age, with the peak at 30 to 39 years. Why might this be the case? These relationships can be explained in part by some of the patterns in victimization we have discussed earlier in this text. Younger people are more likely to be victimized and to offend. The fact that the homicide

FIGURE 10.1 Homicide rates by province, 2006.

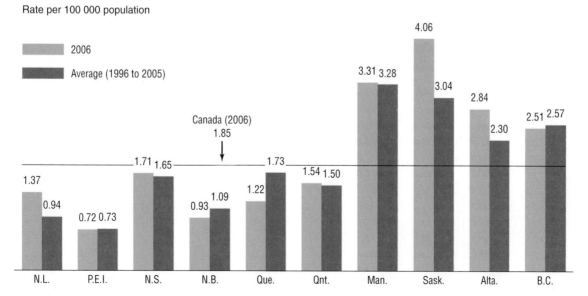

Rate per 100 000 population

- 2006
- Average (1996 to 2005)

Canada (2006) 1.85

	N.L.	P.E.I.	N.S.	N.B.	Que.	Ont.	Man.	Sask.	Alta.	B.C.
2006	1.37	0.72	1.71	0.93	1.22	1.54	3.31	4.06	2.84	2.51
Average	0.94	0.73	1.65	1.09	1.73	1.50	3.28	3.04	2.30	2.57

Source: Statistics Canada, Homicide in Canada, 2006, Catalogue no. 85-002-XIE, Vol. 27, no. 8, page 4.

victimization rate peaks at a younger age for males is related to the fact that males are more likely to be assaulted and/or killed by strangers or acquaintances. On the other hand, women are more likely to suffer victimization at the hands of someone they know: husband, boyfriend, intimate partner. Young males go out in public often; older females are more likely to be dating or in relationships that might set them up for possible victimization. Alcohol and drug use also enters into the picture: Over half of victims reportedly used an intoxicant prior to the offence. Furthermore, male victims are more likely than females to have been under the influence of an intoxicant.[6]

Race plays a role as well—in both offending and victimization rates. While approximately 3 percent of the Canadian population identifies as Aboriginal, in 2005, 17 percent of homicide victims, and 23 percent of those accused of committing homicide, were Aboriginal.[7]

Research indicates that homicide tends to be intra-racial.[8] Bill Meloff and Robert Silverman report that 68 percent of all the homicides committed by youth involve Caucasians killing Caucasians, and that when Aboriginal youth kill, the victim is an Aboriginal person 87 percent of the time.[9] Although homicide may be an intra-racial crime, it is not an intra-gender crime. The data show that males were most often killed by males

> **Did You Know?**
>
> . . . that the U.S. rate of homicide is about three times the Canadian rate?

(89 percent), and nine out of ten female victims were murdered by males.[10]

Homicide Rates over Time Researchers have asked what happens to homicide rates over time when the composition of the population changes. Homicide statistics were first collected in Canada in 1961. Since that time there have been two major trends in homicide rates. Following a period of stability between 1961 and 1966, the homicide rate more than doubled over the next ten years when it finally reached a peak of 3.03 homicide victims per 100 000 population in 1975. Since then, there have been annual fluctuations, but generally the homicide rate has been declining (see Figure 10.2). It may be that the age structure of society has played a role in the declining rate of crime generally, and homicide specifically: As the baby boomers age, crime decreases. Researchers have also pointed to the influence of the economy on changing homicide rates and the changes that ethnic composition of a society has on homicide rates.

The Nature of Homicide

Homicide victims and suspects are disproportionately young, male, and unmarried. These characteristics are associated with the lifestyle and routine activities (as discussed in Chapter 9)—less structured lifestyles, higher levels of physical aggression, consumption of drugs and alcohol—which place young men in situations that can escalate into

FIGURE 10.2 Homicide rate, 1961–2006.

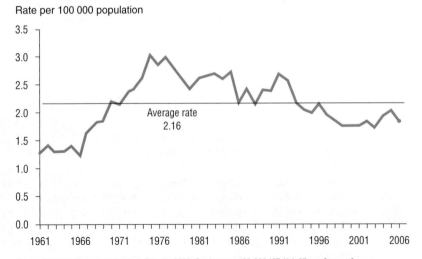

Source: Statistics Canada, Homicide in Canada, 2006, Catalogue no. 85-002-XIE, Vol. 27, no. 8, page 2.

incidents of violence. The literature on the construction of masculinity and the role of socialization in perpetuating ideas about how "real men" use aggression and violence contributes to an understanding of homicide. David Luckenbill pointed to the importance of social context to incidents that result in homicide. Often what begin as relatively minor incidents that start with a "funny look" or "joking comment" escalate into "character contests." For the individuals involved, violence becomes a means of "saving face."[11]

Many homicides are perpetrated by individuals known to the victim, and many of these attacks occur in the victim's home. The pattern of homicides in Canada seems consistent with both routine activities theory and the subcultural theories we discussed in Chapter 6. People hanging out together, participating in routine activities that involve interaction with each other can result in violent incidents like homicide when the interaction takes a turn that is interpreted by one or the other party as necessitating a violent response. Some members of society learn that violence is an appropriate response to resolving problems and dealing with conflict. If we consider that some segments of society are more likely to develop this approach to dealing with others, higher rates of

> ### Did You Know?
>
> ... that almost 80 percent of children murdered in Canada are killed by one or both parents?

violence and homicide among members of these groups is more understandable. Quite simply, disrespecting (however this is defined or interpreted) a member of a group that is quick to resort to violence in order to save face increases one's chances of falling victim to a violent crime. Depending on the circumstances and the way the event unfolds, homicide may be the end result. Nonetheless, homicides committed by strangers do occur, although they are less prevalent than those committed by people known to the victim.

Stranger Homicides The rate of **stranger homicide**—a killing in which killer and victim have had no known previous contact—was 17 percent in 2006[12] The impact of stranger homicides on the quality of urban life—especially the fear of crime they engender—is far greater than their relatively small numbers would suggest.[13] Most homicides are of the type we've just described—people who know each other getting into a disagreement or altercation that escalates. Unfortunately, the homicides that receive media attention, like those committed by Paul Bernardo, Jesse Imeson, or Greg Despres, create unwarranted fears of homicidal strangers among the populace.

Relatives and Acquaintances Most homicides occur among relatives and acquaintances. In Canada in 2006 four out of five victims (in solved

A mural made in honour of the memory of more than 140 children killed between 1995 and 2000 by a mass murderer in Pereira, Colombia.

homicides) knew the attacker. Almost half (49 percent) of the victims were killed by an acquaintance, and another 33 percent were killed by a family member. In cases of spousal homicide, chances are much greater that the female partner is the victim. In other words, women are much more likely than men to be killed by their spouse. The spousal homicide rate against females is five times higher than the rate for males (0.71 per 100 000 female spouses, and 0.14 per 100 000 male spouses).[14] Of these homicides, those in which women killed their mates have received particular attention. Criminologists take special interest in the factors behind such crimes.[15] Researchers have found a high incidence of long-term abuse suffered by women who subsequently kill their mates.[16] They also suggest that mate homicides are the result of a husband's efforts to control his wife and the wife's efforts to retain her independence.[17] Women are often particularly at risk when they leave their abusive partners. The motive in these cases is most often male jealousy and loss of control. In Canada, the courts have considered such long-term abuse at the hands of a spouse a legal defence in the killing of an abusive partner.

Children are also at risk of death at the hands of family members. In 2005, 20 child victims were killed by a parent, and 13 of these victims were under the age of 12 years. The numbers for 2005 are the lowest since 1964.[18] Research suggests that as the age of the child victim increases, so does the level of violence used to fatally injure the child.[19] Also, the closer the family relation to the victim (e.g., mother and child), the more passive the form of homicide (e.g., asphyxiation or abandonment), whereas the more distant a relative is to the victim, the more violent the method used (e.g., stabbing).[20] In most murders of a child under age 15, a family member killed the child, while murder victims aged 15 to 17 are more likely to be killed by an acquaintance of the victim or by someone unknown to the law enforcement authorities.[21] Whether killed by a family member or an acquaintance, boys are more often the victims of violent deaths than are girls.[22]

Mass and Serial Murders Criminological researchers have paid special attention to two types of murder that are particularly disturbing to the community: **serial murder,** the killing of several victims over a period of time, and **mass murder,**

In January 1982 serial killer Clifford Olson was sentenced to life imprisonment for the torture and murder of 11 boys and girls in British Columbia.

the killing of multiple victims in one event or in very quick succession. The literature on the subject is enormous.[23] Some serial murderers, including Clifford Olson and Robert Pickton, accused of numerous murders, have become infamous.

Clifford Olson is currently serving time for the murder of 11 young people in British Columbia. After Olson lured the youngsters into meeting with him, he then drugged, sexually assaulted, and murdered them. Robert Pickton was found guilty of killing several women and is accused of killing over 20 more missing women from the Vancouver area. He allegedly lured the women to his pig farm (where he was known to throw parties), assaulted them, killed them, and then hid the evidence. If convicted of all these murders, Pickton will be the worst serial killer in Canadian history.

John Martin Crawford was convicted in the murders of three Aboriginal women from the Saskatoon area, although it is suspected he killed more. Crawford targeted the women, it is believed, because they were young, Aboriginal, and worked in the sex trade industry. He would brutally assault his victims, sexually assault them, and then murder them. The judge in Crawford's case commented that "the accused has shown no remorse, absolutely none, no regrets, there's been no effort to explain his actions, and in fact, we know from the tapes that he laughed about the killings."[24]

Pedro Alonso Lopez, however, is considered the deadliest serial killer of all time, having killed over 300 people in Colombia, Peru, and Ecuador. Lopez has been dubbed the "Monster of the Andes."[25] Although the most notorious serial killers are men, female serial killers do exist. They are considered to be more difficult to apprehend and to have more complex motivations than their male counterparts.[26]

Over the past two decades, an unusual number of mass murders have occurred. In 1989 Marc Lépine opened fire on female engineering students in Montreal, killing 14 and wounding many others. In 1991, an unemployed young man drove his pickup through the glass window of a Texas café and opened fire with a semi-automatic pistol, leaving 22 dead. James Huberty walked into a McDonald's in California and killed 20 people. In 1996, Thomas Hamilton entered a school in Dunblane, Scotland, shot and killed 16 kindergarten students and their teacher, and wounded 12 others.[27] In 1998, 5 of the 16 persons shot at a Jonesboro, Arkansas, middle school died. In 1999, there were 15 victims of a massacre at Columbine High School in Littleton, Colorado. In 2002 18 people were killed in a school shooting in Erfurt, Germany. In 2007 Virginia Tech University was the scene of a horrific mass murder that resulted in the killing of 32 students in two attacks, two hours apart.

It is popularly believed that multiple murderers are mentally ill; their offences, after all, are often quite bizarre. In many such cases, psychiatrists have found severe pathology.[28] Yet juries are reluctant to find these offenders not guilty by reason of insanity. Albert Fish, who cooked and ate the children he murdered, died in the electric chair.[29] Edmund Kemper, who killed hitchhikers as well as his own mother (he used her head as a dartboard), received a life term.[30]

The criminologists Jack Levin and James Fox do not agree with the hypothesis that all mass and serial murderers are mentally diseased (e.g., psychotic) and therefore legally insane or incompetent. On the contrary, they say, serial killers are **sociopaths,** persons who lack internal controls, disregard common values, and have an intense desire to dominate others. But psychological characteristics alone cannot explain the actions of these people. They are also influenced by the social environment in which they function: the openness of our society, the ease of travel, the availability of firearms, the lack of external controls and supervision, and the general friendliness and trust of North Americans in dealing with each other and with strangers.[31]

The public is fascinated with the phenomena of mass and serial murder.[32] Levin and Fox suggest that the recent increase in mass and serial murders, despite a general decline in the murder rate, is to some extent attributable to the publicity given to mass murders and the resulting copycat phenomenon, the repetition of a crime as a result of the publicity it receives.[33] When one person killed at random by poisoning Tylenol capsules with cyanide, others copied the idea. This phenomenon has prompted experts to recommend that the media cooperate with the criminal justice system when the circumstances demand discretion.[34] Yet cooperation may be hard to achieve when media help is needed to alert the public to a health hazard (as in the Tylenol cases), and because the media are protected by rights to freedom of expression.

Gang Murder Up to this point we have dealt largely with homicides committed by single offenders. But what about homicides by gangs of offenders? Are there any differences between the two types? On the basis of an analysis of data contained in 700 homicide investigation files, researchers found that gang murders "differ both qualitatively and quantitatively from non-gang homicides. Most distinctly, they differ with respect to ethnicity [more likely to be intra-ethnic], age [gang killers are five years younger], number of participants [two-and-a-half times as many participants], and relationship between the participants [gang killers are twice as likely not to know their victims]."[35] But similarities can also be seen. The causes of gang homicides, like those of single offenders, are often attributable to social disorganization, economic inequality, and deprivation.[36] One in six homicides in Canada is gang-related, and almost two-thirds of gang-related homicides are motivated by the "settling of accounts."[37]

Since the 1950s, the nature of gang murder has changed dramatically. As we discuss in Chapter 6, besides the major increase in killings, gang homicides have also gotten more brutal. Drive-by and crossfire shootings of intended victims and innocent bystanders are no longer uncommon. Over the past decade in Canada, the number of gang-related homicides has steadily increased. Although the increase may in part be explained by a change in method of collecting data (notably, a revision was made to the Homicide Survey in 2005 to identify those homicides in which gang-related activity was "suspected" by police and not just "determined"), in 2006 there were 104 homicides (17 percent of all homicides) that were considered gang-related, an increase from the 75 confirmed gang homicides in 2004. The largest increases occurred in Ontario, where the number of gang-related homicides increased from 17 in 2004 to 28 in 2006, Quebec (18 in 2004 to 25 in 2006), and Alberta (15 in 2004 to 21 in 2006). Gang-related homicides occurred predominantly in Toronto, Edmonton, Montreal, and Calgary.[38] Once, gang wars, with a few related homicides, took place over "turf," territory that members protected with knives, rocks, or metal chains as weapons. Now the wars are over drugs, and the weapons are assault rifles and semi-automatic guns.[39]

A Cross-National Comparison of Homicide Rates

The criminal homicides we have been discussing are those committed in Canada. By comparing homicide rates in this country with those of other countries, we can gain a broader understanding of that crime. In the World Crime Survey ending with the year 1995, the United Nations revealed that the average rate of intentional homicide was 7.2 per 100 000 for developed (industrialized Western) countries and 3.5 per 100 000 for developing countries.[40] As Table 10.1 shows, Canada's homicide rate was close to that of Scotland, lower than Sweden and New Zealand, but higher than the rates of several other countries including England and Wales, Denmark, and Japan. Canada's homicide rate was about one-third of that of the United States in 2006. Other data show that the number of homicides per 100 000 children under age 15 in the United States was five times the number in the other countries combined. The rate of child homicides involving firearms was 16 times greater in the United States than in the other countries combined.[41]

One cross-national study found a moderate association between inequality of income and rate of homicide. It likewise revealed a relationship between a youthful population and the homicide rate. The analysis, the study concluded, "suggests that homicide rates are higher in poorer countries, in more culturally diverse countries, in countries which spend less on defense, in less-democratic societies, and in countries where fewer young people are enrolled in school."[42] Another researcher who compared the homicide rates in 76 countries

TABLE 10.1 Homicide Rates for Selected Countries, 2006.

Country	Rate per 100 000 population
Turkey[1]	6.23
United States	5.69
Germany[1]	2.90
Switzerland[1]	2.73
Sweden[1]	2.64
New Zealand	2.37
Finland	2.12
Canada	**1.85**
Scotland[2]	1.83
Hungary[1]	1.64
England and Wales[3]	1.41
France	1.39
Northern Ireland[3]	1.32
Australia	1.06
Denmark	0.90
Japan[1]	0.64
Hong Kong	0.51
Singapore	0.38

[1] Figures reflect 2005 data.

[2] Figures reflect 2005/2006 data.

[3] Figures reflect 2006/2007 data.

Source: Homicide in Canada, 2006, Statistics Canada, Catalogue no. 85-002-XIE. Vol. 27, no. 8, page 3.

with the rate in the United States found that when he took into consideration the differences in the age and sex distributions of the various populations, the United States had a higher rate than all but 15 countries,[43] most of which were experiencing civil war or internal strife.

A comparison of homicide rates with historical and socioeconomic data from 110 nations over a five-year period led researchers to the following conclusions:

- Combatant nations experience an increase in homicides following cessation of hostilities (violence has come to be seen as a legitimate means of settling disputes).

- The largest cities have the highest homicide rates; the smallest have the lowest homicide rates; but, paradoxically, as a city grows, its homicide rate per capita does not.

- The availability of capital punishment does not result in fewer homicides and in fact often results in more; abolition of capital punishment decreases the homicide rate.[44]

We have seen that murder rates are not distributed equally among countries or within a single country, or even within neighbourhoods. As noted earlier, in Canada homicide rates tend to be highest in the West; in the United States, homicide rates tend to be higher in the West and the South.[45] A greater proportion of males, young people, Aboriginals in Canada, and blacks in the United States are perpetrators and victims of homicide, which tends to be committed against someone the killer knows, at or near the home of at least one of the persons involved, in the evening or on a weekend. Gang murders are increasing dramatically. A number of experts have found that homicides are related to the everyday patterns of interactions in socially disorganized slum areas.[46]

ASSAULT

The crimes of homicide and serious **assault** share many characteristics. Both are typically committed by young males, and a disproportionate number of arrestees are members of minority groups. Assault victims, too, often know their attackers. Spatial and temporal distributions are also quite comparable. Assault rates, like those of homicide, are highest in urban areas, during the summer months, in the evening hours, and in the West.

Though the patterns are the same, the legal definitions are not. A murder is an act that causes the death of another person and that is intended to cause death. In 1983 amendments to the Canadian Criminal Code resulted in the creation of three levels of assault. Common assault (level 1) is the least serious and the most common form of assault. Level 2 assaults are those involving a deadly weapon or which cause bodily harm, while aggravated assault (level 3) refers to incidents where one individual wounds, maims, disfigures, or endangers the victim's life. The overall rate of assault in 2006 was 735 per 100 000 people.[47]

> **Did You Know?**
>
> . . . that common assaults (level 1) make up 60 percent of all assaults?

Anger at street encounters often escalates to assault or even homicide. Here a crowd gathers as a street argument develops.

Criminologists have looked closely at situations in which assaults are committed. One researcher identified six stages of a confrontational situation that leads to an assault:

1. One person insults another.
2. The insulted person perceives the significance of the insult, often by noting the reactions of others present, and becomes angry.
3. The insulted person contemplates a response: fight, flight, or conciliation. If the response chosen is a fight, the insultee assaults the insulter then and there. If another response is chosen, the situation advances to stage 4.
4. The original insulter, now reprimanded, shamed, or embarrassed, makes a countermove: fight or flight.
5. If the choice is a fight, the insulter assaults (and possibly kills) the insultee.
6. The "triumphant" party either flees or awaits the consequences (e.g., police response).[48]

We can see that crucial decisions are made at all stages, and that the nature of the decisions depends on the context in which they are made. At stage 1, nobody is likely to offer an insult in a peaceful group or situation. At stage 2, the witnesses to the scene could respond in a conciliatory manner. (Let us call this a conflict-resolution situation.) At stage 3, the insulted person could leave the scene with dignity. (A confrontational person would call it flight; a conflict-resolution-minded person would call it a dignified end to a confrontational situation.) Stage 4 is a critical stage, since it calls for a counter-response. The original aggressor could see this as the last chance to avoid violence and withdraw with apologies. That would be the end of the matter. In a confrontational situation, however, the blows will be delivered now, if none have been dealt already.

A similar pattern was proposed by James Tedeschi and Richard Felson, who developed a theory of aggression as instrumental behaviour— that is, goal-oriented behaviour carried out intentionally with the purpose of obtaining something. This is a different way of thinking about aggression. For years, criminologists and psychologists have generally accepted that aggression (and the violence that often goes with it) happens when a person reaches a "breaking point." There is little premeditation or thought given to some aggressive or violent behaviour. But for Tedeschi and Felson, all aggression occurs after the person has thought about it first, even though these thoughts may be disorganized or illogical and may last for just a fraction of a second.[49]

> **Did You Know?**
>
> . . . that victimization survey data indicate that the rate of assault (all three levels) is about 7500 per 100 000?

The overall rate of assault reported in the 2004 General Social Survey is significantly higher than the numbers reported by the police.[50] However, victimization data likely still underestimate the real incidence of assault. Many people involved in an assault consider the event a private matter, and are reluctant to report it as a result, particularly if the assault took place within the family or household. Consequently, until quite recently little was known about family-related violence. But the focus of recent research is changing that situation rapidly.

FAMILY-RELATED CRIMES

In 1962, five physicians exposed the gravity of the "battered child syndrome" in the *Journal of the American Medical Association*.[51] When they reviewed X-ray photographs of patients in the emergency rooms of 71 hospitals across the United States over the course of a year, they found 300 cases of child abuse, of which 11 percent resulted in death and over 28 percent in permanent brain damage. Shortly thereafter, the women's movement rallied to the plight of the battered wife and, somewhat later, to the personal and legal problems of wives who were sexually assaulted by their husbands.[52]

In the 1960s and 1970s, various organizations, fighting for the rights of women and children, exposed the harm that results from physical and psychological abuse in the home. They demanded public action. They created public awareness of the extent of the problem and drew attention to historically rooted views that promoted the idea that women were the "property" of men. The law was complicit in perpetuating these views by historically upholding husbands' "right to consortium" (which meant wives had a legal obligation with respect to the "consummation of marriage, cohabitation, maintenance of conjugal rights, sexual fidelity, and general obedience and respect for his wishes") and the "right to chastise" their wives.[53] The "right to consortium" was addressed by the 1983 amendment to the Criminal Code, which made it illegal for a husband to rape his wife; the "right to chastise" has been one of the many focuses of the women's movement, as it draws attention to the violence women experience at the hands of their spouses, in their homes, and through which far too many suffer in silence.

Within three decades, family violence, the "well-kept secret," has come to be recognized as a major social problem.[54] Family violence shares some of the characteristics of other forms of violence, yet the intimacy of marital, cohabitational, or parent-child relationships sets family violence apart. The physical and emotional harm inflicted in violent episodes tends to be spread over longer periods of time and to have a more lasting impact on all members of the living unit. Moreover, such events tend to be self-perpetuating.

Spouse Abuse

In May 1998, Motley Crüe drummer Tommy Lee was sentenced to six months in jail and three years probation for battering his wife, former *Baywatch* beauty Pamela Anderson. Lee was also ordered to perform 200 hours of community service and donate US$5000 to a battered women's shelter. He had been arrested in February 1998 after Anderson called 911 to report a domestic dispute in which Lee had kicked her in the back while she was holding seven-week-old Dylan Jagger. Lee was charged with spousal abuse, child abuse, and unlawful possession of a firearm. As the result of a plea agreement, all charges except for the spousal abuse charge were dropped.

Media celebrity and former star athlete O. J. Simpson was convicted in 1989 of assaulting his wife, Nicole Brown Simpson. He served no time in prison, nor was he required to undergo counselling. On June 13, 1994, Nicole Brown Simpson and her friend Ronald Goldman were found lying dead in pools of their own blood, victims of a vicious knife attack. O. J. Simpson was accused of their murder. Following a lengthy, highly publicized, and much-discussed trial, O. J. Simpson was found not guilty by a jury of his peers. The verdict had a wide-reaching impact on various aspects of the criminal justice system. It also made abused women fear for their lives. Concerned that a man who was a convicted batterer could be found not guilty of killing his ex-wife, despite what was perceived by many as convincing evidence, they wondered if they could eventually share the same fate as Nicole Brown Simpson.[55]

The Extent of Spouse Abuse   Spouse abuse and sexual assault (which we discuss later in this chapter) are crimes for which there is a large dark figure. For a variety of reasons, victims of spousal abuse and sexual assault, the vast majority of which are women, are reluctant to report these incidents. As feminist criminologists point out, violence against women is a serious problem that has been exacerbated both by the discipline and society in general. Mainstream criminology was relatively silent on the topic; referring to official statistics which underreported these crimes, criminologists maintained that violence against women was a relatively rare event. The law was complicit in perpetuating beliefs that discounted the extent and nature of violence against women by not adequately acknowledging the violent and criminal nature of such acts.

As a result of the women's movement and growing awareness of male violence against women, legislative reforms in Canada occurred in 1983. These legislative reforms have impacted

A spectator holds up a sign offering advice to Boston Red Sox batter Wilfredo Cordero as he pinch-hits for Reggie Jefferson in a game with the Toronto Blue Jays. The fans at Fenway Park, Boston, greeted him with boos as he stepped up to the plate.

on our understanding of domestic violence, public awareness and response to it, and police enforcement of these laws. In 1983, a national directive was issued to police officers that encouraged them to lay charges in cases of wife assault. Up to this point, the decision to charge an offender was left to the victim. Understandably, a wife in an abusive relationship, scared of her abuser and dependent on him for financial support, would be reluctant to lay charges. After 1983, that decision was placed in the hands of police officers, whose training was also modified to incorporate sensitivity to domestic violence and skills for intervention in such cases. In 1993, Statistics Canada released the findings of the Violence Against Women Survey, which included responses from over 12 000 women across Canada. The survey found that half (51 percent) of Canadian women had experienced at least one incident of physical or sexual violence since the age of 16. It also found that 29 percent of ever-married women had been assaulted by a spouse.[56]

Gendered Violence: The Nature of Spouse Abuse   Spouse abuse and sexual assault are examples of gendered violence: Male violence against women is understood as a manifestation of patriarchy—the systemic and individual power that men exercise over women.[57] As we know from previous chapters, men are victims of violence—in particular, assaults committed by strangers and casual acquaintances. However, the violence committed against women takes a different form and is perpetrated largely by the men in their lives. The Violence Against Women Survey also confirmed that women face the greatest risk from men they know: 45 percent of all women experience violence by men known to them (dates, boyfriends, marital partners, friends, family, neighbours, etc.), while 23 percent experience violence by a stranger. There are definite differences in the forms violent victimization (and perpetration) take for males and females. Violence is gendered.

Violence against women takes many forms, including sexual harassment in the workplace, date rape, violent sexual assaults, and wife abuse.[58] In a patriarchal society like ours, male domination over women is insidious and pervasive. From this perspective, spousal abuse (along with sexual assault) is on one (extreme) end of a continuum of male dominance, that has on the relatively mild end telling sexist jokes or whistling at women walking past a male-dominated work site. The continuum analogy illustrates the pervasiveness of the acceptability in our society of subjecting women to behaviours that wouldn't be acceptable if the targets were men.

Consider this (true) scenario: As a relatively young, female sessional instructor in a university criminology class (she had earned her PhD several years prior), one of this book's authors was presenting information on the Violence Against Women Survey, when she was rudely interrupted by guffawing in the back of the auditorium. When she questioned the source of the noise, a young man, she was confronted with the following question/statement: "Are you for real? Do you expect us to believe that 29 percent of married women have been assaulted by their husband? How did they measure 'assault'? By something minor like slapping? I think you should check your facts."

Despite the fact that this story is not about spousal assault (and despite the fact that this student perceives slapping as "minor"), it is relevant to our discussion for several reasons. First, how likely is it that this student would have confronted an older (white-haired) male professor in the same manner? Second, when we consider that this is not an isolated incident, it is perhaps easier to see how the continuum just mentioned

becomes more relevant. This male student felt justified in his behaviour, and while his question was legitimate, its delivery was disrespectful and implied that the lecturer did not know what she was talking about. For other men, similar justifications may escalate into more serious forms of behaviour, at the base of which is the belief that male domination is acceptable. Escalation of this type of thinking contributed to Marc Lépine's murderous rage that sent 14 "feminists back to their maker." It likely contributes to rationalizations for slipping rohypnol into a young woman's drink when it becomes clear she isn't going to voluntarily "put out" after a date. And, more relevant to this particular section, it contributes to wife assault.

In a patriarchal society messages supporting what we have termed gendered violence are pervasive. Television, movies, and music contribute to beliefs concerning the respective roles of men and women in relationships. In addition, these culturally constructed ideas regarding femininity and masculinity are reinforced in the home. Experts have found that interpersonal violence is learned and transmitted from one generation to the next.[59] Studies demonstrate that children who are raised by aggressive parents tend to grow up to be aggressive adults.[60] Other factors play a role in spousal assault as well. Researchers have demonstrated how stress, frustration, and severe psychopathology take their toll on family relationships.[61] A few researchers have also explored the role of body chemistry; one investigation ties abuse to the tendency of males to secrete adrenaline when they feel sexually threatened.[62] The relationship between domestic violence and the use of alcohol and drugs has also been explored. Abusive men with severe drug and alcohol problems are more likely to abuse their wives or girlfriends and to inflict more injury when they are drunk or high.[63]

Sexual Symmetry Spouse abuse has often been attributed to the imbalance of power between male and female partners. According to some researchers, the historical view of wives as possessions of their husbands persists even today.[64] Recent acts of violence perpetrated by women, however, have changed the public perception of some women. As Elizabeth Comack documents, media attention to the violent acts committed by women such as Karla Homolka and Kelly Ellard (who attacked Reena Virk) created a belief among many that women are just as "violent and nasty" as men.[65] Sexual symmetry in intimate violence refers to the belief that men are as likely as women to be victims of abuse and women are as likely as men to be perpetrators of both minor and serious acts of violence. Research using the Conflict Tactics Scale (CTS), which measures violence and abuse in intimate relationships, offers support for the notion that women and men exhibit equivalent rates of both minor and severe types of violence. However, further examination of the CTS, and domestic violence, reveals this is not the case. While both husbands and wives perpetrate acts of violence, the consequences of their acts differ.[66]

Elizabeth Comack, Vanessa Chopyk, and Linda Wood examined 1002 cases from police incident reports involving men and women charged with violent crime in Winnipeg during a five-year period, with the goal of discerning whether a qualitative difference existed between men's and women's violence. In contrast to the sexual symmetry argument, the researchers found that the violence tactics used by men and women differed: Men were more likely to use their physical strength or force against their female partners, while women were more likely to resort to the use of weapons during the course of a violent event. The researchers also found that violence that occurs between intimate partners is not "mutual combat": In cases where the male was accused of using violence, female partners used violence in only 23 percent of cases. On the other hand, in cases where the female was the accused perpetrator of violence, men responded with violence in 65 percent of cases. Further evidence against the sexual symmetry argument concerns the extent of injury suffered by the accused: 48 percent of the women accused, as opposed to only 7 percent of the men accused, were injured during the course of the violent incident.[67] Finally, in these cases of partner violence, the accused woman called the police in 35 percent of cases, whereas only 7 percent of accused males called the police. In other words, even though the women in 35 percent of cases ended up being charged with a violent offence, they were the ones who had called the police for help, lending further support to the idea that violence between the genders is asymmetrical.

General Social Survey data similarly confirm that intimate violence is gendered. Women are more frequently the victims in spousal assault incidents and are more likely to be on the receiving end of more severe forms of violence.[68] Certainly, women are capable of violence and they do commit violent acts. However, sexual symmetry does not exist and deferring to the argument that women are just as violent as men undermines efforts to adequately address the gendered nature of violence in society.

Efforts to reduce spousal and other forms of violence start with an examination of the role of patriarchy in perpetuating male dominance. Encouraging critical reflection on the ways in which men's and women's roles are culturally constructed and reinforced by institutional processes and individual behaviours is a good place to start. In doing this, we can work toward reducing the number of incidents that occur at the lower, less extreme end of the continuum, and in so doing, reduce the more serious forms of gendered violence that are all too common today.

Child Abuse

Spouse abuse is closely related to child abuse. One-half to three-quarters of men who batter women also beat their children, and many sexually abuse them as well. Children are also injured as a result of reckless behaviour on the part of their fathers while the latter are abusing their mothers. In fact, the majority of abused sons over 14 suffer injuries trying to protect their mothers.[69] Other studies suggest that between 45 and 70 percent of children exposed to domestic violence are also victims of physical abuse.[70]

The Extent of Child Abuse   A pathologist testifying in an inquest into the 2002 death of 19-month old Sherry Charlie in Port Alberni, British Columbia, stated the baby was the victim of battered child syndrome, and had been beaten many times in her short life. Dr. Dan Straathof testified that Sherry had 11 broken ribs and severe bruises in various stages of healing. He said she died as a result of three blows to the head. Sherry's great uncle, Ryan George, was found guilty of beating the child to death three weeks after she and her brother were placed in George's home by an Aboriginal child welfare agency.

In October 2006, an inquiry began into the death of three-year old Halaina Lascelle, who died on Texada Island, British Columbia, in April 2001. Halaina had been transferred from foster care into the care of her aunt and uncle. Her uncle, who walked into Halaina's bedroom and slit her throat as she lay in bed, was convicted of second-degree murder.

Inquiries into both deaths determined that cutbacks in British Columbia's child protection system, as well as leadership and organizational changes, contributed to the tragic deaths of the two young girls. These problems are not unique to that province, nor are the types of neglect and abuse that preceded the deaths as rare as we might want to believe.

According to the Canadian Incidence Study of Reported Child Abuse and Neglect, an estimated 217 319 child investigations were conducted in Canada in 2003, of which 47 percent (103 297) were substantiated. Overall, the incidence rate of substantiated child maltreatment in Canada was 21.71 per 1000 children.[71] When looking at these numbers, it is, of course, critical that we keep in mind that these are the cases that came to the attention of child welfare services. While it is difficult to estimate the number of cases that failed to come to the attention of these agencies, it is safe to assume the number of actual cases of child maltreatment is significantly higher than these official estimates. Furthermore, in an additional 13 percent of the investigations conducted by child welfare agencies participating in the study, there was insufficient evidence to substantiate maltreatment, but the investigators remained suspicious that maltreatment did in fact occur.

As Figure 10.3 illustrates, neglect is the most common primary form of substantiated maltreatment (30 percent), followed by exposure to domestic violence (28 percent), physical abuse (24 percent), emotional abuse (15 percent), and sexual abuse (3 percent). Within these categories of maltreatment, there are gendered patterns of abuse. Girls account for about half (49 percent) of victims but are overrepresented in cases of sexual abuse (63 percent) and emotional maltreatment (54 percent). Boys, on the other hand, are more often victims of physical abuse (54 percent), neglect (52 percent), and exposure to domestic violence (52 percent). Age also interacts with abuse: Older children are more likely to experience physical and sexual abuse (70 and 67 percent of

FIGURE 10.3 Primary category of substantiated child maltreatment in Canada, 2003.*

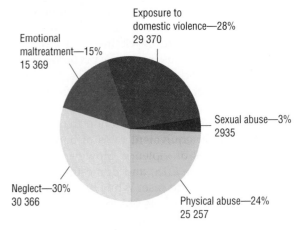

* Quebec is excluded from these results.

Source: "Canadian Incidence Study of Reported Child Abuse and Neglect—2003. Major Findings," Ministry of Public Works and Government Services Canada, 2005. Reproduced with the permission of the Minister of Public Works and Government Services Canada, 2008.

physical and sexual abuse victims, respectively, were between the ages of 8 and 15). Younger children are more likely to experience exposure to domestic violence (60 percent of victims were aged seven or younger). Based on concern regarding Aboriginal overrepresentation in the foster care system, the Canadian Incidence Study of Reported Child Abuse and Neglect examined maltreatment among children of Aboriginal heritage: 15 percent of cases (nearly 15 000) of substantiated maltreatment involved Aboriginal children.

The Nature of Child Abuse When child abuse first began to be investigated in the early 1960s, the investigators were predominantly physicians, who looked at the psychopathology of the abusers. They discovered that a high proportion of abusers suffered from alcoholism, drug abuse, mental retardation, poor attachment, low self-esteem, or sadistic psychosis. Later the search for causes moved in other directions. Some researchers pointed out that abusive parents did not know how to discipline children or, for that matter, even how to provide for basic needs, such as nutrition and medical attention. Claims have been made that abusers have themselves been abused; to date, however, the evidence in regard to this hypothesis is mixed.[72]

The list of factors related to child abuse is long. We know, for example, that the rate of child abuse in lower-income families is high.[73] This finding is probably related to the fact that low-income parents have few resources for dealing with the stresses to which they are subjected, such as poor housing and financial problems. When they cannot cope with their responsibilities, they may become overwhelmed. Alternately, it is possible that low-income families are more likely to come to the attention of social control agencies including the police, social services, and child welfare agencies. In other words, family-related abuse occurs in higher-income families, but these families may have the resources to more effectively keep the abuse hidden from outsiders. Since child abuse among poor families is likely to be handled by a public agency, these cases tend to appear in official statistics. Moreover, the risk of abuse is twice as great for children living with single parents as for children living with both parents.[74] The rate of child abuse may also be related to the acceptance of physical responses to conflict situations in what has been termed the "subculture of violence" (see Chapter 6).

When child abuse is reported to the authorities, the case goes through the criminal justice system just like any other case. However, certain factors are associated with how, and to what extent, these types of cases are prosecuted. One study suggests that, particularly in the case of child sexual abuse, those offenders who are charged with abusing multiple victims are much more likely to be prosecuted than are offenders charged with abusing only one victim. Also, offenders who are strangers to the victim are more likely to be prosecuted than are offenders related to the victim. Cases in which serious abuse was involved and medical evidence of abuse existed were also more likely to be prosecuted.[75]

Some researchers have found that formal action—arrest and prosecution—is the most effective means for limiting repeat offences in the case of battered wives. The situation seems to be different when children are involved. Several advocates for children oppose any involvement of the criminal justice system. They believe that the parent-child attachment remains crucial to the child's development, and they fear that punishment of parents can only be detrimental to the child's need for a stable family environment. Only in the most extreme cases would they separate children from parents and place them in shelters or in foster homes. The preference is to prevent child abuse by other means, such as self-help groups (e.g., Parents Anonymous), babysitting assistance, and crisis phone lines.

The results of various types of intervention are characterized by the title of a report on child maltreatment: "Half Full and Half Empty."[76] Rates of repeated abuse are high; yet some families have had positive results, and advances have been made in identifying the best treatment for various types of problems. Although our understanding of the problem has indeed increased, we need to know a great deal more about the offence before we can reduce its occurrence.[77]

Abuse of the Elderly

We don't have laws that specifically deal with the abuse of the elderly. Rather, sections of the Criminal Code, such as those dealing with physical and sexual assaults, intimidation and harassment, and crimes of property, fraud, or theft by power of attorney are referred to when dealing with specific cases of elder abuse. Generally, elder abuse refers to the "mistreatment of older people by those in a position of trust, power, or responsibility for their care" and as with child abuse, neglect is commonly associated with abuse.[78] Elder abuse occurs in both private and institutional contexts. While abuse can take a variety of forms, the four main categories of abuse often used when discussing the topic of elder abuse include psychological, financial/material, physical, and neglect.

Family (or domestic) violence laws are a relatively new approach to dealing with elder abuse. In addition to use of the Criminal Code, provinces in Canada have taken the initiative to pass special

Fatal child abuse cases attract media attention. Abuse and neglect result in too many unnecessary deaths of children every year. Most victims are under six years of age.

adult protection laws (some of which are mandatory, others voluntary), which give a specific provincial health or social service department the responsibility to respond to abuse or neglect cases that are brought to its attention.[79] For example, Nova Scotia, New Brunswick, Prince Edward Island, Newfoundland and Labrador, British Columbia, and the Yukon have such laws in place. Quebec has a special provision in its provincial human rights legislation that provides a means for dealing with cases of elder abuse.

As with the case of other types of family-related violence, it is difficult to ascertain the full extent of elder abuse. One national study in Canada found that about 4 percent of older adults living in private homes had experienced abuse or neglect. The most prevalent mistreatment reported was material abuse, most often involving widowed older adults living alone and perpetrated by a distant relative or a non-relative rather than by a close family member. The second most prevalent form of abuse, according to this study, was chronic verbal aggression, a component of psychological abuse: Victims were usually abused by their spouse. Third in terms of prevalence was physical abuse. Again, in the majority of cases the abusers were spouses of the victims.[80] The General Social Survey found that 5 percent of the 4000 seniors interviewed experienced emotional, financial, physical, or sexual abuse from an adult child, caregiver, or spouse in the previous five years.[81]

In addition to a lack of legislation focusing on this kind of behaviour, definitions of abuse vary among agencies, and resources for effectively dealing with the issue are often lacking. Furthermore, lack of sensitivity to the issue, including policy and attitudinal barriers, contribute to the double victimization of elderly abuse victims who are "shut out" of the system, and whose concerns are not legitimated.

As a result of these issues, abuse of the elderly has become an area of special concern to social scientists. The population group that is considered to be elderly is variously defined. The majority of researchers consider 65 the age at which an individual falls into the category "elderly." As health care in North America has improved, longevity has increased. And as life expectancy increases, it is inevitable that the population of elderly people will continue to grow. As the baby boomers, who make up about 35 percent of the population, age and

enter the ranks of the elderly, the issue of elder abuse will become more pronounced.

Elderly persons who are being cared for by their adult children are at a certain risk of abuse. A large-scale study found that family members were suspected in two-thirds of reported abuse cases, most often adult children and then spouses.[82] The extent of the problem, however, is still largely unknown. The abused elderly frequently do not talk about their abuse for fear of the embarrassment of public exposure, possible retaliation by the abuser, rejection by loved ones, or fear of having to leave their home. Among the causes of such abuse are caregivers who themselves grew up in homes where violence was a way of life, the stress of caregiving in a private home rather than an institution, generational conflicts, and frustration with gerontological (old-age) problems of the care receiver, such as illness and senility.[83]

We can see that criminologists share a growing concern about family-related violence. Child abuse has received the attention of scholars for three decades. Spousal abuse has been studied for two decades. The abuse of the elderly has begun to receive attention much more recently. Family abuse is not new; our awareness of the size and seriousness of the problem is. The same could be said about yet another offence. It was not until the 1960s that women's advocates launched a campaign on behalf of victims of sexual assault. Since then, sexual assault has become a major topic in criminological literature and research.

SEXUAL ASSAULT

The common law defined **rape** as an act of enforced intercourse by a man of a woman (other than the attacker's wife) without her consent. Intercourse includes any sexual penetration, however slight. The exclusion of wives from the crime of rape rested on several outdated legal fictions, among them the propositions that the marriage vows grant implicit permanent rights of sexual access (the "right to consortium") and that spouses cannot testify against each other.

Canadian law up until 1983 reflected a belief in the husband's right to consortium. Under the old rape law, rape was defined like this: "A male person commits rape when he has sexual intercourse with a female person who is not his wife, (a) without her consent, or (b) with her consent if the consent (i) is extorted by threats or fear of bodily harm, (ii) is obtained by personating her husband, or (iii) is obtained by false and fraudulent representations as to the nature and quality of the act." Older laws universally classify rape as a sex crime. But rape has always been much more than that. It is inherently a crime of violence, an exercise of power.

Oddly, as Susan Brownmiller forcefully argues, it really started as a property crime. Men as archetypal aggressors (the penis as a weapon) subjugated women by the persistent threat of rape. That threat forced each woman to submit to a man for protection and thus to become a wife, the property of a man. Rape then was made a crime to protect one man's property—his wife—from the sexual aggressions of other men.[84] But even that view regards rape as a violent crime against the person, one that destroys the freedom of a woman (and nowadays of a man as well) to decide whether, when, and with whom to enter a sexual relationship.

Well over a thousand books, scholarly articles, and papers have been produced on the topic of rape and sexual assault. Much that was obscure and poorly understood has now been clarified by research generated largely by the initiatives of the feminist movement, including the 1980 report of the Canadian Advisory Council on the Status of Women, the 1993 Statistics Canada Violence Against Women Survey, and other governmental and private funding agencies. While most of the crimes in the Criminal Code have more or less retained their original form, the law on rape has changed rapidly and drastically. The name of the crime, its definition, the rules of evidence and procedure, society's reaction to it—all have changed.[85] Nevertheless, Canadians still regard sexual assault as one of the most serious crimes.

Characteristics of the Sexual Assault Event

According to the Uniform Crime Reports, there were 22 136 sexual assaults in Canada in 2006. This figure represents 7 percent of the total number of violent crimes.[86] There are actually three

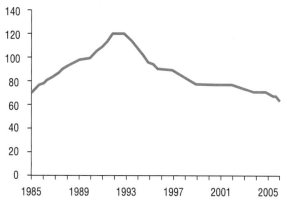

FIGURE 10.4   Reported sexual assault in Canada, 1985–2006.

Rate per 100 000 population

Source: "Crime Statistics in Canada, 2005," Statistics Canada, Catalogue no. 85-002, Vol. 26, no. 4. page 7; "Crime Statistics in Canada, 2006," Statistics Canada, Catalogue no. 85-002-XIE, Vol. 27, no. 5, Minister of Industry, 2007, page 9.

different categories or levels of sexual assault in Canada. These categories were created in 1983 when the old rape law was repealed. Level 1 sexual assault involves the least amount of physical injury to the victim. In 2006, 97 percent of the reported sexual assaults were categorized as level 1. Level 2 sexual assault refers to sexual assault with a weapon, threats to use a weapon, or causing bodily harm. Level 3 sexual assault is considered the most serious and refers to sexual assaults that wound, maim, disfigure, or endanger the lives of victims. In 2006, level 2 and level 3 sexual assaults accounted for about 3 percent of all sexual assaults.

As Figure 10.4 shows, the reported sexual assault rate peaked in the early 1990s and has been declining ever since.[87] As with other types of violence (with the exception of homicide), sexual assaults are seriously underreported.

Estimates based on victimization survey data indicate that about 10 percent of all sexual assaults are reported to the police. More than 80 percent of victims are female, and more than half are between 15 and 25 years of age.[88] Victims are reluctant to report the assaults for many reasons, some of which include embarrassment, self-blame, fear

Did You Know?

... that according to victimization survey data (GSS), over 70 percent of women who are sexually assaulted know their attacker? Forty-one percent were assaulted by an acquaintance, 10 percent by a friend, and 20 percent by a family member. About 20 percent were sexually assaulted by a stranger.

of reprisal from the attacker, not wanting the police involved, and feeling that it is a personal matter.[89]

While Canadian law has changed to reflect the fact that men can and do rape their wives, this does not stop husbands from doing so. We know little about this type of sexual assault except that it often occurs in marriages that are characterized by other forms of violence. And while the number of sexual assaults reported to police has been declining over the years, estimates are that one in four Canadian women will be sexually assaulted during her lifetime. In British Columbia the numbers are even more staggering: Almost one out of two women there have been sexually assaulted.[90]

Recently, researchers have developed a three-category typology of sexual assault. Stranger sexual assault occurs when the victim has had little or no prior contact with the offender. Predatory sexual assault involves a man who, using deception or force, intends and plans to sexually assault his victim by pretending to engage in legitimate dating behaviour. The third category of sexual assault occurs when a legitimate dating situation turns bad, when force is eventually used to gain sex from a woman who is an unwilling participant—"date rape."[91] In these situations, the offenders sometimes use the "date-rape drug" Rohypnol, commonly referred to as "Roofies." Rohypnol falls into the same class of drugs as marijuana. It is a sedative that is said to be ten times the strength of Valium. Twenty to 30 minutes after it is consumed, often after being dropped into a drink at a social gathering, this tasteless, odourless drug produces in its victim muscle relaxation, a slowing of psychomotor responses, and amnesia.[92] A survey of female undergraduates at Canadian universities revealed that four out of five of these women said they had been victims of violence in a dating relationship; 29 percent who reported abuse also reported incidents of sexual assault.[93] Estimates are that only 1 percent of all date rapes are reported to the police.[94]

Sexual offences are the least likely violent crime to result in charges. Many stranger sexual assault offenders remain at large because they commit their acts in ways that produce little tangible evidence as to their identities. They maintain a distance from the victim by not interacting with her before the attack. The serial offender also attacks strangers, but because he finds his victims repeatedly in the same places, his behaviour is more predictable and so leads to a better arrest rate.[95]

Who Are the Perpetrators of Sexual Assault?

Explanations of sexual assault fall into two categories, psychological and sociocultural. While research in these areas has expanded over the last two decades, the causes of sexual assault remain speculative.

Psychological Factors   Several experts view sexual offenders as suffering from mental illness or personality disorders. They argue that some of these offenders are psychotic, sociopathic, or sadistic, or that they feel deficient in masculinity. Most rapists show hostile feelings toward women, have histories of violence, and tend to attack strangers. They commit the offence because of anger, a drive for power (expressed as sexual conquest), or the enjoyment of maltreating a victim (sadism). Some view women as sex objects whose role is to satisfy them.

Sara Lively, 24, left, and Michelle Coler, 21, test their drinks for date-rape drugs at a college pub. Many universities and colleges are buying coasters that test for date-rape drugs in drinks.

> **Did You Know?**
>
> … that a survey found that 60 percent of Canadian university-aged males admitted they would commit sexual assault if they were certain they would not get caught?

Sociocultural Factors   Psychological explanations assume that men who sexually assault are maladjusted in some way. But several studies done in the 1980s demonstrate that they are indistinguishable from other groups of offenders.[96] These studies generally conclude that sexual assault is culturally related to societal norms that approve of aggression as a demonstration of masculinity (as we saw in Chapter 6) or that sexual assault is the mechanism by which men maintain their power over women.

The social significance of sexual assault has long been a part of anthropological literature. A cross-cultural study of 95 tribal societies found that 47 percent were sexual-assault-free, 35 percent intermediate, and 18 percent sexual-assault-prone. In the sexual-assault-prone societies, women had low status and little decision-making power, and they lived apart from men. The author of this study concluded: "Violence is socially, not biologically, programmed."[97]

Despite anthropologists' traditional interest in gender relationships, it was not until the feminist movement and radical criminology focused on the subject that the relationship of sexual assault, gender inequality, and socioeconomic status was fully articulated. Writing from the Marxist perspective, which we explore in Chapter 9, Julia and Herman Schwendinger posited that "the impoverishment of the working class and the widening gap between rich and poor" create conditions for the prevalence of sexual violence.[98] A test of this hypothesis showed that while the incidence of sexual violence was not related to ethnic inequality, it was significantly related to general income inequality.[99]

A more recent study analyzed these findings and concluded that economic inequality was not the sole determinant of violent crime in our society. Sexual assault was found to be an added "cost" of many factors, including social disorganization.[100] In sum, many factors have been associated with the crime of sexual assault: psychological problems, social factors, and even sociopolitical factors. Some experts suggest that boys are socialized to be aggressive and dominating, that the innate male sex drive leads to sexual assault, and that pornography encourages men to commit sexual assault by making sex objects of women, degrading women, and glamorizing violence against them. Sexual assault has been explained in such a wide variety of ways that it is extremely difficult to plan preventive strategies and to formulate crime-control policy. Moreover, it has created major difficulties in the criminal justice system.

Sexual Assault and the Legal System

The difficulties of sexual assault prosecutions have their roots in the English common law. Sir Matthew Hale, a seventeenth-century jurist, explained in *Pleas of the Crown* (1685, 1736) how a jury was to be cautious in viewing evidence of rape: "[It] must be remembered . . . that it is an accusation easily to be made and hard to be proved, and harder to be defended, by the party accused, tho never so innocent."[101] This instruction, which so definitively protects the defendant, up until recently in Canada characterized the manner in which rape cases were tried. Although the law has changed over the years to counteract stereotypes that have perpetuated culturally constructed rape myths, many of these myths continue to linger in the functioning of the criminal justice system and its treatment of sexual assault victims.

Difficulties of Prosecution   Victims of sexual assault have often been regarded with suspicion by the criminal justice system. The victim's testimony has not sufficed to convict the defendant, no matter how unimpeachable that testimony may have been. There had to be "corroborating evidence," such as semen, torn clothes, bruises, or eyewitness testimony.

Another major issue has been that of consent. Did the victim encourage, entice, or maybe even agree to the act? Was the attack forced? Did the victim resist? Martin Schwartz and Todd Clear sum up the reasons for such questions: "There is a widespread belief in our culture that women 'ask for it,' either individually or as a group." They compared sexual assault victims to victims of other offences: "Curiously, society does not censure the robbery victim for walking around with $10, or the burglary victim for keeping all of those nice things in his house, or the car theft victim for showing off his flashy new machine, just asking for someone to covet it."[102]

Because defendants in sexual assault cases so often claim that the victim was in some way responsible for the attack, sexual assault victims in the courtroom tend to become the "accused," required to defend their good reputations, their propriety, and their mental soundness. The severity of the assault, the injuries the victim sustains, whether or not the assailant was a stranger, and the victim's social support network all play a role in terms of the sexual assault reporting process.[103] In sum, so many burdens have traditionally been placed on the victim that no one seriously wonders why so few sexual assaults are reported and why so few men accused of sexual assault are convicted.

Legislative Changes   The feminist movement has had a considerable impact on laws and attitudes concerning sexual assault in our country. Certainly, the 1983 changes to the Criminal Code can be credited to the work of feminists, but several changes in the 1990s also resulted in the creation of a more "victim-friendly" court procedure. It didn't, however, start that way. In 1991 in making rulings in the cases of *Seaboyer* and *Gayme*,[104] the Supreme Court of Canada struck down the "rape shield" provision (section 276 of the Criminal Code), which was one of the outcomes of the 1983 changes. The goal of the rape shield provision was to prevent a victim's sexual conduct from being used to discredit her testimony, but in striking it down, the Supreme Court expressed concern that the provision went too far and could deny the accused a fair trial.[105] The decision was criticized for giving trial judges discretion over whether to admit evidence of the complainant's past sexual history in court cases.

As a result, Parliament introduced Bill C-49 in 1992, which was designed to amend the 1983 legislation. Under the legislation, "rules of evidence now state that evidence that the complainant has engaged in sexual activity, whether with the accused or with any other person, is not admissible to support an inference that the complainant is either more likely to have consented to the sexual activity in question or is less worthy of belief."[106] Bill C-49 defines "consent" in sexual assault cases as "the voluntary agreement of the complainant to engage in the sexual activity in question" (s. 243.1[1]). Consent is not obtained when the complainant is incapable of consenting because of intoxication or when the complainant expresses, by word or conduct, a lack of agree-

ment to engage in the activity. The law also stipulated the defences available to men accused of sexual assault. Specifically, he must show he took "reasonable steps" in the context to establish the woman was consenting.[107]

Another debate ensued following the Supreme Court's ruling in the *O'Connor*[108] case in 1995, when it ruled that confidential records, as well as personal diaries, letters, and other documents, could be accessed for cases before the courts. Critics were concerned because of the highly personal nature of these documents and the fact that the files are often used for therapeutic reasons and are not kept with the explicit purpose of recording allegations. In response to the concerns raised by critics, Parliament passed Bill C-46 in 1997, which limited the access of defendants to confidential records of complainants in sexual assault cases.[109]

The recent history of our laws relating to sexual assault point out the tensions that exist between the courts and Parliament, and between the responsibility of the law to guarantee the accused a fair trial while at the same time protecting the privacy of the complainant. But as these examples illustrate, law reform has limits. Unfortunately, prejudices die hard.

Community Response

Women's advocates have taken an interest not only in legislative reform but also in the community's response to the victims of sexual assault. A number of groups have come into existence over the decades to help women in abusive relationships and those who experience sexual assault. Too numerous to count, crisis centres exist in communities large and small across the country, offering assistance—emotional and financial in the form of living arrangements for victims of domestic and sexual assault. The Canadian Association of Sexual Assault Centres offers support to victims and works to educate the public. One program in Nova Scotia is the SANE (Sexual Assault Nurse Examiner) program, which provides timely, sensitive care to sexual assault victims in the critical hours following an assault, offering emotional support and physical assessment to victims.[110] A variety of groups handle crises, monitor agencies (hospitals, police, courts) that come in contact with victims, educate the public about the problems of victims, and even provide lessons in self-defence.

The number of these centres and their activities has increased dramatically over the decades. The mass media reports on their successes. Federal, provincial, and municipal support for such services has increased. As the centres have become more professional, they have formed boards of directors, prepared detailed budgets to comply with the requirements of funding agencies, have hired social workers and mental health personnel, and have developed their political action component. But even with increased support, the demand for the services of sexual assault crisis centres far outweighs the available resources.

ROBBERY

Portland (April 26, 1999)—Ethan is shrieking. It would be funny, but he is bleeding from the scrotum, and that's just not funny. In the adrenaline rush, he has shoved his dad's gun into his waistband and accidentally shot himself. His best friend Tom has stopped the car, a Chevy Suburban they paid someone [US]$80 to steal for what was supposed to be their big finale. The Oregon teens had planned a major heist, Ethan would later say, maybe half a million that they would tote in athletic bags from the money room at a Nordstrom department store. But that plan didn't work out; in fact, the whole night had gone right to hell. (Why didn't they stick to knocking over Burger Kings?) Tom had worked as a clerk at Nordstrom and—duh— someone recognized him when he and Ethan ambled in. So they walked out without taking a thing. They should have gone home, but after weeks of planning, they were primed. They settled on Rustica, a neighborhood Italian place with a nice sourdough. The petrified manager handed over $500, and it was in the heady aftermath that not far away Ethan shot himself.[111]

Typical robbers? No. Thomas Curtis and Ethan Thrower were two high school superstars who had their fun completing a string of armed robberies.

Robbery is the threatened or actual use of force or of a weapon to take or attempt to take property from a victim. It is considered a violent offence, and therefore different from theft, because of the force or threat to use force, and the resultant fear invoked in the victim. In 2006 robbery made up 10 percent of all violent crimes in Canada. The number of robberies committed in 2006 was over

20 percent lower than when it reached its peak in 1991.[112]

Canadian robbers differ from their American counterparts in the use of weapons. Over half (58 percent) of robberies in Canada were committed without a weapon, while in the United States offenders display weapons, mostly guns and knives, in about 50 percent of all robberies. Robbery is more likely to occur at the hands of a stranger than a family member or acquaintance, because of the tendency for this crime to occur in public. About 8 percent of robberies occur in private residences, whereas over 46 percent occur in public places such as parking lots (6 percent), streets, roads, or highways (32 percent), open areas (4 percent), and on public transportation (4 percent). Commercial areas, which include bars, office buildings, hallways, nightclubs, and restaurants, account for about 41 percent of robberies.[113]

Characteristics of Robbers

Criminologists have classified the characteristics of robbers as well as the characteristics of robberies. John Conklin detected four types of robbers:

- The *professional robber* carefully plans and executes a robbery, often with many accomplices; steals large sums of money; and has a long-term, deep commitment to robbery as a means of supporting a hedonistic lifestyle.

- The *opportunistic robber* (the most common) has no long-term commitment to robbery; targets victims for small amounts of money ($20 or less); victimizes elderly women, drunks, cab drivers, and other people who seem to be in no position to resist; and is young and generally inexperienced.

- The *addict robber* is addicted to drugs, has a low level of commitment to robbery but a high level of commitment to theft, plans less than professional robbers but more than opportunistic robbers, wants just enough money for a fix, and may or may not carry a weapon.

- The *alcoholic robber* has no commitment to robbery as a way of life, has no commitment to theft, does not plan his or her robberies, usually robs people after first assaulting them, takes few precautions, and is apprehended more often than other robbers.[114]

According to the Uniform Crime Reports, 89 percent of those arrested for robbery are males and about three out of eight people charged with robbery are under the age of 18.[115]

The Consequences of Robbery

Robbery is a property crime as well as a violent crime. It is the combination of the motive for economic gain and the violent nature of robbery that makes it so serious.[116] While robbery results in millions of dollars of financial loss each year, loss of money is not its only consequence. The psychological and physical trauma caused by robbery, not to mention the fear and anxiety felt by victims and society at large, know no boundaries.

EMERGING PROBLEMS

Some of the more pressing issues we face today include global terrorism, hate crimes, and deadly shootings in schools. In recent years, largely as a result of media attention, these crimes have had a dramatic impact on the public's perception that violence has reached epidemic proportions. In reality, these crimes account for an extremely low proportion of all violent crimes, and rates for two of them (terrorism and violence in schools) have even gone down.

New York City firefighters carry their fatally injured department chaplain from the wreckage of the World Trade Center on September 11, 2001. Chaplain Mychal Judge was crushed to death while giving a man his last rites.

Terrorism

Terrorism is a resort to violence or a threat of violence on the part of a group seeking to accomplish a purpose against the opposition of constituted authority. Terrorism is a complex phenomenon and often overlaps with interpersonal crimes of violence. It is, after all, individuals who carry out the goals of the terrorist groups. For example, in the 1960s the FLQ (Front de Libération du Québec) in Quebec robbed banks to finance its revolutionary activity. Is this an example of terrorism?[117] Terrorism has existed throughout history; depending on who is victorious, history can make heroes out of terrorists. During World War II, Europeans who resisted the Germans were considered terrorists; today they are considered heroes.[118]

Although there are similarities between terrorism of the past and that which occurs today, a major difference is the important role played by the media in terrorist activities today. Crucial to the terrorists' scheme is the exploitation of the media to attract attention to the cause. Many clandestine organizations around the world have sought to draw attention to their causes—the Irish Republican Army (IRA), committed to the cause of uniting the British counties of Northern Ireland with the Republic of Ireland; Islamic fundamentalists committed to the protection of Islam in its purist form against any Western influence; various Palestinian factions opposed to Israeli occupation or to any Mideast peace settlement; radical groups all over the world seeking an end to capitalism or colonialism or the imposition of one or another form of totalitarian rule. Certainly, the image of the World Trade Center towers crumbling after being hit by hijacked airplanes remains vivid in the minds of people around the world.

From the outset, the member states of the United Nations have been concerned about international terrorism because it endangers or takes innocent lives and jeopardizes fundamental freedoms, such as the freedom to travel and to congregate for public events. The UN effort to control international terrorism concentrates on removal of the underlying grievances that provoke people to sacrifice human lives, including their own, in an attempt to effect radical changes.[119] This approach to the control of terrorism is not concerned with the individual motivations of terrorists. Some of them may be highly motivated idealists; others are recruited for substantial rewards. The control effort is directed, rather, at the conditions that give rise to terrorism and at the removal of such conditions.

To the extent that some grievances have been reduced by political action, such as the granting of independence to colonies and the political accord reached in Northern Ireland in November 1999, terrorism has declined. But other problems remain, especially in the Balkans, India, Central America, Africa, and the West Bank and Gaza Strip occupied by Israel. Crimes of a terrorist nature occur virtually every day and are likely to continue wherever the underlying problems are not resolved. Terrorist activities include but are not restricted to assassinations, hostage taking, and interference with or destruction of ships, aircraft, or means of land transport. When funding by clandestine supporters is not forthcoming, terrorists have carried out robberies to finance their operations.

Osama bin Laden, the reputed mastermind of the September 11, 2001, attacks on the United States, is referred to as the "new model terrorist" and the "chief executive officer" of a network of terrorist groups. He is considered one of the most significant sponsors of Islamic extremist activities in the world today. In fact, bin Laden's so-called terrorist network is considered the most prominent threat to North American security in spite of the recent killing and capture of key Al Qaeda leaders and operatives. As of 2008, bin Laden remains a fugitive. His name is on the FBI's "Ten Most Wanted Fugitives" list, and the United States government has offered a US$25 million reward for his capture.[120]

The Extent of Terrorism In one year alone (1985) terrorists were responsible for four letter bombs, five barricade-hostage incidents, nine hijackings, 17 specific threats, 54 kidnappings, 70 attempted attacks, 84 armed assaults, and 165 bombings and arsons.

Of these crimes, 12 were committed in Belgium, 14 in Chile, 29 in Colombia, 12 in Cyprus, 35 in West Germany, 12 in France, 29 in Greece, 17 in Italy, 47 in Lebanon, 10 in Peru, 18 in Portugal, 15 in Spain, 10 in the United Kingdom, and 148 in other countries that experienced fewer than 10 incidents each. Regionally, Western Europe was hardest hit (182), followed by the Middle East (70) and South America (62). The remaining incidents were spread all over the other regions, with Asia and the Far East suffering the fewest incidents. Of the targets, 151 were political, 80 were diplomatic, 79 were economic, and the remainder were seemingly random public places, specific persons, and various facilities.[121] It is noteworthy that 31 of the 408 terrorist acts were committed on behalf of governments.

Among the most active terrorist groups were the Islamic Jihad (35 acts), the Fatah Revolutionary Council (24), the West German Red Army Faction (19), the Portuguese Popular Forces of 25 April (15), and the Chilean Manuel Rodriguez Popular Front (14). In the course of these acts of terrorism, 265 persons were killed, among them 46 Americans, 16 French, 15 British, 11 Germans, 11 Italians, 10 Israelis, and 9 staff members of international organizations. The terrorists suffered fewer deaths.

The incidence of terrorism may seem slight in the light of overall national crime statistics. But the worldwide destructive impact of such acts is considerable. So, too, are the costs of increased security to combat terrorism. The American airline industry alone spends US$500 million a year for security.[122] After the 1983 bombing of the U.S. embassy complex in Beirut, Lebanon, with the loss of the lives of 241 marines and sailors, the strengthening of U.S. embassy security all over the world cost well over US$3 billion. Canadians face increased hassles and restrictions in travelling to the United States, with these problems and

In 2000 Ajaib Singh Bagri and Ripudaman Singh Malik were charged with killing 331 people in two separate bombings on the same day in June 1985. One bomb killed 329 people on board Air India Flight 182, most of them Canadians. The other bomb killed two baggage handlers at Tokyo's Narita Airport. Bagri and Malik were both acquitted of the charges in 2005.

delays at border crossings costing us more than $8 billion a year.[123]

International Efforts to Control Terrorism

Many years ago, the world community agreed on several international conventions to combat terrorism.[124] These conventions, which provide for widespread international cooperation in the prevention of airplane hijacking and the pursuit and extradition (surrender to a requesting country) of offenders, produced a dramatic drop in the number of such incidents.

By 1989, several governments that had been supporting "freedom fighters" (elsewhere called "terrorist groups") had grown disenchanted with the groups' exercise of arbitrary violence against uninvolved civilian targets, such as airplane passengers, and had ceased to support such groups. In addition, the end of the cold war and breakup of the Soviet bloc have deprived many of these groups of funding; consequently, they are on the decline. Rising in their stead is a new type of terrorist group, more difficult to monitor, and perhaps even more dangerous. The old-style politically motivated mayhem has been replaced with ethnically and religiously inspired violence.

As a result of terrorist activities and specifically the events of September 11, 2001, Canadian Parliament passed Bill C-36 and Bill C-42. Bill C-36 gives police broad new powers of arrest without warrant, enables the government to place a ban on the release of information related to terrorist investigations, increases the period for which a person can be detained, and, as an omnibus bill, includes acts to amend the Criminal Code, the Official Secrets Act, the Canadian Evidence Act, and other acts. Although Canada has relatively few internal problems with terrorism, the government responded to American and international concerns that our close proximity to the United States might implicate Canada in future terrorist acts should precautions not be taken. Bill C-42 gives the federal government the power to designate an area as vital to national security.[125] In practical terms, this means the military can force everyone to leave the area and can then seal it off. The Anti-Terrorism Act dictates that individuals can be forced to testify in investigative hearings and that such hearings must be public.[126] The United States also instituted anti-terrorism legislation in the form of the Patriot Act, which gives domestic law enforcement and international

A Ku Klux Klan rally.

intelligence agencies increased powers to fight terrorism. Civil libertarians have expressed concern over the potential of such legislation to jeopardize civil rights.

Hate Crimes

In June 1998, James Byrd, an African American, was dragged to his death in Jasper, Texas. Byrd was hitchhiking on a Saturday night when John William King and two friends chained him to their truck and pulled him, alive, for over three kilometres. His head was finally severed from his body. King, who was sentenced to death in March 1999, and his two friends were Ku Klux Klan (KKK) members.

An equally barbaric hate crime occurred in October 1998. Russell Henderson and Aaron McKinney posed as homosexuals and lured gay college student Matthew Shepard out of a bar in Wyoming. They robbed, pistol-whipped, and burned him with cigarettes before leaving him tied to a fence in near-freezing temperatures. Shepard died five days later in a hospital. The murder trial of Henderson and McKinney incited further displays of hate, with anti-gay demonstrators shouting and waving signs that read "God Hates Fags."[127]

Although the American examples presented here are extremely violent, **hate crimes** can and do occur in Canada, despite our official policy of multiculturalism, and despite our claims to value tolerance and diversity. In fact, in a recent national victimization survey, one out of 11 visible-minority citizens expressed concern about becoming a victim of hate crime.[128] Hate-motivated offences are those that not only harm the immediate victim, but may affect an entire community because they target what the immediate victim—and the group itself—represent. Hate crimes are motivated by hate, not vulnerability, and are carried out due to the hatred of a person's sex, ethnicity, race, religion, sexual orientation, age, disability, or language.

According to the General Social Survey (GSS), in 2004, victims believed hate motivation was the reason for the crime in 4 percent of all incidents. Among hate-motivated crimes, 65 percent were related to the victim's race or ethnicity, 26 percent were because of the victim's sex, 14 percent were because of religion, and 12 percent were related to sexual orientation of the victim.[129] Overall, 8 percent of violent offences were believed to be motivated by hate, compared to 2 percent of household offences.[130]

Twelve major police forces across Canada participated in a pilot survey of hate crime in 2001 and 2002, the goal of which was to determine the viability of including hate crimes in the Uniform Crime Reports.[131] These police forces recorded a total of 928 hate crime incidents during the years of the survey. Of this total, 57 percent were motivated by race and ethnicity; the groups that reported the most incidents were blacks and South Asians. One out of ten hate crimes recorded by the police were related to sexual orientation; police report that these victims are more likely to suffer a violent victimization, such as an assault, than are other victimized groups.[132]

In terms of types of hate crime, police reports indicate that 29 percent of offences fell into the categories of mischief and vandalism,

25 percent were assaults, 20 percent involved the uttering of threats, and 13 percent involved hate propaganda.[133]

While hate crimes are committed by individuals, sometimes these individuals belong to groups that promote hatred and encourage such acts. The estimated number of organized hate groups in Canada is about 40. According to the Southern Poverty Law Center, the number of hate groups in the United States increased from 474 in 1997 to 762 in 2004.[134] It also appears that groups are recruiting more violent members to carry out their messages of hate. One of the most recent tools used to attract potential members is the Internet. As of 2000, the Media Awareness Network and Hatewatch.org reported the existence of 500 hardcore hate sites on the Internet.

Although hate crimes make up only a small percentage of overall criminality, the viciousness of the acts and their impact on broad population groups give them prominence in the media and pose extraordinary challenges to the criminal justice system. Police departments have formed bias-crime units to further the investigation of these crimes.

Violence in Schools

In the nineteenth century, school violence was seen in the form of teachers' inflicting abuse on students, primarily by slapping a student's hand with a ruler. Parents and members of the community looked upon this "violence" as a way to remind students that they must respect authority. Time

In the police pilot survey of hate crimes in Canada, hate crimes motivated by religion made up the second largest category of offences; in this case, anti-Semitism comprised most offences, followed by attacks against Muslims. Jewish people and institutions were the largest single group identified in hate-motivated crimes, accounting for 25 percent of the 928 recorded incidents.

Shocked Erfurt, Germany, residents on April 26, 2002, have just learned of a high school shooting in which 18 died.

An Epidemic of Hate Crimes?

The media, academics, advocacy groups, and politicians have created what has been described as a hate-crime epidemic. But is the problem really as great as we have been led to believe? One estimate is that 60 000 hate crimes are committed each year in Canada.(1) GSS victimization survey respondents reported a total of 250 000 hate-related criminal offences in 2004 (4 percent of total criminal offences reported). Following the September 11 attacks on the United States, Statistics Canada reported a 350 percent increase in hate crimes in Canada, most of which were committed against Muslims (this number declined significantly a few weeks later).(2). Consider that the media can shape public opinion and reinforce the idea that there is an epidemic through the use of these types of headlines:

- "A Cancer of Hatred Afflicts America"(3)
- "Rise in Hate Crimes Signals Alarming Resurgence of Bigotry"(4)

Books and articles are often inflammatory, argue James Jacobs and Jessica Henry.(5) The authors suggest that some scholars simply assume a grave problem exists, in spite of an overwhelming lack of evidence. This can be a dangerous assumption, for the idea of hate crime divides the community and becomes a self-fulfilling prophecy. "Crime sells—so does racism, sexism, and homophobia. Garden-variety crime has become mundane."(5)

Advocacy groups representing blacks, Jews, gays and lesbians, women, and the disabled have embraced the idea of a hate-crime epidemic, much of which is based on dubious statistics. For example, results of a pilot survey conducted by the Canadian Centre for Justice Statistics in collaboration with 12 major police forces across the country (representing 43 percent of the total volume of crime in Canada) indicate there were 928 reported criminal hate offences between 2001 and 2002. Is this an epidemic?

North American history shows attacks on racial and ethnic groups started from the moment European settlers arrived and made Aboriginal peoples a target. Historically, blacks, Jews, Catholics, and recent immigrants have also been targeted. The 1990s brought a greater intolerance for this behaviour, but, Jacobs and Henry say, there still is no epidemic.

Yet it matters little whether the spate of hate crimes is real or merely perceived; significant developments have taken place in consequence. Throughout the 1980s, media reports of increasing numbers of hate-motivated crimes (also known as "bias crimes") pressured the government to amend the Criminal Code to reflect the growing concern with this type of crime. In 1996, sentencing provisions were amended so that if a judge determined hatred was a motivation in an attack that hatred would be considered an aggravating factor and would result in a more severe sentence. In 2004, a new hate crime bill passed the Senate, giving hate speech based on sexual orientation the same illegal status as that based on colour, race, religion, and ethnic origin.

Many bias crimes fall into the categories of simple assaults, vandalism, and harassment. Because these are relatively less serious crimes, they ordinarily get little attention. They can, however, have a major impact on the community by increasing the level of fear and hostility between groups. So extra attention to them is warranted.

Statistical analyses are important to understanding the pervasiveness of these behaviours and the seriousness of the issue of hate crime. But behind the numbers are stories about the lives of real people. Whether it is the case of a teen distributing hate literature at a high school, sidewalks spray-painted with swastikas, the firebombing of Jewish institutions, the beating and murder of an elderly Pakistani man, or the murder of Sikh cleric Nirmal Singh Gill, the stories and experiences are disturbing, and the actions behind these victimizations are intolerable in a country that values diversity.

Sources

1. Julian V. Roberts, "Disproportionate Harm: Hate Crime in Canada," Department of Justice, Canada, Working Document 1995-11e, 1995.
2. Maire Gannon and Karen Mihorean, "Criminal Victimization in Canada, 2004," Statistics Canada, Catalogue no. 85-002-XPE, Vol. 25, no. 7, Minister of Industry, 2005.
3. Spencer Rumsey, "A Cancer of Hatred Afflicts America," *Newsday,* May 27, 1993, p. 129.
4. Benjamin J. Hubbard, "Commentary on Tolerance," *Los Angeles Times,* Apr. 4, 1993, p. B9.
5. James B. Jacobs and Jessica S. Henry, "The Social Construction of a Hate Crime Epidemic," *Journal of Criminal Law and Criminology,* **86** (1996): 366–391.

Questions for Discussion

1. Bill C-250 made propaganda directing hatred against people of any sexual orientation illegal in Canada. This includes hate speech. However, a "notwithstanding clause" permits hate speech if it is religiously motivated. Do you agree with this exemption?
2. Victimization data suggest that the majority of hate crimes take the form of intimidation/harassment, vandalism, and assault. Do you think these crimes are serious enough to warrant the extra attention they receive?

The Taber, Alberta, school that was the scene of a fatal shooting in 1999.

has brought a new look to school violence. Students increasingly are viewed not as the victims but rather as the agents of violence. In response to increasing attacks on safety, schools with high levels of violence developed security plans.[135] In recent years media accounts of school shootings have caused a widespread panic, and many people have lost faith in the ability of the educational system to keep children safe.

Consider the following incidents:

- May 28, 1975, at Brampton, Ontario's Centennial Secondary School, 16-year old Michael Slobodian kills one teacher, fatally wounds a fellow student, and injures 13 others before killing himself. He was the first recorded high school killer in Canada.

- Five months later, Robert Poulin, 18, kills one student and injures four others at an Ottawa high school before killing himself.

- April 28, 1999, a 17-year-old student is shot dead and another is wounded at W. R. Myers High School in Taber, Alberta, by a 14-year-old boy.

- Dwayne Williams, 20, is shot in the back and leg at a community talent show at Scarborough's Lester B. Pearson Collegiate on February 5, 2000.

- Kimveer Gill opens fire at Dawson College in Montreal, killing one student and injuring 20 before killing himself on September 13, 2006.

- May 23, 2007, 14-year-old Jordan Manners is shot and killed at C. W. Jeffreys secondary school in Toronto

The media has made much of the fact that schools have been turned into killing fields, but what is the reality? What do experts tell us? A National School Safety Center research report shows that the probability of being killed by lightning is twice as high as that of being killed at school.[136] Yet that is little consolation to the victims of school massacres and their families.

The public looks for scapegoats. Who did what wrong? And what happened to the days when throwing a spitball or an eraser got a student in big trouble? The answer must come from specialists in criminology. All too often, policy and legislation in matters of crime and criminal justice are the result of publicity given to emotion-charged media reports rather than of research data from scientific studies. Experts need to look into the causes of school violence. What do the events have in common? Some say that students are growing up with violence. One survey of inner-city children in the United States showed that 43 percent of 7- to 19-year-olds have witnessed a homicide.[137]

What can be done specifically, not only in the aftermath of such events, but also in terms of preventive measures? The shootings we've described are relatively rare examples of extreme violence occurring in school settings. Most violence that occurs in schools is more frequent and much less severe. Bullying is a problem in our schools today. Its frequency and pervasiveness are major concerns because of the physical and emotional harm bullying causes victims and because it has been implicated in the escalation of stress, pain, and alienation, which has led to some of the school shootings. Following most, if not all, cases of school and college shootings, investigations reveal individual profiles characterized by ostracism, alienation, and a desire to strike out at others.

It follows, then, that perhaps our best defence against these kinds of incidents is to focus on the "little" problems of bullying before they escalate into larger and more extreme issues of violence. A recent Canadian survey found that 20 percent of children in kindergarten to grade 8 were bullied more than once or twice over a school term; 8 percent were bullied at least once a week. Twenty-seven percent of students from minority groups in this age group report being bullied because of their ethnicity.[138] The survey revealed that 42 percent of boys and 23 percent of girls in grades 6 to 9 report bullying others in the past two months; for students in grades 9 to 12, the numbers are 41 percent for boys and 21 percent for girls.[139]

Another survey conducted on a representative sample of 3200 Toronto youth in grades 7 to 9

Gun Control

In 2001 Gary Mauser's report for the Fraser Institute argued there is no definitive evidence linking Canadian gun laws to either crime rates or suicide rates. Canada has had gun-control legislation since 1934, when it was required that handguns be registered. The early 1940s witnessed the creation of a gun registry for long guns. Since 1977, police have scrutinized all firearm purchasers, and beginning in the same year, a variety of weapons were prohibited. In 1991, as a result of calls for change following the Montreal Massacre, large-capacity magazines and many semi-automatic rifles were prohibited or restricted. Then, in 1995, the Firearms Act was passed, requiring all firearm owners to be licensed and their firearms to be registered.

The latest changes to Canada's firearm legislation have caused a good deal of controversy and debate, not unlike the debates in the United States. Canadians are divided on the necessity of gun registration considering our already restrictive gun-control laws and policies. In 2001 a majority of Canadians favoured stricter laws, but by 2002 the majority were in favour of scrapping the gun registry. In 2004, the gun registry was modified to focus more on the criminal use of guns. At this time, registry offences were decriminalized.

Yet, gun-control legislation aside, cultural differences between Canada and the United States might be an influential factor in helping to explain differences in firearm-related violence in the two countries. Canadians do use guns for self-defence: Mauser estimates that Canadians use guns to protect themselves between 60 000 and 80 000 times a year; 19 000 to 37 500 of these are for defence against human threats. Armed Americans used their guns against potential offenders 2.5 million times a year, killing 1500 to 2800 of these potential criminals each year (more than the estimated 250 to 1000 killed annually by police officers). Is this evidence of a violent culture? Some would say yes.

Researchers point out that in 2002, 66.7 percent of the homicides committed in the United States involved the use of a gun. Significantly, the proportion of U.S. homicides committed *without* a firearm in is greater than the *overall* homicide rates of all but one other Western nation (Finland). The suggestion is that guns, culture, and a variety of factors likely interact in complex ways to contribute to the high rate of criminal violence in the United States, whether committed with or without guns.

Sources

James C. Hackler, *Canadian Criminology: Strategies and Perspectives*, 4th ed. (Toronto: Pearson Prentice-Hall, 2007), p. 249; Gary Mauser, "Canadians Do Use Firearms in Self-Protection," *Canadian Journal of Criminology* (October 1996): 485–488; James Fyfe, "Police Use of Deadly Force: Research and Reform," *Justice Quarterly*, 5 (1988): 157–176.

Question for Discussion

1. Can gun-control laws effectively reduce gun-related criminal activity? Would stricter gun control in the United States significantly reduce gun-related violence in that country? Has it impacted on gun-related violence in Canada?

found that 40 percent reported having been victimized in the previous year: 28 percent were victims of theft, 21 percent of bullying at school, over 5 percent received threats of extortion, and 3 percent reported being hit so violently that medical attention was required. Furthermore, two-thirds of all students who were bullied were victims more than once. About 16 percent of the youth reported being bullied on more than 12 occasions in the previous year.[140]

If we consider school-related violence and victimization as falling on a continuum from less severe forms of assault and harassment (like bullying) to those that are more severe, and if perpetual victimization contributes to the escalation of stress, frustration, and alienation that is often linked to serious acts of school-related violence, targeting bullying and reducing or preventing this kind of behaviour will likely have a significant impact on more serious types of violence. Certainly it will contribute to the welfare, safety, and school experiences of our youth.

Of course, another tactic to take in dealing with violent school incidents is to increase security measures. While Canadian schools have moved in this direction to some extent (e.g., school lockdown drills are becoming commonplace), we have not embraced this strategy to the extent that many American school jurisdictions have. Nonetheless, such "high-tech" solutions may be in our future.

VIOLENCE AND GUN CONTROL

The tragedies of the recent school shootings have fuelled the gun-control debate, but this is not the first time episodes of gun violence have led to calls for stricter gun laws. The Montreal Massacre of 1989, where gunman Marc Lépine shot and killed 14 women engineering students, resulted in a tightening of gun laws in Canada. The tragedy also contributed to the gun-control debate, which resulted in the 1995 Firearms Act. While debates about gun laws are often heavily influenced by ideology, comparisons between Canada and the United States are worth considering because of the two countries' different stances on gun control, and the resulting differences in behaviours of citizens.

Some researchers suggest Canada has a less violent culture, independent of the greater restrictions on firearms and use of handguns in particular.[141] On the other hand, violence in the United States is frequently attributed to historical conditioning (the need of frontier people to survive in a hostile environment), social factors (poverty, inequities, and other inner-city problems), and the laxity of the criminal justice system (failure to apprehend and convict enough criminals and to imprison long enough those who are convicted). Although firearm availability is not in itself a cause of violence, it can be an important contributing factor. As a result, some researchers have focused on one common element in the relatively larger proportion of violent crime that occurs in the United States compared to Canada—the availability of firearms.

The Extent of Firearm-Related Offences

In 2006, shooting was the second most common method used to commit homicide in Canada (stabbing was the most common): 31 percent of all homicides involved a firearm (35 percent were stabbings). There were 190 victims killed by a firearm in Canada, 33 fewer than the previous year. Handguns accounted for over half (57 percent) of all firearm-related homicides. Rifles/shotguns and sawed-off rifles/shotguns accounted for 19 percent and 13 percent of firearm-related deaths respectively.[142] As Figure 10.5 illustrates, firearm-related homicides have been generally declining over the past several decades.

In comparison, firearm-related crime is still more prevalent in the United States than in Canada and other developed Western nations. According to the Task Force on Firearms of the National Commission on the Causes and Prevention of Violence, the rate of homicide by gun is 40 times higher in the United States than in England and Wales, and the rate of robbery by gun in the United States is 60 times higher. Current estimates indicate there

FIGURE 10.5   Rate of firearm homicides in Canada, 1975–2006.

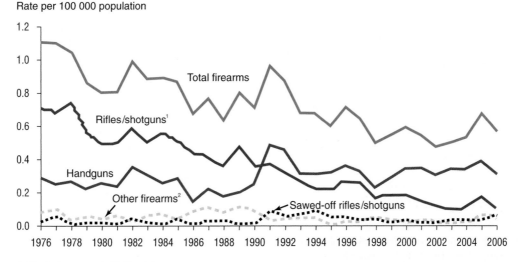

Rate per 100 000 population

1. Excludes sawed-off rifles/shotguns.
2. Includes firearm-like weapons (e.g., nail gun, pellet gun) and unknown type of firearm.

Source: Homicide in Canada, 2006, Statistics Canada, Catalogue no. 85-002-XIE, Vol. 27, no. 8, page 4.

are over 200 million firearms in circulation in the United States, including about 70 million handguns.[143] However, according to estimates based on the 2004 Uniform Crime Reports, the total firearm-crime rate decreased from 225.5 per 100 000 in 1993 to 115.5 per 100 000 in 2004.[144]

REVIEW

1. What is the extent and nature of homicide?

First-degree murder (p. 238), **second-degree murder** (p. 238), and **manslaughter** (p. 238) all share the common element of violence, though they differ in many ways: in the harm they cause, the intention of the perpetrator, the punishment they warrant, and other legal criteria. Social scientists have been exploring the frequency with which homicides (and other types of violent crimes) are committed in our society and elsewhere, their distribution through time and place, and the role played by circumstances, including the environment and behaviour patterns, in facilitating or preventing them.

Such categories as **mass murder** (p. 242), **serial murder** (p. 242), and gang murder are shorthand designations for frequently occurring crime patterns that have not been specifically identified in the Criminal Code.

2. What is the nature and extent of assault?

Assault (p. 245) is similar in nature, though not as extreme, as homicide. Both are typically committed by young males, and a disproportionate number of arrestees are members of minority groups. Assault victims and sexual assault victims often know their attackers. Assault rates, like those of homicide, are highest in urban areas, during the summer months, in the evening hours, and in the West.

3. What types of crimes occur in families?

Another pattern of crime that also is not defined as such in the Criminal Code has become so important that it may be considered in conjunction with the other crimes of violence: family-related crime. This pattern encompasses a variety of violent crimes that include the abuse of spouses, children, and the elderly.

4. What are robbers like?

Robbery (p. 257) is the threatened or actual use of force or of a weapon to take or attempt to take property from a victim. It is considered a violent offence, and therefore different from theft, because of the force or threat to use force, and the resultant fear invoked in the victim. Canadian robbers use weapons less frequently than do their American counterparts. Robbers fall into several categories, including professional, opportunistic, addict, and alcoholic.

5. What are some current examples of criminal behaviours we are concerned about?

Some of the more pressing problems we face today are global **terrorism** (p. 258), **hate crimes** (p. 260), and school violence. The media attention given to these crimes has had a dramatic effect on the public's perception that violence has reached epidemic proportions.

6. To what extent do Canadians use guns to commit crimes?

Firearm-related crime is more prevalent in the United States than in Canada and other developed Western nations. The gun-control controversy demonstrates that both the definitions of crimes and the social and environmental characteristics associated with them must be studied in order to develop control and prevention strategies.

CRIMINOLOGY & PUBLIC POLICY

Just how far is too far? Consider the next chapter of possible privacy invasion that we may be subjected to. We may not be far behind the move in the United States toward a system called "Total Information Awareness" that would give the government access to an ultra-large-scale database of personal information from all communications (phone calls, e-mails, and Web searches), to financial records, medical records, and travel history. This type of surveillance could potentially play a valuable role in the detection and prevention of criminal events. In effect, such a system would take our current "sex offender registry" several steps further, monitoring the activities of everyone—criminal or not—in society. (*Source:* http://www.darpa.MIL/iao/)

Questions for Discussion Should we be concerned that a program like Total Information Awareness is a "Big Brother" program that may spy on innocent civilians? Without very specific limitations on its use, what is to prevent such a program from expanding to gather information on targeted criminal organizations, political groups, and suspected insurgents? What about the rights of innocent citizens? Is this type of surveillance a fair trade-off: invasion of privacy in exchange for increased public safety?

YOU BE THE CRIMINOLOGIST

You are the superintendent of schools for your district. Your schools have not experienced any violent incidents, but because of the media hype surrounding school shootings in recent years, you are under pressure to take preventive measures. What actions would you take and what programs would you develop to make your schools safe and gun-proof? How would you implement these preventive measures? What are their advantages and disadvantages? How would you target your audience? What are the likely positive and negative reactions to the preventive measures?

Visit the Online Learning Centre: www.mcgrawhill.ca/olc/adler

CRIMES AGAINST PROPERTY

CHAPTER **11**

CHAPTER QUESTIONS

1. What are some different types of theft and how does theft differ from larceny?

2. What forms does fraud take?

3. What makes a crime "high-tech"?

4. How is break-and-enter different from theft?

5. What is a fence?

6. What do we know about arsonists?

7. How do the rates of property crime in different parts of the world compare?

Whyte Avenue in Edmonton, Alberta, has been the scene of riots during celebrations such as Canada Day and the Stanley Cup play-offs. This young man taunts members of a police line-up trying to maintain order on the avenue known for its night life and party atmosphere.

The classic motion picture *The Gods Must Be Crazy* introduces us to a society of happy indigenous people on the Kalahari Desert, remote from the hustle and bustle of modern life. Such tools as they have are shared and can easily be replaced from an abundance of sticks and stones.

High up, a "noisy bird" passes over the camp of these happy people. The pilot of the noisy bird casually throws an empty Coke bottle out of the cockpit. It lands in the middle of the camp. The people stare at this foreign object. They handle it delicately and then discover what a useful object it is: It holds water; it can be used for rolling dough, for hammering, for many things. Everybody needs it and wants it. Fights ensue over who can have it. The peace and tranquillity of this little society are shattered. These people have discovered the concept of property, and they are experiencing all the troubles that go with the possession of property, including property crime.

The film has a happy ending. The indigenous people finally get rid of the bottle, and life returns to normal.

We have explored some of the patterns of social interaction and the routine activities of daily life that set the stage for offenders to commit violent crimes and for other people—family members, acquaintances, strangers, airplane passengers—to become victims. We know that if we are to develop effective policies to prevent and control violent crime, we must have a thorough understanding of the characteristics of specific offences; we need to know where, when, and how they are committed, and which individuals are most likely to commit them. The same is true for property offences. To develop crime-prevention strategies, we need to study the characteristics that differentiate the various types of offences that deprive people of their property.

Do such offences as pickpocketing, shoplifting, cheque forgery, theft by use of stolen credit cards, car theft, computer crimes, and burglary have different payoffs and risks? What kinds of resources are needed (weapons, places to sell stolen property)? Are any specific skills needed to carry out these offences? The opportunities to commit property crime are all but unlimited. Studies demonstrate that if these opportunities are reduced, the incidence of crime is reduced as well.

The traditional property crimes are theft, or stealing; obtaining property by fraud of various sorts, including false pretences, confidence games, forgery, and unauthorized use of credit cards; break-and-enter, which does not necessarily involve theft; and arson, which not only deprives the owner of property but also endangers lives. New crime types, such as software piracy, online frauds, and computer viruses, are associated with high-technology equipment. We shall defer until Chapter 12 discussion of the crimes by which criminals deprive people of their property through organizational manipulations—individual white-collar crimes, corporate crimes, and organized crime.

269

THEFT

Theft, or stealing, which in common law was referred to as larceny, is the prototype of all property offences. It is also the most prevalent crime in our society; it includes such contemporary forms as purse-snatching, pickpocketing, shoplifting, and vehicle theft.

The Elements of Larceny

The common law definition of **larceny**, the essence of which is reflected in our Criminal Code definition of theft, contained the following elements:

- A trespassory
- Taking and
- Carrying away of
- Personal property
- Belonging to another
- With the intent to deprive the owner of the property permanently

Each of these elements has a long history that gives it its meaning. The first element is perhaps the easiest. There must be a trespass. "Trespass," a Norman-French term, has a variety of meanings. In the law of larceny, however, it simply means any absence of authority or permission for the taking. Second, the property must be taken: The perpetrator must exert authority over the property, as by putting a hand on a piece of merchandise or getting into the driver's seat of the targeted car.

Third, the property must be carried away. The slightest removal suffices to fulfill this element: moving merchandise from a counter, however slightly; loosening the brakes of a car so that it starts rolling, even a centimetre. Fourth, the property in question, at common law, has to be personal property. (Real estate is not subject to larceny.) Fifth, the property has to belong to another, in the sense that the person has the right to possess that property. Sixth, the taker must intend to deprive the rightful owner permanently of the property. This element is present when the taker (thief) intends to deprive the rightful owner of the property forever. In its modern form, however, the law no longer requires proof that the thief intended to deprive the owner "permanently" of the property.

The Extent of Theft

Larceny, except for the most petty varieties, was a capital offence in medieval England.[1] Courts interpreted all its elements quite strictly—that is, in favour of defendants—so as to limit the use of capital punishment. Only once did the courts expand the reach of larceny, when they ruled that a transporter who opens a box entrusted to him and takes out some items has committed larceny by "breaking bulk." For the other forms of deceptive acquisition of property, such as embezzling funds and obtaining property by false pretences, Parliament had to enact separate legislation.

In Canada, we refer to the crime described thus far not as larceny but as **theft.** The criminal justice system separates theft into two categories according to the value of the goods taken—theft over and under $5000. Property crimes like theft make up the majority of reported criminal incidents in Canada; the property crime rate in Canada is almost four times the violent crime rate (3588 versus 951 per 100 000 in 2006). Of the 633 254 thefts that occurred in Canada in 2006, 97 percent fell into the theft under $5000 category.[2] Estimates from the 2004 GSS victimization survey indicate that Canadians were victims of personal property theft at a rate of 93 per 1000, about double the UCR rate of reported theft.[3] Figure 11.1 shows the distribution of property crime in Canada by offence category.

In most cases of theft, offenders are likely driven by an instrumental motive: the desire for financial or material gain. Theft, therefore, is one of the crime types to which choice-based theories are applicable.

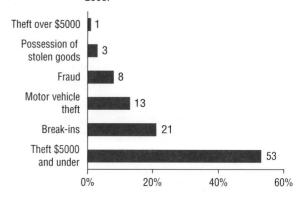

FIGURE 11.1 Distribution of property crime known to police, 2006.

Note: Because of rounding, figures may not total 100 percent.

Source: Adapted from "Crime Statistics in Canada, 2006," Statistics Canada, Catalogue no. 85-002-XIE, vol. 27, no. 5.

A thirsty individual walks past an unattended, unlocked car and notices a case of beer in the front seat. If, in routine-activities theory terms, the offender is motivated, then the lack of guardianship and the availability of the target may fulfill the requirements for a crime to occur. Yet, not every individual who finds him- or herself in this situation will take the case of beer. In fact, most people do not steal. This leads us to ask: Who are the thieves among us?

Who Are the Thieves?

Nobody knows exactly how many of the total number of thefts are committed by amateurs who lead rather conventional lives and how many are the work of professionals. According to some criminologists, the two types differ considerably.[4]

The Amateur Thief   Amateur thieves are occasional offenders who tend to be opportunists. They take advantage of a chance to steal when little risk is involved. Typically, their acts are carried out with little skill, are unplanned, and result from some pressing situation, such as the need to pay the rent or a gambling debt.[5] In other words, amateurs resolve some immediate crisis by stealing. Most occasional offenders commit few crimes; some commit only one crime. Many are youth who do not go on to commit crimes in adulthood.

Amateur thieves do not think of themselves as professional criminals, nor are they recognized as such by those who do think of themselves as professionals. The lives of amateur thieves are quite conventional: Amateurs work, go to school, have conventional friends, and find little support or approval for their criminal behaviour.[6]

The Professional Thief   Professional thieves make a career of stealing. They take pride in their profession. They are imaginative and creative in their work and accept its risks. The most common crimes committed by professional thieves are pickpocketing, shoplifting, forgery, confidence swindling, and break-and-enter (burglary). Professional thieves also are involved in art theft, auto vehicle theft, and fraud or theft by use of stolen or forged credit cards, among other crimes.

Thomas Bartholomew Moran, a professional thief who died in a Miami rescue mission in 1971, has been considered the best of American pickpockets. His career began in 1906, when, as a teenager, he started to pick women's purses. Under the careful guidance of Mary Kelly, a well-known pickpocket, he soon sharpened his skills until he could take wallets from pants, jewelled pins from clothing, and watches from vests without alerting the victims. He devoted his life to shoplifting, forgery, and other forms of theft. In 1912, he boarded the *Titanic,* with the intention of profiting handsomely from proximity to

the more than 300 first-class passengers whose collective wealth exceeded [US]$250 million. His immediate ambitions were dimmed, however, when the *Titanic* brushed an iceberg in the North Atlantic [and sank] only two hours and forty minutes later. But Moran was among the 705 passengers who managed to find space in one of the ship's twenty lifeboats, and his career in crime continued to flourish for the better part of the 59 remaining years of his life.[7]

The most influential study of professional thieves was conducted by Edwin Sutherland in 1937. Sutherland found that professional thieves share five characteristics:

1. They have well-developed technical skills for their particular mode of operation.
2. They enjoy status, accorded to them by their own subculture and by law enforcement.
3. They are bound by consensus, a sharing of values with their own peers.
4. Not only do they learn from each other, but they also protect each other.
5. They are organized, however loosely.[8]

Subsequent studies have tended to confirm Sutherland's findings.

The Female Thief

On August 9, 2001, in Sudbury, Ontario, Kimberly Rogers, a single mother who was eight months pregnant, died in her apartment. She had been confined there under house arrest during a stifling heat wave after having been convicted of welfare fraud for collecting social assistance as a full-time university student.[9]

This case is exceptional in its tragic conclusion. It is not exceptional and in fact is representative of the contextual factors that contribute to many cases of theft and fraud among women.

We saw in Chapter 10 that violence is gendered: Patterns and types of offending and victimization are related to one's gender. Similarly, patterns and types of property crimes like theft are gendered. Let us be clear: both women and men steal. However, in general, women tend to steal different things than men and for different reasons. Margaret Jackson observes that "over 80 percent of all incarcerated women in Canada are in prison for poverty-related offences."[10] Holly Johnson and Karen Rogers explain women's participation in property offences in terms of "their traditional roles as consumers and, increasingly, as low-income, semi-skilled sole-support providers for their families."[11] Reflective of the significant increase in female-headed households and the stresses associated with poverty, particularly as government cutbacks have removed important sources of support, increasing numbers of women are being charged with theft, shoplifting, cheque forgery, and welfare fraud.[12]

Official statistics indicate that women are most likely to be charged with property offences. Recent data reveal that 35 percent of all Criminal Code charges against women involved crimes against property; 28 percent were for theft or fraud. In comparison, 24 percent of all Criminal Code charges against men involved crimes against property; 16 percent were for theft or fraud.[13] As with their male counterparts, females who come in conflict with the law tend to be young, poor, undereducated, and unskilled. However, for young women the added responsibility of single parenthood intensifies their financial burden. While not all crime is rationally motivated, it seems that in the case of the female thief survival is a motivating factor that helps explain the relatively high rate of property offences as a proportion of all female crime. Relatively minor property crimes, like theft under $5000 and shoplifting, are reflective of social structural factors that make crime a viable option for some women.

Shoplifting

Shoplifting, the stealing of goods from retail merchants, is a very common crime that costs Canadian retailers about $3 billion a year, or more than $7 million a day. A recent survey revealed that every twelfth shopper is a shoplifter and that men and women are equally likely to be offenders.[14] Perhaps shoplifting is so frequent because it is a low-risk offence, with a detection rate of perhaps less than 1 percent.[15] One retail expert describes the "basic shoplifter" as an "opportunist," someone who, presented with an opportunity to steal

and get away with it, will.[16] The 2004 Canadian Retail Security Report revealed that 31 percent of retail losses were due to theft by shoplifters and organized crime, 48 percent resulted from internal or employee theft, and the remaining 21 percent were due to administrative errors.[17] In contrast, in 1995, these numbers were 50 percent, 30 percent, and 20 percent respectively, indicating a shift toward employee theft.[18]

Shoppers are extremely reluctant to report shoplifters to the store management.[19] According to one study, of those apprehended for shoplifting, approximately 45.5 percent are actually prosecuted. More than half of shoplifting events occur between the hours of 12:00 P.M. and 6:00 P.M.[20] A Sears Canada representative, in the retail business for over 15 years, confirms that young people often steal for the thrill of it, but adds that some poor people and drug abusers steal for the money, while professionals steal for a living. He adds that, in his experience there is no such thing as a typical "shop thief" (the term the industry chooses to use instead of shoplifter, the former term indicating the seriousness of the crime): "I've seen doctors do it, lawyers do it, I've even seen a nun get caught."[21]

The case of shoplifting exemplifies two theories discussed in Chapters 6 and 9. The increasing proportion of employee theft as a total of all shoplifting suggests that Sutherland's interpretation of the importance of social learning as a contributing factor both in learning the techniques to commit crime and also the rationalizations to do so may be relevant. Employees who see or hear about fellow employees stealing from the company likely also witness that nothing is done about it, and in this process piece together that not only is such behaviour "acceptable" among other employees, but it is condoned. Certainly this doesn't apply in every situation, and not all employees steal from their employer, but the processes Sutherland outlined as the route to which young people learn deviant and criminal behaviours is applicable to this crime type. Similarly, rational-choice theories, which focus on the decision-making processes a potential criminal uses prior to committing an offence, also have relevance in the case of shoplifting. For shoplifters the benefits of stealing outweigh the costs, since detection, apprehension, and prosecution for this crime type are relatively low.

Mary Owen Cameron found that professional shoplifters largely conform to Sutherland's five characteristics of professional thieves mentioned earlier, but that amateurs do not. She estimates that of all shoplifters, only 10 percent are professionals— people who derive most of their income from the sale of stolen goods.[22] A broad range of motivations may lead to shoplifting. Among amateurs, need and greed as well as opportunity may precipitate the event.[23] In contrast to this rational choice-based suggestion, other researchers point to depression and other emotional disturbances and to the use of various prescription drugs.[24]

To most people, shoplifting is a rather insignificant offence. After all, how much can be stolen? On an individual basis, usually not very much: The average theft amount for each incident was roughly $82 for a "customer" and $203 for an employee.[25] But, the incidents quickly add up. Table 11.1 lists some of the most frequently stolen items.

At the upscale Beverly Hills Saks Fifth Avenue on December 12, 2001, actress Winona Ryder is seen from a security surveillance tape released by the Los Angeles County Courts. On November 6, 2002, a jury found the two-time Oscar nominee guilty of grand theft and felony vandalism for stealing designer clothes worth about US$5000.

TABLE 11.1 Most Frequently Shoplifted Items by Store Type

Type of Retailer	Merchandise
Auto parts	Hard parts
Bookstores	Electronics, CDs, cassettes, videos
Consumer electronics/ computer stores	Portable CD players, car alarms, cordless phones
Department stores	Clothing: shirts
Discount stores	Clothing: undergarments, CDs
Drugstores/pharmacies	Cigarettes, batteries, over-the-counter remedies
Fashion merchandise stores	Sneakers
General merchandise stores	Earrings
Grocery stores/supermarkets	Over-the-counter remedies, health and beauty aids, cigarettes
Home centres/hardware stores	Assorted hand tools
Music stores	Compact discs
Shoe stores	Sneakers
Specialty stores	Bedsheets
Specialty apparel stores	Assorted clothes, shoes
Sporting goods stores	Nike shoes
Theme parks	Key chains, jewellery
Toy stores	Action figures
Video stores	Video games
Warehouse stores	Pens, movie videos

Source: Read Hayes, 1996 Retail Theft Trends Report: An Analysis of Customer Theft in Stores (Winter Park, FL: Loss Prevention Specialists, 1996). Reprinted by permission of the author.

As shoplifters decrease store profits, the price of goods goes up; stepped-up security adds even more to costs. Stores typically hire more and more security personnel, although it has been demonstrated that physical or electronic methods of securing merchandise are more cost effective than the deployment of guards.[26] It is only the amateur shoplifter who is deterred by the presence of guards or store personnel, not the professional.[27]

Given the significantly high costs of shoplifting to retailers, what can be done to reclaim what was stolen? One option used by several large department stores in Canada, including Kmart, the Bay, and Zellers, is the use of civil recovery. Civil recovery is an administrative process that enables store owners to utilize the civil law in an attempt to collect restitution from shoplifters directly, whether the shoplifters are customers or store employees. This civil action operates parallel to the criminal process, meaning that stores can both report instances of shoplifting to the police and also file separate civil complaints against the shoplifters to obtain restitution. Those apprehended for shoplifting can then either pay the civil penalty imposed upon them or appear before a civil court. For example, beginning in 1994, Zellers attempted to recover about $325 in costs from each shoplifter through civil court, including small claims court.[28] Research has shown that for amateur shoplifters (as opposed to professionals), the use of civil recovery does not have a significant impact on their initial offence, but does have an impact on preventing them from reoffending.[29]

Other ways of preventing theft include "target hardening" and situational crime prevention measures: making goods difficult to access, using dummy goods for displays while keeping the "real" goods locked in cabinets, monitoring goods with electronic systems, using closed-circuit cameras, or following Home Depot's lead in using "spider wrap," which consists of wrapping cables around the product. When the cables are cut to remove the product, an alarm sounds.

Motor Vehicle Theft

Vehicle theft varies considerably by province, as shown in Figure 11.2.[30] In 2006 about 160 000 auto thefts were reported to police.[31] In the past decade, motor vehicle theft has dropped about 20 percent, but so has the number of recovered vehicles. In 1966, for example, 5 percent of all stolen vehicles were never recovered, compared to 24 percent in 1997. This seems to suggest a more sophisticated car thief has come into existence in recent decades, specifically organized crime groups who steal vehicles for profit. The Insurance Bureau of Canada estimates that motor vehicle theft costs about $1 billion a year.[32]

One car is stolen every three minutes in Canada. This works out to about 480 car thefts a day. About four in ten vehicle thefts occur in parking lots, the most common location from which vehicles are stolen. Next are streets and single homes, including garages and driveways. In 2001, these locations all accounted for 87 percent of all motor vehicle thefts. More vehicle thefts (38 percent) occur between 6:00 A.M. and noon than any other time period, and about 42 percent of offenders are between the ages of 12 and 17.[33]

These young car thieves use stolen vehicles for racing, a show of status among peers, for joyriding, or for the "kick" of destroying them. At the other end of the spectrum are older, professional auto thieves who steal designated cars on consignment for resale in an altered condition (with identifying numbers changed) or for disposition in "chop shops," which strip the cars for the resale value of their parts.[34] Some estimate that a vehicle is worth three times its value when sold illegally for parts by professional car thieves.[35] For example, the thief who steals a Jeep Cherokee "earns" a tax-free $150 to $500 upon delivery. The ringleader of the organized crime group pays about $2500 for the Jeep to be packed in a container and shipped abroad. When the Jeep arrives at its destination, it is sold for twice its Canadian value. Reports are that in Eastern Europe it will be sold for about $100 000, which means the profit for the crooks is $97 000! If sold in North America, the profit will be less—about $40 000—but it saves the thieves the trouble of making international connections.[36] The types of vehicles stolen have changed over the years. It is interesting to note that sport utility vehicles and pickup trucks are becoming just as popular with thieves as they are with consumers. Table 11.2 lists the ten most stolen cars in Canada in 2006.

A variety of strategies are used to steal vehicles for financial gain. The "strip and run" occurs when a

TABLE 11.2 Top 10 Most Stolen Cars, 2006

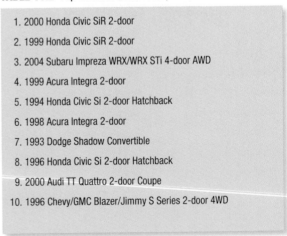

1. 2000 Honda Civic SiR 2-door
2. 1999 Honda Civic SiR 2-door
3. 2004 Subaru Impreza WRX/WRX STi 4-door AWD
4. 1999 Acura Integra 2-door
5. 1994 Honda Civic Si 2-door Hatchback
6. 1998 Acura Integra 2-door
7. 1993 Dodge Shadow Convertible
8. 1996 Honda Civic Si 2-door Hatchback
9. 2000 Audi TT Quattro 2-door Coupe
10. 1996 Chevy/GMC Blazer/Jimmy S Series 2-door 4WD

Source: INSURANCE BUREAU OF CANADA.

FIGURE 11.2   Motor vehicle theft rate by province, 2006.

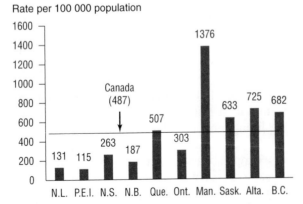

Rate per 100 000 population

Source: Adapted from "Crime Statistics in Canada, 2006," Statistics Canada, Catalogue no. 85-002-XIE, vol. 27, no. 5, page 6.

This police officer carries away "chopped" parts of stolen cars following the investigation into and discovery of a "chop shop."

One of the most successful of the high-tech options for car protection may be electronic tracking systems, including the relatively new Boomerang vehicle tracking system, created by a Montreal company. A small transmitter is installed in the vehicle; when the car is reported stolen, the Boomerang tracking station can find the transmitter's signal using signals sent through the cell phone system in less than an hour, sometimes in a matter of minutes. Operational since 2003, Boomerang Tracking, Inc., reports a recovery rate of 95 percent for stolen vehicles equipped with the device.[38] This system is different from the popular Lo-Jack system used in the United States. Lo-Jack uses a satellite-based global position system (GPS) that is not yet available in Canada but will make its way to this country before long.

Another effective means of dealing with motor vehicle theft, based in prevention by increasing the cost associated with attempting to steal a vehicle, is the Bait Car Program (check out www.baitcar.com to view offenders caught on tape in an actual bait car). A bait car is a vehicle owned by the police and is intended to be stolen. After a bait car is stolen, the location, speed, and direction of travel of the vehicle are monitored by police dispatchers through GPS tracking. The dispatcher coordinates a police response; once officers are in position behind the bait car, the engine is disabled through the click of a computer mouse button, and the car thieves are arrested. While cities across the country are using these programs, the Vancouver program, launched in 2004, is lauded as playing a role in the 35 percent reduction in vehicle thefts in British Columbia between 2004 and 2007.[39]

In addition to these innovative means of reducing vehicle theft, in some jurisdictions car owners can voluntarily display a decal or a special customized licence plate on their vehicles signifying one of two things: that the car is normally not driven between the hours of 1:00 A.M. and 5:00 A.M. or that the vehicle is normally not driven in particular areas. As a member of this program, the car owner consents to vehicle stops if the car is being driven under the conditions described above.[40]

Such efforts (as we saw in Chapter 9) are examples of target hardening—that is, designing the target (the car) in such a way that it is harder to steal. Other means of providing for greater car protection include safer parking facilities. Ronald Clarke has demonstrated that parking lots with

thief steals a car, strips it for its parts, and then abandons the vehicle. The frame of the car is all that is left. The "scissors job" occurs when scissors are jammed into certain ignition locks in mostly American-made cars, allowing the thief to easily start the car. A "valet theft" takes place when a thief dresses and poses as a valet attendant, opens the car door for the driver, takes the keys, and quickly drives away. Another strategy for vehicle theft is simply the "insurance fraud" scheme, in which a car owner reports his or her car stolen and hides the car for approximately 30 days. Once 30 days have passed without the car's being recovered, insurance claims are often paid without question. After the claim is paid, the cars are often miraculously "found," but are in very poor condition. The owner will then use the money from the insurance claim to purchase a newer car.[37]

The invention of the ignition key made it harder to steal cars. In recent years, manufacturers of automobiles have tried to make cars more theft-proof. Steering-shaft locks, cut-off switches, better door locks, and alarm systems have increased the security of protected cars.

Crime on the Oceans: Whose Problem?

While no accurate estimates of worldwide losses from modern-day piracy are possible, knowledgeable experts think the total is probably near US$250 million a year. The thieves make off with tonnes of cement, coffee, sugar, tomato paste, ladies' undergarments, steel, and whatever other cargo they think they can fence on shore. Even more common is the direct attack on the safe in the captain's cabin—pirates may be able to collect $50 000 in cash during a 15-minute job. In 1991, more than 120 pirate attacks were reported worldwide, and it is likely that only 40 percent of the total are reported to authorities.(1)

A downturn of maritime commerce in Nigeria resulted in a decrease of piracies off Lagos. A sharp decrease also occurred in the Malacca Straits, a result of improved security measures. But piracies began to increase again in the mid-1990s, near ports in Cameroon and Angola, and particularly in the Brazilian ports of Santos and Rio de Janeiro. Most affected are vessels at anchor in the roadsteads.

THE LACK OF POLICING

Unfortunately, the world does not yet have an international marine enforcement agency to police the oceans. There is no one to spot a vessel dumping nuclear waste into the high seas or into an exclusive economic zone. Who can intercept arms or narcotics smugglers? Even powerful nations like the United States have trouble policing their own zones. The problems are much worse for small nations that cannot afford to maintain marine police forces of any size.(2) Most regions affected by piracy and terrorism are in areas of notoriously underpoliced territorial waters.

THE SCOPE OF CRIME ON THE OCEANS

All these problems are magnified when we realize that piracy is only one of many crimes committed on the oceans. Following are examples of other crimes:

- Frauds in the marine shipping industry have caused severe damage to international trade and threatened the collapse of entire national economies in Africa and Latin America.
- The international drug trade uses the oceans for about half its shipments from the points of origin or manufacture to the points of distribution.

- Currently about 30 000 American boats are listed in the FBI's Stolen Boat File as having been stolen and not recovered.

Sources

1. G. O. W. Mueller and Freda Adler, *Outlaws of the Ocean* (New York: Hearst Marine Books, 1985), p. 150; Alan Farnham, "Pirates," *Fortune*, July 15, 1991, pp. 113–118.
2. Roger Villar, *Piracy Today* (London: Conway Maritime Press, 1985), p. 59.

Questions for Discussion

1. What crimes against property are committed by those who engage in maritime fraud?
2. Who should be responsible for controlling crime on the oceans? Where should offenders be dealt with if they are caught?
3. In your opinion, what is the best way to control and prevent crime on the oceans?

---

attendants experience far fewer motor vehicle thefts than unattended lots.[41]

It is not our purpose to classify all theft by the type of property stolen. We have singled out automobile theft to demonstrate the socioeconomic significance of this type of theft, its dependence on the economic situation, and the challenge of changing the situational conditions that encourage people to commit it. With the exception of some brazen pickpockets, people who commit thefts tend to avoid personal contact with their victims. Other criminals seek such contact in order to deprive victims of their property by deception.

FRAUD

Fraud, which makes up about 8 percent of all reported property crime in Canada, is the acquisition of the property of another person through cheating or deception.[42] In England, such crimes owed their existence to the interaction of five circumstances: the advancement of trade and commerce, the inventiveness of swindlers in exploiting these economic advances, the demand of merchants for better protection, the unwillingness of the royal courts to expand the old concept of larceny, and the willingness of Parliament to designate new crimes in order to protect mercantile interests. In brief, medieval England developed a market economy that required the transport of goods by wagon trains across the country, from producer or importer to consumer. Later on, when the Crown sought to encourage settlement of colonies overseas, stock companies were created to raise money for such ventures. People with money to invest acquired part ownership in these companies in the expectation of profit.

Just as some dishonest transporters withheld some of the property entrusted to them for transport, some dishonest investment clerks used funds

Nancy Swedberg, winner of the Mrs. Calgary beauty pageant, was later forced to give up her crown after being charged with 68 counts of fraud, totalling $1.5 million.

entrusted to them for their own purposes. Merchants suffered greatly from such losses, yet the royal courts refused to extend the definition of larceny to cover this new means of depriving owners of their property. But merchants demanded protection, and from time to time, as need arose, Parliament designated new, non-capital offences so that the swindlers could be punished.

Obtaining Property by False Pretences

The essence of the crime of **obtaining property by false pretences** is that the victim is made to part with property voluntarily, as a result of the perpetrator's untrue statements regarding a supposed fact. Assume the doorbell rings. A gentleman greets you politely and identifies himself as a representative of a charitable organization, collecting money for disaster victims. On a typed list are the names of all the households in your building, with a dollar amount next to each name. Each household has supposedly contributed an average of $20. Not wanting to be considered cheap, you hand the gentleman a $20 bill. He promptly writes "$20" next to your name and thanks you.

Of course, the gentleman does not represent the charitable organization, there may not even be such a charity, there may not have been a disaster, and you may have been the first victim on his list. The man has obtained property from you by false pretences. He has not committed a common law larceny because he did not engage in any "trespassory taking" of property.

Cheating was made a crime relatively late in history (in 1757 in England). Until that time, the attitude was that people should look out for their own interests. Today obtaining property by false pretences is a Criminal Code offence.

Confidence Games and Frauds

Confidence games refer to situations where the offender gains the confidence of the victim, induces in the victim the expectation of a future gain, and— by abusing the trust thus created—makes the victim part with some property. In a sense, confidence games are an aggravated form of obtaining property by false pretences.

To illustrate: A woman (A) sees a shiny object lying on the sidewalk. As she stoops to pick it up, a man (B) grabs it. A dispute ensues over who should have the "lost diamond ring." A third person (C) comes by and offers to mediate. He happens to be a jeweller, he says. C takes a jeweller's loupe out of his pocket, examines the diamond ring, and pronounces it worth $500. At this point, B generously offers his share in the ring to A for a mere $100. A pays—and gets what turns out to be a worthless object. By the time she discovers this fact, B and C are long gone.

Frauds of this sort have been with us for centuries. But frauds change with commercial developments. Some of the more prevalent fraud schemes of today would have been unimaginable a few decades ago, simply because the commercial opportunities for their occurrence had not yet been invented.

Cheque Forgery

Those motivated to deprive others of their property have always exploited new opportunities to do so. The invention of "instant cash," or credit, by means of a cheque issued by a creditable, trustworthy person provided just such new opportunities. Ever since cheques were invented, they have been abused. It is a criminal offence to use a counterfeit or stolen cheque or to pass a cheque on a non-existing account, or even on one with insufficient funds, with intent to defraud. The intent may be demonstrated by the defendant's inability or unwillingness to reimburse the payee within a specified time period.

Another fraud, called **cheque forgery,** consists of altering a cheque with intent to defraud. The criminologist Edwin Lemert found that most cheque forgers—or "hot-cheque artists," as they are frequently called—are amateurs who act in times of financial need or stress, do not consider themselves criminals, and often believe that nobody really gets hurt.[43] With the increase in cheque forgeries over the past few decades, the primary means of dealing with the problem has been the introduction of identification requirements needed when either cashing a cheque at a financial institution or presenting a cheque for payment. The downside of this approach is the annoyance to cheque users of having to put up with increased restrictions.[44] Some retailers have begun using a system where a cheque presented for payment is run through a machine that verifies whether or not the funds presented as payment on the cheque are in fact available at the time of sale.

Credit Card Crimes

Just as the introduction of cheques for payment for goods and services opened up opportunities for thieves to gain illegitimate financial advantage, so did the introduction of "plastic money." Many believe that the widespread use of credit cards, debit cards, and charge cards is quickly making ours a cashless society.[45] In 2006 there were 61.1 million Visa and MasterCard credit cards in circulation in Canada. Visa and MasterCard reported losses from credit card fraud of over $185 million in Canada in 2006.[46] This amount has been increasing as the volume of cards in circulation goes up. Losses from credit card crime are expected to surpass all other retailer-reported losses, such as those from bad cheques, counterfeit currency, and shoplifting.

Credit card fraud during the 1980s was associated primarily with counterfeiting and lost or stolen cards. Now many cards are stolen while in transit from the issuer to the cardholder. In other instances, an offender may simply use false information about a real person to obtain a genuine card. Or a person may make a purchase by mail order or telephone using a genuine card number but have the goods delivered to an address other than the address of the card owner.[47] Traffickers in stolen cards sell them for cash, with the amount based on the credit limit of the account—a $2000 credit line might bring $250.[48] The availability of new and relatively inexpensive technological equipment, however, keeps transforming the nature of the fraud. Stolen, lost, or expired credit cards are now modified with computers and encoding devices so that they appear to be valid. Totally counterfeit credit cards are also fabricated with the help of laser copiers or other duplicating techniques. And, more recently, credit card account numbers are being stolen from the Internet.

The economic rewards of credit card fraud are quick and relatively easy. The risks are low. Usually merchants do not ask for personal identification;

This office supply store employee has noticed that every time there is a news story about identity theft, shoppers flood to his store to buy paper shredders.

cards are issued in banks that are often in other provinces or countries; and authorization procedures are weak. Originally, the users of stolen credit cards had the inconvenience of selling the merchandise they obtained with the cards. But when banks introduced the practice of cashing the cheques of strangers as long as the transactions were guaranteed by a credit card, perpetrators gained direct access to cash and no longer had to resort to dealers in stolen goods.[49]

Several fraud-prevention initiatives have been developed in response to the prevalence of credit card fraud. The use of laser-engraved photography and signatures on credit cards makes impersonation more difficult. Other initiatives are the use of increased authorization levels on credit card transactions, as well as reduced floor limits above which transactions must be authorized to be guaranteed. Better technology has been developed to quickly transmit data on cards that have been reported lost and stolen to retailers worldwide. Further, with the ever-increasing "card not present" situations, such as when a person is purchasing items over the Internet, additional methods are being developed to verify the identity of the cardholder.[50]

The popularity of debit cards has provided opportunity for debit card fraud as well. Canadians are among the highest users of debit cards for purchases in the world, making an average of 95.1 debit card purchases per person in 2005 (only Sweden uses them more, at an average of 97.2 transactions per person per year). The biggest debit card scam in Canada's history unfolded in Toronto in 2005, where a gang of Eastern Europeans installed false fronts on bank ATMs. The false fronts contained miniature cameras (allowing the thieves to see customer PINs as they are entered) and false card readers (which records bank account information as the bank card is passed through it). The thieves used the card reader and bank account information to make an exact duplicate of the bank card. They hit dozens of machines at the same time; at one point it was estimated they had pocketed $4 million. Eventually, 58 gang members were charged for stealing over $10 million. According to experts, part of the problem is that Canadian banks are still using a security system that is easy to crack. Estimates are that about 27 000 Canadians have been victims of this kind of crime; in 2003 over $44 million was stolen because of debit card fraud.[51]

As online banking and online purchasing continue to rise in popularity, we can expect to see an increase in online banking fraud. About 23 percent of Canadians say the Internet is the primary means through which they conduct the majority of their banking transactions, while 42 percent do at least some banking online.[52] In 2003, 192 million online banking transactions occurred in Canada. As with credit card fraud, fraud committed online will surely rise as thieves become adept at using technology and cracking security codes.

Insurance Fraud

Insurance fraud is a problem in Canada. An estimated $500 million is paid out by home, car, and business insurers for claims containing elements of fraud each year.[53] The Insurance Bureau of Canada's Coalition Against Insurance Fraud estimates that fraud costs Canadians up to $2.3 billion every year.[54] Of all insurance claims, the estimate is that 10 to 15 percent are exaggerated or fraudulent.[55] Auto insurance, in particular, has been the target of many dishonest schemes. Auto insurance schemes include:

- *Staged claims.* Parts of a car are removed, reported stolen, and later replaced by the owner.

- *Owner dumping.* The car is reported stolen; it is stripped by the owner, and the parts are sold.

- *Abandoned vehicles.* The car is left in a vulnerable spot for theft; then it is reported stolen.[56]

- *Staged accidents.* No collision occurs, but an "accident scene" is prepared with glass, blood, and so forth.

- *Intended accidents.* All parties to the "accident" are part of the scheme.

- *Caused accidents.* The perpetrator deliberately causes an innocent victim in a targeted car to crash into his or her car (often in the presence of "friendly" witnesses).[57]

There are many types of insurance fraud besides those involving automobiles. One Canadian study found "elements of fraud" in one in four personal injury claims.[58] Exaggeration of the extent of one's injury—opportunistic fraud—was the most prevalent. Examples include a health care professional exaggerating the severity of a patient's legitimate injury in order to increase the claim amount, or a person who is actually injured exaggerating the extent of his or her injuries or required recuperation time.[59] Less common are premeditated personal injury claims, which occur when someone devises a way to make an insurance claim, such as intentionally falling down a neighbour's stairs (and then collecting benefits from the insurance company for a non-existent injury).[60]

One rapidly growing type of fraud involves filing fraudulent health insurance claims. Various terms have been created to describe the schemes that are used in medical fraud. "Overutilization" involves billing for superfluous and unnecessary tests and other services.[61] "Ping-Ponging" occurs when physicians refer patients to several practitioners when symptoms do not warrant such referrals. "Family ganging" takes place when a doctor extends several unnecessary services to all members of a patient's family. "Steering" is a practice in which doctors direct patients to the clinic's pharmacy to fill unneeded prescriptions. Finally, "upgrading" occurs when a patient is billed for services more extensive than those that were actually performed.[62] A recent accusation of "double billing" in Alberta occurred when information was brought to light regarding almost 10 000 cases where two agencies—the Workers' Compensation Board and Alberta Health and Wellness—were both billed for the same medical procedure.[63]

Credit card crimes and insurance schemes are comparatively recent types of fraud, but they are not the last opportunities for swindlers to deprive others of their property. Computer crime, for example, is a growing concern, and technological advances continue to offer new possibilities for theft. Opportunities will always challenge the imagination of entrepreneurs—illegitimate as well as legitimate. In regard to the illegitimate entrepreneurs, the problem invariably is whether they are in violation of existing criminal laws or whether new legislation will have to be drawn up to cover their schemes.

Cracking Down on Insurance Fraud: Manitoba Public Insurance

The Insurance Bureau of Canada, an organization that keeps track of the types and numbers of insurance frauds that occur each year, presented in 2006 its first annual Scam-ademy Awards. Showcasing the "losers who tried to cheat Canadian insurance companies and their customers—and got caught," the awards reveal perhaps the least sophisticated in a growing number of insurance fraud schemes in Canada.

The "Fraudster Award for Worst Picture" went to "Around the World in 80 Cars." Described as a scam that stretched from Canada to the Middle East, these fraud artists were car thieves and identity thieves who, through creating false identities and false credit reports, leased over 80 high-end cars, which they then shipped to buyers in countries throughout the Middle East. After doing so, they tried to report them as stolen in an attempt to collect on insurance as well. They were caught, and at least five were charged.

"Worst Performance by Actors in Supporting Roles" went to "Same Time Next Week," whereby apparently poor drivers, all driving rental cars, always crashed at

the same time of day and the same day of the week—12 times. The plot was always the same: One car with two people always hit another car with three or four in it. They all used the same paralegals and went to the same clinics for treatment, making false claims.

In another case (awarded "Worst Foreign Production"), two men drove a Hummer, stolen in Ontario, to Mexico, where they acquired insurance for it from a Mexican insurer. One of the men then reported it stolen and filed an insurance claim, while the other was cruising around Acapulco in it.

And the "Fraudster for Worst Director" was awarded to a man who repeatedly reported the theft of his vintage cars. The insurance company noted that he had made three such claims in six years. Upon visiting his home, they found a variety of stolen cars and car parts, including some of the cars he reported stolen.

In response to these kinds of fraudulent claims, Manitoba Public Insurance launched an advertising campaign that encourages honest citizens to report suspicions of insurance fraud. Manitoba's justice system is taking a tough stance on

insurance fraud: Between March 1, 2005, and February 28, 2006, $38 000 in fines and $67 000 in restitution were ordered. Anonymous calls to the TIPS line in 2005 resulted in 1500 investigations that led to $700 000 in savings and six people being charged with various fraud offences. Overall, Manitoba Public Insurance claims to have saved ratepayers $12.5 million in 2005, in part because of the TIPS line.

Sources

1. Insurance Bureau of Canada, "Insurance Scam-ademy Awards," www.ibc.ca/en/Insurance_Crime/Scam-ademy/, accessed October 23, 2007.
2. "Fighting Fraud Helps Keep Autopac Rates Low: Manitoba Public Insurance," July 13, 2006, www.insurance-canada.ca/consinfoauto/Manitoba-PIC-Fighting-fraud-607.php, accessed September 9, 2007.

Questions for Discussion

1. What type of punishment is appropriate for an insurance fraud offender?
2. What other types of laws and policies can be created in an attempt to prevent insurance fraud?

HIGH-TECH CRIMES: CONCERNS FOR TODAY AND TOMORROW

Six telemarketers have been charged in connection with an Internet gaming scam. Prosecutors say the scam took in almost $5 million from more than 500 investors. The six worked for Gecko Holdings. They offered investors stock in Gecko, telling them it was an on-line gambling business about to go public. Investors were promised that their shares, priced at two dollars, would double or triple the value in a few months. But the stock never went public. Instead, prosecutors say, the owners took off with the money. The six are charged with 26 counts each of mail and wire fraud.[64]

Crimes evolve with the environments we live in. The rise of computers and other high-technology equipment has paved the way for the genesis of

new crime types. These present yet another set of challenges for potential victims, law enforcement personnel, criminologists, and other criminal justice professionals.

What exactly is high-technology crime? While there may be debates over the definition of this phenomenon, it is generally agreed that **high-tech crime** involves an attempt to pursue illegal activities through the use of advanced electronic media. We shall define "high technology" as "a form of sophisticated electronic device—computer, cellular telephone, and other digital communication—that is in common use today."[65] The new waves of computer crime are perhaps the most illustrative examples of high-technology crime, although sophisticated credit card fraud schemes and cellular telephone scams are also modern problems. In this section, we will refer to crimes relying on modern electronic technology as "high-tech crimes."

Characteristics of High-Tech Crimes

High-tech crimes have affected the nature of property crimes by taking on the following few distinct characteristics.

Role of Victims, Type of Property Criminals engaging in high-tech crimes no longer need actual direct contact with their victims; computers equipped with modems have unlimited range, enabling offenders to victimize people thousands of kilometres away. The reach of motivated offenders has been considerably extended. Physical movement has been replaced by electronic travel, especially with the recognition that computers are global networks.

The type of property that is stolen or affected is also very different in nature. While other property crimes (arson, vandalism, theft, break-and-enter) victimize concrete targets, high-tech crimes involve less-visible and tangible kinds of property such as information, data, and computer networks. In addition, many victims of high-tech crime realize they have been victimized only long after the crime has taken place. In most other property crimes, there is often little time between the actual crime and the realization that a crime has taken place (as in cases of break-and-enter or arson, for example).

Profits of Crime The profits from high-tech crimes are vast. The rise in the incidence of computer crime, for example, is a testament to its efficacy and the profit to be made. The British Banking Association in London, England, estimates the cost of computer fraud worldwide at about US$8 billion a year.[66] With the increasing sophistication of equipment, computer hackers are able to steal greater amounts with greater ease, and sometimes a single act can victimize multiple people or places at once.

Detection High-tech crime is also attractive to some individuals because they find evading detection and prosecution relatively easy. Few law enforcement agencies are equipped to detect the high-tech crimes occurring within their jurisdictions. Furthermore, since the nature of high-tech crime allows perpetrators to carry out their illegal activities without any geographic limitations, tracing high-tech criminal activity to the responsible individual is very difficult. Identifying the crime location becomes harder to do since street corners and physical space have been replaced by airwaves, cyberspace, and other electronic media. Often, by the time illegal activity has been detected, the criminals have already moved on to a new target.

Degree of Criminal Complexity Another important aspect of high-technology crimes involves the complicated nature of the crimes being committed. Every day, new crimes are being developed and refined by highly skilled computer users. Traditional law enforcement techniques are not designed to deal with such novel and complex crimes. High-tech criminals are, in a sense, sophisticated criminals. Stealing credit card numbers from the Internet for illicit purposes requires a certain degree of proficiency in Internet navigation, knowledge of how to break into the system to commit the thefts, and, finally, experience in using the stolen credit card numbers for criminal gain—all the while avoiding detection.

International Component Phone companies and computer network systems often advertise that using their services will allow individuals to communicate with people located at the other end of the globe. Such ease of electronic travel is appealing to high-tech criminals, who now participate in a modern phenomenon: global criminality. High-tech crimes can easily go beyond national boundaries, making them transnational crimes, a criminal activity of serious concern for targeted countries. Using a computer, a high-tech criminal can make illegal international money transfers, steal information from a computer located in another country, or diffuse illicit information (such as child pornography or terrorist propaganda) worldwide. The ability to detect and successfully deal with such criminal activities is a major challenge for law enforcement agencies around the world.

Computers and the Internet: Types of Crime

High-tech criminals have also created their own crime types. While some seek the same ends as more traditional property offenders (financial gain), modern technology allows for novel and totally new crimes.[67]

There are three main categories of computer crimes. First, the computer can be used as a storage or communication device whereby information can be created, stored, manipulated, and communicated electronically. In this instance, the computer is incidental, since it is not required for the crime itself but is used in some way that is connected to the criminal activity. An example is financial records kept on a drug dealer's computer.

Second, the computer can be used as an instrument or a tool of crime. In this case, the computer is used to commit traditional offences, such as the creation of counterfeit money or official documents, or newer computer crime offences, such as the distribution of child pornography, confidence schemes, and illegal gambling networks on the Internet.

Finally, a computer can be used as a weapon to commit attacks on the confidentiality, integrity, and availability of information, including theft of information, theft of services, and damage to computer systems.[68] This type of computer crime involves the widespread problem of viruses and other forms of siege attacks, such as those referred to as "denial of service" attacks. The purpose of a denial-of-service attack is to prevent the normal operation of a digital system. It is often committed by "cyber vandals." An increasing number of electronic siege attacks employing some form of denial of service have been initiated against organizations worldwide in recent years.[69]

Computer Network Break-ins There are several types of computer network break-ins. The first is commonly known as "hacking." It is not practised for criminal gain and can therefore be considered more mischievous than malicious. Nevertheless, network intrusions have been made illegal. A hacker's reward is being able to tell peers that he or she has managed to break into a network, demonstrating superior computing ability, especially the ability to bypass security measures. Hackers, for the most part, seek entry into a computer system and "snoop around," often leaving no sign of entry. It can be likened to an individual's stealthily gaining entry into another person's house, going through a few personal belongings, and carefully leaving without taking anything.

Another type of break-in is the one done for illegal purposes. A criminal might break into a large credit card company to steal card numbers or into a network to steal data or sensitive information. Other criminal acts include computer vandalism, whereby individuals break into a system, alter its operating structure, delete important files, change passwords, or plant viruses that can destroy operating systems, software programs, and data. *Spyware* software is installed onto a user's computer without his or her consent. It monitors or controls the user's computer use and may be used to send pop-up ads, redirect the computer to websites, monitor Internet surfing, or record the user's keystrokes, which, in turn, could lead to identity theft.[70]

Mail Bombings While computers can be used to steal money and information, they can also be used for more aggressive purposes. Like the bully told to rough up the new kid in the school yard, computers can be instructed to attack other machines. A common method is that of mail bombings. Mail bombs are the products of computer programs that instruct a computer to literally bombard another computer with information, often irrelevant e-mail. Mail bombs are capable of shutting down computers, and even entire networks, if the amount of information is too large for the receiving computer to digest.

Perhaps less damaging but still very aggressive, *mouse-trapping* is one of the most extreme marketing tactics on the Internet. Through this technique, browser tricks can keep a visitor captive at a site, often by disabling the "back" button or by generating pop-up windows. The goal is to extract maximum value from one-time visits by bombarding visitors with a never-ending supply of traffic-exchange banners and pay-per-click links.[71]

Password Sniffers Entry into a computer system often requires a password or some other form of user identification to protect the information it contains. Password sniffers are programs that carefully record the names and passwords of network users as they log in. With such confidential information, unauthorized users are able to gain unlawful access to the computer and the information it contains. Passwords can also be sold to other users for illegal purposes. *Phishing* involves con artists sending fraudulent e-mail messages to users that appear to come from trusted websites, like a bank or credit card company. They ask a user to send personal information, which they then use to access other information, such as credit card numbers, passwords, and account data. *Pharming*

occurs when Internet hackers redirect Internet traffic from one website to different, identical-looking sites in order to trick the user into entering personal information and a password into the database on the fake website.

Software Piracy   It is estimated that approximately US$7.5 billion worth of American software is illegally copied and distributed annually worldwide. Software piracy ranges from friends sharing and occasionally copying software to international fraudulent schemes whereby software is replicated and passed on as the original product, sometimes at a lower price. Recent research indicates that employees contribute significantly to the presence of illegal software in the workplace, either by bringing software from home (40 percent), downloading unauthorized copies from the Internet (24 percent), or sharing programs with other employees (24 percent).[72] The duplication process is relatively simple, and once mastered, any software can be pirated and copies sold worldwide. Software developers are constantly trying to stay ahead of the pirates by attempting to render their software resistant to such duplication. The advent of the compact disc and digital video disc unfortunately makes casual software piracy relatively easy.

Pornography Online   The Internet provides a forum for the display of information. Some individuals, however, see this venue as a means to dis-

Child pornography is easy to find on the Internet if you know where to go—for example, newsgroups, chat rooms, and bulletin boards. Popular search engines are highly suggestive but rarely bring you to illegal images. Garry Geisel, pictured here, has challenged the legal system, defending his practice of taking pictures of naked girls as young as 14.

tribute or seek illegal information such as child pornography. We discuss child pornography in more detail in Chapter 13 because of its categorization as a sexual morality offence. We could also have discussed it in Chapter 10 because it is a violent offence as well, causing immeasurable harm—physical, psychological, and emotional—to children and youth. We discuss it here, however, because of the role that technology plays in propagating pornographic materials and in facilitating the commission of these kinds of criminal acts.

Finding and downloading such material from the Internet is a simple task, even for amateur computer users. While law enforcement agencies occasionally intercept child pornography and those who engage in its dissemination over the airwaves, most offenders are never caught. Also, such material can be strategically hidden or altered to appear to be something else. "Morphing" is a practice that involves using computers to digitally alter pictures. Using such a method, an individual can superimpose two images or cut and paste parts of one image onto another. This technique has become a tool for child pornographers to evade prosecution. They simply attach the head of an adult to a child's body, and claim the image indeed portrays an adult.

Many cases of online pedophilia have been reported as well. Adults make contact with young people in online chat groups or through other online avenues and either seduce them into meeting in person, or make arrangements to meet under false pretences. Cases like that of Patrick Naughton are not infrequent. Naughton, a successful computer guru, who in 1990 helped develop the popular Java programming language at Sun Microsystems, was charged with online pedophilia after he arranged to meet a 13-year-old girl with whom he initiated contact in an online chat room. When he arrived at the rendezvous point, Naughton was met by law enforcement officials. The "13-year-old girl" turned out to be a male police officer.[73]

In another Internet-related pedophilia case, Canadian schoolteacher Christopher Neil was accused of sexually abusing several young boys in Cambodia, Thailand, and Vietnam. Police initiated an investigation into Neil's activities after photos allegedly showing him sexually abusing the boys appeared on the Internet. About 200 such photos were found on the Internet. Although the face of the perpetrator was digitally obscured, German

Christopher Neil was accused of sexually assaulting boys in Thailand. Neil posted pictures of the assaults on the Internet, but with his face digitally scrambled. When officials deciphered the images, he was arrested.

police computer experts were able to unscramble the photos, allegedly of Neil.[74]

Pornography is finding itself online in other ways as well. In fact, Web pages are being "page-jacked." A recent scheme involved two hackers who cloned legitimate Web pages, including sites such as Audi and Paine Webber. When computer users attempted to reach the legitimate sites, they were "page-jacked" to pornographic websites. When attempting to escape the pornographic sites by clicking on the "Back" or "Home" buttons on their browsers, users were then "mouse-trapped" and sent to additional pornographic websites.[75]

Going after such offenders becomes difficult if different countries are involved in the illegal act. Let us suppose an individual in country A posts pornographic material on the Internet, and in country A, such material is legal. If the same material is retrieved in country B (although the source is country A), where the material is considered illegal, who is to blame, and where has the crime occurred? Jurisdictional questions about information found on the Internet remain largely unresolved. They will surely become more complex with the increasing traffic of illicit information and images.

Credit Card Fraud Computers and the Internet are used more and more to conduct business. It has become commonplace to order merchandise, make payments, and conduct personal banking online. This use of credit cards is very appealing to people involved in credit card fraud. Computers can facilitate credit card fraud in two ways. First, a conventionally stolen credit card can be used to order merchandise online and, because no time is wasted going from store to store, a perpetrator can maximize his or her gain before

the card is inactivated. Detection is also reduced since there is no physical contact with sales staff who might alert authorities should they suspect fraud. Second, credit card numbers can be stolen from the Internet as customers are making legitimate purchases. Programs similar to those that are designed to steal passwords from unsuspecting users are often used for this purpose. Another way of stealing credit card numbers is for offenders to access computers located in credit bureaus or financial institutions.

> **Did You Know?**
>
> . . . that the RCMP warns that identify theft is one of the fastest-growing crimes in Canada? One in four Canadians have either been the victim of identify theft, or knows someone who has.

Currently, no one really knows the actual cost of computer crime. Estimates, however, suggest that in the United States alone the costs range from US$500 million to US$5 billion per year. Computer crime is underdetected and underreported. Furthermore, computer crime is not considered a major priority for many police departments. Greater attention and resources are focused on violent-crime-reduction efforts and, more recently, on community policing. Combating computer crime is not a priority for several reasons: It is difficult to police the Internet, and the necessary resources are not available to adequately handle this type of crime. There is no public outcry against computer crime, since the public is more interested in violent crime. Finally, many police officers feel that they did not choose their profession to police computer crime, but rather to help people and arrest the criminals.[76] Despite these problems, training programs on combating computer crime are being designed and implemented in some police departments.

Characteristics of the High-Tech Criminal

While all the crimes and deviant acts discussed so far rely heavily on technology, there are still human offenders behind them. Do these people, however, resemble other property criminals, or do they have distinct characteristics? It is true that modern technology is so widespread that virtually anyone is capable of high-tech crime, but it also remains a fact that most high-tech offenders, especially computer hackers, fit a rather unique profile. These

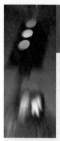

Whose Identity Is It Anyway?

Kim Bradbury thought she was speaking to another annoying telemarketer when she heard it was her credit card company calling. It turned out they were calling to warn her. "Someone has applied for a credit card in your name," said the caller, "and it doesn't match other addresses we have for you."

It was later discovered that a lab assistant at Ms. Bradbury's former place of employment had stolen a box of personnel records. More than three dozen of these records were used to obtain about 75 credit cards, buy at least $100 000 in merchandise, open 20 cellular telephone accounts, and rent three apartments.

"People take this situation lightly, but once it happens to you it's a nightmare," said Ms. Bradbury, a biologist and the mother of two children. "I feel so violated, and I'm very, very angry."

Law enforcement authorities are becoming increasingly worried about the rise in identity theft, the pilfering of people's personal information for use in obtaining credit cards, loans, and other goods. Law enforcement officials and consumer advocates say the Internet is making identity theft one of the signature crimes of the digital era. The rise in identity theft is attributed to the ease with which social security data can be collected on the Internet.

Even a cursory tour through cyberspace turns up a host of vendors peddling personal information. One online company, Net Detective 8.0, promotes itself as "an amazing new tool that allows you to find out *everything* you ever wanted to know about your friends, family, neighbors, employees, and even your boss!"

If an identity thief needs to know someone's social security number, for example, it is easy enough to buy it on the Internet. One website, docusearch. com, will retrieve a person's social security number in one day for a $49 fee. Dan Cohn, the director of docusearch.com, said he got the numbers from "various sources" but that none of his company's services have contributed to identity theft. "Social security numbers are pretty much public numbers anyway," Mr. Cohn observed.

Social security numbers matched with other personal information enable identity thieves to apply for credit cards on the Internet, often with minimal scrutiny from issuers. And if an identity thief uses a credit card to briefly build up a solid credit history by paying off monthly bills, he or she then has the credibility to apply for big-ticket items like loans for cars and rental property.

Consumers rarely face monetary losses related to identity theft because merchants or banks are typically the ones stuck with bogus credit card charges. In addition, credit card issuers are generally vigilant about monitoring customers' buying patterns and flagging questionable transactions very quickly.

The real damage felt by consumers like Ms. Bradbury and other victims of identity theft is not monetary—it is emotional. Victims say they not only must face the reality that their financial privacy has been compromised by an anonymous thief, but also they often endure lengthy, painstaking struggles to clean up credit records that have been tarnished by identity thieves. In some of the worst cases, when identity thieves commit crimes and use their false identities to mislead police, victims of identity theft find themselves saddled with false criminal records.

Source

Adapted from Timothy L. O'Brien, "Officials Worried over a Sharp Rise in Identity Theft," *New York Times,* Apr. 3, 2002. Reprinted with permission.

Questions for Discussion

1. Are Canadians' social insurance numbers safer than Americans' social security numbers?
2. Some lawmakers have suggested that it should be made more difficult—if not illegal—to purchase information like social security numbers from the Internet. Do you agree? Do you think, given the global reach of cyberspace, that this would be an enforceable law?
3. Do the owners of the information websites have any responsibility to monitor the dissemination of this type of information? Or are they just supplying information that the public can find elsewhere anyway?

---

individuals are usually young (14 to 19 years old) white males from middle-class backgrounds. They often possess superior levels of intelligence (IQ over 120), but on a social level they tend to be withdrawn and associate mainly with peers who share their fascination for electronic gadgets and computer-related activities. Some youths also believe that they are part of a counterculture, fighting censorship, liberating information, and challenging big business and major corporations.[77] In a way, they perceive themselves as modern-day Robin Hoods.

The Criminal Justice Problem

High-tech crimes pose a special problem to law enforcement agencies for two reasons. First, these crimes are not easily detected since the offenders can quietly commit them from any computer terminal, usually in the comfort of their own homes. Second, while a few organizations have mobilized to attack high-tech crime, most law enforcement agencies are not equipped to deal with the phenomenon: "Technology changes at an astounding rate while law enforcement techniques, which traditionally are

David L. Smith, the 30-year-old computer programmer from New Jersey who created the "Melissa" virus.

reactionary, do not."[78] It is clear that the police forces of the future need to address this problem by concentrating on detection and by arming themselves with the technological tools necessary to deal with it.

BREAK-AND-ENTER

A "burg," in Anglo-Saxon terminology, was a secure place for the protection of oneself, one's family, and one's property. If the burg protects a person from theft and assault, what protects the burg? The burghers, perhaps. But there had to be a law behind the burghers. And that was the law of burglary, which made it a crime to break and enter the dwelling of another person at night with the intention of committing a crime therein. (Of course, it had to be at night, for during the day the inhabitants could defend themselves, or so it was thought.) The common law defined **burglary** as:

- The breaking
- And entering
- Of the dwelling house
- Of another person
- At night
- With the intention to commit a felony or larceny inside

By "breaking," the law meant any trespass (unauthorized entry), but usually one accompanied by a forceful act, such as cracking the lock, breaking a windowpane, or scaling the roof and entering through the chimney. The "entering" was complete as soon as the perpetrator extended any part of his or her body into the house in pursuit of the objective of committing a crime in the house.

The house had to be a "dwelling," but that definition was extended to cover the "curtilage," the attached servants' quarters, carriage houses, and barns. The dwelling also had to be that of "another." And as we mentioned, the event had to occur at "night," between sundown and sunup.

The most troublesome element has always been the "intention to commit a felony or larceny" (which in current terms in Canada refers to an indictable offence, a theft, even a petty theft or summary offence) inside the premises. How can we know what a burglar intends to do? The best evidence of intent is what the burglar actually does inside the premises: Steal jewellery? Commit a sexual assault? Set the house afire? Any crime the burglar commits inside is considered evidence of criminal intention at the moment the burglar broke and entered the dwelling.[79]

Today burglary, or **break-and-enter** as it is referred to in Canada, is no longer limited to night attacks, and it refers to unlawful entry and intent to commit a crime in a range of structures, including residences, businesses, and other places.

> **Did You Know?**
>
> . . . that the maximum punishment for break-and-enter is life imprisonment (Section 348 [1] of the Criminal Code)?

The rate of break-ins in 2006 reached its lowest level in over 30 years and has dropped 50 percent since reaching its peak rate in 1991. Break-and-enters represent about 21 percent of all property crimes. Most of these reported break-and-enters occurred in residences (147 002) and businesses (79 042).[80] While the original definition required the crime be committed at night, today most break-and-enters occur during the daytime hours. When contemplating a residential break-and-enter, offenders consider factors such as whether the occupant is home. Since many homeowners work during the day or are absent for other reasons (attending school, running errands), daytime provides a prime opportunity for a break-in.

Criminologists ask questions about the characteristics of offenders who commit break-and-enter and of the places that are targeted. Neal Shover described the "good burglar" as one having competence, personal integrity, a specialty in burglary, financial success, and an ability to avoid prison.[81] Another study demonstrated that people who commit break-and-enters are versatile, committing a wide range of offences, but that they do specialize in break-and-enter for short periods of time. Compared with males who commit break-and-enter, females begin offending at a later age, more often commit break-and-enters with others, and have fewer contacts with the criminal justice system.[82]

Recent research on break-and-enter asks questions not only about who is likely to commit this offence or what distinguishes one burglar from another. In addition, as we saw in Chapter 9, criminologists are looking, for instance, at the process that leads to the break-and-enter of a particular house in a specific neighbourhood—that is, how a potential offender discriminates between individual areas and targets when there are so many alternatives—and ways to make the process of break-and-enter more difficult for anyone contemplating the crime.

FENCING: RECEIVING STOLEN PROPERTY

We are treating break-and-enter as a property crime. An occasional burglar enters with the intention of committing sexual assault, arson, or some other serious crime inside the building. But most burglars are thieves; they are looking for cash and for other property that can be turned into cash. Burglars and thieves depend on a network of fences to turn stolen property into cash.

Jonathan Wild controlled the London underworld from about 1714 until his hanging in 1725. For over two-and-a-half centuries he has captured the imagination of historians, social scientists, and writers. Henry Fielding wrote *The Life of Mr. Jonathan Wild, the Great,* and Mack the Knife in John Gay's *Beggar's Opera* was modelled on Wild. Wild was known as a "thief-taker." Thief-takers made an occupation of capturing thieves and claiming the rewards offered for their arrest. By law, thief-takers were allowed to keep the possessions of the thieves they caught, except objects that had been stolen, which were returned to their owners.

Wild added a devious twist to his trade: He bought stolen goods from thieves and sold them back to their rightful owners. The owners paid much more than the thief could get from the usual fences, so both Wild and the thief made a considerable profit. To thieves, he was a fellow thief; to honest people, he was a legitimate citizen helping them get back their property. Playing both roles well, he ran competing fencing operations out of business, employed about 7000 thieves, and became the most famous fence of all time.[83]

A **fence** is a person who buys stolen property, on a regular basis, for resale. Fences, or dealers in stolen property, operate much like legitimate businesses: They buy and sell for profit. Their activity thrives on an understanding of the law governing the receiving of stolen property, on cooperation with the law when necessary, and on networking. The difference between a legitimate business and a fencing operation is that the channelling of stolen goods takes place in a clandestine environment (created by law enforcement and deviant associates) with high risks and with a need to justify one's activities in the eyes of conventional society.

Carl Klockars's *Professional Fence* and Darrell Steffensmeier's *Fence,* each focusing on the life of a particular fence, present us with fascinating accounts of this criminal business. The proprietors of such businesses deal in almost any commodity. "Oh, I done lots of business with him," said Klockars's fence, Vincent Swazzi. "One time I got teeth, maybe five thousand teeth in one action. You know, the kind they use for making false teeth—you see, you never know what a thief's gonna come up with." And many fences are quite proud of their positions in the community. Said Swazzi, "The way I look at it, this is actually my street. I mean I am the mayor. I walk down the street an' people come out the doors to say hello."[84]

Until recently, it was believed that professional thieves and fences were totally interdependent and that their respective illegal activities were mutually reinforcing. Recent research, however, demonstrates a change in the market for stolen goods. D'Aunn Webster Avery, Paul F. Cromwell, and James N. Olson conducted extensive interviews with 38 active burglars, shoplifters, and their fences and concluded that it is no longer the professional fence who takes care of stolen goods but, rather, occasional receivers—otherwise honest citizens—who buy from thieves directly or at flea markets.[85] This willingness to buy merchandise that the buyers must at least suspect has been stolen may indicate that the general public is more tolerant of stealing than previous generations were.

ARSON

The crimes against property that we have discussed so far involve the illegitimate transfer of possession. The property in question is "personal property" rather than real property, or real estate. Only two types of property crime are concerned with real property. Break-and-enter is one; the other is arson.

The common law defined **arson** as the malicious burning of or setting fire to the dwelling of another person. Modern criminal law distinguishes degrees of severity of the offence and has increased its scope to include other structures and even personal property, such as automobiles. The most severe punishments are reserved for arson of dwellings, because of the likelihood that persons in the building may be injured or die.

Arson always has been viewed as a more violent crime than break-and-enter. In comparison with break-and-enter, however, arson is a fairly infrequent offence. Keeping in mind that arson is a crime that is highly underreported (because it is often unclear whether the fire was accidentally or intentionally set), a total of 13 504 arson offences were reported in Canada in 2006.[86] It is safe to assume that the actual number of arson incidents is likely to be far higher than the reported figure.[87]

Homes and commercial locations make up the majority of arson targets, while adults males make up the bulk of charged offenders. Youth, however represent 42 percent of those charged.[88] Arson is a serious crime, putting lives at risk, leaving people homeless, and destroying businesses. In 2007 alone, the total financial loss of only three arson incidents was about $25 million. A neighbourhood in Ottawa's Chinatown was targeted, resulting in $2 million damage and leaving 33 people homeless. Thirty-four horses died in a fire set at a Toronto racetrack, which resulted in $3.2 million in damages, and the MacEwan area in Edmonton suffered $20 million in damages when 18 homes were destroyed, 76 damaged, and a 149-unit condo under construction was destroyed.[89]

The motives of adult arsonists are somewhat different from those of juveniles. Though here, too, we find disturbed offenders (pyromaniacs) and people who set fires out of spite. We are also much more likely to encounter insurance fraudsters, as well as organized-crime figures who force compliance or impose revenge by burning establishments (the "torches").[90] One classification of fire setters by motive includes:

- Revenge, jealousy, and hatred
- Financial gain (mostly insurance fraud)
- Intimidation and/or extortion (often involving organized crime)
- Need for attention
- Social protest
- Arson to conceal other crimes
- Arson to facilitate other crimes
- Vandalism and accidental fire setting[91]

Why do children set fires?[92] Recent research suggests that the motive may be psychological pain, anger, revenge, need for attention, malicious mischief, or excitement.[93] Juvenile fire setters have been classified into three groups: the playing-with-matches fire setter, the crying-for-help fire setter, and the severely disturbed fire setter.[94] Many juvenile fire setters are in urgent need of help.

As arson continues to be a serious problem, policy makers have been developing two distinct approaches for dealing with it. The offender-specific approach focuses on educational outreach in schools and the early identification of troubled children, for purposes of counselling and other assistance.[95] The offence-specific (geographic) approach focuses on places. It seeks to identify areas with a high potential for arson. The aim is to deploy arson specialists to correct problems and to stabilize endangered buildings and neighbourhoods.[96]

COMPARATIVE CRIME RATES

The rates of property crime are much higher than those of the violent crime we discuss in Chapter 10. It is interesting to compare these rates for various regions of the world. If we compare the property-owning, consumer-oriented countries of the industrialized Western world with the still largely agricultural but rapidly urbanizing countries of developing nations, we note a significant discrepancy: The rate of theft per 100 000 in the developed countries was 4200, while the rate in developing countries was 600.[97]

Recall the Coca-Cola bottle that disrupted the lives of the indigenous people in *The Gods Must Be Crazy*. We just may have discovered the secret of that bottle: If there is no Coke bottle, no one is going to steal it. The more property people have, especially portable property, the more opportunity other people have to make off with it. Europeans have an old saying: "Opportunity makes thieves." The foremost opportunity for theft may simply be an abundance of property.

REVIEW

1. What are some different types of theft and how does theft differ from larceny?

Many of the property crimes we discussed in this chapter deal directly with the removal of property from the victim, so that the offender can increase his or her wealth. **Theft** (p. 270) describes those situations where property is stolen from an individual; **shoplifting** (p. 272) refers to the stealing of goods from retailers. **Fraud** (p. 276) refers to the acquisition of the property of another person through cheating or deception.

2. What forms does fraud take?

Fraud includes **obtaining property by false pretences** (p. 277), **confidence games** (p. 277), **cheque forgery** (p. 277), and **insurance fraud** (p. 279). Each new form of legitimate trade provides an opportunity for criminal behaviours as thieves learn to use technology and trickery to deceive unsuspecting citizens. Along with the development of credit cards and debit cards came the opportunity for **credit card fraud** (p. 278) and debit card fraud.

3. What makes a crime "high-tech"?

High-tech crime (p. 280) involves an attempt to pursue illegal activities through the use of advanced electronic media. It is evident that most high-tech offenders are quite sophisticated and, given the vastness of such technology as the Internet, a new challenge lies ahead for social scientists and criminal justice professionals alike.

4. How is break-and-enter different from theft?

Not all crimes against property are aimed at acquiring such property. **Break-and-enter** (p. 286) refers to the invasion of a residence or other structure usually—but not necessarily—to commit a theft inside.

5. What is a fence?

A **fence** (p. 287) is a person who buys stolen property, on a regular basis, for resale.

6. What do we know about arsonists?

Arson (p. 288) is the malicious burning of structures or personal property, which endangers the existence of the structure and its occupants. Motivations for arson differ for adults and juveniles and range from psychological or emotional problems to more rational motivations.

7. How do the rates of property crime in different parts of the world compare?

It seems that the more property a nation produces and possesses (developed nations versus developing nations), the greater the opportunity for and prevalence of property crimes.

CRIMINOLOGY & PUBLIC POLICY

On October16, 2007, the Speech from the Throne was delivered in the House of Commons and in it Stephen Harper's Conservative government vowed to reintroduce several "get tough on crime" bills that had failed to pass during the previous year. Part of the tough-on-crime agenda includes "tough new laws to tackle property crime." Property crime has been declining consistently every year since it peaked in 1991. Furthermore, as we have seen elsewhere in this book, part of the explanation for the decrease in crime we are experiencing is a direct result of the aging of the baby boomers. The government wants to pass legislation that will limit the discretion of judges to sentence convicted criminals to house arrest rather than jail time for some crimes, including some property crimes. Critics of the proposed move to toughen laws and sentences on property crime say that there would be little deterrent effect, but instead the move would increase the Canadian prison population, costing taxpayers hundreds of millions of dollars to build new prisons. Furthermore, lawmakers are assuming that property crimes are committed by rational offenders who weigh the perceived benefits of such crimes against the possible consequences.

Questions for Discussion   Do you think toughening property laws is an effective means of reducing crime? Are property offenders rational offenders who can be deterred by the prospect of tougher sentences? Is house arrest a "slap on the wrist" for property criminals, as the Conservative government implies? Is the threat of imprisonment an effective deterrent to theft? Fraud? Arson?

YOU BE THE CRIMINOLOGIST

Computers are now part of our everyday lives at work, or in school, or at home as vehicles to pay bills, shop online, or simply surf the Internet. With the growing use of computers in all facets of our lives, the potential for misuse increases as well. This chapter has discussed some of the most pressing issues at the heart of computer crimes, including online credit card fraud, the use of the Internet in promoting child pornography, viruses and worms that invade the hard drives of computers, and software piracy. Select at least two forms of computer crime. What, in your opinion, are the causes of and the motivations for committing such crimes? What specifically does the offender stand to gain? Describe ways to counteract the problem. What can be done to prevent this emerging type of property crime?

Visit the Online Learning Centre: www.mcgrawhill.ca/olc/adler

WHITE-COLLAR, CORPORATE, AND ORGANIZED CRIME

CHAPTER **12**

CHAPTER QUESTIONS

1. What is white-collar crime?

2. What is corporate crime?

3. What is organized crime?

Once the seventh largest company in the United States, Enron filed for bankruptcy after multiple disclosures of fraud. Enron's collapse in December 2001 shocked Wall Street.

Y BM Magnex International, incorporated in Alberta in 1994 and listed on the Toronto Stock Exchange in 1996, was forced to halt its trading when in May 1998 the FBI raided its U.S. offices. The firm, whose board included former Ontario premier David Peterson, was being investigated for money-laundering ties to the Russian mob. Documents filed in a U.S. court suggested Canada was chosen for the illegal dealings because of the belief that securities regulations in Canada were more lenient than elsewhere in the world. Following the revelation of organized crime ties, the company went into receivership, leaving its investors in serious trouble. The Ontario Securities Commission fined the former directors of the company a total of $1.2 million and barred several of them from ever serving on boards of other public Canadian firms again.[1]

White-collar, corporate, and organized crimes all involve business enterprises.[2] It is the use of a legitimate or illegitimate business enterprise for illegal profit that distinguishes organizational crimes from other types of offences. Organizational offences are also different in another important respect. Unlike violent crimes and property offences, which the Canadian Criminal Code classifies quite neatly, organizational offences are a heterogeneous mix of crimes, from homicide, fraud, and conspiracy to racketeering and the violation of a host of environmental statutes. Organized crime is also, as the name implies, organizational in nature, usually involving hierarchies of individuals working toward the goal of making money. These organized crime groups have as their goal economic gain by fulfilling the existing demand for illegal goods and services. In this chapter we explore the various kinds of organizational crime.

DEFINING WHITE-COLLAR CRIME

With a daily barrage of media reports on the latest corporate scandal—from allegations of insider trading by Martha Stewart to reports on the six-and-a-half-year sentence given to former financier and newspaper magnate Conrad Black for fraud and obstruction of justice—it is only natural to think that we are in the midst of an unprecedented wave of white-collar and corporate crime. Anecdotal evidence aside, there is no empirical evidence that much, if anything, has changed.

Not surprisingly, politicians seized the opportunity to call for corporate reforms in light of almost daily accusations of illegalities. With little reflection, U.S. President George W. Bush signed the Sarbanes-Oxley Act of 2002 to quell public concerns over the legitimacy and integrity of the markets. This act adopts tough provisions to deter and punish corporate and accounting fraud and corruption. Responding to pressure to adopt similar reforms, Canadian securities regulators in 2002 began a consultative process with a variety

Martha Stewart, an icon of good homemaking, was accused of selling thousands of shares of ImClone Systems Inc., stock just prior to the company's announcement that it failed to receive U.S. Food and Drug Administration approval for an anticancer drug. Was this insider trading? Did she trade on material, non-public information?

of organizations across the country to move in the direction of adopting similar policies to those in the Sarbanes-Oxley Act. Reflective of significant structural and philosophical differences between the two countries' financial markets, the changes are not as "rule-based" as those in the United States. Canada's principles-based regulatory environment is more concerned with developing a "culture of compliance" among corporations, rather than imposing hard-and-fast rules, which tend to encourage corporate leaders to manipulate the system and rules, looking for "loopholes." The market participants and regulators who consulted on the issues "felt that Canadian regulators should establish general principles of disclosure, accountability, and transparency that would allow companies room for judgment in determining what they have to do to meet those principles."[3] As we discuss later in the chapter, several changes were implemented, including changes to the Criminal Code, most of which were in effect by 2005.

For those who think that the problem of white-collar and corporate crime is young, consider that in ancient Greece, public officials reportedly violated the law by purchasing land slated for government acquisition. Much of what we today define as white-collar crime, however, is the result of laws passed within the last 120 years. For example, the Combines Investigation Act, the oldest antitrust statute in the Western world, was passed in 1889; in 1986 it was renamed the Competition Act. This act is our primary legislation governing the actions of businesses. It prohibits certain criminal offences (e.g., price-fixing and bid-rigging conspiracies) and contains non-criminal provisions that allow the review of mergers and a variety of business practices. The act also contains provisions to eliminate or reduce anti-competitive behaviours. Other federal acts that govern competitive behaviour in Canada include the Consumer Packaging and Labelling Act, the Textile Labelling Act, and the Precious Metals Marking Act, as well as amendments to the Competition Act.[4] These acts represent only a portion of the legislation that affects businesses in Canada.

As countries passed legislation governing business practices, criminologists also recognized that companies and their employees were not immune from criminal behaviours. In 1940, Edwin H. Sutherland provided criminologists with the first scholarly account of white-collar crime. He defined it as crime "committed by a person of respectability and high social status in the course of his occupation."[5]

Sutherland's definition, however, is not entirely satisfactory. The accounting firm Arthur Andersen, which was convicted for obstruction of justice in the Enron case, demonstrates that white-collar crime can be committed by a corporation as well as by an individual. Employees of Arthur Andersen shredded documents relating to the Enron Corporation. After the conviction, Arthur Andersen befell the same fate—bankruptcy—as the company it was trying to protect. As Gilbert Geis has noted, Sutherland's work is limited by his own definition. He has a "striking inability to differentiate between the corporations themselves and their executive management personnel."[6] Other criminologists have suggested that the term "white-collar crime" not be used at all; we should speak instead of "corporate crime" and "occupational crime."[7] Generally, however, **white-collar crime** is defined as a violation of the law committed by a person or group of persons in the course of an otherwise respected and legitimate occupation or business enterprise.[8]

Just as white-collar and corporate offences include a heterogeneous mix of corporate and individual crimes, from fraud, deception, and corruption to pollution of the environment, victims of white-collar crime range from the savvy investor to the unsuspecting consumer. No one person or group is immune.[9] The Vatican lost millions of dollars in a fraudulent stock scheme; fraudulent charities have swindled fortunes from unsuspecting investors; and banks have been forced into bankruptcy by losses due to deception and fraud.[10] Perhaps just as important, public perceptions of the legitimacy of financial institutions and markets have been undermined, at least in part, by allegations of corporate abuses.

Crimes Committed by Individuals

As we have noted, white-collar crime occurs during the course of a legitimate occupation or business enterprise. Over time, socioeconomic developments have increasingly changed the dimensions of such

crimes.[11] Once, people needed only a few business relationships to make their way through life. They dealt with an employer or with employees. They dealt on a basis of trust and confidence with the local shoemaker and grocer. They had virtually no dealings with government.

This way of life has changed significantly and very rapidly during the past few decades. People have become dependent on large bureaucratic structures; they are manipulated by agents and officials with whom they have no personal relationship. This situation creates a basis for potential abuses in four sets of relations:

• Employees of large entities may abuse their authority for private gain by making their services to members of the public contingent on a bribe, a kickback, or some other favour.

• Taking advantage of the complexity and anonymity of a large organization, such as a corporation, employees may abuse the systems available to them or the power they hold within the structure for purposes of unlawful gain, as by embezzlement.

• Members of the public who have to deal with a large organization do not have the faith and trust they had when they dealt with individual merchants. If they see an opportunity to defraud a large organization, they may seize it in the belief that the organization can easily absorb the loss and nobody will be hurt.

• Since the relation of buyer to seller (or of service provider to client) has become increasingly less personal in an age of medical group practice, large law firms, and drugstore chains, opportunities for **occupational crimes**—crimes committed by individuals for themselves in the course of rendering a service—have correspondingly increased. Health care insurance fraud, misuse of clients' funds by lawyers and brokers,

Vincent Lacroix, president of Norbourg, leaves the courthouse after being found guilty of losing $130 million in investors' money.

substitution of inferior goods—all such offences are occupational crimes.[12]

Types of White-Collar Crimes

White-collar crimes are as difficult to detect as they are easy to commit.[13] The detection mechanisms on which police and government traditionally rely seem singularly inadequate for this vast new body of crimes. Moreover, though people have learned through the ages to be wary of strangers on the street, they have not yet learned to protect themselves against vast enterprises. Much more scientific study has to be undertaken on the causes, extent, and characteristics of white-collar crimes before we can develop workable prevention strategies.[14]

Eight categories of white-collar offences committed by individuals can be identified:

- Investment-related crimes
- Bankruptcy fraud
- Fraud against the government
- Consumer fraud
- Insurance fraud
- Tax fraud
- Bribery, corruption, and political fraud
- Insider-related fraud[15]

Let us briefly examine each type of crime.

Investment-Related Crimes   Stocks and securities refer to investments that people purchase. Examples of offences that involve stocks and securities include trading on insider information and stock manipulation. *Insider trading* refers to the use of material, non-public, financial information to obtain an unfair advantage in trading securities.[16] A person who has access to confidential corporate information may make significant profits by buying or selling stock on the strength of that information. The prototype case of insider trading is that of Michael Cowpland, the founder of Corel Corp. The Ontario Securities Commission brought charges against him when it was discovered he sold $20 million in shares of Corel four weeks before the company issued an earnings warning to its investors, resulting in a huge decline in share value. The allegation against Cowpland was that he sold the shares based on

Conrad Black, former financier and newspaper magnate, was sentenced to over six years in prison for fraud and obstruction of justice.

his "inside" knowledge that Corel would fall short of quarterly sales figures.[17]

Stock manipulation occurs when, for example, brokers who have a stake in a particular security may make misleading or even false statements to clients to give the impression that the price of the stock is about to rise and thus to create an artificial demand for it. Stock scandals fall into this category. Bre-X Minerals Ltd., a Canadian gold-mining company, ended up costing its investors billions of dollars when, following the reports from its lead geologist, the company claimed to have rights to the largest deposit of gold ever reported. Unfortunately, the reports were false; there was no gold. The company went bankrupt, the lead geologist committed suicide by jumping out of a helicopter, and investors in the company lost out.[18]

In Canada, the organization that deals with stock market regulation is the Toronto Stock Exchange (TSX), a non-profit organization governed by a 15-member board. The TSX is overseen by the Ontario Securities Commission; it investigates market manipulation and insider trading, as well as other instances of securities fraud.

Bankruptcy Fraud   The filing of a bankruptcy petition results in proceedings in which the property and financial obligations of an insolvent person or

Nortel, the Canadian telecommunications equipment giant, has been plagued in recent years with a series of financial losses, accompanied by layoffs, disgruntled shareholders, and questionable accounting activities. Frank Dunn, the company's former CEO, was one of several executives accused of fraud and breaking securities laws in relation to the company's accounting and financial filings.

corporation are disposed of. Bankruptcy proceedings are governed by laws enacted to protect insolvent debtors. Unscrupulous persons have devised numerous means to commit **bankruptcy fraud**—any scam designed to take advantage of loopholes in the bankruptcy laws. While there are many methods for committing this type of fraud, one of the most common involves employees of an already established firm who, motivated by a desire for quick profits, bilk the company of its money and assets and file for bankruptcy. Such a scam is typically used when the company is losing money or has lost its hold on a market.

Bankruptcy fraud also occurs at the individual level, as in the case of a Markham, Ontario, man charged in June 2007 with offences under the Criminal Code and the Bankruptcy and Insolvency Act, for impersonating his deceased wife and selling her property worth $406 415.[19] The Office of the Superintendent of Bankruptcy Canada reported 79 218 consumer bankruptcies and 6756 business bankruptcies in 2006.[20] One estimate is that 10 percent of all bankruptcy filings involve fraud.

Fraud against the Government Governments at all levels are victims of a vast amount of fraud, which includes collusion in bidding, payoffs and kickbacks to government officials, expenditures by a government official that exceed the budget, the filing of false claims, the hiring of friends or associates formerly employed by the government, and offers of inducements to government officials.

Consider, for example, the sponsorship scandal, revealed in 2002, surrounding the Liberal government. A fund set up by the government several years earlier was earmarked to raise the profile of Canada in Quebec and help promote federalism. Auditor General Sheila Fraser investigated the sponsorship program at the behest of then–prime minister Jean Chrétien; Fraser's report was scathing, showing that $100 million was paid to a variety of communications agencies that did nothing to benefit Canadians and or promote federalism. She described the Liberal government's abuse of the system as "scandalous" and "appalling," claiming that the "Publics Works officials broke just about every rule in the book" when it came to awarding contracts to Groupaction (one of the advertising firms). The report also revealed that five Crown corporations and agencies (the RCMP, Via Rail, the Old Port of Montreal, the Business Development Bank of Canada, and Canada Post) "played a role in transferring money through questionable means."[21]

Justice John Gomery was chosen to lead a public inquiry into the handling of the sponsorship program. As the public inquiry progressed, three men also faced criminal charges. Two of the men, Jean Brault, who ran Groupaction, and Paul Coffin, who ran another advertising company, both pled guilty to a variety of fraud charges. Brault admitted paying salaries to Liberal party workers who never did any work for his company. A third man, Chuck Guité, was tried and found guilty of fraud-related charges; the court heard he authorized over $2 million in contracts to Groupaction without proper competition and in one case doubled the value of a contract to $500 000 without demanding any additional work.[22]

As a result of the scandal, opposition parties united in removing the Liberals from power. In a motion of no confidence, they argued that the Liberals no longer had the moral authority to govern the country.

What fuelled these influential individuals to abuse their positions of trust and spend millions of Canadian taxpayer dollars fraudulently? Lack of transparency in government actions encourages abuse of power. Hidden from public view, operating behind closed doors, with access to a significant amount of money, for some the temptation to steal is too much. If we add to that combination, a legal and historical context that is traditionally hesitant to pursue white-collar criminals and is lenient in its treatment of them, the situation seems ripe for a scandal like this one. It certainly raises questions about the extent of similar unethical and

> **Did You Know?**
>
> ... that the cost to taxpayers of the inquiry into the sponsorship scandal was more than $14 million?

Justice John Gomery, head of the inquiry into the sponsorship scandal, begins a news conference. Gomery recommended sweeping changes that would increase government transparency and accountability.

illegal behaviours that have not been discovered. In response to the sponsorship scandal, Stephen Harper's government introduced the Accountability Act, which would directly address unethical actions and make government transparent. Gomery's response was that the act would not go far enough to prevent the kinds of behaviours that resulted in the sponsorship scandal. Still, many say it's a step in the right direction.

Clearly, there is more to government-related fraud than the manipulation of contractors and consultants.[23] As we saw in Chapter 11, health insurance fraud, in the form of double billing or doctors billing the government for services that are never delivered, bilk provincial and federal governments of significant amounts of money each year.

Consumer Fraud Consumer fraud is the act of causing a consumer to surrender money through deceit or a misrepresentation of a material fact. These offences include a wide range of activities, including health care fraud, Internet auction fraud, and homeowner scams (see Table 12.1). Consumer frauds often appear as confidence games and may take some of the following forms:

• *Home-improvement fraud.* Consumers have been defrauded through the promise of low-cost home renovation. The homeowners give sizable down payments to the contractors, who have no plans to complete the job. In fact, contractors often leave the jurisdiction or declare bankruptcy.

• *Deceptive advertising.* Consumers are often lured into a store by an announcement that a product is priced low for a limited period of time. Once in the store, the customer is told that the product is sold out, and he or she is offered a substitute, typically of inferior quality or at a much higher price. Such schemes are known as "bait-and-switch advertising." Another tactic is to inflate the regular price of a product before advertising a reduced sale price for the product. In 2005, Canada's Competition Tribunal found that Sears Canada misrepresented the extent of tire savings in tire advertisements to consumers, which is in violation of the Competition Act. Sears had sold less than 2 percent of the tires at full regular price before they were advertised on sale, and the company was found guilty of misleading customers by referring to "inflated" regular prices when promoting the sale.[24]

• *Telemarketing fraud.* You are no doubt familiar with the old adage "If a deal sounds too good to be true, it probably is!" Each day, countless phone calls are made to homes with a very familiar opening script: "Congratulations! You are a grand prize winner." "Please donate money to _____ fund or _____ charity." Telemarketers lure consumers by making attractive offers (e.g., vacations, prizes, discounts on household items) that are nothing more than scams. Once you pay, your name is often added to a "sucker list" that may be sold to other scam telemarketers.

Of course, not all telemarketing is fraudulent. But the unsuspecting customer is often not in a position to determine the validity of such claims and offers. Figure 12.1 outlines some common telemarketing scams.

• *Land fraud.* Consumers are easy prey for land fraud swindlers. Here the pitch is that a certain piece of vacation or retirement property is a worthy investment, many improvements to the property will be made, and many facilities will be made available in the area. Consumers often make purchases of worthless or overvalued land.

• *Business opportunity fraud.* The objective of business opportunity fraud is to persuade a consumer to invest money in a business concern through misrepresentation of its actual worth. Work-at-home frauds are common: Victims are told they can make big money by addressing envelopes at home or performing some other simple task. Consumers lose large sums of money investing in such ventures.

TABLE 12.1 Scams Homeowners Should Watch Out For

• Loss of identity through stolen mail

• Unsolicited salespeople arriving at your door

• Moving companies that move your belongings to a "fence" instead of your next address

• Bogus lotteries and sweepstakes

• Work-at-home scams

Insurance Fraud There are many varieties of **insurance fraud:** Policyholders defraud insurers, insurers defraud the public, management defrauds

FIGURE 12.1 Common telemarketing scams.

ADVANCE-FEE LOAN OR CREDIT SCHEMES
Telemarketers seek out people with bad credit and offer them loans or credit cards in exchange for fees. Victims offered loans never receive them. Victims offered credit cards usually only get a standard application form or generic information on how to apply.

FOREIGN LOTTERY SCHEMES
Telemarketers offer victims the opportunity to "invest" in tickets in well-known foreign lotteries (e.g., Australia), or give them a "one in six" chance of winning a substantial prize. This is a common cross-border offence since it plays upon the ignorance of victims of the rules (or even the existence) of foreign lotteries. If offenders purport to sell real lottery chances but deceive victims about their chances of winning, it may be both a gambling offence and fraud. If real chances are sold without deception, it may still be a gambling offence.

INVESTMENT SCHEMES
Victims are sold "investments" in a wide range of merchandise or securities that appear to offer high profit margins. The fraud lies in misrepresenting the true value (or actual existence) of what is being sold, and/or the true extent of the risk in buying it. Common "opportunities" have involved stocks or securities, investment-grade gemstones, precious or strategic metals or minerals, and business opportunities such as oil and gas ventures, pizza ovens, and ostrich farms. These schemes commonly defraud victims more than once. Once funds have been committed, the victim can be induced to make additional payments to increase the value of the "investment" or avoid its loss. Since legitimate investments normally tie up assets for extended periods, victims often do not realize for some time that they have been defrauded.

PRIZE PROMOTION
Telemarketers "guarantee" that the victims have won valuable prizes or gifts, such as vacations or automobiles, but require victims to submit one or more payments for non-existent shipping, taxes, customs or bonding fees, or anything else the offender thinks plausible. Some schemes never provide their victims with any prize or gift, while others provide inexpensive items, often called "gimme gifts" by U.S. telemarketers and "cheap gifts" by Canadian telemarketers.

TELEFUNDING SCHEMES
These prey on the charity of victims by soliciting donations for worthy causes such as anti-drug programs or victims of natural disasters. The pitch may simply ask for donations or it may include other inducements, such as donor eligibility for valuable prizes, which never materialize (see "prize promotion" schemes). Charitable donors do not usually expect something in return for their contribution, and may thus never become aware that they have been defrauded.

TRAVEL-RELATED SCHEMES
Fraudulent telemarketers purporting to be travel agencies offer substantial travel packages at comparatively low cost. The use of travel as a commodity makes the long-distance nature of the transaction plausible. The fraud usually involves lies, misrepresentations, or non-disclosure of information about the true value of travel and accommodations, limitations or restrictions on when or where purchasers may go, or what awaits them at the destination. In some cases, the travel proves to be a complete fabrication or has so many terms and conditions as to be completely unusable.

Source: http://www.fbi.gov.

the public, and third parties defraud insurers. Policyholder fraud is most often accomplished by the filing of false claims for life, fire, marine, or casualty insurance. Sometimes an employee of the insurance company is part of the fraud and assists in the preparation of the claim. The fraud may be simple—a false death claim—or it may become complex when multiple policies are involved.

Criminologists Paul Tracy and James Fox conducted a field experiment to find out how many auto-body repair shops in Massachusetts inflate repair estimates to insurance companies, and by how much. These researchers rented two Buick Skylarks with moderate damage, a Volvo 740 GLE with superficial damage, and a Ford Tempo with substantial damage. They then obtained 191 repair estimates, some with a clear understanding that the car was insured, others with the understanding that there was no insurance coverage. The results were unequivocal: Repair estimates for insured vehicles were significantly higher than those for non-covered cars. This finding is highly suggestive of fraud.[25]

Tax Fraud Our revenue system relies on the honesty of Canadian citizens who must annually report their income to the government. **Tax fraud,** which is a crime, refers to an attempt to evade or defeat a tax, non-payment of a tax, or willful filing of a fraudulent tax return. What must the government prove? In order to sustain a conviction, the government must present evidence of income tax due and owing, willful avoidance of payment, and an affirmative act toward tax evasion.[26] Income tax fraud provides several challenges to Canada Revenue Agency and the Auditor General of Canada. Many Canadians regularly underreport their income in an attempt to avoid paying higher taxes, so the sheer numbers of people involved in this activity provide an investigative and enforcement challenge. And although the government conducts random audits of citizens, the reality is that the temptation for this type of behaviour is high, and the chances of getting caught relatively low. Added to this

> **Did You Know?**
>
> ... that tax evasion costs Canadians between $38 billion and $53 billion a year?

difficulty in detecting errors in reporting is the challenge of discerning honest mistakes from deliberate tax evasion.

There is also a fairly substantial "underground economy" in Canada. This economy is comprised of individuals who often work for cash (e.g., tips given to servers), which is not entered into the employer's records, and is not necessarily entered on the recipient's tax return either. Some industries are particularly prone to cash business.

The construction industry provides opportunities for contractors to give customers a price reduction in return for cash payment: These payments are then pocketed and not entered into the company's books. Some studies show that 15 percent or more of the construction industry regularly embarks on this practice.[27] Part of the difficulty in cracking down on these kinds of behaviours is the level of support—or lack of disapproval—among the public when it comes to "cheating the government." Animosity and frustration among many Canadians about perceived high levels of taxation, including the goods and services tax (GST), has created a feeling that Canadians are justified in "ripping off the government."[28]

Bribery, Corruption, and Political Fraud

Judges who fix traffic tickets in exchange for political favours, municipal employees who speculate with city funds, businesspeople who bribe local politicians to obtain favourable treatment—all are part of the corruption in our municipal, provincial, and federal governments. The objectives of such offences vary—favours, special privileges, services, business. The actors include officers of corporations as well as of government; indeed, they may belong to the police or the courts.

Bribery and other forms of corruption are ingrained in the political machinery of all levels of government. Examples abound: Mayors of large cities attempt to obtain favours through bribes; manufacturers pay off political figures for favours; municipal officials demand kickbacks from contractors.[29] Earlier we saw the manner in which government employees used their influence to

Protestors wait for Paul Coffin, one of the executives charged in the federal sponsorship scandal, after his conviction. Coffin had been invited to give a lecture on "ethics."

award millions of dollars in contracts to advertising companies in the sponsorship scandal.

Recently, the House of Commons Ethics Committee investigated former prime minister Brian Mulroney in what has been termed the "Mulroney-Schreiber affair." Businessman Karlheinz Schreiber allegedly paid kickbacks to politicians, including $300 000 paid to Mulroney, in exchange for political lobbying that would benefit through the sale of goods (produced by Schreiber's companies) to the federal government. Of course, political bribery and other forms of corruption do not stop at the nation's borders. Kickbacks to foreign officials are common practice, and countries develop reputations for facilitating corruption and tolerating corruption.[30]

Corruption can be found in private industry as well. One firm pays another to induce it to use a product or service; a firm pays its own board of directors or officers to dispense special favours; two or more firms, presumably competitors, secretly agree to charge the same prices for their products or services.

Insider-Related Fraud Insider-related fraud involves the use and misuse of one's position for pecuniary gain or privilege. This category of offences includes embezzlement, employee-related thefts, and sale of confidential information.

Embezzlement is the conversion (misappropriation) of property or money with which one is entrusted or for which one has a fiduciary responsibility. Consider the case of Canadian businessman Albert Walker. In 2005 Walker returned to Canada from Britain to serve the remainder of a sentence for murder he was serving in that country. In the early 1990s, the former mortgage broker and financier had fled to Britain after embezzling $3 million from his clients. Once in Britain, he killed a man whose identity he had assumed. In addition to completing the murder sentence, Walker also had 37 charges of theft and fraud to contend with.[31]

Employee-related thefts of company property are responsible for a significant share of industry losses. Estimates place such losses in the billions each year. In one example of employee fraud, former Edmonton bank manager Nicholas Lysyk defrauded the Bank of Montreal, his employer, of $16 million by falsifying loans to fictitious customers.[32] He pled guilty to 63 counts of fraud over $5000 and was sentenced to over seven years in prison.

Criminologists John Clark and Richard Hollinger have estimated that the 35 percent rate of employee pilferage in some corporations results primarily from vocational dissatisfaction and a perception of exploitation.[33] And not only goods and services are taken; time and money are at risk as well. Phony payrolls, fictitious overtime charges, false claims for business-related travel, and the like, are common.

Finally, in a free marketplace where a premium is placed on competition, corporations must guard against the *sale of confidential information* and trade secrets. The best insurance policy is employee loyalty. Where there is no loyalty, or where loyalty is compromised, abuse of confidential information is possible. The purchase of confidential information from employees willing to commit industrial espionage is estimated to be a multimillion-dollar business.[34]

CORPORATE CRIME

The idea of white-collar crime is straightforward. Employees in a business step over the line by pocketing corporate funds. Tax avoiders become tax evaders. Home owners file fraudulent insurance claims. The crimes of white-collar criminals make fascinating television and movie scripts, from complex insider trading scandals to smoke-filled, boiler-room stock frauds. The motivations for these acts and behaviours are likely similar to those for acts we refer to as conventional street crime: desire, need, greed, and thrill-seeking adventure. Of course, the white-collar criminal because of his or her occupational position has a different set of opportunities and avenues to reach these goals. Common footing is a desire for more money and more material goods; the differences that exist are in the manner reaching those similar goals takes. Still, not everyone who has a job or job-related opportunities commits white-collar crime. It may be that certain occupational settings are conducive to law breaking behaviours. We turn now to a discussion of another type of white-collar crime: corporate crime.

Corporate crime, like the white-collar crime committed by individuals, also takes place in the course of a respected and legitimate business enterprise. Corporate crime is different from the white-collar crimes we've discussed up to now in that it refers to crimes committed by one or more employees of a corporation with the aim of furthering the interests of the corporation. Often the interests of the individuals involved are furthered as well. Corporate crime can take many forms depending on its objective. For example, it includes price-fixing and the illegal restraint of trade and competition, false advertising, and the violation of environmental regulations.

Frequency and Problems of Definition

While most white-collar crime that is committed by individuals is prohibited under the Criminal Code, corporate crimes are prohibited by a wide variety of municipal, provincial, and federal laws. Enforcement of these laws is the responsibility of government inspectors, but as Laureen Snider points out, they "generally have fewer powers than police to detain suspects and search for evidence."[35] The federal Ministry of Consumer and Corporate Affairs is the agency in charge of prosecuting allegations of corporate crime. As Snider reports, the ministry receives more complaints than it can investigate, so it focuses its efforts on prosecuting those that are most serious. Under the Competition Act, many charges of false advertising are laid annually, but fines are usually less than $400 per charge. Aside from these types of charges, between 1952 and 1975 there were 89 other prosecutions under the Competition Act. Out of these, eight were acquitted, two were dismissed at a preliminary hearing, and 22 defendants were served with what amounted to a warning not to repeat their actions. Fifty-seven defendants were convicted; they were fined amounts ranging from $300 to $50 000, with an average fine of $7500.[36] If we consider that corporate crime can yield a company millions of dollars, these fines are relatively insignificant, and are likely

How Much Corporate Power Is Too Much?

In a recent report on the rise of power in the world's top 200 corporations, it was noted that corporations are larger (in gross domestic product [GDP] terms) than many sizable countries (see most recent revenue/GDP data in the following list). For example, the report stated that "General Motors is now bigger than Denmark; DaimlerChrysler is bigger than Poland; Royal Dutch/Shell is bigger than Venezuela; IBM is bigger than Singapore; and Sony is bigger than Pakistan."

Country/Corporation	GDP/Sales (US$ million)
1. United States	11 667 510.00
2. Japan	4 623 398.00
3. Germany	2 714 418.00
4. United Kingdom	2 140 898.00
5. France	2 002 582.00
6. Italy	1 672 302.00
7. China	1 649 329.00
8. Spain	991 441.60
9. Canada	979 764.20
10. India	691 876.30
11. Korea, Rep.	679 674.30
12. Mexico	676 497.30
13. Australia	631 255.80
14. Brazil	604 855.10
15. Russian Federation	582 395.00
16. Netherlands	577 259.60
17. Switzerland	359 465.30
18. Belgium	349 829.80
19. Sweden	346 404.10
20. Turkey	301 949.80
21. Austria	290 109.50
22. Wal-Mart Stores	**258 681.00**
23. Indonesia	257 641.50
24. Saudi Arabia	250 557.30
25. Norway	250 168.00
26. Denmark	243 043.30
27. Poland	241 832.50
28. Exxon Mobil	**213 199.00**
29. South Africa	212 777.30
30. Greece	203 401.00
31. General Motors	**195 645.20**
32. Finland	186 597.00
33. Ireland	183 559.60
34. Portugal	168 281.40

Country/Corporation	GDP/Sales (US$ million)
35. Ford Motor	**164 496.00**
36. Thailand	163 491.50
37. Hong Kong, China	163 004.70
38. Iran, Islamic Rep.	162 709.30
39. Argentina	151 501.20
40. General Electric	**134 187.00**
41. Malaysia	117 775.80
42. Israel	117 548.40
43. ChevronTexaco	**112 937.00**
44. Venezuela, RB	109 321.90
45. Czech Republic	107 046.80
46. Singapore	106 818.30
47. Hungary	99 712.02
48. New Zealand	99 686.83
49. ConocoPhillips	**99 468.00**
50. Colombia	97 383.93
51. Pakistan	96 114.84
52. Citigroup	**94 713.00**
53. Chile	94 104.94
54. Intl. Business Machines	**89 131.00**
55. Philippines	86 428.60
56. Algeria	84 649.01
57. American Intl. Group	**81 300.00**
58. Egypt, Arab Rep.	75 147.83
59. Romania	73 166.83
60. Hewlett-Packard	**73 061.00**
61. Nigeria	72 105.84
62. Peru	68 394.96
63. Verizon Communications	**67 752.00**
64. Ukraine	65 149.34
65. Home Depot	**64 816.00**
66. Berkshire Hathaway	**63 859.00**
67. Altria Group	**60 704.00**
68. McKesson	**57 129.20**

Country/Corporation	GDP/Sales (US$ million)
69. Bangladesh	56 844.49
70. Cardinal Health	56 829.50
71. State Farm Insurance Co	56 064.60
72. Kroger	53 790.80
73. Fannie Mae	53 766.90
74. Boeing	50 485.00
75. Morocco	50 054.92
76. AmerisourceBergen	49 657.30
77. Target	48 163.00
78. Bank of America Corp.	48 065.00
79. Pfizer	45 950.00
80. Vietnam	45 210.45
81. J.P. Morgan Chase & Co.	44 363.00
82. Time Warner	43 877.00
83. Procter & Gamble	43 377.00
84. Costco Wholesale	42 545.60

Country/Corporation	GDP/Sales (US$ million)
85. Johnson & Johnson	41 862.00
86. Dell	41 444.00
87. Sears Roebuck	41 124.00
88. Slovak Republic	41 091.85
89. SBC Communications	40 843.00
90. Kazakhstan	40 743.19
91. Valero Energy	37 968.60
92. Marathon Oil	37 137.00
93. MetLife	36 261.00
94. Safeway	35 552.70
95. Albertson's	35 436.00
96. Morgan Stanley	34 933.00
97. AT&T	34 629.00
98. Medco Health Solutions	34 264.50
99. Croatia	34 199.98
100. United Parcel Service	33 485.00

Source: Ranking based on corporation revenue data from Fortune, October 1, 2005, and GDP data from *World Bank World Development Indicators (WDI) Report, 2005.*

The authors conclude that

1. of the 100 largest economies in the world, 51 are corporations; only 49 are countries (based on a comparison of corporate sales and country GDPs);
2. the top 200 corporations' sales are growing at a faster rate than overall global economic activity. Between 1983 and 1999, their combined sales grew from the equivalent of 25 percent to 27.5 percent of world GDP;
3. the top 200 corporations' combined sales are bigger than the combined economies of all countries minus the biggest 10;
4. the top 200's combined sales are 18 times the size of the combined annual income of the 1.2 billion people (24 percent of the total world population) living in "severe" poverty;
5. while the sales of the top 200 are the equivalent of 27.5 percent of world economic activity, they employ only 0.78 percent of the world's workforce;
6. between 1983 and 1999, the profits of the top 200 firms grew 362.4 percent, while the number of people they employ grew by only 14.4 percent;
7. a full 5 percent of the top 200's combined workforce is employed by Wal-Mart, a company notorious for union-busting and widespread use of part-time workers to avoid paying benefits. The discount retail giant is the top private employer in the world, with 1 140 000 workers—more than twice as many as number two, DaimlerChrysler, which employs 466 938;
8. U.S. corporations dominate the top 200, with 82 slots (41 percent of the total). Japanese firms are second, with only 41 slots;
9. of the U.S. corporations on the list, 44 did not pay the full standard 35 percent federal corporate tax rate during the 1996–1998 period. Seven of the firms actually paid less than zero in federal income taxes in 1998 (because of rebates). These include Texaco, Chevron, PepsiCo, Enron, WorldCom, McKesson, and the world's biggest corporation—General Motors;
10. between 1983 and 1999, the share of total sales of the top 200 made up by service sector corporations increased from 33.8 percent to 46.7 percent. Gains were particularly evident in financial services and telecommunications sectors, in which most countries have pursued deregulation.

Activists often refer to these data in arguing that the grant of corporate personhood—pretending that corporations are persons—poses many risks and a distinct danger. The risks are that corporate persons will be given too many rights and achieve too great a share of power. With this power, some argue, comes the danger that corporations will victimize their stakeholders.

Questions for Discussion

1. What are these risks and what is this danger?
2. How can the evils of personhood be accommodated?
3. How does the combination of economic influence and political power pose a near-insurmountable challenge for the regulation of large multinational corporations?

perceived as modest licensing fees at best for the companies. Hardly a deterrent!

Despite what many people think, corporate crimes cause more financial and personal harm than do conventional crimes like assaults, theft, and robbery.[37] Corporate crime "causes more deaths in a month than all of the mass murderers do in a decade."[38] Another estimate places occupational deaths in Canada as accounting for more than ten times as many deaths as murder.[39] Illegal and unsafe working conditions have been implicated in far too many deaths in Canada. Yet the problems of workplace deaths and corporate crime continue. Why?

Corporate Liability   One problem with corporate crime is defining it. We have regulations and laws in place that make a variety of corporate actions illegal. But what is a corporate action, legal or illegal? Who claims responsibility for these behaviours? What makes corporate crime unique is that it is committed by a "corporation" which technically is a legal fiction. The law chooses to treat corporations as "juristic persons," which means they are held to the same standard of law as "natural persons." However, the reality of the situation is that it is impossible to imprison a "corporation" for a wrongdoing. What if a senior official of a corporation engages in unlawful activity? Can we say that the corporation committed the crime? If so, what can be done about it?[40]

Initially corporations were considered incapable of committing crimes. After all, crimes require mens rea, an awareness of wrongdoing. Since corporations are bodies without souls, they were deemed to be incapable of forming the requisite sense of wrongdoing. Nor could a corporation be imprisoned for its crimes. Further, corporations were not authorized to commit crimes; they were authorized only to engage in the business for which they had been chartered. So, how should the "blameworthiness" or "culpability" of a corporation be conceived? To illustrate the complexity of this issue, let's look at some examples where corporate liability posed problems for assigning responsibility for tragic events.

In 1989, the supertanker *Exxon Valdez* ran aground in Prince William Sound, Alaska, spilling 250 000 barrels of oil. The spill became North America's largest ecological disaster. Prosecutors were interested in determining the liability of the captain, his officers, and his crew. But there were additional and far-reaching questions. Was the Exxon Corporation liable? If so, was this a corporate crime? The same problem presented itself with the filing of criminal charges against Arthur Andersen, the company that shredded documents relating to the Enron Corporation's collapse. Should the firm bear the brunt of the crimes of its employees?

In Newfoundland the oil platform *Ocean Ranger* sank in a terrible storm, killing 84 people. An inquiry into the incident found that the drilling companies as well as the Newfoundland and federal governments were responsible. Among other things, the *Ocean Ranger* failed to meet safety requirements, was inadequately designed and constructed, and lifesaving equipment was inadequate. Who should pay for the loss of life in incidents such as these?

We discuss corporate crime by focusing on three categories of victims: customers, employees, and the environment. Next, we explore possible explanations for white-collar crime committed by individuals and corporate crime, and then discuss issues surrounding regulation of corporations and enforcement of laws governing corporations.

The Costs of Corporate Crime

Corporate crime is more financially costly than conventional street crimes.[41] Costs associated with this type of crime are often immeasurable. How does one place a monetary estimate on human lives, health, or the environment? These are precisely the kinds of costs corporate crime incurs on society. Let's discuss some of these costs through the use of a few examples.

Costs to Consumers   Price-fixing refers to a practice where companies collude and control the market price of a particular commodity, thus ensuring there is no competition and they can make as much money as they want. It is estimated that between 1958 and 1978 the cost of overcharging by oil companies cost Canadians over $12 billion because of lack of competition and price-fixing. Price-fixing is illegal, and while it is difficult to estimate the true extent of this corporate practice, most believe it is a fairly common activity. Customers are victimized financially by price-fixing since they pay more for products and services than they should have to.

Customers are also victimized when unsafe products are marketed to an unsuspecting public. The seriousness of these actions becomes more pronounced when the faulty products are deliberately sold, as in the case of the Ford Pinto. The problem with the Ford Pinto was with its design. The gas tank was placed in such a manner that if the vehicle was hit from behind, even at very low speeds, gasoline would pour into the passenger area, resulting in a blazing inferno. One author estimates that these exploding gas tanks caused somewhere between 500 and 900 deaths in the early 1970s.[42] In a very businesslike "cost/benefits" analysis, driven by the desire for profit, Ford calculated that the flawed Pinto would probably result in about 180 burn deaths, 180 serious burn injuries, and 2100 burned vehicles each year. Based on these numbers, the company projected the financial loss in civil suits related to these incidents to be approximately US$50 million. On the other hand, installing safety features to correct the design flaw, which would cost about US$10 per vehicle, would cost the company about US$137 million. The company chose the least expensive alternative and knowingly accepted the likelihood of deaths and injuries as a result of its decision.

This is the relatively straightforward version of the Ford Pinto story. Gary Schwartz has offered a more detailed cost-benefit analysis of the situation and presents a cogent argument that Ford's decision was made not only with its own interest in mind, but also those of the consumer. Schwartz suggests that the US$10 per car (to fix the flaw) works out to an amount far more significant than a surface analysis would have us believe. In fact, he calculates that the overall cost of rectifying the problem would actually be passed on to the consumer and would likely have cost consumers far more than they would be willing to pay for the loss of life that might result from the defective car design. In other words, he posits that Ford's decision was based not only on the cost of fixing the cars, but also the cost associated with losing a significant proportion of the market and consumer support.[43] Of course, his analysis raises the issue of what exactly a human life is worth. One million dollars? Twenty million? Should we even talk in these terms? Nonetheless, the Ford Pinto stands

In Mexia, Texas, Jim and Kathy Taylor hold a photo of their daughter Jessica, a cheerleader who died in a tire blowout crash on her way to a game. Their lawyer, Randell Roberts, holds a Firestone tire from the SUV. Subsequently, Firestone recalled 6.5 million of its most widely used product.

out as a disturbing example of corporate greed and the placement of profit before human life.

The case of the Ford Pinto is not an exception but rather is representative of what amounts to far too many cases of corporate crime and the costs incurred by customers who unknowingly become victims in the race for profit. More recently, the Ford SUV/Firestone-Bridgestone tire scandal served as a reminder of the pervasiveness of corporate greed and disregard for human life. Well over 100 lives have been lost as a direct result of faulty tires and rollover accidents involving the top-heavy Ford Explorers. The movies *Erin Brockovich* and *A Civil Action* retell stories involving corporations disregarding the health and lives of children and others in order to make a buck.

Costs to Employees While customers sustain their share of injuries, financial costs, and loss of life, so do employees. Danger in the workplace is a risk employees are well aware of, particularly those in certain industries. However, often the injuries suffered, diseases developed, and deaths that occur are a result of negligence or carelessness on the part of employers. One estimate is that more than one-third of all on-the-job injuries are due to illegal working conditions and that another quarter are due to legal, but unsafe, conditions.[44]

In many cases, employers have ignored warnings and orders to rectify dangerous situations; in others employers cover up their role in creating work hazards. The problem emerges: Who is ultimately responsible for the unsafe working conditions? Which corporate executive, manager, or board member should be held responsible? Even when responsibility is placed on the company, the situation is compounded by the fact that penalties for these actions, or for the lack of action, are light.

Consider, for example, the case of a petroleum company in Calgary, fined $15 000 for violating safety regulations that resulted in the deaths of three men who, without protective equipment or training, were required to enter and clean a tank containing toxic fumes. Then there is the case of asbestos poisoning. Despite company, government, and medical knowledge regarding the disease-causing nature of this chemical, workers were not informed of the risk to their health. Many who worked with asbestos died from lung diseases.

An attempt was made to hold company managers criminally responsible for the deaths of 26 miners in the Westray Mine disaster in Plymouth, Nova Scotia. Despite many occupational health and safety warnings in the months leading up to the explosion that trapped the miners, nothing was done to fix the problems. Following the explosion, the company and four mine managers were fined $10 000 for 52 violations of the Occupational Health and Safety Act. An RCMP criminal investigation resulted in the company and two managers being charged with manslaughter and criminal negligence. Nothing ever resulted from the charges.[45]

Costs to the Environment Some corporate crimes result in disastrous consequences for the environment. The effects are far ranging; sometimes they are immediate, as in the case of disease and death to plants, animals, birds, fish, and humans. Some of the effects are long lasting; the true effect may not be realized for years to come. An example of the latter instance is illustrated in the case of Aboriginal peoples living on the Grassy Narrows and Whitedog reserves in Ontario between 1962 and 1970. Although for centuries Ojibwa families were provided with clear water to drink and fish to eat from the English-Wabigoon river system, this changed when Dryden Chemicals Ltd, a pulp and paper company, began pumping tonnes of mercury into the Wabigoon River. The company used mercury to make chlorine for bleaching paper.

In this photo from 1976 are residents of the Whitedog Indian reserve, one of the reserves affected by the mercury spewed into the English-Wabigoon river system by a Dryden pulp and paper firm. These individuals protested the mercury contamination in 12-hour shifts.

The mercury pollution spread east into the English River, then to the Winnipeg River, and eventually to Lake Winnipeg, but not before contaminating fish in the river. In 1970, a lab test revealed that fish from the river system in the area contained mercury 33 times the safe eating level. When members of the reserve were tested in 1975, hair and blood samples showed that 37 of the 89 members tested had blood mercury levels five times the level considered safe for humans.[46] Prolonged exposure to mercury can cause damage to the brain, spinal cord, kidneys, liver, and to a developing fetus. Severe, prolonged exposure can cause personality changes, coma, and death.

Another example of contaminated water occurred in 2000 in Walkerton, Ontario, when *E. coli* bacteria from cattle manure washed into the drinking water system of the small rural community. Over 2500 people got sick and seven died. In this case, the culprit was not a corporation, but rather the government. A judicial inquiry following the tragedy revealed that government policy regarding drinking water safety was flawed. In addition to this issue, which resulted in 121 recommendations to improve regulations governing water safety, two untrained men who ran the Walkerton water system were blamed for not monitoring and treating the water supply properly.[47]

In the Grassy Narrows and Walkerton examples, we see an overlap between government and corporate negligence, as well as a disastrous impact on the environment and human life. Humans, however, are not the only ones affected by environmental disasters. When the tanker *Exxon Valdez* ran aground on an Alaskan reef in 1989, over 500 million

Dangerous Ground: The World of Hazardous Waste Crime

What kind of person would illegally dump hazardous waste into the waterways and landscapes of [North] America? Many would guess it might be a sinister organized crime operator. Some past published works on hazardous waste crime have, in fact, described this area of crime as being synonymous with syndicate crime.

This is the introduction to criminologist Donald J. Rebovich's controversial book *Dangerous Ground: The World of Hazardous Waste Crime,* in which he reports the results of an empirical study of hazardous waste offenders in four states. He continues:

Surprisingly enough, the study has found that, most commonly, the criminal dumper is an ordinary, profit-motivated businessman who operates in a business where syndicate crime activity may be present but by no means pervasive. The research uncovers a criminal world of the hazardous waste offender unlike any theorized in the past. It is a world where the intensity, duration, and methods of the criminal act will be more likely determined by the criminal opportunities available in the legitimate marketplace than by the orders of a controlling criminal syndicate.

Rebovich's portrait of hazardous waste crime replaces our ideas about midnight dumping and masked dumpers with

straightforward descriptions of hazardous waste treatment/storage/disposal (TSD) facilities failing to comply with regulations:

The mark of a successful hazardous waste criminal—one who can maintain his criminal lifestyle for a lengthy duration—is his skill in effectively analyzing the potential threats to his livelihood and his versatility in adapting to those threats. For many TSD-facility operators, the serious game of working the system was played out by eluding the regulatory inspectors by capitalizing on either the inspectors' unfamiliarity with treatment apparatus or their lack of diligence in inspecting thoroughly.

TSD-facility offenders did have to contend with monitoring devices, installed by regulators, that were used to gauge volume and properties of effluents released into local sewer systems to determine compliance with existing discharge standards. The mechanisms were intended to sample effluents randomly but, in reality, offenders found the system seriously flawed and did not hesitate to seize their opportunities to work the system in a new way. . . . The tests were simply rigged to elicit a false impression of the toxicity of the substances discharged into the sewer.

Rebovich makes this prediction:

The characteristics of future hazardous waste offenders, and the crimes that they

commit, will more than likely be determined by developments in several areas external to the criminal act: (1) pressure from the general public and public interest groups for stricter enforcement, (2) legislative expansion of the scope of legal coverage, (3) redesigned enforcement, and (4) future availability of affordable disposal outlets. These areas can be seen as the components of an equation that could lead to a reduction in hazardous waste crime.

Source

Donald J. Rebovich, *Dangerous Ground: The World of Hazardous Waste Crime* (New Brunswick, N.J.: Transaction, 1992). Copyright © 1992 by Transaction Publishers. Reprinted by permission of the publisher.

Questions for Discussion

1. Illegal hazardous waste practices may be punished by fining the company or industry. Should individuals be punished as well?
2. Some TSD-facility operators have claimed that they were forced to use illegal practices because it is economically impossible to take care of hazardous wastes under current regulations. What is your reaction to such a defence?

litres of crude oil were dumped into the water and over 1100 kilometres of shoreline were contaminated by the spill. The impact on the habitat of millions of living organisms is immeasurable.

These three examples are the tip of the iceberg when it comes to **environmental crimes.** We cannot know the full extent of regulation violations that result in air, water, and soil pollution every day. Part of the reason we don't have accurate data on these crimes is that regulation and enforcement of laws relating to environmental and corporate crimes are lacking.

Government Control of Corporations and Enforcement of Regulations

The legal system includes few effective laws and mechanisms to curb destruction of the environ-

ment. The emission of noxious fumes into the air and the discharge of pollutants into the water have until recently been regarded as common law nuisances, commanding usually no more than a small fine. Industrial polluters could easily absorb such a fine and regard it as a kind of business tax. In the case of Grassy Narrows, the Aboriginals were initially told to stop eating the fish and their commercial industries were shut down. But when it became clear that these measures were impacting on tourism and business in the area, these initial warnings were scaled back. Ontario government officials continued to stall on the issue, while the Ojibwa people protested what was happening. Despite clear evidence that Dryden Chemicals played a key role in this environmental and human disaster, it was five years later, in 1975, that the provincial government ordered the company to halt mercury emissions. Scientists estimated that it would take 50 to 100 years for the existing mercury in the sediment of the rivers to dissipate.[48]

Since the tragedy, the federal government has contributed more than $9 million in compensation to the First Nations people affected by the mercury contamination for economic and social development initiatives. The Mercury Disability Board was created in 1986 in response to the situation; it oversees the administration of a trust fund to individuals who have developed symptoms of mercury poisoning. In 1985 an agreement was signed committing the government and companies involved to pay a one-time compensation payment ($16.67 million, $2.75 million of which was paid by the Canadian government) to the Ojibwa people.[49] Efforts to compensate victims of disasters are admirable, but the question remains: Why was nothing done at the time the tragedy was unfolding to prevent the extent of damage and loss that occurred?

In the Walkerton case, the two men in charge of the water supply system were criminally charged with public endangerment, fraud, and breach of trust for their role in the incident. However, they pled guilty and in return the charges were reduced to risking public safety by failing to monitor and treat the water properly. One of the men, the former manager of the Walkerton utilities commission, was sentenced in 2004 to one year in jail; the other, the water foreman, received a sentence of six months to be spent confined to his home. Many believe the two men are scapegoats, saving politicians and officials higher up in the chain of command from being held accountable. In fact, Justice Dennis O'Connor, who headed the inquiry into the ordeal, said as much when he reported the following two key findings: (1) Ontario's Conservative government failed to put safeguards in place when water-testing was privatized in 1996, despite numerous warnings; and (2) Cutbacks at the province's environment ministry undermined the province's ability to deal with problems at Walkerton's water utility.[50]

The results of both of these cases illustrate the manner in which corporations and government in Canada have evaded full accountability. In the mercury contamination case, the company that made millions of dollars during the course of the poisoning contributed to the financial compensation to victims. A cost-benefit analysis of the type performed by Ford in the case of its Pinto likely would reveal that in the grand scheme of money-making ventures, the money paid to the Ojibwa people was a pittance. In the case of Walkerton, the scapegoating of two men for the actions (or lack thereof) of an entire system, including government regulatory agencies, politicians, and municipal organizations, makes the point that accountability from those truly responsible was lacking. What do we do?

Enforcing Legislation To some extent, the difficulties of enforcing legislation designed to protect the environment are enormous. For a moment, let's return to the example of the *Exxon Valdez*. What legislation could have prevented the disaster? Developing effective laws to protect the environment is a complex problem. It is far easier to define the crimes of murder and theft than to define acts of pollution, which are infinitely varied. A particular challenge is the separation of harmful activities from socially useful ones. Moreover, pollution is hard to quantify. How much of a chemical must be discharged into the water before the discharge is considered noxious and subjects the polluter to punishment? Discharge of a litre or two by one polluter may not warrant punishment, and a small quantity may not even be detectable. But what do we do with 100 polluters, each of whom discharges 10 litres?

Many other issues must be addressed as well. For instance, should accidental pollution warrant the same punishment as intentional or negligent pollution? The two men in Walkerton did not intentionally contribute to the contamination of the drinking water: They were untrained and, like many other (about 1200 to 1800) water-system operators in Ontario, were "grandfathered" into their jobs after earning two decades of on-the-job experience.[51] Since many polluters are corporations, what are the implications of penalties that force a company to install costly anti-pollution devices? To cover the costs, the corporation may have to increase the price of its product, and so the consumer pays. Should the company be allowed to lower plant workers' wages instead? Should the plant be forced or permitted to shut down, thereby increasing unemployment in the community? The company may choose to move its plant to another jurisdiction or country that is more hospitable.

Legislation in Canada Canadian legislators have developed a range of regulations and legislation to protect the environment, although the environmental regulatory framework is complicated by the fact that there is overlap between all three levels of government. We will restrict our discussion to some of the major federal efforts to regulate environmental crime, but keep in mind that provinces and municipalities have their own additional regulations and, in recent years, have become very active in the area of environmental regulation.

- *Canadian Environmental Protection Act (CEPA).* First enacted in 1988 and then amended in 1999, the CEPA is the primary federal statute dealing with environmental matters. It regulates toxic substances through their full life cycle, from the stage of research and development, to production and marketing, to use and disposal. The CEPA also regulates the import of substances into Canada, and regulates hazardous wastes. It provides broad enforcement power with substantial maximum fines and penalties and mandatory remediation mechanisms, such as environmental protection orders. In addition, in certain situations, the CEPA requires public participation and, in some cases, consultation with Aboriginal peoples.[52]

- *Canadian Environmental Assessment Act.* This act applies to federal and private projects that involve federal government funds or lands, that require federal government approvals, and other projects that might result in adverse international environmental effects or that might impact Aboriginal lands. Essentially, a project must be assessed for its effect on the environment before approval is granted.

- *Canadian Criminal Code.* The Criminal Code provides the government with the ability to criminally prosecute "organizations" for "egregious environmental violations (i.e., those causing bodily injury or death)." There is also a provision for the prosecution of employers who put their employees at risk of bodily harm, but this section can be interpreted to include people whose directions result in "environmental discharges that cause injury." Other circumstances can also result in criminal liability.[53]

In terms of the enforcement of environmental regulations, there are four general types of liabilities negligent corporations could be subject to:

- *Criminal enforcement.* According to one report, the number of prosecutions of individuals and companies for environmental offences has increased significantly in recent years.[54] At the same time, the penalties being imposed have increased in severity, though they still tend not to approach the maximum penalties possible (i.e., fines of $10 million per day for each day the offence continues). Increased effort to deter potential offenders by publicizing convictions and embarrassing offenders is another strategy being used. In addition, some offenders have been imprisoned (although only rarely).

- *Environmental penalties (EPs).* Similar to administrative monetary penalties, the stated purpose of EPs is to encourage compliance with regulations. In practice they serve a similar function to fines. In Ontario, EPs can potentially penalize offenders for up to $100 000 for each day the offence continues.

- *Administrative orders.* These are directives from government authorities to offending companies or individuals to take remedial actions to address an environmental concern or issue. Failure to comply can result in prosecution.

- *Civil actions.* Individuals or corporations that cause environmental damage to another's property or that cause harm to a person may be held responsible for the damage.

In addition to these categories of liability, directors and officers of corporations can be held personally liable to fine and, in extreme cases, imprisonment, "for causing or permitting damage to the environment regardless of whether their corporation has been prosecuted or convicted."[55]

There appear, then, to be a variety of regulations and avenues for enforcement in place, providing, of course, violations are detected. But Canada is part of an international community that shares one environment—the earth. We must also think about the global interconnections and how our shared space is affected by environmentally irresponsible behaviours elsewhere as well. In developing nations, problems of punishing and preventing pollution are enormous. Industries preparing to locate there have the power to influence governments and officials, surreptitiously and officially, into passing legislation favourable to the industry. The desire to industrialize outweighs the desire to preserve the environment. Some countries find ways to address the problem, only to relinquish controls when they prove irksome. While Japan was trying to establish its industrial dominance, for example, it observed a constitutional provision stating, "The conservation of life environment shall be balanced against the needs of economic development."[56] This provision was removed in 1970 when Japan had achieved economic strength.

We have offered a basic overview of some of the environmental regulations that exist in our country. Let's turn now to a discussion of the laws in place that deal with corporate crime generally. When we look at the context within which these laws are expected to operate, the relative lack of regulation and enforcement should become clearer. We will also integrate a theoretical examination of the complex interaction between context, regulation, and explanation of white-collar and corporate crime.

Regulating Corporations: Explaining Corporate Crime

Some writers have stated that corporations are like machines in that they have no conscience, which in human terms means they function much like a psychopathic personality.[57] These authors conclude that, as a result of this tendency, corporations must be subject to "checks by government and international regulatory bodies in order to control their destructive behaviour."[58]

Corporate misconduct is covered by a broad range of federal and provincial regulations and laws. At the start of this chapter, we discussed the Combines Investigation Act, renamed the Competition Act in 1986, which governs a variety of corporate actions, including price-fixing and false advertising. Other laws directed at corporate crime include the

John Forzani of the sporting goods retailer Forzani Group. The company agreed to pay $1.7 million in penalties after an investigation by the federal Competition Bureau suggested consumers were misled about sales prices at the company's Sport Chek and Sport Mart stores.

Food and Drugs Act (preventing the sale of contaminated food and drugs), Hazardous Products Act (preventing the sale of dangerous items), Weights and Measures Act (preventing dishonest scales), laws that protect investors, and laws that protect workers on the job.[59] The problem with these laws, as we've discussed, is in their enforcement and, in some cases, the severity of consequences. Also at issue is the question of assigning responsibility or blame for the violation of these laws. As "artificial yet legal/juristic persons," can corporations assume responsibility for the actions of the individuals within them? Or should individuals who make decisions on behalf of corporations be held responsible?

From a sociological perspective, we would be remiss if we didn't consider the fact that corporations exert considerable influence and structural restraints on individuals. It is possible—quite likely, in fact—that there are very moral, charitable individuals working in the corporate world, and, as James Hackler points out, they probably feel quite uncomfortable witnessing some of the damaging, criminal decisions and events that unfold around them. Hackler argues that "the structure of the business environment pressures even socially responsible people to be immoral."[60] The bottom line for corporations is profit. These are not altruistic organizations. "They may do things to improve their reputation, but no virtuous act will be performed by a corporation unless it is publicized or is profitable. Businesses do engage in philanthropy, but such actions are tax deductible and are intended to improve their image, leading eventually to improved profits."[61]

While it is not our aim to let corporate executives "off the hook" for their criminal activities, the context within which they are expected to operate warrants some examination. We look now at three elements of the social environment within which individuals working in corporations make decisions and act.

Corporate Culture Corporations exist to make profits. Some companies directly or indirectly encourage deviant and criminal behaviours if they encounter difficulties attaining their objectives. Employees might be asked to carry out cost-reduction policies that border on law-breaking. If they express hesitation with their tasks, they might be told that "this is the way we do things around here." "Shaving time," for example, occurs when managers illegally alter retail employee pay records or time sheets. When they express discomfort with carrying out these directives from supervisors, managers are threatened with their jobs.[62] Individuals are more likely to comply with the orders to commit illegal acts if they are under the impression that company employees at all levels embark on similar behaviours. In other words, attitudes supporting illegal behaviours among company supervisors and executives inadvertently promote similar thinking and behaviour among lower-level employees.

What we are talking about is a subculture, not unlike the subcultures we discussed earlier in this text when the topic was street crime. Cultural deviance and subcultural theories argue that lower-class youth are socialized into norms that promote behaviours considered deviant and criminal by mainstream culture. Crime occurs when obedience to subcultural norms and values causes people to break the rules of conventional society. The same process—socialization—occurs in many corporations. Norms promoting "win at all cost" permeate throughout the corporate hierarchy; new employees quickly learn what is not only acceptable but encouraged within the organization. If the values, beliefs, and behaviours are deviant, we shouldn't be too surprised to hear of criminal activities at the individual level or the corporate level. If a line-level employee at the bottom of the corporate hierarchy learns of price-fixing and false advertising being carried out by superiors, the message sent says breaking rules is okay. The employee might be less hesitant to pilfer or take home office supplies, to pocket petty cash, or to take advantage of any variety of other criminal opportunities.

Organizational Structure The pyramid structure of most corporations is conducive to diffusion of responsibility for actions, good or bad. The people at the bottom of the hierarchy answer to people directly above them in the hierarchy. These people answer to those above them, and so forth. The layers in this organizational structure provide insulation from responsibility for company wrongdoing for those at the top, who can legitimately claim that they don't directly supervise everyone in the chain of command and, therefore, cannot be held accountable for the actions taken by each link in the chain. While theoretically the directors and officials at the top of the hierarchy who permit a law violation to occur through negligence are liable to suit by the corporation itself, through a shareholders' action, in reality the courts are reluctant to

impose a duty on these directors to uncover corporate wrongdoing.[63]

Although we have simplified this process somewhat in our brief discussion, the point is that executives make decisions and set the tone for a corporation, while those executing the decisions are far removed from the decision makers. This provides the opportunity for director "disengagement" from criminal activities. Corporate workers who participated in studies on the issue complained of pressure from superiors to support incorrect viewpoints, sign false documents, and overlook superiors' wrongdoing. As John Hagan reports, about half of those surveyed "thought that their superiors frequently did not wish to know how results were obtained as long as the desired outcome was accomplished."[64]

If we stop for a moment and consider all we've covered so far in this chapter, it seems that one very good explanation for white-collar crime at the individual and corporate level is a theory we discussed much earlier in this text—rational choice. White-collar criminals and corporate directors are clearly intelligent people who have jobs—often very good jobs—that provide ample opportunity to deviate. They are responsible, clever people who are able to weigh costs and benefits and calculate risks. The context within which white-collar offences are dealt with in Canada would seem to indicate that, with low rates of detection and lower rates of prosecution, and even lower rates of punishment, committing a white-collar offence is a fairly cost-effective, low-risk endeavour. Throw into this context, a work environment that provides a subculture that promotes profit-making at any cost, and we seem to have a recipe for white-collar crime. The question we probably should be asking is why more people do not commit white-collar crimes, and why more corporations are not doing the same. The prognosis for reducing crimes of this type becomes even more dismal when we consider the broader cultural and economic context within which business is conducted in Canada.

Capitalism While the internal environment of corporations promotes profit, the external environment within which corporations operate is one that further emphasizes money making. We all benefit from living in a capitalist society, but capitalism tends to promote greed, selfishness, and crime. Capitalism and free enterprise create enormous competitive demands on businesses, including the pressure to make profits. Following the rules, respecting environmental protection regulations, and keeping workplaces safe for employees costs money. These costs detract from profit. If one company is abiding by the laws and its competitor isn't, the former company is losing money. The pressure is on to deviate, just to keep up.

Corporate takeovers are commonplace, as are the shutdown and selling out of small family-run businesses as corporate giants barge into small towns across the country. We've all heard *caveat emptor:* buyer beware. We are always on guard when purchasing an item, always looking for a sale. Consider the exchange between a customer and used car salesman, or garage sale host and customer. The drive for profit permeates much of our society; as consumers, we expect to be taken advantage of by companies. That is why we must beware.

As James Hackler points out, somewhere along the way, "structures arose that made it possible for those with power and wealth to abuse that power."[65] Conflict theorists shed some light on white-collar and corporate crime. The people who make laws tend to come from the same class as business owners. Some criminologists point to the close connection that exists between government officials, the lawmakers, and business interests. If lawmakers and white-collar lawbreakers come from the same social class, attend the same schools, and play tennis at the same country clubs, perhaps we should not be surprised at the low levels of detection and prosecution of white-collar criminal cases.

Conflict theorists, who draw on the notion of class in their explanations of criminal behaviour (see Chapter 8), would point out the close class connections between political and business elites. In other words, government is complicit in the criminal actions of white-collar and corporate criminals. Law-making is one area of concern; law enforcement is another. The public is more concerned with the young gang member who is selling drugs on the street corner than with the pharmacist who is replacing a more expensive drug with a cheaper one and pocketing the difference. Judges are more likely to identify with an older, successful, respectable male company executive charged with fraud than with an Aboriginal youth charged with assault. There is a perception among members of the public that white-collar criminals are not "real criminals" because they are not using guns and knives to commit their crimes. It is for these reasons that the criminal justice system and government authorities believe that the stigma and humiliation of being charged with an offence is enough punishment for white-collar and corporate offenders.

White-collar crimes are clearly about offences committed by individuals working in respectable occupations. But not everyone working in these occupations receives the same amount of respect, status, or power. Feminist scholars draw our attention to the fact that most corporate executives are male, and a variety of professions are still male-dominated. As a result, white-collar crime is gendered. When women commit white-collar offences, they are more likely to be of the "individual" type, such as women pilfering or committing fraud commensurate with their lower positions in business hierarchies. If only about 15 percent of corporate executive officers are women, it follows that the female corporate criminal is also relatively rare.[66]

An examination of white-collar and corporate crime reveals the complexity of the demands placed on individuals and corporations in a capitalist economy, the pressures companies exert on their employees, and the significance the drive for profit has on people. It may be that subcultural socialization within businesses prepares individuals for criminal action, but at the same time rational decision making enters into the picture, particularly since laws and their enforcement are relatively lax. Finally, conflict and feminist theories help us to understand how class and gender affect the types of white-collar offences available to men and women.

The Future of White-Collar and Corporate Crime

We know very little about the extent of economic criminality in Canada. There is no national database for the assessment of corporate criminality, and corporations are not likely to release information about their own wrongdoing. The situation is worse in other countries, especially in the developing countries of Africa south of the Sahara, where few national crime statistics are kept and where corporations are least subject to governmental control. Yet the evidence in regard to corporate crime is gradually coming in.[67]

According to Marshall Clinard and Peter Yeager, what makes it so difficult to curb corporate crime is the enormous political power corporations wield in the shaping and administration of the laws that govern their conduct. This is particularly the case with multinational corporations that wish to operate in developing countries. The promise of jobs and development by a giant corporation is a temptation too great for the governments of many such countries to resist. They would rather have employment opportunities that pollute the air and water than unemployment in a clean environment. Government officials in some developing countries can be bribed to create or maintain a legal climate favourable to the business interests of the corporation, even though it may be detrimental to the people of the host country.

The work of Sutherland, Clinard, and Yeager, and other traditional scholars, as well as a group of radical criminologists,[68] highly publicized revelations of scandalous corporate activities in recent years (see Table 12.2), and investigative reporting

A catastrophic explosion at the Union Carbide plant in Bhopal, India, on December 2, 1984, spewed clouds of deadly gas, causing nearly 6500 fatalities and more than 20 000 injuries.

by the press have all contributed to public awareness of large corporations' power to inflict harm on population groups.

TABLE 12.2 Corporate Icons under Attack

WorldCom
• WorldCom has admitted orchestrating one of the largest accounting frauds in history.
• The company admitted that it had inflated its profits by US$3.8 billion between January 2001 and March 2002.The firm was already shrouded in scandal after the departure of its founder and chief executive, Bernie Ebbers, in April. Mr. Ebbers borrowed hundreds of millions from the firm to underwrite the inflated prices he had paid for the company's own shares.

Enron
• When energy giant Enron reported its third-quarter results in October 2001, it revealed a large, mysterious black hole that sent its share price tumbling.
• The U.S. financial regulator—the Securities and Exchange Commission (SEC)—launched an investigation into the firm and its results. Enron then admitted it had inflated its profits, sending shares even lower. Enron is now bankrupt.
• Once it became clear that the firm's success was in effect an elaborate scam, a chorus of outraged investors, employees, pension holders, and politicians wanted to know why Enron's failings were not spotted earlier. The U.S. government is now thought to be studying the best way of bringing criminal charges against the company.

Arthur Andersen
• Attention quickly turned to Enron's auditors—Arthur Andersen. The obvious question was why did the auditors—charged with verifying the true state of the company's books—not know what was going on?
• Andersen reacted by destroying Enron documents, and on June 15, 2002, a guilty verdict was reached in an obstruction of justice case. The verdict signalled an end to the already mortally wounded accountancy firm. This wasn't the first time Andersen's practices had come under scrutiny—it had previously been fined by the SEC for auditing work for waste-disposal firm Waste Management in the mid-1990s.
• The Andersen case raises a wider question about accounting in the United States and how it might restore its reputation as the guarantor of the honest presentation of accounts. Notably, the verdict in the Andersen case was overturned by the United States Supreme Court in 2005.

Xerox
• In April 2002, the SEC filed a civil suit against photocopy giant Xerox for misstating four years' worth of profits, resulting in an overstatement of close to US$3 billion. Xerox negotiated a settlement with the SEC with regard to the suit.
• As part of that agreement, Xerox agreed to pay a US$10 million fine and restate four years' worth of trading statements, while neither admitting, nor denying, any wrongdoing. The penalty is the largest ever imposed by the SEC against a publicly traded firm in relation to accounting misdeeds.

The passage of environmental protection regulations in Canada and the strengthening of penalties for environmental and corporate crime in recent years are a step in the right direction. Although historically resources have been lacking, the RCMP has made enforcement of white-collar laws one of its top priorities. While the future is promising in this regard, the fact still remains: White-collar crime in a capitalist society, more often than not, pays.

Another type of crime that appears lucrative to would-be offenders, and presents challenges to law enforcement, is organized crime. As the name implies, organized crime shares with corporate crime a structured, organizational framework, and a hierarchical division of labour. The similarities don't end there. Integral to the success of organized crime is the complicit participation of legitimate businesses, corrupt politicians, and law enforcement officials susceptible to bribery. We turn now to a discussion of organized crime.

ORGANIZED CRIME

It's enough to make John Gotti turn in his grave—the feds are administering the last rites to his once-powerful Gambino crime family.

Only five days after the godfather's funeral, FBI agents yesterday pounced on 14 alleged family members and associates wanted for murder and racketeering crimes stretching back to the late '80s—a time when the Gambinos ruled New York's gangland with iron fists.

"It's a whole different world than it was," U.S. Attorney Jim Comey said, pointing proudly to a pyramid chart of rubbed-out Gambino mobsters with black crosses stamped on their faces.

"'This thing of ours'—La Cosa Nostra—is very, very different today."

The freshest black cross was on the head of one of the late Dapper Don's longest serving capos, Louis "Big Louie" Vallario, who was one of four men indicted for the 1989 execution of Staten Island businessman Fred Weiss.

One of the Gambinos' rising stars, Michael "Mikey Scars" DiLeonardo, was also arrested for the execution-style slaying. It was allegedly carried out as a favor to Gotti, who feared Weiss was cooperating with the feds.

Comey said the three indictments unsealed yesterday represented a "further dismantling of the Gambino family's leadership" and sent a signal that the feds will prevent the family from re-establishing its "violent, extortionate grip" over New York.

New York FBI assistant director Kevin Donovan described the busts as the "latest chapter in the decade-long saga of the decline of the Gambinos."

"Making money the mob way has always meant instilling fear through intimidation and violence, and it is not true that the victims of mob violence are just other mobsters," Donovan said.

Since Gotti was put away for the last time in June 1992, the Gambinos' grip over legitimate industries, such as garbage carting and the waterfront, has been pried loose.

And the family's ability to rebuild was dealt a further blow this month, when Peter Gotti, who took over from his ailing brother this year, was arrested along with 16 other soldiers and associates.

As part of the indictments unsealed yesterday, the feds claim to have busted a large-scale theft racket centered on a vegetable store in The Bronx, called Top Tomato. It was owned by Salvatore Sciandra, brother of Gambino member Carmine Sciandra, the indictment says.

Sciandra's wife, Margaret, and her mother, Mildred Scarpati, are also facing up to five years in prison after being charged with conspiracy to defraud Allstate Insurance by filing a bogus car-loss claim.

Three Gambino associates were also charged with extorting two Manhattan garment businesses.[69]

Earlier we noted that all forms of organizational criminality have in common the use of business enterprises for illegal profit. We have recognized some significant problems not only with existing definitions and conceptualizations of white-collar and corporate crime but also with the criminal justice response to such offences. Similar problems

Johnny "Pops" Papalia was the long-time head of the Hamilton Mafia. He was assassinated in 1997.

arise in efforts to deal with organized crime. It, too, depends on business enterprises. And like corporate crime, **organized crime** comes in so many varieties that attempts to define it precisely lead to frustration.

The difficulty of gaining access to information on organized crime has also hindered attempts to conceptualize the problems posed by this kind of law violation. Finally, law enforcement efforts have been inadequate to control the influence of organized crime. As will be evident, a greater effort must be made to uncover the nature, patterns, and extent of organized crime.

Defining Organized Crime

Broadly speaking, organized crime is understood to be a relatively structured hierarchical system, the goal of which is to provide consumers with goods for which there is a demand—including drugs, weapons, prostitution, some kinds of pornography, and gambling. But a specific definition is more elusive.

Despite the difficulties in definition, researchers, police, informants, and government sources provide some insights into the world of organized crime. Margaret Baere provides a continuum of organized criminal activity. She states that "organized crime is a process or method of committing crimes, not a distinct type of crime in itself." She goes on to write that this ongoing activity is one "involving a continuing criminal conspiracy, with a structure greater than any single member, with the potential for corruption and/or violence to facilitate the criminal process."[70]

Canadian legislators have struggled with formalizing a legal definition of organized crime groups and activities. It would be safe to say that defining the phenomenon is a work in progress. For example, in 1997, Parliament passed Bill C-95, which amended the Criminal Code to create the offence of "participation in a criminal organization through the commission or furtherance of certain indictable offences for the benefit of the organization." At this point it was still *not* an offence to belong to a criminal organization, although both a *criminal organization* and a *criminal organization offence* were defined within the legislation. Table 12.3 lists three definitions of organized crime that have influenced Canadian law enforcement agencies over the years.

TABLE 12.3 Definitions That Apply to Organized Crime Activities

- *Bill C-95 (1997):* A criminal organization is defined as: "any group, association or other body consisting of five or more persons, whether formally or informally organized, having as one of its primary activities the commission of an indictable offence . . . and any or all of the members of which engage in or have within the preceding five years engaged in the commission of a series of such offences."

- *Solicitor General of Canada (1998):* Organized crime is "economically motivated illicit activity undertaken by any group, association or other body consisting of two or more individuals, whether formally or informally organized where the negative impact of said activity could be considered significant from an economic, social, violence generation, health and safety and/or environmental perspective."

- *Bill C-24 (2002):* A criminal organization means "(1) a group, however organized, that is composed of three or more persons and, (2) that has as one of its main purposes or main activities the facilitation or commission of one or more serious offences, (3) that, if committed, would likely result in the direct or indirect receipt of a material benefit, including a financial benefit, by the group or by any one of the persons who constitute the group."

Sources: Department of Justice Canada, "New Criminal Anti-Gang Measures," www.justice.gc.ca/en/news/nr/1997/prgangbk.html; "Royal Assent of Bill C-24 Organized Crime Legislation," www.justice.gc.ca/en/news/nr/2001/doc_28213. html, accessed November 20, 2007; Samuel Porteous, *Organized Crime Impact Study: Highlights,* prepared for the Ministry of the Solicitor General of Canada, 1998.

An all-encompassing definition of organized crime must be general if it is to include the different types of groups that engage in the provision of illicit goods and services to consumers. Relatively unorganized street-level groups engage in these behaviours, as do highly organized groups. Leaving the realm of legal definitions for a moment, some of the general characteristics of organized crime include the following:

- It is a *conspiratorial activity* involving the coordination of many people in the planning and execution of illegal acts.

- It is about making money: *Economic gain* is the primary goal, although status and prestige are also important to organized crime group members. It is through the provision of illegal goods and services that these groups make their money.

- It is connected with *legitimate activities.* Often organized crime groups use legitimate businesses as fronts that facilitate the laundering of money attained illegally.

- It is *predatory,* using intimidation, corruption, exploitation, and violence in its dealings with associates, customers, victims, and group members who "need" disciplining.

One reason for using these general characteristics to describe organized crime is because the organized crime landscape changes and evolves over time, which can make restrictive definitions less applicable as groups change. As the opening to this section reveals, more traditional, Italian Mafia-type groups are reported to be waning somewhat in influence as other groups take over certain markets. Before we discuss the changes and diversity within the world of organized crime, let's first take a brief look at the history of organized crime in North America.

The History of Organized Crime

For many of us, the term "organized crime" conjures up images of Tony Soprano types, *Godfather* quotes and quips, or grisly movie scenes where scores are evened with broken knees, and professional hit men "whack" unsuspecting enemies. Popular culture and media representations have contributed to this stereotypical view, referred to by some criminologists as the "Mafia myth." Certainly, the Italian Mafia, with centuries-old roots in Sicily, attained a position of power in modern-day North American society, but this wasn't always the case, nor is it necessarily the case today.

The first "organized" gangs in North America originated in the slum districts of New York City, and consisted of Irish immigrants. The "Forty Thieves," the first group with a definite leadership structure in place, consisted of pickpockets, muggers, and thieves. The group preyed on other immigrants living on the Lower East Side of Manhattan from the 1820s until just prior to the Civil War. Italian immigrants, operating under the "Black Hand" (because their letters of extortion were signed with a black handprint), modelled their organizational structure on the Sicilian Mafia, and became active in the U.S. around 1890.

It was around this time, the late nineteenth century, when members of the Sicilian Mafia found their way to Canada and Australia as well. By the early 1900s, Mafia groups had surfaced in Ontario: Toronto, Hamilton, and the Niagara Peninsula became the centres of Canadian Mafia activity.[71] Prohibition had a significant impact on the "organization" and proliferation of organized crime. The Volstead Act in the United States passed in 1919 signalled the beginning of a new black market commodity: liquor. In order to meet the demand for liquor, and to effectively supply customers with the product, crime groups needed to cooperate rather than fight with

Réal Simard, former mafia hit man, leaves court after being found guilty of second-degree murder.

each other over turf and markets. Recognizing the need for cooperation, Lucky Luciano made alliances with other ethnically based crime groups and eventually created a unified crime syndicate, La Cosa Nostra (LCN).

LCN, and its primary ethnic component, the Italian Mafia was well-entrenched in Montreal, Toronto, and Vancouver by the 1930s. During the Prohibition years, Moose Jaw, Saskatchewan, became a hub for liquor distribution within Canada, but also across the border. Underground tunnels in the city facilitated the illicit transportation and distribution of alcohol between Canada and the United States (these tunnels also play a role in the history of Chinese immigrants in the city). Known as "Little Chicago," Moose Jaw was notorious for its link to organized crime in the United States (reinforced by its physical link to Chicago via the Canadian Pacific Railway's Soo Line).[72]

Montreal played a pivotal role in the establishment of the Italian Mafia in Canada. According to O. D. Carrigan, when the U.S. government placed pressure on the Mafia during the early 1950s, the group moved its gambling headquarters to Montreal.[73] As Margaret Baere explains, Montreal was chosen over Toronto because of geographical proximity, but also because the political corruption characteristic of Maurice Duplessis's provincial government in Quebec produced conditions hospitable to organized crime activities.[74]

The early history of organized crime in Canada is directly related to the Italian Mafia. What is the perceived current state of organized crime in our country?

The Diversity of Organized Crime

Organized crime is not synonymous with the Mafia. Some scholars doubt the existence of a Sicilian-based

North American crime syndicate. To the criminologist Jay Albanese, for instance,

> it is clear ... that despite popular opinion which has for many years insisted on the existence of a secret criminal society called "the Mafia," which somehow evolved from Italy, many separate historical investigations have found no evidence to support such a belief.[75]

Whether the Italian Mafia-based stronghold on organized crime is real or exaggerated, evidence indicates that during the course of the past 10 to 15 years, the organized crime landscape has changed. As mob bosses fall victim to hit men hired by rivals, and as law enforcement efforts result in imprisonment of key participants, other groups move in to share in the lucrative nature of supplying illicit goods and services. The evolving nature of the underworld has led some criminologists to characterize organized crime as a group of ethnically diverse gangs or groups who operate independently. These groups might alternately form and/or break alliances with other groups depending on what the market demands, and in response to police enforcement tactics. This conception of organized crime describes a more variable picture of the enterprise than more traditional conceptions.

Fred Desroches recently conducted a study on higher-level drug trafficking in Canada. His depiction of organized crime is one consisting of criminal networks that connect small groups of independent illicit drug entrepreneurs who use pre-existing friendship, family, criminal, business, and ethnic networks to select partners, employees, suppliers, and distributors.[76] He suggests that with the exception of a few groups like outlaw bikers, most drug-dealing organized crime groups in Canada are relatively small, comprised of three to nine members, and rely on secrecy, trust, and friendship rather than violence and corruption. He concludes that the illicit drug trade in Canada is characterized by open competition among a large number of these small criminal groupings.

While Desroches focuses on the illicit drug trade, evidence indicates that organized crime generally in Canada is also characterized by diversity. Although our coverage of active organized crime groups in the country is by no means exhaustive, it should provide some insight into the different types of groups that exist and have evolved over the years.

Italian-Based Mafia   As we discussed earlier, these groups have a long history of involvement in organized crime in North America. Part of their success has to do with their reliance on ethnicity, family loyalty, and a code of secrecy. Throughout history, these strong families have served each other and Sicily. Information has established that the structure of an Italian-based organized crime group is similar to that of a Sicilian family. Family members are joined by "adopted" members; the family is then aided at the functional level by non-member auxiliaries.[77] The use of military designations such as *caporegima* ("lieutenant") and "soldier" does not alter the fact that a criminal organization is rather more like a closely knit family business enterprise than like an army.[78] On the basis of testimony presented by Joseph Valachi in 1963, the U.S. Task Force on Organized Crime was able to construct an organization chart of the typical Mafia, or Cosa Nostra, family (see Figure 12.2).

The activities of the Mafia appear to have shifted from the once extremely violent bootlegging and street-crime operations to a far more sophisticated level of criminal activity.[79] In Canada, three main Italian-based organized crime groups are active: the Sicilian Mafia, the 'Ndrangheta, and the U.S. branch of La Cosa Nostra. These groups are prominent primarily in Ontario and Quebec, although they are active in varying levels in other provinces as well. They are involved in a variety of illegal activities, including drug trafficking, smuggling, money laundering, illegal gambling, extortion, loan sharking, stock market manipulation, and prostitution. Working relationships are maintained with several other criminal organizations, including some outlaw biker groups, as well as Asian and Eastern European-based organized crime groups.

Italian-based Mafia groups maintain a relatively low profile in Canada, engaging in legitimate business in order to conceal their illegally attained profits and hide their criminal activities.[80]

Asian-Based Organized Crime Groups Probably most well-known among these groups are the Triads, Chinese groups that came into existence in the seventeenth century as resistance fighters against the Manchu invaders. Over time they developed into crime groups and have established themselves in Canada and the United States. These groups use a "cell system," which sees small individual groups or cells operating separately and

FIGURE 12.2 Organization chart of the typical Mafia family.

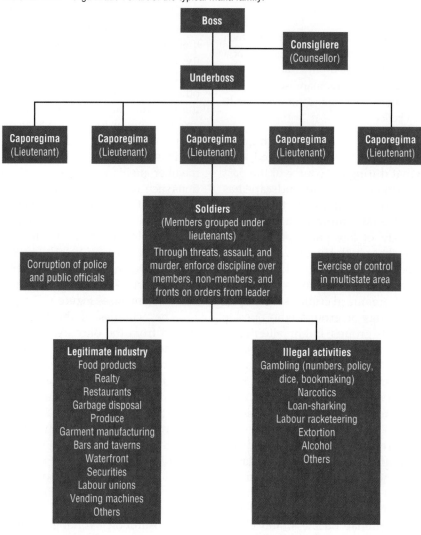

Source: President's Commission on Law Enforcement and Administration of Justice, *Task Force Report: Organized Crime* (Washington, D.C.: U.S. Government Printing Office, 1967), p. 9.

secretly within the larger organization. Other Asian-based groups are said to follow this same cell structure. Generally, they participate in trafficking of drugs, primarily heroin, cocaine, and ecstasy, and are actively involved in the large-scale cultivation and exportation of marijuana through residential growing operations across Canada, particularly in British Columbia. According to Criminal Intelligence Services Canada, 95 percent of the heroin smuggled into Canada originates in Southeast Asia.[81] Based primarily in Montreal, Toronto, Vancouver, Calgary, and Edmonton, the groups are also involved in illicit trade in drugs, firearms, and illegal human migrants. Other

activities include home invasions, kidnapping, theft, loan-sharking, and the production of counterfeit currency, software, and credit cards. As with the Italian-based crime groups, these groups also conceal their illegitimately accrued profits by laundering the money through legitimate business investments.

Eastern European Organized Crime Groups
Influenced by the change from a communist to capitalist economy, organized crime groups are seizing opportunities within the former Soviet Union and continue to expand their activities in Canada and the United States. Power tends to be

Organized crime groups are heavily involved in a variety of illegal enterprises, including prostitution. Often these groups use legitimate businesses as a front for their illegal activities.

As the group continues to expand, the Hell's Angels take over smaller outlaw biker groups. In this photo, members of the Winnipeg chapter of Los Bravos wait to meet with the Hell's Angels who took them under their wing in 2000.

concentrated among groups from the former Soviet Union but also the Ukraine, Belarus, and several other regions. In Canada the groups operate primarily out of southern Ontario but are increasingly active in larger urban centres in Quebec and British Columbia.[82] The groups are fairly flexible, moving into areas and markets that appear vulnerable for exploitation. Their crimes range from street-level crime to fraud that requires sophisticated technological expertise. They participate in the range of activities characteristic of other organized crime groups, including prostitution, smuggling, theft, drug trafficking, and money laundering. In addition, these groups are actively involved in the theft and exportation of vehicles, and are extensively involved in smuggling goods from Canada into the former Soviet Union and other European countries.

> **Did You Know?**
>
> . . . that 40 percent of illicit massage parlours operating in Toronto are believed to be controlled by Russian organized crime groups?

Outlaw Motorcycle Groups   It all started in California on July 4, 1947, when an American Motorcycle Association (AMA)–sponsored motorcycle event resulted in a clash between groups within the AMA. Two groups involved in the violence were the Booze Fighters and the Hell's Angels. Police officers and bikers were injured and the small town where the event took place was left a mess. Following this incident, the AMA declared that 99 percent of its members were law-abiding, clean-living folks who loved the sport; 1 percent of the members were troublemakers. The so-called troublemakers developed badges proclaiming their affiliation with the 1 percent. The incident and its aftermath have been credited

with solidifying a major organized crime society in North America.

Outlaw biker groups are tightly knit, highly structured groups that violently control their territories. They use violence to expand their membership, intimidate other clubs, discipline members, and intimidate the public. The groups engage in extortion, prostitution, drug trafficking (marijuana, hashish, cocaine), and the manufacture and sale of illicit drugs such as ecstasy, methamphetamine, and PCP. The Hell's Angels is the largest and most well-established group in Canada, with over 30 chapters across the country.[83] This does not stop other groups from vying for influence and territory. Quebec in particular has witnessed extremely violent clashes between the Hell's Angels and the Bandidos, although other groups like the Rock Machine have also contributed to the violence. Despite conflicts with each other, outlaw biker groups have developed strong connections with the Italian-based Mafia in eastern Canada and with Asian groups as well.

Aboriginal Crime Groups   There is some debate about the level of organization of Aboriginal groups in Canada. One study suggests that Aboriginal groups in Ontario are politically motivated and organized in the smuggling of cigarettes and firearms.[84] Groups in the West, however, appear less organized. Groups like the Manitoba Warriors, the Alberta Warriors, Indian Posse, Redd Alert, and Native Syndicate are generally involved in street crime, including drug trafficking, prostitution, break-and-enter, robberies, assaults, intimidation, and vehicle theft. These groups are notorious for the use of violence in their criminal activities but also in their recruitment techniques. Aboriginal gangs are also well-established in prison populations, using these

The Business of Organized Crime

Have you ever asked yourself (or anyone else) what the world's largest business is? Oil? Autos? Computers? Steel? It's none of these. Drug and arms trafficking by major crime syndicates take first and second place.(1) The United Nations estimates that the combined annual sales from organized crime range from US$700 billion to US$1000 billion. Trafficking in narcotics alone exceeds US$300 billion each year.(1, p. 22)

Much of the expansion of organized crime in recent years has been made possible by the fragile political and economic situation of developing and transitional countries. A prime example is post–cold war Russia. Enticed by the weakened judicial system, reduced law enforcement, and a susceptible bureaucracy, organized-crime groups such as the Russian and Sicilian Mafias have established a firm hold on the ex-Soviet states. Organized crime has moved in, shielded by the need for foreign capital investment. The Russian Mafia alone, with over 3 million members in 5700 gangs, controls approximately one-quarter of the commercial and retail

banks, as well as tens of thousands of other legitimate businesses. Gangs traffic in everything from raw material to nuclear weapons.

The infiltration of organized crime into legitimate businesses poses a particularly significant threat to the emerging economic order of transitional economies. Politically and economically, the Mafia is becoming part of the business culture in certain markets. "Instead of being a threat to the legal order, the Mafia is becoming its rival and even its replacement. Wherever and whenever the state fails to fulfill the basic needs of its people, this creates a vacuum which the criminals can exploit."(2)

The effects of the infiltration of organized crime are unmistakable. On November 21, 1994, member states of the United Nations gathered in Naples, Italy, at the World Ministerial Conference on Organized Crime. One conclusion was very clear. "Traditionally insular and clannish, the world powers of crime—the Hong Kong–based Triads, the Cali Cartel of Colombia, the Italian Mafia, the Japanese Yakuza, the Russian Vory v. Zakonye and affiliated

newcomers, and rapidly expanding West African crime groups—are now making deals with each other and taking tentative steps to maximize their operations."(1) The cooperative nature of organized crime has changed the realities of law enforcement efforts. The policing of organized crime is no longer a regional or local endeavour. To control the effects of the single largest business in the world, law enforcement efforts must also be transnational and cooperative.

Among the steps called for at the conference:

• Global assessment and regular monitoring of organized transnational crime.
• New legislation, both substantive (against the crimes) and procedural (against the criminals).
• Special cooperative programs and preventive strategies.
• A concerted attack on money laundering to chip away at the economic advantage of organized transnational crime and criminals.

Here is why the steps are needed. Each national criminal group, as the table in this

arenas as avenues for recruitment and drug distribution. In fact, the Redd Alert began as a prison gang and then, as members were released, developed a street presence. A discussion of Aboriginal gangs must include recognition and analysis of the crucial role Aboriginal overrepresentation in the criminal justice system plays in the genesis and perpetuation of these groups.[85]

Attempting to Control Organized Crime

Specific legislation and law enforcement programs have allowed governmental agencies to assert some measure of control over organized crime. Attempts to control organized crime are numerous and include amendments to the law, shifting of resources within law enforcement agencies to focus on organized crime, increasing the power of police to arrest, and the power of courts to prosecute organized criminals. For example, Bill C-69 gives police more power to seize goods suspected of

being purchased with the proceeds of crime. Section 312 of the Criminal Code makes it an offence to possess anything derived from an indictable offence. Bill C-24 provided for $200 million over five years to give police new measures to fight organized crime. In addition, Canada is party to agreements with the United States and the international community in an effort to reduce organized crime. As the diversity of organized crime groups operating within our borders reveals, an international effort is necessary to effectively deal with organized crime groups.

In the United States, cases have been successfully prosecuted under the **Racketeer Influenced and Corrupt Organizations (RICO) Act** of 1970.[86] This statute attacks racketeering activities by prohibiting the investment of any funds derived from racketeering in any enterprise that is engaged in interstate commerce. In addition, the **Federal Witness Protection Program,** established under the Organized Crime Control Act of 1970, has

Organization	Size	Major Activities	International Ties
Colombian cartels	Hundreds of men	Drug trafficking—manage entire cycle from production to distribution	U.S. and Sicilian Cosa Nostra, Chinese Triads, Japanese Yakuza
Chinese Triads (Hong Kong and Taiwan)	150 000 in 5 groups	Drugs, usury, illegal immigration, gambling, racketeering, prostitution, money laundering	Colombian cartels, Japanese Yakuza, U.S. groups
Russian Mafia	3 million in 5700 gangs	Trafficking in everything—army weapons, nuclear materials, drugs, money laundering, prostitution, counterfeiting	Settlements in the U.S., Colombian cartels, Sicilian Cosa Nostra
Sicilian Cosa Nostra	5000 members	International drug trafficking clearinghouse, money laundering on a grand scale, arms trafficking, extortion	U.S. Cosa Nostra, Colombian cartels, Mafia families in western Europe, Russian Mafia, Chinese Triads
U.S. Cosa Nostra	3000 soldiers in 25 families	Drug and arms trafficking, illegal gambling, prostitution, extortion, business activities	Colombian cartels, Russian Mafia, Sicilian Cosa Nostra
Japanese Yakuza	60 000 full-time, 25 000 associates, in 1246 clans	Amphetamine traffic in Asia and U.S., extortion, prostitution	Chinese Triads, Colombian cartels, German groups, Russian Mafia, U.S. Cosa Nostra

box shows, is allied with most of the others across the globe.

Sources

1. ANSA News Agency Dossier on Organized Crime, *U.N. World Ministerial Conference on Organized Transnational Crime*, Naples, Italy, Nov. 21–23, 1994.
2. "Russian Organized Crime," *Jane's Intelligence Review*, **8**, May 1, 1996: 195.

Questions for Discussion

1. Why is organized crime the world's largest business?
2. What efforts to control the rise of organized crime seem most promising?

made it easier for witnesses to testify in court by guaranteeing them a new identity, thus protecting them against revenge. Currently 14 000 witnesses are in the program.[87]

Yet, some would argue that enforcement and law-making is simply not enough. We must look at the causes or motivations for organized crime and if we can address the motivation to engage in this activity, then we can reduce or eliminate organized crime. The history of organized crime points to blocked opportunities for particular groups of people as a contributing factor to its existence. Individuals engaged in organized crime seek the same goals as many of us do in our work: money, status, prestige. Robert Merton might suggest that organized criminals are prototypical "innovators"—individuals whose access to legitimate means is limited because of immigrant status, poverty, or disadvantage generally. Yet, these are individuals who aspire to the so-called "American Dream" and are willing to do whatever it takes to reach culturally prescribed goals. Victims of the social structure, they astutely hone into a demand for goods and services and seek to make money by fulfilling that demand.

Steven Messner and Richard Rosenfeld added to Merton's theory by pointing out the ways in which societal institutions promote the achievement of the "American Dream": the pursuit of money and success has become a major emphasis throughout society, including such institutions as school, work, and family. Even religious organizations are run like businesses today. Should we be surprised, then, when organized criminals likewise pursue successful and lucrative careers, albeit through illegitimate means?

Individuals or groups left out of the legitimate opportunity structure are one component to the issue of organized crime. The other component—perhaps more important—is the demand for illicit goods. If we reflect on the genesis of organized crime, the event that is credited with making

"I TAKE IT YOU'RE ALSO IN THE FEDERAL WITNESS-PROTECTION PROGRAM."

ScienceCartoonsPlus.com

organized crime organized was the prohibition of alcohol. When certain goods and services are prohibited—goods for which a demand exists—groups will inevitably arise to fulfill the demand. How do we deal with organized crime then? By legalizing all illicit goods and thereby reducing the demand?

Of course, such a suggestion is preposterous and would never sell to the public. But it is a valid suggestion, if we consider the raison d'être for organized crime. However, it is also highly likely that legalization of "all illicit goods and services" would create a black market for *cheaper* illicit goods and services, and so the demand continues in one form or another. Another option is to continue with our enforcement tactics and, most importantly, increase international cooperation in the passing of laws and in creating agreements between countries that crack down on money laundering. But if the problem is structural in nature, regardless of how many Gottis we put away in prison, other up and coming youngsters will rise to fill their positions.

REVIEW

1. What is white-collar crime?

Organizational crimes are characterized by the use of a legitimate or illegitimate business enterprise for illegal profit. As corporations grew in the nineteenth and twentieth centuries, they amassed great wealth, and many corporations abused their economic power. Government stepped in to curb such abuses by legislation. In 1889, the federal government passed the Combines Investigation Act, which was renamed the Competition Act in 1986. Edwin Sutherland, who provided the first scholarly insight into the wrongdoing of corporations, originated the concept of **white-collar crime** (p. 293).

2. What is corporate crime?

Subsequent scholars have distinguished white-collar crime, committed by individuals, from **corporate crime** (p. 299), committed by business organizations. Corporate or individual white-collar offences include securities-related crimes, such as **bankruptcy fraud** (p. 295) of various kinds, fraud against the government, **consumer fraud** (p. 296), **insurance fraud** (p. 296), **tax fraud** (p. 297), political fraud; and **insider-related fraud** (p. 298). In the twentieth century, corporations have been subjected to criminal liability for an increasing number of offences, including **environmental crimes** (p. 305).

3. What is organized crime?

Organized crime (p. 313) refers to groups, often organized much like legitimate businesses, and sometimes linked to these businesses, which fulfill demands for illicit goods and services. These groups, such as the Italian-based Mafia, Asian-based groups, Eastern European groups, outlaw bikers, and Aboriginal gangs, are also known for their use of violence. Controlling organized crime is challenging, particularly because these groups permeate international boundaries. However, Canadian legislators and law enforcement agencies have passed a number of laws and dedicated significant resources to enforcing these laws. The **Federal Witness Protection Program** (p. 318) and the **Racketeer Influences and Corrupt Organizations (RICO) Act** (p. 318) in the United States help officials in dealing with this type of crime. Because there will always be a demand for illegal goods and services, eliminating organized crime is highly unlikely.

CRIMINOLOGY & PUBLIC POLICY

"Sutherland challenged the traditional image of criminals and the predominant etiological theories of crime of his day. The white-collar criminals he identified were middle-aged men of respectability and high-social status. They lived in affluent neighborhoods, and they were well respected in the community. Sutherland was not the first to draw attention to such criminals. In earlier decades, scholars such as W. A. Bonger (1916) and E. A. Ross (1907) and popular writers such as Upton Sinclair (1906) and Lincoln Steffens (1903) pointed out a variety of misdeeds by businessmen and elites. However, such people were seldom considered by those who wrote about or studied crime and were not a major concern of the public or policy makers when addressing the crime problem." (*Source:* David Weisburd and Elin Waring, *White-Collar Crime and Criminal Careers* [Cambridge: Cambridge University Press, 2001], p. 8.)

Questions for Discussion Professors David Weisburd and Elin Waring make the point, in the introduction to their book *White-Collar Crime and Criminal Careers,* that much of the conventional wisdom of white-collar offenders is untrue. These researchers previously established that white-collar offenders are not "elite" offenders as Sutherland conceived. White-collar criminals generally come from the middle class and have multiple contacts with the criminal justice system. White-collar offenders have criminal careers as well! What can you conclude from the similarity between and among white-collar and street criminals? Should criminologists expect meaningful differences in the life course of either offender? Should policy makers ensure different or similar treatment in the criminal process?

YOU BE THE CRIMINOLOGIST

For obvious reasons, the extent of corporate crime and organized crime is difficult to assess and measure. But criminologists do not shy away from significant challenges. How would you approach the problem of assessing and measuring crimes committed by corporations and organized criminals? Would you administer a survey? Embark on a participant observation study as Daniel Wolf did (described in Chapter 2, see page 27). What might be some of the advantages or drawbacks of collecting your information in this manner? Would you rely on official statistics? Why or why not?

Visit the Online Learning Centre: www.mcgrawhill.ca/olc/adler

PUBLIC ORDER CRIMES

CHAPTER **13**

CHAPTER QUESTIONS

1. What is drug abuse? Is it related to crime?

2. What is the relationship between alcohol and crime?

3. How do we legislate sexual morality?

Strip clubs and X-rated shops tend to be concentrated in the seedier parts of towns.

In cities across the country and around the world, people buying and selling illicit goods and services congregate in certain areas that are easily identifiable by theatre marquees advertising live sex shows. Shops feature everything from child pornography to sadomasochistic slide shows; prostitutes openly solicit clients; drunks propped up in doorways clutch brown bags; drug addicts deal small amounts of whatever they can get to sell to support their habits. The friendly locals will deliver virtually any service to visitors, for a price.

The activities involved—prostitution, drunkenness, sex acts between consenting adults for money, drug use—were commonly called "victimless" crimes. Perhaps that is because it was assumed that people who engaged in them rationally chose to do so and did not view themselves as victims. Often no one complains to the police about being victimized by such consensual activity. But contemporary forms of such activities and their ramifications may entail massive victimizations: How many murders are committed during drug gang wars? How many thefts are committed by addicts seeking to support their habits? How much damage is done to persons and property by drunken drivers? Does pornography encourage physical abuse? And what of the future of children sold for prostitution?

DRUG ABUSE AND CRIME

A woman arrives at an airport in a major urban centre with very few belongings, no hotel reservations, no family or friends in the country, and a passport showing eight recent trips from Bogotá, Colombia. A pat-down and strip search reveal a firm, distended abdomen, which is discovered to hold 88 balloons filled with cocaine.[1] Elsewhere, a heroin addict admits that "the only livin' thing that counts is the fix . . . : Like I would steal off anybody—anybody, at all, my own mother gladly included."[2] In large cities, crack cocaine has transformed some of the toughest gangs into ghetto-based drug-trafficking organizations that guard their turf with automatic weapons and assault rifles.[3]

On a college campus in the west, a crowd sits in the basement of a fraternity house drinking beer and smoking pot through the night. At a beachfront house in Nova Scotia, three young professional couples gather for a barbecue. After dinner they sit down at a card table in the playroom. On a mirror, someone lines up a white powdery substance into rows about 3 mm wide and 2.5 cm long. Through rolled-up paper they breathe the powder into their nostrils and await the "rush" of the coke. In the north, a group of young Aboriginal teens inhale paint thinner instead of attending school.

These incidents demonstrate that when we speak of the "drug problem," we are talking about a wide variety of conditions that stretch beyond our borders, that involve all social classes, that in one way or another touch most people's lives, and that cost society significant sums of money. The drug scene includes manufacturers, importers, primary distributors (for large geographical areas), smugglers (who transport large quantities of drugs from their place of origin), dealers (who sell drugs on the street and in crack houses), corrupt criminal justice officials, users who endanger other people's lives through negligence (train engineers, pilots, physicians), and even unborn children (see Table 13.1). As the comparatively easy-to-produce synthetic "designer drugs" like ecstasy and methamphetamine become more popular, the typical drug producer and supplier is changing—from more organized groups with international connections, to local organized and not-so-organized crime groups who have, for example, their own "meth labs."

The drug problem is further complicated by the wide diversity of substances abused, their varying effects on the mind and body, and the kinds of dependencies users develop. There is also the much-debated issue of the connection between drug use and crime—an issue infinitely more complex than the stereotype of maddened addicts committing heinous acts because they either were under the influence of drugs or needed to get the money to support a habit. Many of the crimes we have discussed in earlier chapters are part of what has been called the drug problem. Let us examine this problem in detail.

The History of Drug Laws: Constructing the Immoral and Illegal

The use of chemical substances that alter physiological and psychological functioning dates back to the Old Stone Age.[4] Egyptian relics from 3500 B.C. depict the use of opium in religious rituals. By 1600 B.C., an Egyptian reference work listed opium as an analgesic, or painkiller. The Incas of South America are known to have used cocaine at least 5000 years ago. Cannabis, the hemp plant from which marijuana and hashish are derived, also has a 5000-year history.[5]

Since antiquity, people have cultivated a variety of drugs for religious, medicinal, and social purposes. The modern era of drug abuse in Canada and the United States began with the use of drugs for medicinal purposes. By the nineteenth century, the two components of opium, which is derived from the sap of the opium poppy, were identified and given the names "morphine" and "codeine." Ignorant of the addictive properties of these drugs, physicians used them to treat a wide variety of human illnesses. So great was their popularity that they found their way into almost all patent medicines used for pain relief and were even incorporated in soothing syrups for babies (Mother Barley's Quieting Syrup and Mumm's Elixir were very popular).

During the Civil War in the United States, the use of injectable morphine to ease the pain of battle casualties was so extensive that morphine addiction among veterans came to be known as the "soldier's disease."[6] By the time the medical profession and the public recognized just how addictive morphine was, its use had reached epidemic proportions. Then in 1898, the Bayer Company in Germany introduced a new opiate, supposedly a non-addictive

TABLE 13.1 Roles and Functions in the Drug Distribution Business Compared with Those in Legitimate Industry

Approximate Role Equivalents in Legal Markets	Roles by Common Names at Various Stages of the Drug Distribution Business	Major Functions Accomplished at This Level
Grower producer	Coca farmer, opium farmer, marijuana grower	Grow coca, opium, marijuana: the raw materials
Manufacturer	Collector, transporter, elaborator, chemist, drug lord	All stages for preparation of heroin, cocaine, marijuana as commonly sold
Traffickers		
Importer	Multikilo importer, mule, airplane pilot, smuggler, Trafficker, money launderer	Smuggling of large quantities of substances into the country
Wholesale distributor	Major distributor, investor, "kilo connection"	Transportation and redistribution of multikilograms and single kilograms
Dealers		
Regional distributor	Pound and ounce men, weight dealers	Adulteration and sale of moderately expensive products
Retail store owner	House connections, suppliers, crack-house supplier	Adulteration and production of retail-level dosage units (bags, vials, grams) in very large numbers
Assistant manager, security chief, or accountant	"Lieutenant," "muscle men," transporter, crew boss, crack-house manager/proprietor	Supervises three or more sellers, enforces informal contracts, collects money, distributes multiple dosage units to actual sellers
Sellers		
Store clerk, salesmen (door-to-door and phone)	Street drug seller, runner, juggler	Makes actual direct sales to consumer; private seller responsible for both money and drugs
Low-Level Distributors		
Advertiser, security guards, leaflet distributor	Steerer, tout, cop man, lookout, holder runner, help friend, guard, go-between	Assists in making sales, advertises, protects seller from police and criminals, solicits customers; handles drugs or money but not both
Servant, temporary employee	Run shooting gallery, injector (of drugs), freebaser, taster, apartment cleaner, drug bagger, fence, money launderer	Provides short-term services to drug users or sellers for money or drugs; not responsible for money or drugs

Source: Bruce D. Johnson, Terry Williams, Kojo A. Dir, and Harry Sanabria, "Drug Abuse in the Inner City: Impact on Hard-Drug Users and the Community," in *Drugs and Crime,* vol. 13: *Crime and Justice,* Michael Tonry and James Q. Wilson, eds. (Chicago: University of Chicago Press, 1990), p. 19. © 1990 by the University of Chicago. All rights reserved. Reprinted by permission of the University of Chicago Press.

substitute for morphine and codeine. It came out under the trade name Heroin; yet it proved to be even more addictive than morphine.[7]

When cocaine, which was isolated from the coca leaf in 1860, appeared on the drug scene, it, too, was used for medicinal purposes. (Its use to unblock the sinuses initiated the "snorting" of cocaine into the nostrils.) Its popularity spread, and soon it was used in other products: Peruvian Wine of Coca ($1 a bottle in the Sears, Roebuck catalogue);

a variety of tonics; and, the most famous of all, Coca-Cola, which was made with coca until 1903.[8]

As the consumption of opium products (narcotics) and cocaine spread, Canada and many U.S. states passed a variety of laws to restrict the sale and use of these substances. In Canada, early drug legislation was closely connected to anti-Asiatic sentiment in the West. Chinese immigrants were brought in to work on the railway and other large construction projects because they were willing to work for one-half to two-thirds what European workers received. These single men, once the work was completed, were perceived as a threat to the jobs of others. These "others" also believed that the Chinese immigrant men were immoral: They gambled and smuggled opium into the country. Although both activities were legal at the time, religious groups and moral crusaders targeted these behaviours as unsavoury.

As a result of these economic and political factors, in 1907 the Asiatic Exclusion League initiated a riot that involved about 20 000 people and targeted the businesses and shops of Chinese and Japanese people in Vancouver. In response, the government sent Deputy Minister of Labour Mackenzie King to investigate the effects of the riot, and ascertain the extent of damage to the buildings and businesses. During his investigation he learned of the opium use among the Chinese population and concluded that the only way to eliminate the problems that sparked the riot was to eliminate the Chinese. One way to do so was to criminalize an activity associated with this group: opium use. Following the submission of his report to government officials, the Opium Act of 1908 was passed with little discussion. Interestingly, while opium use was criminalized by this act, the types of opiates used in medicine were not.[9] In 1911, the Opium and Drug Act expanded the list of prohibited substances and widened police power of search and seizure.

By the 1920s, the public was calling for harsher penalties for drug users. Fuelling their concern was a series of sensationalistic *Maclean's* magazine articles written by Judge Emily Murphy under the pen name "Janey Canuck." The articles were exaggerated, biased accounts that were blatantly racist, but that nonetheless struck a chord with citizens and legislators alike. Murphy compiled the articles and additional writings into *The Black Candle*, published in 1922. The book aroused public opinion to the point where the government, in response to the pressure, passed the Opium and Narcotic Drug Act of 1923, which made cannabis hemp illegal.[10]

Earlier in the text we've discussed how factors other than "criminal behaviour" influence society's reaction to events and situations. Anti-drug legislation in Canada was influenced by a variety of factors and actors, including anti-Asiatic sentiments based in part on labour market and political factors. Moral entrepreneurs such as Emily Murphy and Mackenzie King played a significant role in influencing condemnation of the use of opium and rallying public support for legislation that would control its use. In addition, bureaucratic concerns entered into the picture. Specifically, the RCMP was on the brink of ruin and possible dissolution in the early 1900s. Honing in on the need to control narcotics, which up to this point was under the purview of the Division of Narcotic Control branch of the Department of Health, the RCMP convinced the public they could wage a war on drugs (and, as James Hackler points out, save their jobs).[11] The result? The Mounties became leaders in the moral crusade against illicit drug use in Canada.

In the United States, growing concern over the increase in addiction led in 1914 to the passage of the Harrison Act, and in 1937 to the Marijuana Tax Act, which, like the corresponding Canadian legislation, was designed to regulate the domestic use, sale, and transfer of opium and coca products. However, as discussed in Chapter 12, by restricting the importation and distribution of drugs, such legislation paved the way for the drug smuggling and black-market operations that are so deeply entrenched today.

Since these initial laws were passed, Canadian federal laws were passed to clarify sections of the drug laws and revise penalties. The Food and Drug Act (FDA) and the Narcotic Control Act (NCA) determined definition, enforcement, and punishment of illicit substances until 1996, when the government repealed the NCA and part of the FDA, replacing them with the Controlled Drugs and Substances Act. Depending on the substance involved, the role of the accused (possession, trafficking, exporting), and his or her prior offences, maximum punishments outlined in the act range from a fine of $1000 or $2000 and/or a prison term of six months for less serious offences, all the way to life imprisonment for more serious offences.[12] Part of Prime Minister Stephen Harper's get-tough-on-crime campaign involves implementing "mandatory minimum" sentences for serious drug offences. The current practice of providing maximum sentencing options only is perceived to be lenient by the government representatives seeking change.

The Extent of Drug Abuse

In 2006 police reported drug offences increased by 2 percent over the previous year. Cocaine-related offences contributed significantly to the increase:

The total number of cocaine-related charges (22 074) was 13 percent higher than in 2005. Other drug offences, including charges related to crystal meth, rose 8 percent. Although cannabis offences decreased by 4 percent in 2006, historically, the substance (other than alcohol) most frequently used in Canada has been marijuana. This was the case in 2006. Of the 96 164 police-reported drug offences for the year, 45 percent were for cannabis possession and an additional 16 percent were for trafficking, importing, or producing cannabis.[13]

The Canadian Addiction Survey, which is based on interviews with about 14 000 Canadians aged 15 and over, reports that almost 45 percent of Canadians report using cannabis at least once in their lifetime. Fourteen percent report using the substance in the year prior to the survey.[14] The researchers found that young people are more likely to have ever used cannabis: 70 percent of those between 18 and 24 reported using it at least once. Younger people are also more likely to have used cannabis recently; almost 30 percent of 15- to 17-year-olds and about 47 percent of 18- and 19-years-old had used cannabis in the past year.[15]

Rates of use for illicit drugs other than cannabis are significantly lower. Hallucinogens were used by 11 percent of the respondents at some point during their lifetime, 10 percent had used cocaine, about 6 percent had used speed, and 4 percent had used ecstasy. Lifetime use of inhalants, heroin, steroids, and drugs by injection was about 1 percent. The survey results reveal that one in six Canadians has used an illicit drug other than cannabis; however, few had used these drugs during the previous year.[16]

It is difficult to measure how many people use drugs in any given period. Official crime reports show a decline in the overall rate of drug-related incidents beginning in the 1980s. The decline continued until the early 1990s, when drug-related incidents began to climb. The cannabis offence rate, for example, rose approximately 80 percent from 1992 to 2002, largely a result of an increased number of possession offences. Trafficking offences, however, declined over the same time period.

Drug-related crime reports represent one type of crime where politics, definition, and enforcement influence the numbers. The former Liberal federal government proposed a bill that would have moved the country one step closer to decriminalization of marijuana. As a result, people in possession of small amounts of marijuana would no longer be charged with a criminal offence. However, when the Conservatives came into power in 2006, quashing the bill was one of their first orders of business. As a result, experts suggest that many Canadians, thinking the decriminalization bill had passed, were "spark[ing] up in public without fear of reprisal."[17] Many people were charged with an offence that would have been non-existent had the shift in political party control not occurred. The point here is that with drug laws and enforcement, as with other public order offences, a variety of factors—political, economic, historical—affect the criminalization of substances and behaviours, and influence statistics. Table 13.2 provides some facts on the use and abuse of illicit and licit drugs, and Figure 13.1 on page 329 outlines drug use among youth in grades 7 and 12.

Patterns of Drug Abuse

New and more potent varieties of illicit substances, as well as increasing levels of violent crime associated with drug abuse, have led researchers to ask many questions about the phenomenon. Is drug abuse a symptom of an underlying mental or psychological disorder that makes some people more vulnerable than others? Some investigators argue that the addict is characterized by strong dependency needs, feelings of inadequacy, a need for immediate gratification, and lack of internal controls.[18] Or is it possible that addicts lack certain body chemicals and that drugs make them feel better by compensating for that deficit?

Perhaps the causes are environmental. Is drug abuse a norm in deteriorated inner cities, where youngsters are learning how to behave from older addicted role models? Do people escape from the realities of poverty by retreating into drug abuse?[19] If so, how do we explain drug abuse among the upper classes?

Just as there are many causes of drug abuse, there are many addict lifestyles—and the lifestyles may be linked to the use of particular substances. In the United States during the 1950s, heroin abuse began to increase markedly in the inner cities, particularly among young black and Hispanic males.[20] In fact, it was their drug of choice throughout the 1960s and early 1970s. Heroin addicts spend their days buying heroin, finding a safe place to shoot the substance into a vein with a needle attached to a hypodermic syringe, waiting for the euphoric

TABLE 13.2 Canadians' Use of Illicit Drugs, Alcohol, and Tobacco

Illicit Drug Use

- The National Longitudinal Survey on Youth found that 3 percent of Canadian youth have tried marijuana by the age of 12. By the age of 15, the proportion increases to 38 percent.

- In contrast, in 1990, only 25 percent of grade 10 youth had ever tried marijuana.

- In 2003, cannabis accounted for 71 percent of the total drug crimes known to police. In 2006, this number dropped to 60 percent.

- Lifetime use of cannabis is higher than average (45 percent) in British Columbia (52 percent) and Alberta (49 percent) and lower than average in Ontario (40 percent), Newfoundland and Labrador (39 percent), and Prince Edward Island (37 percent). Past-year use is significantly higher in British Columbia (17 percent) and Quebec (16 percent) than the national average (14 percent).

- Those who have never been married are more likely to have smoked marijuana (58 percent) than those who are currently married (41 percent).

- Lifetime cannabis use increases with education. About 35 percent of those without high school diplomas reported use, compared to 52 percent among those with some post-secondary education. Use then declines among those with a university degree (44 percent).

- About 51 percent of university students report using marijuana at some point in their lives, 32 percent have used it within the last year, and 17 percent in the last month.

- The national rate of lifetime use of illicit drugs other than cannabis (17 percent) is highest among men (21 percent); 18- to 19-year-olds (31 percent) and 20- to 24-year-old (28 percent); residents of Quebec (18 percent), British Columbia (23 percent), and Alberta (19 percent); as well as single (24 percent) and previously married respondents (14 percent).

- The national rate of past-year illicit drug use, other than cannabis (3 percent), is also highest among men (4 percent), 18- to 19-year-olds (18 percent) and 20- to 24-year-olds (12 percent), residents of Quebec (4 percent) and B.C. (4 percent), and single respondents (9 percent).

- Regional differences in some types of drug use exist. A study conducted in the Northwest Territories reports that over 11 percent of the population there reports sniffing solvents or aerosols, compared to 0.8 percent for Canada as a whole. Sniffing these substances was also more prevalent in Nunavut (21 percent).

- The rate of solvent or aerosol use among Aboriginal peoples was 24 times the national rate. Among Aboriginals, the rate was much higher for those living in Nunavut (26 percent) compared to the Northwest Territories (13 percent), and higher among men (14 percent) than women (9 percent).

Alcohol Use

- The Canadian Addiction Survey found that 79 percent of Canadians consumed alcohol in the 12 months prior to the survey. About 6 percent engaged in heavy drinking (defined as consuming five or more drinks in one sitting for men, and four or more drinks in one sitting for women) once a week; 26 percent reported this pattern at least once a month.

- Most "heavy and hazardous" drinkers, according to the survey, are males under the age of 25.

- The prevalence of heavy and hazardous drinking is much higher in Northern Canada. According to the Northwest Territories Addiction Survey, of the 78 percent of respondents 15 and over who indicated they had consumed alcohol in the year prior to the survey, 46 percent reported consuming five or more drinks on a single occasion at least once a month, and 15 percent stated they had engaged in such heavy drinking at least once a week.

- The 2005 Ontario Student Drug Use Survey (OSDUS) showed that 62 percent of students in grades 7 to 12 reported drinking alcohol in the previous year, ranging from 31 percent of grade 7 students to 82 percent of grade 12 students. These numbers actually represent a decrease from 2003, which indicated that 66 percent of students consumed alcohol.

- Another survey reports that 34 percent of boys and 23 percent of girls in grade 10 report weekly alcohol use in 2002. Furthermore, 46 percent of boys and 42 percent of girls in grade 10 indicated they had been "really drunk" at least twice.

- Alcohol consumption has risen by at least 13 percent since 1997.

- About 5000 Canadians die each year prematurely from the effects of alcohol, which is five times greater than all the illicit drug deaths put together.

Tobacco Use

- According to the Canadian Tobacco Use Monitoring Survey, 21 percent of Canadians aged 15 and over were current smokers in 2003. This number dropped to 19 percent in 2005—the lowest level in more than four decades. In 1965, when monitoring began, an estimated 50 percent of the population smoked.

- Canadian smokers smoke less. In 1981 smokers smoked an average of 21 cigarettes a day, compared to 15 per day in 2005.

- In the 1970s more than half of all teens aged 15 to 19 smoked. The rate for teens dropped but then began to climb again in the early 1990s, remaining stable at around 28 percent since the mid-1990s. In 2005, this rate dropped to 18 percent.

- From 2000 to 2005, smoking among 12- to 17-year-olds dropped from 14 percent to 8 percent.

- Smoking has also dropped among college students: 17 percent smoked in 1998 compared to 13 percent in 2004.

- People between the ages of 18 and 34 form the highest proportion of smokers, making up 28 percent of the smoking population. The proportion of male smokers is higher than the proportion of female smokers: 23 percent versus 20 percent.

- Smoking rates are lowest in British Columbia (18 percent) and Ontario (21 percent).

- Smoking rates in the territories are high: 30 percent in the Yukon, 36 percent in the Northwest Territories, and 53 percent in Nunavut.

Sources: "Smoking in Canada Being Snuffed Out," CBC News, February 15, 2007, www.cbc.ca.new.background.smoking/stats.html, accessed October 30, 2007; "Smoking Statistics," Heart and Stroke Foundation of Canada, ww2.heartandstroke.ca/Page.asp?PageID=110&Article ID=1076&Src=news, accessed October 30, 2007; "Smoking in Canada: An Overview," Health Canada, www.hc-sc.gc.ca/hl-vs/tobac-tabac/research-recherche/stat/ctums-esutc/fs-if/2003; "Alcohol Consumption Rises by 13% since 1997," CTV News, www.ctv.ca/servlet/ArticleNews/print/CTVNews/20051215/alcohol_statscan_2005, accessed October 30, 2007; "Statistical Overview of Alcohol Use," Alcohol Policy Network, www.apolnet.ca/resources/stats/stats_overview.html, accessed October 30, 2007; E. M. Adlaf, P. Beging, and E. Sawka, eds., *Canadian Addiction Survey (CAS): A National Survey of Canadians' Use of Alcohol and Other Drugs: Prevalence of Use and Related Harms: Detailed Report.* (Ottawa: Canadian Centre on Substance Abuse, 2005); "1996 NWT Alcohol & Drug Survey" Northwest Territories Bureau of Statistics, www.stats.gov.nt.ca./Statinfo?Health/alcdrug/report.html, accessed October 30, 2007.

feeling, or rush, that follows the injection, and ultimately reaching a feeling of overall well-being known as "a high," which lasts about four hours.[21] The heroin abuser's lifestyle is typically characterized by poor health, crime, arrest, imprisonment, and temporary stays in drug treatment programs.[22] Today AIDS, which is spread, among other ways, by the shared use of needles, has become the most serious health problem among heroin addicts.

During the 1960s, marijuana became one of the major drugs of choice, particularly among white, middle-class young people who identified themselves as anti-establishment. Their lifestyles were distinct from those of the inner-city heroin addicts. Young marijuana users tended to live for the moment. Disillusioned by what they perceived as a rigid and hypocritical society, they challenged its

FIGURE 13.1 Alcohol and drug use among youth.

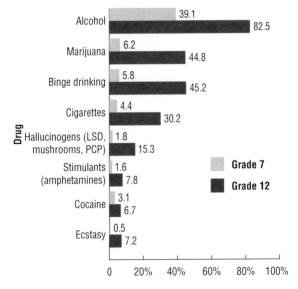

Drug	Grade 7	Grade 12
Alcohol	39.1	82.5
Marijuana	6.2	44.8
Binge drinking	5.8	45.2
Cigarettes	4.4	30.2
Hallucinogens (LSD, mushrooms, PCP)	1.8	15.3
Stimulants (amphetamines)	1.6	7.8
Cocaine	3.1	6.7
Ecstasy	0.5	7.2

Source: The Ontario Drug Use Survey. Centre for Addiction and Mental Health; reprinted with permission.

The countercultural Woodstock Music and Art Fair in 1969 drew over 450 000 people to open fields in New York state. The rock concert, where drugs and "free love" flowed, lasted for four days.

Actor Robert Downey Jr. in a Malibu, California, courtroom just prior to being sentenced to six months in jail for violating parole on a prior drug conviction. Subsequently, in 2002, he was once again in trouble when authorities allegedly found drugs in his Palm Springs hotel room.

norms through deviant behaviour. Drugs—first marijuana, then hallucinogens (principally LSD), amphetamines, and barbiturates—came to symbolize the counterculture.[23]

In the 1960s and 1970s, attitudes toward recreational drug use became quite lax, perhaps as a result of the wide acceptance of marijuana.[24] By the 1980s, cocaine, once associated only with deviants, had become the drug of choice among the privileged, who watched (and copied) the well-publicized drug-oriented lifestyles of some celebrities and athletes. Typical cocaine users were well-educated, prosperous, upwardly mobile professionals in their 20s and 30s. They were lawyers and architects, editors and stockbrokers. They earned enough money to spend at least $100 an evening on their illegal recreational activities. By and large, they were otherwise law-abiding, even though they knew their behaviour was against the law.

The popularity of cocaine waned toward the end of the 1980s. The same is not true for crack, however, which spread to the inner-city population that had abused heroin in the latter part of the 1980s.[25] Crack is cheaper than powdered cocaine, fast-acting, and powerful. Though individual doses are inexpensive, once a person is hooked on crack, a daily supply can run between $100 and $250.

Drug addicts continually search for new ways to extend their highs. In 1989, a mixture of crack

and heroin, called "crank," began to be used. Crank is smoked in a pipe.[26] It is potentially very dangerous—first, because it prolongs the brief high of crack alone and, second, because it appeals to younger drug addicts who are concerned about the link between AIDS and the sharing of hypodermic needles. The history of drug abuse is evolutionary. "Crank" is now the name of methamphetamine—also known as "ice," "crystal," "chalk," and "speed." Ecstasy is a relatively new addition to the list of synthetic drugs available to users. Also referred to as "E," it gained popularity with the rise of the "rave" culture in the late 1990s.

> **Did You Know?**
>
> . . . that the maximum penalty for methamphetamine offences is life imprisonment?

Crime-Related Activities

Many researchers have examined the criminal implications of addiction to heroin and, more recently, cocaine. From 1992 to 2002 about one in ten homicides in Canada involved activities such as trafficking or the settling of drug-related accounts. Cocaine was involved in 60 percent of drug-related homicide incidents, cannabis in 20 percent, heroin in 5 percent, and other unspecified drugs in 15 percent. Heroin and cocaine involvement in homicide incidents was highest in British Columbia; about 58 percent of heroin-related homicide incidents and 33 percent of cocaine-related incidents occurred in the province.[27] In another study, police officers reported that 51 percent of arrestees were under the influence of a psychoactive substance.[28] The officers in the study also reported that 32 percent of thefts were committed under the influence of drugs. Official statistics on drug-related offences make it quite clear that street crime is significantly related to drug use and abuse. For example, 26 percent of all drug-related homicides in Canada were gang-related.[29]

The nature of the drug-crime relationship, however, is less clear. Is the addict typically an adolescent who never committed a crime before he or she became hooked, but who thereafter was forced to commit crimes to get money to support the drug habit? In other words, does drug abuse lead to crime?[30] Or does criminal behaviour precede drug abuse? Another possibility is that both drug abuse and criminal behaviour stem from the same factors (biological, psychological, or socio-logical).[31] The debate continues, and many questions are still unanswered. But on one point most researchers agree: Whatever the temporal or causal sequence of drug abuse and crime, the frequency and seriousness of criminality increase as addiction increases. Drug abuse may not "cause" criminal behaviour, but it does enhance it.[32]

Until the late 1970s, most investigators of the drug-crime relationship reported that drug abusers were arrested primarily for property offences. Recent scholarly literature, however, presents a different perspective. There appears to be an increasing amount of violence associated with drugs, and it may be attributable largely to the appearance of crack and more recently crystal meth. Beginning in the 1980s and continuing to today, drug wars became more frequent. Rival drug dealers settle disputes with guns, power struggles within a single drug enterprise lead to assaults and homicides, one dealer robs another, informers are killed, their associates retaliate, and bystanders, some of them children, get caught in the crossfire.[33]

The International Drug Economy

The drug problem is a worldwide phenomenon, beyond the power of any one government to deal with.[34] Nor are drugs a concern simply of law enforcement agencies. Drugs influence politics, international relations, peace and war, and the economies of individual countries and of the world. Let us take a look at the political and economic impact of the international drug trade, specifically as it concerns cocaine, heroin, and marijuana. Figure 13.2 shows the sources of these drugs and some shipping routes.

Cocaine   Today the largest cocaine producer is Peru, although harvests have been decreasing since 1995. Annual harvests of 95 600 to 130 200 tonnes of coca leaves yield from 160 to 215 tonnes of pure cocaine. Cocaine production in Colombia has increased in recent years, with a cocaine base production of 516 tonnes in 2000.[35] Colombia also exports more than any other country—over half the world's supply—because much of the raw coca of Peru and other coca producers, such as Bolivia, is refined into cocaine in Colombia. The "cocaine cartel," which controls production and distribution, is said to be composed of no more than 12 families, located principally in Colombia and Bolivia. However, organized-crime interests in other South American countries are establishing themselves in the market.

Each year nearly half of all cocaine seized was shipped to the United States on private planes.

FIGURE 13.2   Worldwide drug-smuggling routes, 1993.

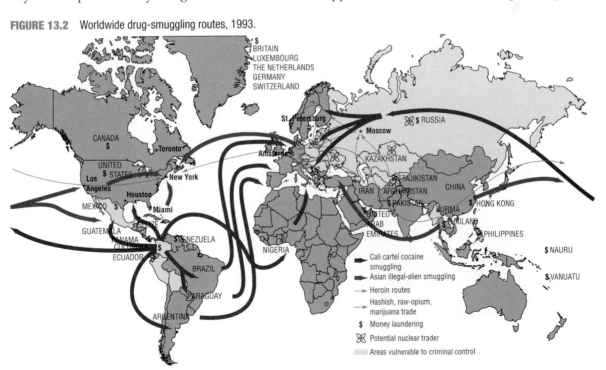

Small planes evade controls and land on little-used airstrips or drop their cargos offshore to waiting speedboats.[36] Boats carrying drugs then mingle with local pleasure craft and bring the cargo to shore. Wholesalers who work for the Colombian cartels take care of the distribution. Some of the estimated 100 000 Colombians living illegally in the United States are thought to belong to the distribution apparatus.

Heroin "Just five years ago, almost all of the heroin seized came from Asia. Today, 32 percent of heroin seized can be traced to South America, with an estimated 20 000 hectares of opium poppies being cultivated in Colombia alone." This statement, made by the former head of the U.S. Justice Department's Drug Enforcement Administration, sheds light on the recent expansion in scope of Colombia's cash crop. This diversification is a direct result of simple economics—while 1 kilogram of cocaine sells for US$10 000 to US$40 000 on the streets, an equal amount of South American heroin fetches anywhere from US$85 000 to US$180 000.

Production of heroin in all countries is organized by local warlords, illegitimate traders, and corrupt administrators; it is increasingly coming under the control of "triads"—organized-crime families of Chinese origin based in Hong Kong and Taiwan. More and more, heroin in the United States comes from Mexico. Most of the heroin from the Golden Crescent and Golden Triangle enters the United States on commercial aircraft, whereas Mexican heroin comes overland. In Europe and in the United States, the traditional Sicilian Mafia families have assumed significant roles in the refining and distribution of heroin.

Marijuana While the popularity of various illegal substances has waxed and waned as patterns of drug use change over time, marijuana has sustained its popularity over the decades. Canadians use marijuana more than any country in Europe, Asia, or Latin America, according to the United Nations' 2007 World Drug Report.[37] A 2007 Angus Reid survey found that 55 percent of Canadians think marijuana should be legalized.

Use, however, is not the extent of Canada's role in the marijuana market or the illicit drug market generally. Canada is a major source of marijuana for both the national and international markets. One of the most lucrative markets in British Columbia is marijuana production; in 2007 alone the marijuana harvest generated about $7 billion.[38] The RCMP report that today almost all large-scale grow operations are linked to organized crime groups. Outlaw motorcycle gangs have traditionally controlled the production and distribution of the substance, but increasingly, Asian-based criminal organizations and gangs are taking over. However, while large grow operations serve as a source of the drug for an extensive market, marijuana is also grown by individuals for their personal use. An economist from Simon Fraser University estimates that marijuana is grown in at least 17 500 homes in British Columbia alone.

As Douglas Belkin reports, in Vancouver, large profits, lenient laws, lax enforcement, and an established smuggling and money-laundering infrastructure have attracted organized crime. The city's prominent role as a base for the global distribution of illicit drugs was recently highlighted following the arrest of Yong Long Ye, who allegedly imported drugs from the United States and Southeast Asia and exported them across North America and to Australia.[39] Canada's role in the production and

> **Did You Know?**
>
> . . . that "khat" comes from the young leaves of the Catha Edulis shrub, which is native to East Africa and Southern Arabia? It contains chemicals that can cause grandiose delusions, paranoia, and hallucinations. "Kat" or "qat" is growing in popularity among some immigrant groups.

A Lahu hill tribe girl in Myanmar holds opium poppies as she assists her tribe in eradicating illegal poppies.

distribution of marijuana is increasingly affecting the international drug trade, as is its contribution to the ecstasy trade.

Ecstasy Ecstasy (methylenedioxymethamphetamine), first developed as an appetite suppressant in 1914, became available on the street in the late 1970s and early 1980s. One of the easiest illegal drugs to obtain, its effects are similar to those of amphetamines and hallucinogens. Most often consumed in pill form, ecstasy is distributed almost everywhere, but became very popular at social events like raves. Unlike methamphetamine ("crystal meth"), which can be produced from a variety of easily obtainable ingredients, ecstasy is more difficult to produce. Because ingredients are difficult to get, manufacturers of the drug often use substitutes, which reduce the quality of the drug, and often produce more dangerous combinations with unknown effects.

For organized-crime groups, many of which are actively involved in the production and distribution of ecstasy, producing less pure forms of the drugs by using cheaper substitutes is more lucrative. Lacing pills of ecstasy with the less expensive and easier-to-produce methamphetamine increases profits and makes the pills more addictive, thus creating a better market for suppliers. Since 2003, following the reported success of U.S. and European government efforts to reduce the supply of ecstasy entering the United States from the Netherlands and Belgium, Canadian organized-crime groups have moved in to fill the void. Produced in large quantities in Canada, the pills are then smuggled into the northern U.S. states for distribution throughout that country. A news release from the White House in January 2008 reports that over the past several years there has been a ten-fold increase in the amount of ecstasy found entering the United States from Canada.[40] Furthermore, of the seized pills tested, 55 percent contained methamphetamine. Similarly, 10 000 ecstasy pills headed for New York that were seized by Canadian police in 2006 were found to contain 80 percent methamphetamine.[41] As Michael Chettleburgh points out, when sold in this type of impure state, the profit margin for organized criminals is significant. The street price for one pill is about $20; it costs about 3 cents to produce an impure pill.[42]

Money Laundering The illegal drug economy is vast. Annual sales are estimated to be between US$300 billion and US$500 billion. Profits are enormous, and no taxes are paid on them. Because the profits are "dirty money," they must undergo **money laundering.** Typically, the cash obtained from drug sales in Canada and the United States is physically smuggled to other countries because it cannot be legally exported without disclosure (see Table 13.3), although the International Monetary Fund estimates that between $22 billion and $55 billion is laundered annually in Canada.[43]

Smuggling cash is not easy—$1 million in $20 bills weighs about 45 kilograms—yet billions of dollars are exported, in false-bottomed suitcases and smugglers' vests, to countries that allow numbered bank accounts without identification of names (the Cayman Islands, Russia, Vanuatu, and West African countries, among others).

New methods of laundering drug profits, not involving physical transfer of cash, have recently been devised, such as fake real estate transactions;

TABLE 13.3 A Typical Money-Laundering Scheme

La Mina, the Mine, reportedly laundered US$1.2 billion for the Colombian cartels over a two-year period.

Currency from selling cocaine was packed in boxes labelled "jewellery" and sent by armoured car to Ropex, a jewellery maker in Los Angeles.

↓

The cash was counted and deposited in banks but few suspicions were raised because the gold business is based on cash.

↓

Ropex then wire-transferred the money to New York banks in payment for fictitious gold purchased from Ronel, allegedly a gold bullion business.

↓

Ronel shipped Ropex bars of lead painted gold to complete the fake transaction. Ropex used the alleged sale of this gold to other jewellery businesses to cover further currency conversions.

↓

Ronel then transferred the funds from U.S. banks to South American banks where the Colombian cartel could gain access to them.

Source: Adapted from "Getting Banks to Just Say 'No,'" *Business Week*, Apr. 17, 1989, p. 17; and Maggie Mahar, "Dirty Money: It Triggers a Bold New Attack in the War on Drugs," *Barron's*, 69 (June), 1989: 6–38, at p. 7. From the U.S. Department of Justice, Drugs, Crime and the Justice System (Washington, D.C.: U.S. Government Printing Office, 1992).

purchase of gold, antiques, and art; and cybercurrency (microchip-based electronic money), which utilizes the Internet. Such transactions permit electronic transfer of drug funds worldwide with minimum chance of detection. Once deposited in foreign accounts, the funds are "clean" and can be returned to legitimate businesses and investments. They may also be used for illegal purposes, such as the purchase of arms for export to terrorist groups.

The Political Impact The political impact of the drug trade on producer countries is devastating. In the late 1970s and early 1980s, the government of Bolivia became completely corrupt. The minister of justice was referred to as the "minister of cocaine." In Colombia, drug lords and terrorists combined their resources to wrest power from the democratically elected government. Thirteen supreme court judges and 167 police officers were killed; the minister of justice and the ambassador to Hungary were assassinated.

The message was that death was the price for refusal to succumb to drug corruption. In 1989, a highly respected Colombian presidential candidate who had come out against the cocaine cartel was assassinated. The government remained fragile and the situation precarious. Over the years, the scandal aroused by liaisons between notorious drug lords and high-ranking government officials has endured. One of the scandals, perhaps most injurious to diplomatic relations with the United States, was that involving Colombia's former president Ernesto Samper. Samper received US$6 million toward his 1994 campaign fund from the renowned Cali cartel—the leader in cocaine trafficking. Despite his exoneration by Colombia's House of Representatives, the United States government sent an unequivocal message to President Samper by revoking his U.S. visa and decertifying Colombia (the United States "certifies" countries considered an ally in the drug war).

Nor is Colombia alone in its efforts to cope with the drug problem. Before General Manuel Noriega was arrested in a U.S. invasion of Panama to face charges of drug smuggling, he had made himself military dictator of Panama. By 1996 (seven years later), however, little had really changed. Corruption and crime rule in all drug-producing countries. Government instability is the necessary consequence. Coups replace elections. The populations of these countries are not immune to addiction themselves. Several South American countries, including Colombia, Bolivia, and Peru, are now experiencing major addiction problems; Peru alone has some 60 000 addicts. The Asian narcotics-producing countries, which thought themselves immune to the addiction problem, also became victims of their own production. Pakistan now has about 200 000 addicts.[44]

One of the more remarkable aspects of the expansion of the drug trade has been the spread of addiction and the drug economy to developing nations and to the newly democratic, formerly socialist countries. Of all political problems, however, the most vicious is the alliance that drug dealers have forged with terrorist groups in the Near East, in Latin America, and in Europe.[45]

Drug Control

As we discussed earlier in this chapter, factors other than the pharmacological properties of substances influence their legal and illegal status. In particular, we looked at the role that political and economic factors played, in conjunction with racial biases, in the criminalization of opium in the early 1900s. Contemporary government drug policies are similarly subject to external factors. Under Canada's former Liberal government we witnessed a move toward the decriminalization of marijuana for medicinal purposes, as well as decriminalization of the possession of small amounts of the substance. Considering the results of one study, which found that the percentage of Canadians who have used illicit drugs jumped from 28.5 percent in 1994 to 45 percent in 2004, it seems decriminalization is not at odds with public sentiment and experience.[46]

Following, in part, the U.S. anti-drug strategy that focuses on law enforcement as a means of reducing the amount of drugs and suppliers on the streets, the Canadian government announced a $63.8 million two-pronged anti-drug campaign in October 2007. One prong focuses on prevention of drug abuse and treatment for abusers, and the other focuses on enforcement of drug laws and tougher punishments for those convicted of drug offences. Part of the government's plan is to provide $21.6 million to "fund the battle against drug producers and traffickers."[47]

The push for mandatory minimum sentences for drug offences is one strategy for deterring drug producers and traffickers. Emulating the United States' "war on drugs," the Canadian government has announced plans to introduce legislation that would set mandatory minimum prison sentences for marijuana growers and traffickers. The proposed bill, if passed, could result in a six-month mandatory sentence for growing as little as one marijuana plant for the purposes of trafficking. Critics of the proposed legislation point to the failure of the American war on drugs as an effective tool of social control. Drug policy in the United States has resulted in one of the highest rates of incarceration in the world and has not reduced recidivism rates or rates of drug use and addiction.[48]

More funding for law enforcement officers and prosecutors to crack down on marijuana grow operations and manufacturing sites is another focus. Increased enforcement will also include targeting drug smuggling across the border and new legislation to control substances used in drug production.[49]

Law enforcement is one of the primary methods used to control illicit substances in Canada. Critics, however, contend that too much money is spent on enforcement instead of prevention. For example, the B.C. Centre for Excellence in HIV/AIDS reports that in 2004–2005, 73 percent of the $368 million spent on targeting illicit drugs in the country went toward law enforcement initiatives. The remainder of the money was spent on treatment (14 percent), research (7 percent), prevention (2.6 percent), and harm-reduction (2.6 percent).[50]

The problem with emphasizing law enforcement is that it tends not to be effective.[51] The fact is that a demand exists for illicit substances; taking a few suppliers out of the loop by imprisoning them for long periods simply provides an opportunity for others to fill the demand for the goods. The issue is a systemic one; imprisoning individuals does not target the source of the problem: demand for drugs. Enforcement and imprisonment efforts are also problematic for the criminal justice system. Following a crackdown on drugs, courts become backed up and correctional facilities are expected to handle an increasing number of prisoners. Part of the impetus for the former Liberal government's move to decriminalize marijuana possession was the overcrowding of prisons with relatively minor offenders (people convicted for using and possessing marijuana), and the burdening and stigmatization of (primarily) young people with criminal records for such possession.

Recognizing the need for prevention and treatment as well as enforcement, the federal government currently spends $1.2 billion on substance abuse programs, and the two-pronged approach mentioned earlier will invest an additional $9.6 million per year in community initiatives that address factors that lead to illicit drug use. Some proposed uses for the funding are a nationwide awareness campaign targeting youth and parents, the development of new treatment programs, expansion of treatment programs already in operation, and expansion of rehabilitation facilities.[52]

The federal government, with its dual pronged funding, is attempting to find a drug-control strategy that balances prevention and punishment. Let's look now at the various components such a strategy might include.

Treatment The treatment approach to drug control is not new. During the late 1960s and into the 1970s, hope for the drug problem centred on treatment programs. These programs took a variety of forms, depending on the setting and modality—for example, self-help groups (Narcotics Anonymous, Cocaine Anonymous), psychotherapy, detoxification ("drying out" in a hospital), "rap" houses (neighbourhood centres where addicts can come for group therapy sessions), various community social-action efforts (addicts clean up neighbourhoods, plant trees, and so on), and—the two most popular—residential therapeutic communities and methadone maintenance programs.[53]

The therapeutic community is a 24-hour, total-care facility where former addicts and professionals work together to help addicts become drug-free. In methadone maintenance programs, addicts are given a synthetic narcotic, methadone, which prevents withdrawal symptoms (physical and psychological pain associated with giving up drugs), while addicts reduce their drug intake slowly over a period of time. Throughout the program, addicts receive counselling designed to help them return to a normal life.

It is difficult to assess the success of most treatment programs. Even if individuals appear to be drug-free within a program, it is hard to find out what happens to them once they leave it (or even during a week when they do not show up). In addition, it may well be that the addicts who succeed in drug treatment programs are those who have already resolved to stop abusing drugs before they voluntarily come in for treatment; the real hard-core users may not even make an effort to become drug-free.

A program to divert drug offenders (users and purchasers) from criminal careers is the drug court, in which the judge has the option to divert non-violent drug offenders to a counselling program in lieu of incarceration. Drug treatment courts are an intensive, court-monitored alternative to incarceration. Participants follow a structured program of treatment and community service, which requires them to participate in intensive group and individual therapy, including meeting with a judge on a weekly basis. The first drug court was created in Toronto in 1998. Since that time, drug courts have been established in Vancouver, Regina, Winnipeg, Ottawa, Edmonton, and Calgary. The goals of drug courts are to help non-violent offenders overcome their addictions and improve their social stability, thereby reducing criminal behaviours associated with substance abuse. Although drug courts are relatively new in Canada, evaluations indicate that the recidivism rate for those sentenced through drug courts is about 11 percent.[54]

Education While drug treatment deals with the problem of addiction after the fact, education tries to prevent people from taking illegal drugs in the first place. The idea behind educational programs is straightforward: People who have information about the harmful effects of illegal drugs are likely to stay away from them. Sometimes the presentation of the facts has been coupled with scare techniques. Some well-known athletes and entertainers have joined the crusade with public-service messages ("a questionable approach," says Howard Abadinsky, "given the level of substance abuse reported in these groups").[55]

The educational approach has several drawbacks. Critics maintain that most addicts are quite knowledgeable about the potential consequences of taking drugs but think of them as just a part of the "game."[56] Most people who begin to use drugs believe they will never become addicted, even when they have information about addiction.[57] Inner-city youngsters do not lack information

about the harmful effects of drugs. They learn about the dangers from daily exposure to addicts desperately searching for drugs, sleeping on the streets, going through withdrawal, and stealing family belongings to get money.[58] The Drug Abuse Resistance Education (DARE) program is an example of an educational program that targets children in elementary school. The objectives of the program are to educate young people on the dangers of drug addiction, and they are also provided with skills for resisting peer pressure to experiment with drugs, legal and illegal. Evaluations of the program, however, are mixed, causing some critics to call for changes to the content and manner in which it is delivered.[59]

Legalization Despite increases in government funding for an expanded effort to enforce drug legislation and reduce drug use and abuse, these goals have not been achieved and likely won't be for a long time. There is much evidence that all the approaches, even the "new" ones, have been tried before with little or no effect. Some experts are beginning to advocate a very different approach—legalization. Their reasoning is that since the drug problem seems to elude all control efforts, why not deal with heroin and cocaine the same way we deal with alcohol and tobacco? In other words, why not subject these drugs to some government control and restrictions, but make them legally available to all adults?[60]

> **Did You Know?**
>
> . . . that the 1973 Le Dain Commission recommended that the government "gradually withdraw from the use of the criminal law against the non-medical user of drugs rather than extend its application"?

They argue that current drug-control policies impose tremendous costs on taxpayers without demonstrating effective results. In addition to spending less money on crime control, the government would make money on tax revenue from the sale of legalized drugs. This is, of course, a hotly debated issue. Drug use is at the centre of debates that draw on arguments about health, criminal behaviour, and morals. Given these conflicts, legalization surely offers no easy solution and has had little public support.

Another approach, often confused with legalization, is **decriminalization**. Decriminalization reduces the penalty for an act, but does not make it legal. Legalization would condone the use of drugs to the point where the government would regulate and control its use; decriminalization does not give the act the state's approval but rather transforms the criminal status of the behaviour to a civil violation. For example, under the former Liberal government's proposed bill that would have decriminalized marijuana to some extent, being caught with more than a small amount of marijuana would result in a fine rather than a criminal charge, possible conviction, and criminal record.

Harm Reduction   The **harm-reduction approach** is one favoured by many Canadian drug researchers and some criminologists. Harm reduction stems from a recognition that our past and current drug laws stem from factors that are not necessarily directly related to the harm the substances cause the users. For example, alcohol and

tobacco rate higher in terms of harm to users than opiates. Yet, alcohol and tobacco producers have much to gain financially from their production and sale.[61] So do illicit drug providers. Who decides which drugs should be legal? Legalization of certain drugs has worked to the advantage of certain vested interests. At the same time, prohibition clearly did not work with alcohol. Why are we repeating past mistakes by prohibiting and criminalizing the use of substances, which may pharmacologically be less damaging than alcohol and tobacco? Tables 13.4 and 13.5 describe Vancouver's Four Pillars Drug Strategy and some of the results from its evaluation.

TABLE 13.4 Vancouver's Four Pillars Drug Strategy

The four pillars of our city's drug policy are:

Prevention

Promoting healthy families and communities, protecting child and youth development, preventing or delaying the start of substance use among young people and reducing harm associated with substance use. Successful prevention efforts aim to improve the health of the general population and reduce differences in health between groups of people.

Treatment

Offering individuals access to services that help people come to terms with problem substance use and lead healthier lives, including outpatient and peer-based counselling, methadone programs, daytime and residential treatment, housing support and ongoing medical care.

Harm Reduction

Reducing the spread of deadly communicable diseases, preventing drug overdose deaths, increasing substance users' contact with health care services and drug treatment programs and reducing consumption of drugs in the street.

Enforcement

Recognizing the need for peace and quiet, public order and safety in the Downtown Eastside and other Vancouver neighbourhoods by targeting organized crime, drug dealing, drug houses, problem businesses involved in the drug trade, and improving coordination with health services and other agencies that link drug users to withdrawal management (detox), treatment, counselling and prevention services.

Source: City of Vancouver, "Four Pillars Drug Strategy," 2008, www.city.vancouver. bc.ca/fourpillars/, accessed April 5, 2008.

TABLE 13.5 Evaluation of Vancouver's Supervised Injection Site (Insite)

Research results show:*

- 7278 unique individuals registered at Insite.
- Women made up 26 percent of clients.
- Aboriginal people made up 18 percent of clients.
- Heroin was used in 41 percent of injections.
- Cocaine was used in 27 percent of injections.
- Morphine was used in 12 percent of injections.
- 453 overdoses resulted in no fatalities.
- 4084 referrals were made with 40 percent of them made to addiction counselling.
- Referral to withdrawal management: 368.
- Referral to methadone maintenance: 2 per week.
- Daily average visits: 607.
- Average number of visits per month, per person: 11.
- Busiest day: May 25, 2005 (933 visits in 18 hours).
- Number of nursing care interventions: 6227.
- Number of nursing interventions for abscess care: 2055.

Additional findings:

- Insite has not led to an increase in drug-related crime.
- It has reduced the number of people injecting in public and the amount of injection-related litter in the downtown eastside.
- Insite is attracting the highest-risk users—those more likely to be vulnerable to HIV infection and overdose.
- Insite has reduced overall rates of needle sharing in the community.

*All totals or averages are for the two-year period from April 1, 2004, to March 31, 2006.

Source: Vancouver Coastal Health, "Insite Supervised Injection Site," www.vch.ca/ sis/research.htm, accessed April 5, 2008.

This man enters Insite, Canada's only safe injection site. Insite, which is located in Vancouver, is an example of the harm-reduction approach to dealing with drug-addicted individuals.

Harm reduction acknowledges that users and abusers are people who have a contribution to make to society. They should not be criminalized, but should be helped. Harm reduction includes the provision of clean needles to users, and the provision of methadone programs for individuals who want to take steps to deal with their addictions. Vancouver's Downtown Eastside safe-injection site is an example of harm reduction in practice. It has been operating since 2003, with an exemption under Section 56 of the Controlled Drugs and Substances Act. The approach promotes making safer options more available to people who abuse drugs, including clean needles and individual or group counselling. The underlying philosophy of this approach is that criminalizing addicts and throwing them in jail will increase rather than decrease the harm being done to people and to society. We should show compassion and care toward our fellow human beings, and respect their choices and decisions. As Pat O'Malley and Stephen Mugford argue, "the addict should not be cast out of the society."[62] Rather, we should make moves toward normalizing the user, which is not necessarily a move toward condoning excessive drug use, but rather an acknowledgement that such use and abuse exists and our current approaches are not working.

ALCOHOL AND CRIME

Alcohol is another substance that contributes to social problems. One of the major differences between alcohol and the other drugs we have been discussing is that the sale and purchase of alcohol

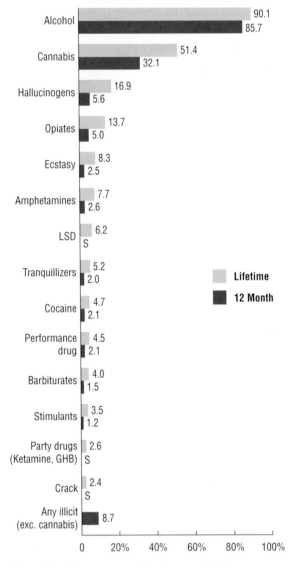

FIGURE 13.3 Lifetime and 12-month prevalence of alcohol and other drug use among Canadian undergraduates, 2004.

Notes: S – data suppressed due to unreliability.

Source: Edward M. Adlaf, Andrée Demers, and Louis Gliksman, eds., *Canadian Campus Survey, 2004* (Toronto: Centre for Addition and Mental Health, 2005).

are legal. For Canadians over the age of 15 years, each person consumes an average of 85 litres of beer, 12 litres of wine, and 7 litres of spirits per year.[63] Alcohol is consumed at recreational events, business meetings, lunches and dinners at home, and celebrations; in short, drinking alcohol has become the expected behaviour in many social situations. See Figure 13.3 for a look at alcohol and drug use among Canadian undergraduates.

The History of Legalization

Alcohol consumption is not new to our culture; in colonial days alcohol was considered safer and healthier than water. Still, the history of alcohol consumption is filled with controversy. Many people through the centuries have viewed it as wicked and degenerate. By the turn of the twentieth century, social reformers linked liquor to prostitution, poverty, the immigrant culture, and corrupt politics.

Various lobbying groups in the United States, such as the Women's Christian Temperance Union and the American Anti-Saloon League, bombarded politicians with demands for the prohibition of alcohol.[64] Canadian affiliate groups did the same. Prince Edward Island was the first province to forbid the sale of alcohol in 1900. Other provinces followed suit over the next two decades.

Historians generally agree that no legislation has ever been more widely violated or more unpopular than prohibition laws. Vast numbers of people continued to consume alcohol. It was easy to manufacture and to import. The illegal business brought tremendous profits to suppliers, and it could not be controlled by enforcement officers, who were too inefficient, too few, or too corrupt. The unlawful sale of alcohol was called "bootlegging." The term originated in the early practice of concealing liquor in one's boot to avoid payment of liquor taxes.

Bootlegging created empires for such gangsters as Al Capone and Lucky Luciano, as we saw in Chapter 12. Private saloons, or "speakeasies," prospered. Unpopular and unenforceable, prohibition laws throughout Canada were mostly repealed by 1924 (although Prince Edward Island was the last to repeal in 1948). The sale and consumption of alcohol is legal throughout the country, but its use and abuse present many social problems.

Crime-Related Activities

The alcohol-related activities that have become serious social problems are violent crime, drunk driving, and public intoxication.

Violence Surveys of federal inmates provide some insight into the alcohol/drug-crime relationship:

- Substance-abuse is identified as a contributing factor to the criminal behaviours of 70 percent of offenders. Of these, 61 percent abuse alcohol; 47 percent abuse both alcohol and drugs.[65]

- Alcohol-dependent inmates are more likely to have committed a violent crime.

- Fifty-five percent of the inmates reported that they were under the influence of drugs, alcohol, or both the day they committed the offence for which they are incarcerated;[66] 39 percent of assault offenders were under the influence of alcohol at the time they committed the crime.[67]

- Supplementing the information based on offender profiles and surveys, victimization data suggests that in about half of physical (51 percent) and sexual (48 percent) assaults, the victim believed the incident was related to the perpetrator's use of alcohol or drugs.[68]

Many other offences show a significant relationship between alcohol and violence. The role of alcohol in violent family disputes has been increasingly recognized. Findings from the Violence Against Women Survey suggest that 51 percent of violent partners were under the influence of alcohol when the assault occurred.[69]

Many explanations have been offered for the relationship between alcohol and violence.[70] Some studies focus on the individual. When people are provoked, for example, alcohol can reduce restraints on aggression.[71] Alcohol also escalates aggression by reducing awareness of consequences.[72] Other studies analyze the social situation in which drinking takes place. Experts argue that in some situations aggressive behaviour is considered appropriate or is even expected when people drink together.[73]

Drunk Driving The effect of alcohol on driving is causing continuing concern. Impaired driving offences include driving with a blood alcohol rate of over 80 mg, impaired operation of a vehicle causing death or bodily harm, and failure/refusal to provide a breath/blood sample. Statistics indicate the extent of the problem:

- The rate of impaired driving reached a peak in 1981 and then generally declined over the next two decades.

- Since then, the rate of impaired driving according to police statistics has hovered between a high of 255 per 100 000 in 2002 to a low of 243 per 100 000 in 2005.

- In 2006 this rate dropped to 228 per 100 000.

- A study based on Transport Canada data showed that there were 1069 fatal alcohol-related crashes in Canada in 2000, which means that alcohol was involved in 34 percent of total traffic deaths during that year.

- More than 80 percent of those who died in alcohol-relate deaths in 2000 were males; 25 percent were 26 to 35 years old.[74]

- In 2006 there were 74 331 impaired driving incidents reported to the police.[75]

Mothers Against Drunk Driving (MADD) is a group we've discussed earlier. Its members tend to be people who themselves have been injured or whose family members have been injured or killed in an accident involving an intoxicated driver. The organization has grown to more than 300 chapters.[76] Remove Intoxicated Drivers (RID) and Students Against Drunk Drivers (SADD) have joined the campaign.

MADD has called public attention to a major health and social problem, demanded action, and got it. Canadian Senator Marjory LeBreton, who lost her daughter and grandson because of impaired driving, is vice-chair of MADD in Canada. People today are far more aware of the dangers of drinking and driving than they were 20 years ago. Young people going out delegate a designated driver for their group; bars often provide free pop or coffee to those designated. Community organizations provide services like "Operation Rednose" during holiday seasons. Such services drive the intoxicated person and his or her vehicle home. Advertisements, many sponsored in part by MADD, drive home the point that drinking and driving has devastating effects. Police CheckStop programs target drunk drivers as well.

Some objectives of legislation have been to limit the "happy hours" during which bars serve drinks at reduced prices, to shorten hours when alcoholic beverages can be sold, to make hosts and bartenders liable for damages if their guests or patrons drink too much and become involved in an accident, to limit advertisements, and to put health warnings on bottles. Our laws have increased penalties for drunk driving to include automatic licence suspension, higher minimum fines, and even mandatory jail sentences.

Bill C-275, known as "Carley's law," was first introduced in the House of Commons for debate in 2004. Carley was a 13-year-old girl who was killed by a hit-and-run impaired driver in Abbotsford, British Columbia, in 2003. The man was driving without a licence (it had been suspended) and had received 11 driving prohibitions and citations since 1997. Angered by the initial sentence of 18 months in jail the driver received, and more angered when the sentence was reduced to 14 months plus three years probation, activists pushed for minimum sentences for hit-and-run offenders. Carley's law, if passed, would see the sentence for hit-and-run drivers who kill someone increased to a minimum of seven years imprisonment, with a possible maximum sentence of life imprisonment. Although Carley's law was defeated, her family and supporters continue to work for reform.

As far as "get-tough" impaired driving legislation goes, results are mixed. One study found that such measures did indeed lower the number of traffic deaths, while other investigations did not show positive results.[77] Nevertheless, drunk driving has achieved widespread attention, and even modern technology is being used in the effort to find solutions: Japanese and American technicians have come up with a device that locks the ignition system and can be unlocked only when the attached Breathalyzer (which registers alcohol in the blood) indicates that the driver is sober.[78]

SEXUAL MORALITY OFFENCES

All societies endeavour to regulate sexual behaviour, although what specifically is considered not permissible has varied from society to society and from time to time. The legal regulation of sexual conduct in Anglo-American law has been greatly influenced by both the Old and the New Testaments. In the Middle Ages, the enforcement of laws pertaining to sexual morality was the province of church courts. Today, to the extent that immorality is still illegal, it is the regular criminal courts that enforce such laws.

Did You Know?

. . . that the legal age of consent for sexual activity is 14 in Canada?

Morality laws have always been controversial, whether they seek to prevent alcohol abuse or to prohibit certain forms of sexual behaviour or its public display or depiction. Sexual activity other than intercourse between spouses for the purpose of procreation has been severely penalized in many societies and until only recently in Canada. It was only in 1965 that Canada's laws regarding "deviant" sexual behaviour came into question and sparked much controversy. During a police investigation, Everett Klippert stated he was a homosexual, which according to the Canadian Criminal Code meant he was guilty of gross indecency. Because psychiatrists attested that Klippert was likely to repeat this criminal behaviour, he was sentenced to life imprisonment as a dangerous offender. The sentence was upheld by the Supreme Court in 1967. The decision caused an uproar in the country and led Pierre Trudeau, then the federal justice minister, to state that "the state has no place in the bedrooms of the nation."[79]

In 1969, after heated debate, Bill C-150 decriminalized homosexuality by stating that sexual acts between consenting adults in private were legal. And in 1971, Everett Klippert was released from prison. The history regarding sexual behaviours and their legality is a testament to the highly contentious nature of the topic of "deviant sexuality." At one time, sexual intercourse between unmarried persons (known as "lewd cohabitation"), seduction of a female by promise of marriage, and all forms of "unnatural" sexual relations were serious crimes.

The idea behind the changes to the law is that the sexual relations of consenting adults should be beyond the control of the law, not only because throughout history such legal efforts have proved ineffective but also because the harm to society, if any, is too slight to warrant the condemnation of law. As revealed by Trudeau's famous statement and outrage over the Klippert case, Canada is one of the more progressive countries in the world when it comes to recognizing same-sex unions. By 2005, same-sex marriages were legal in the country.

Nonetheless, some sexual offences remain offensive to the public and in the eyes of the law. Let us take a close look at two existing offences involving sexual morality: prostitution and pornography.

Prostitution

Prostitution refers to the consensual exchange of sex for money and money for sex. In Canada, it is not a crime to be a prostitute. Doing the act is not illegal, but negotiating the arrangement for it in public is illegal under Section 213 of the Criminal Code (see Table 13.6). It is the public aspect of prostitution that lawmakers and the public seem to find most problematic. In other words, "outdoor"

Same-sex marriage supporters show their support by staging a "one big kiss" demonstration.

TABLE 13.6 Criminal Code Excerpt on Prostitution

213. (1) Every person who in a public place or in any place open to public view
    (a) stops or attempts to stop any motor vehicle
    (b) impedes the free flow of pedestrian or vehicular traffic or ingress to or egress from premises adjacent to that place or
    (c) stops or attempts to stop any person or in any manner communicates or attempts to communicate with any person for the purpose of engaging in prostitution or of obtaining the sexual services of a prostitute is guilty of an offence punishable on summary conviction.

(2) Definition of "public place"
    (a) In this section, "public place" includes any place to which the public have access as of right or by invitation, express or implied, and any motor vehicle located in a public place or in any place open to public view.

Source: Public Works and Government Services Canada.

prostitution is more of an issue for society than "indoor" prostitution (i.e., call girls, escort services, and individuals who have higher-end, wealthier clients). While our discussion primarily focuses on female prostitutes, male prostitutes exist and are growing in numbers. Male prostitutes face many of the same issues as their female counterparts, but they also experience unique challenges.[80]

The Uniform Crime Reports recorded 5701 incidents of prostitution in 2006.[81] The number of prostitution-related incidents would be extremely high if we were to include all acts of sexual favours granted in return for some gratuity. Even if the number were limited to straightforward cash transactions (including credit card transactions), there is no way of arriving at a figure. Many persons may act as prostitutes for a while and then return to legitimate lifestyles. There are part-time and full-time prostitutes, male and female prostitutes, itinerant and resident prostitutes, and street hookers and high-priced escorts who do not consider themselves prostitutes.[82]

Many law enforcement agencies do not relish the task of suppressing prostitution. In some jurisdictions, the police have little time to spend on vice control, given the extent of violent and property crimes. Thus, when prostitutes are arrested, it is likely to be in response to demands by community groups, business establishments, or church leaders to "clean up the neighbourhood." Occasionally, the police find it expedient to arrest prostitutes because they may divulge information about unsolved crimes, such as narcotics distribution, theft, receiving stolen property, or organized crime.

Prostitution encompasses a variety of both acts and actors. The prostitute, female or male, is not alone in the business of prostitution. A **pimp** provides access to prostitutes and protects and exploits them, living off their proceeds. There are still madams who maintain houses of prostitution. And finally, there are the patrons of prostitutes, popularly called "johns."

The vast majority (over 90 percent) of recorded prostitution-related offences involve communicating to buy or sell sex, as opposed to charges relating to the operation of a bawdy house or pimping charges, and most people charged are adults. Youth are involved in prostitution, but the tendency is for social services agencies to intervene when these individuals come to the attention of the authorities, rather than lay criminal charges. Prostitution is a policing-sensitive crime and, as a result, is influenced by the amount of effort and emphasis the police are willing to devote to policing this crime type. A crackdown on prostitution in a particular area will obviously affect the recorded crime rate for this offence. Criminal Code definitions also affect enforcement. For example, prior to 1985, the law condemned "solicitation" for the purposes of buying and/or selling sex. After 1985, the terminology changed to the present-day "communication" offence. This change in definition affected enforcement of the law. Since 1985, more men have been charged with "communicating" than was the case with the old "solicitation" law.[83]

Nonetheless, despite increasing numbers of men being charged with prostitution-related offences, women are penalized more harshly when they are charged and convicted. About 39 percent of women convicted received a prison sentence, compared to 3 percent of men convicted of the same offence. When the punishment is a fine, men outnumber women: 56 percent of men versus 32 percent of women received this more lenient disposition.[84]

While often referred to as a "victimless" crime because of the consensual nature of the agreement to buy and sell sex, prostitution is a dangerous occupation for the women and men who are selling their bodies. Between 1991 and 1995, 63 known prostitutes were murdered. Almost all (60) were female. Most of the deaths were directly related to the trade: 50 prostitutes were believed to have been killed by clients, and eight by pimps or in a drug-related incident. Street workers are at a much higher risk of physical and sexual assault, but because of the illegal nature of their trade are reluctant to report their victimizations.[85]

Researchers have found that many prostitutes come from broken homes and poor neighbourhoods and are school dropouts. Yet all social classes contribute to the prostitution hierarchy. High-priced call girls, many of them well-educated women, may operate singly or out of agencies. Some television channels carry commercials advertising the availability of call girls, their phone numbers, and sometimes their specialties. At the next lower level of the prostitution hierarchy are the massage-parlour prostitutes. When Shirley, a

For years, the Mustang Ranch, near Reno, was one of the many legal brothels in Nevada. The property was forfeited to the U.S. government in 1999 after guilty verdicts were obtained against the ranch's owner in a fraud and racketeering trial. The 104-room brothel was auctioned off on eBay in 2003 and moved 10 kilometres east of the original site to the Wild Horse Adult Resort & Spa, where the buildings were renovated and became the second brothel located at that complex. Plans are to restore the land where the original Mustang Ranch was located to natural conditions.

masseuse, was asked, "Do you consider yourself a prostitute?" she answered: "Yes, as well as a masseuse, and a healer, and a couple of other things."[86] One rung lower on the prostitution ladder are the "inmates" of the houses of prostitution, often called "bawdy houses," "bordellos," "whorehouses," "cathouses," or "red-light houses."

According to people "in the life" (prostitution), the streetwalkers are the least-respected class in the hierarchy. They are the "working girls" or "hookers." They are found clustered on their accustomed street corners, on thoroughfares, or in truck and bus depots, dressed in bright attire, ready to negotiate

a price with any passerby. Sexual services are performed in vehicles or in nearby "hot-sheet" hotel rooms. Life for these prostitutes—some of whom are transvestite males—is dangerous and grim. Self-reports suggest that many are drug addicts and have been exposed to HIV.[87] Another variety of prostitution is the bar ("B") girls who entertain customers in cocktail lounges and make themselves available for sexual activities for a price.

Popular, political, and scientific opinions on prostitution have changed, no doubt largely because prostitution has changed. Around the turn of the twentieth century, it probably was true that a large number of prostitutes had been forced into the occupation by unscrupulous men. There is a good deal of evidence that today the need for money, often fuelled by drug addiction, together with few legitimate opportunities to obtain it, prompts many young women and men to become prostitutes.

Feminist Perspectives Much of the research conducted on prostitution is feminist in nature. Concerned with the plight of sex trade workers, feminists are divided on the issue of prostitution. Radical feminists argue that prostitution is directly related to patriarchy and the power politics of the male gender: Prostitution is degrading not only to prostitutes but to all women and should therefore be eradicated. For radical feminists, prostitution is most certainly not a victimless crime. Rather, it permits men to "unconscionably oppress and coerce women in order to satisfy their own fantasies."[88] Liberal feminists, on the other hand, are more apt to see prostitution as a business transaction that benefits both parties to the arrangement. Socialist or Marxist feminists point out that prostitutes are oppressed and victimized both by patriarchy (men) and capitalism. In other words, they are "doubly marginalized"—first by their gender, and second by the fact that they are relegated to poorer-paying occupations in society. Prostitutes are those women who are on the lowest rungs of the socioeconomic ladder and who are therefore driven to sell their bodies to survive.

Feminist approaches each contribute meaningfully to a discussion of prostitution and each provides different insight into the issue. While feminists engage in heated debate about which

Global Sexual Slavery: Women and Children

"I thought I was going to work as a waitress," a young Dominican, transported to Greece, told BBC television, her eyes welling with tears. "Then they said if I didn't have sex, I'd be sent back to Santo Domingo without a penny. I was beaten, burned with cigarettes. I knew nobody. I was a virgin. I held out for five days, crying, with no food. [Eventually] I lost my honor and my virginity for $25."(1)

This woman's story is a common one. While some women in foreign countries become prostitutes by choice, many are forced into it. The growing sex trade around the world needs a constant supply of bodies, and it is getting them however it can. The statistics are horrifying: For the brothels of Bombay, some 7000 adolescents from Nepal's Himalayan hill villages are sold to slave traders each year. In Brazil, the number of girls forced into prostitution in mining camps is estimated at 25 000. Japan's bars feature approximately 70 000 Thai "hostesses" working as sex slaves. Some 200 000 Bangladeshi women have been kidnapped into prostitution in Pakistan.(1)

The numbers of underage prostitutes are equally shocking, whether the children were sold into slavery or are trying to survive in a harsh world by selling their bodies: 800 000 in Thailand; 400 000 in India; 250 000 in Brazil; and 60 000 in the Philippines. Child prostitution recently has increased in Russian and East European cities, with an estimated 1000 youngsters working in Moscow alone.(2) In Vietnam, fathers may act as pimps for their daughters to get money for the family to survive:

> Dr. Hoa, [a] pediatrician from Vietnam, said she asked the fathers of her young patients why they sold their daughters' services. "One father came with his 12-year-old daughter," Dr. Hoa recalled. "She was bleeding from her wounds and as torn as if she had given birth. He told me, 'We've earned $300, so it's enough. She can stop now.'"(3)

The physical wounds suffered by underage prostitutes are part of the terrible irony of the growing market for sex with children. Customers request children under the mistaken belief that they are less likely to be infected with the virus that causes AIDS. In fact, because children are so likely to incur injuries in intercourse, they are more vulnerable to infection.(2)

Experts at a 1993 conference on the sex trade and human rights cited the global AIDS epidemic, pornography, peep shows, and "sex tours" as factors responsible for the increasing demand for child prostitutes.(3) Organized sex tours form a large part of the market for bodies of any age; Taiwan, South Korea, the Philippines, and Thailand have been favourite destinations for sex tourists, and many other places are gaining in popularity.

A UNICEF report from January 2002 estimates that 1 million children are brought into the multibillion-dollar global trade every year.(4)

Sources

1. Margot Hornblower, "The Skin Trade," *Time,* June 21, 1993, pp. 45–51.
2. Michael S. Serrill, "Defiling the Children," *Time,* June 21, 1993, pp. 53–55.
3. Marlise Simons, "The Sex Market: Scourge on the World's Children," *New York Times,* Apr. 9, 1993, p. A3.
4. UNICEF Press Release, Jan. 18, 2002, UNICEF Media, Geneva, Switzerland.

Questions for Discussion

1. How would you begin to fight the exploitation of women and children in the sex market?
2. What are some of the forces at work that would make such a fight difficult?

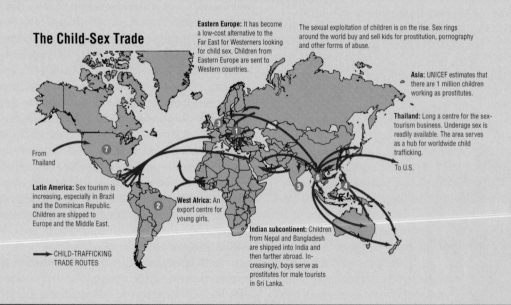

The Child-Sex Trade

Eastern Europe: It has become a low-cost alternative to the Far East for Westerners looking for child sex. Children from Eastern Europe are sent to Western countries.

The sexual exploitation of children is on the rise. Sex rings around the world buy and sell kids for prostitution, pornography and other forms of abuse.

Asia: UNICEF estimates that there are 1 million children working as prostitutes.

Thailand: Long a centre for the sex-tourism business. Underage sex is readily available. The area serves as a hub for worldwide child trafficking.

To U.S.

From Thailand

Latin America: Sex tourism is increasing, especially in Brazil and the Dominican Republic. Children are shipped to Europe and the Middle East.

West Africa: An export centre for young girls.

Indian subcontinent: Children from Nepal and Bangladesh are shipped into India and then farther abroad. Increasingly, boys serve as prostitutes for male tourists in Sri Lanka.

→ CHILD-TRAFFICKING TRADE ROUTES

perspective is most applicable, they are all united by their shared objective: promoting a world in which women enjoy an equal share of the rights and power.[89] Perhaps some of the differences between feminist views stem from the stereotypical description of a "prostitute" employed by many feminists. Sarah Bromberg presents a typology of prostitutes that describes nine different situations that can lead to prostitution among women. The categories range from women who are poor and destitute and prostitute themselves to survive, to situations where women choose to temporarily do the work until they find something better, to those who voluntarily choose prostitution because it suits their needs.[90] Prostitution is a complicated social issue, and clearly a complicated feminist issue as well.

Whatever view we take of adult prostitutes as victims of a supposedly victimless criminal activity, one subgroup clearly is a victimized class: children, female and male, who are enticed and sometimes forced into prostitution, especially in large cities. Some are runaways, picked up by procurers at bus depots; some are simply "street children"; and others have been abused and molested by the adults in their lives.[91]

Pornography

Physical sexual contact is a basic component of prostitution. **Pornography** requires no contact at all; it simply portrays sexually explicit material. Section 163 of the Criminal Code makes it an offence to publish or circulate any obscene "thing." "Obscene" is defined as the undue exploitation of sex and crime, horror, cruelty, and violence.

The Problem of Definition The term "pornographic" is derived from the Greek *pornographos* ("writing of harlots," or descriptions of the acts of harlots). The term "obscene" comes from the Latin *ob* ("against," "before") plus *caenum* ("filth"), or possibly from *obscena* ("offstage"). In Roman theatrical performances, disgusting and offensive parts of plays took place offstage, out of sight but not out of hearing of the audience.[92] Courts and legislators have used the two terms interchangeably, but nearly all decisions deal with pornography (with the implication of sexual arousal) rather than with obscenity (with its implication of filth).[93] Part of the difficulty of enforcing the law is the subjective nature of "obscenity"; what is obscene to one person may not be to another. In determining what is obscene, judges are to consider whether the material in question violates community standards. Adult nudity is not considered obscene; a picture of adult-and-child sex is.

Libertarian movements in Canada and the United States in the 1960s fought for less stringent definitions of pornography, but despite these efforts, Canada retained its relatively restrictive definition of pornography. In the 1980s, feminists and conservative groups began to press legislators to strengthen the obscenity law by criminalizing violent and degrading pornography. A Special Committee on Pornography and Prostitution was formed (the Fraser Commission) to investigate the issue; its recommendation was to criminalize such material. While lawmakers did not implement such changes, the courts, following their mandate to penalize behaviours that violate community standards, began incorporating a feminist approach in judgments beginning around the mid-1980s.[94]

More recent changes to laws governing pornography focus on the exploitation of children. In 1993 a child pornography law was passed, making Canada a country with some of the harshest penalties in the world for this crime. Under the Criminal Code, offenders who possess images of children under the age of 18 engaging in sexual activity can be sentenced for up to five years in prison.[95] Section 163.1(1) of the Criminal Code defines **child pornography** as:

> a photographic, film, video, or other visual representation, whether or not it was made by electronic or mechanical means (i) that shows a person who is or is depicted as being under the age of 18 years and is engaged in or is depicted as engaged in explicit sexual activity or (ii) the dominant characteristic of which is the depiction, for a sexual purpose, of a sexual organ or the anal region of a person under the age of 18 years.

> ### Did You Know?
>
> ... that at least 146 Canadians have been charged overseas for sexually abusing children, particularly in countries such as Cambodia and Thailand, where children are easy targets for abusers? Many more have bribed their way out of being charged.

Pornography has a place in society—there exists a demand for material that sexually arouses its audience. However, the law steps in when pornography is of the type that produces harm and is exploitative of its subjects. Pornography that uses violence, degradation, or children is a clear example of the latter type. A recurring debate surrounding pornography concerns the existence of a link between its use and violent behaviour.

Pornography and Violence An extensive amount of research has investigated the association between pornography, on the one hand, and violence and crime, on the other. This research has focused on public attitudes toward pornography, experiences with pornography, the association between the availability of pornography and crime rates, the experience of sex offenders with pornography, and the relation between pornography and behaviour. Generally, the research has found little or no evidence that links explicit sexual materials to criminal behaviours.[96] Additional research has also found that non-violent and non-degrading pornography is not significantly associated with crime and aggression. Some of the research did conclude, however, that exposure to pornographic materials

> (1) leads to a greater acceptance of rape myths and violence against women; (2) results in pronounced effects when the victim is shown enjoying the use of force or violence; (3) is arousing for rapists and for some males in the general population; and (4) has resulted in sexual aggression against women in the laboratory.[97]

The Feminist View: Victimization For some feminists, these conclusions support the call for greater restrictions on the manufacture and dissemination of pornographic material. For them pornography is viewed as an expression of male culture through which women are commodified and exploited. The historian Joan Hoff has coined the term "pornerotic," meaning

> any representation of persons that sexually objectifies them and is accompanied by actual or implied violence in ways designed to encourage readers or viewers that such sexual subordination of women (or children or men) is acceptable behaviour or an innocuous form of sex education.[98]

Hoff's definition also suggests that pornography, obscenity, and erotica may do far more than offend sensitivities. Such material may victimize not only the people who are depicted but all women (or men or children, if they are the people shown). Pornographers have been accused of promoting the exploitation, objectification, and degradation of women. Many people who call for the abolition of violent pornography argue that it also promotes violence toward women. Reflective of this feminist view, in *R. v. Butler* in 1992, the Supreme Court of Canada defined material as obscene if it contains sexual violence, is degrading or dehumanizing, or involves sexual portrayals of children.

However, as we saw in our discussion on prostitution, there are also some liberal feminists who argue that in combination, a respect for free speech and the principle "a woman's body, a woman's right," means that pornography isn't the evil is it often made out to be. As one feminist writer explains: "as a woman I am appalled by *Playboy* . . . but as a writer I understand the need for free expression."[99] Proponents of another view, termed "pro-sex" feminism, argue that pornography has personal and political benefits for women. Examples of some of the personal benefits are that pornography provides sexual information, breaks cultural and political stereotypes so that each woman can interpret sex for herself, and can be good therapy. Politically, pornography is free speech applied to the sexual realm. Additionally, legitimizing pornography would protect women sex workers, who are stigmatized by society.[100] The debate between feminists ensues. Andrea Dworkin gets at the extent of the division between feminists when she says that "no one who defends pornography can be a feminist." And, as Page Mellish of Feminists Fighting Pornography states, "there's no feminist issue that isn't rooted in the porn problem."[101] One of the main issues in the debate over

> **Did You Know?**
>
> . . . that Canada's child-sex tourism law was passed in 1997 and toughened in 2002 so that the foreign country where the allegations of sexual abuse took place no longer had to consent to the charges? Since that time, only one individual has been convicted under the law. Donald Bakker received a 10-year sentence for 10 sexual assaults on girls between the ages of seven and 12 in Cambodia, where he videotaped the abuse.

Cyberporn: Where Do We (Should We) Draw the Line?

- Toronto police targeted 241 pedophile suspects in the Greater Toronto Area who allegedly paid to view pornographic images on the Internet that investigators described as "evil." Among those arrested were a police officer, a teacher, and a doctor.(1)
- A man was charged with possession of child pornography (two counts), accessing child pornography, distributing and making child pornography and theft of telecommunications after he attracted the attention of the police by driving on the wrong side of the road. When stopped, the man, naked from the waste down, was found to be downloading pornography by cracking into a computer in a nearby home while driving.(2)
- A 23-year-old woman started her own porn website as a hobby. She expects to make about $50 000 a week on the site in the next year. This money will allow her to cut back on making movies and dancing at clubs. She is one of many women in the porn industry who have set up their own websites as alternative businesses.(3)
- Some men find themselves "addicted" to cyberporn, spending as much as 80 hours per week online. Their real sex lives and relationships are damaged as online sex becomes more important and fulfilling than the

real thing, leading some marriages to end in divorce.(4)

The Internet provides an ever-increasing number of avenues for the distribution of pornography. For entrepreneurs setting up porn sites, the Internet is proving quite lucrative. However, some of those who use it find themselves in legal trouble when they go beyond legal pornography to child pornography or use sex chat rooms to solicit sex with children. Even those who stick to legal porn may face problems related to their jobs or their personal relationships. It is unlikely that pornography—both legal and illegal—on the Internet will decrease in the years to come.

Of all the issues regarding pornography on the Internet, one of the most hotly debated is censorship. While some programs can limit access to porn sites, they do not prevent the exploitation of children or keep those who wish to access the sites from doing so. Child pornographers are creative and adaptable, shying away from explicit child pornography. Many frequent preteen and teen nudism news groups and sites, where thousands of photographs of nude children await them in an apparently "constitutionally protected" cyberspace. The question remains as to what can be done to limit children's access to pornographic sites as well as to prevent their exploitation

on the Internet while still protecting freedom of speech. Where should courts draw the line?

Sources

1. Josh Rubin, "Teacher, Doctor Nabbed in Porn Probe: Police Make Plea for Resources to Stop Spread of 'Evil,'" TheStar.com, Jan. 16, 2003.
2. "Police Warn of Wi-Fi Theft by Porn Downloaders," CTV.ca, November 23, 2003, www.ctv.ca, accessed Oct. 30, 2007.
3. John Leland, "More Bang for the Buck: How Sex on the Internet Has Transformed the Business of Pornography," *Newsweek,* Oct. 11, 1999, p. 73.
4. Greg Gutfield, "The Sex Drive: Web Pornography Has Turned Computers into Sex Objects, and Men, by the Millions, Are Hooking Up, Should You?" *Men's Health,* Oct. 1, 1999, p. 116.

Questions for Discussion

1. Why do you think seemingly normal individuals procure child pornography on the Internet or become "addicted" to cyberporn?
2. What can society do to limit the damage to children by child pornographers who use the Internet as a means of distribution? What should be done with those who are caught?

pornography is that between individual freedom and social control.

The Legal View: Enforcing Pornography Laws In 1995, John Robin Sharpe was arrested and charged with two counts of possession of child pornography and two counts of distributing child pornography. In addition to pictures of boys under the age of 14 engaged in sex, he had written a collection of stories titled *Kiddie Kink Classics.* He fought the charges claiming the stories and images had "artistic merit." The Supreme Court of Canada heard the case in January 2000, but after a lengthy

debate, it was sent back to British Columbia courts for retrial. In the end, Sharpe was found not guilty of possessing written child pornography, but was found guilty on two counts of possessing pornographic pictures of children. He was sentenced to four months of house arrest. The case drew attention to the broad interpretation by the courts of child pornography laws, leading to the creation of Bill C-20, which toughened Canada's child pornography laws and clarified the type of written material that constitutes child pornography.[102]

Enforcing child pornography laws is difficult. The Toronto Child Exploitation police unit has been operating since 2000. In their first three years of operation, they made 27 arrests and seized 84 computers with millions of pornographic images.[103] While they have extensive lists of suspects, numbering in the thousands, resources are insufficient to investigate even a small portion of them. Compounding this problem is the frustration of what are perceived as weak sentences, despite Canada's tough laws governing child pornography. For example, convicted pedophile Tony Marr was in possession of 64 000 pornographic images when police arrested him. He received a conditional sentence and probation.[104]

Child pornography is an international phenomenon, which makes it even more difficult to police. Compounding the lack of resources and the elusiveness of offenders is the increasing ease with which they can access, create, and distribute pornographic material over the Internet.

Pornography and the Internet Any child with basic knowledge of a computer and a minimal amount of curiosity can, with a few clicks of a mouse, open a doorway to the world of cyberporn: pictures of adults having sexual intercourse, adults having intercourse with animals, video clips of adults having sex with children, and guides to bordellos, massage parlours, and various pleasure districts—both local and international.[105]

Censorship of the Internet has been a heavily debated issue in recent times. Almost everyone agrees that access of minors to pornographic material over the Internet should be restricted, but the primary point of contention remains: Who should be responsible for policing access to such material? Parents? Educators? The government? Responding to increasing awareness and concern about Internet predators, legislators passed Bill C-15A, which became law in July 2002. It deals specifically with child pornography and exploitation on the Internet, including cyber-luring—using the Internet to communicate with children for sex.

As we have discussed throughout this text, law creation is one thing, human behaviour another, and law enforcement yet another. Passing Bill C-15A was certainly a step in the right direction as far as legal definitions of behaviour are concerned. But changes in law do not necessarily translate into changes in behaviour. To start with, 38 percent of young people using the Internet say their parents know nothing or very little about their online activities. Furthermore, one in four children has had a stranger ask to meet them in person.[106] Project Snowball, an initiative launched by Toronto police, targeted more than 2000 Canadians suspected of viewing pornographic images on the Internet that fall under the child pornography legislation.[107] American investigators have traced over 250 000 suspected pedophiles around the world through credit-card details on child porno sites. This is likely just the tip of the iceberg.

Anyone with a computer and a modem can access cyber pornography. Pornography of all sorts—from child pornography to bondage and S & M—is available on binary files in newsgroups, chat rooms, bulletin boards, and individual websites. Canadian Internet service providers have agreed to voluntarily block access to child pornography websites using filtering technology.

One of the biggest issues surrounding government regulation of pornography on the Internet is the lack of global cooperation. Legislation on pornography varies around the world, and thus means that pornography can be easily sent across borders. Strategies are currently being developed by several international agencies to increase communication, provide hotlines for users to report illegal material, make laws more unified, and prevent the exploitation of children on a global scale.

Another significant issue is the fine line between what some call eroticism and others call child pornography. Perhaps the most famous photographer of young girls—David Hamilton—prides himself on belonging to an elite group of art photographers. His books—which no doubt appeal to child pornographers—are carried by most large chain bookstores and are "on" the Internet. But is this art or child pornography? Is it constitutionally protected or should it be criminally prosecuted? These two questions will be at the forefront of a debate about pornography on and off the Web.

In the wake of the continued controversy over "cybersmut," several computer programs have been developed to assist parents and educators in regulating children's access to the Internet. Programs such as Net Nanny, Cyber Patrol, and Surf Watch are designed to block access to sites deemed inappropriate for children.

These programs, however, are far from effective. The software must be continually updated to keep up with the new sites added on a daily basis. If activated by certain keywords, access may also be limited to potentially educational sites (such as those related to sexual harassment). Also, the cost of implementing such programs in a particular school district could run into tens of thousands of dollars.

Another approach is to report online child exploitation in an effort to shut down illegal websites. Cybertip.ca is a national program created by Child Find Manitoba in 2002. The first online service in Canada to report instances of child exploitation, the website collects complaints and incident reports about child sexual exploitation or luring on the Internet and forwards the most serious to appropriate law enforcement agencies.[108] As of 2005, the group had influenced the shutdown of over 400 websites hosting illegal material and ten arrests—all the result of the public coming forward to launch complaints and reports. While the group and its website are perceived by many as reducing harm to children, opponents of censorship consider the website and its activities a violation of rights to freedom of expression. Nonetheless, in December 2006, a group of Canada's largest Internet service providers, including Bell, MTS Allstream, Rogers, Shaw, Telus, and Videotron, entered into an agreement with Cybertip.ca to voluntarily block access to child pornography websites using filtering technology.[109]

Visit the Online Learning Centre: www.mcgrawhill.ca/olc/adler

REVIEW

1. What is drug abuse? Is it related to crime?

Intoxicating substances have been used for religious, medicinal, and recreational purposes throughout history. Lifestyles of people who use them are as varied as the drugs they favour.

Governments have repeatedly tried to prevent the abuse of these substances. The drug problem today is significant, and it grows more serious every year. Heroin and cocaine in particular are associated with many crimes. A vast international criminal empire has been organized to promote the production and distribution of drugs. These groups are experts at **money laundering** (p. 333). Efforts of law enforcement and health agencies to control the drug problem take the forms of interna-tional cooperation in stemming drug trafficking, treatment of addicts, education of the public, and arrest and incarceration of offenders. Some observers, comparing the drug problem with the wide evasion of prohibition laws and the consequent rise in crime, believe that drugs should be legalized. **Decriminalization** (p. 336) is an option for dealing with currently illicit substances, as is a **harm-reduction approach** (p. 337). Such alternatives to criminalization are a cause of debate among citizens and politicians.

2. What is the relationship between alcohol and crime?

Legalization of alcoholic beverages, however, has not solved all problems related to alcohol. The abuse of alcohol has been reliably linked to violence, and the incidence of drunk driving has increased so alarmingly that citizen groups have formed to combat the problem.

3. How do we legislate sexual morality?

The legal regulation of sexual conduct has undergone striking changes in recent decades. Many sexual "offences" once categorized as serious crimes no longer concern society or government. In this sphere, research has done much to influence public opinion and, consequently, legislation. **Prostitution** (p. 341), which refers to the sale and/or purchase of sex, is technically not illegal in Canada, although a variety of prostitution-related offences exist. **Pornography** (p. 345), and in particular **child pornography** (p. 345) and its dissemination over the Internet, remain hotly debated issues.

CRIMINOLOGY & PUBLIC POLICY

"Child pornography law presents the opportunity for a case study of how censorship law responds to and shapes a cultural crisis. We have two corresponding events. On the one hand, we have the 'discovery' in the late 1970s of the twin problems of child sexual abuse and child pornography, and the continuation of the problems to the point where they have reached the level of an ongoing, 'ever-widening' crisis. On the other hand, we have child pornography law. Born in the same period, created to solve the problem of child sexual abuse, child pornography law too has grown dramatically in the past two decades, expanding and proliferating along with the underlying problem that it targets. Yet, curiously, the law's expansion has not solved the problem, but only presided over its escalation. As child pornography law has expanded since the late 1970s, so has a 'culture of child abuse,' a growing 'panic' about the threat to children.

"What, if any, is the relationship between these two concurrent phenomena—the expansion of child pornography law and the growing problem of child sexual abuse, including child pornography? Does their correlative temporal connection allow us to draw any conclusions about a possible causal relationship?

"There is a standard, conventional explanation for this correlation. This account casts law in a reactive stance: As the sexual exploitation of children, or at least our awareness of the problem, has risen, legislatures and courts have responded by passing and upholding tougher child pornography laws. As the crisis has surged, so has the law. In this view, cultural horror drives law to play a game of catch-up. Law is always a step behind the problem, racing to keep pace with a burgeoning social crisis.

"I am sure that is at least part of what is going on. But in this Article, I propose two alternative readings—readings that do not exclude the conventional account described above, but supplement it. In the first reading, I explore the possibility that certain sexual prohibitions invite their own violation by increasing the sexual allure of what they forbid. I suggest that child pornography law and the eroticization of children exist in a dialectic of transgression and taboo: The dramatic expansion of child pornography law may have unwittingly heightened pedophilic desire.

"I then turn to a second reading, which reveals the previous one to be an only partially satisfactory account. In the second reading, I view law and the culture it regulates not as dialectical opposites, but as intermingled. Child pornography law may represent only another symptom of and not a solution to the problem of child abuse or the cultural fascination with sexual children. The cross purposes of law and culture that I describe above (law as prohibition, which both halts and incites desire) may mask a deeper harmony between them: The legal discourse on prohibiting child pornography may represent yet another way in which our culture drenches itself in sexualized children.

"The point of this Article is that laws regulating child pornography may produce perverse, unintended consequences and that the legal battle we are waging may have unrecognized costs. I do not doubt, however, that child pornography law has substantial social benefits. In fact, I do not doubt that these benefits might outweigh the costs detailed. I nonetheless focus on these costs as a means to unsettle the confident assumption of most courts, legislators, and academics that the current approach to child pornography law is unequivocally sound. I question their conviction that the more regulation we impose the more harm we avert. Ultimately, I raise questions about the nature of censorship itself." (*Source:* Amy Adler, "The Perverse Law of Child Pornography," Columbia Law Review, **101**, 2001: 209. Copyright 2001 by Columbia Law Review Association, Inc. Reproduced with permission of Columbia Law Review Association, Inc., in the format Textbook via Copyright Clearance Center.)

Questions for Discussion What do you think of Prof. Adler's thesis? Is it possible that child pornography laws further the very victimization that they are designed to inhibit?

YOU BE THE CRIMINOLOGIST

Significant debate continues over how to reduce drug use and what to do with users and dealers. If you were to make a recommendation to the government on how to design the next drug-control strategy, what would you recommend? On what evidence would you base your recommendations? Would you emphasize social control and tougher laws? Would you provide more funding for treatment programs or safe injection sites? Focus on education? Target organized crime groups? Some combination? Or would you recommend an altogether new approach? What would it look like?

Visit the Online Learning Centre: www.mcgrawhill.ca/olc/adler

INTERNATIONAL AND COMPARATIVE CRIMINOLOGY

CHAPTER 14

CHAPTER QUESTIONS

1. How does comparative
criminology differ from other
types of criminology?

2. How do we do comparative
criminology?

3. What is the role of theory testing
in comparative criminology?

4. What is the objective of
comparative criminology?

Neo-Nazi groups march in Germany on the anniversary of the death of Rudolf Hess, one of Hitler's best-known associates and one of the few Nazis to serve a long prison term.

"**K**ill one (Sikh) and you're a murderer. Kill many and you're a conqueror. Kill them all and you're a god," boasted Daniel Miloszewski in a secretly recorded conversation with an undercover police officer. Daniel and four accomplices, members of the White Power neo-Nazi group, were later sentenced to between 12 and 15 years in prison for the beating death of 65-year-old Nirmal Singh Gill outside a British Columbia gurdwara. Neo-Nazi skinheads have become notorious for their random assaults on blacks, Jews, gays, immigrants, minority groups— anybody they perceive as different and whom they therefore dislike. They revere Hitler and his terror, delight in overt racist music, display swastikas and Nazi flags, and serve as shock troops for more established racist organizations. In the United States alone, between 3300 and 3500 skinheads are scattered in 160 or so groups. They have become so dangerous that the FBI had to withdraw some undercover agents who had infiltrated their ranks.[1]

Few people had heard of skinheads prior to May 1985, when groups from Britain, Belgium, Denmark, and France staged a riot at a soccer game in Belgium, which left 38 people of colour dead and another 200 wounded. Since then, skinheads have become a daily news item in many countries.

Recently, an estimated 70 000 youths, in 33 countries, on six continents, adhered to the neo-Nazi skinhead movement, with the largest concentrations in Germany, Hungary, the Czech Republic, the United States, Poland, the United Kingdom, Brazil, Italy, and Sweden (listed in descending order).[2]

Hardest hit has been Germany, the birthplace of Nazism, where the homes of Jewish families have been firebombed and hundreds of foreign workers and asylum seekers have been attacked or killed. The skinheads attack with screams of "Heil Hitler," waving their favourite symbol, the old German imperial flag.

Their ideology, if that is the word, is primitive. . . . They know nothing about Hitler, or the war, beyond the fact that Hitler exterminated people who were "different," which is what they like to do themselves. They do not even know about the "ethnic cleansing" perpetrated recently in Bosnia. They do not read newspapers. They read killer comic books and listen to Oi music, which is a kind of heavy-metal rock about the pleasures of "genocide."[3]

In 1990–1991 it had been the mosques of the London region. By 1994–1995 the torch was turned on some 70 African-American churches in the southern United States, nearly all with the hallmark of hate crime. In France, hate has now reversed. The new "enemy," born of the suburban ghettos, is of mostly African origin, a ragtag subcultural group. Their common language is "hip-hop." Their roots are "in the Bronx and Kingston, Jamaica; in South-Central Los Angeles and Brixton, London; in Dakar and Algiers, in Islam and the N.B.A."[4] Its hallmarks are rage, graffiti, drug dealing, and firearms. For the time being, this movement has been dubbed the "guerrilla renaissance." What has caused the rise of neo-Nazism and the formation of skinhead groups, of torchers of houses of worship, and of "guerrilla renaissance," almost simultaneously, in so many different parts of the world? Who defines the often bizarre ideology of such groups? Do adherents communicate with each other across borders?

353

To answer these questions, criminologists must engage in comparative research. But so far, there are few answers. For the skinheads, criminologist Mark Hamm has begun this process with his work *American Skinheads—The Criminology and Control of Hate Crime*, which presents the phenomenon in an international perspective. He traces American developments to earlier occurrences in England and to the ideological background of Nazism in Germany.[5] Yet much more comparative research remains to be done to explain the almost simultaneous occurrence of identical crime problems in many parts of the world.

We begin this chapter on comparative criminology with an attempt to define it. We look next at the history of comparative criminology in order to identify its purpose and goals. Later in the chapter we focus on the prerequisites for comparative criminological research, the process itself, and the challenges globalization is posing to comparative criminology.

WHAT IS COMPARATIVE CRIMINOLOGY?

Comparison is something all human beings do every day. In choosing a home, for example, you compare such elements as number of rooms and price; location; access to transportation, shopping, and recreation; age of the structure; beauty of the surroundings; and so on. This comparison can become a science if it is done in a systematic manner. And so it is with comparative criminology.[6]

The Definition of Comparative Criminology

What is **comparative criminology?** Simply put, it is the cross-cultural or cross-national study of crime and crime control applying the comparative method in the science of criminology.[7]

Many criminologists use comparisons. Just think of a study comparing one group with another group, a control group. But this is not what we mean by comparative criminology; it requires comparison across cultures or nations. A comparative study of victimization rates between Saskatchewan and Ontario is not comparative criminology, because the two provinces are part of one nation and of one basic culture. But if we were to compare the role of alcohol in the escalation of violence among the Cree, in Alberta, with that among the people of the rest of the province, we might well have a cross-cultural comparison, because the Cree have a distinct legal system and a culture of their own.

The History of Comparative Criminology

Comparative criminology is not new. When the Romans had a crime problem in the fifth century B.C., they sent a delegation to the more advanced nation of Greece to learn better techniques for dealing with crime, such as the publication of laws. In the late Middle Ages and during the Renaissance (fourteenth to sixteenth centuries), all of continental Europe became a vast comparative laboratory as laws that had developed in the various principalities and cities were compared against the rediscovered laws of the old Roman Empire.

It was also during this era that crime-control methods became ever more brutal. The situation did not change until the eighteenth century, when—again through comparison, cooperation, and transfer—the work of the classical school (see Chapter 3) began to introduce rationality and humanitarian principles

Luther and Johnny Htoo, 12-year-old twin Myanmar messianic guerrilla leaders. Luther prepares to fire an M-16 rifle.

into crime control in Europe and North America. In the nineteenth century, as communications improved, policy makers and scholars of criminology compared approaches and introduced into one another's systems what seemed to work. Such ideas as the juvenile court, the penitentiary, the reformatory, probation, and parole gained worldwide acceptance as a result of comparison. Yet the comparisons of the nineteenth and early twentieth centuries lacked scientific rigour; they were impressionistic and often emotional. For example, the juvenile court, first established in Chicago in 1899, seemed such a good idea that it gained acceptance in many parts of the world. But as later experience showed, it did not necessarily work everywhere.

The founders of criminology, were, for the most part, comparatists. They would gather at international meetings and trade ideas; they would visit each other and stimulate criminological thought. But truly comparative studies, measuring up to scholarly standards, could not be done until criminology itself became a science. Throughout the first half of the twentieth century, internationalism met resistance from isolationism. Comparatists were regarded as dreamers, and the comparative approach was seen as not very practical.

The Global Village: Advantages   Now circumstances have changed drastically. Comparative criminologists have become a necessity, simply because the world has become a "global village." Consider these figures: in 1960, U.S. exports amounted to US$19 659 million. By 2004, that figure had increased to US$0.8 trillion. Similarly, in 1960, imports amounted to US$15 073 million. By 2004 that figure had increased to US$1.5 trillion. And that is only part of the global trade picture.

World economies have become totally integrated and interdependent. The Japanese car you own was probably manufactured in the United States, and your North American car may have parts made in more than 30 countries. Your shirt may come from Hong Kong, your shoes from Italy, and your Swiss watch from the American Virgin Islands. The situation is no different abroad, where Coke and Pepsi and American fast-food chains are only the most visible aspects of economic globalization.

Communications likewise have become global. Sitting in your living room before a TV, you participate in world events as they happen. Phone and fax and computer networking have made instant

personal and business communications possible. Transportation advances, especially since the introduction of jumbo jets, together with the opening of frontiers, have made it possible for millions of people to move across oceans within hours. Air-traffic volume increased from 33.4 billion passenger miles in 1960 to close to 5 trillion by the end of 2003.

Europe is feeling the effects of globalization even more intensely than the rest of the world. The collapse of Communist dictatorships in central and eastern Europe[8] and the virtual abolition of frontiers within Europe[9] have brought crime problems until now unheard of in Europe. Consequently, national criminology had to become international criminology. Criminology has in fact been globalized.[10]

The Global Village: Disadvantages   While many aspects of the global village are beneficial, others have brought great problems. Instant communication promotes not only the spread of benefits, in goods, lifestyles, and useful knowledge, but also the dissemination of dysfunctional ideas and values—like the skinhead phenomenon. Economic globalization, as much as it promotes useful commerce, also aids organized crime and fosters the global spread of frauds that were once confined to smaller localities or single countries.

Jet planes transport not just legitimate travellers but also illegal aliens, criminal entrepreneurs, drug dealers, money launderers, and terrorists. Airlines themselves have become the targets and tools of international criminals. Moreover, the industrialization of the world brings not just economic benefits but threats to the world ecology so severe that, unless checked, they could compromise the food, water, and clean air supply for all people. It is little wonder, then, that criminologists, too, must look across borders to study crime and crime-control efforts, and to search for internationally acceptable solutions to common problems.

The Goals of Comparative Research

Before the 1970s, there was very little literature on comparative research in criminology. Since then, however, it has been growing rapidly. That is attributable to (1) a realization that we will learn more about crime if we test our theories under diverse cultural conditions and (2) renewed interest in trying to discover what we can learn from the experience of other nations.[11]

Comparative criminology, then, has both theoretical and practical goals. It helps us better understand crime causation and find successful means of crime control so that no nation need repeat costly mistakes made elsewhere.

Presently, a large number of UN and affiliated organizations are engaged in the task of establishing international measures to deal with dangers that threaten people of all cultures. (See Table 14.1.)

TABLE 14.1 United Nations Organizations and Affiliates: Solving Worldwide Crime Problems

Center for International Crime Prevention, in the Office for Drug Control and Crime Prevention (of the UN Secretariat at Vienna, Austria): Reports to the UN Commission on Crime Prevention and Criminal Justice and conducts the quinquennial UN Congress on the Prevention of Crime and the Treatment of Offenders; provides extensive reports, research, documentation, and technical assistance; is responsible for UN standards and guidelines in criminal justice; conducts worldwide statistical surveys.

UNICRI—United Nations Interregional Crime and Justice Research Institute (located in Turin, Italy): Research arm of the UN Secretariat in crime prevention and criminal justice; is responsible for extensive research and publications.

UNAFEI—United Nations Asia and Far East Institute for the Prevention of Crime and the Treatment of Offenders (Fuchu, Japan): Services the region with training, technical assistance, research, and publications.

ILANUD—United Nations Latin American Institute for the Prevention of Crime and the Treatment of Offenders (San José, Costa Rica): Services the region with training, technical assistance, research, and publications.

UNAFRI—United Nations African Regional Institute for the Prevention of Crime and the Treatment of Offenders (Kampala, Uganda): Services the region with training and technical assistance.

HEUNI—Helsinki European Institute for Crime Prevention and Control; affiliated with the United Nations (Helsinki, Finland): Provides extensive research, training, research publications, and technical assistance services on behalf of European countries for both developed and developing countries.

AIC—Australian Institute of Criminology (Canberra, Australia): Under agreement with the UN, provides research, publication, training, and technical assistance services for Oceania, including Australia and New Zealand.

Arab Security Studies and Training Centre (Riyadh, Saudi Arabia): In close cooperation with the UN, provides extensive educational and training services, research, publications, and development and technical assistance to Arab countries.

International Centre for Criminal Law Reform and Criminal Justice Policy (Vancouver, B.C.): Newly established, by agreement with the UN, to provide services within its sphere of expertise.

ISPAC—International Scientific and Professional Advisory Council of the United Nations Crime Prevention and Criminal Justice Programme (Milan, Italy): By agreement with the UN, provides advisory services to the UN with respect to data and information, both in general and on specific subjects falling within the mandate of the UN.

UNCJIN—United Nations Crime and Justice Information Network (Albany, NY): In close cooperation with *WCJLN*—World Criminal Justice Library Network (Newark, NJ)—assembles, integrates, and disseminates criminal justice information and data worldwide, with a view to complete electronic accessibility.

NIJ—The National Institute of Justice, of the U.S. Department of Justice: By an agreement with the United Nations signed in 1995, joined the Network of UN-affiliated institutes to make the services of the National Criminal Justice Reference Service—especially its UNOJUST computer services—available to the UN community through its International Center.

NGOs—Non-governmental organizations in consultative status with the United Nations Economic and Social Council: International organizations whose expertise is made available to the UN. They include many major scientific, professional, and advocacy groups, such as:

- International Association of Penal Law
- International Penal and Penitentiary Foundation (special status)
- International Society of Criminology
- International Society of Social Defense
- Institute of Higher Studies in Criminal Sciences
- Centro Nazionale di Prevenzione e Difesa Sociale
- International Association of Chiefs of Police
- International Prisoners Aid Association
- Amnesty International

NGO Alliances in Crime Prevention and Criminal Justice (New York, NY, and Vienna, Austria): Made up of the headquarters' representatives of NGOs; provide coordination and research services to the UN.

UN agencies: Concerned with various aspects of crime and justice. The agencies include:

- Centre for Human Rights (Geneva, Switzerland)
- UNICEF—United Nations Children's Fund (New York, NY)

The United Nations Centre for International Drug Control: Concerned with various aspects of international drug control and drug abuse prevention. The programs include:

- Division on Narcotic Drugs
- International Narcotic Drug Control Board
- UN Fund for Drug Abuse Control

Regional intergovernmental organizations: Have organizational units and/or conduct programs concerned with crime prevention and criminal justice. Examples include:

- Council of Europe
- European Union (EU)
- Organization of American States
- Organization of African Unity
- North Atlantic Treaty Organization

Group of seated Afghani men gathers for Shura (or elders) meeting near Kandahar, Afghanistan.

Before we discuss the implementation of comparative research, we must look at the methods used by comparative criminologists.

ENGAGING IN COMPARATIVE CRIMINOLOGICAL RESEARCH

Comparative research requires special preparatory work to ensure that research data and information are in fact comparable. Empirical research presents additional obstacles.

Preparatory Work

Studying Foreign Law Before beginning a comparative study, the researcher must become familiar with the laws of the country or culture to which the comparison extends. Every country belongs to one or more of the world's great families of law, or legal systems (see Table 14.2):

- *The civil law system.* This system grew out of the Roman legal tradition, was refined by scholars, and was codified under Napoleon in the early nineteenth century. Today it is

TABLE 14.2 Dominant Criminal Justice Systems

Roman (Civil) Law	Common Law	Other Legal Systems
Law and procedure governed by separate, comprehensive, systematized codes, which are forward-looking, wishing to anticipate new problems.	Law and procedure governed by laws and precedents, which, if codified at all, simply organize past exerpeinces.	*Islamic Law.* Called the "Sharia"; based in part on the Koran; of divine origin; covers all aspects of a Muslim's life; interpreted by judges and legal scholars; reasoning by analogy.
Codes based on scholarly analysis and conceptualizations.	Laws reflect experience of practitioners, on a case-by-case basis.	*Customary Law.* Also called "tribal law"; administered by elders; often exists side by side with civil or common law.
Supreme courts interpret nuances of law.	Supreme courts develop law.	
Legal proceedings must establish entire truth.	Truth finding strictly limited by pleadings and rules of evidence.	*Socialist Law.* Basically civil law; legal propositions subject to social/political policy.
Judges free to find and interpret facts.	Rules of evidence limit fact-finding process. Parties produce evidence.	*Mixed Systems.* A mix of civil and common law; may exist within a province or in a nation as a whole.
Very little lay participation.	Grand and petit juries play strong role.	
Originally, no presumption of guilt or innocence. Now presumption of innocence recognized.	Presumption of innocence.	

found in systematic codes of law. The countries of continental Europe belong to this family of law, as do their former colonies in Africa, Latin America, and Asia, including Japan and China (now socialist), which chose the civil law system when they modernized.

- *The common law system.* Common law originated in England and then spread to the various English colonies. Today it is the legal system not only of the United Kingdom but also of the United States, Canada (except Quebec), Australia, New Zealand, India, many of the Caribbean islands, and African and Asian countries that were once English colonies. Although common law is now found in written form, it originated from case law, and case precedents still play a determining role.
- *Other legal systems.* (See Table 14.2.)

Having identified the legal system to which the country under study belongs, the comparatist studies the applicable law and its precise interpretation. Foreign legal systems, just like that of Canada, contain penal codes, codes of criminal procedure, constitutions, and case reports. But they also include special legislation on such topics as environmental protection and money laundering. In federal countries, both federal and provincial or state legislation may have to be studied.

Then there is the problem of finding the country's laws. For the English-speaking researcher, this need not be an insurmountable task. The laws, court decisions, and textbooks of English-speaking countries, for the most part, are accessible in libraries. The constitutions,[12] criminal codes,[13] and codes of criminal procedure[14] of many other countries are available in English. For a number of non-English-speaking countries, there are English-language texts about their criminal law or procedure.[15] But since there is always a gap between the law on the books and the law in action, the comparatist must also consult the criminal justice research literature.

Understanding Foreign Criminal Justice Systems Laws function within a country's criminal justice system. It is the practitioners of the system who make the laws function. There are reports from around the world based on their experience.[16] There is also a considerable amount of periodical literature and statistical information in English describing the functioning of criminal justice systems in a variety of countries (see Table 14.3).[17]

TABLE 14.3 English-Language Periodical Literature for Comparative Criminology

Abstracting Services
Criminal Justice Abstracts
Criminology, Penology, and Police Science Abstracts

Periodicals
Advances in Criminological Theory
Crime Prevention and Criminal Justice Newsletter (UN)
Criminal Justice International
Criminal Justice—The International Journal of Policy and Practice (2001)
Criminal Law Forum: An International Journal
Dutch Penal Law and Policy
EuroCriminology
European Journal of Crime, Criminal Law and Criminal Justice
European Journal on Criminal Policy and Research
Forensic Science International
Forum on Crime and Society
Home Office Research and Planning Unit Research Bulletin
International Annals of Criminology
International Criminal Justice Review
International Criminal Police Review
International Journal of Comparative and Applied Criminal Justice
International Journal of Law and Psychiatry
International Journal of Offender Therapy and Comparative Criminology
International Journal of the Addictions
International Journal on Drug Policy
International Review of Victimology
Japanese Journal of Sociological Criminology
Police Practice and Research: An International Journal
Revue de Science Criminelle et de Droit Penal Comparée
Revue Internationale de Criminologie et de Police Technique
Revue Internationale de Droit Penal
Studies in Conflict and Terrorism
Studies on Crime and Crime Prevention (Norway)
Terrorism
UNAFEI Resource Material Series
Violence, Aggression and Terrorism
Violence and Victims

Contemporary cross-cultural texts and treatises contain descriptions of the developments in criminology and criminal justice for over 50 countries.[18] In addition to the descriptions of entire criminal justice systems, there are accounts of the functioning of subsystems. For example, a five-volume series examines the area of delinquency and juvenile justice in more than two dozen countries and regions throughout the world.[19] Other aspects of criminal justice have been investigated by specialists in such areas as policing,[20] corrections,[21] and the incidence of female criminality.[22]

Learning about a Foreign Culture Comparatists may have an understanding of their own culture. To do comparative work, they must study a foreign culture: They must become familiar with its history, politics, economy, and social structure. Scholars of comparative criminology—such as Marshall B. Clinard, working in Switzerland as well as India and other developing countries;[23] Louise I. Shelley, working in eastern European socialist countries and elsewhere;[24] and William Clifford, having worked in several African countries as well as Japan[25]—have successfully demonstrated that the immersion in the cultures under study that comparative research requires can be accomplished without losing the objectivity of the detached scientific researcher.

Collecting Data Research, as we emphasized in Chapter 2, requires factual information. Although some countries do not yet have the resources for systematically collecting information on their crime problems,[26] the great majority send statistics to the International Criminal Police Organization (Interpol), which publishes the data biannually,[27] or participate in the United Nations Surveys of Crime Trends, Operation of Criminal Justice Systems and Crime Prevention Strategies. The UN surveys, published periodically, began with data for the year 1970 and by now include statistics from well over 100 countries on prevalence of crime and the operation of criminal systems.[28]

Several other international databases are available to the researcher, including the homicide statistics of the World Health Organization;[29] the private-initiative Comparative Crime Data File, which covers 110 sovereignties (published 1984);[30] and the Correlates of Crime (published 1989).[31]

International (or nation-by-nation) crime statistics suffer from the same problems as Canadian UCR statistics, only magnified several times.[32]

Consequently, to obtain a more accurate picture of the crime situation in various countries, researchers have devised two additional statistical instruments:

1. The International Crime Victim Survey (ICVS). Beginning in 1989 and working through 1997, a group of researchers from various countries and research centres has conducted three victimization surveys in numerous developed (industrialized) and developing countries; 130 000 people were interviewed around the world, in 40 languages.[33]

2. A self-report study has measured delinquency among 14- to 21-year-old subjects in 12 countries, extending to property, violence, and drug criminality. This 1992 survey did not include developing countries.[34]

A comparison between the "official" crime rates of the UN surveys and the victimization rates shows that the two are reasonably related, although victimization studies usually show higher crime rates and tend to fluctuate over the years more than the UN survey rates. (See Figure 14.1.) One may cautiously conclude that the UN survey rates provide a fairly reasonable account of crime rates for most countries.

Comparative Research

Up to this point we have reviewed the general approach to doing comparative criminological research: studying foreign law, criminal justice systems, cultures, and available data. Comparative criminological research begins only after these requirements have been met. It is at this point that the comparatist sets sail for uncharted seas. The comparatist meets two problems right at the outset: the interdependence of all crime and criminal justice phenomena, and culture specificity.

Interdependent Phenomena Think of an elaborately assembled mobile hanging from the ceiling. All the parts are in perfect balance. If you remove a single part, the whole mobile will shift out of balance. It is the same with problems of crime and justice in any society: The existence of

FIGURE 14.1 Police and victim survey data. Comparison between police data of UN Crime and Justice Survey (UNCJS) and victim data (ICVS), percent change in reported crime 1988–1995.

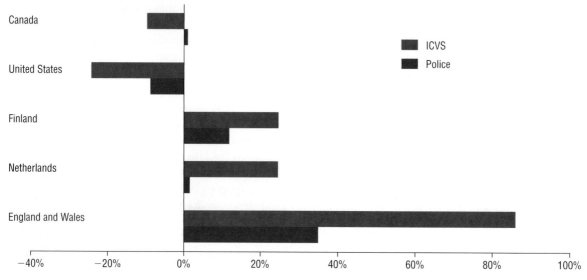

Source: Global Report on Crime and Justice (New York: United Nations, 1999), p. 69.

each is related to all the others and is explainable by reference to the others. Bicycle thefts may exist in countries like China, Denmark, and the Netherlands—all of which rely heavily on bicycle transportation—as well as in Canada or Mexico. But such theft plays a different role in the various countries, generates different responses, and leads to different consequences.

Is the bicycle theft problem comparable around the world? What could be learned from a comparison, and what factors must be considered? Would it be more useful to compare the Chinese bicycle theft problem with the Italian automobile theft problem? How do these problems fit in their countries' respective crime and justice mobiles?

The preferred means of transportation during rush hour in the streets of Beijing, China.

Culture-Specific Phenomena   The task of a comparative criminologist is like that of a surgeon about to transplant a heart or a liver. The surgeon studies a great variety of factors to be sure the donor's organ is compatible with the recipient's body. If we want to compare Japan's low crime rates with the higher crime rates in Canada, we must consider many factors, such as the role of shame in Japanese society. Misconduct brings shame not only on individual Japanese wrongdoers, but also on their families, schools, and companies: Could shaming, as a sanction, play a role in Canadian criminal justice, or is it too culture-specific? It is easier to ask such questions than it is to answer them, since research experience in comparative criminology is still limited.

Comparative Research Tools and Resources

The first book entitled *Comparative Criminology* appeared as recently as 1965. Its author, the late German-English scholar Hermann Mannheim, relied on his vast cross-cultural experience in criminology but offered no guide to the comparative method.[35] Researchers and teachers of the field now have at their disposal a variety of reference works,[36] textbooks,[37] scholarly books,[38] and book-length informative coverage of United Nations activities in the field, of which the *Global Report on Crime and Justice* is the most significant.[39]

The Special Problems of Empirical Research

Criminologists who cannot find or rely upon comparative data must generate their own, usually by parallel field investigations proceeding more or less simultaneously. They confront three problems: first, the identification of comparable problems; second, the identification of sources of information; and third, the selection of a research method compatible in the countries under comparison.

Identification of Comparable Problems Researchers of New York University's Comparative Criminal Law Project, in the 1960s, compared the prevalence of delinquency in several cultures. To their surprise, they learned that Egypt had a high rate of delinquency for railroad offences. Only local assistance could provide a plausible answer:

The long railroad line running parallel to the Nile River is a favoured haunt for local youths. Their delinquent acts were recorded as railroad offences, rather than as delinquency.[40] These "railroad offences" had to be made comparable to non-railroad delinquencies in both Egypt and the other countries under comparison.

Identification of Sources of Information The social groups of one society may not be comparable to those of another. Canadian junior high school students may represent Canadian youngsters of that age range as a whole, but Haitian junior high school students would not. What groups are comparable to such favourite research subjects as college students, blue-collar workers, and self-employed small-business-people? What is a fair cross section of any country's population? Police records may be highly reliable in Belgium, but are they in Mali and Malawi or in Armenia? And if they are not, what comparable substitutes can the comparatist find? Such problems challenge the researcher's ingenuity.

Selection of Compatible Research Methods Criminologist James Finckenauer, studying attitudes toward legal and other values among American and Russian youngsters, was at first confronted with the reluctance of Russian administrators to ask youngsters to report (even anonymously) their own delinquencies. The Soviet culture had blocked any such initiative. The problem was overcome only by indirect questions to the youngsters, such as "How wrong would it be (to do this, that, or the other)?" This was followed by further semi-direct

The proliferation of supermarkets, like this one in Moscow, Russia, is a phenomenon of socioeconomic development that brings about an increase in crime.

questions, such as "Do your peers (parents, and so on) view you as a good kid, bad kid, or something in between?" It was only after the end of communism in 1992 that Finckenauer could administer a self-report delinquency questionnaire.

Certain research methods simply are unknown in many other countries or, if known, are frowned upon. In a study of perceptions of police power in four cultures, for example, the commanding officer of a foreign police department was asked to have some questionnaires distributed to his officers. At first the officer responded, "You don't seem to understand our police! It is we who ask the questions!" Finally, he agreed and distributed the questionnaires. After the results were analyzed, the researchers were astonished to find that all the answers were identical. Apparently, all the questionnaires had been reviewed and "corrected" by a lawyer to make sure they were "accurate."[41]

THEORY TESTING

As we noted earlier, the cross-cultural testing of criminological theories has become one of the major goals of comparative criminology. Recent studies have extended to several of the crime-causation theories discussed in this book. Yet cross-cultural theory testing requires utmost caution.[42]

Validation of Major Theories

After Sheldon and Eleanor Glueck had completed *Unraveling Juvenile Delinquency* (1950),[43] their work was criticized as too culture-specific because it was based on a sample of American children. In response, scholars replicated the Glueck research in different cultural settings—Puerto Rico, Germany, and Japan. As the Gluecks themselves put it, "all these [studies] . . . have provided the most definite of all proofs, that of applicability to other samples by other researchers."[44] These cross-cultural validations of the Gluecks' delinquency-prediction system are some of the earliest empirical, comparative criminological studies.

More recently, criminologist Obi Ebbe has reviewed the Gluecks' studies and found their theories applicable to juvenile delinquents in Nigeria.[45] He has also examined the cross-cultural validity of other American theories, such as differential association, social control, and culture conflict. During the last few years, other scholars have tested

opportunity theory,[46] situational characteristics of crime,[47] routine-activity theory,[48] differential opportunity theory,[49] social control and strain theory,[50] the synnomie explanation of low crime rates,[51] and Durkheim's anomie theory.[52] Most of these studies have shown the theories to have moderate to significant validity.[53]

The Socioeconomic Development Perspective

Cross-cultural researchers have devoted particular attention to the recently developed hypothesis that modernization and urbanization lead to increases in crime[54] as well as to the general question of whether socioeconomic development necessarily brings an increase in crime.[55] Several have noted a connection between rapid development and an increase in certain types of crime, especially property crime.[56] Other research has demonstrated that sudden urbanization and industrialization have not led to increased crime in some countries,[57] but that unguided socioeconomic and political changes, such as the current transformation from a socialist to a market economy in central and eastern Europe, do produce an increase in crime.[58] The complexity of the relation between development and crime has prompted some comparative criminologists to warn that, as yet, there is no universal theoretical framework linking crime and development.[59]

PRACTICAL GOALS

Learning from Others' Experiences

With increasing globalization, the similarity of crime problems increases as well. It is natural that criminologists would look at the experiences of other countries in their search for solutions, especially the experiences of countries that seem to have found workable solutions.[60] For the worldwide drunk-driving problem, for example, comparative research has been done in Australia, Norway, and the United States.[61] As for gun control, one study investigated the situation in seven nations;[62] another, in 26.[63] Insurance fraud researchers have looked at the situation in eight countries;[64] insider-trading researchers, in three.[65]

A recent symposium compared differential methods of dealing with ecological crime in the United States, Germany, Austria, Japan, and

Taiwan.[66] Comparative criminological research has also been done on violent crime, such as homicides of children,[67] spousal homicides,[68] homicides among young males,[69] and urban violence.[70] For the past 25 years, much attention has been devoted to the comparative study of the problem of juvenile delinquency.[71]

By now there is also a considerable body of cross-cultural research on various aspects of crime-control policy. One of the earliest studies in this area examined the perception of police power among divergent population groups in four countries.[72] The perception of law was studied in six cultures,[73] and teenagers' perception of crime and criminal justice was the subject of a more recent two-country study.[74]

Issues in policing[75] as well as sanctions[76] occupy the attention of comparatists in their search for "what works." Victimologists have been particularly active in cross-cultural study.[77]

Developing International Strategies

Comparative criminology reveals that most crime problems are not unique to a single country. So we are challenged to develop strategies jointly with other countries in order to establish crime-prevention and crime-control programs to benefit all. This is particularly necessary for those crime problems that have international implications. For the sake of convenience, we can group crime problems reaching beyond national borders into three categories:

- Internationally induced local crime problems
- Transnational crime
- International crime

Internationally Induced Local Crime Problems The skinhead phenomenon is a prime example of the simultaneous appearance of a similar type of crime in various parts of the world.[78] As yet, little is known about what causes such simultaneous appearances, although instantaneous reporting in the mass media may aid the process,[79] and some international organizational connections also may play a role. Recently, the Internet has come to play a role in connecting people pursuing common criminal goals. (Yet none of these factors was present in another simultaneous occurrence of

a crime problem—namely, piracy in several widely separated waterways of the world in the mid-1970s, perpetrated in large part by rootless young offenders.[80]) The skinheads are part of the broader problem of crimes of discrimination against minorities, which itself is fuelled by vastly increased intra-continental and intercontinental migrations. The appearance of new ethnic minorities within heretofore monoethnic communities often results in the victimization of minorities. These population migrations have also resulted in the migration of crime perpetrated by migrants—often against their fellow migrants, but also against the indigenous population. Consequently, criminologists have had to look for new ways to deal with these new forms and dimensions of crime.[81]

Internationally induced local crime problems can be far greater than hate crimes or other forms of crime associated with culture conflict and migration. Consider that drugs produced abroad and distributed locally create a vast problem of crime: Not only is drug dealing illegal, but a considerable portion of street crime is associated with narcotics. Ultimately, it could be said that there are very few crime problems that are not associated with persons and events abroad over which we have no direct control. Although the problem is a vast, yet largely uncharted territory, a number of criminal activities with foreign connections have recently been identified and given the title "transnational crime."

Transnational Crime Criminologists use the term **transnational crime** to refer to criminal activities, transactions, or schemes that violate the laws of more than one country or have a direct impact on a foreign country. Neither individually, nor by type, nor collectively by category do transnational crimes conform to the definitions and categorizations found in penal codes.

In a recent questionnaire sent to all the world's national governments, and in a subsequent report on the results, the United Nations, for the first time in history, demonstrated the existence and prevalence of transnational crime.[82] Eighteen categories of transnational criminality emerged. While it is conceivable that all these activities could be committed within a single jurisdiction and/or by individual perpetrators, it is the hallmark of all that they are typically perpetrated by means of transnational activities and by organized groups of perpetrators.[83]

1. *Money laundering.* This category ranks number one on the list because of its massive impact on the economy of the entire world. Money laundering is an activity aimed at making illegally obtained funds seem legitimate, so that such funds can be spent or invested in the legitimate economy without arousing suspicion. Consider that a substantial part of the financial gain of the world's citizens is ill-gotten—for example, by bribery, by corruption, by black-market activities and transactions outside the tax laws, and especially by dealing in contraband.

The drug barons and others who have illegitimate income have devised many schemes to launder dirty money, including bogus real estate transactions, purchases of gold (many times consisting of lead bars with a coating of gold), and sales (real or fictitious) of art and antiques. But the standard method remains the physical transfer of cash out of the country (by planes or ships or by trucks and trailers with false bottoms), deposit of such cash abroad, followed by a series of international (electronic) transfers, at the end of which the source is untraceable, and the money seems clean and legitimately invested in the economy (see Figure 14.2).

FIGURE 14.2 The operational principles of money laundering are as follows: First, move the funds from direct association with the crime; second, disguise the trail to foil pursuit; and third, make the money available to the criminal once again with its origins hidden.

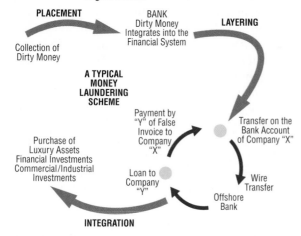

Source: United Nations Office for Drug Control and Crime Prevention, *United Nations Global Programme against Money Laundering* (New York: United Nations, 1998), pp. 18–19.

The true dimensions of money laundering are largely unknown. Estimates are as low as US$500 billion and as high as US$1 trillion annually.[84] Nevertheless, policy research (especially the Financial Transactions Task Force of the Group of Seven [highly industrialized countries]) has resulted in some remedies.

2. *Terrorist activities.* Americans had been largely unaware of the international scope of terrorist activities, primarily because their homeland had remained unaffected. This naiveté changed with the growing awareness that Americans, and American interests and installations abroad, have become targets of international terrorists. But only the bombing of the World Trade Center in New York City in February 1993 by an organized group of Middle Eastern terrorists alerted Americans to the vulnerability of their own country. Similarly, Russians were shocked when Chechen rebels took 800 people hostage in a Moscow theatre in October 2002. Rescue efforts killed 41 terrorists and 123 hostages. Of course, the victimization of air transport to and from the United States is a continuing reminder of terrorists' capability to harm American interests. The most horrific demonstration of air terrorism was the use of four hijacked jets by Al Qaeda terrorists to completely destroy the World Trade Center towers and damage the Pentagon on September 11, 2001, with a loss of nearly 3000 lives.[85]

Much scholarly inquiry has been directed at understanding and explaining international terrorism.[86] And there have been legislative responses. As a matter of fact, a network of international conventions is in place to deal with international terrorism. International judicial and police cooperation have been vastly improved. Yet there is no international machinery in operation to ensure the arrest or adjudication of international terrorists, and criminologists have yet to arrive at theoretically sound explanations that would help deal with a problem that knows no boundaries.

3. *Theft of art and cultural objects.* This category obtained a number three ranking because of its potential for robbing entire cultures and nations of their cultural heritage. Tombs and monuments have been plundered since the time of the pharaohs. But with the development of modern tools and the high demand for cultural objects, as well as the ease of transport, international thieves

What Should Be Done to Prevent International Corporate Fraud?

"Massive fraud," "World's biggest banking crash," and "Financial deception of 'epic proportions.'" Journalists had a field day characterizing the magnitude of the collapse of the Bank of Credit and Commerce International (BCCI), which failed in July 1991. But let's talk numbers instead of adjectives:

- Founded in Pakistan, the international financial institution owed some US$2 billion when it folded.
- A senior official admitted to playing a major role in frauds totalling US$1.242 billion.
- Thousands of creditors, both businesses and individuals, lost every penny of the money they had deposited.
- In 1991, BCCI agreed to forfeit US$550 million to begin compensating depositors worldwide and to salvage institutions the corporation owned secretly in the United States.
- The U.S. investigation that preceded the prosecution of a single person accused of participating in the scandal cost a whopping US$20 million.
- In England alone, BCCI had a staff of 1200 and 45 000 customers—personnel who lost their jobs and customers who lost their life savings when the bank failed.

Big numbers. What are the crimes that led to this scandal of "epic proportions"? In the United States, BCCI pleaded guilty to federal and state charges of racketeering, fraud, and money laundering. Individuals were charged with withholding information in a scheme to defraud federal and state bank regulators and depositors. In Britain, charges against bank officials include false accounting, furnishing false information, and conspiracy to defraud.

HOW IT WORKED

A picture of the corporation's operations has unfolded since the crash:

BCCI's reported profits had been "falsely inflated" by [US]$614 million between January 1983 and December 1985. The misuse of clients' funds by the bank amounted to another [US]$627 million by the end of 1985. . . . By the early 1980s the bank needed to demonstrate its profitability and a healthy balance sheet to maintain the confidence of banking regulators and current and potential investors. In desperation, the bank's founder and his senior officers turned to the trading of commodities as a likely source of funds and began a series of high-risk speculations trading in futures. Most of these were in options on large-scale purchases of silver, which went badly wrong when the price of the metal turned sharply downwards. As money was lost upon money, the frauds became more widespread. The methods involved to maintain the pretense of solidity included filing accounts in which commissions on silver-trading deals that had never taken place were recorded as profits. . . . Accounts were falsified and large sums of customers' money diverted using a financial labyrinth to fool auditors into thinking the bank was solvent when it was actually hugely in deficit.(1)

A HARD LESSON

While the settlement in the United States provided funds for the compensation of some depositors, many more will never see their money again. Some consider this a "school of hard knocks" lesson about the inability of the criminal justice system to deal effectively with international fraud. Gathering the documents needed to provide evidence ranges from difficult to impossible. After one trial in the United States, a *Chicago Tribune* editorial commented, "International financial transactions can be made so complex as to effectively conceal what is really going on; key officials can always flee the jurisdiction and take vital evidence with them."(2) One lawyer summed up his observation of the outcomes of big international cases very succinctly: "No one gets caught but huge sums of money disappear."(3)

Most recently, the Daewoo Group in Korea imploded in a 22.9 trillion won accounting fraud scandal—the largest in history. The fraud, resulting in countless victims across a wide range of stakeholders, highlights the inadequacy of effective governance structures and controls, not to mention the abject failure of the gatekeepers (e.g., accountants, lawyers, etc.).

What should be done to prevent international corporate fraud? This question remains the subject of lively debate. How should liability and culpability be assessed? What kinds of punishments ensure just deserts and deter future offences? What international bodies must be created to investigate, prosecute, and punish corporate offenders? These are the debatable issues.

Sources

1. Ben Fenton and Sonia Purnell, "Bank Official Admits $750m Fraud, 'Financial Juggler' Was at the Heart of BCCI Scandal," *Daily Telegraph*, Sept. 28, 1993, p.1.
2. "BCCI Still a Mystery," *Chicago Tribune*, Aug. 27, 1993, p. 23.
3. Peter Blackman, "The BCCI Problem; System's Flaws Stymie Probes of Foreign Banks," *New York Law Journal*, Aug. 26, 1993, p. 5.

Questions for Discussion

1. How could depositors be protected from losing their money in international scams like BCCI?
2. Would an international criminal court be better able to deal with massive international fraud?
3. What steps need to be taken by international jurisdictions to prevent cases such as the BCCI from reoccurring?

have developed systems that can strip an entire region or country of its heritage—as well as the work of contemporary artists. There is no country that has not been victimized. An estimated US$4.5 billion worth of fine art is stolen every year for sale on the international market. A database lists 45 000 stolen art objects, with an increase of 2000 items a month.[87] With few exceptions,[88] criminologists have paid scant attention to this phenomenon, though the art industry

Pandemonium in a Moscow theatre where 41 Chechen terrorists held 800 people hostage for 57 hours.

has endeavoured to come up with some practical solutions.[89]

4. *Theft of intellectual property.* Theft of intellectual property includes the unauthorized use of the rights of authors and performers, and of copyrights and trademarks. There is obviously a high temptation to reproduce works of protected originators at a fraction of franchise (or similar) costs, especially in countries with relatively unregulated economies. Yet the destructive impact on the economies of producing or originating countries is immediately apparent—though hard to assess in monetary terms. One type of theft of intellectual property, namely the illegal copying of software, has been quantified by the U.S. Software Publishers Association: It amounts to an astounding loss of US$7.5 billion annually.[90] Despite international agreements, this transnational crime category is a problem without a solution.

5. *Illicit traffic in arms.* Local, regional, or national armed conflicts, which plague us today in every part of the globe, would not be imaginable without an international network of weapons producers and suppliers. This is a shadowy world beyond the reach of statistical assessment. Criminological information on the illegal arms trade is also lacking. Yet the largest portion of the world's homicides is potentially traceable to the illegal trade in arms.

The most lethal part of the world's illegal arms trade centres on the transfer of nuclear materials. It is clear now that during the past few years, several relatively small quantities of nuclear material, including pure plutonium, have been diverted from nuclear facilities in former Soviet republics and offered for sale in Germany and other countries west of Russia.

First indications are that the diversions of nuclear material that have occurred so far were carried out by small groups of individuals, rather than organized crime, for motives of individual gain (or possibly to assist in financing totally underfunded former Soviet laboratories and scientists). Most of the efforts were amateurish, and none of the material apparently reached a viable buyer. Indeed, most ended up in sting operations. However, quantities of nuclear material seized by authorities are not insubstantial. In September 1999, Georgian authorities seized a kilogram of uranium 235 at the Georgian-Turkish border.[91] In several cases, the thieves, transporters, and the public have been exposed to radiation hazards—in itself a not insubstantial danger.[92] Criminologists have been caught by surprise. As yet, there have been few criminological responses.[93] At this point, governments have cooperated to control nuclear materials at the source.

6. *Aircraft hijacking.* The system for curbing and responding to the illegal interception of aircraft is in place and has proved somewhat effective. The number of hijackings has declined significantly, yet incidents still occur with regularity.

The airline industry had been plagued by aircraft hijackings in the 1970s and into the 1980s.

While a few such incidents were attributable to individuals who demanded ransom, most were political statements with typical terrorist characteristics, seeking to demonstrate the ability of the terrorist organization to strike at vulnerable targets almost anywhere in the world.

Since the entire world community was affected, especially diplomats and politicians, whose mobility depends on air travel, the reaction to the flood of hijackings was swift. The industry itself reacted by increasing security measures.

The criminological literature on this phenomenon is considerable, centring on the profiles of hijackers, causes, regions, carriers involved, and the like, all of which has led to the improvement of controls.

7. *Sea piracy.* Virtually forgotten until the mid-1970s, sea piracy has resurfaced on two fronts since then:

- The illegal narcotics drug smuggling from South and Central America into the United States initially relied heavily on yachts and fishing vessels captured at sea or in port, after owners and crews were killed. Several thousand vessels were victimized. As the drug trade became prosperous, smugglers began to rely on purchased or illegally chartered vessels.

- At the roadstead of Lagos, Nigeria, and the narrow shipping channel of the Malacca Straits—as well as in several other comparable sea lanes—the opportunity of deriving some benefit by attacking commercial vessels at anchor or slow speed attracted thousands of marginalized young men in Africa, Southeast Asia, and Latin America. Such piracies (often not piracies in the international law sense, since they occurred in the territorial waters of states) reached a high level of frequency (one a day in the 1980s), but are on the decline now, thanks largely to the research and policy activities of the International Maritime Bureau (London) of the International Chamber of Commerce (Paris), the International Maritime Organization (UN), and research by a number of criminologists.[94] (See "Debatable Issues," Chapter 11, p. 276.)

While the problem has been ameliorated, it has by no means ended. Prudent shipping lines order "piracy watches" on their vessels in affected waters. National and regional maritime law enforcement agencies maintain closer watch, and the International Maritime Bureau maintains a special branch office in Kuala Lumpur, Malaysia, to monitor developments.

8. *Land hijacking.* The inclusion of land hijacking in the list of transnational crimes was a surprise. At the national level, hijacking of trucks had been well documented as a form of robbery or theft. But the world economy has changed. Long-distance trucking from Eastern to Western Europe or from the central Asian republics to the Baltic States now is a reality and involves a high percentage of goods transported transnationally. The opportunity to divert such cargos has increased proportionately.

It is telling that only four countries responded to this item on the UN questionnaire. At this point, the evidence is entirely episodic but seems to point to the involvement of organized groups. Predictably, the problem will increase as a result of the openness of borders, the growth of organized crime (especially in Eastern Europe), and the lack of data and criminological analysis.

9. *Insurance fraud.* The insurance industry is internationally linked, especially through reinsurance and other methods of spreading risks and benefits. Thus, local insurance fraud ultimately affects all insurers, and all insured, worldwide. The global dimensions of the problem have not been calculated, but for the United States alone, the loss likely amounts to US$100 billion annually.[95]

10. *Computer crime.* Just as computers serve legitimate commerce, governments, and researchers, the global Internet is also accessible for criminal schemes, exploitation, and use by organized crime. Current estimates of losses through computer crime range up to US$8 billion annually.[96] Unfortunately, on this issue we lack information, though criminologists take an increasing interest in the development of legal and other protections.

11. *Environmental crime.* Well into the middle of the twentieth century, harming the environment was regarded as a matter to be controlled by local authorities. It was not until the United Nations Congress on the Environment (Stockholm, 1972) that the global dimensions of environmental destruction, and thus the need for its control, were recognized. In the decades since Stockholm, much has been achieved in recognizing environmental dangers, quantifying them, and devising control mechanisms (by treaties, legislation, and ultimately, technology) in order to avert these dangers. Criminological research has contributed a great deal in this regard.[97]

12. *Trafficking in persons.* Original forms of trafficking in persons included the slave trade and the white slave trade (traffic in women). While the slave trade may be a matter of the past, the traffic in persons is on the increase, including

- the transport of illegal immigrants, often resulting in involuntary servitude;
- the transport of women and young children for purposes of prostitution;
- the transport of migratory labourers to work under slavelike conditions;
- the transport of household workers from developing countries;
- the transfer of children for adoptions not sanctioned by law.

For the most part, laws are in place to prevent the illegal trafficking in persons. Their enforcement is another matter. The problem is bound to increase as the populations of a stagnant Third World press to emigrate to the relatively prosperous countries.

Much of the illegal population flow is controlled by organized crime.[98] The newcomers in the industrialized countries, being largely unemployable, are forming a new marginalized class, likely to be exploited but also contributing to crime and unrest.

13. *Trade in human body parts.* The first kidney transplant was performed in 1954, the first lung transplant in 1963, and the first heart transplant in 1967. By now close to half a million kidneys have been transplanted. Transplant surgery has become a highly specialized branch of medicine, and the supply of transplantable organs has spawned a very large industry. In the United States, 69 transplant agencies have been established, and federal and state laws seek to control their activities.

Yet, at any given moment, 35 000 people are waiting for a transplant (and the number increases by 14 percent annually); thus, the demand far outstrips the supply. (The number of potential donors in the United States is estimated

at about 12 000.) An illegitimate industry has sprung up to provide a service. Recipients are flown to a country where organs can be procured virtually on demand. "Donors" may in fact have been murdered for their organs, or they are children of poor parents sold for their organs, at extremely low prices.

14. *Illicit drug trafficking.* Illicit traffic in narcotic drugs is entirely controlled by organized-crime networks, loosely related with each other geographically, as well as at the various levels of production and marketing and by type of narcotic drugs.[99] The criminological literature exploring this phenomenon from every angle is vast but by no means clear in terms of policy implications.[100] With the Single Convention on Narcotic Drugs (1961), the Convention on Psychotropic Substances (1971), and the United Nations Convention against Illicit Traffic in Narcotic Drugs and Psychotropic Substances (1988), a theoretically perfect international legal structure to control this traffic is in place. Yet its application and enforcement suffer from the following shortcomings:

- The UN structure to oversee this treaty scheme is inadequate, primarily due to underfunding.
- Similarly underfunded are comparable national and regional programs.
- Nations differ vastly in their emphases (interdiction versus repression and control versus tolerance versus treatment approaches).
- Some of the most important countries of origin suffer from corruption at all levels— due to the vast income base of the trade— thus affecting enforcement.
- Corruption similarly affects law enforcement in many countries.
- Most developing and newly democratic countries lack the legal and technical infrastructure necessary to implement the treaties.

No other form of transnational and organized crime is as costly in terms of human and national financial suffering as the illicit trade in narcotic drugs.

15. *Fraudulent bankruptcy.* The internationalization of commerce has turned fraudulent bankruptcy from a local to a transnational crime. The dimensions of the phenomenon are largely unknown. Evidence is anecdotal but includes information that organized crime, after acquiring an enterprise, may subject it to bankruptcy when the gains from bankruptcy exceed the expectations of profit. There is a need to strengthen national enforcement efforts and to coordinate these efforts internationally.

16. *Infiltration of legal business.* This is the logical and temporal sequence of money laundering, the principal objective of which is seemingly legitimate investment. At this point, the existing information permits no quantitative or qualitative assessment of the phenomenon, but it must be considered that the drug trade alone has between US$200 billion and US$500 billion to invest in the market. At this rate, one could theoretically predict a time at which the world's economy would be controlled by organized crime.[101]

17. *Corruption and bribery of public officials, party officials, and elected representatives.* While bribery of party officials is not punishable in several countries, all other forms of bribery encompassed by this title are prohibited by penal codes. The problem lies with the enforceability of such laws, in both developed and developing countries, particularly with respect to international investments and trade. Disguised as "commissions," "consultancies," and agency or attorneys' fees, bribes have become a necessary cost of doing business worldwide. Nor is the practice universally condemned. Traders and investors have often proclaimed that it cannot be their business to improve the business or political ethics in countries with which they have commercial relations.[102] A recently established international organization, Transparency International (Berlin), has undertaken the formidable task of investigating international business ethics. Among its accomplishments are

- publishing a country-by-country bribery index;

- pressing for national legislation abolishing the tax deductibility of bribes;

- seeking international governmental cooperation in criminalizing the bribing of officials;

- strengthening international cooperation among non-governmental organizations, such as the International Chamber of Commerce;

- creating independent watchdog mechanisms.

18. *Other offences committed by organized criminal groups.* This catchall category permitted governments to report problems that could not be easily included in the 17 other categories. For example, both North America and Western Europe are experiencing large-scale automobile theft, with the stolen vehicles being transported abroad. These activities are controlled by international organized criminal groups. They affect not just individual owners, but the insurance industry of each country.

This review of the 18 categories of transnational criminality demonstrates the vast impact these criminal activities have on individuals, various branches of the economy, and the world economy itself. Individuals and individual commercial enterprises can do relatively little to protect themselves from these dangers, and increased international cooperation among nations has been recognized as absolutely necessary. But international action must be preceded by research. Thus, comparative criminological research will increasingly focus on transnational crime.[103]

International Crime International crimes are the major criminal offences so designated by the community of nations for the protection of interests common to all humankind. They may be found in precedent (much like the Anglo-American common law of crimes) or in written form in international conventions. They can be tried in the courts of countries that recognize them, or they can be tried by international courts. The war crimes tribunals that tried German and Japanese war criminals after World War II were such courts. In 1993, the UN Security Council ordered the establishment of an international tribunal to sit in the Netherlands for war crimes committed on the territory of the former Yugoslavia; a court for the trial of persons charged with genocide in Rwanda was added. These courts have issued several hundred indictments—the exact number is unknown because they are sealed. Several trials were held, leading to convictions as well as acquittals. Two accused didn't live long enough to receive a verdict in their trials. For example, General Momir Talic, the chief of staff of the Bosnian Serb army, who was arrested in Austria on August 24, 1999, and indicted for genocide and crimes against humanity, died of lung cancer in a military hospital in Belgrade, 16 months into his trial. Some other powerful indicted war

Investigators excavate one of many mass grave sites in the former Yugoslavia, October 1995.

criminals are still in hiding, but they cannot leave the small territories under their control, for fear of likewise being taken into custody under outstanding international arrest warrants. Indeed, the former president of Yugoslavia, Slobodan Milosevic, while on trial for war crimes at the Amsterdam Tribunal of the United Nations, died in his prison cell in March 2006. He was facing 66 charges of genocide, crimes against humanity, and war crimes related to his reign during Yugoslavia's breakup in the 1990s.

In May 2002, a long-standing dream of establishing a permanent **international criminal court (ICC)** became a reality after more than 60 nations, including Canada, ratified the treaty. The court, which will try only cases involving the most heinous crimes, became effective on July 1, 2002. The ICC will be a court of last resort—it will only try future cases that other countries cannot or will not handle. The jurisdiction of the new court extends

only to the most serious international crimes, such as crimes against humanity, genocide, and war crimes. While such an agreement was impossible during the era of the cold war, the governments of the world, meeting in Rome in 1998, agreed by a vast majority vote to establish the Permanent International Court. Under U.S. President Bill Clinton, the United States signed the treaty in 2000. However, in a decision that has provoked outrage among human rights organizations around the world, in May 2002, George W. Bush's administration withdrew from the treaty, declaring it to be against American interests. The handful of other nations that have not yet approved of the treaty are Pakistan, China, India, and a few small— so-called rogue—countries. Many fear that the power of the court will be greatly weakened without the support of these countries. Except for the few major international crimes over which the international court has jurisdiction, all others are triable only before national criminal courts.

Which crimes are listed as international crimes? The Draft Code of Crimes lists the following as crimes against the peace and security of humanity:

- Crimes against humanity
- Aggression (by one state against another)
- Threat of aggression
- Intervention (in the internal or external affairs of another state)
- Colonial domination and other forms of alien domination
- Genocide (destroying a national, ethnic, racial, or religious group)
- Apartheid (suppression of a racial or an ethnic group)
- Systematic or mass violations of human rights
- Exceptionally serious war crimes
- Recruitment, use, financing, and training of mercenaries (soldiers of fortune)
- International terrorism
- Illicit traffic in narcotic drugs
- Willful and severe damage to the environment[104]

These crimes occur in many forms. For example, "systematic or mass violations of human

Visit the Online Learning Centre: www.mcgrawhill.ca/olc/adler

rights" may be organized, large-scale rapes of women in occupied territories, as in Bosnia in 1992 and 1993.[105]

In addition to the listed international crimes, many others are recognized by convention; these include the cutting of undersea cables, the transportation of women for purposes of prostitution ("white slavery"), and fisheries offences. There is now a considerable body of research and scholarship on international crimes.[106]

Globalization versus Ethnic Fragmentation

We have entered the twenty-first century. Comparative criminologists view the new millennium with some uneasiness. Globalization raises great hopes for a better future for all human beings. Yet it brings with it grave dangers in terms of the internationalization of crime. Comparative criminology has a significant role to play in the investigation of new forms of transnational crime.

The new millennium presents additional hazards arising from the trend toward balkanization. "Balkanization," the opposite of globalization, is the breakup of nation-states into ethnic entities. Many ethnic groups are striving for the independence and sovereignty denied to them when they were incorporated in larger nation-states, as in the former Soviet Union or Yugoslavia; or when they were joined arbitrarily with other groups in colonial times, as in Africa; or when other accidents of history included them within empires, as in Western Europe. Frequently, such ethnic groups had to abide by laws and customs that were not of their own choosing and had to suppress their own languages and cultures. Now they are searching for identities, territories, and criminal justice systems of their own. Unfortunately, the struggle has brought with it human rights violations, war crimes, and genocide on a massive scale. This is the latest challenge for criminologists and criminal justice specialists working on the international level.

REVIEW

1. How does comparative criminology differ from other types of criminology?

Comparative criminology (p. 354), despite its historical antecedents, is a young science, a subspecialty of criminology. In view of the globalization of the world—brought about by recent technological advances and the enormous increase in international commerce, both legal and illegal—comparative studies in criminology have become a necessity. Comparatists are called upon to assist governments in devising strategies to deal with a wide variety of **international** (p. 369) and **transnational crimes** (p. 363).

2. How do we do comparative criminology?

In this chapter, we traced the history of comparative criminology, sought to define it, and attempted to identify its goals. These goals may be theoretical, like the cross-cultural testing of prominent theories of crime. They can also be very practical, like the search for transplantable crime-fighting strategies or for techniques to deal with specific transnational and international crimes.

There are a number of requirements for successful comparative research: studying foreign law, understanding foreign criminal justice systems, learning about a foreign culture, collecting reliable data, engaging in comparative research, and, when needed, doing cross-cultural empirical research.

3. What is the role of theory testing in comparative criminology?

We paid special attention to three dimensions that pose special challenges to comparative criminology: internationally induced local crime, transnational crime, and international crime. There is much research to be conducted before progress can be expected in these three areas.

4. What is the objective of comparative criminology?

The accomplishments of criminologists who have engaged in comparative studies form the foundation for further research. The tools of comparative criminology should prove useful in helping both individual nations and the United Nations solve some of their common crime problems. The United Nations and its agencies continue to do very practical work to help nations deal with crime on a worldwide basis. For example, in 2002 an **international criminal court** (p. 370) was established after more than 60 nations ratified the treaty.

CRIMINOLOGY & PUBLIC POLICY

Why is it that criminologists rarely if ever study genocide? Have we forgotten the systematic decimation of 1.5 million Armenians by the Young Turks during World War I; the planned killing of 6 million Jews; and the extermination of another 5 million *untermenschen*, including Gypsies, political opponents, mentally ill, retarded, and other "inferior" peoples between 1941 and 1945? How could criminology have neglected an examination of the crimes against humanity that resulted in an estimated 7 to 16 million deaths over the past 60 years since World War II?

Some of the more obvious and yet unacceptable reasons are offered here.

1. Genocide is a political act reflecting the will of sovereignty.

2. Genocide is a breach of international norms and international law.

3. Genocide is committed by the state.

4. The magnitude of victimization in genocide defies belief.

5. Criminology has little to offer the study of genocide.

6. There are problems in denying or in admitting atrocity.

"Consider how the criminology of genocide would add to our knowledge of victimization, homicide, aggression, and violence. Consider, as well, how research on genocide might support the theoretical work of critical and Marxist scholars in their efforts to explain a different conception of the state in relation to crime. Most important, reflect on the contribution that criminologists could make to further our understanding as to how genocide may be prevented. Nowhere are matters of prevention more important than with the crime of genocide.

"It is all too easy to say that criminology's neglect of genocide suggests a disciplinary denial; that our failure to recognize genocide implicitly contributes to the evil of revisionism; and that we should know better than to have the boundaries of our field permanently fixed by the criminal law—especially where extant law is so frail and uncertain. It is all too easy to say these things, because they are true." (*Source:* William S. Laufer, "The Forgotten Criminology of Genocide," *The Criminology of Criminal Law: Advances in Criminological Theory,* 8, 1999).

Questions for Discussion Why do you suppose that the field of criminology neglects the study of genocide? Is it justifiable if genocide is the most serious form of homicide?

YOU BE THE CRIMINOLOGIST

What advice would you give to the federal government regarding how to alleviate the global problem of drug trafficking as it affects Canadian citizens? Should Canada go it alone? Enter into bilateral arrangements? Attempt to find global solutions? Explain your recommendations.

NOTES

Chapter 1

1. Robert M. Gordon, "Criminal Business Organization, Street Gangs and 'Wanna-be' Groups: A Vancouver Perspective," *Canadian Journal of Criminology*, Jan. 2000, pp. 39–60; R. Fasilio and S. Leckie, *Canadian Media Coverage of Gangs: A Content Analysis: Users Report, 1993–94* (Ottawa: Ministry of the Solicitor General, 1993); Fred Mathews, "Youth Gangs" in John A. Winterdyk, *Issues and Perspectives on Young Offenders in Canada*, 3rd ed. (Toronto: Thomson Nelson, 2005).
2. Lisa Khoo, "Up in Smoke? Canada's Marijuana Law and the Debate over Decriminalization," CBC News Online, Nov. 25, 2004, www.cbc.ca.news/background/marijuana/marijuana_legalize.html.
3. J. P. Gibbs, *Norms, Deviance, and Social Control: Conceptual Matters* (New York: Elsevier, 1981), p. 14.
4. "The Mariner Group—Oil Spill History," www.marinergroup.com/oil-spill-history.htm; CNN.com/world, "Chinese Oil Tanker Explodes at Sea," www.cnn.com/2002/WORLD/asiapcf/east/09/11/china.tanker.reut/index.html; Toby Reynolds, "South Africa Blocks Oil Spill from Wetlands," www.swissinfo.org/sen/Swissinfo.html.Environmental; Timeline, www.mapreport.com/subtopics/d/l.html; Incident News, www.incidentnews.gov/, National Ocean Service, National Oceanic and Atmospheric Administration, Apr. 11, 2002.
5. Raffaele Garofalo, *Criminologia* (Naples, 1885), published in English as *Criminology*, trans. Robert W. Millar (Boston: Little, Brown, 1914; rpt., Montclair, N.J.: Patterson Smith, 1968).
6. Paul Topinard, "L'Anthropologie criminelle," *Revue d'anthropologie*, **2** (1887).
7. Edwin H. Sutherland, *Principles of Criminology*, 2nd ed. (Philadelphia: Lippincott, 1934), originally published as *Criminology*, 1924.
8. Some legal scholars argue that criminologists should study only law-breaking.
9. Jack D. Douglas and Frances C. Waksler, *The Sociology of Deviance* (Boston: Little, Brown, 1982).
10. Garofalo, *Criminologia*, p. 5.
11. Émile Durkheim, *Rules of Sociological Method*, trans. S. A. Solaway and J. H. Mueller (Glencoe, Ill.: Free Press, 1958), p. 64.
12. Freda Adler, "Our American Society of Criminology, the World, and the State of the Art—The American Society of Criminology 1995 Presidential Address," *Criminology*, **34** (1995): 1–9.

Chapter 2

1. American Law Institute, Model Penal Code, sec. 2.01(1). The American Law Institute, dedicated to law reform, is an association of some of the most prestigious American lawyers. Between 1954 and 1962 this group sought to codify the best features of the penal codes of the various states. The resultant Model Penal Code (MPC) has had considerable influence on law reform in many states, and has been adopted nearly in full by New Jersey and Pennsylvania. We shall have frequent occasion to refer to the MPC as "typical" American criminal law. See also Gerhard O. W. Mueller, "The Public Law of Wrongs—Its Concepts in the World of Reality," *Journal of Public Law*, **10** (1961): 203–260; Michael Moore, *Act and Crime—The Philosophy of Action and Its Implications for Criminal Law* (Oxford: Clarendon Press, 1993).
2. Nanci Adler, *The Gulag Survivor: Beyond the Soviet System* (New Brunswick, N.J.: Transaction Publishers, 2002).
3. For a recent look at the insanity defence, and its many challenges, see Richard Moran, *Knowing Right from Wrong: The Insanity Defense of Daniel McNaughtan* (New York: Free Press, 2000).
4. Daniel R. Wolf, *The Rebels: A Brotherhood of Outlaw Bikers* (Toronto: University of Toronto Press, 1991).
5. Edwin H. Sutherland, *The Professional Thief* (Chicago: University of Chicago Press, 1937).
6. Public Works and Government Services, *Ethical Conduct for Research Involving Humans* (Tri-Council Policy Statement, 2003), Catalogue No: MR21-18/2003E.
7. "Russel Ogden v. SFU: The Russel Ogden Case," www.sfu.ca/~plays/OgdenPge.htm, accessed Jan. 10, 2008.
8. Vincent F. Sacco and Leslie W. Kennedy, *The Criminal Event: An Introduction to Criminology* (Toronto: Nelson Canada, 1994).
9. Michael Couzens, "Getting the Crime Rate Down: Political Pressure and Crime Reporting," *Law and Society Review*, **8** (1974): 457–493.
10. Patrick Jackson, "Assessing the Validity of Official Data on Arson," *Criminology*, **26** (1988): 181–195.
11. Maire Gannon and Karen Mihorean, "Criminal Victimization in Canada, 2004," Statistics Canada, Catalogue no: 85-002-XPE, vol. 25, no. 7.
12. James Levine, "The Potential for Crime Over-reporting in Criminal Victimization Surveys," *Criminology*, **14** (1976): 307–330.
13. James S. Wallerstein and Clement J. Wyle, "Our Law-Abiding Law-Breakers," *Probation*, **25** (March–April 1947): 107–112.
14. Martin Gold, "Undetected Delinquent Behavior," *Journal of Research in Crime and Delinquency*, **3** (1966): 27–46.
15. D. Wayne Osgood, Lloyd Johnston, Patrick O'Malley, and Jerald Bachman, "The Generality of Deviance in Late Adolescence and Early Adulthood," *American Sociological Review*, **53** (1988): 81–93.
16. Franklin Dunford and Delbert Elliott, "Identifying Career Offenders Using Self-Reported Data," *Journal of Research in Crime and Delinquency*, **21** (1983): 57–86.
17. Josine Junger-Tas, Gert-Jan Terlouw, and Malcolm W. Klein, eds., *Delinquent Behavior among Young People in the Western World* (Amsterdam: Kugler, 1994).

18. M. Fréchette and Marc Le Blanc, "La délinquance cachée à l'adolescence," *Inadaptation juvénile,* Cahier 1 (Montreal: Université de Montréal, 1979); M. Fréchette and Marc Le Blanc, "Pour une pratique de la criminologie: configurations de conduites délinquantes et portraits de délinquants," *Inadaptation juvenile,* Cahier 5 (Montreal: Université de Montréal, 1980); Julian Tanner and Scott Wortley, as cited in Larry J. Siegel and Chris McCormick, eds., *Criminology in Canada: Theories, Patterns, and Typologies* (Toronto: Thomson Nelson, 2006), p. 61.

19. Michael Hindelang, Travis Hirschi, and Joseph Weis, *Measuring Delinquency* (Beverly Hills, Calif.: Sage, 1981).

20. Edmonton Police Service, "Report to the Edmonton Police Commission, June 9, 2006, www.edmontonpolice. commission.com/pdfs/meetings/june2006-5.7.4.pdf, accessed Apr. 16, 2007.

21. Gordon Kent, "Council to Double Fines for Whyte Avenue Rowdiness," *The Edmonton Journal,* Apr. 10, 2007.

22. Maire Gannon, "Crime Statistics in Canada, 2005," Statistics Canada, Catalogue no: 85-002-XIE, vol. 26, no. 4.

23. Gannon and Mihorean, "Criminal Victimization in Canada, 2004."

24. Valerie Pottie Bunge, Holly Johnson, and Thierno A. Baldé, "Exploring Crime Patterns in Canada," *Crime and Justice Research Paper Series,* Statistics Canada, Catalogue no: 85-561-MIE, no. 005.

25. Gannon, "Crime Statistics in Canada, 2005."

26. Gannon and Mihorean, "Criminal Victimization in Canada, 2004."

27. Derral Cheatwood, "The Effects of Weather on Homicide," *Journal of Quantitative Criminology,* 11 (1995): 51–70. Ellen Cohn, "The Effect of Weather and Temporal Variations on Calls for Police Service," *American Journal of Police* 15 (1996): 23–43.

28. Jim Dooley, "Man, 83, Accused of Stabbing Wife at Least 100 Times," *Honolulu Advertiser,* March 1 2007.

29. Jennifer Thomas, "Youth Court Statistics, 2003–2004," *Juristat,* Statistics Canada (Minister of Industry, June 2005), Catalogue no: 85-002-XPE, vol. 25, no. 4.

30. Mikhail Thomas, "Adult Criminal Court Statistics, 2003–2004," *Juristat,* Statistics Canada, Catalogue no. 85-002-XIE, vol. 24, no. 12.

31. Michael Gottfredson and Travis Hirschi, "The True Value of Lambda Would Appear to Be Zero: An Essay on Career Criminals, Criminal Careers, Selective Incapacitation, Cohort Studies, and Related Topics," *Criminology,* 24 (1986): 213–234.

32. Michael Gottfredson and Travis Hirschi, "Science, Public Policy, and the Career Paradigm," *Criminology,* 26 (1988): 37–55. For a test of those contentions, see Sung Joon Jang and Marvin D. Krohn, "Developmental Patterns of Sex Differences in Delinquency among African American Adolescents: A Test of the Sex-Invariance Hypothesis," *Journal of Quantitative Criminology,* 11 (1995): 195–222.

33. James Q. Wilson and Richard Herrnstein, *Crime and Human Nature* (New York: Simon & Schuster, 1985), pp. 126–147.

34. Alfred Blumstein, Jacqueline Cohen, and David Farrington, "Criminal Career Research: Its Value for Criminology," *Criminology,* 26 (1988): 1–35.

35. Dawn R. Jeglum Bartusch, Donald R. Lynum, Terrie E. Moffitt, and Phil A. Silva, "Is Age Important? Testing a General versus a Developmental Theory of Antisocial Behavior," *Criminology,* 35 (1997): 13–48.

36. Alfred Blumstein, Jacqueline Cohen, Jeffrey Roth, and Christy Visher, *Criminal Careers and "Career Criminals"* (Washington, D.C.: National Academy Press, 1986). On the relationship between crime and age, see Robert J. Sampson and John H. Laub, *Crime in the Making: Pathways and Turning Points through Life* (Cambridge, Mass.: Harvard University Press, 1993); Neal Shover and Carol Y. Thompson, "Age, Differential Expectations, and Crime Desistance," *Criminology,* 30 (1992): 89–104; David F. Greenberg, "The Historical Variability of the Age-Crime Relationship," *Journal of Quantitative Criminology,* 10 (1994): 361–373; Daniel S. Nagin, David P. Farrington, and Terrie E. Moffitt, "Life-Course Trajectories of Different Types of Offenders," *Criminology,* 33 (1995): 111–139; and Julie Horney, Wayne Osgood, and Ineke Haen Marshall, "Criminal Careers in the Short-Term: Intra-individual Variability in Crime and Its Relation to Local Life Circumstances," *American Sociological Review,* 60 (1995): 655–673.

37. Marvin Wolfgang, Robert Figlio, and Thorsten Sellin, *Delinquency in a Birth Cohort* (Chicago: University of Chicago Press, 1972). For a discussion of how each delinquent act was weighted for seriousness, see Thorsten Sellin and Marvin Wolfgang, *The Measurement of Delinquency* (New York: Wiley, 1964). See also Douglas A. Smith, Christy A. Visher, and G. Roger Jarjoura, "Dimensions of Delinquency: Exploring the Correlates of Participation, Frequency, and Persistence of Delinquent Behavior," *Journal of Research in Crime and Delinquency,* 28 (1990): 6–32.

38. Marvin E. Wolfgang, Terence Thornberry, and Robert Figlio, *From Boy to Man, from Delinquency to Crime* (Chicago: University of Chicago Press, 1987).

39. Paul E. Tracy, Marvin E. Wolfgang, and Robert M. Figlio, *Delinquency Careers in Two Birth Cohorts* (New York: Plenum, 1990), pp. 275–280.

40. Anthony Matarazzo, Peter J. Carrington and Robert D. Hiscott, "The Effect of Prior Dispositions on Current Disposition: An Application of Societal-Reaction Theory," *Journal of Quantitative Criminology,* 17 (2001): 169–200.

41. Helen Boritch, *Fallen Women: Female Crime and Criminal Justice in Canada* (Toronto: Nelson, 1997).

42. Gannon and Mihorean, "Criminal Victimization in Canada, 2004."

43. Boritch, *Fallen Women.*

44. Uniform Crime Reports, 2003, p. 201.

45. Delbert Elliott and Suzanne Ageton, "Reconciling Race and Class Differences in Self-Reported and Official Estimates of Delinquency," *American Sociological Review,* 45 (1980): 95–110; and Roy L. Austin, "Recent Trends in Official Male and Female Crime Rates: The Convergence Controversy," *Journal of Criminal Justice,* 21 (1993): 447–466.

46. John Hagan, John Simpson, and A. R. Gillis, "Class in the Household: A Power Control Theory of Gender and Delinquency," *American Journal of Sociology,* 92 (1987): 788–816. See also Gary F. Jensen, John Hagan, and A. R. Gillis, "Power-Control vs. Social Control Theories of Common Delinquency: A Comparative

Analysis," in *New Directions in Criminological Theory*, eds. Freda Adler and William S. Laufer (New Brunswick, N.J.: Transaction, 1993), pp. 363–398.

47. Merry Morash and Meda Chesney-Lind, "A Reformulation and Partial Test of the Power Control Theory of Delinquency," *Justice Quarterly*, **8** (1991): 347–377. For an examination of sexual abuse of girls and how it leads to later delinquency, as well as a discussion of how the double standard influences female criminality, see Meda Chesney-Lind, *The Female Offender: Girls, Women, and Crime* (Thousand Oaks, CA: Sage, 1997). For a discussion about the role family controls have on female delinquency, see Karen Keimer and Stacy De Coster, "The Gendering of Violent Delinquency," *Criminology*, **37** (1999): 277–318. For an application of strain theory to female crime, see Lisa Broidy and Robert Agnew, "Gender and Crime: A General Strain Theory Perspective," *Journal of Research in Crime and Delinquency*, **34** (1997): 275–306. For a discussion of the implications of the feminization of poverty and welfare on property crime and assault, see Anne Campbell, Steven Muncer, and Daniel Bibel, "Female–Female Criminal Assault: An Evolutionary Perspective," *Journal of Research in Crime and Delinquency*, **35** (1998): 413–428; and Lance Hannon and James DeFronzo, "Welfare and Property Crime," *Justice Quarterly*, **15** (1998): 273–288.

48. Cesare Lombroso and William Ferrero, *The Female Offender* (London: T. Fisher Unwin, 1895).

49. Sheldon Glueck and Eleanor T. Glueck, *Five Hundred Delinquent Women* (New York: Knopf, 1934).

50. Otto Pollack, *The Criminality of Women* (Philadelphia: University of Pennsylvania Press, 1950).

51. Freda Adler, *Sisters in Crime* (New York: McGraw-Hill, 1975), pp. 6–7.

52. Rita Simon, *The Contemporary Woman and Crime* (Rockville, Md.: National Institute of Mental Health, 1975).

53. Meda Chesney-Lind, "Female Offenders: Paternalism Reexamined," in *Women, the Courts, and Equality*, eds. Laura Crites and Winifred Hepperle (Newbury Park, Calif.: Sage, 1987).

54. Darrell J. Steffensmeier, "Crime and the Contemporary Woman: An Analysis of Changing Levels of Female Property Crimes, 1960–1975," *Social Forces*, **57** (1978): 566–584; Lee H. Bowker, *Women, Crime, and the Criminal Justice System* (Lexington, Mass.: Heath, 1978). For a description of the typical female offender, see Nancy T. Wolfe, Francis T. Cullen, and John B. Cullen, "Describing the Female Offender: A Note on the Demographics of Arrests," *Journal of Criminal Justice*, **12** (1984): 483–492; and Holly Johnson, "Getting the Facts Straight," in E. Adelberg and C. Currie, eds., *Too Few to Count* (Vancouver: Press Gang Publishers, 1987), pp. 23–46.

55. Mary E. Gilfus, "From Victims to Survivors to Offenders: Women's Routes of Entry and Immersion into Street Crime," *Women and Criminal Justice*, **4** (1992): 63–89; and Sally S. Simpson and Lori Ellis, "Doing Gender: Sorting Out the Caste and Crime Conundrum," *Criminology*, **33** (1995): 47–81. For a discussion of the internalization of gender roles by female prisoners, see Edna Erez, "The Myth of the New Female Offender: Some Evidence from Attitudes toward Law and Justice," *Journal of Criminal Justice*, **16** (1988): 499–509. See also Helen Boritch, *Fallen Women: Female Crime and Criminal Justice in Canada* (Toronto: Nelson, 1997).

56. G. Nettler, *Explaining Crime* (New York: McGraw-Hill, 1984); J. Fox and T. Hartnagel, "Changing Social Roles and Female Crime in Canada," *Canadian Review of Sociology and Anthropology*, **16** (1979): 96–104; Nanci Koser Wilson, "The Masculinity of Violent Crime—Some Second Thoughts," *Journal of Criminal Justice*, **9** (1981): 111–123; Ronald L. Simons, Martin G. Miller, and Stephen M. Aigner, "Contemporary Theories of Deviance and Female Delinquency: An Empirical Test," *Journal of Research in Crime and Delinquency*, **17** (1980): 42–57.

57. For a discussion of a unisex theory of crime, see Coramae Richey Mann, *Female Crime and Delinquency* (Tuscaloosa: University of Alabama Press, 1984). For an analysis of the relation of both gender and race to crime, see Vernetta D. Young, "Women, Race, and Crime," *Criminology*, **18** (1980): 26–34; Gary D. Hill and Elizabeth M. Crawford, "Women, Race, and Crime," *Criminology*, **28** (1990): 601–626; and Sally S. Simpson, "Caste, Class, and Violent Crime: Explaining Differences in Female Offending," *Criminology*, **29** (1991): 115–136. For a discussion of female crime in countries around the world, see Freda Adler, ed., *The Incidence of Female Criminality in the Contemporary World* (New York: New York University Press, 1984). See also Freda Adler and Rita James Simon, eds., *The Criminology of Deviant Women* (Boston: Houghton Mifflin, 1979). For other sources on the subject of female crime, see Victoria E. Brewster and M. Dwayne Smith, "Gender Inequality and Rates of Female Homicide Victimization across U.S. Cities," *Journal of Research in Crime and Delinquency*, **32** (1995): 175–190; R. Barri Flowers, *Female Crime, Criminals and Cellmates: An Exploration of Female Criminality and Delinquency* (Jefferson, N.C.: McFarland & Company, 1995); R. Emerson Dobash, Russell P. Dobash, and Lesley Noaks, eds., *Gender and Crime* (Cardiff: University of Wales Press, 1995); and Ruth Triplett and Laura B. Myers, "Evaluating Contextual Patterns of Delinquency: Gender-Based Differences," *Justice Quarterly*, **12** (1995): 59–84. For an examination of women who commit murder, see Coramae Richey Mann, *When Women Kill* (Albany, N.Y.: SUNY Press, 1996).

58. Pat Carlen, ed., *Criminal Women* (Cambridge: Polity Press, 1985); Karlene Faith, *Unruly Women: The Politics of Confinement and Resistance* (Vancouver: Press Gang Publishers, 1993); Danielle Leberge, "Women's Criminality, Criminal Women, Criminalized Women?: Questions in and for a Feminist Perspective," *Journal of Human Justice*, **2** (1991): 37–56; Carol Smart, *Feminism and the Power of Law* (London: Routledge, 1989).

59. Charles Tittle, Wayne Villemez, and Douglas Smith, "The Myth of Social Class and Criminality: An Empirical Assessment of the Empirical Evidence," *American Sociological Review*, **43** (1978): 643–656; Charles R. Tittle and Robert F. Meier, "Specifying the SES/Delinquency Relationship," *Criminology*, **28** (1990): 271–299. For a discussion of the relationship between crime and aspects of social class that influence juveniles' personality and behaviour, see G. Roger Jarjoura and Ruth A. Triplett, "Delinquency and Class: A Test of the Proximity Principle," *Justice Quarterly*, **14** (1997): 763–792. For an elaboration

on the relationship between socioeconomic status (SES) and delinquency, see Bradley R. Entner Wright, Avshalom Caspi, Terrie E. Moffitt, Richard A. Miech, and Phil A. Silva, "Reconsidering the Relationship between SES and Delinquency: Causation but Not Correlation," *Criminology*, **37** (1999): 175–194.

60. Delbert Elliott and Suzanne Ageton, "Reconciling Race and Class Differences in Self-Reported and Official Estimates of Delinquency," *American Sociological Review*, **45** (1980): 95–110.

61. Delbert Elliott and David Huizinga, "Social Class and Delinquent Behavior in a National Youth Panel: 1976–1980," *Criminology*, **21** (1983): 149–177.

62. M. Fréchette and Marc Le Blanc, "La délinquance cache à l'adolescence," *Inadaptation juvenile*, Cahier 1 (Montreal: Université de Montréal, 1979); M. Fréchette and Marc Le Blanc, "Pour une pratique de la criminologie: configurations de conduites délinquantes et portraits de délinquants," *Inadaptation juvenile*, Cahier 5 (Montreal: Université de Montréal, 1980); John Evans and Alexander Himelfarb, "Counting Crime," in *Criminology: A Canadian Perspective*, 5th ed., ed. Rick Linden (Toronto: Nelson, 2004).

63. Shelley Trevethan, Gisèle Carrière, Barry MacKillop, Anne Finn, David Robinson, Frank J. Porporino, and William A. Millson, *A One-Day Snapshot of Inmates in Canada's Adult Correctional Facilities* (Minister of Industry, 1999), Catalogue No: 85-601 XIE. ISBN: 0-660-17627-0. Data on socioeconomic factors from U.S. Department of Justice, *Report to the Nation on Crime and Justice*, pp. 48–49.

64. Research Branch, "The Changing Federal Offender Population: Profiles and Forecasts, 2006," www.csc-scc.gc. ca/text/rsrch/special_reports/highlights-2006-eng. shtml, accessed Apr. 18, 2007.

65. Correctional Service of Canada, Aboriginal Initiatives Branch, "Facts and Figures: Demographic Overview of Aboriginal Peoples in Canada and Aboriginal Offenders in Federal Corrections," http://198.103.98.138/text/ prgrm/correctional/abissues/know/10_e.shtml, accessed May 6, 2007.

66. J. Phillip Johnston, "Academic Approaches to Race-Crime Statistics Do Not Justify Their Collection," *Canadian Journal of Criminology*, **36** (1994): 166–174; Julian V. Roberts, "Crime and Race Statistics: Toward a Canadian Solution," *Canadian Journal of Criminology*, 36 (1994): 175–185; J. V. Roberts and A. N. Doob, "Race, Ethnicity, and Criminal Justice in Canada," in M. Tonry, ed., *Ethnicity, Crime, and Immigration. Crime and Justice: A Review of Research* (Chicago: University of Chicago Press, 1997), pp. 469–522; Joan Petersilia, "Racial Disparities in the Criminal Justice System: A Summary," *Crime and Delinquency*, **31** (1985): 15–34.

67. Task Force on Aboriginal Peoples in Federal Corrections, *Final Report* (Ottawa: Minister of Supply and Services, 1989); Royal Commission on Aboriginal Peoples, *Report of the Royal Commission on Aboriginal Peoples 1, Looking Forward, Looking Back* (Ottawa: Minister of Supply and Services Canada, 1996); C. P. LaPrairie, *Examining Aboriginal Corrections in Canada* (Ottawa: Supply and Services Canada, 1996); M. Reed and J. V. Roberts, "Adult Correctional Services in Canada, 1996–1997," *Juristat* **18** (1998): 1–12.

68. National Crime Prevention Centre, *Aboriginal Canadians: Violence, Victimization, and Prevention* (Ottawa: Department of Justice, 2001); Nathalie L. Quann and Shelley Treventhan, *Police Reproted Aboriginal Cirme in Saskatchewan* (Ottawa: Statistics Canada, 2000); Larry J. Siegel and Chris McCormick, *Criminology in Canada: Theories, Patterns, and Typologies* (Toronto: Thomson Nelson, 2006).

69. National Crime Prevention Centre, *Aboriginal Canadians: Violence, Victimization and Prevention* (Ottawa: Department of Justice, 2001).

Chapter 3

1. Quote: attributed to Socrates by Plato, wording unconfirmed by researchers; see *Respectfully Quoted*, ed. Suzy Platt (Washington, D.C.: Library of Congress, 1989), p. 42.

2. Leon Radzinowicz, *Ideology and Crime* (New York: Columbia University Press, 1966), p. 2; Marc Ancel, *Introduction to the French Penal Code*, ed. G. O. W. Mueller (South Hackensack, N.J.: Fred B. Rothman, 1960), pp. 1–2.

3. Thorsten Sellin, *Slavery and the Penal System* (New York: Elsevier, 1976); Thorsten Eriksson, *The Reformers: An Historical Survey of Pioneer Experiments in the Treatment of Criminals* (New York: Elsevier, 1976).

4. Marcello T. Maestro, *Cesare Beccaria and the Origins of Penal Reform* (Philadelphia: Temple University Press, 1973), p. 16.

5. George Rude, *The Crowd in the French Revolution* (New York: Oxford University Press, 1959), appendix.

6. Harry Elmer Barnes, *The Story of Punishment: A Record of Man's Inhumanity to Man*, 2nd ed. (Montclair, N.J.: Patterson Smith, 1972), p. 99.

7. Cesare Beccaria, *On Crimes and Punishment*, 2nd ed., trans. Edward D. Ingraham (Philadelphia: Philip H. Nicklin, 1819), pp. 15, 20, 22–23, 30–32, 60, 74–75, 80, 97–98, 149, 156. For a debate on the contribution of Beccaria to modern criminology, see G. O. W. Mueller, "Whose Prophet Is Cesare Beccaria? An Essay on the Origins of Criminological Theory," *Advances in Criminological Theory*, **2** (1990): 1–14; Graeme Newman and Pietro Marongiu, "Penological Reform and the Myth of Beccaria," *Criminology*, **28** (1990): 325–346; and Piers Beirne, "Inventing Criminology: The 'Science of Man,' in Cesare Beccaria's *Dei delitti e delle pene*," *Criminology*, **29** (1991): 777–820.

8. Marcello T. Maestro, *Voltaire and Beccaria as Reformers of Criminal Law* (New York: Columbia University Press, 1942), p. 73.

9. Jeremy Bentham, *A Fragment on Government and an Introduction to the Principles of Morals and Legislation*, ed. Wilfred Harrison (Oxford: Basil Blackwell, 1967), p. 21.

10. Barnes, *The Story of Punishment*, p. 102.

11. Quoted in Leon Radzinowicz, *A History of English Criminal Law and Its Administration from 1750*, vol. 1 (New York: Macmillan, 1948), p. 330.

12. Charles Darwin, *Origin of Species* (1854; Cambridge, Mass.: Harvard University Press, 1859); Charles Darwin, *The Descent of Man and Selection in Relation to Sex* (1871; New York: A. L. Burt, 1874).

13. Havelock Ellis, *The Criminal,* 2nd ed. (New York: Scribner, 1900), p. 27.
14. Christopher Hibbert, *The Roots of Evil* (Boston: Little, Brown, 1963), p. 187.
15. Arthur E. Fink, *The Causes of Crime: Biological Theories in the United States, 1800–1915* (Philadelphia: University of Pennsylvania Press, 1938), p. 1.
16. Hermann Mannheim, *Comparative Criminology* (Boston: Houghton Mifflin, 1965), p. 213.
17. George B. Vold, *Theoretical Criminology* (New York: Oxford University Press, 1958), pp. 44–49.
18. Gina Lombroso Ferrero, *Criminal Man: According to the Classification of Cesare Lombroso,* with an Introduction by Cesare Lombroso (1911; Montclair, N.J.: Patterson Smith, 1972), pp. xxiv–xxv.
19. Cesare Lombroso and William Ferrero, *The Female Offender* (New York: Appleton, 1895), pp. 151–152.
20. Cesare Lombroso, *Crime, Its Causes and Remedies* (Boston: Little, Brown, 1918).
21. Marvin Wolfgang, "Cesare Lombroso," in *Pioneers in Criminology,* ed. Hermann Mannheim (London: Stevens, 1960), p. 168.
22. Thorsten Sellin, "The Lombrosian Myth in Criminology," *American Journal of Sociology,* **42** (1937): 898–899. For Lombroso's impact on American anthropological criminology, see Nicole Hahn Rafter, "Criminal Anthropology in the United States," *Criminology,* 30 (1992): 525–545.
23. Wolfgang, "Cesare Lombroso."
24. Thorsten Sellin, "Enrico Ferri: Pioneer in Criminology, 1856–1929," in *The Positive School of Criminology: Three Lectures by Enrico Ferri,* ed. Stanley E. Grupp (Pittsburgh: University of Pittsburgh Press, 1968), p. 13.
25. Raffaele Garofalo, *Criminology,* trans. Robert Wyness Millar (Montclair, N.J.: Patterson Smith, 1968), pp. 4–5.
26. Marc Ancel, *Social Defense: The Future of Penal Reform* (Littleton, Colo.: Fred B. Rothman, 1987).
27. Charles B. Goring, *The English Convict: A Statistical Study* (London: His Majesty's Stationery Office, 1913), p. 145. For a critique of Goring's work, see Piers Beirne, "Heredity versus Environment," *British Journal of Criminology,* 28 (1988): 315–339.
28. E. A. Hooten, *The American Criminal* (Cambridge, Mass.: Harvard University Press, 1939), p. 308.
29. E. A. Hooten, *Crime and the Man* (Cambridge, Mass.: Harvard University Press, 1939), p. 13.
30. Ernst Kretschmer, *Physique and Character* (New York: Harcourt Brace, 1926).
31. William H. Sheldon, *Varieties of Delinquent Youth: An Introduction to Constitutional Psychiatry* (New York: Harper, 1949). See also Emil M. Hartl, Edward P. Monnelly, and Ronald D. Elderkin, *Physique and Delinquent Behavior: A Thirty-Year Follow-Up of William H. Sheldon's Varieties of Delinquent Youth* (New York: Academic Press, 1982).
32. Eleanor Glueck and Sheldon Glueck, *Unraveling Juvenile Delinquency* (Cambridge, Mass.: Harvard University Press, 1950). See also Sheldon Glueck and Eleanor Glueck, *Of Delinquency and Crime* (Springfield, Ill.: Charles C. Thomas, 1974), p. 2. For a recent reanalysis of the Gluecks' data, see John H. Laub and Robert J. Sampson, "Unravelling Families and Delinquency: A Reanalysis of the Gluecks' Data," *Criminology,* 26 (1988): 355–380. For the life and work of Eleanor Touroff Glueck, see John H. Laub and Jinney S. Smith, "Eleanor Touroff Glueck: An Unsung Pioneer in Criminology," *Women in Criminal Justice,* **6** (1995): 1–22.
33. S. L. Washburn, book review, "Varieties of Delinquent Youth, An Introduction to Constitutional Psychiatry," *American Anthropologist,* 53 (1951): 561–563.
34. Richard L. Dugdale, *The Jukes: A Study in Crime, Pauperism, Disease, and Heredity,* 5th ed. (New York: Putnam, 1895), p. 8.
35. Henry H. Goddard, The Kallikak Family: A Study in the Heredity of Feeble-Mindedness (New York: Macmillan, 1912), p. 50.
36. "The Black Donnellys: Canada's Tragic Roustabouts," www.crimelibrary.com/notorious_murders/family/donnelly/2.html, accessed Jan. 31, 2008.
37. "Goler Clan," http://en.wikipedia.org/wiki/Goler_clan, accessed Jan. 31, 2008.
38. *Buck v. Bell,* 274 U.S. 200, 207 (1927).
39. Isaac Ray, *The Medical Jurisprudence of Insanity* (Boston: Little, Brown, 1838).
40. Philippe Pinel, *A Treatise on Insanity* (1806; New York: Hafner, 1962).
41. Peter Scott, "Henry Maudsley," *Journal of Criminal Law, Criminology, and Police Science,* **46** (March–April 1956): 753–769.
42. Henry H. Goddard, *The Criminal Imbecile* (New York: Macmillan, 1915), pp. 106–107.
43. Adolphe Quételet, *A Treatise on Man,* facs. ed. of 1842 ed., trans. Salomon Diamond (1835; Gainesville, Fla.: Scholars Facsimiles and Reprints, 1969), p. 97.
44. Quételet, *A Treatise on Man,* p. 103. For Quételet's influence on modern scholars, see Derral Cheatwood, "Is There a Season for Homicide?" *Criminology,* 26 (1988): 287–306.
45. Gabriel Tarde, *Penal Philosophy,* trans. R. Howell (Boston: Little, Brown, 1912), p. 252.
46. Gabriel Tarde, *Social Laws: An Outline of Sociology* (New York: Macmillan, 1907).
47. Émile Durkheim, *The Rules of Sociological Method,* ed. George E. G. Catlin (Chicago: University of Chicago Press, 1938), p. 71.

Chapter 4

1. Gonzalo Moreno, "More Gruesome than Fiction," Jan. 29, 2007, www.thecannon.ca/news_details.php?id=3175, accessed June 6, 2007.
2. See Ronald Blackburn, *The Psychology of Criminal Conduct: Theory, Research, and Practice* (Chichester, England: Wiley, 1993); and Hans Toch, *Violent Men: An Inquiry into the Psychology of Violence,* rev. ed. (Washington, D.C.: American Psychological Association, 1992).
3. See, e.g., Cathy Spatz Widom, "Cycle of Violence," *Science,* **244** (1989): 160–165; and Nathaniel J. Pallone and J. J. Hennessey, *Criminal Behavior: A Process Psychology Analysis* (New Brunswick, N.J.: Transaction, 1992).
4. See, e.g., Sigmund Freud, *A General Introduction to Psychoanalysis* (New York: Liveright, 1920); and Sigmund Freud, *The Ego and the Id* (London: Hogarth, 1927).

5. August Aichhorn, *Wayward Youth* (New York: Viking, 1935).

6. Kate Friedlander, *The Psycho-Analytic Approach to Juvenile Delinquency* (New York: International Universities Press, 1947).

7. See Hans Eysenck, *The Rise and Fall of the Freudian Empire* (New York: Plenum, 1987).

8. Lawrence Kohlberg, "The Development of Modes of Moral Thinking and Choice in the Years Ten to Sixteen," Ph.D. dissertation, University of Chicago, 1958.

9. Lawrence Kohlberg, "Stage and Sequence: The Cognitive-Developmental Approach to Socialization," in *Handbook of Socialization Theory and Research*, ed. David A. Goslin (Chicago: Rand McNally, 1969).

10. Carol Gilligan has studied moral development in women—extending Kohlberg's role-taking theory of moral development. She found that moral reasoning differed in women. Women, according to Gilligan, see morality as the responsibility to take the view of others and to ensure their well-being. See Carol Gilligan, *In a Different Voice: Psychological Theory and Women's Development* (Cambridge, Mass.: Harvard University Press, 1982).

11. G. L. Little, "Meta-analysis of MRT Recidivism Research on Post-incarceration Adult Felony Offenders," *Cognitive-Behavioral Treatment Review,* **10** (2001): 4–6; William S. Jennings, Robert Kilkenny, and Lawrence Kohlberg, "Moral Development Theory and Practice for Youthful Offenders," in *Personality Theory, Moral Development, and Criminal Behavior,* eds. William S. Laufer and James M. Day (Lexington, Mass.: Lexington Books, 1983). See also Daniel D. Macphail, "The Moral Education Approach in Treating Adult Inmates," *Criminal Justice and Behavior,* **15** (1989): 81–97; Jack Arbuthnot and Donald A. Gordon, "Crime and Cognition: Community Applications of Sociomoral Reasoning Development," *Criminal Justice and Behavior,* **15** (1988): 379–393; and J. E. LeCapitaine, "The Relationships between Emotional Development and Moral Development and the Differential Impact of Three Psychological Interventions on Children," *Psychology in the Schools,* **15** (1987): 379–393.

12. Carol Gilligan, *In a Different Voice: Psychological Theory and Women's Development* (Cambridge, MA: Harvard University Press, 1982), p. 18.

13. John Bowlby, *Attachment and Loss,* 2 vols. (New York: Basic Books, 1969, 1973). See also Bowlby's "Forty-Four Juvenile Thieves: Their Characteristics and Home Life," *International Journal of Psychoanalysis,* **25** (1944): 19–52.

14. John Bowlby, *The Making and Breaking of Affectional Bonds* (London: Tavistock, 1979). See also Michael Rutter, *Maternal Deprivation Reassessed* (Harmondsworth, Eng.: Penguin, 1971).

15. Heather Juby and David P. Farrington, "Disentangling the Link between Disrupted Families and *Delinquency:* Sociodemography, Ethnicity and Risk Behaviours," *British Journal of Criminology* **41** (2001): 22–40; Joan McCord, "Some Child-Rearing Antecedents of Criminal Behavior," *Journal of Personality and Social Psychology,* **37** (1979): 1477–1486; Joan McCord, "A Longitudinal View of the Relationship between Paternal Absence and Crime," in *Abnormal Offenders, Delinquency, and the Criminal Justice System,* eds. John Gunn and David P. Farrington (London: Wiley, 1982). See also Scott W. Henggeler, Cindy L. Hanson, Charles M. Borduin, Sylvia M. Watson, and Molly A. Brunk, "Mother-Son Relationships of Juvenile Felons," *Journal of Consulting and Clinical Psychology,* **53** (1985): 942–943; and Francis I. Nye, *Family Relationships and Delinquent Behavior* (New York: Wiley, 1958).

16. Sheldon Glueck and Eleanor T. Glueck, *Unraveling Juvenile Delinquency* (New York: Commonwealth Fund, 1950); Lee N. Robins, "Aetiological Implications in Studies of Childhood Histories Relating to Antisocial Personality," in *Psychopathic Behaviour,* eds. Robert D. Hare and Daisy Schalling (Chichester, Eng.: Wiley, 1970); Lee N. Robins, *Deviant Children Grow Up* (Baltimore: Williams & Wilkins, 1966).

17. Joan McCord, "Instigation and Insulation: How Families Affect Antisocial Aggression," in *Development of Antisocial and Prosocial Behavior: Research Theories and Issues,* eds. Dan Olweus, Jack Block, and M. Radke-Yarrow (London: Academic Press, 1986).

18. Albert Bandura, *Aggression: A Social Learning Analysis* (Englewood Cliffs, N.J.: Prentice-Hall, 1973); Albert Bandura, "The Social Learning Perspective: Mechanism of Aggression," in *Psychology of Crime and Criminal Justice,* ed. Hans Toch (New York: Holt, Rinehart & Winston, 1979).

19. Leonard D. Eron and L. Rowell Huesmann, "Parent-Child Interaction, Television Violence, and Aggression of Children," *American Psychologist,* **37** (1982): 197–211; Russell G. Geen, "Aggression and Television Violence," in *Aggression: Theoretical and Empirical Reviews,* vol. 2, eds. Russell G. Geen and Edward I. Donnerstein (New York: Academic Press, 1983).

20. Leonard D. Eron and L. Rowell Huesmann, "The Control of Aggressive Behavior by Changes in Attitudes, Values, and the Conditions of Learning," in *Advances in the Study of Aggression,* vol. 1, eds. Robert J. Blanchard and D. Caroline Blanchard (Orlando, Fla.: Academic Press, 1984).

21. *National Television Violence Study: Executive Summary* 1994–1995 (Studio City, Calif.: Mediascope, 1996); O. Wiegman, M. Kuttschreuter, and B. Baarda, "A Longitudinal Study of the Effects of Television Viewing on Aggressive and Prosocial Behaviors," *British Journal of Social Psychology,* **31** (1992): 147–164; B. S. Centerwall, "Television and Violence: The Scale of the Problem and Where to Go from Here," *Journal of the American Medical Association,* **267** (1992): 3059–3063; J. E. Ledingham, C. A. Ledingham, and John E. Richardson, *The Effects of Media Violence on Children* (Ottawa: National Clearinghouse on Family Violence, Health and Welfare, 1993); M. I. Tulloch, M. L. Prendergast, and M. D. Anglin, "Evaluating Aggression: School Students' Responses to Television Portrayals of Institutionalized Violence," *Journal of Youth and Adolescence,* **24** (1995): 95–115.

22. See Gerald R. Patterson, R. A. Littman, and W. Brickler, *Assertive Behavior in Children: A Step toward a Theory of Aggression,* monograph of the Society for Research in Child Development, no. 32 (1976).

23. Bandura, *Aggression.*

24. Tanya Thomas, "Violence in Hockey," *SNN Student Magazine*, Feb. 2003, www.snn-rdr.ca/snn/2003feb/hockey.html, accessed Feb. 9, 2008.

25. C. Ray Jeffery, "Criminal Behavior and Learning Theory," *Journal of Criminal Law, Criminology and Police Science*, 56 (1965): 294–300.

26. Ernest L. Burgess and Ronald L. Akers, "A Differential Association-Reinforcement Theory of Criminal Behavior," *Social Problems*, 14 (1966): 128–147. See also Reed Adams, "Differential Association and Learning Principles Revisited," *Social Problems*, 20 (1973): 458–470.

27. See D. W. Andrews and J. Stephen Wormith, "Personality and Crime: Knowledge Destruction and Construction in Criminology," *Justice Quarterly*, 6 (1989): 149–160.

28. William S. Laufer, Dagna K. Skoog, and James M. Day, "Personality and Criminality: A Review of the California Psychological Inventory," *Journal of Clinical Psychology*, 38 (1982): 562–573; R. D. Hare, "Psychopathy and the Personality Dimensions of Psychoticism, Extraversion and Neuroticism." *Personality and Individual Differences*, 3 (1982): 35–42.

29. Richard E. Tremblay, "The Prediction of Delinquent Behavior from Childhood Behavior: Personality Theory Revisited," in *Facts, Frameworks, and Forecasts: Advances in Criminological Theory*, vol. 3, ed. J. McCord (New Brunswick, N.J.: Transaction, 1992); R. D. Hare, "The Hare PCL-R: Some Issues Concerning Its Use and Misuse," *Legal and Criminological Psychology*, 3 (1998): 101–119.

30. Michael L. Gearing, "The MMPI as a Primary Differentiator and Predictor of Behavior in Prison: A Methodological Critique and Review of the Recent Literature," *Psychological Bulletin*, 36 (1979): 929–963.

31. Edwin I. Megargee and Martin J. Bohn, *Classifying Criminal Offenders* (Beverly Hills, Calif.: Sage, 1979); William S. Laufer, John A. Johnson, and Robert Hogan, "Ego Control and Criminal Behavior," *Journal of Personality and Social Psychology*, 41 (1981): 179–184; Edwin I. Megargee, "Psychological Determinants and Correlates of Criminal Violence," in *Criminal Violence*, eds. Marvin E. Wolfgang and Neil A. Weiner (Beverly Hills, Calif.: Sage, 1982); Edwin I. Megargee, "The Role of Inhibition in the Assessment and Understanding of Violence," in *Current Topics in Clinical and Community Psychology*, ed. Charles Donald Spielberger (New York: Academic Press, 1971); Edwin I. Megargee, "Undercontrol and Overcontrol in Assaultive and Homicidal Adolescents," Ph.D. dissertation, University of California, Berkeley, 1964; Edwin I. Megargee, "Undercontrolled and Overcontrolled Personality Types in Extreme Antisocial Aggression," *Psychological Monographs*, 80 (1966); and Edwin I. Megargee and Gerald A. Mendelsohn, "A Cross-Validation of Twelve MMPI Indices of Hostility and Control," *Journal of Abnormal and Social Psychology*, 65 (1962): 431–438.

32. See, e.g., William S. Laufer and James M. Day, eds., *Personality Theory, Moral Development, and Criminal Behavior* (Lexington, Mass.: Lexington Books, 1983).

33. Daniel J. Tennenbaum, "Personality and Criminality: A Summary and Implications of the Literature," *Journal of Criminal Justice*, 5 (1977): 225–235. See also G. P. Waldo and Simon Dinitz, "Personality Attributes of the Criminal: An Analysis of Research Studies, 1950–1965," *Journal of Research in Crime and Delinquency*, 4 (1967): 185–202; and R. D. Martin and D. G. Fischer, "Personality Factors in Juvenile Delinquency: A Review of the Literature," *Catalog of Selected Documents in Psychology*, vol. 8 (1978), ms. 1759.

34. Samuel Yochelson and Stanton Samenow, *The Criminal Personality* (New York: Jason Aronson, 1976).

35. Laufer et al., "Personality and Criminality"; Harrison G. Gough and Pamela Bradley, "Delinquent and Criminal Behavior as Assessed by the Revised California Psychological Inventory," *Journal of Clinical Psychology*, 48 (1991): 298–308.

36. See Anne Campbell and John J. Gibbs, eds., *Violent Transactions: The Limits of Personality* (Oxford: Basil Blackwell, 1986); Lawrence A. Pervin, "Personality: Current Controversies, Issues, and Direction," *Annual Review of Psychology*, 36 (1985): 83–114; and Lawrence A. Pervin, "Persons, Situations, Interactions: Perspectives on a Recurrent Issue," in Campbell and Gibbs, *Violent Transactions*.

37. See Hans J. Eysenck, *Crime and Personality* (London: Routledge & Kegan Paul, 1977); H. J. Eysenck, "Personality and Crime: Where Do We Stand?" *Psychology, Crime and Law*, 2 (1996): 143–152; Hans J. Eysenck, "Personality, Conditioning, and Antisocial Behavior," in Laufer and Day, *Personality Theory*; Hans J. Eysenck, "Personality and Criminality: A Dispositional Analysis," in *Advances in Criminological Theory*, vol. 1, eds. William S. Laufer and Freda Adler (New Brunswick, N.J.: Transaction, 1989); and Hans J. Eysenck and Gisli H. Gudjonnson, *The Causes and Cures of Crime* (New York: Plenum, 1990).

38. *The Life and Death of Edmond Yu*, Documentary by David Hawkins.

39. Seymour L. Halleck, *Psychiatry and the Dilemmas of Crime* (New York: Harper & Row, 1967); Nicholas N. Kittrie, *The Right to Be Different: Deviance and Enforced Therapy* (Baltimore, Md.: Johns Hopkins Press, 1971).

40. Karl Menninger, *The Crime of Punishment* (New York: Viking, 1968).

41. See Daniel L. Davis et al., "Prevalence of Emotional Disorders in a Juvenile Justice Institutional Population," *American Journal of Forensic Psychology*, 9 (1991): 5–17.

42. S. Hodgins and G. Coté, "Prevalence of Mental Disorders among Penitentiary Inmates in Quebec," *Canada's Mental Health*, (March 1990): 1–4.

43. L. A. Teplin, "The Criminalization Hypothesis: Myth, Misnoer, or Management Strategy," in S. A. Shah and B. D. Sales, eds., *Law and Mental Health: Major Developments and Research Needs* (Rockville, Md.: U.S. Department of Health and Human Services, 1991), pp. 149–183.

44. J. Monahan and H. J. Steadman, "Crime and Mental Disorder: An Epidemiological Approach," in M. Tonry and N. Morris, eds., *Crime and Justice: An Annual Review of Research* (Chicago: University of Chicago Press, 1983).

45. R. Roesch, "Mental Health Interventions in Pretrial Jails," in G. M. Davies, S. Lloyd-Bostock, M. McMurran, and C. Wilson, eds., *Psychology and Law: Advances in Research* (Berlin: De Greuter, 1995), p. 520–531.

46. K. M. Abram and L. A. Teplin, "Co-occurring Disorders Among Mentally Ill Jail Detainees: Implications for Public Policy," *American Psychologist*, **46** (1991): 1036–1045.

47. R. Roesch and S. L. Golding, "The Impact of Deinstitutionalization," in D. P. Farrington and J. Gunn, eds., *Aggression and Dangerousness* (New York: Wiley, 1985).

48. Eric Silver, "Extending Social Disorganization Theory: A Multilevel Approach to the Study of Violence among Persons with Mental Illness," *Criminology*, **38** (2000): 1043–1074.

49. Canadian Mental Health Association, "Violence and Mental Illness," www.cmha.ca/bins/, accessed May 26, 2007.

50. Katherine Janson, "Over the Edge" *W-Five*. CTV News, Apr. 21, 2007, www.ctv.ca/servlet/ArticleNews/print/CTVNews/20070420/wfive_overtheedge_070, accessed Feb. 10, 2008.

51. R. R. Corrado, I. Cohen, S. D. Hart, and R. Roesch, "Comparative Examination of the Prevalence of Mental Disorders among Jailed Inmates in Canada and the United States," *International Journal of Law and Psychiatry*, **23** (2000): 633–647.

52. J. Bonta, M. Law, and K. Hanson, "The Prediction of Criminal and Violent Recidivism Among Mentally Disordered Offenders: A Meta-Analysis," *Psychological Bulletin* (1998): 123–142; R. Borum, "Improving the Clinical Practice of Violence Risk Assessment: Technology Guidelines and Training," *American Psychologist*, **51** (1996): 945–946.

53. R. D. Hare, "Diagnosis of Antisocial Personality Disorder in Two Prison Populations," *American Journal of Psychiatry*, **140** (1983): 887–890; Rick Linden, ed., *Criminology: A Canadian Perspective*, 5th ed. (Toronto: Thomson Nelson, 2004).

54. R. D. Hare. "The Hare PCL-R: Some Issues Concerning Its Use and Misuse." *Legal and Criminological Psychology*, **3** (1998): 101–119; R. D. Hare. *Psychopathy: Theory and Research* (New York: Wiley, 1970).

55. Hervey Cleckley, *The Mask of Sanity*, 5th ed. (St. Louis: Mosby, 1976), pp. 271–272. Copyright 1976, 1988. Published by Emily S. Cleckley, 3024 Fox Spring Road, Augusta, GA 30909.

56. This quotation and the next one are taken from a newspaper article written for the *Vancouver Sun*, Jan. 14, 1982, by M. Farrow as well as Robert Hare's work *Without Conscience: The Disturbing World of the Psychopaths Among Us* (New York: Guilford Press, 1998), p. 132–134.

57. Hervey Cleckley, *The Mask of Sanity*, 5th ed. (St. Louis: Mosby, 1976), pp. 271–272. Copyright 1976, 1988. Published by Emily S. Cleckley, 3024 Fox Spring Road, Augusta, GA 30909. p. 57; Robert D. Hare, *Psychopathy: Theory and Research* (New York: Wiley, 1970); M. Philip Feldman, *Criminal Behavior: A Psychological Analysis* (New York: Wiley, 1978); William McCord and Joan McCord, *Psychopathy and Delinquency* (New York: Wiley, 1956).

58. *The American Psychiatric Association's Diagnostic and Statistical Manual of Mental Disorders*, 3rd rev. ed. (DSM III-R) (Washington, D.C., 1987), classifies psychopathy as "antisocial personality." See Benjamin Karpman, "On the Need of Separating Psychopathy into Two Distinct Clinical Types: The Symptomatic and the Idiopathic," *Journal of Criminal Psychopathology*, **3** (1941): 112–137.

59. Eysenck and Gudjonsson, *The Causes and Cures of Crime*. See also Robert D. Hare, "Research Scale for the Assessment of Psychopathology in Criminal Populations," *Personality and Individual Differences*, **1** (1980): 111–119.

60. See, generally, A. J. Reiss, Jr., K. A. Klaus, and J. A. Roth, eds., *Biobehavioral Influences*: vol. 2, *Understanding and Preventing Violence* (Washington, D.C.: National Academy Press, 1994); M. Hillbrand and N. J. Pallone, "The Psychobiology of Aggression: Engines, Measurement, Control," *Journal of Offender Rehabilitation*, **21** (1994): 1–243; J. T. Tedeschi and R. B. Felson, *Violence, Aggression, and Coercive Actions* (Washington, D.C.: American Psychological Association, 1994).

61. J. Puig-Antich, "Biological Factors in Prepubertal Major Depression," *Pediatric Annals*, **12** (1986): 867–878.

62. See, e.g., Guenther Knoblich and Roy King, "Biological Correlates of Criminal Behavior," in McCord, *Facts, Frameworks, and Forecasts*; Diana H. Fishbein, "Biological Perspectives in Criminology," *Criminology*, **28** (1990): 17–40; David Magnusson, Britt af Klinteberg, and Hakan Stattin, "Autonomic Activity/Reactivity, Behavior, and Crime in a Longitudinal Perspective," in McCord, *Facts, Frameworks, and Forecasts*; Frank A. Elliott, "Violence: The Neurologic Contribution: An Overview," *Archives of Neurology*, **49** (1992): 595–603; L. French, "Neuropsychology of Violence," *Corrective and Social Psychiatry and Journal of Behavior Technology Methods and Therapy*, **37** (1991): 12–17; and Elizabeth Kandel and Sarnoff A. Mednick, "Perinatal Complications Predict Violent Offending," *Criminology*, **29** (1991): 519–530.

63. Edward O. Wilson, *Sociobiology: The New Synthesis* (Cambridge, Mass.: Harvard University Press, 1975).

64. C. Ray Jeffery, *Biology and Crime* (Beverly Hills, Calif.: Sage, 1979).

65. P. A. Brennan and S. A. Mednick, "Genetic Perspectives on Crime," *Acta Psychiatria Scandinavia*, **370** (1993): 19–26.

66. See Sarnoff A. Mednick, Terrie E. Moffitt, and Susan A. Stack, *The Causes of Crime: New Biological Approaches* (New York: Cambridge University Press, 1987).

67. A. Sandberg, G. F. Koepf, and T. Ishihara, "An XYY Human Male," *Lancet* (Aug. 1961): 488–489.

68. Herman A. Witkin, et al., "Criminality, Aggression, and Intelligence among XYY and XXY Men," in *Biosocial Bases of Criminal Behavior*, eds. Sarnoff A. Mednick and Karl O. Christiansen (New York: Wiley, 1977).

69. Johannes Lange, *Verbrechen als Schicksal* (Leipzig: Georg Thieme, 1929).

70. Cf. Gregory Carey, "Twin Imitation for Antisocial Behavior: Implications for Genetic Environment Research," *Journal of Abnormal Psychology*, **101** (1992): 18–25.

71. See Karl O. Christiansen, "A Preliminary Study of Criminality among Twins," in Mednick and Christiansen, *Biosocial Bases of Criminal Behavior*.

72. David C. Rowe and D. Wayne Osgood, "Heredity and Sociological Theories of Delinquency: A Reconsideration," *American Sociological Review*, **49** (1986): 526–540; David C. Rowe, "Genetic and Environmental Components of Antisocial Behavior: A Study of 256 Twin Pairs," *Criminology*, **24** (1986): 513–532.

73. Sarnoff A. Mednick, William Gabrielli, and Barry Hutchings, "Genetic Influences in Criminal Behavior: Evidence from an Adoption Court," in *Prospective Studies of Crime and Delinquency*, ed. K. Teilmann et al. (Boston: Kluwer-Nijhoff, 1983).

74. These and other studies are reviewed in Mednick et al., *The Causes of Crime.*

75. Hannah Bloch and Dick Thompson, "Seeking the Roots of Violence," *Time,* Apr. 19, 1993, pp. 52–53.

76. Daniel Goleman, "New Storm Brews on Whether Crime Has Roots in Genes," *New York Times,* Sept. 15, 1992, p. C1.

77. Bloch and Thompson, "Seeking the Roots of Violence."

78. Goleman, "New Storm Brews on Whether Crime Has Roots in Genes."

79. Study Group on Serious and Violent Juvenile Offenders, Office of Juvenile Justice and Delinquency Prevention (Washington, D.C.: NIJ, 1998); Fox Butterfield, "Study Cites Biology's Role in Violent Behavior," *New York Times,* Nov. 13, 1992, p. A7.

80. Goleman, "New Storm Brews on Whether Crime Has Roots in Genes."

81. Jana Grekul, "The Social Construction of the Feeble-minded Threat: Implementation of the Sexual Sterilization Act in Alberta, 1929–1972," unpublished doctoral dissertation, University of Alberta, 2002.

82. Hugo Munsterberg, *On the Witness Stand* (New York: Doubleday, 1908); and Henry H. Goddard, *Feeble-Mindedness: Its Causes and Consequences* (New York: Macmillan, 1914).

83. Edwin H. Sutherland, "Mental Deficiency and Crime," in *Social Attitudes,* ed. K. Young (New York: Henry Holt, 1931).

84. Robert H. Gault, "Highlights of Forty Years in the Correctional Field—and Looking Ahead," *Federal Probation,* **17** (1953): 3–4.

85. Arthur Jensen, *Bias in Mental Testing* (New York: Free Press, 1979).

86. Ibid.; Richard J. Herrnstein, *IQ in the Meritocracy* (Boston: Atlantic–Little, Brown, 1973).

87. J. P. Rushton, *Race, Evolution and Behaviour: A Life History Perspective,* 2nd ed. (Port Huron, MI: Charles Darwin Research Institute, 2000); Doug Wahlsten, "Genetics and the Development of Brain and Behaviour," in *Handbook of Developmental Psychology,* J. Valsiner and K. J. Connolly, eds. (London: Sage, 2003).

88. Travis Hirschi and Michael J. Hindelang, "Intelligence and Delinquency: A Revisionist Review," *American Sociological Review,* **42** (1977): 571–586.

89. Travis Hirschi, *Causes of Delinquency* (Berkeley: University of California Press, 1969).

90. Marvin E. Wolfgang, Robert F. Figlio, and Thorsten Sellin, *Delinquency in a Birth Cohort* (Chicago: University of Chicago Press, 1972).

91. Albert J. Reiss and Albert L. Rhodes, "The Distribution of Juvenile Delinquency in the Social Class Structure," *American Sociological Review,* **26** (1961): 720–732.

92. See M. Rutter, T. E. Moffitt, and A. Caspi, "Gene-Environment Interplay and Psychopathology: Multiple Varieties but Real Effects," *Journal of Child Psychology and Psychiatry,* **47** (2006): 226–261; T. E. Moffitt, A. Caspi, and M. Rutter, "Measured Gene-Environment Interactions in Psychopathology: Concepts, Research Strategies, and Implications for Research, Intervention, and Public Understanding of Genetics," *Perspectives on Psychological Science,* **1** (2006): 5–27. See also James Q. Wilson and Richard Herrnstein, *Crime and Human Nature* (New York: Simon & Schuster, 1985); Deborah W. Denno, "Sociological and Human Developmental Explanations of Crime: Conflict or Consensus?" *Criminology,* **23** (1985): 711–740; Deborah W. Denno, "Victim, Offender, and Situational Characteristics of Violent Crime," *Journal of Criminal Law and Criminology,* **77** (1986): 1142–1158.

93. James C. Hackler, *Canadian Criminology: Strategies and Perspectives,* 4th ed. (Toronto: Prentice Hall, 2007).

94. "Taking the Chitling Test," *Newsweek,* July 15, 1968.

95. Sandra Scarr and Richard Weinberg, "I.Q. Test Performance of Black Children Adopted by White Families," *American Psychologist,* **31** (1976): 726–739.

96. See Doris J. Rapp, *Allergies and the Hyperactive Child* (New York: Simon & Schuster, 1981).

97. Diana H. Fishbein and Susan Pease, "The Effects of Diet on Behavior: Implications for Criminology and Corrections," *Research on Corrections,* **1** (1988): 1–45.

98. Stephen Schoenthaler, "Diet and Crime: An Empirical Examination of the Value of Nutrition in the Control and Treatment of Incarcerated Juvenile Offenders," *International Journal of Biosocial Research,* **4** (1982): 25–39.

99. Heather M. Little, "Food May Be Causing Kids' Problems," *Chicago Tribune,* Oct. 29, 1995, p. 1; Abram Hoffer, "The Relation of Crime to Nutrition," *Humanist in Canada,* **8** (1975): 2–9.

100. Benjamin F. Feingold, *Why Is Your Child Hyperactive?* (New York: Random House, 1975).

101. James W. Swanson and Marcel Kinsbourne, "Food Dyes Impair Performance of Hyperactive Children on a Laboratory Test," *Science,* **207** (1980): 1485–1487.

102. "Toddler Dies after Being Thrown in Lake by Dad in Diabetic Seizure," *Chicago Tribune,* July 10, 1995, p. 9.

103. Matti Virkkunen, "Insulin Secretion during the Glucose Tolerance Test among Habitually Violent and Impulsive Offenders," *Aggressive Behavior,* **12** (1986): 303–310.

104. E. A. Beeman, "The Effect of Male Hormones on Aggressive Behavior in Mice," *Physiological Zoology,* **20** (1947): 373–405.

105. D. A. Hamburg and D. T. Lunde, "Sex Hormones in the Development of Sex Differences," in *The Development of Sex Differences,* ed. Eleanor E. Maccoby (Stanford, Calif.: Stanford University Press, 1966).

106. Booth and D. W. Osgood, "The Influence of Testosterone on Deviance in Adulthood: Assessing and Explaining the Relationship," *Criminology,* **31** (1993): 93–117; L. E. Kreuz and R. M. Rose, "Assessment of Aggressive Behavior and Plasma Testosterone of a Young Criminal Population," *Psychosomatic Medicine,* **34** (1972): 321–332; R. T. Rada, D. R. Laws, and R. Kellner, "Plasma Testosterone Levels in the Rapist," *Psychosomatic Medicine,* **38** (1976): 257–268.

107. Katherina Dalton, *The Premenstrual Syndrome* (Springfield, Ill.: Charles C. Thomas, 1971).

108. Julie Horney, "Menstrual Cycles and Criminal Responsibility," *Law and Human Behavior,* **2** (1978): 25–36.

109. P. Easteal, "Women and Crime: Premenstrual Issues," *Trends and Issues,* No. 31 (Canberra: Australian Institute of Criminology, 1991).

110. *Regina v. Charlson,* 1 A11. E.R. 859 (1955).

111. L. P. Chesterman et al., "Multiple Measures of Cerebral State in Dangerous Mentally Disordered Inpatients," *Criminal Behavior and Mental Health,* **4** (1994): 228–239; Lee Ellis, "Monoamine Oxidase and Criminality: Identifying an Apparent Biological Marker for Antisocial Behavior," *Journal of Research in Crime and Delinquency,* **28** (1991): 227–251.

112. H. Forssman and T. S. Frey, "Electroencephalograms of Boys with Behavior Disorders," *Acta Psychologica et Neurologia Scandinavica,* **28** (1953): 61–73; H. de Baudouin et al., "Study of a Population of 97 Confined Murderers," *Annales Medico-Psychologique,* **119** (1961): 625–686.

113. Sarnoff A. Mednick, Jan Volavka, William F. Gabrielli, and Turan M. Itil, "EEG as a Predictor of Antisocial Behavior," *Criminology,* **19** (1981): 219–229.

114. See, e.g., Adrian Raine, Monte Buchsbaum, and Lori LaCasse, "Brain Abnormalities in Murderers Indicated by Positron Emission Tomography," *Biological Psychiatry,* **42** (1997): 495–508; Adrian Raine, J. Reid Meloy, Susan Bihrle, Jackie Stoddard, Lori LaCasse, and Monte S. Buchsbaum, "Reduced Prefrontal and Increased Subcortical Brain Functioning Assessed Using Positron Emission Tomography in Predatory and Affective Murderers," *Behavioral Sciences and the Law,* **16** (1998): 319–332; Jan Volavka, "Electroencephalogram among Criminals," in Mednick et al., *The Causes of Crime.* See also J. Volavka, *Neurobiology of Violence* (Washington, D.C.: American Psychiatric Press, 1995).

115. Larry N. Chartrand, "Aboriginal Youth and the Criminal Justice System," in *Understanding Youth Justice in Canada,* ed. Kathryn Campbell (Toronto: Prentice Hall, 2005).

116. Caroline L. Tait and Sir Mortimer B. Davis, "Fetal Alcohol Syndrome Among Aboriginal People in Canada: Review and Analysis of the Intergenerational Links to Residential Schools" (Aboriginal Healing Foundation, 2003).

117. Paul Szabo, "Fetal Alcohol Syndrome: The Real Brain Drain," March, 2000; A. P. Streissguth, H. M. Barr, J. Kogan and F. L. Bookstein, *Understanding the Occurrence of Secondary Disabilities in Clients with Fetal Alcohol Syndrome (FAS) and Fetal Alcohol Effects (FAE)* (Ottawa: Centers for Disease Control and Prevention, 1996 [unpublished]).

118. DSM III-R, 314.01. See also Michael Rutter, "Syndromes Attributed to 'Minimal Brain Dysfunction' in Children," *American Journal of Psychiatry,* **139** (1980): 21–33.

119. T. Moffitt, R. McGee, and P. Silva. "Self-Reported Delinquency, Neuropsychological Deficit, and History of Attention Deficit Disorder," paper presented at annual meeting of the American Society of Criminology, Montreal, 1987.

120. Edward Sagarin, "Taboo Subjects and Taboo Viewpoints in Criminology," in *Taboos in Criminology,* ed. E. Sagarin (Beverly Hills, Calif.: Sage, 1980), pp. 8–9.

121. Diana H. Fishbein, "Biological Perspectives in Criminology," *Criminology,* **28** (1990): 27–40.

122. Wilson and Herrnstein, *Crime and Human Nature.* Infants develop attachment to mothers, or mother substitutes, for comfort, security, and warmth.

Chapter 5

1. Ysabel Rennie, *The Search for Criminal Man* (Lexington, Mass.: Lexington Books, 1978), p. 125.

2. James T. Carey, *Sociology and Public Affairs: The Chicago School* (Beverly Hills, Calif.: Sage, 1975), pp. 19–20.

3. See the discussion of sociological theory in Frank P. Williams III and Marilyn D. McShane, *Criminological Theory* (Englewood Cliffs, N.J.: Prentice-Hall, 1988).

4. Émile Durkheim, *The Division of Labor in Society* (New York: Free Press, 1964).

5. Émile Durkheim, *Rules of Sociological Method* (New York: Free Press, 1966).

6. Émile Durkheim, *Suicide* (Glencoe, Ill.: Free Press, 1951), pp. 241–276.

7. Ibid., p. 247.

8. Robert K. Merton, "Social Structure and Anomie," *American Sociological Review,* **3** (1938): 672–682. For a complete history of the social structure and anomie paradigm, see recent reflections of Merton in Robert K. Merton, "Opportunity Structure: The Emergence, Diffusion, and Differentiation of a Sociological Concept, 1930s–1950s," in *Advances in Criminological Theory: The Legacy of Anomie,* vol. 6, eds. Freda Adler and William S. Laufer (New Brunswick, N.J.: Transaction, 1994), pp. 3–78. Several measures of anomie have been developed. Probably the best-known indicator of anomie at the social level was formulated by Bernard Lander in a study of 8464 cases of juvenile delinquency in Baltimore, Maryland, between 1939 and 1942. Lander devised a measure that included the rate of delinquency, the percentage of non-white population in a given area, and the percentage of owner-occupied homes. According to Lander, those factors were indicative of the amount of normlessness (anomie) in a community. See Bernard Lander, *Towards an Understanding of Juvenile Delinquency* (New York: Columbia University Press, 1954), p. 65.

9. Canadian Council on Social Development, "Census Shows Growing Polarization of Income in Canada, 2003," http://ccsd.ca/pr/2003/censusincome.htm, accessed Jan. 1, 2006.

10. "Jim Carrey Movies," www.fluge.com/jim-carrey-star.html, accessed Feb. 14, 2008.

11. Robert K. Merton, *Social Theory and the Social Structure* (New York: Free Press, 1957), p. 187.

12. Albert J. Reiss Jr. and Albert L. Rhodes, "The Distribution of Juvenile Delinquency in the Social Class Structure," *American Sociological Review,* **26** (1961): 720–732. For the relationship between economic changes and crime, see Pamela Irving Jackson, "Crime, Youth Gangs, and Urban Transition: The Social Dislocations of Postindustrial Economic Development," *Justice Quarterly,* **8** (1991): 380–397.

13. F. Ivan Nye, James F. Short, and Virgil J. Olson, "Socioeconomic Status and Delinquent Behavior," *American Journal of Sociology,* **63** (1958): 381–389.

14. Charles R. Tittle, Wayne J. Villemez, and Douglas A. Smith, "The Myth of Social Class and Criminality: An Empirical Assessment of the Empirical Evidence," *American Sociological Review,* **43** (1978): 652; and Charles R.

Tittle and Robert F. Meier, "Specifying the SES/Delinquency Relationship by Social Characteristics of Contexts," *Journal of Research in Crime and Delinquency,* **28** (1991): 430–455.

15. Gary F. Jensen and Kevin Thompson, "What's Class Got to Do with It? A Further Examination of Power-Control Theory," *American Journal of Sociology,* **95** (1990): 1009–1023.

16. John Braithwaite, "The Myth of Social Class and Criminality Reconsidered," *American Sociological Review,* **46** (1981): 41. See also Delbert S. Elliott and Suzanne S. Ageton, "Reconciling Race and Class Differences in Self-Reported and Official Estimates of Delinquency," *American Sociological Review,* **45** (1980): 95–110; Michael W. Neustrom and William M. Norton, "Economic Dislocation and Property Crime," *Journal of Criminal Justice,* **23** (1995): 29–39; and James De Frongo, "Welfare and Homicide," *Journal of Research in Crime and Delinquency,* **34** (1997): 395–406.

17. William R. Avison and Pamela L. Loring, "Population Diversity and Cross-National Homicide: The Effects of Inequality and Heterogeneity," *Criminology,* **24** (1986): 733–749; Harvey Krahn, Timothy F. Hartnagel, and John W. Gartrell, "Income Inequality and Homicide Rates: Cross-National Data and Criminological Theories," *Criminology,* **24** (1986): 269–295; and Richard Fowles and Mary Merva, "Wage Inequity and Criminal Activity: An Extreme Bounds Analysis for the United States, 1975–1990," *Criminology,* **34** (1996): 163–182.

18. Krahn et al., "Income Inequality," p. 288.

19. S. Baron, "Serious Offenders" in *Canadian Delinquency,* eds., J. H. Creechan and R. A. Silverman (Scarborough, Ontario: Prentice-Hall Canada, 1995).

20. John Hagan and Bill McCarthy, "Anomie, Social Capital, and Street Criminology," in *The Future of Anomie Theory,* eds. Nikos Passas and Robert Agnew (Boston: Northeastern University Press, 1997).

21. John Hagan, "The Social Embeddedness of Crime and Unemployment," *Criminology,* **31** (1993): 465–492.

22. See, e.g., Shaun L. Gabbidon and Helen Taylor Greene, *Race and Crime* (Thousand Oaks, Calif.: Sage, 2005).

23. Bradley R. Entner Wright, Avshalom Caski, Terrie E. Moffitt, Richard A. Miech, and Phil A. Silva, "Reconsidering the Relationship between SES and Delinquency Causation but Not Correlation," *Criminology,* **37** (1999): 175–194.

24. Terence P. Thornberry and Margaret Farnsworth, "Social Correlates of Criminal Involvement: Further Evidence on the Relationship between Social Status and Criminal Behavior," *American Sociological Review,* **47** (1982): 505–518; Thomas J. Bernard, "Control Criticisms of Strain Theories: An Assessment of Theoretical and Empirical Adequacy," *Journal of Research in Crime and Delinquency,* **21** (1984): 353–372; and Delbert S. Elliott and David Huizinga, "Social Class and Delinquent Behavior in a National Youth Panel," *Criminology,* **21** (1983): 149–177.

25. John Braithwaite, *Inequality, Crime, and Public Policy* (London: Routledge & Kegan Paul, 1979), p. 219.

26. Nikos Passas, "Anomie, Reference Groups, and Relative Deprivation," in *The Future of Anomie Theory,* eds. Nikos Passas and Robert Agnew (Boston: Northeastern Press, 1997), pp. 64–65.

27. Gwynne Nettler, *Explaining Crime* (New York: McGraw-Hill: 1984).

28. Stephen A. Cernkovich, Peggy C. Giordano, and Jennifer L. Rudolph, "Race, Crime, and the American Dream," *Journal of Research in Crime and Delinquency,* **37** (2000): 131–170.

29. Thomas J. Bernard, "Merton versus Hirschi: Who Is Faithful to Durkheim's Heritage?" in *Advances in Criminological Theory,* vol. 4, pp. 81–91; Nikos Passas, "Continuities in the Anomie Tradition," in *Advances in Criminological Theory,* vol. 4, pp. 91–112; Scott Menard, "A Developmental Test of Mertonian Anomie Theory," *Journal of Research in Crime and Delinquency,* **32** (1995): 136–174.

30. Gary F. Jensen, "Salvaging Structure through Strain: A Theoretical and Empirical Critique," in *Advances in Criminological Theory,* vol. 4, pp. 139–158; Velmer S. Burton Jr., Francis T. Cullen, T. David Evans, and R. Gregory Dunaway, "Reconsidering Strain Theory: Operationalization, Rival Theories, and Adult Criminality," *Journal of Quantitative Criminology,* **10** (1994): 213–239.

31. Ian Taylor, Paul Walton, and Jock Young, *The New Criminology* (New York: Harper & Row, 1973), p. 107.

32. Elizabeth Comack, "Women and Crime" in *Criminology: A Canadian Perspective,* 2nd ed., ed. Rick Linden (Toronto: Harcourt Brace Jovanovich Canada, 1992).

33. Ngaire Naffine, *Feminism and Criminology* (Sydney: Allen and Unwin, 1997); Elizabeth Comack, "Women and Crime" in *Criminology: A Canadian Perspective.*

34. James C. Hackler, *Canadian Criminology: Strategies and Perspectives,* 4th ed. (Toronto: Prentice Hall, 2007).

35. Stephen Baron, doctoral dissertation.

36. Freda Adler, *Nations Not Obsessed with Crime* (Littleton, Colo.: Fred B. Rothman, 1983).

37. Steven F. Messner and Richard Rosenfeld, *Crime and the American Dream* (Belmont, Calif.: Wadsworth, 1994).

38. Mitchell B. Chamlin and John K. Cochran, "Assessing Messner and Rosenfeld's Institutional Anomie Theory: A Partial Test," *Criminology,* **33** (1995): 411–429.

39. James C. Hackler, "Strain Theories," in *Criminology: A Canadian Perspective,* 5th ed., ed. Rick Linden (Toronto: Thomson Nelson, 2004). p. 310.

40. Freda Adler, "Synnomie to Anomie: A Macrosociological Formulation," in *Advances in Criminological Theory,* vol. 4, pp. 271–283.

41. Robert Agnew, "Foundations for a General Strain Theory of Crime and Delinquency," *Criminology,* **30** (1992): 47–87.

42. Robert Agnew, "The Contribution of Social-Psychological Strain Theory to the Explanation of Crime and Delinquency," in *Advances in Criminological Theory,* pp. 113–137. See also John P. Hoffman and Alan S. Miller, "A Latent Variable Analysis of General Strain Theory," *Journal of Quantitative Criminology,* **14** (1998): 83–110.

43. Raymond Paternoster and Paul Mazerolle, "General Strain Theory and Delinquency: A Replication and Extension," *Journal of Research in Crime and Delinquency,* **31** (1994): 235–263; see also Robert Agnew, Timothy Brezina, John Paul Wright, and Francis T. Cullen, "Strain, Personality Traits, and Delinquency: Extending General Strain Theory," *Criminology,* **40** (2002): 43–71;

Paul Mazerolle and Jeff Maahs, "General Strain and Delinquency: An Alternative Examination of Conditioning Influences," *Justice Quarterly*, **17** (2000): 753–773; Timothy Brezina, "Adapting to Strain: An Examination of Delinquent Coping Responses," *Criminology*, **34** (1996): 39–60; and Robert Agnew and Helene Raskin White, "An Empirical Test of General Strain Theory," *Criminology*, **30** (1992): 475–499. For an examination of gender and delinquent behavior from a general strain theory perspective, see Paul Mazerolle, "Gender, General Strain and Delinquency: An Empirical Examination," *Justice Quarterly*, **15** (1998): 65–91.

44. Aboriginal Head Start, "Program Overview," www. phac-aspc.gc.ca/dca-dea/programs-mes/ahs_overview_e.html, accessed June 6, 2007.

45. "Fact Sheet—Aboriginal Head Start in Urban and Northern Communities," www.ainc-inac.gc.ca/ps/ecde/unc_e.html, accessed June 14, 2007.

46. Ministry of Government Services, "McGuinty Government Helps Students Stay in School," Jan. 16, 2007, http://ogov.newswire.ca/ontario/GPOE/2007/01/16/c6146.html, accessed June 14, 2007.

47. "Toronto Youth Job Corps," www.jvstoronto.org/index. php?page+toronto-youth-job-corps/, accessed June 6, 2007.

48. Employment, Immigration and Industry, "Alberta Job Corps," http://employment.alberta.ca/hre/ets/reg/Display.asp?EntityCode=HLEVEL_3&EntityKey=, accessed June 6, 2007.

49. Albert K. Cohen, *Delinquent Boys: The Culture of the Gang* (Glencoe, Ill.: Free Press, 1955).

50. For example, James F. Short Jr. and Fred L. Strodtbeck, *Group Process and Gang Delinquency* (Chicago: University of Chicago Press, 1965).

51. Kenneth Polk and Walter B. Schafer, eds., *School and Delinquency* (Englewood Cliffs, N.J.: Prentice-Hall, 1972); Alexander Liazos, "School, Alienation, and Delinquency," *Crime and Delinquency*, **24** (1978): 355–370.

52. Travis Hirschi, *Causes of Delinquency* (Berkeley: University of California Press, 1969).

53. Delbert S. Elliott and Harwin L. Voss, *Delinquency and Dropout* (Lexington, Mass.: Lexington Books, 1974).

54. I. Gomme, "Predictors of Status and Criminal Offences Among Male and Female Adolescents in an Ontario Community," *Canadian Journal of Criminology*, **27** (1985): 147–160.

55. M. Le Blanc,"Delinquency as an Epiphenomenon of Adolescents," in *Current Issues in Juvenile Justice*, ed. N. Corrado, M. Le Blanc, and J. Trepanier (Toronto: Butterworths, 1983).

56. Linda Pagani, Bernard Boulerice, Frank Vitaro, and Richard E. Tremblay, "Effects of Poverty on Academic Failure and Delinquency in Boys: A Change and Process Model Approach," *Journal of Child Psychology and Psychiatry*, **40** (1999): 1209–1219.

57. G. Roger Jarjoura, "Dropping Out of School Enhances Delinquent Involvement? Results from a Large-Scale National Probability Sample," *Criminology*, **31** (1993): 149–172.

58. L. Davies, "In Search of Resistance and Rebellion Among High School Drop-Outs," *Canadian Journal of Sociology*, **19** (1994): 331–350.

59. L. Davies. "Class Dismissed? Student Opposition in Ontario High Schools." *Canadian Review of Sociology and Anthropology*, **31** (1994): 422–445.

60. P. Solomon, *Black Resistance in High School: Forging a Separatist Culture.* (Albany, NY: State University of New York Press, 1992). See also Sandra Bell, *Young Offenders and Juvenile Justice: A Century After the Fact,* 2nd ed. (Toronto: Thomson Nelson, 2002).

61. Albert J. Reiss and Albert L. Rhodes, "Deprivation and Delinquent Behavior," *Sociological Quarterly*, **4** (1963): 135–149.

62. Marvin Krohn, R. L. Akers, M. J. Radosevich, and L. Lanza-Kaduce, "Social Status and Deviance," *Criminology*, **18** (1980): 303–318.

63. Mark Warr, "Organization and Instigation in Delinquent Groups," *Criminology*, **34** (1996): 11–37.

64. David F. Greenberg, "Delinquency and the Age Structure of Society," *Contemporary Crisis*, **1** (1977): 189–223.

65. John I. Kitsuse and David C. Dietrick, "Delinquent Boys: A Critique," *American Sociological Review*, **24** (1959): 208–215.

66. David J. Bordua, "Delinquent Subcultures: Sociological Interpretations of Gang Delinquency," *Annals of the American Academy of Political and Social Science*, **338** (1961): 119–136.

67. Albert K. Cohen and James F. Short Jr., "Research in Delinquent Subcultures," *Journal of Social Issues*, **14** (1958): 20–37.

68. Richard A. Cloward and Lloyd E. Ohlin, *Delinquency and Opportunity* (Glencoe, Ill.: Free Press, 1960).

69. Michael C. Chettleburgh. Young Thugs: Inside the Dangerous World of Canadian Street Gangs (Toronto: Harper Collins Publishers Ltd., 2007).

70. James R. David, *Street Gangs* (Dubuque, Iowa: Kendall/Hunt, 1982).

71. Hirschi, *Causes of Delinquency*, p. 227.

72. John M. Hagedorn, "Homeboys, Dope Fiends, Legits, and New Jacks," *Criminology*, **32** (1994): 197–219.

73. James Short, Ramon Rivera, and Ray Tennyson, "Perceived Opportunities, Gang Membership, and Delinquency," *American Sociological Review*, **30** (1965): 56–57.

74. John Hagan and Bill McCarthy, *Mean Streets: Youth Homelessness and Crime.* (New York: Cambridge University Press, 1997); John Hagan and Bill McCarthy, "Anomie, Social Capital, and Street Criminology" in *The Future of Anomie Theory*, ed. Nikos Passas and Robert Agnew (Boston: Northeastern University Press, 1997).

75. Lecture by Ko-lin Chin, Rutgers University, Nov. 22, 1993. See also K. Chin, *Chinese Subculture and Criminality: Nontraditional Crime Groups in America*, Criminology and Penology Series, vol. 29 (Westport, Conn.: Greenwood, 1990); Mark Warr, "Organization and Instigation in Delinquent Groups," *Criminology*, **34** (1996): 11–37; Kevin M. Thompson, David Brownfield, and Ann Marie Sorenson, "Specialization Patterns of Gang and Nongang Offending: A Latent Structure Analysis," *Journal of Gang Research*, **3** (1996): 25–35.

76. Finn-Aage Esbensen and David Huizinga, "Gangs, Drugs, and Delinquency in a Survey of Urban Youth," *Criminology*, **31** (1993): 565–587; Terence P. Thornberry, Marvin D. Krohn, Alan J. Lizotte, and Deborah Chard-Wierschem,

"The Role of Juvenile Gangs in Facilitating Delinquent Behavior," *Journal of Research in Crime and Delinquency,* **30** (1993): 55–87; Malcolm Klein, Cheryl L. Maxson, and Lea C. Cunningham, "'Crack,' Street Gangs, and Violence," *Criminology,* **29** (1991): 623–650.

77. Jana Grekul and Patti LaBoucane-Benson, "Aboriginal Gangs and Their (Dis)placement: Contextualizing Recruitment, Membership, and Status," *Canadian Journal of Criminology and Criminal Justice,* **50(1)** (2008).

78. Michael C. Chettleburgh, *Young Thugs: Inside the Dangerous World of Canadian Street Gangs* (Toronto: Harper Collins Publishers Ltd., 2007), p. 23.

79. Scot Wortley and Julian Tanner, Metropolis Conference, 2005, as cited in "Feature Focus 2006: Youth Gangs & Guns," Royal Canadian Mounted Police, www.rcmp-grc.gc.ca/focus/youth_gun/vancouver26_e.htm, accessed Feb. 14, 2008.

80. K. Chin and J. Fagan, "Social Order and Gang Formation in Chinatown," in *Advances in Criminological Theory,* vol. 6, eds. Freda Adler and William S. Laufer (New Brunswick, N.J.: Transaction, 1994).

81. John P. Hoffman and Timothy Ireland, "Cloward and Ohlin's Strain Theory Reexamined: An Elaborated Theoretical Model," in *Advances in Criminological Theory,* vol. 6.

Chapter 6

1. Robert M. Gordon, "Criminal Business Organizations, Street Gangs and 'Wanna-be' Groups: A Vancouver Perspective," *Canadian Journal of Criminology* (Jan., 2000): 39–60.

2. Edwin H. Sutherland, *Principles of Criminology,* 3rd ed. (Philadelphia: Lippincott, 1939).

3. James S. Short, "Differential Association as a Hypothesis: Problems of Empirical Testing," *Social Problems,* **8** (1960): 14–15.

4. Travis Hirschi, *Causes of Delinquency* (Berkeley: University of California Press, 1969), p. 95.

5. Sandra Bell, *Young Offenders and Juvenile Justice: A Century After the Fact,* 2nd ed. (Toronto: Thomson Nelson: 2002).

6. Beth Bjerregaard and Carolyn Smith, "Patterns of Male and Female Gang Membership," working paper no. 13, Rochester Youth Development Study (Albany, N.Y.: Hindelang Criminal Justice Research Center, 1992), p. 20. For contradictory findings, see Mark D. Reed and Pamela Wilcox Roundtree, "Peer Pressure and Adolescent Substance Abuse," *Journal of Quantitative Criminology,* **13** (1997), 143–180. For the relationship of delinquents to their delinquent siblings, see Janet L. Lauritsen, "Sibling Resemblance in Juvenile Delinquency: Findings from the National Youth Survey," *Criminology,* **31** (1993): 387–409.

7. Robert A. Stebbins, "Interactionist Theories" in *Criminology: A Canadian Perspective,* 5th ed., ed. Rick Linden (Toronto: Thomson Nelson, 2004).

8. Mark Warr, "Age, Peers, and Delinquency," *Criminology,* **31** (1993): 17–40.

9. Jana Grekul and Patti LaBoucane-Benson, "Aboriginal Gangs and Their (Dis)placement: Contextualizing Recruitment, Membership, and Status," *Canadian Journal of Criminology and Criminal Justice,* **50(1)** (2008).

10. Charles Tittle, *Sanctions and Social Deviance* (New York: Praeger, 1980).

11. Daniel R. Wolf, *The Rebels: A Brotherhood of Outlaw Bikers* (Toronto: University of Toronto Press, 1991) p. 11.

12. Clayton A. Hartjen, *Crime and Criminalization* (New York: Praeger, 1974), p. 51.

13. Jack Katz, *Seductions of Crime: Moral and Sensual Attractions in Doing Evil* (New York: Basic Books, 1990).

14. Ross L. Matsueda, "The Current State of Differential Association," *Crime and Delinquency,* **34** (1988): 277–306; and Craig Reinarman and Jeffrey Fagan, "Social Organization and Differential Association: A Research Note from a Longitudinal Study of Violent Juvenile Offenders," *Crime and Delinquency,* **34** (1988): 307–327.

15. Thorsten Sellin, *Culture Conflict and Crime,* Bulletin 41 (New York: Social Science Research Council, 1938); Avison and Loring, "Population Diversity and Cross-National Homicide"; Mark R. Pogrebin and Eric D. Poole, "Culture Conflict and Crime in the Korean-American Community," *Criminal Justice Policy Review,* **4** (1990): 69–78; and Ira Sommers, Jeffrey Fagan, and Deborah Baskin, "The Influences of Acculturation and Familism on Puerto Rican Delinquency," *Justice Quarterly,* **11** (1994): 207–228.

16. Marvin E. Wolfgang and Franco Ferracuti, *The Subculture of Violence* (London: Tavistock, 1967).

17. Elijah Anderson, *Code of the Street* (New York: W. W. Norton & Company, 1999); T. Brezina, Robert Agnew, and F. T. Cullen, "The Code of the Street: A Quantitative Assessment of Elijah Anderson's Subculture of Violence Thesis and Its Contribution to Youth Violence Research," *Youth Violence and Juvenile Justice,* **2(4)** (2004): 303–328; Liqun Cao, Anthony Adams, and Vickie J. Jensen, "A Test of the Black Subculture of Violence Thesis: A Research Note," *Criminology,* **35(2)** (1997): 367–379; Lance Hannon, "Race, Victim-Precipitated Homicide, and the Subculture of Violence Thesis," *Social Science Journal,* **41** (2004): 115–121; Howard S. Erlanger, "The Empirical Status of the Subcultures of Violence Thesis," *Social Problems,* **22** (1974): 280–292. For the relationship of the thesis to routine activities, see Leslie W. Kennedy and Stephen W. Baron, "Routine Activities and a Subculture of Violence: A Study on the Street," *Journal of Research in Crime and Delinquency,* **30** (1993): 88–112. For a look at regional differences in punitiveness, see Marian J. Borg, "The Southern Subculture of Punitiveness? Regional Variation in Support for Capital Punishment," *Journal of Research in Crime and Delinquency,* **34** (1997): 25–45.

18. Timothy F. Hartnagel, "Crime among the Provinces," *Canadian Journal of Criminology,* **30** (1997): 387–402.

19. Colin Loftin and Robert Hill, "Regional Subculture of Violence: An Examination of the Gastril-Hackney Thesis," *American Sociological Review,* **39** (1974): 714–724. See also Colin Loftin and David McDowall, "Regional Culture and Patterns of Homicide," *Homicide Studies,* **7(4)** (2003): 353–367.

20. Melanie Nimmo, *The "Invisible" Gang Members: A Report on Female Gang Association in Winnipeg* (Canadian Centre for Policy Alternatives, June 2001).

21. Royal Canadian Mounted Police, "Feature Focus 2006: Youth Gangs & Guns," 2006, www.rcmp-grc.gc.ca/

focus/youth_gun/toronto2o_e.htm, accessed Feb. 14, 2008.

22. "What Is Youth Violence," Canadian Health Network, Public Health Agency of Canada, www. canadian-health-network.ca/servlet/ContentServer?cid= 1069439907509, accessed Feb. 18, 2008.

23. Marvin E. Wolfgang, Robert M. Figlio, and Thorsten Sellin, *Delinquency in a Birth Cohort* (Chicago: University of Chicago Press, 1972); Simon I. Singer, "Victims of Serious Violence and Their Criminal Behavior: Subcultural Theory and Beyond," *Violence and Victims,* 1 (1986): 61–70. See also Neil Alan Weiner and Marvin E. Wolfgang, "The Extent and Character of Violent Crime in America, 1969–1982," in *American Violence and Public Policy,* ed. Lynn Curtis (New Haven, Conn.: Yale University Press, 1985), pp. 17–39.

24. Steven Messner, "Regional and Racial Effects on the Urban Homicide Rate: The Subculture of Violence Revisited," *American Journal of Sociology,* 88 (1983): 997–1007.

25. Scott H. Decker, "Collective and Normative Features of Gang Violence," *Justice Quarterly,* 13 (1996): 243–264.

26. Jeffrey Fagan, "The Social Organization of Drug Use and Drug Dealing among Urban Gangs," *Criminology,* 27 (1989): 633–666.

27. Joseph B. Treaster, "Jamaica's Gangs Take Root in U.S.," *New York Times,* Nov. 13, 1988, p. 15.

28. Criminal Intelligence Service Canada, "Highlights of the 2004 Annual Report on Organized Crime in Canada," http://cisc.gc.ca.

29. Canadian Press, "Police Keep Heat on Notorious Québec Bike Gangs," March 26, 2006, www.ctv.ca/servlet/ArticleNews/story/CTVNews/20060325/bike_gangs_cp_060325/, accessed July 9, 2007.

30. Walter B. Miller, "Lower-Class Culture as a Generating Milieu of Gang Delinquency," *Journal of Social Issues,* 14 (1958): 5–19.

31. Jana Grekul and Patti LaBoucane-Benson, "An Investigation into the Formation and Recruitment Processes of Aboriginal Gangs in Canada," *Aboriginal Peoples Collection,* Winter 2007, Cat. No.: JS42-110/2002 ISBN No.: 0-662-66993-2 (Ottawa: Aboriginal Corrections Policy Unit, Public Safety and Emergency Preparedness Canada, 2007).

32. R. W. Connell, *Gender and Power* (Standord, CA: Stanford University Press, 1987); J. Messerschmidt, *Capitalism Patriarchy, and Crime: Toward a Socialist Feminist Criminology* (Totowa, NJ: Rowman & Littlefield, 1986).

33. Miller, "Lower-Class Culture."

34. Stephen A. Cernovich, "Value Orientations and Delinquency Involvement," *Criminology,* 15 (1978): 443–458.

35. Gresham Sykes and David Matza, "Techniques of Neutralization: A Theory of Delinquency," *American Sociological Review,* 22 (1957): 664–673.

36. Barbara Kantrowitz, "Wild in the Streets," *Newsweek,* Aug. 2, 1993, p. 46.

37. *Gang Aftermath,* Bearpaw Media Productions, Native Counseling Services of Alberta, 2005.

38. Ibid.

39. Christie Blatchford, Joe Friesen and Timothy Appleby, "Slain Teenager Veered Blithely into Crossfire," *Globe and Mail,* Dec. 29, 2005, www.theglobeandmail.com/servlet/story/RTGAM.20051228.wcreba1228a/BNStory/, accessed Aug. 4, 2007.

40. CBC News, "Biker Gangs in Canada," *In Depth,* Apr. 5, 2007, www.cbc.ca/news/background/bikergangs/, accessed July 9, 2007.

41. Gerard Young, "Gang Violence Hits Home," *Times Colonist,* Sept. 18, 2004, www.canada.com/components/, accessed July 24, 2007.

42. Jeffrey Fagan, "The Political Economy of Drug Dealing among Urban Gangs," in *Drugs and the Community,* eds. Robert Davis, Arthur Lurigio, and Dennis Rosenbaum (Springfield, Ill.: Charles C. Thomas, 1993), pp. 19–54.

43. toronto.ctv.ca, "'City Is Safer' after Gang Crackdown: T. O. Chief," June 13, 2007, www.ctv.ca/servlet/ArticleNews/print/CTVNews/20070613/gang_raids_070613/2007/, accessed June 24, 2007.

44. Scott Wortley and Julian Tanner, "Social Groups or Criminal Organizations? The Extent and Nature of Youth Gang Activity in Toronto," Jim Phillips and Bruce Kids, eds., *From Enforcement and Prevention to Civic Engagement: Research on Community Safety* (Toronto: Centre of Criminology, 2004).

45. *Gang Aftermath.*

46. Beth Bjerregaard and Alan J. Lizotte, "Gun Ownership and Gang Membership," *The Journal of Criminal Law and Criminology,* 86 (1995): 37–58; Alan J. Lizotte, James M. Tesoriero, Terence P. Thornberry, and Marvin D. Krohn, "Patterns of Adolescent Firearms Ownership and Use," *Justice Quarterly,* 11 (1994): 51–74. On the extent of gang organizations, see Scott H. Decker, Tim Bynum, and Deborah Weisel, "A Tale of Two Cities: Gangs as Organized Crime Groups," *Justice Quarterly,* 15 (1998): 395–425.

47. Criminal Intelligence Service Saskatchewan, *2005 Intelligence Trends: Aboriginal-Based Gangs in Saskatchewan,* 1 (Winter 2005).

48. Brian Mellor, Leslie MacRae, Monica Pauls and Joseph P. Hornick, *Youth Gangs In Canada: A Preliminary Review of Programs and Services* (Ottawa: Canadian Research Institute for Law and the Family for Public Safety and Emergency Preparedness Canada, Sept. 2005).

49. CPS, *Results of the 2002 Canadian Police Survey on Youth Gangs* (Ottawa: Public Safety and Emergency Preparedness Canada, Dec. 2003).

50. Criminal Intelligence Service Saskatchewan, *2005 Intelligence Trends: Aboriginal-Based Gangs in Saskatchewan,* 1 (Winter 2005): p. 2.

51. Ibid. p. 3.

52. Mellor, MacRae, Pauls, and Hornick, *Youth Gangs in Canada.*

53. Ibid., p. 2.

54. Ibid., p. 2.

55. Grekul and LaBoucane-Benson, "An Investigation into the Formation and Recruitment Processes of Aboriginal Gangs in Canada."

56. John P. Sullivan and Martin E. Silverstein, "The Disaster within Us: Urban Conflict and Street Gang Violence in Los Angeles," *Journal of Gang Research,* 2 (1995): 11–30 (p. 28).

57. Albert K. Cohen and James F. Short Jr., "Research in Delinquent Subcultures," *Journal of Social Issues,* 14 (1958): 20–37.

58. Anne Campbell, *The Girls in the Gang* (New York: Basil Blackwell, 1984), p. 267.
59. Melanie Nimmo, *The "Invisible" Gang Members: A Report on Female Gang Association in Winnipeg* (Canadian Centre for Policy Alternatives, June 2001).
60. Ibid.
61. Ibid. p. 6.
62. Ibid. p. 6.
63. *New Mexico Street Gangs, 1994: Update* (Albuquerque: New Mexico Department of Public Safety, 1994); Dana Peterson, Jody Miller, and Fin-Aage Esbenson, "Impact of Sex Composition on Gangs and Gang Member Delinquency," *Criminology*, **39(2)** (2001): 411–440.
64. *Gang Aftermath.*
65. Personal communication with a member of the Edmonton Police Service Gang Unit.
66. Leanne Dalley-Trim, "'The Boys' Present . . . Hegemonic Masculinity: A Performance of Multiple Acts," *Gender and Education*, **19** (March 2007): pp. 199–217.
67. Mimi Schippers, "Recovering the Feminine Other: Masculinity, Femininity, and Gender Hegemony," *Theoretical Sociology*, **36** (2007): 85–102.
68. R. W. Connell as cited in Mimi Schippers, "Recovering the Feminine Other," p. 87.
69. David Lauderback, Joy Hansen, and Dan Waldorf, "'Sisters Are Doin' It for Themselves': A Black Female Gang in San Francisco," *Gang Journal*, **1** (1992): 57–72.
70. Melanie Nimmo, *The "Invisible" Gang Members.*
71. Ibid., p. 16.
72. Ibid.
73. Ibid.
74. Beth Bjerregaard and Carolyn Smith, *Rochester Youth Development Study: Patterns of Male and Female Gang Membership*, working paper no. 13 (Albany, N.Y.: Hindelang Criminal Justice Research Center, 1992).
75. C. Ronald Huff, ed., *Gangs in America* (Newbury Park, Calif.: Sage, 1990).
76. Seth Mydans, "Not Just the Inner City: Well-to-Do Join Gangs," *New York Times*, Apr. 10, 1990, p. A10.
77. Dan Korem, *Suburban Gangs: Affluent Rebels* (Richardson, Tex.: International Focus, 1994).
78. As quoted in Mydans, "Not Just the Inner City."
79. Michael C. Chettleburgh, *Young Thugs: Inside the Dangerous World of Canadian Street Gangs* (Toronto HarperCollins, 2007), p.150.
80. See www.nizkor.org.
81. Richard T. Schaefer and Edith Smith, *Sociology*, 1st Canadian ed. (Toronto: McGraw-Hill Ryerson, 2004), p. 269; CBC News, "Internet Use by Hate Groups Increasing: Expert," Apr. 5, 2006, www.cbc.ca/canada/story/2006/04/05/web-terror-wiesenthal.html, accessed June 27, 2007.
82. Statistics Canada, "Pilot Survey of Hate Crime," *The Daily*, June 1, 2004, www.statcan.ca/Daily/English/040601/d040601a.htm, accessed June 27, 2007.
83. "Hate Crime Statistics 2003," Federal Bureau of Investigation Report, U.S. Department of Justice, Nov. 2004.
84. Albert K. Cohen, "Middle-Class Delinquency and the Social Structure," in *Middle-Class Delinquency*, ed. E. W. Vaz (New York: Harper & Row, 1967), pp. 207–221.
85. Chettleburgh, *Young Thugs*, p. 111.
86. Korem, *Suburban Gangs*, p. 50.
87. A. W. Leschied and Alison Cunningham, *Seeking Effective Interventions for Serious Young Offenders: Interim Results of a Four-year Randomized Study of Multisystemic Therapy in Ontario, Canada* (London, Ontario: Centre for Children and Families in the Justice System, 2002).
88. Personal communication with program facilitator.
89. Edmonton Police Service Gang Unit, "Overview of the Current Gang Situation in the City of Edmonton," March 2005.
90. Edmonton Police Service, *Who Are Your Children Hangin' With? A Resource Guide on Youth and Gangs.*
91. Public Safety Canada, "Gang Strategy Announced for Saskatoon," July 7, 2006, http://publicsafety.gc.ca/media/nr/2006/nr20060707-01-en.asp, accessed June 27, 2007.
92. "Highlights," http://tacklingcrime.gc.ca/highlights_e.asp, accessed June 27, 2007.

Chapter 7

1. William Golding, *Lord of the Flies* (New York: Coward-McCann, 1954), p. 31.
2. Jack P. Gibbs, "Social Control, Deterrence, and Perspectives on Social Order," *Social Forces*, **56** (1977): 408–423. See also Freda Adler, *Nations Not Obsessed with Crime* (Littleton, Colo.: Fred B. Rothman, 1983).
3. Travis Hirschi, *Causes of Delinquency* (Berkeley: University of California Press, 1969).
4. Donald J. Black, *The Behavior of Law* (New York: Academic Press, 1976), p. 105. See Allan V. Horwitz, *The Logic of Social Control* (New York: Plenum, 1990), for an exceptional evaluation of Black's work.
5. Sheldon L. Messinger and Rosann Greenspan, "Changes in Social Control" *Qualitative Sociology*, **9** (Spring 1986): 58–62.
6. Stanley Cohen, *Visions of Social Control: Crime, Punishment and Classification* (Cambridge New York: Polity Press, 1985).
7. Elizabeth K. Brown, "The Dog That Did Not Bark," *Punishment and Society*, **8** (2006): 287–312.
8. Ibid., p. 289.
9. Community Safety & Crime Prevention Council, "Youth Crime: Fact Sheet Canada, 2007," www.preventingcrime.net.
10. Nanette J. Davis and Bo Anderson, *Social Control: The Production of Deviance in the Modern State* (New York: Irvington, 1983); S. Cohen and A. Scull, eds., *Social Control and the State* (New York: St. Martin's Press, 1983).
11. W. I. Thomas and Florian Znaniecki, *The Polish Peasant in Europe and America* (Boston: Gorham, 1920).
12. Matthew G. Yeager, "Immigrants and Criminality: A Meta Survey," www.cyberus.ca/~myeager/art-1.htm, accessed March 4, 2008.
13. Robert E. Park, "Human Ecology," *American Journal of Sociology*, **42** (1936): 1–15.
14. Clifford R. Shaw, Frederick M. Forbaugh, Henry D. McKay, and Leonard S. Cottrell, *Delinquency Areas* (Chicago: University of Chicago Press, 1929).
15. Clifford R. Shaw and Henry D. McKay, *Juvenile Delinquency and Urban Areas* (Chicago: University of Chicago

Press, 1942); see also the revised and updated edition: Clifford R. Shaw and Henry D. McKay, *Juvenile Delinquency and Urban Areas: A Study of Delinquency in Relation to Differential Characteristics of Local Communities in American Cities* (Chicago: University of Chicago Press, 1969); and Frederick M. Thrasher, *The Gang* (Chicago: University of Chicago Press, 1927).

16. Ralph B. Taylor, "The Impact of Crime on Communities," *The Annals of the American Academy,* **539** (1995): 28–45.

17. Ralph B. Taylor, Steve D. Gottfredson, and Sidney Brower, "Attachments to Place: Discriminant Validity and Impacts of Disorder and Diversity," *American Journal of Community Psychology,* **13** (1985): 525–542.

18. Michael Marriott, "Living in 'Lockdown,'" *Newsweek,* Jan. 23, 1995, p. 57.

19. Lynn Newhart Smith and Gary D. Hill, "Victimization and Fear of Crime," *Criminal Justice and Behavior,* **18** (1991): 217–239; see also Fred E. Markowitz, Paul E. Bellair, Allen E. Liska, and Jianhong Liu, "Extending Social Disorganization Theory: Modeling the Relationships between Cohesion, Disorder, and Fear," *Criminology,* **39** (2001): 293–319; and Randy L. LaGrange, Kenneth F. Ferraro, and Michael Supancic, "Perceived Risk of Fear of Crime: Role of Social and Physical Incivilities," *Journal of Research in Crime and Delinquency,* **29** (1992): 311–334. For research that measures safety and perceived safety resources in the context of other environmental concerns (as an alternative to measuring fear of crime), see John J. Gibbs and Kathleen J. Hanrahan, "Safety Demand and Supply: An Alternative to Fear of Crime," *Justice Quarterly,* **10** (1993): 369–394.

20. Ralph Taylor and Jeanette Covington, "Community Structural Change and Fear of Crime," *Social Problems,* **40** (1993): 374–392.

21. Douglas A. Smith, "The Neighborhood Context of Police Behavior," in *Communities and Crime,* eds. Albert J. Reiss and Michael Tonry (Chicago: University of Chicago Press, 1986), pp. 313–341; Terance D. Miethe, Michael Hughes, and David McDowall, "Social Change in Crime Rates: An Evaluation of Alternative Theoretical Approaches," *Social Forces,* **70** (1991): 165–185; E. Britt Paterson, "Poverty, Income Inequality, and Community Crime Rates," *Criminology,* **29** (1991): 755–776; Josefina Figueira-McDonough, "Community Structure and Delinquency: A Typology," *Social Service Review,* **65** (1991): 65–91; and Denise C. Gottfredson, Richard J. McNeil, and Gary D. Gottfredson, "Social Area Influence on Delinquency: A Multilevel Analysis," *Journal of Research in Crime and Delinquency,* **28** (1991): 197–226.

22. Dina R. Rose and Todd R. Clear, "Incarceration, Social Capital, and Crime: Implications for Social Disorganization Theory," *Criminology,* **36** (1998): 441–479.

23. Correctional Services for Aboriginal Inmates, "Special Report: Inmate Services and Conditions of Custody in Saskatchewan Correctional Centres," Oct. 2002.

24. Rose and Clear, "Incarceration, Social Capital, and Crime: Implications for Social Disorganization Theory."

25. Colin Goff, *Criminal Justice in Canada,* 4th ed. (Toronto: Thomson Nelson, 2008), p. 137.

26. Robert J. Sampson and Dawn Jeglum Bartusch, *Attitudes toward Crime, Police, and the Law: Individual and Neighborhood Differences* (National Institute of Justice Research Preview, June 1999).

27. Steve J. South and Gary D. Deane, "Race and Residential Mobility: Individual Determinants and Structural Constraints," *Social Forces,* **72** (1993): 147–167.

28. See Faith Peeples and Rolf Loeber, "Do Individual Factors and Neighborhood Context Explain Ethnic Differences in Juvenile Delinquency?" *Journal of Quantitative Criminology,* **10** (1994): 141–157; and Thomas A. Petee, Gregory S. Kowlaski, and Don W. Duffield, "Crime, Social Disorganization, and Social Structure: A Research Note on the Use of Interurban Ecological Models," *American Journal of Criminal Justice,* **19** (1994): 117–132; for generalizability of social disorganization theory to nonurban areas, see D. Wayne Osgood and Jeff M. Chambers, "Social Disorganization Outside the Metropolis: An Analysis of Rural Youth Violence," *Criminology,* **38** (2000): 81–115.

29. Community Safety & Crime Prevention Council, "Youth Crime: Fact Sheet Canada, 2007," www.preventingcrime.net.

30. Robert J. Bursik and Harold G. Grosmick, *Neighborhoods and Crime* (New York: Lexington Books, 1993).

31. "Vancouver's Downtown Eastside Community Development Project: Lessons for Crime Prevention and Community Safety" (City of Vancouver, Sept. 2006).

32. Ibid.

33. "Graffiti Gallery (Graffiti Art Programming)," The Murals of Winnipeg, http://themuralsofwinnipeg.com/Mpages/ArtistProfile.php?ID = 71, accessed March 3, 2008.

34. Community Safety and Crime Prevention Council, "The Cost of Crime, 2007," *Together We Make a Difference: Crime Prevention: Local Actions That Reduce Crime and Victimization,* www.preventingcrime.net.

35. Albert J. Reiss, "Delinquency as the Failure of Personal and Social Controls," *American Sociological Review,* **16** (1951): 206.

36. Jackson Toby, "Social Disorganization and Stake in Conformity: Complementary Factors in the Predatory Behavior of Hoodlums," *Journal of Criminal Law, Criminology, and Police Science,* **48** (1957): 137.

37. Walter C. Reckless, "A New Theory of Delinquency and Crime," *Federal Probation,* **25** (1961): 42–46; Walter C. Reckless, Simon Dinitz, and E. Murray, "Self-Concept as an Insulator against Delinquency," *American Sociological Review,* **21** (1956): 744–746; Frank R. Scarpitti, Ellen Murray, Simon Dinitz, and Walter C. Reckless, "The Good Boy in a High Delinquency Area: Four Years Later," *American Sociological Review,* **25** (1960): 555–558. See also K. Heimer and R. L. Matsueda, "Role-Taking, Role Commitment, and Delinquency: A Theory of Differential Social Control," *American Sociological Review,* **59** (1994): 365–390.

38. Walter C. Reckless, "A Non-causal Explanation: Containment Theory," *Excerpta Criminologia,* **2** (1962): 131–132.

39. Francis Ivan Nye, *Family Relationships and Delinquent Behavior* (New York: Wiley, 1958).

40. L. Edward Wells and Joseph H. Rankin, "Broken Homes and Juvenile Delinquency: An Empirical Review," *Criminal Justice Abstracts,* **17** (1985): 249–272.

41. Stephen Demuth and Susan L. Brown, "Family Structure, Family Processes, and Adolescent Delinquency: The Significance of Parental Absence Versus Parental Gender," *Journal of Research in Crime and Delinquency,* **41(1)** (2004): 58–81; L. Edward Wells and Joseph H. Rankin, "Direct Parental Controls and Delinquency," *Criminology,* **26(2)** (1988): 263–285; Ruth Seydlitz, "Complexity in the Relationships among Direct and Indirect Parental Controls and Delinquency," *Youth & Society,* **24(3)** 1993: 243–275. L. Edward Wells and Joseph H. Rankin, "Direct Parental Controls and Delinquency," *Criminology,* **26** (1988): 263–285. See also Douglas Smith and Raymond Paternoster, "The Gender Gap in Theories of Deviance: Issues and Evidence," *Journal of Research in Crime and Delinquency,* **24** (1987): 140–172; and John Hagan, A. R. Gillis, and John Simpson, "The Class Structure of Gender and Delinquency: Toward a Power-Control Theory of Common Delinquent Behavior," *American Journal of Sociology,* **90** (1985): 1151–1178. See Joan McCord, "Some Child-Rearing Antecedents of Criminal Behavior in Adult Men," *Journal of Personality and Social Psychology,* **36** (1979): 1477–1486. For an examination of the family backgrounds of female offenders, see Jill Leslie Rosenbaum, "Family Dysfunction and Female Delinquency," *Crime and Delinquency,* **35** (1989): 31–44.
42. Gary F. Jensen, "Delinquency and Adolescent Self-Conceptions: A Study of the Personal Relevance of Infraction," *Social Problems,* **20** (1972): 84–103.
43. Clarence Schrag, *Crime and Justice American Style* (Washington, D.C.: U.S. Government Printing Office, 1971), pp. 82–89.
44. Hirschi, *Causes of Delinquency.*
45. See John Bowlby, *Attachment and Loss,* 2 vols. (New York: Basic Books, 1969, 1973); John Bowlby, "Forty-Four Juvenile Thieves: Their Characteristics and Home Life," *International Journal of Psychoanalysis,* **25** (1944): 19–25; and John Bowlby, *The Making and Breaking of Affectional Bonds* (London: Tavistock, 1979).
46. Hirschi, *Causes of Delinquency.*
47. Ibid., p. 145.
48. Roger Belgrave, "Sheridan's Police Program Earns Award from Peers," Jan. 5, 2008, www.bramptonlife.com/printArticle-40782, accessed March 3, 2008.
49. Hirschi, *Causes of Delinquency.*
50. Big Brothers Big Sisters of Halton, www.bbbshalton.ca/en/Home/Volunteering/clubtutor.aspx, accessed March 3, 2008.
51. "Teen Curfews," *Street Cents,*www.cbc.ca/streetcents/archives/guide/2001/15/s05_01html, accessed July 9, 2007.
52. Ibid.
53. Michael J. Hindelang, "Causes of Delinquency: A Partial Replication and Extension," *Social Problems,* **20** (1973): 471–487.
54. George Kupfer, "Middle Class Delinquency in a Canadian City," Unpublished Ph.D. dissertation, Department of Sociology, University of Washington. As reported in Rick Linden, *Criminology: A Canadian Perspective,* 5th ed. (Toronto: Thomson Nelson, 2004), p. 381.
55. Josine Junger-Tas, "An Empirical Test of Social Control Theory," *Journal of Quantitative Criminology,* **8** (1992): 18–29.
56. Teresa Lagrange and Robert Silverman, "Perceived Strain and Delinquency Motivation: An Empirical Evaluation of General Strain Theory," Paper presented at the American Society of Criminology meeting, Boston, Nov., 1995.
57. Leslie Samuelson, Timothy Hartnagel, and Harvey Krahn, "Crime and Social Control Among High School Dropouts," *Journal of Crime and Justice,* **18** (1990): 129–161.
58. Rick Linden, "Social Control Theory" in Rick Linden, ed., *Criminology: A Canadian Perspective,* 5th ed. (Toronto: Thomson Nelson, 2004), p. 382.
59. Ibid., p. 383
60. John Hagan and Bill McCarthy, *Mean Streets: Youth Homelessness and Crime* (New York: Cambridge University Press, 1997).
61. Marvin D. Krohn and James L. Massey, "Social Control and Delinquent Behavior: An Examination of the Elements of the Social Bond," *Sociological Quarterly,* **21** (1980): 529–544.
62. Michael D. Wiatrowski, David Griswold, and Mary K. Roberts, "Social Control Theory and Delinquency," *American Sociological Review,* **46** (1985): 525–541.
63. Robert Agnew, "Social Control Theory and Delinquency: A Longitudinal Test," *Criminology,* **23** (1985): 47–61. See also Scott Menard, "Demographic and Theoretical Variables in the Age-Period-Cohort Analysis of Illegal Behavior," *Journal of Research in Crime and Delinquency,* **29** (1992): 178–199; Stephen A. Cernovich and Peggy C. Giordano, "School Bonding, Age, Race, and Delinquency," *Criminology,* **30** (1992): 261–291; Kimberly L. Kempf, "The Empirical Status of Social Control Theory," in *New Directions in Criminological Theory,* eds. Freda Adler and William S. Laufer (New Brunswick, N.J.: Transaction, 1993), pp. 143–185; Marc LeBlanc and Aaron Caplan, "Theoretical Formalization, a Necessity: The Example of Hirschi's Bonding Theory," in *New Directions in Criminological Theory,* pp. 237–336; and Orlando Rodriguez and David Weisburd, "The Integrated Social Control Model and Ethnicity: The Case of Puerto Rican American Delinquency," *Criminal Justice and Behavior,* **18** (1991): 464–479.
64. David F. Greenberg, "The Weak Strength of Social Control Theory," *Crime and Delinquency,* **45** (1999): 66–81.
65. Kimberly K. Leonard and S. H. Decker, "The Theory of Social Control: Does It Apply to the Very Young?" *Journal of Criminal Justice,* **22** (1994): 89–105; Karen S. Rook, "Promoting Social Bonding: Strategies for Helping the Lonely and Socially Isolated," *American Psychologist,* **39** (1984): 1389–1407.
66. Milton Rokeach, *The Nature of Human Values* (New York: Free Press, 1973).
67. See Donald J. Shoemaker, *Theories of Delinquency: An Examination of Explanations of Delinquent Behavior,* 2nd ed. (New York: Oxford University Press, 1990), pp. 172–207, for an evaluation of social control theory.
68. Rick Linden, "Social Control Theory" in Rick Linden, ed., *Criminology: A Canadian Perspective,* 5th ed. (Toronto: Thomson Nelson, 2004), p. 386.
69. John Hagan, A. R. Gillis, and John Simpson, "The Class Structure of Gender and Delinquency: Toward a Power Control Theory of Common Delinquent Behavior," *American Journal of Sociology,* **90** (1985): 1151–1178.

70. M. Morash and M. Chesney-Lind, "Girls' Crime and Women's Place: Toward a Feminist Model of Female Delinquency," *Crime and Delinquency*, **35** (1989): 5–29; M. Chesney-Lind and R. Shelden, *Girls, Delinquency and Juvenile Justice*, 2nd ed. (Belmont, CA: West/Wadsworth, 1998).

71. M. Reitsma-Street, "Girls Learn to Care, Girls Policed to Care," In C. Baines, P. Evans, and S. Neysmith, eds., *Women's Caring* (Toronto: McClelland and Stewart, 1991).

72. Sandra Bell, *Young Offenders and Juvenile Justice: A Century After the Fact*, 2nd ed. (Toronto: Thomson Nelson, 2002), p. 186.

73. Ibid.

74. Brenda Sims Blackwell, "Perceived Sanction Threats, Gender, and Crime: A Test and Elaboration of Power Control Theory," *Criminology*, **38** (2000): 439–488.

75. Ngaire Naffine, *Female Crime: The Construction of Women in Criminology* (Sydney: Allen and Unwin, 1987).

76. David Matza, *Delinquency and Drift* (New York: Wiley, 1964), p. 21.

77. Gresham Sykes and David Matza, "Techniques of Neutralization: A Theory of Delinquency," *American Sociological Review*, **22** (1957): 664–670. For a more recent look at techniques of neutralization, see John Hamlin, "The Misplaced Role of Rational Choice in Neutralization Theory," *Criminology*, **26** (1988): 425–438.

78. Richard A. Ball, "An Empirical Exploration of Neutralization Theory," *Criminologica*, **4** (1966): 103–120. See also N. William Minor, "The Neutralization of Criminal Offense," *Criminology*, **18** (1980): 103–120.

79. Robert Gordon, James F. Short Jr., D. Cartwright, and Fred L. Strodtbeck, "Values and Gang Delinquency: A Study of Street Corner Groups," *American Journal of Sociology*, **69** (1963): 109–128.

80. Alan Liska, Marvin D. Krohn, and Steven F. Messner, "Strategies and Requisites for Theoretical Integration in the Study of Crime and Deviance," in *Theoretical Integration in the Study of Deviance and Crime: Problems and Prospects*, eds. S. F. Lessner, M. D. Krohn, and A. Liska (New York: SUNYA, 1989), p. 4. See also R. J. Hepburn, "Testing Alternative Models of Delinquency Causation," *Journal of Criminal Law and Criminology*, **67** (1977): 450–460; T. Ross Matsueda, "Testing Control Theory and Differential Association: A Causal Modeling Approach," *American Sociological Review*, **47** (1982): 489–497; Frank S. Pearson and Neil A. Weiner, "Toward an Integration of Criminological Theories," *Journal of Criminal Law and Criminology*, **76** (1985): 116–150; Terrie E. Moffitt, "Adolescence-Limited and Life-Course-Persistent Antisocial Behavior: A Developmental Taxonomy," *Psychological Review*, **100** (1993): 674–701; Terrie E. Moffitt et al., "Childhood-Onset versus Adolescent-Onset Antisocial Conduct Problems in Males: Natural History from Ages 3 to 18 Years," *Development and Psychopathology*, **8** (1996): 399–424; and Terrie E. Moffitt, "Adolescence-Limited and Life-Course-Persistent Offending: A Complementary Pair of Developmental Theories," in ed. T. P. Thornberry, *Developmental Theories of Crime and Delinquency: Advances in Criminological Theory*, **7** (1997).

81. Robert J. Sampson and John H. Laub, *Crime in the Making: Pathways and Turning Points through Life* (Cambridge, Mass.: Harvard University Press, 1993); R. J. Sampson and J. H. Laub, "Understanding Variability in Lives through Time: Contributions of Life-Course Criminology," *Studies on Crime and Crime Prevention*, **4** (1995): 143–158.

82. Terence P. Thornberry, A. J. Lizotte, and M. D. Krohn, "Delinquent Peers, Beliefs, and Delinquent Behavior: A Longitudinal Test of Interactional Theory," *Criminology*, **32** (1994): 47–83; Terence P. Thornberry, Alan J. Lizotte, Marvin D. Krohn, Margaret Farnsworth, and Sung Juon Jung, "Testing Interactional Theory: An Examination of Reciprocal Causal Relationships among Family, School, and Delinquency," *Journal of Criminal Law and Criminology*, **82** (1991): 3–35; see also Madeline G. Aultman and Charles F. Wellford, "Toward an Integrated Model of Delinquency Causation: An Empirical Analysis," *Sociology and Social Research*, **63** (1979): 316–317; and Thornberry, *Developmental Theories of Crime and Delinquency*.

83. D. S. Nagin and D. P. Farrington, "The Onset and Persistence of Offending," *Criminology*, **30** (1992): 501–524; D. S. Nagin and D. P. Farrington, "The Stability of Criminal Potential from Childhood to Adulthood," *Criminology*, **30** (1992): 235–260; D. P. Farrington, "Explaining the Beginning, Progress, and Ending of Antisocial Behavior from Birth to Adulthood," *Advances in Criminological Theory*, **3** (1992): 253–286.

84. Delbert S. Elliott, Suzanne S. Ageton, and R. J. Canter, "An Integrated Theoretical Perspective on Delinquent Behavior," *Journal of Research in Crime and Delinquency*, **16** (1979): 3–27; S. Menard and Delbert S. Elliott, "Delinquent Bonding, Moral Beliefs, and Illegal Behavior: A Three Wave Panel Model," *Justice Quarterly*, **11** (1994): 173–188.

85. David J. Hawkins and Joseph G. Weis, "The Social Development Model: An Integrated Approach to Delinquency Prevention," *Journal of Primary Prevention*, **6** (1985): 73–97.

86. Michael R. Gottfredson and Travis Hirschi, *A General Theory of Crime* (Stanford, Calif.: Stanford University Press, 1990); Michael Gottfredson and Travis Hirschi, "A Propensity-Event Theory of Crime," in *Advances in Criminological Theory*, vol. 1, eds. W. Laufer and F. Adler (New Brunswick, N.J.: Transaction, 1989); B. J. Arneklev, H. G. Grasmick, and C. R. Tittle, "Low Self-Control and Imprudent Behavior," *Journal of Quantitative Criminology*, **9** (1993): 225–247; D. Brownfield and A. M. Sorenson, "Self Control and Juvenile Delinquency: Theoretical Issues and an Empirical Assessment of Selected Elements of a General Theory of Crime," *Deviant Behavior*, **14** (1993): 243–264; T. Hirschi and M. Gottfredson, "Commentary: Testing the General Theory of Crime," *Journal of Research in Crime and Delinquency*, **30** (1993): 47–54.

87. Travis Hirschi and Michael Gottfredson, "The Significance of White-Collar Crime for a General Theory of Crime," *Criminology*, **27** (1989): 359–371; Darrell Steffensmeier, "On the Causes of 'White Collar' Crime: An Assessment of Hirschi and Gottfredson's Claim," *Criminology*, **27** (1989): 345–358.

88. Alex R. Piquero, John MacDonald, Adam Dobrin, Leah E. Daigle, and Frances T. Cullen, "Self-Control, Violent

Offending, and Homicide Victimization: Assessing the General Theory of Crime," *Journal of Quantitative Criminology,* **21(1)** (2005): 55–71; Alexander T. Vazsonyi and Jennifer M. Crosswhite, "Test of Gottfredson and Hirschi's General Theory of Crime in African-American Adolescents," *Research in Crime and Delinquency,* **41(4)** (2004): 407–432; Alexander T. Vazsonyi, Janice E. Clifford Wittekind, Lara M. Belliston, and Timothy D. Van Loh, "Extending the General Theory of Crime to 'The East:' Low Self-Control in Japanese Late Adolescents," *Journal of Quantitative Criminology,* **23(3)** (2004): 189–216.

89. Marc LeBlanc, "A Generic Control Theory of the Criminal Phenomenon," in Terence P. Thornberry, ed., *Developmental Theories of Crime and Delinquency.* (New Brunswick, N.J.: Transaction Publishers, 1997), pp. 215–285.

90. Teresa LaGrange and Robert Silverman, "Low Self-Control and Opportunity: Testing the General Theory of Crime as an Explanation for Gender Differences in Delinquency," *Criminology,* **37(1)** (1999): 41–72.

91. Dina Perrone, Christopher J. Sullivan, Travis C. Pratt, and Satenik Margaryan, "Parental Efficacy, Self-Control, and Delinquency: A Test of a General Theory of Crime on a Nationally Representative Sample of Youth," *International Journal of Offender Therapy and Comparative Criminology,* **48(3)** (2004): 298–312.

92. Robert Agnew, *Why Do Criminals Offend? A General Theory of Crime and Delinquency* (Los Angeles, CA: Roxbury, 2004).

93. See W. Timothy Austin, "Crime and Custom in an Orderly Society: The Singapore Prototype," *Criminology,* **25** (1987): 279–294; J. M. Day and William S. Laufer, eds., *Crime, Values, and Religion* (Norwood, N.J.: Ablex, 1987); and Freda Adler and William S. Laufer, "Social Control and the Workplace," in *US-USSR Approaches to Urban Crime Prevention,* ed. James Finckenauer and Alexander Yakovlev (Moscow: Soviet Academy of State and Law, 1987).

94. Community Solution to Gang Violence, www.csgv.ca.

95. David J. Hawkins, Richard F. Catalano, Gwen Jones, and David Fine, "Delinquency Prevention through Parent-Training: Results and Issues from Work in Progress," in *From Children to Citizens:* vol. 3, *Families, Schools, and Delinquency Prevention,* eds. James Q. Wilson and Glenn C. Loury (New York: Springer Verlag, 1987), pp. 186–204.

Chapter 8

1. Gonzalo Moreno, "More Gruesome than Fiction," Jan. 29, 2007, http://thecannon.ca/news_details.php?id=3175, accessed June 6, 2007; Petti Fong, "Crown appeals Pickton Convictions," Jan. 7, 2008, www.thestar.com/printArticle/291715, accessed March 24, 2008.

2. Richard T. Schaefer and Jana Grekul, *Sociology Matters,* 1st Canadian ed. (Toronto: McGraw-Hill Ryerson, 2007), pp. 161–162.

3. Howard S. Becker, *Outsiders: Studies in the Sociology of Deviance* (New York: Macmillan, 1963), p. 9.

4. For an excellent discussion of how society controls deviance, see Nicholas N. Kittrie, *The Right to Be Different* (Baltimore: Johns Hopkins University Press, 1972).

5. William I. Thomas, *The Unadjusted Girl* (1923; New York: Harper & Row, 1967).

6. George Herbert Mead, "The Psychology of Punitive Justice," *American Journal of Sociology,* **23** (1918): 577–602. See also Charles Horton Cooley, "The Roots of Social Knowledge," *American Journal of Sociology,* **32** (1926): 59–79.

7. Herbert Blumer, "Sociological Implications of the Thought of George Herbert Mead," in *Symbolic Interactionism,* ed. Blumer (Englewood Cliffs, N.J.: Prentice-Hall, 1969), pp. 62, 65, 66.

8. Frank Tannenbaum, *Crime and the Community* (Boston: Ginn, 1938), p. 27.

9. Edwin M. Lemert, *Social Pathology* (New York: McGraw-Hill, 1951).

10. Edwin M. Lemert, *Human Deviance, Social Problems, and Social Control* (Englewood Cliffs, N.J.: Prentice-Hall, 1967), chap. 3.

11. Lemert, *Social Pathology,* pp. 75–76.

12. Lemert, *Human Deviance,* p. 46. See also Albert K. Cohen, *Deviance and Control* (Englewood Cliffs, N.J.: Prentice-Hall, 1966), pp. 24–25.

13. Erving Goffman, *Stigma: Notes on the Management of Spoiled Identity* (Englewood Cliffs, N.J.: Prentice-Hall, 1963).

14. Gerhard O. W. Mueller, "Resocialization of the Young Adult Offender in Switzerland," *Journal of Criminal Law and Criminology,* **43** (1953): 578–591, at p. 584.

15. "'Redneck' Government Was anti-Indian, Ipperwash Inquiry Hears," CBC News, May 19, 2005, www.cbc.ca/canada/story/2005/05/19/ipperwash-050510.html, accessed March 3, 2008.

16. Kai T. Erickson, "Notes on the Sociology of Deviance," in *The Other Side: Perspectives on Deviance,* ed. Howard S. Becker (New York: Free Press, 1964), p. 11.

17. Edwin Schur, *Labeling Deviant Behavior* (New York: Harper & Row, 1971), p. 21.

18. Edwin M. Schur, *Crimes without Victims* (Englewood Cliffs, N.J.: Prentice-Hall, 1965).

19. M. Ray, "The Cycle of Abstinence and Relapse among Heroin Addicts," *Social Problems,* **9** (1961): 132–140.

20. David Matza, *Becoming Deviant* (Englewood Cliffs, N.J.: Prentice-Hall, 1969), pp. 44–53.

21. Robert A. Stebbins, *Commitment to Deviance: The Nonprofessional Criminal in the Community* (Westport, CT: Greenwood, 1976).

22. Becker, *Outsiders,* pp. 18, 20.

23. D. L. Rosenhan, "On Being Sane in Insane Places," *Science,* **179** (1973): 250–258. See also Bruce G. Link, "Understanding Labeling Effects in the Area of Mental Disorders: An Assessment of the Effects of Expectations of Rejection," *American Sociological Review,* **52** (1987): 96–112; and Anthony Walsh, "Twice Labeled: The Effect of Psychiatric Labeling on the Sentencing of Sex Offenders," *Social Problems,* **37** (1990): 375–389.

24. Carol Warren and John Johnson, "A Critique of Labeling Theory from the Phenomenological Perspective," in *Theoretical Perspectives on Deviance,* eds. J. D. Douglas and R. Scott (New York: Basic Books, 1973), p. 77; James P. Spradley, *You Owe Yourself a Drunk: An Ethnography of Urban Nomads* (Boston: Little, Brown, 1979), p. 254.

25. Richard D. Schwartz and Jerome H. Skolnick, "Two Studies of Legal Stigma," *Social Problems,* **10** (1962): 133–138.

26. Anthony Platt, *The Child Savers* (Chicago: University of Chicago Press, 1969). For a further discussion of the effects of stigmatization by the criminal justice system, see Charles W. Thomas and Donna M. Bishop, "The Effect of Formal and Informal Sanctions on Delinquency: A Longitudinal Comparison of Labeling and Deterrence Theories," *Journal of Criminal Law and Criminology,* **75** (1984): 1222–1245.

27. William J. Chambliss, "The Saints and the Roughnecks," *Society,* **11** (1973): 24–31.

28. Walter R. Gove, "Deviant Behavior, Social Intervention, and Labeling Theory," in *The Uses of Controversy in Sociology,* eds. Lewis A. Coser and Otto N. Larsen (New York: Free Press, 1976), pp. 219–227; Ross L. Matsueda, "Reflected Appraisals, Parental Labeling, and Delinquency: Specifying a Symbolic Interactionist Theory," *American Journal of Sociology,* **97** (1992): 1577–1611.

29. Ronald L. Akers, "Problems in the Sociology of Deviance," *Social Forces,* **46** (1968): 455–465.

30. Ronald L. Akers, *Deviant Behavior: A Social Learning Approach,* 2nd ed. (Belmont, Calif.: Wadsworth, 1977); David Ward and Charles R. Tittle, "Deterrence or Labeling: The Effects of Informal Sanctions," *Deviant Behavior,* **14** (1993): 43–64.

31. Jack P. Gibbs, "Conceptions of Deviant Behavior: The Old and the New," *Pacific Sociological Review,* **9** (Spring 1966): 9–14.

32. Charles Wellford, "Labelling Theory and Criminology: An Assessment," *Social Problems,* **22** (1975): 343; Charles F. Wellford and Ruth A. Triplett, "The Future of Labeling Theory: Foundations and Promises," in *Advances in Criminological Theory,* vol. 4, eds. Freda Adler and William S. Laufer (New Brunswick, N.J.: Transaction, 1993).

33. Alexander Liazos, "The Poverty of the Sociology of Deviance: Nuts, Sluts, and Perverts," *Social Problems,* **20** (1972): 103–120.

34. Howard S. Becker, "Labelling Theory Reconsidered," in *Outsiders: Studies in the Sociology of Deviance,* rev. ed., ed. Becker (New York: Free Press, 1973), pp. 177–208. See also Schur, *Labeling Deviant Behavior,* for an excellent review of labeling theory.

35. Robert J. Sampson and John H. Laub, "A Life-Course Theory of Cumulative Disadvantage and Stability of Delinquency," in T. Thornberry, ed., *Developmental Theories of Crime and Delinquency: Advances in Criminology Theory,* **7** (1997).

36. Compare this perspective with the emerging notion of criminology as peacemaking; see Harold E. Pepinsky and Richard Quinney, eds., *Criminology as Peace-Making* (Bloomington: Indiana University Press, 1991).

37. Émile Durkheim, *The Division of Labor in Society* (New York: Free Press, 1947), p. 80.

38. Ibid., p. 102.

39. Roscoe Pound, *An Introduction to the Philosophy of Law* (Boston: Little, Brown, 1922), p. 98.

40. Richard Quinney, *Crime and Justice in Society* (Boston: Little, Brown, 1969), pp. 26–30.

41. William Chambliss, "The State, the Law, and the Definition of Behavior as Criminal or Delinquent," in *Handbook of Criminology,* ed. Daniel Glaser (Chicago: Rand McNally, 1974), pp. 7–44.

42. Austin Turk, "Law as a Weapon in Social Conflict," *Social Problems,* **23** (1976): 276–291.

43. George Vold, *Theoretical Criminology* (New York: Oxford University Press, 1958), pp. 204, 209.

44. Ralf Dahrendorf, *Class and Class Conflict in Industrial Society* (Stanford, Calif.: Stanford University Press, 1959). See also Ralf Dahrendorf, "Out of Utopia: Toward a Reorientation of Sociological Analysis," *American Journal of Sociology,* **64** (1958): 127.

45. Austin Turk, *Criminality and Legal Order* (Chicago: Rand McNally, 1969), pp. 25, 33, 41–42, 48. See also Thomas O'Reilly-Fleming et al., "Issues in Social Order and Social Control," *Journal of Human Justice,* **2** (1990): 55–74.

46. Austin Turk, *Political Criminality: The Defiance and Defense of Authority* (Beverly Hills, Calif.: Sage, 1982), p. 15.

47. Turk, "Law as a Weapon."

48. William J. Chambliss, "A Sociological Analysis of the Law of Vagrancy," *Social Problems,* **12** (1966): 67–77. For an opposing view on the historical development of criminal law, see Jeffrey S. Adler, "A Historical Analysis of the Law of Vagrancy," *Criminology,* **27** (1989): 209–229; and a rejoinder to Adler: William J. Chambliss, "On Trashing Criminology," ibid., pp. 231–238.

49. Alan Lizotte, "Extra-Legal Factors in Chicago's Criminal Courts: Testing the Conflict Model of Criminal Justice," *Social Problems,* **25** (1978): 564–580. See also Kathleen Daly, "Neither Conflict nor Labeling nor Paternalism Will Suffice: Intersections of Race, Ethnicity, Gender, and Family in Criminal Court Decisions," *Crime and Delinquency,* **35** (1989): 136–168; and Elizabeth Comack, ed., "Race, Class, Gender and Justice," *Journal of Human Justice,* **2** (1990): 1–124.

50. Freda Adler, "Socioeconomic Variables Influencing Jury Verdicts," *New York University Review of Law on Social Change,* **3** (1973): 16–36. See also Martha A. Myers, "Social Background and the Sentencing Behavior of Judges," *Criminology,* **26** (1988): 649–675.

51. Celesta A. Albonetti, Robert M. Hauser, John Hagan, and Ilene H. Nagel, "Criminal Justice Decision-Making as a Stratification Process: The Role of Race and Stratification Resources in Pretrial Release," *Journal of Quantitative Criminology,* **5** (1989): 57–82.

52. Austin Turk, "Law, Conflict, and Order: From Theorizing toward Theories," *Canadian Review of Sociology and Anthropology,* **13** (1976): 282–294.

53. Georg Rusche and Otto Kirchheimer, *Punishment and Social Structure* (New York: Columbia University Press, 1939), p. 93.

54. Friedrich Engels, "To the Working Class of Great Britain," Introduction to *The Condition of the Working Class in England (1845),* in Karl Marx and Friedrich Engels, *Collected Works,* vol. 4 (New York: International Publishers, 1974), pp. 213–214, 298.

55. Karl Marx and Friedrich Engels, *The Communist Manifesto* (1848; New York: International Publishers, 1979), p. 9.

56. Willem Adriaan Bonger, *Criminality and Economic Conditions,* trans. Henry P. Horton (Boston: Little, Brown, 1916).

57. Ibid., p. 669.

58. M. Van Bemmelen, "Willem Adriaan Bonger," in *Pioneers in Criminology,* ed. Hermann Mannheim (London: Stevens, 1960), p. 361.

59. Ian Taylor, Paul Walton, and Jock Young, *The New Criminology: For a Social Theory of Deviance* (London: Routledge & Kegan Paul, 1973), pp. 264, 281. See also Jock Young, "Radical Criminology in Britain: The Emergence of a Competing Paradigm," *British Journal of Criminology,* **28** (1988): 159–183.

60. Gresham Sykes, "The Rise of Critical Criminology," *Journal of Criminal Law and Criminology,* **65** (1974): 206–213.

61. Richard Quinney, "Crime Control in Capitalist Society: A Critical Philosophy of Legal Order," *Issues in Criminology,* **8** (1973): 75–95; Richard Quinney, "There's a Lot of Us Folks Grateful to the Lone Ranger: Some Notes on the Rise and Fall of American Criminology," *Insurgent Sociologist,* **4** (1973): 56–64.

62. Richard Quinney, "Crime Control in Capitalist Society," in *Critical Criminology,* ed. Ian Taylor, Paul Walton, and Jock Young (London: Routledge & Kegan Paul, 1975), p. 199.

63. Richard Quinney, *Class, State, and Crime: On the Theory and Practice of Criminal Justice,* 2nd ed. (New York: David McKay, 1977), p. 10.

64. Richard Quinney, *Critique of Legal Order: Crime Control in a Capitalist Society* (Boston: Little, Brown, 1974), pp. 11–13.

65. William Chambliss and Robert Seidman, *Law, Order, and Power* (Reading, Mass.: Addison-Wesley, 1971), p. 503.

66. Ibid., p. 504.

67. Barry Krisberg, *Crime and Privilege: Toward a New Criminology* (Englewood Cliffs, N.J.: Prentice-Hall, 1975).

68. Herman Schwendinger and Julia Schwendinger, "Delinquency and Social Reform: A Radical Perspective," in *Juvenile Justice,* ed. Lamar Empey (Charlottesville: University of Virginia Press, 1979), pp. 246–290.

69. Elliot Currie, "A Dialogue with Anthony M. Platt," *Issues in Criminology,* **8** (1973): 28.

70. Steven F. Messner and Marvin D. Krohn, "Class, Compliance Structures, and Delinquency: Assessing Integrated Structural-Marxist Theory," *American Journal of Sociology,* **96** (1990): 300–328.

71. Lance H. Selva and Robert M. Bohm, "A Critical Examination of the Informalism Experiment in the Administration of Justice," *Crime and Social Justice,* **29** (1987): 43–57; Timothy Carter and Donald Clelland, "A Neo-Marxian Critique, Formulation, and Test of Juvenile Dispositions as a Function of Social Class," *Social Problems,* **27** (1979): 96–108; David Greenberg and Drew Humphries, "The Co-optation of Fixed Sentencing Reform," *Crime and Delinquency,* **26** (1980): 216–225.

72. Jackson Toby, "The New Criminology Is the Old Sentimentality," *Criminology,* **16** (1979): 516–526; Jim Thomas and Aogan O'Maolchatha, "Reassessing the Critical Metaphor: An Optimistic Revisionist View," *Justice Quarterly,* **6** (1989): 143–171; David Brown and Russell Hogg, "Essentialism, Radical Criminology and Left Realism," *Australian and New Zealand Journal of Criminology,* **25** (1992): 195–230.

73. Carl B. Klockars, "The Contemporary Crises of Marxist Criminology," *Criminology,* **16** (1979): 477–515.

74. Ibid.

75. Richard F. Sparks, "A Critique of Marxist Criminology," in *Crime and Justice: An Annual Review of Research,* ed. Norval Morris and Michael Tonry (Chicago: University of Chicago Press, 1980), p. 159.

76. Milton Mankoff, "On the Responsibility of Marxist Criminology: A Reply to Quinney," *Contemporary Crisis,* **2** (1978): 293–301.

77. Austin T. Turk, "Analyzing Official Deviance: For Non-partisan Conflict Analysis in Criminology," in *Radical Criminology: The Coming Crisis,* ed. James A. Inciardi (Beverly Hills, Calif.: Sage, 1980), pp. 78–91. See also Sykes, "The Rise of Critical Criminology," p. 212.

78. Philip L. Reichel and Andrzej Rzeplinski, "Student Views of Crime and Criminal Justice in Poland and the United States," *International Journal of Comparative and Applied Criminal Justice,* **13** (1989): 65–81.

79. Quinney, *Class, State, and Crime,* p. 40.

80. Elizabeth Comack, "Feminism and Criminology," *Criminology: A Canadian Perspective,* Rick Linden, ed., 5th ed. (Toronto: Thomson Nelson, 2004), p. 165.

81. Marie-Andrée Bertrand, "The Myth of Sexual Equality Before the Law," Fifth Research Conference on Delinquency and Criminality, Montreal, Centre de Psychologies et de Pédagogie, 1967, pp. 129-61; Frances Heidensohn, "The Deviance of Women: A Critique and an Enquiry," *British Journal of Sociology.* **19(2)** (1968): 160–175.

82. Helen Boritch, *Fallen Women: Female Crime and Criminal Justice in Canada* (Toronto: Nelson, 1997); Dorothy Chunn and Robert Menzies, "Canadian Criminology and the Woman Question," in *International Feminist Perspectives in Criminology: Engendering a Discipline,* Nicole Hahn Rafter and Frances Heidensohn, eds. (Buckingham: Open University Press, 1996); Holly Johnson. "Getting the Facts Straight: A Statistical Overview," in *Too Few to Count: Canadian Women in Conflict with the Law,* Ellen Adelberg and Claudia Currie, eds. (Vancouver: Press Gang, 1987); Sandra Bell, *Young Offenders and Juvenile Justice: A Century After the Fact,* 2nd ed. (Toronto: Thomson Nelson, 2002), p. 177.

83. C. Lombroso and W. Ferrero, *The Female Offenders* (London: Fischer Unwin, 1895).

84. W. I. Thomas, *The Unadjusted Girl* (New York: Harper and Row, 1967).

85. Otto Pollack, *The Criminality of Women* (New York: A. S. Barnes, 1961).

86. Meda Chesney-Lind, *The Female Offender: Girls, Women, and Crime* (Thousand Oaks, CA: Sage, 1997); Holly Johnson, *Dangerous Domains* (Scarborough, ON: Nelson Canada, 1996).

87. Diane Hudson. "You Can't Commit Violence against an Object: Women, Psychiatry, and Psychosurgery," in *Women, Violence, and Social Control,* J. Hanmer and M. Maynard, eds. (Houndsmills, Eng.: Macmillan Press, 1987); Dorothy E. Chunn and Shelley A. M. Gavigan, "Women and Crime in Canada," in *Canadian Criminology: Perspectives on Crime and Criminality,* Margaret Jackson and Curt Griffiths, eds. (Toronto: Harcourt Brace Jovanovich Canada, 1991); Robert J. Menzies, Dorothy E. Chunn, and Christopher D. Webster, "Female Follies: The Forensic Psychiatric Assessment of Women Defendants," *International Journal of Law and Psychiatry,* **15** (1992): 179–193.

88. Meda Chesney-Lind, "Girls, Delinquency, and Juvenile Justice: Toward a Feminist Theory of Young Women's

Crime," in *The Criminal Justice System and Women*, Barbara Raffel Price and Natalie Sokoloff, eds. (New York: McGraw-Hill, 1995).

89. Pat Carlen, ed., *Criminal Women* (Cambridge: Polity Press, 1985); Elizabeth Comack, "Feminism and Criminology," in *Criminology: A Canadian Perspective*, Rick Linden, ed., 5th ed. (Toronto: Thomson Nelson, 2004), p. 165.

90. Carol LaPrairie, "Native Women and Crime: A Theoretical Model," in *Too Few to Count: Canadian Women in Conflict with the Law*, Ellen Adelberg and Claudia Currie, eds. (Vancouver: Press Gang, 1987); Carol LaPrairie, "The Role of Sentencing in the Over-Representation of Aboriginal People in Correctional Institutions," *Canadian Journal of Corrections*, **32** (1990): 429–440.

91. Marie-Andrée Bertrand, "Self-Image and Delinquency: A Contribution to the Study of Female Criminality and Women's Image," *Acta criminological: Études sur la conduite antisociale*, **2** (1969): 71–144; Ngaire Naffine, *Feminism and Criminology* (Sydney: Allen and Unwin, 1997).

92. James C. Hackler, *Canadian Criminology: Strategies and Perspectives*, 4th ed. (Toronto: Pearson Prentice-Hall, 2007), p. 205.

93. Carol Smart, *Women, Crime, and Criminology: A Feminist Critique* (London: Routledge & Kegan Paul, 1976).

94. Elizabeth Comack, "Feminism and Criminology."

95. Allison Morris, *Women, Crime and Criminal Justice* (Oxford: Basil Blackwell, 1987) p. 64.

96. Freda Adler, *Sisters in Crime* (New York: McGraw-Hill, 1975); Rita Simon, *Women and Crime* (Lexington, Mass.: D. C. Heath, 1975).

97. Helen Boritch, *Fallen Women: Female Crime and Criminal Justice in Canada* (Toronto: Nelson, 1997).

98. Elizabeth Comack, "The Feminist Engagement with Criminology" in *Criminalizing Women*, Gillian Balfour and Elizabeth Comack, eds. (Halifax: Fernwood Publishing Company Limited, 2006), p. 31.

99. Naffine, *Feminism and Criminology*.

100. John Hagan, A. R. Gillis, and John Simpson, "The Class Structure of Gender and Delinquency: Toward a Power-Control Theory of Common Delinquent Behavior," *American Journal of Sociology*, **90** (1985): 1151–1178; John Hagan, A. R. Gillis, and John Simpson, "Class in the Household: A Power-Control Theory of Gender and Delinquency," *American Journal of Sociology*, **92(4)** (1987): 788–816.

101. Comack, "Feminism and Criminology," p. 169.

102. Ibid.

103. Kathleen Daly and Meda Chesney-Lind, "Feminism and Criminology," *Justice Quarterly*, **5** (1988): 497–538.

104. Ruth Alexander, *The "Girl Problem": Female Sexual Delinquency in New York, 1900–1930* (Ithaca, New York: Cornell University Press, 1995); Dorothy Chunn, *From Punishment to Doing Good: Family Courts and Socialized Justice in Ontario 1880–1940* (Toronto: University of Toronto Press, 1992); Sibylle Artz, Diana Nicholson, and Carmen Rodriguez, "Understanding Girls' Delinquency: Looking Beyond Their Behaviour," in *Understanding Youth Justice in Canada*, Kathryn Campbell, ed. (Toronto: Pearson Prentice-Hall, 2005); R. Corrado, C. Odgers, and I. Cohen, "The Incarceration of Female Young Offenders: Protection for Whom?" *Canadian Journal of Criminology*,

42(2) (2000): 189–207; J. Sprott and A. Doob, "It's All in the Denominator: Trends in the Processing of Girls in Canada's Youth Courts," *Canadian Journal of Criminology and Criminal Justice*, **45(1)** (2003): 73–80.

105. J. R. Schwendinger and H. Schwendinger, *Rape and Inequality* (Beverly Hills: Sage, 1983).

106. Sylvia Hale, *Controversies in Sociology: A Canadian Introduction* (Toronto: Copp Clark Pitman Ltd, 1990).

107. James Messerschmidt, *Capitalism, Patriarchy and Crime* (Totowa, NJ: Rowman and Littlefield, 1986).

108. Jane Roberts Chapman, "Violence against Women as a Violation of Human Rights," *Social Justice*, **17** (1990): 54–71.

109. Meda Chesney-Lind, "Feminism and Criminology," *Justice Quarterly*, **5** (1988): 497–538; Pat Carlen, "Women, Crime, Feminism, and Realism," *Social Justice*, **17** (1990): 106–123.

110. Zillah Eisenstein, "Some Notes on the Relations of Capitalist Patriarchy," in *Capitalist Patriarchy and the Case for Socialist Feminism*, Zillah Eisenstein, ed. (New York: Monthly Review Press, 1979), pp. 5–14.

111. Sally Simpson, "Feminist Theory, Crime and Justice," *Criminology*, **27** (1989): 605–632; Meda Chesney-Lind, "Judicial Enforcement of the Female Sex Role: The Family Court and the Female Delinquent," *Issues in Criminology*, **8** (1973): 51–69.

112. Elizabeth Comack, "The Feminist Engagement with Criminology," in *Criminalizing Women*, Gillian Balfour and Elizabeth Comack, eds. (Halifax: Fernwood Publishing Company Limited, 2006).

113. D. Howarth, *Discourse* (Buckingham: Open University Press, 2000).

114. Comack, "The Feminist Engagement with Criminology," p. 42.

115. Ibid., p. 43.

116. Ibid., p. 55.

117. Martin D. Schwartz and Walter S. DeKeseredy, "Left Realist Criminology: Strengths, Weaknesses and the Feminist Critique," *Crime, Law and Social Change*, **15** (1991): 51–72; John Lowman and Brian D. MacLean, eds., *Realist Criminology: Crime Control and Policing in the 1990s* (Toronto: University of Toronto Press, 1990); Walter S. DeKeseredy and Martin D. Schwartz, "British and U.S. Left Realism: A Critical Comparison," *International Journal of Offender Therapy and Comparative Criminology*, **35** (1991): 248–262.

118. John Lea and Jock Young, *What Is to Be Done about Law and Order?* (London: Penguin Books; 1984); John Lea, "Left Realism: A Defence," *Contemporary Crises*, **11(4)** (1987): 357–370; Jock Young, "Left Idealism, Reformism, and Beyond: From New Criminology to Marxism," in *Capitalism and the Rule of Law: From Deviancy Theory to Marxism*, Bob Fine, Richard Kinsey, John Lea, Sol Picciotto, and Jock Young, eds. (London: Hutchinson and Company, 1979), pp. 13–28); Thomas O'Reilly-Fleming, "Left Realism as Theoretical Retreatism or Paradigm Shift: Toward Post-Critical Criminology" in *Post-Critical Criminology*, Thomas O'Reilly-Fleming, ed. (Scarborough, ON: Prentice-Hall Canada, 1996), pp.1–25.

119. Larry Tifft and Dennis Sullivan, as quoted in Larry J. Siegel and Chris McCormick, *Criminology in Canada:*

Theories, Patterns, and Typologies (Toronto: Thomson Nelson, 2006), p. 274.

120. Harold Pepinsky and Richard Quinney, eds., *Criminology as Peace-Making* (Bloomington: Indiana University Press, 1991); Richard Quinney, "Socialist Humanism and the Problem of Crime," *Crime, Law and Social Change,* **23** (1995): 147–156; Robert Elias et al., Special Issue, "Declaring Peace on Crime," *Peace Review: A Transnational Quarterly,* **6** (1994): 131–254.

121. John Braithwaite, *Crime, Shame and Reintegration* (Cambridge: Cambridge University Press, 1989).

122. James C. Hackler, *Canadian Criminology: Strategies and Perspectives,* 4th ed. (Toronto: Pearson Prentice-Hall, 2007), p. 291.

123. Bryan R. Hogeveen, "Unsettling Youth Justice and Cultural Norms: The Youth Restorative Action Project," *Journal of Youth Studies,* **9(1)** (Feb. 2006): 58.

124. Ibid., p. 59.

125. Ibid., pp. 58–59.

126. Ibid., p. 50.

127. Ibid., p. 59.

128. Ibid., p. 62.

129. Bryan Hogeveen and Andrew Woolford, "Critical Criminology and Possibility in the Neo-liberal Ethos," *Canadian Journal of Criminology and Criminal Justice* (Sept. 2006): 681–701.

130. Ibid, p. 684; George Pavlich, *Governing Paradoxes of Restorative Justice* (London: Glasshouse Press, 2005).

131. Hogeveen and Woolford, "Critical Criminology and Possibility in the Neo-liberal Ethos," p. 684. See also Andrew Woolford and R. S. Ratner, "Nomadic Justice? Restorative Justice on the Margins of Law," *Social Justice,* **30**(2003): 177–194.

132. Ibid., p. 684.

133. R. S. Ratner, "Criminology in Canada: Conflicting Objectives" Unpublished manuscript, 1971, as cited in Joane Martel, Bryan Hogeveen, and Andrew Woolford, "The State of Critical Scholarship in Criminology and Socio-legal Studies in Canada," *Canadian Journal of Criminology and Criminal Justice* (Sept., 2006): 633–646.

134. Hogeveen and Andrew Woolford, "Critical Criminology and Possibility in the Neo-liberal Ethos," p. 695.

135. Robert Menzies and Dorothy E. Chunn, "Discipline in Dissent: Canadian Academic Criminology at the Millennium," *Canadian Journal of Criminology and Criminal Justice,* **41** (1999): 285–297.

136. R. S. Ratner, "Pioneering Critical Criminology in Canada," *Canadian Journal of Criminology and Criminal Justice,* (Sept. 2006): 648.

137. Joane Martel, "Policing Criminological Knowledge: The Hazards of Qualitative Research on Women in Prison," *Theoretical Criminology,* **8** (2004): 157–189.

138. Joane Martel, Bryan Hogeveen, and Andrew Woolford, "The State of Critical Scholarship in Criminology and Socio-legal Studies in Canada," *Canadian Journal of Criminology and Criminal Justice* (Sept., 2006): 635. See also George Pavlich, "Experiencing Critique," *Law and Critique,* **16** (2005): 95–112.

139. Ibid, p. 641.

140. Ibid, p. 641.

141. Hogeveen and Woolford, "Critical Criminology and Possibility in the Neo-liberal Ethos," p. 682.

Chapter 9

1. Kim Rossmo, "Geographic Profiling," Paper presented at the NCIS Conference, 1998.

2. "Suburban Digest," *Denver Post,* Apr. 10, 1996, p. B-2.

3. City News, "Cops Bust Huge GTA-Based Auto Theft Rings," Aug. 30, 2007, www.citynews.ca/news/news_14246. aspx, accessed March 11, 2008.

4. Paul J. Brantingham and Patricia L. Brantingham, "Introduction: The Dimensions of Crime," in *Environmental Criminology,* ed. Brantingham and Brantingham (Prospect Heights, Ill.: Waveland, 1991), p. 8. For a discussion on the application of environmental criminology to urban planning, see Paul J. Brantingham and Patricia L. Brantingham, "Environmental Criminology: From Theory to Urban Planning Practice," *Studies on Crime and Crime Prevention,* **7** (1998): 31–60.

5. André M. Guerry, *Essai sur la Statistique Morale de la France* (Paris: Crochard, 1833).

6. Adolphe Quételet, *A Treatise on Man* (Edinburgh: Chambers, 1842), reprinted excerpt Adolphe Quételet, "Of the development of the propensity to crime," in *Criminological Perspectives: A Reader,* ed. John Muncie, Eugene McLaughlin, and Mary Langan (Thousand Oaks, Calif.: Sage, 1996), p. 19.

7. Ronald Clarke and Derek Cornish, "Modeling Offenders' Decisions: A Framework for Research and Policy," in *Crime and Justice,* vol. 6, ed. Michael Tonry and Norval Morris (Chicago: University of Chicago Press, 1985), pp. 147–185; Derek B. Cornish and Ronald V. Clarke, eds., *The Reasoning Criminal* (New York: Springer Verlag, 1986).

8. Jeremy Bentham, *On the Principles and Morals of Legislation* (New York: Kegan Paul, 1789) [reprinted 1948]; Gary S. Becker, "Crime and Punishment: An Economic Approach," *Journal of Political Economy,* **76** (1968): 169–217.

9. Lawrence E. Cohen and Marcus Felson, "Social Change and Crime Rate Trends: A Routine Activity Approach," *American Sociological Review,* **44** (1979): 588–608; Marcus Felson, "Linking Criminal Choices, Routine Activities, Informal Control, and Criminal Outcomes," in *The Reasoning Criminal: Rational Choice Perspectives on Offending,* ed. Derek B. Cornish and Ronald V. Clarke (New York: Springer-Verlag, 1986), pp. 119–128.

10. Marcus Felson, *Crime and Everyday Life: Insights and Implications for Society* (Thousand Oaks, Calif.: Pine Forge Press, 1994), pp. 20–21, 35.

11. Mangai Natarajan, "Telephones as Facilitators of Drug Dealing," paper presented at the Fourth International Seminar on Environmental Criminology and Crime Analysis, July 1995, Cambridge, England; Mangai Natarajan, Ronald V. Clarke and Mathieu Belanger, "Drug Dealing and Pay Phones: The Scope for Intervention," *Security Journal,* **7** (1996): pp. 245–251.

12. Lawrence W. Sherman, Patrick R. Gartin, and Michael E. Buerger, "Hot Spots of Predatory Crime: Routine Activities and the Criminology of Place," *Criminology,* **27** (1989): 27–55; Ronald V. Clarke and Patricia M. Harris, "A Rational Choice Perspective on the Targets of Automobile

Theft," *Criminal Behaviour and Mental Health,* **2** (1992): 25–42. See also the following articles in Ronald V. Clarke and Marcus Felson, eds., *Routine Activity and Rational Choice, Advances in Criminological Theory,* vol. 5 (New Brunswick, N.J.: Transaction, 1993): Raymond Paternoster and Sally Simpson, "A Rational Choice Theory of Corporate Crime," pp. 37–58; Richard W. Harding, "Gun Use in Crime, Rational Choice, and Social Learning Theory," pp. 85–102; Richard B. Felson, "Predatory and Dispute-Related Violence: A Social Interactionist Approach," pp. 103–125; Nathaniel J. Pallone and James J. Hennessy, "Tinderbox Criminal Violence: Neurogenic Impulsivity, Risk-Taking, and the Phenomenology of Rational Choice," pp. 127–157; Max Taylor, "Rational Choice, Behavior Analysis, and Political Violence," pp. 159–178; Pietro Marongiu and Ronald V. Clarke, "Ransom Kidnapping in Sardinia, Subcultural Theory and Rational Choice," pp. 179–199; Bruce D. Johnson, Mangai Natarajan, and Harry Sanabria, "'Successful' Criminal Careers: Toward an Ethnography within the Rational Choice Perspective," pp. 201–221.

13. George Rengert and John Wasilchick, *Suburban Burglary: A Time and a Place for Everything* (Springfield, Ill.: Charles C Thomas, 1985).

14. Paul F. Cromwell, James N. Olson, and D'Aunn Webster Avary, *Breaking and Entering: An Ethnographic Analysis of Burglary* (Newbury Park, Calif.: Sage, 1991), pp. 45–46.

15. Ronald Clarke and Marcus Felson, *Routine Activity and Rational Choice Theory (Advances in Criminological Theory)* (New Brunswick, N.J.: Transaction, 2004); Richard T. Wright and Scott H. Decker, *Burglars on the Job: Streetlife and Residential Break-Ins* (Boston: Northeastern University Press, 1994), pp. 63–68; Alex Piquero and George F. Rengert, "Studying Deterrence with Active Residential Burglars: A Research Note," *Justice Quarterly,* **16** (1999): 451–472.

16. Richard T. Wright and Scott Decker, *Armed Robbers in Action: Stickups and Street Culture* (Boston: Northeastern University Press, 1994). For a feminist analysis of Wright and Decker's ethnographic work on street robbers, see Jody Miller, "Up It Up: Gender and the Accomplishment of Street Robbery," *Criminology,* **36** (1998): 37–66.

17. Philip J. Cook, *Robbery in the United States: An Analysis of Recent Trends and Patterns,* U.S. Department of Justice (Washington, D.C.: U.S. Government Printing Office, 1983).

18. Wayland Clifton Jr., *Convenience Store Robbery in Gainesville, Florida* (Gainesville, Fla.: Gainesville Police Department, 1987), p. 15.

19. Lawrence E. Cohen and Marcus Felson, "Social Change and Crime Rate Trends: A Routine Activity Approach," *American Sociological Review,* **44** (1979): 588–608.

20. Ronald V. Clarke, *Hot Products: Understanding, Anticipating and Reducing Demand for Stolen Goods,* Policing and Reducing Crime Unit, Police Research Series Paper 112 (London: Home Office, 1999). For discussions of what drives shoplifters, see Read Hayes, "Shop Theft: An Analysis of Shoplifter Perceptions and Situational Factors," *Security Journal,* **12** (1999): 7–18; and David P. Farrington, "Measuring, Explaining, and Preventing Shoplifting: A Review of British Research," *Security Journal,* **12** (1999): 9–28. For

details on measuring and preventing crime against retail business, see a special issue of *Security Journal,* **7** (1996): 1–75.

21. Bonnie S. Fisher, John J. Sloan, Francis T. Cullen, and Chunmeng Lu, "Crime in the Ivory Tower: The Level and Sources of Student Victimization," *Criminology,* **36** (1998): 671–710. For additional research supporting the routine-activity approach, see also Verna A. Henson and William E. Stone, "Campus Crime: A Victimization Study," *Journal of Criminal Justice,* **27** (1999): 295–308.

22. Hans von Hentig, "Remarks on the Interaction of Perpetrator and Victim," *Journal of Criminal Law and Criminology,* **31** (1941): 303–309.

23. Hans von Hentig, *The Criminal and His Victim* (New Haven, Conn.: Yale University, 1948).

24. See Benjamin Mendelsohn, "The Origin of the Doctrine of Victimology," in *Victimology,* ed. Israel Drapkin and Emilio Viano (Lexington, Mass.: Lexington Books, 1974), pp. 3–4.

25. Frederic Wertham, *The Show of Violence* (Garden City, N.Y.: Country Life Press, 1948), p. 259.

26. Ezzat A. Fattah, "Victims and Victimology: The Facts and the Rhetoric," *International Review of Victimology,* **1** (1989): 44–66, at p. 44.

27. Ezzat A. Fattah, "The Rational Choice/Opportunity Perspective as a Vehicle for Integrating Criminological and Victimological Theories," in Clarke and Felson, *Routine Activity and Rational Choice,* pp. 230–231. For an examination of the relationship between lifestyle factors and the victimization of prostitutes, see Charisse Coston and Lee Ross, "Criminal Victimization of Prostitutes: Empirical Support for the Lifestyle/Exposure Model," *Journal of Crime and Justice,* **21** (1998): 53–70.

28. Fattah, "Victims and Victimology," p. 54.

29. Michael J. Hindelang, Michael R. Gottfredson, and James Garofalo, *Victims of Personal Crime: An Empirical Foundation for a Theory of Personal Victimization* (Cambridge, Mass.: Ballinger, 1978), p. 245.

30. Ibid., pp. 251–265.

31. Marvin E. Wolfgang, *Patterns in Criminal Homicide* (Philadelphia: University of Pennsylvania Press, 1958), p. 253.

32. "Shooting Victims Had Gang Connections," CBC News, Nov. 6, 2007, www.cbc.ca/canada/british-columbia/story/2007/11/06/bc-granvilleshooting.html, accessed March 11, 2008; Mark Hume, "Victim Was Gang Target, Police Say," March 10, 2008, www.theglobeandmail.com/servlet/story/LAC.20080310.BCSHOOY10/TPStory/TP, accessed March 11, 2008.

33. James T. Tedeschi and Richard B. Felson, *Violence, Aggression, and Coercive Actions* (Washington, D.C.: American Psychological Association, 1994).

34. Richard B. Felson, "Big People Hit Little People: Sex Differences in Physical Power and Interpersonal Violence," *Criminology,* **34** (1996): 433–452.

35. Dan Olweus, "Aggressors and Their Victims: Bullying at School," in *Disruptive Behaviors in Schools,* ed. N. Frude and H. Gault (New York: Wiley, 1984), pp. 57–76.

36. "Toronto: Crime and Safety in the City," Ipsos-Reid poll, Sept. 9, 2003; "British Columbians on Crime," Ipsos-Reid poll, March 26, 2004.

37. Maire Gannon and Karen Mihorean, "Criminal Victim-ization in Canada, 2004," Statistics Canada, Catalogue no: 85-002-XPE, vol. 25, no. 7.

38. Larry J. Siegel and Chris McCormick, *Criminology in Canada: Theories, Patterns, and Typologies,* 3rd ed. (Toronto: Thomson Nelson, 2006), p. 90.

39. Leslie W. Kennedy and David Forde, "Risky Lifestyles and Dangerous Results: Routine Activities and Exposure to Crime," *Sociology and Social Research,* **74** (1990): 208–211.

40. Vincent F. Sacco and Holly Johnson, *Patterns of Criminal Victimization in Canada* (Ottawa: Statistics Canada, 1990).

41. Ronet Bachman, *Violence Against Women* (Washington, DC: Bureau of Justice Statistics, 1994).

42. Gannon and Mihorean, "Criminal Victimization in Canada, 2004."

43. Holly Johnson and Gary Lazarus, "The Impact of Age on Crime Victimization Rates," *Canadian Journal of Criminology,* **31** (1989): 309–317.

44. Siegel and McCormick, *Criminology in Canada,* p. 94.

45. Walter S. DeKeseredy and Ronald Hinch, *Woman Abuse: Sociological Perspectives* (Toronto: Thompson, 1991); Karen Rodgers, "Wife Assault: the Findings of a National Survey," *Juristat,* **14** (1990); Siegel and McCormick, *Criminology in Canada,* p. 98.

46. Alan Trickett, Dan Ellingworth, Tim Hope, and Ken Pease, "Crime Victimization in the Eighties: Changes in Area and Regional Inequality," *British Journal of Crimi-nology,* **35** (1995): 343–359; Graham Farrell, "Preventing Repeat Victimization," in *Building a Safer Society: Strategic Approaches to Crime Prevention, Crime and Justice,* vol. 19, ed. Michael Tonry and David P. Farrington (Chicago: University of Chicago Press, 1995), pp. 469–534; Dan Ellingworth, Graham Farrell, and Ken Pease, "A Victim Is a Victim Is a Victim? Chronic Victimization in Four Sweeps of the British Crime Survey," *British Journal of Criminology,* **35** (1995): 360–365.

47. Gannon and Mihorean, "Criminal Victimization in Canada, 2004."

48. William Spelman, "Once Bitten, Then What? Cross-Sectional and Time-Course Explanations of Repeat Victimization," *British Journal of Criminology,* **35** (1995): 366–383; Natalie Polvi, Terah Looman, Charlie Humphries, and Ken Pease, "The Time-Course of Repeat Burglary Victimization," *British Journal of Crimi-nology,* **31** (1991): 411–414.

49. Graham Farrell, Coretta Phillips, and Ken Pease, "Like Taking Candy: Why Does Repeat Victimization Occur?" *British Journal of Criminology,* **35** (1995): 384–399.

50. James P. Lynch, Michael L. Berbaum, and Mike Planty, *Investigating Repeated Victimization with the NCVS* (Washington, D.C.: National Institute of Justice, 1998).

51. Colin Goff, *Criminal Justice in Canada,* 4th ed. (Toronto: Thomson Nelson, 2008), p. 131.

52. Josée Savoie, Frédéric Bédard and Krista Collins, "Neighbourhood Characteristics and the Distribution of Crime on the Island of Montréal," Statistics Canada, *Crime and Justice Research Paper Series,* 85-561-MWE, 2006, no. 7.

53. See, e.g., Kate J. Bowers, Shane D. Johnson, and Ken Pease, "Prospective Hot-Spotting: The Future of Crime Mapping?" *British Journal of Criminology,* **44** (2004): 641–658.

54. Dennis W. Roncek and Donald Faggiani, "High Schools and Crime: A Replication," *Sociological Quarterly,* **26** (1985): 491–505.

55. Dennis W. Roncek and Pamela A. Maier, "Bars, Blocks, and Crimes Revisited: Linking the Theory of Routine Activities to the Empiricism of 'Hot Spots,'" *Criminol-ogy,* **29** (1991): 725–753.

56. Richard L. Block and Carolyn R. Block, "Space, Place and Crime: Hot Spot Areas and Hot Places of Liquor-Related Crime," in *Crime and Place: Crime Prevention Stud-ies,* vol. 4, ed. John E. Eck and David Weisburd (Monsey, N.Y.: Criminal Justice Press; Washington, D.C.: The Police Executive Research Forum, 1995), pp. 145–183.

57. Per-Olof Wikström, "Preventing City-Center Street Crimes," in Tonry and Farrington, *Building a Safer Soci-ety,* vol. 19, pp. 429–468.

58. William Spelman, "Abandoned Buildings: Magnets for Crime?" *Journal of Criminal Justice,* **21** (1993): 481–495.

59. Dennis W. Roncek and Ralph Bell, "Bars, Blocks, and Crimes," *Journal of Environmental Systems,* **11** (1981): 35–47; Roncek and Faggiani, "High Schools and Crime."

60. Jeffrey Peck, G. O. W. Mueller, and Freda Adler, "The Vulnerability of Ports and Marinas to Vessel and Equip-ment Theft," *Security Journal,* **5** (1994): 146–153.

61. David Weisburd and Lorraine Green with Frank Gajewski and Charles Bellucci, Jersey City Police Department, "Defining the Street Level Drug Market," in *Drugs and Crime: Evaluating Public Policy Initiatives,* ed. Doris Layton MacKenzie and Craig Uchida (Newbury Park, Calif.: Sage, 1994), pp. 61–76. For a discussion of the role of place managers in controlling drug and disorder problems, see Lorraine Green Mazerolle, Colleen Kadleck, and Jan Roehl, "Controlling Drug and Disorder Problems: The Role of Place Managers," *Criminology,* **36** (1998): 371–404. For an analysis of problem-oriented policing in troubled areas, see Anthony A. Braga, David L. Weisburd, Elin J. Waring, Lorraine Green Mazerolle, William Spelman, and Francis Gajewski, "Problem-Oriented Policing in Violent Crime Places: A Random-ized Controlled Experiment," *Criminology,* **37** (1999): 541–580.

62. Lawrence W. Sherman, "Hot Spots of Crime and Crimi-nal Careers of Places," in Eck and Weisburd, *Crime and Place,* vol. 4, pp. 35–52.

63. See Fattah, "The Rational Choice/Opportunity Perspec-tive," in Clark and Felson, *Routine Activity and Rational Choice,* pp. 225–258.

64. James R. Lasley, "Drinking Routines/Lifestyles and Predatory Victimization: A Causal Analysis," *Justice Quarterly,* **6** (1989): 529–542.

65. Martin D. Schwartz and Victoria L. Pitts, "Exploring a Feminist Routine Activities Approach to Explaining Sex-ual Assault," *Justice Quarterly,* **12** (1995): 9–31.

66. Robert F. Meier and Terance D. Miethe, "Understanding Theories of Criminal Victimization," in *Crime and Justice: A Review of Research,* vol. 17, ed. Michael Tonry (Chicago: University of Chicago Press, 1993), pp. 459–499; Richard Titus, "Bringing Crime Victims Back into Routine Activi-ties Theory/Research," paper presented at Fourth

International Seminar on Environmental Criminology and Crime Analysis, July 1995, Cambridge, England.

67. C. Ray Jeffery, *Crime Prevention through Environmental Design* (Beverly Hills, Calif.: Sage, 1971).

68. Oscar Newman, *Defensible Space: Crime Prevention through Urban Design* (New York: Macmillan, 1972).

69. Patricia L. Brantingham and Paul J. Brantingham, "Criminality of Place: Crime Generators and Crime Attractors," *European Journal on Criminal Policy and Research*, 3 (1995): 5–26; Paul J. Brantingham and Patricia L. Brantingham, "Understanding and Controlling Crime and Fear of Crime: Conflicts and Trade-offs in Crime Prevention Planning," in *Crime Prevention at a Crossroads*, ed. S. P. Lab (Cincinnati: Anderson Publishing, 1997).

70. Patricia L. Brantingham, Paul J. Brantingham, and Wendy Taylor, "Situational Crime Prevention as a Key Component in Embedded Crime Prevention," *Canadian Journal of Criminology and Criminal Justice* (Apr., 2005): 272.

71. Ronald V. Clarke, "Introduction," in *Situational Crime Prevention: Successful Case Studies*, ed. Ronald V. Clarke (New York: Harrow and Heston, 1992), pp. 3–36.

72. Brantingham, Brantingham, and Taylor, "Situational Crime Prevention as a Key Component in Embedded Crime Prevention," p. 273.

73. Derek B. Cornish and Ronald V. Clarke, "Opportunities, Precipitators and Criminal Decisions: A Reply to Wortley's Critique of Situational Crime Prevention," *Crime Prevention Studies*, 16 (2003): 41–96.

74. Brantingham, Brantingham, and Taylor, "Situational Crime Prevention as a Key Component in Embedded Crime Prevention," p. 277.

75. Ibid, p. 280.

76. Ibid.

77. Ronald V. Clarke and Ross Homel, "A Revised Classification of Situational Crime Prevention Techniques," in *Crime Prevention at a Crossroads*, ed. Steven P. Lab (Cincinnati: Anderson, 1997). For a discussion of precipitating factors and opportunity, see Richard Wortley, "A Two-Stage Model of Situational Crime Prevention," *Studies on Crime and Crime Prevention*, 7 (1998): 173–188.

78. See Gresham M. Sykes and David Matza, "Techniques of Neutralization: A Theory of Delinquency," *American Sociological Review*, 22 (1957): 664–670; Harold G. Grasmick and Robert J. Bursik, "Conscience, Significant Others, and Rational Choice," *Law and Society Review*, 34 (1990): 837–861; John Braithwaite, *Crime, Shame and Reintegration* (Cambridge: Cambridge University, 1989).

79. Clifford D. Shearing and Phillip C. Stenning, "From the Panopticon to Disney World: The Development of Discipline," in *Perspectives in Criminal Law: Essays in Honour of John L. J. Edwards*, ed. Anthony N. Doob and Edward L. Greenspan (Aurora: Canada Law Book, 1984), pp. 335–349.

80. Marcus Nieto, *Public Video Surveillance: Is It an Effective Crime Prevention Tool?* (Sacramento: California Research Bureau, 1997).

81. Rick Linden and Renuka Chaturvedi, "The Need for Comprehensive Crime Prevention Planning: The Case of Motor Vehicle Theft," *Canadian Journal of Criminology and Criminal Justice*, (Apr. 2005): 251–270.

82. Ibid, p. 254.

83. Ibid, p. 254–255.

84. Ibid, p. 262–264.

85. Ronald D. Hunter and C. Ray Jeffery, "Preventing Convenience Store Robbery through Environmental Design," in Clarke, *Situational Crime Prevention*, pp. 194–204. See also Lisa C. Bellamy, "Situational Crime Prevention and Convenience Store Robbery," *Security Journal*, 7 (1996): 41–52.

86. All information for this section abstracted from Mary S. Smith, *Crime Prevention through Environmental Design in Parking Facilities*, Research in Brief, for National Institute of Justice (Washington, D.C.: U.S. Government Printing Office, 1996).

87. David Weisburd et al., *Does Crime Just Move Around the Corner? A Study of Displacement and Diffusion in Jersey City, NJ* (Washington, D.C.: National Institute of Justice, 2005).

88. Patricia L. Brantingham and Paul J. Brantingham, "Notes on the Geometry of Crime" in *Environmental Criminology*, eds., Paul Brantingham and Patricia Brantingham (Beverly Hills, CA: Sage, 1981).

89. Kim Rossmo, "Geographic Profiling," Paper presented at the NCIS Conference, 1998.

90. D. Kim Rossmo, *Geographic Profiling* (Boca Raton, FL: CRC Press, 2000).

Chapter 10

1. *Crimes of Violence: A Staff Report Submitted to the National Commission on the Causes and Prevention of Violence* (Washington, D.C.: U.S. Government Printing Office, December 1969), vol. 12, p. xxvii; vol. 11, p. 4.

2. G. O. W. Mueller, "Where Murder Begins," *New Hampshire Bar Journal*, 2 (1960): 214–224; G. O. W. Mueller, "On Common Law Mens Rea," *Minnesota Law Review*, 42 (1958): 1043–1104.

3. Wayne R. LaFave and Austin W. Scott, *Handbook on Criminal Law* (St. Paul, Minn.: West, 1972), pp. 572–577.

4. *Commonwealth v. Welansky*, 316 Mass. 383, N.E. 2d 902 (1944), at pp. 906–907. See G. O. W. Mueller, "The Devil May Care—Or Should We? A Reexamination of Criminal Negligence," *Kentucky Law Journal*, 55 (1966–1967): 29–49.

5. Mia Dauvergne and Geoffrey Li, "Homicide in Canada, 2005," Statistics Canada, Catalogue no. 85-002-XIE, vol. 26, no. 6, Nov. 2006.

6. Mia Dauvergne, "Homicide in Canada, 2001" *Juristat 22(7)*; Geoffrey Li, "Homicide in Canada, 2006," Statistics Canada, Catalogue no. 85-002-XIE, vol. 27, no. 8.

7. Dauvergne and Li, "Homicide in Canada, 2005." The authors of the report note that data on ethnicity exclude about 50 percent of victims and accused persons where police reported Aboriginal origin as unknown.

8. Uniform Crime Reports, 2004, p. 18.

9. W. Meloff and R. Silverman, "Canadian Kids Who Kill," *Canadian Journal of Criminology*, 34 (1992): 15–34.

10. Uniform Crime Reports, 2004, p. 17.

11. David Luckenbill, "Criminal Homicide as a Situated Transaction," *Social Problems*, 25(2) (1977): 176–186.

12. Dauvergne and Li, "Homicide in Canada, 2005."

13. Kenneth Polk, "Observations on Stranger Homicide," *Journal of Criminal Justice*, 21 (1993): 573–582.

14. Dauvergne and Li, "Homicide in Canada, 2005"; Li. "Homicide in Canada, 2006."

15. See, e.g., Colin Loftin, Karen Kindley, Sandra L. Norris, and Brian Wiersema, "An Attribute Approach to Relationships between Offenders and Victims in Homicide," *Journal of Criminal Law and Criminology,* **78** (1987): 259–271.

16. Angela Browne, "Assault and Homicide at Home: When Battered Women Kill," *Advances in Applied Social Psychology,* **3** (1986): 57–79.

17. Martin Daly and Margo Wilson, *Homicide* (New York: Aldine–De Gruyter, 1988), pp. 294–295.

18. Dauvergne and Li, "Homicide in Canada, 2005."

19. Martha Smithey, "Infant Homicide: Victim/Offender Relationship and Causes of Death," *Journal of Family Violence,* **13** (1998): 285–297.

20. Ibid.

21. Lawrence A. Greenfeld, *Child Victimizers: Violent Offenders and Their Victims* (Washington, D.C.: Bureau of Justice Statistics, 1996), p. 3.

22. Etienne G. Krug, James A. Mercy, Linda Dahlberg, and Kenneth Powell, "Firearm- and Non-Firearm-Related Homicide among Children: An International Comparison," *Homicide Studies,* **2** (1998): 83–95.

23. See Michael Newton, *Mass Murder: An Annotated Bibliography* (New York: Garland, 1988).

24. Warren Goulding, *Just Another Indian* (Calgary: Fifth House Ltd., 2001).

25. See www.mayhem.net/crime/serial.html.

26. Michael D. Kelleher and C. L. Kelleher, *Murder Most Rare: The Female Serial Killer* (Westport, Conn.: Praeger, 1998).

27. Daniel Pedersen, "Death in Dunblane," *Newsweek,* Mar. 25, 1996, pp. 24–29.

28. David Abrahamsen, *The Murdering Mind* (New York: Harper & Row, 1973).

29. Mel Heimer, *The Cannibal: The Case of Albert Fish* (New York: Lyle Stuart, 1971).

30. Margaret Cheney, *The Co-ed Killer* (New York: Walker, 1976).

31. Jack Levin and James Alan Fox, *Mass Murder: America's Growing Menace* (New York: Plenum, 1985). See also Ronald M. Holmes and Stephen T. Holmes, "Understanding Mass Murder: A Starting Point," *Federal Probation,* **56** (1992): 53–61.

32. James Fox and Jack Levin, "Multiple Homicide: Patterns of Serial and Mass Murder," in *Crime and Justice: A Review of Research,* ed. Michael Tonry (Chicago: University of Chicago Press, 1998), pp. 407–455.

33. James Alan Fox and Jack Levin, *Overkill: Mass Murder and Serial Killing Exposed* (New York: Plenum, 1994); and Philip Jenkins, "African-Americans and Serial Homicide," *American Journal of Criminal Justice,* **17** (1993): 47–60.

34. Ronald M. Holmes and James de Burger, *Serial Murder* (Newbury Park, Calif.: Sage, 1988), p. 155.

35. Cheryl L. Maxson, Margaret A. Gordon, and Malcolm W. Klein, "Differences between Gang and Nongang Homicides," *Criminology,* **23** (1985): 209–222.

36. G. David Curry and Irving A. Spergel, "Gang Homicide, Delinquency, and Community," *Criminology,* **26** (1988): 381–405.

37. Dauvergne and Li, "Homicide in Canada, 2005"; Li, "Homicide in Canada, 2006."

38. Ibid.

39. Sam Howe Verhovek, "Houston Knows Murder, but This . . . ," *New York Times,* July 9, 1993, p. A8.

40. Groeme Newman, ed., *Global Report on Crime and Justice* (New York: United Nations; Oxford University Press, 1999), p. 50.

41. U.S. Department of Justice, Office of Juvenile Justice and Delinquency Prevention, *Juvenile Offenders and Victims, 1999 National Report* (Washington, D.C.: U.S. Department of Justice, OJJDP, 1999), p. 17. See also Krug et al., "Firearm- and Non-Firearm-Related Homicide among Children."

42. Harvey Krahn, Timothy F. Hartnagel, and John W. Gartrell, "Income Inequality and Homicide Rates: Cross-National Data and Criminological Theories," *Criminology,* **24** (1986): 269–295.

43. Glenn D. Deane, "Cross-National Comparison of Homicide: Age/Sex-Adjusted Rates Using the 1980 U.S. Homicide Experience as a Standard," *Journal of Quantitative Criminology,* **3** (1987): 215–227.

44. Dane Archer and Rosemary Gartner, *Violence and Crime in Cross-National Perspective* (New Haven, Conn.: Yale University Press, 1984).

45. Candice Nelsen, Jay Corzine, and Lin Corzine-Huff, "The Violent West Reexamined; A Research Note on Regional Homicide Rates," *Criminology,* **32** (1994): 149–161.

46. See Scott H. Decker, "Exploring Victim-Offender Relationships in Homicide: The Role of Individual and Event Characteristics," *Justice Quarterly,* **10** (1993): 585–612. See also Scott H. Decker, "Reconstructing Homicide Events: The Role of Witnesses in Fatal Encounters," *Journal of Criminal Justice,* **23** (1995): 439–450.

47. Warren Silver, "Crime Statistics in Canada, 2006," Statistics Canada, Catalogue no. 85-002-XIE, vol. 27, no. 5, p. 9; Edmonton Social Plan, "Crime and Victimization" (Edmonton Community Services, 2006).

48. David F. Luckenbill, "Criminal Homicide as a Situated Transaction," *Social Problems,* **25** (1977): 176–186. Although Luckenbill focused on homicides, the stages he identified are identical in assaults.

49. For a comprehensive, multidisciplinary review of the literature on violence, see James T. Tedeschi and Richard B. Felson, *Violence, Aggression, and Coercive Actions* (Washington, D.C.: American Psychological Association, 1994). See also Barry R. Ruback and Neil Alan Weiner, eds., *Interpersonal Violent Behaviors: Social and Cultural Aspects* (New York: Springer, 1994).

50. Edmonton Social Plan, "Crime and Victimization" (Edmonton Community Services, 2006), p. 53.

51. C. H. Kempe, F. N. Silverman, B. F. Steele, W. Droegemueller, and H. K. Silver, "The Battered-Child Syndrome," *Journal of the American Medical Association,* **181** (1962): 17–24.

52. Elizabeth Pleck, "Criminal Approaches to Family Violence, 1640–1980," in *Family Violence,* ed. Lloyd Ohlin and Michael Tonry, vol. 2 (Chicago: University of Chicago Press, 1989), pp. 19–57.

53. Elizabeth Comack, "Feminism and Criminology," in Rick Linden, *Criminology: A Canadian Perspectives,* 5th ed. (Toronto: Thomson Nelson, 2004), p. 178.

54. For a special journal issue on the subject of family violence, see Richard J. Gelles, ed., "Family Violence," *Journal of Comparative Family Studies*, **25** (1994): 1–142.

55. Lyn Nell Hancock, "Why Batterers So Often Go Free," *Newsweek*, Oct. 16, 1995, pp. 61–62.

56. Statistics Canada, "The Violence Against Women Survey," *The Daily*, Nov. 18, 1993.

57. Elizabeth Comack, "The Feminist Engagement with Criminology," in *Criminalizing Women*, eds., Gillian Balfour and Elizabeth Comack (Halifax: Fernwood Publishing, 2006), p. 33.

58. Ibid., p. 34.

59. Marvin E. Wolfgang and Franco Ferracuti, *The Subculture of Violence: Toward an Integrated Theory in Criminology* (London: Tavistock, 1967).

60. Joan McCord, "Parental Aggressiveness and Physical Punishment in Long-Term Perspective," in *Family Abuse and Its Consequences*, pp. 91–98.

61. Margery A. Cassidy, "Power-Control Theory: Its Potential Application to Woman Battering," *Journal of Crime and Justice*, **18** (1995): 1–15.

62. Donald G. Dutton, *The Domestic Assault of Women* (Boston: Allyn and Bacon, 1988), p. 15.

63. Lenore E. Walker, *The Battered Woman Syndrome* (New York: Springer Verlag, 1984); Brenda A. Miller, Thomas H. Nochajski, Kenneth E. Leonard, Howard T. Blane, Dawn M. Gondoli, and Patricia M. Bowers, "Spousal Violence and Alcohol/Drug Problems among Parolees and Their Spouses," *Women and Criminal Justice*, **1** (1990): 55–72.

64. Carolyn F. Swift, "Surviving: Women's Strength through Connections," in *Abuse and Victimization across the Life Span*, ed. Martha Straus (Baltimore: Johns Hopkins University Press, 1988), pp. 153–169.

65. Comack, "The Feminist Engagement with Criminology," p. 47.

66. Richard B. Felson, "Big People Hit Little People: Sex Differences in Physical Power and Interpersonal Violence," *Criminology*, **34** (1996): 433–452.

67. Elizabeth Comack, Vanessa Chopyk, and Linda Wood, "Aren't Women Violent Too? The Gendered Nature of Violence," in *Marginality and Condemnation: An Introduction to Critical Criminology*, eds. B. Schissel and C. Brooks (Halifax: Fernwood Publishing, 2002).

68. Comack, "Feminism and Criminology," p. 188.

69. Joan Zorza, "The Criminal Law of Misdemeanor Domestic Violence, 1970–1990," *Journal of Criminal Law and Criminology*, **83** (1992): 46–72. See also Candace Kruttschnitt and Maude Dornfeld, "Will They Tell? Assessing Preadolescents' Reports of Family Violence," *Journal of Research in Crime and Delinquency*, **29** (1992): 136–147.

70. J. W. Fantuzzo and W. K. Mohr, "Prevalence and Effects of Child Exposure to Domestic Violence," *Future Child*, **9(3)** (1999): 21–32.

71. Nico Trocmé et al., "Canadian Incidence Study of Reported Child Abuse and Neglect—2003. Major Findings" (Ottawa: Ministry of Public Works and Government Services Canada, 2005).

72. Cathy Spatz Widom and M. Ashley Ames, "Criminal Consequences of Childhood Sexual Victimization," *Child Abuse and Neglect*, **18** (1994): 303–318; Carolyn Smith and

73. Terence P. Thornberry, "The Relationship between Childhood Maltreatment and Adolescent Involvement in Delinquency," *Criminology*, **33** (1995): 451–481.

73. U.S. Department of Justice, OJJDP, Juvenile Offenders and Victims, 1999 National Report, p. 41.

74. Study conducted by Mohammed Ayat, Atiqui Abdelaziz, Najat Kfita, and El Khazouni Zineb, at the request of UNESCO and the Union of Arab Lawyers, Fez, Morocco, 1989.

75. David Levinson, *Family Violence in Cross-Cultural Perspective* (Newbury Park, Calif.: Sage, 1989).

76. Deborah Daro, "Half Full and Half Empty: The Evaluation of Results of Nineteen Clinical Research and Demonstration Projects," *Summary of Nineteen Clinical Demonstration Projects Funded by the National Center on Child Abuse and Neglect, 1978*.

77. See Candace Kruttschnitt and Maude Dornfeld, "Childhood Victimization, Race, and Violent Crime," *Criminal Justice and Behavior*, **18** (1991): 448–463.

78. "Abuse and Neglect of Older Adults. Fact Sheet. NCFV," Public Health Agency of Canada, www.phac-aspc.gc.ca/ncfv-cnivf, accessed Oct. 13, 2007.

79. Canadian Laws on Abuse and Neglect, www.cnpea.ca/canadian_laws_ on_abuse_and_ negle.htm, accessed Oct. 13, 2007.

80. "Abuse and Neglect of Older Adults."

81. Mia Dauvergne, "Family Violence Against Seniors," *Canadian Social Trends* (Ottawa: Statistics Canada, 2003).

82. "Abuse and Neglect of Older Adults."

83. Jordan I. Kosberg and Juanita L. Garcia, eds., "Elder Abuse: International and Cross-Cultural Perspectives," *Journal of Elder Abuse and Neglect*, **6** (1995): 1–197.

84. Susan Brownmiller, *Against Our Will: Men, Women, and Rape* (New York: Simon & Schuster, 1975), pp. 1–9.

85. Duncan Chappell, "Sexual Criminal Violence," in *Pathways to Criminal Violence*, ed. Neil Alan Weiner and Marvin E. Wolfgang (Newbury Park, Calif.: Sage, 1989), pp. 68–108; Comack, "Feminism and Criminology," p. 178.

86. Warren Silver, "Crime Statistics in Canada, 2006," Statistics Canada, Catalogue no. 85-002-XIE, vol. 27, no. 5, p. 9.

87. Ibid.

88. Rebecca Kong, Holly Johnson, Sara Beattie, and Andrea Cardillo, "Sexual Offences in Canada," *Juristat* **23(6)** (2003).

89. Ibid.

90. "Rape Statistics," Women Against Violence Against Women, www.wavaw.ca/informed_stats.php, accessed Sept. 26, 2007.

91. Ida Johnson and Robert Sigler, *Forced Sexual Intercourse in Intimate Relationships* (Brookfield, Vt.: Ashgate, 1997).

92. Clark Staten, "Roofies, The New Date Rape Drug of Choice," Jan. 6, 1996 (see www.emergency.com/roofies.htm).

93. W. DeKeseredy and K. Kelly, "The Incidence and Prevalence of Woman Abuse in Canadian University and College Dating Relationships: Results From a National Survey" (Ottawa: Health Canada, 1993).

94. Diana Russell, *Sexual Exploitation: Rape, Child Abuse and Workplace Harassment* (Beverly Hills, Calif.: Sage, 1984).

95. James L. LeBeau, "Patterns of Stranger and Serial Rape Offending: Factors Distinguishing Apprehended and At Large Offenders," *Journal of Criminal Law and Criminology*, **78** (1987): 309–326.

96. Marolla and D. Scully, *Attitudes toward Women, Violence, and Rape: A Comparison of Convicted Rapists and Other Felons* (Rockville, Md.: National Institute of Mental Health, 1982).

97. Christine Alder, "An Exploration of Self-Reported Sexually Aggressive Behavior," *Crime and Delinquency*, **31** (1985): 306–331; P. R. Sanday, "The Socio-Cultural Context of Rape: A Cross-Cultural Study," *Journal of Social Issues*, **37** (1981): 5–27.

98. Julia R. Schwendinger and Herman Schwendinger, *Rape and Inequality* (Beverly Hills, Calif.: Sage, 1983), p. 220.

99. M. Dwayne Smith and Nathan Bennett, "Poverty, Inequality, and Theories of Forcible Rape," *Crime and Delinquency*, **31** (1985): 295–305.

100. Ruth D. Peterson and William C. Bailey, "Forcible Rape, Poverty, and Economic Inequality in U.S. Metropolitan Communities," *Journal of Quantitative Criminology*, **4** (1988): 99–119.

101. Matthew Hale, *History of the Pleas of the Crown*, vol. 1 (London, 1736), p. 635.

102. Martin D. Schwartz and Todd R. Clear, "Toward a New Law on Rape," *Crime and Delinquency*, **26** (1980): 129–151.

103. Patricia Frazier and Beth Haney, "Sexual Assault Cases in the Legal System: Police, Prosecutor, and Victim Perspectives," *Law and Human Behavior*, **20** (1996): 607–628.

104. *R. v. Seaboyer*; *R. v. Gayme* [1991] 2 S.C.R. 577.

105. Comack, "Feminism and Criminology," pp. 182–183.

106. Ibid.

107. Ibid.

108. *R. v. O'Connor* [1995] 4 S.C.R. 411.

109. Comack, "Feminism and Criminology," pp. 184.

110. Comack, "Feminism and Criminology," pp. 182–183.

111. Nova Scotia Department of Health, "Nurses Provide Emergency Care for Sexual Assault Victims," news release, Oct. 5, 2001, www.gov.ns.ca/news/details.asp?id=20011005003.

112. John Cloud, "Most Likely to Succeed," *Time*, Apr. 26, 1999, p. 72. Copyright © TIME Inc. Reprinted by permission.

113. Warren Silver, "Crime Statistics in Canada, 2006," Statistics Canada, Catalogue no. 85-002-XIE, vol. 27, no. 5.

114. Canadian Centre for Justice Statistics, "Canadian Crime Statistics 2003" (Ottawa: Statistics Canada, 2004), Catalogue no. 85-205-XPE; Larry J. Siegel and Chris McCormick, *Criminology in Canada: Theories, Patterns, and Typologies*, 3rd ed. (Toronto: Thomson Nelson, 2006), p. 325.

115. John Conklin, *Robbery and the Criminal Justice System* (Philadelphia: Lippincott, 1972), pp. 59–78.

116. Edmonton Social Plan, "Crime and Victimization," p. 32; Daniel J. Koenig and Rick Linden, "Conventional or 'Street' Crime," in *Criminology: A Canadian Perspective*, 5th ed., ed. Rick Linden (Toronto: Thomson Nelson, 2004), p. 426.

117. Terry L. Baumer and Michael D. Carrington, *The Robbery of Financial Institutions*, for U.S. Department of Justice (Washington, D.C.: U.S. Government Printing Office, 1986).

118. Siegel and McCormick, *Criminology in Canada: Theories, Patterns, and Typologies*, p. 327.

119. Ibid.

120. Robert J. Kelly and Rufus Schatzberg, "Galvanizing Indiscriminate Political Violence: Mind-Sets and Some Ideological Constructs in Terrorism," *International Journal of Comparative and Applied Criminal Justice*, **16** (1992): 15–41; Jeffrey D. Simon, *The Terrorist Trap: America's Experience with Terrorism* (Bloomington: Indiana University Press, 1993); Brent L. Smith and Gregory P. Orvis, "America's Response to Terrorism: An Empirical Analysis of Federal Intervention Strategies during the 1980s," *Justice Quarterly*, **10** (1993): 661–681.

121. See "Bin-Laden Still Sought a Year after Embassy Bombings in Africa," Aug. 6, 1999, http://cnn.com/US/9908/06/embassy.bombings.

122. Ariel Merari, Tamar Prat, Sophia Kotzer, Anat Kurz, and Yoram Schweitzer, *Inter 85: A Review of International Terrorism in 1985* (Boulder, Colo.: Westview, 1986), p. 106.

123. Harvey J. Iglarsh, "Terrorism and Corporate Costs," *Terrorism*, **10** (1987): 227–230.

124. Siegel and McCormick, *Criminology in Canada: Theories, Patterns, and Typologies*, p. 336.

125. Some of the conventions include the following: Convention on Offences and Certain Other Acts Committed on Board Aircraft, signed at Tokyo on Sept. 14, 1963; Convention for the Suppression of Unlawful Seizure of Aircraft, signed at The Hague on Dec. 16, 1970; Convention for the Suppression of Unlawful Acts against the Safety of Civil Aviation, signed at Montreal on Sept. 23, 1971; Convention on the Prevention and Punishment of Crimes against Internationally Protected Persons, Including Diplomatic Agents, adopted by the General Assembly of the United Nations on December 14, 1973; International Convention against the Taking of Hostages, adopted by the General Assembly of the United Nations on December 17, 1979.

126. Siegel and McCormick, *Criminology in Canada: Theories, Patterns, and Typologies*, p. 334.

127. Ibid., p. 336.

128. James Brooke, "Wyoming City Braces for Gay Murder Trial," *New York Times*, Apr. 4, 1999, p. 14.

129. Maire Gannon and Karen Mihorean, "Criminal Victimization in Canada, 2004," Statistics Canada, Catalogue no. 85-002-XPE, vol. 25, no. 7.

130. Ibid.

131. Ibid.

132. "Pilot Survey of Hate Crime," *The Daily*, June 1, 2004, Statistics Canada, www.statcan.ca/Daily/English/040601/d040601a.htm, accessed Oct. 10, 2007.

133. Ibid.

134. Active Hate Groups in the United States, 2004: Southern Poverty Law Center Intelligence Project, www.splcenter.org/intel/map/hate.jsp.

135. Gordon Crew and Reid Countes, *The Evolution of School Disturbance in America: Colonial Times to Modern Day* (Westport, Conn.: Praeger, 1997).

136. For the latest school safety data, see NSSC Review of School Safety Research, School Safety Statistics January 2006, available at: www.schoolsafety.us/pubfiles/school_crime_and_violence_statistics.pdf. Vincent

Schiraldi, "Hype Aside, School Violence Is Declining." This report appeared in *Newsday*, *The Washington Post*, and other media, Sept. 30, 1998.

137. Mary Jo Nolin, Elizabeth Davies, and Kathryn Chandler, "Student Victimization at School," *Journal of School Health*, **66** (1996): 216.

138. "First Steps to Stop Bullying: Adults Helping Children Aged 4 to 11," Public Safety Canada, www.securitepublique.gc.ca/res/cp/bully_4211-en.asp, accessed Sept. 28, 2007.

139. "First Steps to Stop Bullying: Adults Helping Children Aged 12 to 17," Public Safety Canada, www.securitepublique.gc.ca/res/cp/bully_12217-en.asp, accessed Sept. 28, 2007.

140. "Study: Self-Reported Delinquency among Young People in Toronto," *The Daily*, Sept. 25, 2007, www.statcan.ca/Daily/English/070925/d070925a.htm.

141. James C. Hackler, *Canadian Criminology: Strategies and Perspectives*, 4th ed. (Toronto: Pearson Prentice-Hall, 2007), p. 249.

142. Li, "Homicide in Canada, 2006."

143. Samuel Walker, *Sense and Nonsense about Crime and Drugs: A Policy Guide*, 4th ed. (Belmont, Calif.: West/Wadsworth, 1998).

144. National Crime Victimization Survey, 1993–2004. See Martin Killias, "International Correlations between Gun Ownership and Rates of Homicide and Suicide," *Canadian Medical Association Journal*, **148** (1993): 1721–1776; Peter J. Carrington and Sharon Moyer, "Gun Availability and Suicide in Canada: Testing the Displacement Hypothesis," *Studies on Crime and Crime Prevention*, **3** (1994): 168–178.

Chapter 11

1. Jerome Hall, *Theft, Law, and Society* (Indianapolis: Bobbs-Merrill, 1935).

2. Warren Silver, "Crime Statistics in Canada, 2006," Statistics Canada, Catalogue no. 85-002-XIE, vol. 27, no. 5.

3. Edmonton Social Plan, "Crime and Victimization," (Edmonton Community Services, 2006); Maire Gannon and Karen Mihorean, "Criminal Victimization in Canada, 2004," Statistics Canada, Catalogue no. 85-002-XPE, vol. 25, no. 7.

4. See Abraham S. Blumberg, "Typologies of Criminal Behavior," in *Current Perspectives on Criminal Behavior*, 2nd ed., ed. Blumberg (New York: Knopf, 1981).

5. See John Hepburn, "Occasional Criminals," in *Major Forms of Crime*, ed. Robert Meier (Beverly Hills, Calif.: Sage, 1984), pp. 73–94; and John Gibbs and Peggy Shelly, "Life in the Fast Lane: A Retrospective View by Commercial Thieves," *Journal of Research in Crime and Delinquency*, **19** (1982): 299–330, at p. 327.

6. Lloyd W. Klemke, The *Sociology of Shoplifting: Boosters and Snitches Today* (Westport, Conn.: Praeger, 1992).

7. James Inciardi, "Professional Thief," in Meier, *Major Forms of Crime*, p. 224. See also Harry King and William Chambliss, *Box Man—A Professional Thief's Journal* (New York: Harper & Row, 1972).

8. *The Professional Thief*, annotated and interpreted by Edwin H. Sutherland (Chicago: University of Chicago Press, 1937).

9. Gillian Balfour and Elizabeth Comack, "Introduction," in *Criminalizing Women*, eds. Gillian Balfour and Elizabeth Comack (Halifax: Fernwood Publishing, 2006), p. 16.

10. Ibid., p. 67.

11. Ibid.

12. Ibid.

13. Ibid., p. 64.

14. Jo-Ann Ray, "Every Twelfth Shopper: Who Shoplifts and Why?" *Social Casework*, **68** (1987): 234–239. For a discussion of who gets caught and what kinds of treatment programs exist, see Gail A. Caputo, "A Program of Treatment for Adult Shoplifters," *Journal of Offender Rehabilitation* **27** (1998): 123–137.

15. Abigail Buckle and David P. Farrington, "An Observational Study of Shoplifting," *British Journal of Criminology*, **24** (1984): 63–73.

16. Thana Dharmarajah, "Merchants Battle Shoplifting Plague," *Halo Metrics*, March 26, 2005, www.halometrics.com/web/home/index.php?id=29&rid=1&d=news, accessed Oct. 21, 2007.

17. Ibid.

18. Jim Fox, "Canadian Retailers Take Bite Out of Crime," Retail Council of Canada's Retail Loss Prevention Conference, July 17, 1995, http://findarticles.com/p/articles/mi_m3092/is_n14_v34/ai_17295174/print, accessed Sept. 19, 2007.

19. Donald Hartmann, Donna Gelfand, Brent Page, and Patrice Walder, "Rates of Bystander Observation and Reporting of Contrived Shoplifting Incidents," *Criminology*, **10** (1972): 247–267.

20. *1998–1999 Retail Theft Trends Report: Executive Summary* (Winter Park, Fla.: Loss Prevention Specialists, 1999).

21. Bruce Constantineau, "Shoplifting Wipes Out 100 000 Jobs Across Canada," *Vancouver Sun*, www.ilps.com/index.php?option=com_content&task=view&id=112&Itemid=152, accessed Oct. 21, 2007.

22. Mary Owen Cameron, *The Booster and the Snitch* (New York: Free Press, 1964). See also John Rosecrance, "The Stooper: A Professional Thief in the Sutherland Manner," *Criminology*, **24** (1986): 29–40.

23. Richard Moore, "Shoplifting in Middle America: Patterns and Motivational Correlates," *International Journal of Offender Therapy and Comparative Criminology*, **28** (1984): 53–64. See also Charles A. Sennewald and John H. Christman, *Shoplifting* (Boston: Butterworth-Heinemann, 1992).

24. Trevor N. Gibbens, C. Palmer, and Joyce Prince, "Mental Health Aspects of Shoplifting," *British Medical Journal*, **3** (1971): 612–615.

25. Fox, "Canadian Retailers Take Bite Out of Crime."

26. Barry Poyner and Ruth Woodall, *Preventing Shoplifting: A Study in Oxford Street* (London: Police Foundation, 1987).

27. John Carroll and Frances Weaver, "Shoplifters' Perceptions of Crime Opportunities: A Process-Tracing Study," in *The Reasoning Criminal*, ed. Derek Cornish and Ronald V. Clarke (New York: Springer Verlag, 1986), pp. 19–38.

28. Fox, "Canadian Retailers Take Bite Out of Crime."

29. Joshua Bamfield, "Retail Civil Recovery: Filling a Deficit in the Criminal Justice System?" *International Journal of*

Risk Security and Crime Prevention, **3** (1998): 257–267; Fox, "Canadian Retailers Take Bite Out of Crime."

30. Marnie Wallace, "Motor Vehicle Theft in Canada, 2001," Statistics Canada, Catalogue no. 85-002-XIE, vol. 23, no. 1.

31. Silver, "Crime Statistics in Canada, 2006."

32. "Facts & Figures: CBC Marketplace: Vehicles—Grand Theft Auto," Oct. 28, 2003, www.cbc.ca/consumers/market/files/cars/gta/facts.html, accessed Oct. 21, 2007.

33. Ibid.

34. See Charles McCaghy, Peggy Giordano, and Trudy Knicely Henson, "Auto Theft," *Criminology,* **15** (1977): 367–385.

35. See www.lojack.com/theft.htm.

36. Insurance Bureau of Canada, "Theft Stats: Which Cars Are Stolen?" www.directed.ca/en/Marketing/Thieves%20Stats/index.php?t=3, accessed Oct. 21, 2007.

37. Kevin Blake, "What You Should Know about Car Theft," *Consumer's Research* (Oct. 1995): 26–28.

38. Paul Williams, "Tracking Stolen Vehicles: Boomerang Vehicle Tracking System," www.canadiandriver.com/articles/pw/boomerang.htm, accessed March 23, 2008.

39. "About IMPACT and the Bait Car Program," www.baitcar.com, accessed March 23, 2008.

40. "The Watch Your Car Program," www.ojp.usdoj.gov/BJA/html/wycfaq.htm.

41. Ronald V. Clarke, "Situational Crime Prevention: Theoretical Basis and Practical Scope," in *Crime and Justice: An Annual Review of Research,* vol. 4, ed. Michael Tonry and Norval Morris (Chicago: University of Chicago Press, 1983).

42. Silver, "Crime Statistics in Canada, 2006."

43. Edwin Lemert, "An Isolation and Closure Theory of Naive Check Forgery," *Journal of Criminal Law, Criminology, and Police Science,* **44** (1953–1954): 296–307.

44. Johannes Knutsson and Eckart Kuhlhorn, "Macro Measures against Crime: The Example of Check Forgeries," in *Situational Crime Prevention: Successful Case Studies,* 2nd ed., ed. Ronald V. Clarke (Albany, N.Y.: Harrow and Heston, 1997).

45. W. A. Watts, "Credit Card Fraud: Policing Plastic," *Journal of Financial Crime,* **7** (1999): 67–69.

46. Canadian Bankers Association, "Quick Facts," www.cba.ca/en/viewdocument.asp?fl=3&sl=174&docid=413&pag=1, accessed Oct. 23, 2007.

47. Michael Levi and Jim Handley, *A Research and Statistics Directorate Report: The Prevention of Plastic and Cheque Fraud Revisited* (London: Home Office, 1998).

48. Barry Masuda, "Card Fraud: Discover the Possibilities," *Security Management,* **36** (1992): 71–74.

49. Pierre Tremblay, "Designing Crime," *British Journal of Criminology,* **26** (1986): 234–253.

50. Levi and Handley, *A Research and Statistics Directorate Report.*

51. "Debit Card Fraud," CTV.ca, Jan. 8, 2005, www.ctv.ca/servlet/ArticleNews/story/CTVNews/1105142446966_16/?hub=WFive, accessed Oct. 2, 2007.

52. Canadian Bankers Association, "Quick Facts."

53. Insurance Bureau of Canada, "The Cost of Personal Injury Fraud," 2007, www.ibc.ca/en/Insurance_Crime/Personal_Injury_Fraud/Costs.asp, accessed Oct. 23, 2007.

54. Consumer Info on Auto Insurance, "Fighting Fraud Helps Keep Autopac Rates Low: Manitoba Public Insurance," www.insurance-canada.ca/consinfoauto/Manitoba-PIC-Fighting-fraud-607.php.

55. Ibid.; Leonard Sloane, "Rising Fraud Worrying Car Insurers," *New York Times,* Nov. 16, 1991, p. 48.

56. Sloane, "Rising Fraud Worrying Car Insurers."

57. Edmund J. Pankan and Frank E. Krzeszowski, "Putting a Claim on Insurance Fraud," *Security Management,* **37** (1993): 91–94.

58. "Fraud 'Prevalent' in Auto Insurance Claims: Study," CBC News, Oct. 17, 2001, www.cbc.ca/news/story/2001/10/17/insurancefraud_011017.html, accessed Sept. 20, 2007.

59. Insurance Bureau of Canada, "Personal Injury Fraud," www.ibc.ca/en/Insurance_Crime/Personal_Injury_Fraud/, accessed Oct. 23, 2007.

60. Ibid.

61. P. Jesilow, H. N. Pontell, and G. Geis, "Physician Immunity from Prosecution and Punishment for Medical Program Fraud," in *Punishment and Privilege,* ed. W. B. Groves and G. R. Newman (New York: N.Y. Harrow and Heston, 1987), p. 8.

62. H. N. Pontell, P. Jesilow, and G. Geis, "Policing Physicians: Practitioner Fraud and Abuse in a Government Medical Program," *Social Problems,* **30** (1982): 117–125.

63. "Docs Milking WCB: Single Medical Practice Says It Reviewed 13 354 WCB Cases in a Year," Alberta NDP Opposition, Aug. 4, 2007, www.ndpopposition.ab.ca/site/index.cfm?fuseaction=page.details&ID=7580&t=11& . . . , accessed Sept. 20, 2007.

64. Yahoo! News, Sept. 15, 1999, www.dailynews.yahoo.com.

65. Larry E. Coutorie, "The Future of High-Technology Crime: A Parallel Delphi Study," *Journal of Criminal Justice,* **23** (1995): 13–27.

66. "Survey Finds Computer Crime Widespread in Corporate America," *The News and Observer,* Raleigh, N.C., Oct. 25, 1995.

67. Natalie D. Voss, "Crime on the Internet," *Jones Telecommunications and Multimedia Encyclopedia,* Drive D: Studios, Jones Digital Century (1996), www.digitalcentury.com/encyclo/update/crime.html.

68. Marc Goodman, "Why the Police Don't Care about Computer Crime," *Harvard Journal of Law and Technology,* **10** (1997): 465–494.

69. Richard Overill, "Denial of Service Attacks: Threats and Methodologies," *Journal of Financial Crime,* **6** (1999): 351–353.

70. Federal Trade Commission, "Spyware," www.ftc.gov/bcp/conline/pubs/alerts/spywarealrt.shtm, accessed March 23, 2008.

71. Ibid.

72. Yahoo! News, "Employer Beware . . . National Survey Cites Employees as Significant Contributors to Software Piracy in the Workplace," Sept. 16, 1999, www.biz.yahoo.com/bw/990916/dc_bsa_1.html.

73. Brad Stone, "A High Technology Crash," *Newsweek,* Oct. 4, 1999, p. 54.

74. The Canadian Press, "Thai Police Files Additional Charges against Canadian Pedophile Suspect," Oct. 24, 2007, http://Canadianpress.google.com/article/ALeqM5iC4PDV1J183kTUAZkkhKP2FvFRbg, accessed Oct. 25, 2007.

75. Stephen Labaton, "Net Sites Co-Opted by Pornographers," *New York Times*, Sept. 23, 1999, p. 1.

76. Goodman, "Why the Police Don't Care about Computer Crime."

77. Robert W. Taylor, "Computer Crime," in *Criminal Investigation*, ed. C. R. Swanson, N. C. Chamelin, and L. Tersito (New York: Random House, 1991).

78. Coutorie, "The Future of High-Technology Crime."

79. Kenneth C. Sears and Henry Weihofen, *May's Law of Crimes*, 4th ed. (Boston: Little, Brown, 1948), pp. 307–317.

80. Silver, "Crime Statistics in Canada, 2006"; Gannon and Mihorean,"Criminal Victimization in Canada, 2004."

81. Neal Shover, "Structures and Careers in Burglary," *Journal of Criminal Law and Criminology*, **63** (1972): 540–549.

82. Scott Decker, Richard Wright, Allison Redfern, and Dietrich Smith, "A Woman's Place Is in the Home: Females and Residential Burglary," *Justice Quarterly*, **10** (1993): 143–162.

83. Darrell Steffensmeier, *The Fence: In the Shadow of Two Worlds* (Totowa, N.J.: Rowman & Littlefield, 1986), p. 7.

84. Carl Klockars, *The Professional Fence* (New York: Free Press, 1976), pp. 110, 113.

85. D'Aunn Webster Avery, Paul F. Cromwell, and James N. Olson, "Marketing Stolen Property: Burglars and Their Fences," paper presented at the 1988 Annual Meeting of the American Society of Criminology, Reno, Nev.

86. Silver, "Crime Statistics in Canada, 2006."

87. Patrick G. Jackson, "Assessing the Validity of Official Data on Arson," *Criminology*, **26** (1988): 181–195.

88. Lee Wolff, "Arson in Canada" *Juristat* **12** (1992); "Canadian Crime Statistics, 2003," Statistics Canada (Ottawa: Canadian Centre for Justice Statistics, 2004).

89. "$2-Million Chinatown Fire Was Arson, Investigators Say," CBC News, Oct. 12, 2007, www.cbc.ca/canada/ottawa/story/2007/10/12/arson-chinatowan.html?ref= rss, accessed Oct. 25, 2007; "MacEwan Fire Ruled Arson," edmontonjournal.com, July 24, 2007; Associated Press, "Arson Blamed for Canada Racetrack Fire," June 14, 2007, http://cms.firehouse.com/web/online/Arson-and-Investigation/Arson-Blamed-for-Canada, accessed Oct. 25, 2007.

90. See Wayne W. Bennett and Karen Matison Hess, *Investigating Arson* (Springfield, Ill.: Charles C Thomas, 1984), pp. 34–38.

91. John M. Macdonald, *Bombers and Firesetters* (Springfield, Ill.: Charles C Thomas, 1977), pp. 198–204.

92. Irving Kaufman and Lora W. Heims, "A Reevaluation of the Dynamics of Firesetting," *American Journal of Orthopsychiatry*, **31** (1961): 123–136.

93. Rebecca K. Hersch, *A Look at Juvenile Firesetter Programs*, for U.S. Department of Justice, Office of Justice Programs, Office of Juvenile Justice and Delinquency Prevention (Washington, D.C.: U.S. Government Printing Office, May 1989).

94. Wayne S. Wooden and Martha Lou Berkey, *Children and Arson* (New York: Plenum, 1984), p. 3.

95. See Federal Emergency Management Agency, U.S. Fire Administration, *Interviewing and Counseling Juvenile Firesetters* (Washington, D.C.: U.S. Government Printing Office, 1979).

96. Clifford L. Karchmer, *Preventing Arson Epidemics: The Role of Early Warning Strategies*, Aetna Arson Prevention Series (Hartford, Conn.: Aetna Life & Casualty, 1981).

97. "Third United Nations Survey of Crime Trends, Operations of Criminal Justice Systems and Crime Prevention Strategies," A/CONF. 144/6, July 27, 1990.

Chapter 12

1. "Securities Regulators Levy $1.2 Million in Fines, Penalties in YBM Magnex Case," CBC News, Dec. 4, 2003, www.cbc.ca/news/story/2003/07/02/ybm_030702.html, accessed Nov. 6, 2007.

2. Marshall B. Clinard and Peter C. Yeager, *Corporate Crime* (New York: Free Press, 1980), pp. 59–60.

3. Tara Gray, "Canadian Response to the U.S. Sarbanes-Oxley Act of 2002: New Directions for Corporate Governance," Economics Division, Library of Parliament, Parliamentary Information and Research Service, Oct. 2005, p. 3, www.parl.gc.ca/information/library/PRBpubs/prb0537-e.htm, accessed Sept. 9, 2007.

4. "About the Acts," Competition Bureau Canada, www.competitionbureau.gc.ca/internet/index.cfm?itemID= 148&1g=e, accessed Sept. 23, 2007.

5. Edwin H. Sutherland, "White Collar Criminality," *American Sociological Review*, **5** (1940): 1–20.

6. Gilbert Geis, *On White Collar Crime* (Lexington, Mass.: Lexington Books, 1982), p. 9.

7. Marshall B. Clinard and Richard Quinney, *Criminal Behavior Systems*, 2nd ed. (New York: Holt, Rinehart & Winston, 1982); Marshall B. Clinard, *Corporate Corruption: The Abuse of Power* (Westport, Conn.: Praeger, 1990); Gilbert Geis and Paul Jesilow, eds., "White-Collar Crime," *Annals of the American Academy of Political and Social Science*, **525** (1993): 8–169; David Weisburd, Stanton Wheeler, and Elin Waring, *Crimes of the Middle Classes: White-Collar Offenders in the Federal Courts* (New Haven, Conn.: Yale University Press, 1991); John Braithwaite, "Poverty, Power, White-Collar Crime and the Paradoxes of Criminological Theory," *Australian and New Zealand Journal of Criminology*, **24** (1991): 40–48; Frank Pearce and Laureen Snider, eds., "Crimes of the Powerful," *Journal of Human Justice*, **3** (1992): 1–124; Hazel Croall, *White Collar Crime: Criminal Justice and Criminology* (Buckingham, England: Open University Press, 1991); Stephen J. Rackmill, "Understanding and Sanctioning the White Collar Offender," *Federal Probation*, **56** (1992): 26–33; Brent Fisse, Michael Bersten, and Peter Grabosky, "White Collar and Corporate Crime," *University of New South Wales Law Journal*, **13** (1990): 1–171; Susan P. Shapiro, "Collaring the Crime Not the Criminal: Reconsidering the Concept of White-Collar Crime," *American Sociological Review*, **55** (1990): 346–365; Kip Schlegel and David Weisburd, eds., *White-Collar Crime Reconsidered* (Boston: Northeastern University Press, 1992); David Weisburd, Stanton Wheeler, Elin Waring, et al., *Crimes of the Middle Classes: White-Collar Offenders in the Federal Courts* (New Haven, Conn.: Yale University Press, 1991); David Weisburd, Ellen F. Chayet, and Elin J. Waring, "White-Collar Crime and Criminal Careers: Some Preliminary Findings," *Crime*

and Delinquency, **36** (1990): 342–355; David Weisburd, Elin Waring, and Stanton Wheeler, "Class, Status, and the Punishment of White-Collar Criminals," *Law and Social Inquiry*, **15** (1990): 223–243; Lisa Maher and Elin J. Waring, "Beyond Simple Differences: White Collar Crime, Gender and Workforce Position," *Phoebe*, **2** (1990): 44–54; John Hagan and Fiona Kay, "Gender and Delinquency in White-Collar Families: A Power-Control Perspective," *Crime and Delinquency*, **36** (1990): 391–407.

8. See James W. Coleman, *The Criminal Elite: The Sociological White-Collar Crime*, 2nd ed. (New York: St. Martin's Press, 1989); and Michael L. Benson and Elizabeth Moore, "Are White-Collar and Common Offenders the Same? An Empirical and Theoretical Critique of a Recently Proposed General Theory of Crime," *Journal of Research in Crime and Delinquency*, **29** (1992): 251–272. See also Lori A. Elis and Sally S. Simpson, "Informal Sanction Threats and Corporate Crime: Additive versus Multiplicative Models," *Journal of Research in Crime and Delinquency*, **32** (1995): 399–424. For a view of white-collar offending in which the risks and rewards are considered by potential offenders, see David Weisburd, Elin Waring, and Ellen Chayet, "Specific Deterrence in a Sample of Offenders Convicted of White-Collar Crimes," *Criminology*, **33** (1995): 587–605.

9. Not only are governments at all levels victimized by corporate crimes, governments of all nations are also victimized; see Karlhans Liebl, "Developing Trends in Economic Crime in the Federal Republic of Germany," *Police Studies*, **8** (1985): 149–162. See also Jurg Gerber and Susan L. Weeks, "Women as Victims of Corporate Crime: A Call for Research on a Neglected Topic," *Deviant Behavior*, **13** (1992): 325–347; Elizabeth Moore and Michael Mills, "The Neglected Victims and Unexamined Costs of White-Collar Crime," *Crime and Delinquency*, **36** (1990): 408–418.

10. August Bequai, *White Collar Crime: A 20th-Century Crisis* (Lexington, Mass.: Lexington Books, 1978), p. 3; Linda Ganzini, Bentson McFarland, and Joseph Bloom, "Victims of Fraud: Comparing Victims of White Collar and Violent Crime," *Bulletin of the American Academy of Psychiatry and the Law*, **18** (1990): 55–63.

11. For the relationship between patterns of crimes in the savings and loan industry and those in organized crime, see Kitty Calavita and Henry N. Pontell, "Savings and Loan Fraud as Organized Crime: Toward a Conceptual Typology of Corporate Illegality," *Criminology*, **31** (1993): 519–548.

12. For an international perspective on consumer fraud, see U.S. Senate Committee on Governmental Affairs, *International Consumer Fraud: Can Consumers Be Protected?* (Washington, D.C.: U.S. Government Printing Office, 1994); Gilbert Geis, Henry N. Pontell, and Paul Jesilow, "Medicaid Fraud," in *Controversial Issues in Criminology and Criminal Justice*, ed. Joseph E. Scott and Travis Hirschi (Beverly Hills, Calif.: Sage, 1987); Maria S. Boss and Barbara Crutchfield George, "Challenging Conventional Views of White Collar Crime: Should the Criminal Justice System Be Refocused?" *Criminal Law Bulletin*, **28** (1992): 32–58. See also Richard M. Titus, Fred Heinzelmann, and John M. Boyle, "Victimization of Persons by Fraud,"

Crime and Delinquency, **41** (1995): 54–72. For a description of fraud in an organizational setting presented from the perspective of the perpetrator, fellow employees, and the organization itself, see Steve W. Albrecht, Gerald W. Wernz, and Timothy L. Williams, *Fraud: Bringing Light to the Dark Side of Business* (Burr Ridge, Ill.: Irwin Professional Publishing, 1995).

13. For an outline of a general theory of crime causation applicable to both street crime and white-collar crime, see Travis Hirschi and Michael Gottfredson, "Causes of White-Collar Crime," *Criminology*, **25** (1987): 949–974; James W. Coleman, "Toward an Integrated Theory of White Collar Crime," *American Journal of Sociology*, **93** (1987): 406–439; and James R. Lasley, "Toward a Control Theory of White Collar Offending," *Journal of Quantitative Criminology*, **4** (1988): 347–362.

14. Donald R. Cressey, "The Poverty of Theory in Corporate Crime Research," in *Advances in Criminological Theory*, vol. 1, ed. William Laufer and Freda Adler (New Brunswick, N.J.: Transaction, 1989); for a response, see John Braithwaite and Brent Fisse, "On the Plausibility of Corporate Crime Theory," in *Advances in Criminological Theory*, vol. 2, ed. William Laufer and Freda Adler (New Brunswick, N.J.: Transaction, 1990). See also Travis Hirschi and Michael Gottfredson, "The Significance of White-Collar Crime for a General Theory of Crime," *Criminology*, **27** (1989): 359–371; and Darrell Steffensmeier, "On the Causes of 'White Collar' Crime: An Assessment of Hirschi and Gottfredson's Claims," *Criminology*, **27** (1989): 345–358.

15. Bequai, *White Collar Crime*. Bequai also includes antitrust and environmental offenses, which are corporate crimes, discussed in the next section.

16. Kenneth Polk and William Weston, "Insider Trading as an Aspect of White Collar Crime," *Australian and New Zealand Journal of Criminology*, **23** (1990): 24–38. In a report before U.S. Congress, insider trading scandals were said to have cost the securities industry nearly half a billion dollars in the early 1970s; see U.S. Congress House Select Committee on Crime, *Conversion of Worthless Securities into Cash* (Washington, D.C.: U.S. Government Printing Office, 1973). For a review of the insider trading that persists on Wall Street, see Gene G. Marcial, *Secrets of the Street: The Dark Side of Making Money* (New York: McGraw-Hill, 1995); Martin Mayer, *Nightmare on Wall Street: Salomon Brothers and the Corruption of the Marketplace* (New York: Simon & Schuster, 1993); Nancy Reichman, "Insider Trading," in Michael Tonry and Albert J. Reiss Jr., eds., *Beyond the Law: Crime in Complex Organizations* (Chicago: University of Chicago Press, 1993).

17. "Cowpland Settles Insider Trading Case for $575 000," CBC News, Dec. 4, 2003, www.cbc.ca/money/story/2003/10/20/cowpland201003.html, accessed Sept. 23, 2007.

18. Andrew Alden, "The Bre-X Gold Scandal," http://geology.about.com/cs/mineralogy/a/aa042097.htm?p=1, accessed Sept. 23, 2007.

19. "Bad Man Charged with Bankruptcy Fraud," Myvesta Canada, June 7, 2007, http://myvesta.ca/articles/

articles/2/1/Bad-Man-Charged-With-Bankruptcy-Fraud/Page1.html, accessed Sept. 21, 2007.

20. Office of the Superintendent of Bankruptcy Canada, www.ic.gc.ca/epic/site/bsf-osb.nsf/en/br01702e.html, accessed Oct. 28, 2007.

21. "Indepth: Sponsorship Scandal: Gomery's Reports," CBC News Online, Oct. 26, 2006, www.cbc.ca/includes/printablestory.jsp, accessed Sept. 23, 2007.

22. Ibid.

23. For a discussion of the many ways in which a person may be defrauded, see Phil Berger and Craig Jacob, *Twisted Genius: Confessions of a $10 Million Scam Man* (New York: Four Walls Eight Windows, 1995). For an Australian perspective of fraud, see M. Kapardis and A. Kapardis, "Co-regulation of Fraud Detection and Reporting by Auditors in Australia: Criminology's Lessons for Non-compliance," *Australian and New Zealand Journal of Criminology*, **28** (1995): 193–212.

24. "Landmark Competition Act Ruling Against Sears Canada—Sears Misrepresented Extent of Savings in Tire Advertisements Distributed to Millions of Canadians," Industry Canada, News Release, Jan. 24, 2005, www.ic.gc.ca/cmb/welcomeic.nsf/cdd9dc973c4bf6bc852564ca006418a0/85256a5d0, accessed Sept. 23, 2007.

25. Paul E. Tracy and James A. Fox, "A Field Experiment on Insurance Fraud in Auto Body Repair," *Criminology*, **27** (1989): 589–603.

26. Kathleen F. Brickey, *Corporate Criminal Liability*, 2 vols. (Wilmette, Ill.: Callaghan, 1984). See also Thomas Gabor, *Everybody Does It! Crime by the Public* (Toronto: University of Toronto Press, 1994). For a uniquely British perspective, see Doreen McBarnet, "Whiter Than White Collar Crime: Tax, Fraud, Insurance and the Management of Stigma," *British Journal of Sociology*, **42** (1991): 323–344.

27. "Underground Economy," Building Construction and Trades Department. www.buildingtrades.ca/english/economy.html, accessed Oct. 28, 2007.

28. Lindsay Tedds, "The Underground Economy in Canada," in *Size, Causes, and Consequences of the Underground Economy*, eds. Chris Bajada and Friedrich Schneider (Aldershot, U.K.: Ashgate Publishing, 2005).

29. Ralph Salerno and John S. Tompkins, "Protecting Organized Crime," in *Theft of the City*, ed. John A. Gardiner and David Olson (Bloomington: Indiana University Press, 1984); Edwin Sutherland, *The Professional Thief* (Chicago: University of Chicago Press, 1937).

30. Bequai, *White Collar Crime*, p. 45.

31. "Convicted Killer Albert Walker Returning to Canada," CBC News, Feb. 23, 2005, www.cbc.ca/canada/story/2005/02/23/walker050223.html, accessed Oct. 29, 2007.

32. "Bank Manager Sentenced for $16 Million Fraud," CBC News, Sept. 10, 2004, www.cbc.ca/canada/story/2004/09/10/lysyk_sentence040910.html, accessed Oct. 30, 2007.

33. John Clark and Richard Hollinger, *Theft by Employees in Work Organization* (Washington, D.C.: U.S. Government Printing Office, 1983).

34. Bequai, *White Collar Crime*, p. 89.

35. Laureen Snider, "White Collar Crime," *The Canadian Encyclopedia Historica*, http://thecanadianencyclopedia.

com/PrinterFriendly.cfm?Params=A1ARTA0008557, accessed Sept. 21, 2007.

36. Ibid.

37. Ibid.

38. Laureen Snider, *Bad Business: Corporate Crime in Canada* (Scarborough: Nelson Canada, 1993), p. 1.

39. Charles E. Reasons, Lois L. Ross, and Craig Paterson, *Assault on the Worker: Occupational Health and Safety in Canada* (Toronto: Butterworths, 1981).

40. Nearly a century ago D. R. Richberg asked the question, "Should it not be the effort of all legislation dealing with corporations, to place them as nearly as possible on a plane of equal responsibility with individuals?" D. R. Richberg, "The Imprisonment of the Corporation," *Case and Comment*, **18** (1912): 512–529. Saul M. Pilchen discovered that although notions of corporate criminal culpability have been broadened over the years, initial prosecutions under the federal sentencing guidelines for organizations generally have been limited in scope. Saul M. Pilchen, "When Corporations Commit Crimes: Sentencing under the Federal Organizational Guidelines," *Judicature*, **78** (1995): 202–206. Daniel R. Fischel and Alan O. Sykes, "Corporate Crime," *The Journal of Legal Studies*, **xxv** (1996): 319–349. Ronald L. Dixon believes, "No corporation should be unaware of these statutes or of the theories upon which criminal liability can be established. Corporations must realize that no one is immune from criminal liability, and corporate practices must reflect this fact." Ronald L. Dixon, "Corporate Criminal Liability," in *Corporate Misconduct: The Legal, Societal, and Management Issues*, ed. Margaret P. Spencer and Ronald R. Sims (Westport, Conn.: Quorum Books, 1995). For a British perspective on corporate liability, see "Great Britain, The Law Commission," in *Criminal Law: Involuntary Manslaughter: A Consultation Paper*, no. 135 (London: Her Majesty's Stationery Office, 1994). For a general overview of the corporate crime problem, see Francis T. Cullen, William J. Maakestad, and Gray Cavender, *Corporate Crime under Attack: The Ford Pinto Case and Beyond* (Cincinnati: Anderson, 1987), pp. 37–99.

41. Snider, *Bad Business*.

42. Mark Dowie, "Pinto Madness," *Mother Jones*. Sept./Oct. (1977): 18–32.

43. Gary T. Schwartz, "The Myth of the Ford Pinto Case," *Rutgers Law Review*, **43** (1990–1991): 1013–1068.

44. Reasons, Ross, and Paterson, *Assault on the Worker*.

45. Shaun Comish, *The Westray Tragedy: A Miner's Story* (Halifax: Fernwood, 1993).

46. Richard Schaefer and Jana Grekul, *Sociology Matters*, Canadian ed. (Toronto: McGraw-Hill Ryerson, 2007), p. 307.

47. "Walkerton Marks Five Years Since Water Tragedy," Canadian Press, May 22, 2005, www.ctv.ca/servlet/ARticleNews/story/CTVNews/1116787827492_24/?hub = Health, accessed Nov. 1, 2007.

48. Schaefer and Grekul, *Sociology Matters*, p. 308.

49. "Fact Sheet: English-Wabigoon River Mercury Compensation," Indian and Northern Affairs Canada (INAC), www.ainc-inac.gc.ca/pr/info/ewr_e.html, accessed Nov. 1, 2007.

50. "The Real Walkerton Water Culprits Never Went to Court," Dec. 2004, www.nupage.ca/news_2004/n21de04a.htm, accessed Nov. 1, 2007.

51. "Walkerton Marks Five Years Since Water Tragedy."

52. C. W. Daniel Kirby, Radha Curpen, and Shawn Denstedt, "Environmental Law in Canada," June. 2006, www.osler.com/resources.aspx?id=8745, accessed Nov. 1, 2007.

53. Ibid.; Excerpted from Citizenworks, http://citizenworks.org/enron/accountinglaw.php.

54. Ibid.

55. Ryuichi Hirano, "The Criminal Law Protection of Environment: General Report," Tenth International Congress of Comparative Law, Budapest, 1978. For a discussion of the problems of multinational corporations operating in developing countries, see Richard Schaffer, Beverly Earle, and Filiberto Agusti, *International Business Law and Its Environment*, 2nd ed. (St. Paul, Minn.: West, 1993). For a discussion of corporate crime in Japan, see Harold R. Kerbo and Mariko Inoue, "Japanese Social Structure and White Collar Crime: Recruit Cosmos and Beyond," *Deviant Behavior*, **11** (1990): 139–154.

56. Joel Bakan, *The Corporation: The Pathological Pursuit of Profit and Power* (Toronto: Viking, 2004); Wade Rowland, *Greed Inc. Why Corporations Rule Our World and Why We Let It Happen* (Toronto: Thomas Allen, 2005).

57. Ibid.

58. James Hackler, *Canadian Criminology: Strategies and Perspectives*, 4th ed. (Toronto: Pearson Prentice Hall, 2007), p. 298.

59. Snider, "White Collar Crime."

60. Hackler, *Canadian Criminology*, p. 297.

61. Ibid, p. 295.

62. Ibid, p. 298.

63. Snider, "White Collar Crime

64. Christopher Stone, *Where the Law Ends: The Social Control of Corporate Behavior* (New York: Harper and Row, 1975); John Hagan, "Corporate and White-Collar Crime," in *Criminology: A Canadian Perspective*, 5th ed., ed. Rick Linden (Toronto: Thomson Nelson, 2004), p. 491.

65. Hackler, *Canadian Criminology*, p. 301.

66. Laura D'Andrea Tyson, "Glass Ceiling: What Holds Women Back: New Views," *BusinessWeek Online*, Oct. 28, 2003, www.businessweek.com/careers/content/oct2003/ca20031028_9217_ca011.htm, accessed Nov. 13, 2003; Schaefer and Grekul, *Sociology Matters*, p. 211.

67. Marshall Clinard and Peter Yeager, *Corporate Crime* (New York: Free Press, 1980).

68. See Edwin Sutherland, *White Collar Crime* (1946). Sutherland had earlier published articles on the topic, including "White Collar Criminality," *American Sociological Review*, **5** (1940): 1–12, and "Is White Collar Crime 'Crime'?" *American Sociological Review*, **10** (1945): 132–139; See Gary E. Reed and Peter Cleary Yeager, "Organizational Offending and Neoclassical Criminology: Challenging the Reach of a General Theory of Crime," *Criminology*, **34** (1996): 357–382; Clinard and Yeager, *Corporate Crime*, p. 116. See also Peter C. Yeager, "Analysing Corporate Offences: Progress and Prospects," *Research in Corporate Social Performance and Policy*, **8** (1986): 93–120. For similar findings in Canada, see Colin H. Goff and Charles E.

Reasons, *Corporate Crime in Canada* (Scarborough: Prentice-Hall, 1978); Richard Quinney, *Critique of Legal Order: Crime Control in Capitalist Society* (Boston: Little, Brown, 1974); Richard Quinney, *Class, State, and Crime: On the Theory and Practice of Criminal Justice* (New York: David McKay, 1977); Ian Taylor, Paul Walton, and Jock Young, *The New Criminology: For a Social Theory of Deviance* (London: Routledge & Kegan Paul, 1973); William Chambliss and Robert Seidman, *Law, Order, and Power*, 2nd ed. (Reading, Mass.: Addison-Wesley, 1982).

69. John Lehmann and Al Guart, "Ciao: Gotti Gang Gone," *New York Post*, June 21, 2002, p. 5. Reprinted with permission from *The New York Post*, 2002, copyright NYP Holdings, Inc.

70. Margaret E. Beare, *Criminal Conspiracies: Organized Crime in Canada* (Toronto: ITP Nelson, 1996), pp. 14–15.

71. Ibid.

72. Joe Kissell, "Down and Out in Moose Jaw," http://itotd.com/articles/423/the-tunnels-of-moose-jaw/, accessed Nov. 3, 2007.

73. O. D. Carrigan, *Crime and Punishment in Canada: A History* (Toronto: McClelland & Stewart, 1991).

74. Margaret E. Beare, *Criminal Conspiracies: Organized Crime in Canada* (Toronto: ITP Nelson, 1996).

75. Jay Albanese, *Organized Crime in America* (Cincinnati: Anderson, 1985), p. 25. See also Francis A. J. Ianni, *A Family Business: Kinship and Social Control in Organized Crime* (New York: Russell Sage, 1972); Joseph Albini, *The American Mafia: Genesis of a Legend* (New York: Irvington, 1971); Merry Morash, "Organized Crime," in *Major Forms of Crime*, ed. Robert F. Meier (Beverly Hills, Calif.: Sage, 1984), pp. 191–220. For a response, see Claire Sterling, *Octopus: The Long Reach of the International Sicilian Mafia* (New York: W. W. Norton, 1990); Ralph Blumenthal, *Last Days of the Sicilians: At War with the Mafia* (New York: Pocket Books, 1994). See also Shana Alexander, *The Pizza Connection* (New York: Weidenfeld & Nicolson, 1988).

76. Frederick Desroches, *Crime That Pays: Drug Trafficking and Organized Crime in Canada* (Toronto: Canadian Scholars Press, 2005).

77. For a description of the contemporary leadership of New York's five Italian-American organized-crime families, see Jeffrey Goldberg, "The Mafia's Morality Crisis," *New York Magazine*, Jan. 9, 1995, p. 22. See also Donald Cressey, *Theft of the Nation* (New York: Harper & Row, 1969).

78. Howard Abadinsky, *Organized Crime*, 2nd ed. (Chicago: Nelson Hall, 1985), pp. 8–23; Donald Cressey, in President's Commission, *Task Force Report*, pp. 7–8; Gay Talese, *Honor Thy Father* (New York: World, 1971).

79. James Walston, "Mafia in the Eighties," *Violence, Aggression, and Terrorism*, **1** (1987): 13–39. For a look into organized crime's once mighty and still lingering hand on gambling in the United States, see Jay Albanese, "Casino Gambling and Organized Crime: More Than Reshuffling the Deck," in Albanese, *Contemporary Issues in Organized Crime*; Ronald A. Farrelland and Carole Case, *The Black Book and the Mob: The Untold Story of the Control of Nevada's Casinos* (Madison: University of Wisconsin Press, 1995); Nicholas Pileggi, *Casino: Love and*

Honor in Las Vegas (New York: Simon & Schuster, 1995); David Johnston, *Temples of Chance: How America Inc. Bought Out Murder Inc. to Win Control of the Casino Business* (New York: Doubleday, 1992).

80. Criminal Intelligence Service of Canada, *Annual Report on Organized Crime* (2002, 2003, 2004, 2005, 2006, 2007), www.cisc.gc.ca, accessed Nov. 20, 2007.

81. Ibid.

82. Ibid.

83. "Biker Gangs in Canada," CBC News, *In Depth*, Apr. 5, 2007, www.cbc.ca/news/background/bikergangs, accessed Nov. 20, 2007.

84. E. J. Dickson-Gilmore, Jane Dickson-Gilmore, and Chris Whitehead, "Aboriginal Organized Crime in Canada: Developing a Typology for Understanding and Strategizing Responses," Research and Evaluation Branch (Ottawa: Royal Canadian Mounted Police, 2003).

85. Jana Grekul and Patti LaBoucane-Benson, "Aboriginal Gangs and Their (Dis)placement: Contexualizing Recruitment, Membership, and Status," *Canadian Journal of Criminology and Criminal Justice,* **50** (Jan. 2008).

86. Past efforts to develop civil and criminal causes of action against corporations are found in RICO legislation. See Racketeer Influenced and Corrupt Organizations (RICO) Provisions of the Organized Crime Control Act of 1970 [Act of Oct. 15, 1970, Public Law 91-452, Section 901(a), 84 Stat. 941, 18 U.S.C. §§ 1961 through 1968, effective Oct. 15, 1970, as amended Nov. 2, 1978, Public Law 95-575, Sec. 3(c), 92 Stat. 2465, and Nov. 6, 1978, Public Law 95-598, Sec. 314(g), 92 Stat. 2677]. For a discussion of the pros and cons of RICO, see Donald J. Rebovich, "Use and Avoidance of RICO at the Local Level: The Implementation of Organized Crime Laws," in *Contemporary Issues in Organized Crime,* ed. Jay Albanese (Monsey, N.Y.: Criminal Justice Press, 1995).

87. Fred Montanino, "Protecting Organized Crime Witnesses in the United States," *International Journal of Comparative and Applied Criminal Justice,* **14** (1990): 123–131.

Chapter 13

1. Christopher S. Wren, "A Pipeline of the Poor Feeds the Flow of Heroin," *New York Times,* Feb. 21, 1999, p. 37.

2. Arthur Santana, "For Liz, a Heroin User, Time Is Running Out—Health Officials Estimate 15,000 Addicts in King County," *Seattle Times,* July 12, 1999, p. B1.

3. David Heinzmann, "Violence No Stranger Where Boy Shot; 4-Year-Old Victim of Gun Battle in Good Condition," *Chicago Tribune,* Oct. 9, 1999, p. 5. See also Robert C. Davis and Arthur J. Lurigio, *Fighting Back: Neighborhood Antidrug Strategies* (Thousand Oaks, Calif.: Sage, 1996); Bureau of Justice Statistics, *Guns Used in Crime* (Washington, D.C.: U.S. Department of Justice, 1995); Susan J. Popkin, Lynn M. Olson, Arthur J. Lurigio, et al., "Sweeping Out Drugs and Crime: Residents' Views of the Chicago Housing Authority's Public Housing Drug Elimination Program," *Journal of Research in Crime and Delinquency,* **41** (1995): 73–99.

4. Mark D. Merlin, *On the Trail of the Ancient Opium Poppy* (Rutherford, N.J.: Fairleigh Dickinson University Press, 1984). For a historic account of alcohol consumption, see Harvey A. Siegal and James A. Inciardi, "A Brief History of Alcohol," in *The American Drug Scene: An Anthology,* ed. James A. Inciardi and Karen McElrath (Los Angeles: Roxbury, 1995).

5. Howard Abadinsky, *Drug Abuse: An Introduction* (Chicago: Nelson Hall, 1989), pp. 30–31, 54. For the medicinal benefits of marijuana, see Lester Grinspoon and James Bakalar, "Marijuana: The Forbidden Medicine," in Inciardi and McElrath, *The American Drug Scene.*

6. Michael D. Lyman, *Narcotics and Crime Control* (Springfield, Ill.: Charles C Thomas, 1987), p. 8. See also F. E. Oliver, "The Use and Abuse of Opium," in *Yesterday's Addicts: American Society and Drug Abuse, 1865–1920,* ed. H. Wayne Morgan (Norman: University of Oklahoma Press, 1974).

7. W. Z. Guggenheim, "Heroin: History and Pharmacology," *International Journal of the Addictions,* **2** (1967): 328. For a history of heroin use in New York City, from just after the turn of the twentieth century into the late 1960s, see Edward Preble and John J. Casey, "Taking Care of Business: The Heroin Addict's Life on the Street," *International Journal of the Addictions,* **4** (1969): 1–24.

8. Abadinsky, *Drug Abuse,* p. 52.

9. Shirley Small, "Canadian Narcotics Legislation, 1908–1923: A Conflict Model Interpretation," in *Law and Social Control in Canada,* eds. William K. Greenaway and Stephen L. Brickey (Scarborough, Ont.: Prentice-Hall Canada. 1978).

10. Ibid.

11. James Hackler, *Canadian Criminology: Strategies and Perspectives,* 4th ed. (Toronto: Pearson Prentice Hall, 2007), p. 175.

12. Controlled Drugs and Substances Act, http://laws.justice.gc.ca/en/showdoc/cs/C-38.8/bo-ga:1_I-gb:s_4//en, accessed Nov. 8, 2007.

13. Warren Silver, "Crime Statistics in Canada, 2006," Statistics Canada, Catalogue no. 85-002-XIE, vol. 27, no. 5.

14. David Patton and Edward M. Adlaf, "Cannabis Use and Problems," *Canadian Addiction Survey: A National Survey of Canadians' Use of Alcohol and Other Drugs: Prevalence of Use and Related Harms: Detailed Report* (Ottawa: Canadian Centre on Substance Abuse, 2005).

15. Ibid.

16. Ibid.

17. "Prevention and Punishment Focus of New Drug Law," CTV News, Oct. 4, 2007, www.ctv.ca/servlet/ArticleNews/print/CTVNews/20071003/anti-_drug_071004/2007, accessed Oct. 29, 2007.

18. Lisa Maher, Eloise Dunlap, Bruce D. Johnson, and Ansley Hamid, "Gender, Power, and Alternative Living Arrangements in the Inner-City Crack Culture," *Journal of Research in Crime and Delinquency,* **33** (1996): 181–205; H. Virginia McCoy, Christine Miles, and James A. Inciardi, "Survival Sex: Inner-City Women and Crack-Cocaine," in Inciardi and McElrath, *The American Drug Scene;* Jody Miller, "Gender and Power on the Streets: Street Prostitution in the Era of Crack Cocaine," *Journal of Contemporary Ethnography,* **23** (1995): 427–452; Ann Sorenson and David Brownfield, "Adolescent Drug Use and a General Theory of Crime: An Analysis of a Theoretical Integration," *Canadian Journal of Criminology,* **37** (1995): 19–37. For a summary of psychiatric approaches,

see Marie Nyswander, *The Drug Addict as a Patient* (New York: Grune & Stratton, 1956), chap. 4.

19. Richard Cloward and Lloyd Ohlin, *Delinquency and Opportunity* (New York: Free Press, 1960), pp. 178–186. See also Jeffrey A. Fagan, "The Social Organization of Drug Use and Drug Dealing among Urban Gangs," *Criminology,* **27** (1989): 633–669. See also Marcia R. Chaiken, *Identifying and Responding to New Forms of Drug Abuse: Lessons Learned from "Crack" and "Ice"* (Washington, D.C.: National Institute of Justice, 1993).

20. D. F. Musto, "The History of Legislative Control over Opium, Cocaine, and Their Derivatives," in Hamowy, *Dealing with Drugs.*

21. Marsha Rosenbaum, *Women on Heroin* (New Brunswick, N.J.: Rutgers University Press, 1981), pp. 14–15; Jeannette Covington, "Theoretical Explanations of Race Differences in Heroin Use," in *Advances in Criminological Theory,* vol. 2, ed. William S. Laufer and Freda Adler (New Brunswick, N.J.: Transaction). See also U.S. Senate Judiciary Committee, Subcommittee to Investigate Juvenile Delinquency, *The Global Connection: Heroin Entrepreneurs. Hearings, July 28 and August 5, 1976* (Washington, D.C.: U.S. Government Printing Office, 1976).

22. Freda Adler, Arthur D. Moffett, Frederick G. Glaser, John C. Ball, and Diana Horwitz, *A Systems Approach to Drug Treatment* (Philadelphia: Dorrance, 1974).

23. Norman E. Zinberg, "The Use and Misuse of Intoxicants: Factors in the Development of Controlled Abuse," in Hamowy, *Dealing with Drugs,* p. 262.

24. Abadinsky, *Drug Abuse,* p. 53. See also, as an early treatment, Hope R. Victor, Jan Carl Grossman, and Russell Eisenman, "Openness to Experience and Marijuana Use in High School Students," *Journal of Consulting and Clinical Psychology,* **41** (1973): 78–85; U.S. Narcotics and Dangerous Drugs Bureau, *Marijuana: An Analysis of Use, Distribution and Control* (Washington, D.C.: U.S. Government Printing Office, 1971); California Department of Public Health and Welfare, Research and Statistics Section, *Five Mind-Altering Drugs: The Use of Alcoholic Beverages, Amphetamines, LSD, Marijuana, and Tobacco, Reported by High School and Junior High School Students, San Mateo County, California, Two Comparable Surveys, 1968 and 1969* (San Mateo: California Department of Public Health, 1969); Erich Goode, "Multiple Drug Use among Marijuana Smokers," *Social Problems,* **17** (1969): 48–64.

25. Bruce A. Jacobs, "Crack Dealers' Apprehension Avoidance Techniques: A Case of Restrictive Deterrence," *Justice Quarterly,* **13** (1996): 359–381; Bruce A. Jacobs, "Crack Dealers and Restrictive Deterrences: Identifying Narcs," *Criminology,* **34** (1996): 409–431; Bruce D. Johnson, Andrew Golub, and Jeffrey Fagan, "Careers in Crack, Drug Use, Drug Distribution, and Nondrug Criminality," *Journal of Crime and Delinquency,* **41** (1995): 275–295; Abadinsky, *Drug Abuse,* p. 83. See also Jeffrey A. Fagan, "Initiation into Crack and Powdered Cocaine: A Tale of Two Epidemics," *Contemporary Drug Problems,* **16** (1989): 579–618; Jeffrey A. Fagan, Joseph G. Weis, and Y. T. Cheng, "Drug Use and Delinquency among Inner City Youth," *Journal of Drug Issues,* **20** (1990): 349–400; and James A. Inciardi et al., "The Crack Epidemic Revisited,"

Journal of Psychoactive Drugs, **24** (1992): 305–416. See also B. D. Johnson, M. Natarajan, E. Dunlap, and E. Elmoghazy, "Crack Abusers and Noncrack Abusers: A Comparison of Drug Use, Drug Sales, and Nondrug Criminality," *Journal of Drug Issues,* **24** (1994): 117–141. Smoking crack is certainly not limited to the inner cities of America. For a description of crack use in the tropical paradise of Hawaii, see Gordon James Knowles, "Dealing Crack Cocaine: A View from the Streets of Honolulu," *The FBI Law Enforcement Bulletin,* July 1996: 1–7.

26. Michael Marriott, "Potent Crack Blend on the Streets Lures a New Generation to Heroin," *New York Times,* July 13, 1989, pp. A1, B3.

27. "Trends in Drug Offences and the Role of Alcohol and Drugs in Crime," *The Daily,* Feb. 23, 2004, www.statcan.ca/Daily.English/040223/d040223a.htm, accessed Oct. 29, 2007.

28. Kai Pernanen, Marie-Marthe Cousineau, Serge Brochu, and Fu Sun, *Proportions of Crimes Associated with Alcohol and Other Drugs in Canada* (Ottawa: Canadian Centre on Substance Abuse, 2002).

29. "Trends in Drug Offences and the Role of Alcohol and Drugs in Crime."

30. For a determination of the causal link between drug use and crime, see Bruce L. Benson and David W. Rasmussen, *Illicit Drugs and Crimes* (Oakland, Calif.: The Independent Institute, 1996); James A. Inciardi, Duane C. McBride, and James E. Rivers, *Drug Control and the Courts* (Thousand Oaks, Calif.: Sage, 1996); Inciardi and McElrath, *The American Drug Scene;* Sybille M. Guy, Gene M. Smith, and P. M. Bentler, "The Influence of Adolescent Substance Use and Socialization on Deviant Behavior in Young Adulthood," *Criminal Justice and Behavior,* **21** (1994): 236–255.

31. George Speckart and M. Douglas Anglin found that criminal records preceded drug use; see their "Narcotics Use and Crime: An Overview of Recent Research Advances," *Contemporary Drug Problems,* **13** (1986): 741–769, and "Narcotics and Crime: A Causal Modeling Approach," *Journal of Quantitative Criminology,* **2** (1986): 3–28. See also Cheryl Carpenter, Barry Glassner, Bruce D. Johnson, and Julia Loughlin, *Kids, Drugs, and Crime* (Lexington, Mass.: Heath, 1988). See also Louise L. Biron, Serge Brochu, and Lyne Desjardins, "The Issue of Drugs and Crime among a Sample of Incarcerated Women," *Deviant Behavior,* **16** (1995): 25–43.

32. James A. Inciardi and Anne E. Pottieger, "Kids, Crack, and Crime," *Journal of Drug Issues,* **21** (1991): 257–270; David N. Nurco, Thomas E. Hanlon, Timothy W. Kinlock, and Karen R. Duszynski, "Differential Criminal Patterns of Narcotics Addicts over an Addiction Career," *Criminology,* **26** (1988): 407–423; M. Douglas Anglin and George Speckart, "Narcotics Use and Crime: A Multisample, Multimethod Analysis," *Criminology,* **26** (1988): 197–233; M. Douglas Anglin and Yining Hser, "Addicted Women and Crime," *Criminology,* **25** (1987): 359–397.

33. Paul Goldstein, "Drugs and Violent Crime," in *Pathways to Criminal Violence,* ed. Neil Alan Weiner and Marvin E. Wolfgang (Newbury Park, Calif.: Sage, 1989), pp. 16–48.

34. This section is based on Inciardi, *The War on Drugs.* See also Fernando Cepeda Ulloa, "International Cooperation and the War on Drugs," in *Drug Trafficking in the Americas,* ed. Bruce M. Bagley and William O. Walker III (Coral Gables, Fla.: North-South Center Press, University of Miami, 1996); Ronald Kessler, *The FBI* (New York: Pocket Books, 1993); *United States v. Celio,* 945 F.2d 180 (7th Cir. 1991), where the U.S. Court of Appeals for the Seventh Circuit acknowledged the need for a concerted effort on behalf of various law enforcement agencies to combat international drug-trafficking cartels.

35. Office of National Drug Control Policy, *Source Countries and Drug Transit Zones: Colombia* (Washington, D.C.: U.S. Government Printing Office, 2002).

36. *The Illicit Drug Situation in the United States and Canada* (Ottawa: Royal Canadian Mounted Police, 1984–1986), p. 19. See also William Gately and Yvette Fernandez, *Dead Ringer: An Insider's Account of the Mob's Colombian Connection* (New York: Donald I. Fine, 1994).

37. Douglas Belkin, "Canada's Tolerance on Marijuana Fades," *The Wall Street Journal,* Jan. 11, 2008, http://thefilter.ca/articles/canada/canadas-tolerance-on-marijuana-fades/, accessed Apr. 3, 2008.

38. Ibid.

39. Ibid.

40. "Canadian-Made, Meth-Laced Ecstasy Being Dumped into U.S. Illegal Drug Markets," Office of National Drug Control Policy New & Public Affairs, Press Release, Jan. 3, 2008, www.whitehousedrugpolicy.gov/news/press08/010308.html, accessed Apr. 3, 2008.

41. Adrian Humphreys, "Altered Ecstasy from Canada flooding U.S," *National Post,* Jan. 4, 2008, www.national-post.com/story-printer.html?id=213805, accessed Apr. 3, 2008.

42. Michael Chettleburgh, Public Forum on Gang Prevention, University of Alberta, March 26, 2008.

43. Criminal Intelligence Service of Canada, *Annual Report on Organized Crime.* (2002, 2003, 2004, 2005, 2006, 2007), www.cisc.gc.ca, accessed Nov. 20, 2007.

44. United Nations, "Commission on Narcotic Drugs, Comprehensive Review of the Activities of the United Nations Fund for Drug Abuse Control in 1985," E/CN.7/1986/CRP.4, Feb. 4, 1986. See also Elaine Sciolino, "U.N. Report Links Drugs, Arms, and Terror," *New York Times,* Jan. 12, 1987.

45. John Warner, "Terrorism and Drug Trafficking: A Lethal Partnership," *Security Management,* **28** (1984): 44–46. See, as an early treatment, U.S. Congress, House Public Health and Environment Subcommittee, *Production and Abuse of Opiates in the Far East* (Washington, D.C.: U.S. Government Printing Office, 1971).

46. "Canada's Anti-Drug Strategy a Failure, Study Suggests," CBC News, Jan. 15, 2007, www.cbc.ca/canada/story/2007/01/15/drug-strategy.html, accessed Oct. 29, 2007.

47. "Prevention and Punishment Focus of New Drug Law," CTV.ca, Oct. 4, 2007, www.ctv.ca/servlet/ArticleNews/print/CTV News/20071003/anti_drug_071004/2007, accessed Oct. 29, 2007.

48. Douglas Belkin, "Canada's Tolerance on Marijuana Fades," *The Wall Street Journal,* Jan. 11, 2008, http://thefilter.ca/articles/canada/canadas-tolerance-on-marijuana-fades/, accessed Apr. 3, 2008.

49. "Prevention and Punishment Focus of New Drug Law."

50. "Canada's Anti-Drug Strategy a Failure, Study Suggests."

51. Even before President Bush's drug initiatives, U.S. government agencies recognized the ineffectiveness of narcotic countermeasures during the 1970s; see U.S. Comptroller General, *Gains Made in Controlling Illegal Drugs, Yet the Drug Trade Flourishes* (Washington, D.C.: U.S. Government Printing Office, 1979).

52. "Prevention and Punishment Focus of New Drug Law."

53. See Rae Sibbitt, *The Ilps Methadone Prescribing Project* (London: Home Office, 1996); Paul J. Turnbull, Russell Webster, and Gary Stillwell, *Get It While You Can: An Evaluation of an Early Intervention Project for Arrestees with Alcohol and Drug Problems* (London: Home Office, 1996); Ira Sommers, Deborah R. Baskin, and Jeffrey Fagan, "Getting out of the Life: Crime Desistance by Female Street Offenders," *Deviant Behavior,* **15** (1994): 125–149; Sandra L. Tunis, *The State of the Art in Jail Drug Treatment Programs* (San Francisco: National Council on Crime and Delinquency, 1994).

54. "Government of Canada Announces New Drug Treatment Courts," Health Canada, June 4, 2005, www.medicalnewstoday.com/articles/25626.php, accessed Nov. 13, 2007; "Calgary Drug Court Set to Open Next Month," CBC News, Apr. 9, 2007, www.cbc.ca/canada/edmonton/story/200704/09/drug-court.html, accessed Nov. 13, 2007; Mike Sadava, "Conference's Goal to Improve Drug Courts," *Edmonton Journal,* Oct. 15, 2006, www.canada.com/components/print.aspx?id=4a636eab-5750-4901-aa7b-cfe702bf1, accessed Nov. 13, 2007.

55. Abadinsky, *Drug Abuse,* p. 171.

56. David N. Nurco, Norma Wegner, Philip Stephenson, Abraham Makofsky, and John W. Shaffer, *Ex-Addicts' Self-Help Groups: Potentials and Pitfalls* (New York: Praeger, 1983); Harold I. Hendler and Richard C. Stephens, "The Addict Odyssey: From Experimentation to Addiction," *International Journal of the Addictions,* **12** (1977): pp. 25–42.

57. For a perspective on how corporate America educates employees on the risks of drug abuse, see Mark A. de Bernardo, *What Every Employee Should Know about Drug Abuse* (Washington, D.C.: Institute for a Drug-Free Workplace, 1993); Troy Duster, *The Legislation of Morality: Law, Drugs, and Moral Judgment* (New York: Free Press, 1970), p. 192.

58. Dan Waldorf, "Natural Recovery from Opiate Addiction," *Journal of Drug Issues,* **13** (1983): 237–280.

59. "Canada's Anti-Drug Strategy a Failure, Study Suggests."

60. See James A. Inciardi, Duane C. McBride, Clyde B. McCoy, et al., "Violence, Street Crime and the Drug Legalization Debate: A Perspective and Commentary on the U.S. Experience," *Studies on Crime and Crime Prevention,* **4** (1995): 105–118; Steven Foy Luper, Curtis Brown, et al., *Drugs, Morality, and the Law* (New York: Garland, 1994); Robert J. MacCoun, James P. Kahan, and James Gillespie, "A Content Analysis of the Drug Legalization Debate," *Journal of Drug Issues,* **23** (1993):

615–629; Arnold S. Trebach and James A. Inciardi, *Legalize It? Debating American Drug Policy* (Washington, D.C.: American University Press, 1993).

61. Hackler, *Canadian Criminology*, p. 182.

62. Pat O'Malley and Stephen Mugford, "The Demand for Intoxicating Commodities: Implications for the 'War on Drugs,'" *Social Justice*, **18** (1991): 49–74.

63. E. M. Adlaf, P. Begin, and E. Sawka, eds., *Canadian Addiction Survey (CAS): A National Survey of Canadians' Use of Alcohol and Other Drugs: Prevalence of Use and Related Harms: Detailed Report* (Ottawa: Canadian Centre on Substance Abuse, 2005).

64. James Inciardi, *Reflections on Crime* (New York: Holt, Rinehart & Winston, 1978), pp. 8–10. For an even earlier perspective, see Herbert Berger and Andrew A. Eggston, "Should We Legalize Narcotics?" *Coronet*, **38** (June 1995): 30–34.

65. Correctional Service of Canada, "Our Agenda," Addictions Research, http://198.103.98.138/text/rsrch/addictions/index_e.shtml, accessed Nov. 14, 2007.

66. National Crime Prevention Council, "Substance Abuse: Offender Profiles," Public Health Agency of Canada, Sept. 1995, www.phac-aspc.gc.ca/ncfv-cnivf/family-violence/html/fcprofil_e.html, accessed Nov. 14, 2007.

67. Kai Pernanen, Marie-Marthe Cousineau, Serge Brochu, and Fu Sun, *Proportions of Crimes Associated with Alcohol and Other Drugs in Canada* (Ottawa: Canadian Centre on Substance Abuse, 2002).

68. Norm Desjardins and Tina Hotton, "Trends in Drug Offences and the Role of Alcohol and Drugs in Crime," *Juristat*, Statistics Canada, Catalogue no. 85-002-XPE, vol. 24, no.1, 2004.

69. V. P. Bunge and A. Levett, *Family Violence: A Statistical Profile* (Ottawa: Statistics Canada, Ministry of Industry, 1998).

70. See Maggie Sumner and Howard Parker, *Law in Alcohol: A Review of International Research into Alcohol's Role in Crime Causation* (Manchester, U.K.: Department of Social Policy and Social Work, University of Manchester, 1995); Klaus A. Miczek et al., "Alcohol, Drugs of Abuse, Aggression, and Violence," in *Understanding and Preventing Violence*, ed. Albert J. Reiss Jr. and Jeffrey A. Roth (Washington, D.C.: National Academy Press, 1993).

71. K. E. Leonard, "Alcohol and Human Physical Aggression," *Aggression*, **2** (1983): 77–101. See also Matthew W. Lewis, Jon F. Merz, Ron D. Hays, et al., "Perceptions of Intoxication and Impairment at Arrest among Adults Convicted of Driving under the Influence of Alcohol," *Journal of Drug Issues*, **25** (1995): 141–160.

72. C. M. Steele and L. Southwick, "Alcohol and Social Behavior: I. The Psychology of Drunken Excess," *Journal of Personality and Social Psychology*, **48** (1985): 18–34. See also Peter B. Wood, John K. Cochran, Betty Pfefferbaum, et al., "Sensation-Seeking and Delinquent Substance Use: An Extension of Learning Theory," *Journal of Drug Issues*, **25** (1995): 173–193.

73. S. Ahlstrom-Laakso, "European Drinking Habits: A Review of Research and Time Suggestions for Conceptual Integration of Findings," in *Cross-Cultural Approaches to the Study of Alcohol*, ed. M. W. Everett, J. O. Waddell, and D. Heath (The Hague: Mouton, 1976).

74. Alcohol Policy Network, "Statistical Overview of Alcohol Use," www.apolnet.ca/resources/stats/stats_overview_html, accessed Oct. 30, 2007.

75. Silver, "Crime Statistics in Canada, 2006."

76. Jacobs, *Drunk Driving*, p. xvi.

77. Brandon K. Applegate, Francis T. Cullen, Bruce G. Link, Pamela J. Richards, and Lonn Lanza-Kaduce, "Determinants of Public Punitiveness toward Drunk Driving: A Factorial Survey Approach," *Justice Quarterly*, **13** (1996): 57–79; Stephen D. Mastrofski and R. Richard Ritti, "Police Training and the Effects of Organization on Drunk Driving Enforcement," *Justice Quarterly*, **13** (1996): 291–320.

78. *The Effectiveness of the Ignition Interlock Device in Reducing Recidivism among Driving under the Influence Cases* (Honolulu: Criminal Justice Commission, 1987).

79. "Same-Sex Right," CBC News, Indepth, March 1, 2007, www.cbc.ca/news/background/samesexrights/timeline_canada.html, accessed Nov. 21, 2007.

80. See Michel Dorais, *Rent Boys* (Montreal: McGill-Queen's University Press, 2005), which explores the life experiences of male prostitutes.

81. Silver, "Crime Statistics in Canada, 2006."

82. See Cudore L. Snell, *Young Men in the Street: Help-Seeking Behavior of Young Male Prostitutes* (Westport, Conn.: Praeger, 1995); Sari van der Poel, "Solidarity as Boomerang: The Fiasco of the Prostitutes' Rights Movement in the Netherlands," *Crime, Law and Social Change*, **23** (1995): 41–65; Barbara Sherman Heyl, "The Madam as Teacher: The Training of House Prostitutes," in *Deviant Behavior*, ed. Delos H. Kelly (New York: St. Martin's Press, 1993); Sari van der Poel, "Professional Male Prostitution: A Neglected Phenomenon," *Crime, Law, and Social Change*, **18** (1992): 259–275; David F. Luckenbill, "Deviant Career Mobility: The Case of Male Prostitutes," *Social Problems*, **33** (1986): 283–296.

83. Doreen Duchesne, "Street Prostitution in Canada," *Juristat*, Statistics Canada, 1996, Catalogue no. 85-002-XPE Vol. 17, no. 2.

84. Ibid.; "Street Prostitution" Federal/Provincial Working Group on Prostitution: Report and Recommendations in Respect of Legislation, Policy, and Practices Concerning Prostitution-related Activities," Dec. 1998, Department of Justice Canada, www.justice.gc.ca/en/news/nr/1998/part3.html.

85. Ibid.

86. Jeremiah Lowney, Robert W. Winslow, and Virginia Winslow, *Deviant Reality—Alternative World Views*, 2nd ed. (Boston: Allyn and Bacon, 1981), p. 156. For a law enforcement perspective on countering prostitution in New York City, where female undercover police officers are used to seek out the patrons of prostitutes, see Dean Chang, "Dear John, It's a Bust: Cops Target Sex Clients," *New York Daily News*, June 26, 1994, p. 10.

87. Bureau of Justice Statistics, *HIV in Prisons 1994* (Washington, D.C.: U.S. Department of Justice, 1996); Bureau of Justice Statistics, *HIV in Prisons and Jails, 1993* (Washington, D.C.: U.S. Department of Justice, 1995);

James A. Inciardi, Anne E. Pottieger, Mary Ann Forney, et al., "Prostitution, IV Drug Use, and Sex-for-Crack Exchanges among Serious Delinquents: Risks for HIV Infection," *Criminology*, **29** (1991): 221–236; Joseph B. Kuhns III and Kathleen M. Heide, "AIDS-Related Issues among Female Prostitutes and Female Arrestees," *International Journal of Offender Therapy and Comparative Criminology*, **36** (1992): 231–245; David J. Bellis, "Reduction of AIDS Risk among 41 Heroin Addicted Female Street Prostitutes: Effects of Free Methadone Maintenance," *Journal of Addictive Diseases*, **12** (1993): 7–23; L. Maher and R. Curtis, "Women on the Edge of Crime: Crack Cocaine and the Changing Contexts of Street-Level Sex Work in New York City," *Crime, Law, and Social Change*, **18** (1992): 221–258; Edward V. Morse, Patricia M. Simon, Stephanie A. Baus, et al., "Cofactors of Substance Use among Male Street Prostitutes," *Journal of Drug Issues*, **22** (1992): 977–994.

88. Sarah Bromberg, "Feminist Issues in Prostitution," www.feministissues.com/, accessed Apr. 3, 2008.

89. Ibid.

90. Ibid.

91. R. Karl Hanson, Heather Scott, and Richard A. Steffy, "A Comparison of Child Molesters and Nonsexual Criminals: Risk Predictors and Long-Term Recidivism," *Journal of Research in Crime and Delinquency*, **32** (1995): 325–337; Dennis Howitt, *Paedophiles and Sexual Offences against Children* (Chichester, U.K.: Wiley, 1995); Human Rights Watch: Asia, *Rape for Profit: Trafficking of Nepali Girls and Women to India's Brothels* (New York: Human Rights Watch, 1995).

92. Edward Donnerstein et al., *The Question of Pornography: Final Report of the Attorney General's Commission on Pornography* (Nashville, Tenn.: Rutledge Hill Press, 1986), p. 147.

93. For the now famous Justice Potter Stewart comment on pornography, where he couldn't truly define obscenity, but stated he knew it when he saw it, see *Jacobellis v. Ohio*, 378 U.S. 184 (1964). Joel Feinberg, "Pornography and Criminal Law," in *Pornography and Censorship*, ed. D. Copp and S. Wendell (New York: Prometheus, 1979).

94. Donald A. Downs, "Pornography," *Encarta Online Encyclopedia*, 2007, http://encarta.msn.com.

95. "Landslide," CBC News, *The Fifth Estate*, Nov. 5, 2003, www.cbc.ca/fifth/landslide/laws_printer.html, accessed Oct. 29, 2007.

96. The Report of the Commission on Obscenity and Pornography; R. A. Barron and P. A. Bell, "Sexual Arousal and Aggression by Males: Effects of Type of Erotic Stimuli and Prior Provocation," *Journal of Personality and Social Psychology*, **35** (1977): 79–87. For a more current study, see Scot B. Boeringer, "Pornography and Sexual Aggression: Associations of Violent and Nonviolent Depictions with Rape and Rape Proclivity," *Deviant Behavior*, **15** (1994): 289–304; Dolf Zillman and Jennings Bryant, "Pornography, Sexual Callousness, and the Trivialization of Rape," *Journal of Communication*, **32** (1984): 10–21. See also Berl Kutchinsky, "Evidence Proves That Pornography Does Not Promote

Rape," in the Current Controversies series, *Violence against Women,* ed. Karin L. Swisher, Carol Wekesser, and William Barbour (San Diego: Greenhaven Press, 1994); Cynthia S. Gentry, "Pornography and Rape: An Empirical Analysis," *Deviant Behavior,* **12** (1991): 277–288.

97. Donnerstein et al., *The Question of Pornography,* esp. pp. 38–47. See also Swisher, Wekesser, and Barbour, *Violence Against Women;* Myriam Miedzian, "How Rape Is Encouraged in American Boys and What We Can Do to Stop It," in *Transforming a Rape Culture,* ed. Emilie Buchwald, Pamela R. Fletcher, and Martha Roth (Minneapolis: Milkweed Editions, 1993); Judith A. Reisman, *Images of Children, Crime and Violence in* Playboy, Penthouse *and* Hustler (Washington, D.C.: Office of Juvenile Justice and Delinquency Prevention, Office of Justice Assistance, Research and Statistics, U.S. Department of Justice, 1990).

98. Joan Hoff, "Why Is There No History of Pornography?" in *For Adult Users Only: The Dilemma of Violent Pornography,* ed. Susan Gubar and Joan Hoff (Bloomington: Indiana University Press, 1989), p. 18. See also Franklin Mark Osanka and Sara Lee Johann, "Pornography Contributes to Violence against Women," in Swisher, Wekesser, and Barbour, *Violence against Women.*

99. Wendy McElroy, "A Feminist Overview of Pornography, Ending in a Defense Thereof," www.zetetics.com/mac/freeinqu.htm, accessed Apr. 3, 2008.

100. Ibid.

101. Ibid.

102. "Landslide," CBC News, *The Fifth Estate,* Nov. 5, 2003, www.cbc.ca/fifth/landslide/laws_printer.html, accessed Oct. 29, 2007.

103. Ibid.

104. Ibid.

105. Laura Davis, Marilyn D. McShane, and Frank P. Williams III, "Controlling Computer Access to Pornography: Special Conditions for Sex Offenders," *Federal Probation,* **59** (1995): 43–48; Marty Rimm, "Marketing Pornography on the Information Superhighway: A Survey of 917,410 Images, Descriptions, Short Stories and Animations Downloaded 8.5 Million Times by Consumers in Over 2,000 Cities in Forty Countries, Provinces, and Territories," *Georgetown Law Journal,* **83** (1995): 1849–2008; Great Britain House of Commons, *Computer Pornography* (London: Her Majesty's Stationery Office, 1994). For a perspective on the government's plan to police the Internet's superhighway, see James Aley, "How Not to Help High Tech," *Fortune Magazine,* May 16, 1994, p. 100.

106. "Child Porn Tip Line Launches Nationwide," CTV News, Jan. 24, 2005, www.ctv.ca/servlet/ArticleNews/print/CTVNews/20050124/child_porn_tipline_05, accessed Oct. 30, 2007.

107. Josh Rubin, "Teacher, Doctor Nabbed in Porn Probe: Police Make Plea for Resources to Stop Spread of 'Evil'," Jan. 16, 2003, TheStar.com, www.cyber-rights.org/reports/child.htm, accessed Oct. 30, 2007.

108. "Child Porn Tip Line Launches Nationwide," CTV News.

109. Michael Geist, "Child Pornography Blocking Plan a Risk Worth Taking," Dec. 4, 2006, www.michaelgeist.ca, accessed Oct. 30, 2007.

Chapter 14

1. Peter Applebome, "Skinhead Violence Grows, Experts Say," *New York Times*, July 18, 1993, p. 25; A. P. Kamath, "Would-be 'God' Sentenced for Murder," Rediff on the Net, Nov. 17, 1999, www.rediff.com/news/1999/nov/17us1.htm, accessed Apr. 10, 2008.

2. *The Skinhead International: A World-Wide Survey of Neo-Nazi Skinheads* (New York: Anti-Defamation League of B'nai B'rith, 1995).

3. Jane Kramer, "Neo-Nazis: A Chaos in the Head," *New Yorker*, July 14, 1993, pp. 52–70, at p. 53. See also Marie C. Douglas, "Ausländer Raus! Nazi Raus! An Observation of German Skins and Jugendgangen," *International Journal of Comparative and Applied Criminal Justice*, **16** (1992): 129–134.

4. John Leland and Marcus Mabry, "Toasting the 'Head,' " *Newsweek*, Feb. 26, 1996, pp. 42–43.

5. Mark S. Hamm, *American Skinheads—The Criminology and Control of Hate Crime* (Westport, Conn.: Praeger, 1993).

6. Piers Beirne and David Nelken, eds., *Issues in Comparative Criminology* (Aldershot, U.K.: Dartmouth, 1997), is a useful anthology of scientific issues in comparative criminology.

7. The term "comparative criminology" appears to have been coined by Sheldon Glueck. See Sheldon Glueck, "Wanted: A Comparative Criminology," in *Ventures in Criminology*, ed. Sheldon Glueck and Eleanor Glueck (London: Tavistock, 1964), pp. 304–322.

8. James O. Finckenauer, *Russian Youth: Law, Deviance and the Pursuit of Freedom* (New Brunswick, N.J.: Transaction, 1995); Nanci Adler, "Planned Economy and Unplanned Criminality: The Soviet Experience," *International Journal of Comparative and Applied Criminal Justice*, **17** (1993): 189–201; Wojciech Cebulak, "White-Collar Crime in Socialism: Myth or Reality?" *International Journal of Comparative and Applied Criminal Justice*, **15** (1991): 109–120; Klaus Sessar, "Crime Rate Trends before and after the End of the German Democratic Republic—Impressions and First Analyses," in *Fear of Crime and Criminal Victimization*, ed. Wolfgang Bilsky, Christian Pfeiffer, and Peter Wetzels (Stuttgart, Germany: Ferdinand Enke Verlag, 1993), pp. 231–244; Louise I. Shelley et al., "East Meets West in Crime," *European Journal on Criminal Policy and Research*, 3 (1995): 7–107. As China is undergoing a transformation, mostly economic, changes in that country are noteworthy. See Yue Ma, "Crime in China: Characteristics, Causes and Control Strategies," *Journal of Comparative and Applied Criminal Justice*, 34 (1994): 54–68.

9. Martin Kilias et al., "Cross-Border Crime," *European Journal on Criminal Policy and Research*, 1 (1993): 7–134.

10. William F. McDonald, "The Globalization of Criminology: The New Frontier Is the Frontier," *Transnational Organized Crime*, 1 (1995): 1–12.

11. Piers Beirne and Joan Hill, *Comparative Criminology—An Annotated Bibliography* (New York: Greenwood, 1991), pp. vii–viii.

12. See especially Albert P. Blaustein and G. H. Flenz, *Constitutions of the Countries of the World*, 21 vols. (updated) (Dobbs Ferry, N.Y.: Oceana, 1971 and continuing).

13. The Comparative Criminal Law Project at Wayne State University Law School (formerly at New York University School of Law) has published 21 criminal codes in *The American Series of Foreign Penal Codes*, ed. G. O. W. Mueller, cont. by Edward M. Wise (Littleton, Colo.: Fred B. Rothman, since 1960); G. O. W. Mueller and Fré Le Poole Griffiths, *Comparative Criminal Procedure* (New York: New York University Press, 1969); Albin Eser and George Fletcher, *Justification and Excuse—Comparative Perspectives*, 2 vols. (Freiburg, Germany: Max Planck Institut, 1987); Edward M. Wise and G. O. W. Mueller, eds., *Studies in Comparative Criminal Law*, Comparative Criminal Law Project Publications Series, vol. 9 (Littleton, Colo.: Fred B. Rothman, 1975); Marc Ancel, *Social Defense: The Future of Penal Reform*, Comparative Criminal Law Project Publications Series, vol. 16 (Littleton, Colo.: Fred B. Rothman, 1987). For a historical survey, see G. O. W. Mueller, *Comparative Criminal Law in the United States*, Comparative Criminal Law Project Monograph Series, vol. 4 (South Hackensack, N.J.: Fred B. Rothman, 1970).

14. Seven codes of criminal procedure have appeared in Mueller and Wise, *The American Series of Foreign Penal Codes*.

15. E.g., Shigemitsu Dando, *Japanese Criminal Procedure*, Comparative Criminal Law Project Publications Series, vol. 4 (Littleton, Colo.: Fred B. Rothman, 1965).

16. UNAFEI, 1–26 Harumicho, Fuchu, Tokyo, Japan. There are now 51 volumes.

17. Kristiina Kangaspunta, ed., *Profiles of Criminal Justice Systems in Europe and North America* (Helsinki: HEUNI, 1995); Matti Joutsen, *Criminal Justice Systems in Europe: Finland* (Helsinki: HEUNI, 1995).

18. Dae H. Chang, *Criminology: A Cross-Cultural Perspective*, 2 vols. (Durham, N.C.: Carolina Academic Press, 1976); George F. Cole, Stanislaw J. Frankowski, and Marc G. Gertz, *Major Criminal Justice Systems—A Comparative Survey*, 2nd ed. (Newbury Park, Calif.: Sage, 1987); Richard J. Terrill, *World Criminal Justice Systems*, 2nd ed. (Cincinnati: Anderson, 1985); Robert Heiner, ed., *Criminology—A Cross-Cultural Perspective* (Minneapolis/St. Paul: West, 1996); Obi N. I. Ebbe, ed., *Comparative and International Criminal Justice Systems* (Boston: Butterworth-Heinemann, 1996); Charles B. Fields and Richter H. Moore, eds., *Comparative Criminal Justice: Traditional and Non-traditional Systems of Law and Control* (Prospect Heights, Ill.: Waveland Press, 1996).

19. V. Lorne Stewart, *Justice and Troubled Children around the World*, vols. 1–5 (New York: New York University Press, 1980–1983).

20. David H. Bayley, *Patterns of Policing—A Comparative International Analysis* (New Brunswick, N.J.: Rutgers University Press, 1985).

21. Roy Walmsley, *Prison Systems in Central and Eastern Europe* (Helsinki: HEUNI, 1996).

22. Freda Adler, ed., *The Incidence of Female Criminality in the Contemporary World* (New York: New York University Press, 1984).

23. Marshall B. Clinard, *Cities with Little Crime: The Case of Switzerland* (London: Cambridge University Press, 1978).

24. Louise I. Shelley, *Crime and Modernization: The Impact of Industrialization and Urbanization on Crime* (Carbondale: Southern Illinois University Press, 1981).

25. William Clifford, *Crime Control in Japan* (Lexington, Mass.: Lexington Books, 1976).

26. G. O. W. Mueller, *World Survey on the Availability of Criminal Justice Statistics*, Internet-UNCJIN-ftp238.33.18WSAYL. See also G. O. W. Mueller, "International Criminal Justice: Harnessing the Information Explosion—Coasting Down the Electronic Superhighway," *Journal of Criminal Justice Education* **7**(2) (Fall 1996): 253–261.

27. Interpol, located in Lyons, France, has published the crime statistics supplied to it by member states since 1951.

28. First survey: 1970–1975, A/32/199; second survey: 1975–1980, A/Conf. 121/18; third survey: 1980–1986, A/Conf. 144/6; fourth survey: 1986–1990, A/Conf. 169/15 and Add. 1; fifth survey (see United Nations, *Global Report on Crime and Justice*). See "Window to the World" in Chapter 2.

29. World Health Organization, "Homicide Statistics," in *World Health Statistics* (Geneva: World Health Organization, annually).

30. Dane Archer and Rosemary Gartner, *Violence and Crime in Cross-National Perspective* (New Haven, Conn.: Yale University Press, 1984).

31. Richard R. Bennett, *Correlates of Crime: A Study of Nations, 1960–1984* (Ann Arbor, Mich.: Inter-University Consortium for Political and Social Research, 1989).

32. Richard R. Bennett and James P. Lynch, "Does a Difference Make a Difference?" *Criminology,* **28** (1990): 155–182; Carol B. Kalish, *International Crime Rates* (Washington, D.C.: Bureau of Justice Statistics, 1988).

33. Jan J. M. Van Dijk, Pat Mayhew, and Martin Killias, *Experiences of Crime across the World: Key Findings from the 1989 International Crime Survey* (Deventer, Netherlands: Kluwer, 1990); Richard R. Bennett and R. Bruce Wiegand, "Observations on Crime Reporting in a Developing Nation," *Criminology,* **32** (1994): 135–148; Ugljesa Zvekic and Anna Albazzi del Frate, eds., *Criminal Victimization in the Developing World* (Rome: United Nations Interregional Crime and Justice Research Institute, 1995); Gail Travis et al., "The International Crime Surveys: Some Methodological Concerns," *Current Issues in Criminal Justice,* **6** (1995): 346–361; Van Dijk, Box 0.9 in *Global Report on Crime and Justice*, p. 9.

34. Josine Junger-Tas, Gert-Jan Terlouw, and Malcolm W. Klein, *Delinquent Behavior among People in the Western World* (Amsterdam: RDC Ministry of Justice, Kugler Publ., 1994); Junger-Tas, Box 0.10 in *Global Report on Crime and Justice*, p. 16.

35. Hermann Mannheim, *Comparative Criminology* (Boston: Houghton Mifflin, 1965).

36. See Jerome L. Neapolitan, *Cross-National Crime—A Research Review and Sourcebook* (Westport, Conn.: Greenwald Press, 1997); Dennis Benamati, Phyllis Schultze, Adam Bouloukos, and Graeme Newman, *Criminal Justice Information: How to Find It, How to Use It* (Phoenix, Ariz.: Onyx Press, 1997); Harry R. Dammer and Philip L. Reichel, eds., *Teaching about Comparative/International Criminal Justice—A Resource Manual* (Highland Heights, N.Y.: Academy of Criminal Justice Sciences, 1997).

37. Elmer H. Johnson, ed., *International Handbook of Contemporary Developments in Criminology,* 2 vols. (Westport, Conn.: Greenwood Press, 1983); George F. Cole, Stanislaw J. Frankowski, and Marc G. Gertz, *Major Criminal Justice Systems—A Comparative Survey,* 2nd ed. (Newbury Park, Calif.: Sage, 1987); Richard J. Terrill, *World Criminal Justice Systems: A Survey* (Cincinnati: Anderson, 1984); Obi N. Ignatius Ebbe, *Comparative and International Criminal Justice Systems* (Boston: Butterworth, 1996); Philip L. Reichel, *Comparative Criminal Justice Systems: A Topical Approach* (Upper Saddle River, N.J.: Prentice Hall, 1994); Brunon Holyst, *Comparative Criminology* (Lexington, Mass.: Lexington Books, 1979); Louise I. Shelley, ed., *Readings in Comparative Criminology* (Carbondale: Southern Illinois University Press, 1981).

38. United Nations, *The United Nations Crime Prevention and Criminal Justice Program: Formulation of Standards and Efforts at Their Implementation* (Philadelphia: University of Pennsylvania, 1994); Benedict Alper and Jerry F. Boren, *Crime: International Agenda* (Lexington, Mass.: Lexington Books, 1972); Ethan N. Nadelman, *Cops across Borders* (University Park: Penn State Press, 1993); André Bossard, *Transnational Crime and Criminal Law* (Chicago: Office of International Criminal Justice, 1990).

39. Graeme Newman, ed., *Global Report on Crime and Justice,* United Nations Office for Drug Control and Crime Prevention, Centre for International Crime Prevention (New York: Oxford University Press, 1999). See also, *The United Nations and Crime Prevention: Seeking Security and Justice for All* (New York: UNDPI, 1996); and *The United Nations and Criminal Justice, 1946–1996: Resolutions, Reports, Documents and Publications, International Review of Criminal Policy,* Issue 47–48 (Vienna: United Nations, 1996/97).

40. G. O. W. Mueller, Michael Gage, and Lenore R. Kupperstein, *The Legal Norms of Delinquency: A Comparative Study,* Criminal Law Education and Research Center Monograph Series, vol. 1 (South Hackensack, N.J.: Fred B. Rothman, 1969).

41. Anastassios Mylonas, *Perception of Police Power: A Study in Four Cities,* Comparative Criminal Law Project Monograph Series, vol. 8 (South Hackensack, N.J.: Fred B. Rothman, 1973).

42. Setsuo Miyazawa, "The Enigma of Japan as a Testing Ground for Cross-Cultural Criminological Studies," *Annales Internationales de Criminologie,* **32** (1994): 81–103; B. Hebenton and J. Spencer, "The Contribution and Limitations of Anglo-American Criminology to Understanding Crime in Central-Eastern Europe," *European Journal of Crime, Criminal Law and Criminal Justice,* **2** (1994): 50–61.

43. Sheldon Glueck and Eleanor Glueck, *Unraveling Juvenile Delinquency* (New York: The Commonwealth Fund; Cambridge, Mass.: Harvard University Press, 1950).

44. Sheldon Glueck and Eleanor Glueck, *Of Delinquency and Crime—A Panorama of Years of Search and Research,* Publications of the Criminal Law Education and Research Center, vol. 8 (Springfield, Ill.: Charles C Thomas, 1974), p. 332.

45. Obi N. I. Ebbe, "Juvenile Delinquency in Nigeria: The Problem of Application of Western Theories," *International*

Journal of Comparative and Applied Criminal Justice, **16** (1992): 353–370.

46. Rosemary Gartner, "The Victims of Homicide: A Temporal and Cross-National Comparison," *American Sociological Review,* **55** (1990): 92–106.

47. Gary LaFree and Christopher Birkbeck, "The Neglected Situation: A Cross-National Study of the Situational Characteristics of Crime," *Criminology,* **29** (1991): 73–98.

48. Richard R. Bennett, "Routine Activities: A Cross-National Assessment of a Criminological Perspective," *Social Forces,* **70** (1991): 147–163.

49. Richard R. Bennett and P. Peter Basiotis, "Structural Correlates of Juvenile Property Crime: A Cross-National, Time-Series Analysis," *Journal of Research in Crime and Delinquency,* **28** (1991): 262–287.

50. Sam S. Souryal, "Juvenile Delinquency in the Cross-Cultural Context: The Egyptian Experience," *International Journal of Comparative and Applied Criminal Justice,* **16** (1992): 329–352.

51. Adel Helal and Charisse T. M. Coston, "Low Crime Rates in Bahrain: Islamic Social Control—Testing the Theory of Synnomie," *International Journal of Comparative and Applied Criminal Justice,* **15** (1991): 125–144.

52. Gregory C. Leavitt, "General Evaluation and Durkheim's Hypothesis of Crime Frequency: A Cross-Cultural Test," *Sociological Quarterly,* **33** (1992): 241–263; and Suzanne T. Ortega, Jay Corzine, and Cathleen Burnett, "Modernization, Age Structure, and Regional Context: A Cross-National Study of Crime," *Sociological Spectrum,* **12** (1992): 257–277.

53. Christopher Birkbeck, "Against Ethnocentrism: A Cross-Cultural Perspective on Criminal Justice Theories and Policies," *Journal of Criminal Justice Education,* **4** (1993): 307–323.

54. Shelley, *Crime and Modernization.*

55. David Shichor, "Crime Patterns and Socio-Economic Development: A Cross-National Analysis," *Criminal Justice Review,* **15** (1990): 64–78; and John Arthur, "Development and Crime in Africa: A Test of Modernization Theory," *Journal of Criminal Justice,* **19** (1991): 499–513.

56. "New Perspectives in Crime Prevention and Criminal Justice and Development: The Role of International Cooperation," working paper prepared by the Secretariat, United Nations, 1980, A/Conf. 87/10.

57. Freda Adler, *Nations Not Obsessed with Crime,* Comparative Criminal Law Project Publications Series, vol. 15 (Littleton, Colo.: Fred B. Rothman, 1983).

58. See Note 8.

59. See Ugljesa Zvekic, ed., *Essays on Crime and Development* (Rome: U.N. Interregional Crime and Justice Research Institute, 1990).

60. V. Lee Hamilton and Joseph Sanders, *Everyday Justice: Responsibility and the Individual in Japan and the United States* (New Haven, Conn.: Yale University Press, 1992); Hans Joachim Schneider, "Crime and Its Control in Japan and in the Federal Republic of Germany, a Comparative Study," *International Journal of Offender Therapy and Comparative Criminology,* **36** (1992): 47–63.

61. Dale E. Berger et al., "Deterrence and Prevention of Alcohol-Impaired Driving in Australia, the United States, and Norway," *Justice Quarterly,* **7** (1990): 453–465.

62. David B. Kopel, The Samurai, the Mountie, and the Cowboy: Should America Adopt the Gun Controls of Other Democracies? (Buffalo, N.Y.: Prometheus, 1992).

63. Robert L. Nay, *Firearms Regulations in Various Foreign Countries* (Washington, D.C.: Law Library of Congress, 1990).

64. Michael Clarke, "The Control of Insurance Fraud: A Comparative View," *British Journal of Criminology,* **30** (1990): 1–23.

65. Kenneth Polk and William Weston, "Insider Trading as an Aspect of White Collar Crime," *Australian and New Zealand Journal of Criminology,* **23** (1990): 24–38.

66. Yü-Hsiu Hsü, ed., *International Conference on Environmental Criminal Law* (Taipei: Taiwan/ROC Chapter of the International Association of Penal Law, 1992).

67. Rosemary Gartner, "Family Structure, Welfare Spending, and Child Homicide in Developed Democracies," *Journal of Marriage and the Family,* **53** (1991): 231–240.

68. Margo I. Wilson and Martin Daly, "Who Kills Whom in Spouse Killings? On the Exceptional Sex Ratio of Spousal Homicides in the United States," *Criminology,* **30** (1992): 189–215.

69. Lois A. Fingerhut and Joel C. Kleinman, "International and Interstate Comparisons of Homicide among Young Males," *Journal of the American Medical Association,* **263** (1990): 3292–3295.

70. F. H. McClintock and Per-Olof H. Wikstrom, "The Comparative Study of Urban Violence—Criminal Violence in Edinburgh and Stockholm," *British Journal of Criminology,* **32** (1992): 505–520.

71. Dae H. Chang and Galan M. Janeksela, eds., "Special Issue on Comparative Juvenile Delinquency," *International Journal of Comparative and Applied Criminal Justice,* **16** (1992): 135–170, with contributions by Gaban M. Janeksela, David P. Farrington, Alison Hatch and Curt T. Griffiths, Günther Kaiser, Josine Junger-Tas, Paul C. Friday, James O. Finckenauer and Linda Kelly, Hualing Fu, Michael S. Vaughn and Frank F. Y. Huang, Byung In Cho and Richard J. Chang, Clayton A. Hartjen and Sesharajani Kethineni, Sam S. Souryhal, and Obi N. I. Ebbe.

72. Mylonas, *Perception of Police Power.*

73. Graeme Newman, *Comparative Deviance: Perception and Law in Six Cultures* (New York: Elsevier Scientific, 1976).

74. Russel P. Dobash, R. Emerson Dobash, Scott Balliofyne, Karl Schuman, Reiner Kaulitzki, and Hans-Werner Guth, "Ignorance and Suspicion: Young People and Criminal Justice in Scotland and Germany," *British Journal of Criminology,* **30** (1990): 306–320.

75. Ronald D. Hunter, "Three Models of Policing," *Police Studies,* **13** (1990): 118–124; R. I. I. Mawby, *Comparable Policing Issues: The British and American Experience in International Perspective* (London: Unwin Hyman, 1990).

76. Leslie T. Wilkins, *Punishment, Crime and Market Forces* (Aldershot, England: Dartmouth, 1991); Dennis Wiechman, Jerry Kendall, and Ronald Bae, "International Use of the Death Penalty," *International Journal of Comparative and Applied Criminal Justice,* **14** (1990): 239–259.

77. See Gunther Kaiser, Helmut Kury, and Hans-Jorg Albrecht, eds., *Victims and Criminal Justice,* 3 vols. (Freiburg, Germany: Max Planck Institut, 1991); Emilio

C. Viano, ed., *Critical Issues in Victimology—International Perspectives* (New York: Springer Verlag, 1992).

78. Jack Levin and Jack McDevitt, *Hate Crimes—The Rising Tide of Bigotry and Bloodshed* (New York: Plenum, 1993).

79. See Hans-Dieter Schwind et al., "Causes, Prevention and Control of Violence," *Revue Internationale de Criminologie et de Police Technique,* **43** (1990): 395–520.

80. Gerhard O. W. Mueller and Freda Adler, *Outlaws of the Ocean: The Complete Book of Contemporary Crime on the High Seas* (New York: Hearst Marine Books, 1985); Gerhard O. W. Mueller and Freda Adler, "A New Wave of Crime at Sea," *The World and I* (Feb. 1986): 96–103.

81. Mike King, *Towards Federalism: Policing the Borders of a "New" Europe* (Leicester, United Kingdom: University of Leicester, 1993); H. Lensing, "The Federalization of Europe: Towards a Federal System of Criminal Justice," *European Journal of Crime, Criminal Law and Criminal Justice,* **1** (1993): 212–229; Ethan A. Nadelmann, *Cops across Borders: The Internationalization of U.S. Criminal Law Enforcement* (University Park: Penn State University Press, 1994).

82. See fourth U.N. Survey, 1986–1990, A/Conf.169/15 and Add. 1.

83. See, for example, Jonathan Reuvid, ed., *The Regulation and Prevention of Economic Crime Internationally* (London: Kogan Page, 1995).

84. See Financial Action Task Force on Money Laundering, *Report on Money Laundering Typologies, 2003–2004* (Paris: FATF, 2005). See also Global Programme Against Money Laundering, www.unodc.org/unodc/en/money_laundering.html.

85. Laurence Zuckerman and John Sullivan, "An FAA Study Shows Few Gains in Improving Security at Airports," *New York Times,* Nov. 5, 1999, p. 30.

86. Several journals are devoted entirely to terrorism. See *Terrorism* (New York); *Studies in Conflict and Terrorism* (London); *Violence, Aggression, Terrorism* (Danbury, Conn.).

87. "High-Tech Art Sleuths Snare Thieves," *C. J. International, 9* (1993): 4:6.

88. Truc-Nhu Ho, Art Theft in New York City: An Explanatory Study in Crime Specificity, Ph.D. dissertation, Rutgers University, 1992.

89. Ralph Blumenthal, "Museums Getting Together to Track Stolen Art," *New York Times,* July 16, 1996, pp. C13, C15.

90. Natalie D. Voss, "Crime on the Internet," *Jones Telecommunications and Multimedia Encyclopedia,* Drive D:, Jones Digital Century, 1996.

91. Michael R. Gordon, "Stolen Uranium Intercepted by Georgia in the Caucasus," *New York Times,* Sept. 24, 1999, p. 6.

92. "For Sale—Nukes: Deadly Plutonium from Russia's Vast Nuclear Network Is Turning Up on the European Market. Who Is Buying—and Can They Be Stopped?" *Newsweek,* Aug. 29, 1994, pp. 30–31; Bruce W. Nolan, "Formula for Terror," *Time,* Aug. 29, 1994.

93. Les Johnston, "Policing Plutonium: Issues in the Provision of Policing Services at Nuclear Facilities and for Related Materials in Transit," *Policing and Society, 4* (1994): 53–72; Phil Williams and Paul H. Woessnar, *Nuclear Material Trafficking: An Interim Assessment* (Pittsburgh: Ridgway Center for International Security Studies, 1995).

94. Eric Ellen, "The Dimensions of International Maritime Crime," in *Issues in Maritime Crime: Mayhem at Sea,* ed.

Martin Gill (Leicester, United Kingdom: Perpetuity Press, 1995), pp. 4–11; Martin Gill, *Crime at Sea: A Forgotten Issue in Police Co-operation* (Leicester, United Kingdom: Centre for the Study of Public Order, 1995); Gerhard O. W. Mueller and Freda Adler, "Piraterie: le 'Jolly Roger' flotte à nouveau les Corsaires des Caribes," *Revue Internationale de Criminologie et de Police Technique, 4* (1992): 408–424.

95. National Insurance Crime Bureau, fax of July 29, 1996.

96. British Banking Association estimate. See Larry E. Coutoria, "The Future of High-Technology Crime: A Parallel Delphi Study," *Journal of Criminal Justice,* **23** (1995): 13–27.

97. E.g., Sally M. Edwards, Terry D. Edwards, and Charles B. Fields, eds., *Environmental Crime and Criminality* (New York: Garland, 1996).

98. Ko-lin Chin, *Chinese Subculture and Criminality: Nontraditional Crime Groups in America* (Westport, Conn.: Greenwood, 1990); Alex P. Schmid, ed., *Migration and Crime* (Milan, Italy: International Scientific and Professional Advisory Council of the United Nations Crime Prevention and Criminal Justice Programme, 1998).

99. Michael Woodiwiss, "Crime's Global Reach," in *Global Crime Connections,* ed. Frank Pearce and Michael Woodiwiss (Houndmills, U.K.: Macmillan, 1993), pp. 1–31.

100. Raphael F. Perl, ed., *Drugs and Foreign Policy: A Critical Review* (Boulder, Colo.: Westview Press, 1994); Günther Kaiser, "International Experiences with Different Strategies of Drug Policy," *EuroCriminology, 7* (1994): 3–29.

101. See Frederick T. Martens, "Transnational Enterprise Crime and the Elimination of Frontiers," *International Journal of Comparative and Applied Criminal Justice,* **15** (1991): 99–107; Wojciech Cebulak, "The Antitrust Doctrine: How It Was Internationalized," *International Journal of Comparative and Applied Criminal Justice,* **14** (1990): 261–267.

102. See "Crime Prevention and Criminal Justice in the Context of Development: Realities and Perspectives of International Cooperation," *International Review of Criminal Policy,* **41/42** (1993): 1–19.

103. Gerhard O. W. Mueller, "Transnational Crime: An Experience in Uncertainties," in *Organized Crime: Uncertainties and Dilemmas,* ed. S. Einstein and M. Amir (Chicago: Office of International Criminal Justice, 1999), pp. 3–18.

104. Draft Articles of the Draft Code of Crimes against the Peace and Security of Mankind, adopted by the International Law Commission on First Reading, United Nations, New York, 1991. For a complete listing, see M. Cherif Bassiouni, *International Criminal Law—A Draft International Criminal Code* (Alphen an den Rijn, Netherlands: Sijthoff & Noordhoff, 1980).

105. Shana Swiss and Joan E. Giller, "Rape as a Crime of War," *Journal of the American Medical Association,* **270** (1993): 612–615.

106. For an analysis of all international crimes, see M. Cherif Bassiouni, ed., *International Criminal Law:* vol. 1, *Crimes,* 2nd ed. (Ardsley, N.Y.: Transnational, 1999); M. Cherif Bassiouni, *A Draft International Criminal Code and Draft Statute for an International Criminal Tribunal* (Dordrecht, Netherlands: Martinus Nijhoff, 1987); Farhad Malekian, *International Criminal Law,* 2 vols. (Motala, Sweden: Borgstroms Trycker, 1991); Gerhard O. W. Mueller and Edward M. Wise, *International Criminal Law,* Comparative Criminal Law Project.

GLOSSARY

Accommodate   In regard to achieving the "American Dream," to adjust non-economic needs so that they are secondary to and supportive of economic ones.

Actus reus   An act that is guilty, evil, and prohibited.

Aging-out phenomenon   A concept that holds that offenders commit less crime as they get older because they have less strength, initiative, stamina, and mobility.

Anomie   A societal state marked by normlessness, in which disintegration and chaos have replaced social cohesion.

Arson   At common law, the malicious burning of the dwelling house of another. This definition has been broadened to cover the burning of other structures or even personal property.

Assault   At common law, an unlawful offer or attempt with force or violence to do a corporal hurt to another or to frighten another.

Atavistic stigmata   Physical features of a human being at an earlier stage of development, which—according to Cesare Lombroso—distinguish a born criminal from the general population.

Attachment   The bond between a parent and child or between individuals and their family, friends, and school.

Attention deficit/hyperactivity disorder (AD/HD)   A relatively common form of minimal brain dysfunction with symptoms including lack of attention, poor school performance, poor concentration, acting without thinking, bullying, and lack of response to discipline; some research links AD/HD to the onset and sustenance of a delinquent career.

Bankruptcy fraud   A scam in which an individual falsely attempts to claim bankruptcy (and thereby erase financial debts) by taking advantage of existing laws.

Behavioural modelling   Learning how to behave by fashioning one's behaviour after that of others.

Belief   The extent to which an individual subscribes to society's values.

Biocriminology   The subdiscipline of criminology that investigates biological and genetic factors and their relation to criminal behaviour.

Birth cohort   A group consisting of all individuals born in the same year.

Born criminal   According to Lombroso, a person born with features resembling an earlier, more primitive form of human life, destined to become a criminal.

Break-and-enter   Canadian term for the unlawful entry into a residence, business, or other structure, with the intent to commit a crime.

Burglary   A common law felony; the night-time breaking and entering of the dwelling house of another, with the intention to commit a crime (felony or larceny) therein.

Case study   An analysis of all pertinent aspects of one unit of study.

Cheque forgery   The criminal offence of making or altering a cheque with intent to defraud.

Child pornography   The use of children as subjects in the portrayal of sexually explicit material.

Chromosomes   Basic cellular structures containing genes (i.e., biological material that creates individuality).

Classical school   A criminological perspective suggesting that (1) people have free will to choose criminal or conventional behaviour; (2) people choose to commit crime for reasons of greed or personal need; and (3) crime can be controlled by criminal sanctions, which should be proportionate to the guilt of the perpetrator.

Commitment   A person's support of and participation in a program, cause, or social activity, which ties the individual to the moral or ethical codes of society.

Comparative criminology   The study of crime in two or more cultures in an effort to gain broader information for theory construction and crime-control modelling.

Conditioning   The process of developing a behaviour pattern through a series of repeated experiences.

Conduct norms   Norms that regulate the daily lives of people and that reflect the attitudes of the groups to which they belong.

Confidence game   A deceptive means of obtaining money or property from a victim who is led to trust the perpetrator.

Conflict model   A model of crime in which the criminal justice system is seen as being used by the ruling class to control the lower class. Criminological investigation of the conflicts within society is emphasized.

Conflict theory   A theory that holds that the people who possess the power work to keep the powerless at a disadvantage.

Conformity   Correspondence of an individual's behaviour to society's patterns, norms, or standards.

Consensus model   A model of criminal lawmaking that assumes that members of society agree on what is right and wrong and that law is the codification of agreed-upon social values.

Consumer fraud   An act that causes a consumer to surrender money through deceit or a misrepresentation of a material fact.

Containment theory   A theory positing that every person possesses a containing external structure and a protective internal structure, both of which provide defence, protection, or insulation against delinquency.

Corporate crime   A crime attributed to a corporation, but perpetrated by or on the authority of an officer or high managerial agent.

Cortical arousal   Activation of the cerebral cortex, a structure of the brain that is responsible for higher intellectual functioning, information processing, and decision making.

Credit card fraud   The illegal use of credit cards (or credit card information) by card owners or those who unlawfully gain access to the card information.

Crime   An act in violation of law that causes harm, is identified by law, is committed with criminal intent, and is subject to punishment.

Crime funnel   Metaphor for the manner in which criminal cases are "lost" or filtered out the further one moves into the criminal justice system; for example, fewer people are arrested than commit crimes, fewer go to court and are convicted, and fewer still serve a prison sentence.

Criminal careers A concept that describes the onset of criminal activity, the types and amount of crime committed, and the termination of such activity.

Criminal justice system The interdependent and interactive components of police, courts, and corrections that form a unified whole (a system).

Criminologists Collect information on crime and criminals for study and analysis in accordance with the research methods of modern science.

Criminology The body of knowledge regarding crime as a social phenomenon. It includes within its scope the process of making laws, of breaking laws, and of reacting toward the breaking of laws (Sutherland). Thus, criminology is an empirical, social-behavioural science that investigates crime, criminals, and criminal justice.

Cultural deviance theories Theories positing that crime results from cultural values that permit, or even demand, behaviour in violation of the law.

Cultural transmission A theory that views delinquency as a socially learned behaviour transmitted from one generation to the next in disorganized urban areas.

Culture conflict theory A theory positing two groups may clash when their conduct norms differ, resulting in criminal activity.

Data Collected facts, observations, and other pertinent information from which conclusions can be drawn.

Decriminalization Reduces the penalty for committing an act, but does not make the act legal.

Deviance A broad concept encompassing both illegal behaviour and behaviour that departs from the social norm.

Differential association-reinforcement A theory of criminality based on the incorporation of psychological learning theory and differential association with social learning theory. Criminal behaviour, the theory claims, is learned through associations and is contained or discontinued as a result of positive or negative reinforcements.

Differential association theory A theory of criminality based on the principle that an individual becomes delinquent because of an excess of definitions learned that are favourable to violation of law over definitions learned that are unfavourable to violation of law.

Differential opportunity theory A theory that attempts to join the concept of anomie and differential association by analyzing both legitimate and illegitimate opportunity structures available to individuals. It posits that illegitimate opportunities, like legitimate opportunities, are unequally distributed.

Direct control An external control that depends on rules, restrictions, and punishments.

Displacement In the event that a crime has been prevented, the commission of a quantitatively similar crime at a different time or place.

Dizygotic (DZ) twins Fraternal twins, who develop from two separate eggs fertilized at the same time. *See also* Monozygotic twins.

Drift According to David Matza, a state of limbo in which youths move in and out of delinquency and in which their lifestyles can embrace both conventional and deviant values.

Due process A fundamental mandate that a person should not be deprived of life, liberty, or property without reasonable and lawful procedures.

Ego The part of the psyche that, according to psychoanalytic theory, governs rational behaviour; the moderator between the superego and the id.

Embezzlement The crime of withholding or withdrawing (conversion or misappropriation), without consent, funds entrusted to an agent (e.g., a bank teller or officer).

Environmental criminology An approach to crime that examines the location of a specific crime and the context in which it occurred in order to understand and explain crime patterns.

Equal protection The constitutional guarantee of equal protection of the law to everyone, without regard to race, origin, economic class, gender, or religion.

Eugenics A science, based on the principle of heredity, that has for its purpose the improvement of the race.

Experiment A research technique in which an investigator introduces a change into a process in order to make measurements or observations that evaluate the effects of the change.

Extroversion According to Hans Eysenck, a dimension of the human personality; describes individuals who are sensation-seeking, dominant, and assertive.

False pretences, obtaining property by Leading a victim to part with property on a voluntary basis through trickery, deceit, or misrepresentation.

Federal Witness Protection Program A U.S. federal program, established under the Organized Crime Control Act of 1970, designed to protect witnesses who testify in court by relocating them and assigning to them new identities.

Fence A receiver of stolen property who resells the goods for profit.

Field experiment An experiment conducted in a real-world setting, as opposed to one conducted in a laboratory.

First-degree murder A premeditated, deliberate, intentional killing; also includes the killing of a police officer or correctional office in the line of duty, or a killing in connection with sexual assault, kidnapping, or hijacking.

Fraud An act of trickery or deceit, especially involving misrepresentation.

General strain theory A criminological theory positing that criminal behaviour can result from strain caused by failure to achieve positively valued goals, stress caused by the removal of positively valued stimuli from the individual, or strain caused by the presentation of negative stimuli.

Geography of crime Research based on the idea that crimes tend to cluster in certain areas, known as "hot spots"; for example, high schools, abandoned buildings, and blocks with bars or nightclubs tend to be the sites of higher crime rates than other areas.

Harm-reduction approach An approach that promotes making safer options more available to people who use and abuse drugs; it is based in the belief that drug users and abusers should not be criminalized but rather should be helped.

Hate crimes Crimes motivated by dislike, prejudice, or discrimination against members of groups who share race, ethnicity, religion, sexual orientation, or immigrant status.

High-tech crime The pursuit of illegal activities through the use of advanced electronic media.

Homicide The killing of one person by another.

Hypoglycemia A condition that may occur in susceptible individuals when the level of blood sugar falls below an acceptable range, causing anxiety, headaches, confusion, fatigue, and aggressive behaviour.

Hypothesis   A proposition set forth as an explanation for some specified phenomenon.

Id   The part of the personality that, according to psycho-analytic theory, contains powerful urges and drives for gratification and satisfaction.

Indictable offences   Criminal offences that are considered serious, involve a trial by judge or judge and jury, and for which there is no limitation period on prosecution.

Indirect control   A behavioural influence that arises from an individual's identification with non-criminals and his or her desire to conform to societal norms.

Insider-related fraud   The misuse of one's position for pecuniary gain or privilege. Includes embezzlement, employee-related theft, and sale of confidential information.

Insurance fraud   Making false or exaggerated automobile, health, personal injury, or other insurance claims in order to reap economic benefit.

Internalized control   Self-regulation of behaviour and conformity to societal norms as a result of guilt feelings arising in the conscience.

International crimes   The major criminal offences so designated by the community of nations for the protection of interests common to all humankind.

International criminal court   The United Nations court with jurisdiction over the most heinous international crimes.

Involuntary manslaughter   Homicide in which the perpetrator unintentionally but recklessly causes the death of another person by consciously taking a grave risk that endangers the person's life.

Involvement   An individual's participation in conventional activities.

Justifiable homicide   A homicide, permitted by law, in defence of a legal right or mandate.

Labelling theory   A theory that explains deviance in terms of the process by which a person acquires a negative identity, such as "addict" or "ex-con," and is forced to suffer the consequences of outcast status.

Larceny   The trespassory (unconsented) taking and carrying away of personal property belonging to another with the intent to deprive the owner of the property permanently.

Laws of imitation   An explanation of crime as learned behaviour. Individuals are thought to emulate behaviour patterns of others with whom they have contact.

Longitudinal study   An analysis that focuses on studies of a particular group conducted repeatedly over a period of time.

Macrosociological study   The study of overall social arrangements, their structures, and their long-term effects.

Malice aforethought   The mens rea requirement for murder, consisting of the intention to kill with the awareness that there is no right to kill. *See also* Mens rea.

Manslaughter   Criminal homicide without malice, committed intentionally after provocation (voluntary manslaughter) or recklessly (involuntary manslaughter).

Mass murder   The killing of several persons, in one act or transaction, by one perpetrator or a group of perpetrators.

Mens rea   (Latin, "guilty mind") Awareness of wrongdoing; the intention to commit a criminal act or behave recklessly.

Microsociological study   The study of everyday patterns of behaviour and personal interactions.

Middle-class measuring rod   Evaluation standards used in schools that emphasize middle-class values such as self-reliance, good manners, respect for property, and long-range planning.

Minimal brain dysfunction (MBD)   An attention-deficit disorder that may produce such asocial behaviour as impulsivity, hyperactivity, and aggressiveness.

Money laundering   The process by which money derived from illegal activities (especially drug sales) is unlawfully taken out of the country, placed in a numbered account abroad, and then transferred as funds no longer "dirty."

Monozygotic (MZ) twins   Identical twins, who develop from a single fertilized egg that divides into two embryos. *See also* Dizygotic twins.

Murder   The unlawful (usually intentional) killing of a human being with malice aforethought.

Neuroticism   A personality disorder marked by low self-esteem, excessive anxiety, and wide mood swings (Eysenck).

Non-participant observation   A study in which investigators observe closely but do not become participants.

Occupational crime   A crime committed by an individual for his or her own benefit, in the course of performing a profession.

Organized crime   Relatively structured, hierarchical system involving a variety of groups that provide consumers with goods and services for illegal goods and services, such as drugs, weapons, prostitution, some kinds of pornography, and gambling.

Participant observation   Collection of information through involvement in the social life of the group a researcher is studying.

Penologist   A social scientist who studies and applies the theory and methods of punishment for crime.

Phrenology   A nineteenth-century theory based on the hypothesis that human behaviour is localized in certain specific brain and skull areas. According to this theory, criminal behaviour can be determined by the bumps on the head.

Physiognomy   The study of facial features and their relation to human behaviour.

Pimp   A procurer or manager of prostitutes who provides access to prostitutes and protects and exploits them, living off their proceeds.

Population   A large group of persons in a study.

Pornography   The portrayal, by whatever means, of lewd or obscene (sexually explicit) material prohibited by law.

Positivist school   A criminological perspective that uses the scientific methods of the natural sciences and suggests that human behaviour is a product of social, biological, psychological, or economic forces.

Primary data   Facts and observations that researchers gather by conducting their own measurements for a study.

Prostitution   The practice of engaging in sexual activities for hire.

Psychoanalytic theory   In criminology, a theory of criminality that attributes delinquent and criminal behaviour to a conscience that is either so overbearing that it arouses excessive feelings of guilt or so weak that it cannot control the individual's impulses.

Psychopathy   A condition in which a person appears to be psychologically normal but in reality has no sense of responsibility, shows disregard for truth, is insincere, and feels no sense of shame, guilt, or humiliation (also called sociopathy).

Psychosis   A mental illness characterized by a loss of contact with reality.

Psychoticism   A dimension of the human personality describing individuals who are aggressive, egocentric, and impulsive (Eysenck).

Racketeer Influenced and Corrupt Organizations (RICO) Act   A U.S. federal statute that provides for forfeiture of assets derived from a criminal enterprise.

Radical criminology   A criminological perspective that studies the relationships between economic disparity and crime, maintains that crime is the result of a struggle between owners of capital and workers for the distribution of power and resources, and posits that crime will disappear only when capitalism is abolished.

Random sample   A sample chosen in such a way as to ensure that each person in the population to be studied has an equal chance of being selected. *See also* Sample.

Rape   At common law, a felony consisting of the carnal knowledge (intercourse), by force and violence, by a man of a woman (not his wife) against her will. The stipulation that the woman not be the man's wife is omitted in modern statutes. Known as "sexual assault" in Canada.

Rational-choice perspective   A theory stating that crime is the result of a decision-making process in which the offender weighs the potential penalties and rewards of committing a crime.

Reaction formation   An individual response to anxiety in which the person reacts to a stimulus with abnormal intensity or inappropriate conduct.

Robbery   The taking of the property of another, or out of his or her presence, by means of force and violence or the threat thereof.

Routine activity   A theory stating that an increase or decrease in crime rates can be explained by changes in the daily habits of potential victims; based on the expectation that crimes will occur where there is a suitable target unprotected by guardians.

Sample   A selected subset of a population to be studied. *See also* Random sample.

Second-degree murder   An intentional killing without premeditation and deliberation.

Secondary data   Facts and observations that were previously collected for a different study.

Self-report survey   A survey in which respondents answer in a confidential interview or, most often, by completing an anonymous questionnaire.

Serial murder   The killing of several victims over a period of time by the same perpetrator(s).

Shoplifting   Stealing goods from stores or markets.

Situational crime prevention   An approach to crime prevention that draws on rational choice and routine activity theories, as well as the belief that altering physical spaces (e.g., through improving architectural designs) can decrease victimizations.

Social control theory   An explanation of criminal behaviour that focuses on control mechanisms, techniques, and strategies for regulating human behaviour, leading to conformity or obedience to society's rules, and which posits that deviance results when social controls are weakened or break down, so that individuals are not motivated to conform to them.

Social disorganization theory   A theory of criminality in which the breakdown of effective social bonds, primary-group associations, and social controls in neighbourhoods and communities is held to result in development of high-crime areas.

Social learning theory   A theory of criminality that maintains that delinquent behaviour is learned through the same psychological processes as non-delinquent behaviour (e.g., through reinforcement).

Social norms   Perceived standards of acceptable behaviour prevalent among members of a society.

Sociopath   A person who has no sense of responsibility; shows disregard for truth; is insincere; and feels no sense of shame, guilt, or humiliation.

Somatotype school   A criminological perspective that relates body build to behavioural tendencies, temperament, susceptibility to disease, and life expectancy.

Strain theory   A criminological theory positing that a gap between culturally approved goals and legitimate means of achieving them causes frustration which leads to criminal behaviour.

Stranger homicide   Homicide committed by a person unknown and unrelated to the victim.

Strict liability   Liability for a crime or violation imposed without regard to the actor's guilt; criminal liability without mens rea. *See also* Mens rea.

Subculture   A subdivision within the dominant culture that has its own norms, beliefs, and values.

Subculture of violence   A subculture with values that demand the overt use of violence in certain social situations.

Subculture of violence thesis   An explanation for delinquency that locates the root of violent behaviour in the value systems of subcultures that demand the use of violence in certain situations.

Summary offences   Relatively minor criminal offences (e.g., loitering) that can result in a fine of up to $2000, a six-month jail term, or both; there is a six-month limitation period on prosecution of these crimes.

Superego   In psychoanalytic theory, the conscience, or those aspects of the personality that threaten the person or impose a sense of guilt or psychic suffering and thus restrain the id.

Survey   The systematic collection of information by asking questions in questionnaires or interviews.

Symbolic interactionists   Scholars who view the human self as formed through a process of social interaction; it is through our interactions with others that we learn the symbolic meanings of the world around us, learn how to assign meaning to objects and behaviour, and learn how to react to others.

Synnomie   A societal state, opposite of anomie, marked by social cohesion achieved through the sharing of values.

Target hardening   A crime-prevention technique that seeks to make it more difficult to commit a given offence, by better protecting the threatened object or person.

Terrorism   The use of violence against a target to create fear, alarm, dread, or coercion for the purpose of obtaining concessions or rewards or commanding public attention for a political cause.

Theft   The taking of others' property; known as larceny in common law.

Theories of victimization   Theories that explain the role that victims play in the crimes that happen to them.

Theory A coherent group of propositions used as principles in explaining or accounting for known facts or phenomena.

Transnational crime A criminal act or transaction violating the laws of more than one country, or having an impact on a foreign country.

Uniform Crime Reports (UCR) A standard survey used by police departments to collect and report crime-related information to the Canadian Centre for Justice Statistics, which then releases the information to the public.

Utilitarianism A criminological perspective positing that crime prevention and criminal justice must serve the end of providing the greatest good for the greatest number; based on the rationality of lawmakers, law enforcers, and the public at large.

Variables Changeable factors.

Victimization survey A survey that measures the extent of crime by interviewing individuals about their experiences as victims.

Voluntary manslaughter Homicide in which the perpetrator intentionally, but without malice, causes the death of another person, as in the heat of passion, in response to strong provocation, or possibly under severe intoxication.

White-collar crime A sociological concept encompassing any violation of the law committed by a person or group of persons in the course of an otherwise respected and legitimate occupation or business enterprise.

CREDITS

ILLUSTRATIONS AND TEXT CREDITS

Chapter 1

Figure 1.1 Adapted from Jack D. Douglas and Frances C. Waksler, *The Sociology of Deviance* (Boston: Little, Brown, 1980), p. 11. Copyright © 1982 by Jack D. Douglas and Frances Chaput Waksler. Reprinted by permission of the authors.

Page 19 Lori Wilkinson, "Are Human Rights Jeopardized in 21st Century Canada? An Examination of Immigration Policies Post 9/11" in *Security vs. Freedom: Playing a Zero-Sum Game in the Post 9/11 Era,* ed. Sandra Rollings-Magnuson [Halifax: Fernwood, 2008]; William J. Stuntz, "Local Policing after Terror." Reprinted by permission of The Yale Law Journal Company and William S. Hein Company from the *Yale Law Journal,* 111, 2002: 2137.)

Chapter 2

Table 2.2 Adapted from Statistics Canada, www.statscan.ca/101/cst01/legal02.htm, accessed April 6, 2007.

Figure 2.2 Adapted from "Criminal Victimization in Canada, 2004," Maire Gannon and Karen Mihorean, *Juristat,* Statistics Canada, Catalogue No: 85-002-XPE. Vol. 25, No. 7, November 2005; "Crime Statistics in Canada, 2005," Maire Gannon, *Juristat,* Statistics Canada, Catalogue No: 85-002-XIE, Vol. 26, No.4 July, 2006.

Figure 2.3 Adapted from "Criminal Victimization in Canada, 2004," Maire Gannon and Karen Mihorean, *Juristat,* Statistics Canada, Catalogue No: 85-002-XPE, Vol. 25, No. 7, November 2005.

Table 2.3 Adapted from "Comparison of the GSS and UCR," adapted from Statistics Canada publication *An Overview of the Differences Between Police-Reported and Victim-Reported Crime,* Catalogue 85-542, No. 1, released May 14, 1997, www.statcan.ca/bsolc/english/bsolc?catno=85-542-X.

Figure 2.4 Adapted from Maire Gannon and Karen Mihorean, November 2005. "Criminal Victimization in Canada, 2004," *Juristat,* Statistics Canada, Catalogue No: 85-002-XPE. Vol. 25, No. 7; Statistics Canada, General Social Survey, 1999 and 2004, *Juristat,* Catalogue No. 85-002, Vol. 15, No. 10.

Figure 2.5 Adapted from Maire Gannon and Karen Mihorean, November 2005. "Criminal Victimization in Canada, 2004," *Juristat,* Statistics Canada, Catalogue No: 85-002-XPE. Vol. 25, No. 7; Statistics Canada, General Social Survey, 1993, 1999 and 2004.

Figure 2.6 Adapted from Maire Gannon, "Crime Statistics in Canada, 2005," *Juristat,* Statistics Canada, Catalogue No: 85-002-XIE, Vol. 26, No. 4 July, 2006. Minister of Industry; Statistics Canada, Canadian Centre for Justice Statistics, Uniform Crime Reporting Survey.

Figure 2.7 Valerie Pottie Bunge, Holly Johnson, and Thierno A. Baldé "Exploring Crime Patterns in Canada," *Crime and Justice Research Paper Series,* Statistics Canada, Catalogue no: 85-561-MIE-No.005, ISBN:0-662-40697-4; Statistics Canada, Canadian Centre for Justice Statistics, Uniform Crime Reporting Survey; Warren Silver "Crime Statistics in Canada, 2006." *Juristat.* Statistics Canada. Catalogue No: 85-002-XIE, Vol. 27, No. 5, July, 2007; Statistics Canada. Canadian Centre for Justice Statistics, Uniform Crime Reporting Survey; Persons Charged by Type of Offence, www.40.statcan.ca/101/cst01/legal14c.htm, accessed January 31, 2008.

Figure 2.8 Valerie Pottie Bunge, Holly Johnson and Thierno A. Baldé "Exploring Crime Patterns in Canada," *Crime and Justice Research Paper Series,* Statistics Canada, Catalogue no: 85-561-MIE-No.005, ISBN:0-662-40697-4; Statistics Canada, Canadian Centre for Justice Statistics, Incident-based Uniform Crime Reporting Survey.

Figure 2.9 Adapted from Marnie Wallace, "Crime Statistics in Canada, 2003," *Juristat,* Statistics Canada, Catalogue No: 85-002-XIE, Vol. 24, No. 6. July, 2004.

Page 53 Kevin Haggerty, *Making Crime Count* [Toronto: University of Toronto Press, 2001]; Julian V. Roberts, "Racism and the Collection of Statistics Relating to Race and Ethnicity" in *Crimes of Colour: Racialization and the CJS in Canada,* Wendy Chan and Kilran Mirchandani, eds. [Peterborough, Ontario: Broadview Press, 2002], pp. 101–112; David Rudovsky, "Breaking the Pattern of Racial Profiling," *Trial,* August 2002, Association of Trial Lawyers of America; Larry J. Siegel and Chris McCormick, *Criminology in Canada: Theories, Patterns and Typologies,* Third

2002 by Transaction Publishers. Reprinted by permission of the publisher.

Table 7.2 James C. Howell, *Youth Gangs: An Overview* (Washington, D.C.: U.S. Department of Justice, 1998).

Figure 7.3 Marc LeBlanc, "A Generic Control Theory of the Criminal Phenomenon: The Structural and Dynamic Statements of an Integrative Multilayered Control Theory," in *Developmental Theories of Crime and Delinquency: Advances in Criminological Theory,* vol. 7, T. P. Thornberry, ed. (New Brunswick, NJ: Transaction, 1997), p. 238. Copyright © 1997 by Transaction Publishers. Reprinted by permission of the publisher.

Page 181 John Clark, James Austin, and D. Alan Henry, *Three Strikes and You're Out: A Review of State Legislation* [Washington, D.C.: NJ, 1997]; Janice Tibbetts, "Government to Deliver Canadian Version of 'Three-Strikes' Law," *CanWest News Service,* September 21, 2006, accessed at www.canada.com.)

Chapter 8

Page 211 Ira Basen, "Reality Check: Voting No to Prisoners," CBC Reality Check Team, www.cbc.ca /canadavotes/realitycheck/prisoners.html, accessed June 23, 2007; "Developments in the Law: One Person, No Vote: The Laws of Felon Disenfranchisement," *Harvard Law Review,* 115, 2002: 1939. Reprinted by permission of the Harvard Law Review Association and William S. Hein Company.

Chapter 9

Table 9.1 Marcus Felson and Ronald V. Clarke, *Opportunity Makes the Thief: Practical Theory for Crime Prevention,* Police Research Series Paper 98 (London: Home Office, 1998), p. 9. © Crown Copyright 1998. Reprinted by permission of Her Majesty's Stationery Office.

Figure 9.1 Adapted from Ronald V. Clarke and Derek B. Cornish, "Modeling Offenders' Decisions: A Framework for Research and Policy," in *Crime and Justice,* vol. 6, Michael Tonry and Norval Morris, eds (Chicago: University of Chicago, 1985), p. 169. © 1985 by The University of Chicago. All rights reserved. Reprinted by permission of the University of Chicago Press.

Figure 9.3 George Rengert and John Wasilchick, *Suburban Burglary: A Time and a Place for Everything* (Springfield, IL: Charles C. Thomas, 1985), p. 35. Courtesy of Charles C Thomas Publisher, Ltd., Springfield, Illinois.

Table 9.2 Canadian Resource Centre for Victims of Crime, "Victim's Rights in Canada," January 2006.

Table 9.3 Ronald V. Clarke and Ross Homel, "A Revised Classification of Situational Crime Prevention Techniques," in *Crime Prevention at a Crossroads,* Steven P. Lab, ed. (Cincinnati, OH: Anderson, 1997), with permission. Copyright 1997 Matthew Bender & Company, Inc., a member of the LexisNexis Group. All rights reserved.

Table 9.4 Zachary Fleming, Patricia Brantingham, and Paul Brantingham, "Exploring Auto Theft in British Columbia," in *Crime Prevention Studies,* vol. 3, Ronald V. Clarke, ed. (Monsey, NY: Criminal Justice Press, 1994), p. 62. Reprinted by permission of the publisher.

Chapter 10

Figure 10.1 Statistics Canada, Homicide in Canada, 2006, Catalogue no. 85-002-XIE, Vol. 27, no. 8, page 4.

Figure 10.2 Statistics Canada, Homicide in Canada, 2006, Catalogue no. 85-002-XIE, Vol. 27, no. 8, page 2.

Table 10.1 Homicide in Canada, 2006, Statistics Canada, Catalogue no. 85-002-XIE. Vol. 27, no. 8, page 3.

Table 10.3 "Canadian Incidence Study of Reported Child Abuse and Neglect—2003. Major Findings," Ministry of Public Works and Government Services Canada, 2005. Reproduced with the permission of the Minister of Public Works and Government Services Canada, 2008.

Figure 10.4 "Crime Statistics in Canada, 2005," Statistics Canada, Catalogue no. 85-002, Vol. 26, no. 4. page 7; "Crime Statistics in Canada, 2006," Statistics Canada, Catalogue no. 85-002-XIE, Vol. 27, no. 5, Minister of Industry, 2007, page 9.

Figure 10.5 Homicide in Canada, 2006, Statistics Canada, Catalogue no. 85-002-XIE, Vol. 27. no. 8, page 4.

Page 266 http://www.darpa.MIL/iao/

Chapter 11

Figure 11.1 Adapted from "Crime Statistics in Canada, 2006," Statistics Canada, Catalogue no. 85-002-XIE, vol. 27, no. 5.

Table 11.1 Read Hayes, *1996 Retail Theft Trends Report: An Analysis of Customer Theft in Stores* (Winter Park, FL: Loss Prevention Specialists, 1996). Reprinted by permission of the author.

Figure 11.2 Adapted from "Crime Statistics in Canada, 2006," Statistics Canada, Catalogue no. 85-002-XIE, vol. 27, no. 5, page 6.

Table 11.2 Insurance Bureau of Canada.

Chapter 12

Figure 12.1 http://www.fbi.gov.

Table 12.3 Department of Justice Canada, "New Criminal Anti-Gang Measures," www.justice.gc.ca/en/news/nr/1997/prgangbk.html; "Royal Assent of Bill C-24 Organized Crime Legislation," www.justice.gc.ca/en/news/nr/2001/doc_28213.html, accessed November 20, 2007; Samuel Porteous, *Organized Crime Impact Study: Highlights,* prepared for the Ministry of the Soldier General of Canada, 1998.

Figure 12.2 President's Commission on Law Enforcement and Administration of Justice, *Task Force Report: Organized Crime* (Washington, D.C.: U.S. Government Printing Office, 1967), p. 9.

Page 321 David Weisburd and Elin Waring, *White-Collar Crime and Criminal Careers* [Cambridge: Cambridge University Press, 2001], p. 8.

Chapter 13

Table 13.1 Bruce D. Johnson, Terry Williams, Kojo A. Dir, and Harry Sanabria, "Drug Abuse in the Inner City: Impact on Hard-Drug Users and the Community," in *Drugs and Crime,* vol. 13: *Crime and Justice,* Michael Tonry and James Q. Wilson, eds. (Chicago: University of Chicago Press, 1990), p. 19. © 1990 by the University of Chicago. All rights reserved. Reprinted by permission of the University of Chicago Press.

Table 13.2 "Smoking in Canada Being Snuffed Out," CBC News, February 15, 2007, www.cbc.ca.news.background.smoking/stats.html, accessed October 30, 2007; "Smoking Statistics," Heart and Stroke Foundation of Canada, ww2.heartandstroke.ca/Page.asp?PageID=110&Article ID=1076&Src=news, accessed October 30, 2007; "Smoking in Canada: An Overview," Health Canada, www.hc-sc.gc.ca/hl-vs/tobac-tabac/research-recherche/stat/ctums-esutc/fs-if/2003; "Alcohol Consumption Rises by 13% since 1997," *CTV News,* www.ctv.ca/servlet/ArticleNews/print/CTVNews/20051215/alcohol_statscan_2005, accessed October 30, 2007; E.M. Adlaf, P. Beging, and E. Sawka, eds., *Canadian Addiction Survey (CAS): A National Survey of Canadians' Use of Alcohol and Other Drugs: Prevalence of Use and Related Harms: Detailed Report.* (Ottawa: Canadian Centre on Substance Abuse, 2005); "1996 NWT Alcohol & Drug Survey" Northwest Territories Bureau of Statistics, www.stats.gov.nt.ca/Statinfo?Health/alcdrug/report.html, accessed October 30, 2007.

Table 13.3 Adapted from "Getting Banks to Just Say 'No,'" *Business Week,* Apr. 17, 1989, p. 17; and Maggie Mahar, "Dirty Money: It Triggers a Bold New Attack in the War on Drugs," *Barron's,* 69 (June), 1989: 6–38, at p. 7. From the U.S. Department of Justice, Drugs, Crime and the Justice System (Washington, D.C.: U.S. Government Printing Office, 1992).

Table 13.4 City of Vancouver, "Four Pillars Drug Strategy," 2008, www.city.vancouver.bc.ca/fourpillars/, accessed April 5, 2008.

Table 13.5 Vancouver Coastal Health, "Insite Supervised Injection Site," www.vch.ca/sis/research.htm, accessed April 5, 2008.

Figure 13.3 Edward M. Adlaf, Andrée Demers, and Louis Gliksman, eds., *Canadian Campus Survey, 2004* (Toronto: Centre for Addition and Mental Health, 2005).

Table 13.6 Public Works and Government Services Canada.

Page 350 Amy Adler, "The Perverse Law of Child Pornography," Columbia Law Review, **101,** 2001: 209. Copyright 2001 by Columbia Law Review Association, Inc., in the format Textbook via Copyright Clearance Center.

Chapter 14

Figure 14.1 *Global Report on Crime and Justice* (New York: United Nations, 1999), p. 69.

Figure 14.2 United Nations Office for Drug Control and Crime Prevention, *United Nations Global Programme against Money Laundering* (New York: United Nations, 1998), pp. 18–19.

Page 372 William S. Laufer, "The Forgotten Criminology of Genocide," *The Criminology of Criminal Law: Advances in Criminological Theory,* 8, 1999).

PHOTO CREDITS

Chapter 1

3: CP PHOTO/ Tom Hanson; **5:** © Photodisc/Superstock; **7:** CP PHOTO/1997 (Guelph Mercury); **8:** CP PHOTO/ Dave Chidley; **10:** © Timothy Fadek/Gamma Presse; **11:** © Oka Bidhi/Getty; **13:** © Giraudon/Art resource; **17:** CP PHOTO/*Edmonton Sun*/Walter Tychnowicz.

Chapter 2

21: CP PHOTO/Jacques Boissinot; **23:** © Robert Brenner/PhotoEdit; **26:** © Al Grillo/AP/Wide World Photos; **27:** © Christopher Morris/Corbis; **46:** © Andrew Lichtenstein/The Image Works; **48:** CP PHOTO/*Moose Jaw Times-Herald*/Shelby Parker; **50:** Photo by Scott Olson/Getty Images.

Chapter 3

55: © Pushkin Museum of Fine Arts, Moscow, Scala/Art Resource; **56:** © PhotoEdit; **57:** © Gerhard Hinterleitner/Gamma Presse; **59:** © Granger Collection; **60:** © AP/Wide World Photos; **63:** © The British Museum; **64:** "How to Read Character. A New Illustrated Hand-Book of Physiology, Phrenology and Physiognomy for Students and Examiner," by Samuel Wells, Fowler & Wells Co. NY 1890 (Collection of B. Salz); **66:** Topham/The Image Works; **67:** © Arthur Estabrook Paper, M. E. Grenander Department of Special Collections and Archives, University of Albany; **71:** © Corbis.

Chapter 4

77: © Toronto Star Syndicate (2003) all rights reserved; **78:** © Joel Gordon; **79:** © Corbis; **82, top:** © Martin Rodgers/Stock.Boston; **86:** (CP PHOTO/*Toronto Sun*/Craig Robertson); **82, bottom:** © Gretchen Ertl/AP/Wide World Photos; **91:** (CP PHOTO/*London Free Press*/Derek Ruttan); **92:** SIPA; **99:** © Joe Azel/Aurora Photos; **101:** (CP PHOTO/*The St. Catharines Standard*/Denis Cahill).

Chapter 5

107: CP PHOTO/*Toronto Star*/Ron Bull; **110:** © Collart Herve/Corbis Sygma; **112:** Photo by Robert Nickelsberg/Liaison; **115:** CP PHOTO/*Daily Gleaner*/Stephen MacGillivray; **122:** © Bob Daemmich/Stock.Boston; **123:** © Mark Peterson/Corbis Saba; **126:** CP PHOTO/*London Free Press*/Susan Bradnam.

Chapter 6

129: CP PHOTO/Gerard Kwiatkowski; **130:** © Owen Franken/CORBIS; **131:** © Sankei Shimbun/Corbis Sygma; **132:** © Lisa Terry/Getty Images; **135:** CP PHOTO/*The Whig-Standard*-Michael Lea; **136:** CP PICTURE ARCHIVE/Ryan Remiorz; **142:** © Jim Cooper/AP/Wide World Photos; **144:** CP PHOTO/Ruth Bonneville; **147:** CP PHOTO/Chuck Stoody CANADA; **149:** © A. Ramey/PhotoEdit; **150:** CP PHOTO/Aaron Harris.

Chapter 7

157: © Frederic J. Brown/Agence France Presse; **158:** CP PHOTO 1996 (Stf-Fred Chartrand); **165:** © Dave G. Houser/Corbis; **168:** Taylor S. Kennedy; **170:** CP PHOTO/*Toronto Star*/Michael Stuparyk; **176:** CP PHOTO/Jason Scott; **178:** © Fujiphotos/The Image Works.

Chapter 8

183: © Reuters/CORBIS; **187:** CP PHOTO/*Brantford Expositor*-Brian Thompson CANADA; **191, left:** © Rick Reinhard; **191, right:** © James McCoy/*Buffalo News*/Corbis Sygma; **193:** CP PHOTO/*Winnipeg Free Press*-Wayne Glowacki; **198:** © Stephen Ferry/Getty Images; **206:** CP PHOTO/*Toronto* Star-Rick Madonik; **207:** AP PHOTO/Jerome Delay, File.

Chapter 9

213: © Reuters/CORBIS; **214:** CP PICTURE ARCHIVE/AP/Nick Wass); **217:** © Courtesy Gerhard O.W. Mueller; **218:** © Ion C. Diehl/PhotoEdit; **219:** © Oscar Alolafia/Getty Images; **220:** © Mike Siluk/The Image Works; **223:** *The Canadian Press*/Steve White; **228:** © David Butow/Corbis Saba; **230:** CP PHOTO/Peter McCabe.

Chapter 10

237: © Ceneta Manuel/Gamma Presse; **238:** CP PHOTO/Ryan Remiorz; **239:** © Taylor/*Montgomery Journal*/Gamma Presse; **241:** © Scott Dalton/AP/Wide World Photos; **242:** CP PICTURE ARCHIVE/Regina Leader Post/Roy Antal; **245:** © Dwayne Newton/PhotoEdit; **247:** © Charles Drupa/AP/Wide World Photos; **251:** © Joel Gordon; **254:** © John Todd/AP/Wide World Photos; **258:** © Shannon Stapleton/Reuters/Landov; **259:** Photo by Jeff Vinnick/Getty Images; **260:** AP Photo/Bebeto Matthews; **261, left:** CP PHOTO/*Toronto Star*/Lucas Oleniuk; **261, right:** © Christian Fischer/DDP/SIPA; **263:** CP PHOTO/Chuck Stoody.

Chapter 11

269: CP PHOTO/Jason Scott; **273:** © Los Angeles County Courts/Getty Images; **275:** © George Widman/AP/Wide World Photos; **277:** CP PHOTO/*Calgary Sun*-Jim Wells; **278:** (CP PHOTO/*Toronto Star*-Colin McConnell; **283:** AP Photo/Apichart Weerawong; **284:** CP PHOTO/*Winnipeg Free* Press-Ken Gigliotti; **286:** © Daniel Hulshizer/AP/Wide World Photos.

Chapter 12

291: © Thimas E. Witte/Gamma Presse; **292:** © William Miller/SIPA; **293:** *The Canadian Press*/Ryan Remiorz; **294, top:** AP Photo/M. Spencer Green; **294, bottom:** CP PHOTO/*Halifax Chronicle-Herald*-Ingrid Bulmer; **295:** CP PHOTO/Fred Chartrand; **298:** CP PHOTO/Ryan Remiorz; **303:** © Bob Shaw; **304:** *Toronto Star*; **308:** CP PHOTO/Adrian Wyld; **311:** © Baldev/Corbis

Sygma; **312:** CP PHOTO/*Hamilton Spectator*/Files; **314:** CP PHOTO/Files/*Globe and Mail*/Tim McKenna; **317, left:** AP Photo/Paul Sancya; **317, right:** CP PHOTO/*The Winnipeg Free Press*-Phil Hossack.

Chapter 13

323: Michael Schmelling/AP/Wide World Photos; **329:** © Tom Miner/The Image Works; **330:** © Nick Ut/AP/Wide World Photos; **332:** © Apichart Weerawong/AP/Wide World Photos; **338:** *The Canadian Press*/Richard Lam; **341:** CP PHOTO/Richard Lam; **343:** © Jim Wilson/Woodfin Camp & Associates; **348:** © T.Crosby/Getty Images.

Chapter 14

353: © Chip Hires/Gamma Presse; **354:** © Apichart Weerawong/AP/Wide World Photos; **357:** © Mia Foster/PhotoEdit; **360:** © A.Ramey/Woodfin Camp & Associates; **361:** © Peter Blakely/Corbis Saba; **366:** © Vladimir Sichov/SIPA; **370:** © Philip S. Farnsworth/Getty Images.

NAME INDEX

SUBJECT INDEX